T0212376

Communications
in Computer and Information Science 1289

Commenced Publication in 2007
Founding and Former Series Editors:
Simone Diniz Junqueira Barbosa, Phoebe Chen, Alfredo Cuzzocrea,
Xiaoyong Du, Orhun Kara, Ting Liu, Krishna M. Sivalingam,
Dominik Ślęzak, Takashi Washio, Xiaokang Yang, and Junsong Yuan

Editorial Board Members

More information about this series at http://www.springer.com/series/7899

Jerzy Mikulski (Ed.)

Research and the Future of Telematics

20th International Conference
on Transport Systems Telematics, TST 2020
Kraków, Poland, October 27–30, 2020
Selected Papers

 Springer

Editor
Jerzy Mikulski
University of Economics in Katowice
Katowice, Poland

ISSN 1865-0929 ISSN 1865-0937 (electronic)
Communications in Computer and Information Science
ISBN 978-3-030-59269-1 ISBN 978-3-030-59270-7 (eBook)
https://doi.org/10.1007/978-3-030-59270-7

This Springer imprint is published by the registered company Springer Nature Switzerland AG
The registered company address is: Gewerbestrasse 11, 6330 Cham, Switzerland

Preface

I am very pleased to introduce the proceedings of the 20th Jubilee Conference on Transport System Telematics (TST 2020). This volume of conference proceedings contains the written version of most of the contributions. The present special issue of CCIS consists of 34 selected papers from those which will be presented at the conference. I would like to thank all participants for their contributions to the conference program.

As for previous conferences, "Intelligent Transport Systems (ITS)" was the theme. ITS is the area of computer and communications science focusing on transport. The use of ITS is gaining popularity. The primary purpose of their existence is to improve safety and traffic flow, and to prevent congestion. Identification of the most useful and helpful tools of ITS will allow us to define the preferred directions of development.

The conference aims to bring together researchers and practitioners from various countries, working in different areas of transport, to discuss the current state of knowledge about transport telematics.

The conference has come a long way since the first one in 2001, which included 1 session and had about 20 attendees. TST 2020 continued the trend of increasing size, student attendance, and international participation, that was evident in recent years.

TST 2020 was to be held in May this year, but the COVID-19 epidemic changed everything. At the time of writing, the date was rescheduled for October 2020. Whilst COVID-19 has had an impact on all of us, I am confident that we will be able to continue to work together.

The TST conferences so far were always held stationary, but the current situation has forced us to consider a hybrid way of holding it. Hybrid meetings are becoming a reality in the international arena as webinars, online conferences, and webcasts become more popular. It is difficult to say now what their scale is in Poland. In my opinion, the fashion for these meetings is still ahead of us. The hybrid conference combines the meeting of participants taking part in the event at the place of its organization, with online (virtual) participation of participants located elsewhere in Poland and in the world.

Krakow is pleased to welcome TST conference participants again for the second time, the first being in 2018.

Once again, I wish you all the best in the hopefully gradual recovery back to normality and I look forward to meeting you soon.

August 2020   Jerzy Mikulski

Organization

Organizers

Polish Association of Transport Telematics, Poland

Co-operating Universities

Czech Technical University, Czech Republic
Gdynia Maritime University, Poland
Maritime University of Szczecin, Poland
University of Bielsko-Biała, Poland
University of Economics in Katowice, Poland
University of Lodz, Poland
University of Technology Katowice, Poland
University of Zilina, Slovakia
UNESCO Chair for Science, Technology and Engineering Education
   at the AGH, Poland

Scientific Program Committee

J. Mikulski (Chair)	Polish Association of Transport Telematics, Poland
E. van Berkum	University of Twente, The Netherlands
M. Bregulla	Ingolstadt University of Applied Sciences, Germany
F. Busch	Technische Universität München, Germany
R. van Duin	Delft University of Technology, The Netherlands
P. Engelseth	Molde University College, Norway
G. Gentile	Universita di Roma, Italy
M. Givoni	Tel-Aviv University, Israel
P. Groumpos	University of Patras, Greece
H. Hadj-Mabrouk	Institut Français des Sciences et Technologies des Transports, France
S. Iwan	Maritime University of Szczecin, Poland
A. Janota	University of Zilina, Slovakia
U. Jumar	Institut für Automation und Kommunikation, Germany
A. Kalašová	University of Zilina, Slovakia
R. Kozłowski	University of Lodz, Poland
J. Krimmling	Technische Uniwersität Dresden, Germany
O. Krettek	RWTH Aachen, Emeritus Professor, Germany
M. Luft	University of Technology and Humanities in Radom, Poland

Z. Łukasik	University of Technology and Humanities in Radom, Poland
M. Michałowska	Katowice Business University, Poland
M. Poliak	University of Zilina, Slovakia
P. Pribyl	Czech Technical University, Czech Republic
C. Pronello	Politecnico di Torino, Italy
K. Rástočný	University of Zilina, Slovakia
A. da Silva	Carvalho University of Porto, Portugal
J. Szpytko	AGH University of Science and Technology, Poland
R. Thompson	The University of Melbourne, Australia
R. Toledo-Moreo	Universidad Politécnica de Cartagena, Spain
A. Weintrit	Gdynia Maritime University, Poland
P. Zalewski	Maritime University of Szczecin, Poland
E. Załoga	University of Szczecin, Poland

Contents

Telematics in Road Transport - Details in Applications

Telematics in Rail and Marine Transport

General About Telematics

Introduction

Mobility of Polish Residents

Piotr Gorzelanczyk[(✉)]

Stanislaw Staszic University of Applied Sciences in Pila, Podchorazych 10, Piła, Poland
Piotr.gorzelanczyk@puss.pila.pl

Abstract. The behavior of Polish residents changes from year to year. Currently, residents are moving from the city center beyond its borders, to smaller towns or to the countryside. In order to learn about their current mobility trends, the article presents the results of mobility studies of the inhabitants of Poland. A survey was conducted where they were asked, among others o: main and secondary destination of their journey, way of reaching the destination, distance to destination and duration of the journey. These studies were carried out on a group of inhabitants including: age, sex, place of residence and professional status.

Keywords: Transport · Mobility

1 Mobility Characteristics

Due to the rapid development of civilization and the increase in the automotive index (Fig. 1), more and more people use private cars to quickly reach their destination, which is mainly work or school. Over the last 10 years, the number of registered cars in Poland increased by nearly 50%. Efficient and fast communication is very important, because of the ability to easily change your location time to move from one place to another in a short time. Many elements affect efficient communication.

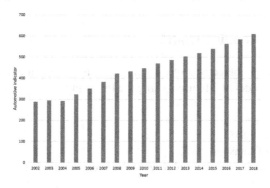

Fig. 1. Automotive index in years 2002 ÷ 2018 [1]

Efficient communication of users depends on their activity. Under which we can distinguish their professional, social, existential, physical and other activities. The activity

J. Mikulski (Ed.): TST 2020, CCIS 1289, pp. 3–14, 2020.
https://doi.org/10.1007/978-3-030-59270-7_1

of residents depends in, among others on the size of the city. We can meet with other activities in the town and with others in the city. Different activities of the inhabitants influence their mobility directions.

When considering this issue, it should be taken into account that society is aging and therefore public transport will have to develop, as well as the development of medical transport.

By the authors of the publication, mobility is defined differently. Szołtysek treats [2] mobility as a daily, routine movement and activities resulting from the reorganization of his personal life, which can include a change of residence or workplace. We can identify her with the movement and any activity of people carried out by means of transport outside their place of residence [3, 4]. On the other hand, Menes [5] presents mobility as mobility associated with the daily movements of residents, usually to work or school.

According to the Treaty on the Functioning of the European Union [6] and the resulting EU transport policy, mobility understood as an element of human activity depends on the person carrying out the journey, the person managing the infrastructure, as well as other users of the transport system related to this mobility [7, 8]. The concept of sustainable development is closely related to the issue of mobility, including economic, environmental and social issues [9–12].

When analyzing the mobility of residents, one should remember about transport challenges, which have been included, among others in the White Paper of 2011 [13] and the Action Plan for Urban Mobility [14]. Taking into account the behavior of urban residents, a policy of sustainable transport development in urban areas should be created. This policy creates plans for sustainable transport development in cities where sustainable urban mobility is the most important element. It is the main goal of the 21st century transport policy [11, 12, 15, 16]. A sustainable transport development plan requires, among others restrictions on daily use of passenger cars for the benefit of increased use of public transport, bicycles or walking [17].

According to the author of the publication, mobility is a daily, routine movement of residents into related to their existence. And this wording is included later in the article.

2 Generalized Mobility Model

Taking into account the objectives of transport activities, we can assume that we can define the mobility model of city users using the following elements [18]:

- user bases - BU,
- mobility structures - SM,
- choice of means of transport - ST,
- a database of characteristics of mobility structure elements - BM,
- travel arrangements - OP.

Taking into account the above elements of mobility, the mobility model - MM, we can present in the form of the equation:

$$MM = \langle BU, SM, ST, BM, OP \rangle \tag{1}$$

In the above model, the set of users takes the form:

$$U = \{1, \ldots, U\} \tag{2}$$

where:

U – is the number of users of the studied mobility .

However, the user was described by vector :

$$\overrightarrow{F(u)} = p(u), gw(u), wz(u), srp(u) \tag{3}$$

where:

$p(u)$ – user's sex
$gw(u)$ – user's age group,
$wz(u)$ – user's state of residence,
$mz(u)$ – user residence,
$srp(u)$ – status on the user's labor market.

The gender of the city user assumed the value (p (u) = 1) for a woman and (p (u) = 2) for a man, while the set of age group numbers:

$$gw = \{1, \ldots, GW\} \tag{4}$$

determines the age of the user. In this case, it was assumed: gw (u) = 1 - up to 18 years, gw (u) = 2 - 18 ÷ 25 years, gw (u) = 3 − 26 ÷ 35 years, gw (u) = 4 - 36 ÷ 45 years, gw (u) = 5 - 46 ÷ 55 years, gw (u) = 6 - over 55 years.

where:
GW – determines the number of all age groups surveyed, in this case equal 6.

In the next step of the algorithm, the residents were divided according to the voivodship of residence in (u). For example (wz (u) = 1) - defines the Lower Silesian Voivodeship, (wz (u) = 2) - Kujawsko-Pomorskie, etc. In this case the formula takes the form:

$$wz = \{1, \ldots, WZ\} \tag{5}$$

where:

WZ – determines the number of all provinces, equal 16.

Then the residents were divided according to their place of residence mz (u). For example (mz (u) = 1) - it specifies a city below 10 thous. residents, (mz (u) = 2) -

determines the town of 10,000 ÷ 50 thousand residents, etc. In this case the formula takes the form:

$$mz = \{1, \ldots, MZ\} \tag{6}$$

where:

MZ – determines the number of all residences equal 6.

Users have been assigned the professional status srp (u). There were distinguished in this case: student (srp (u) = 1), student (srp (u) = 2), working (srp (u) = 3), unemployed (srp (u) = 4), pensioner (srp (u) = 5), other (srp (u) = 6). In this case, the set of professional status takes the form:

$$srp = \{1, \ldots \ldots, SRP\} \tag{7}$$

where: SRP – determines the size of the set, equal to 6.

The next element considered is the user base, which takes the form of the following vector:

$$\overrightarrow{BU} = \{U, F(u)\} \tag{8}$$

The structure of mobility of residents in the mobility model of city users has been presented in the form of:

$$SM = \{PM, PT\} \tag{9}$$

where:

PM – is the mobility point

PT – collection of transport connections.

The places of activity of city users (e.g. place of residence, workplace or school) were taken as the mobility point, i.e. the starting and ending point of travel. They also include an intermediate point (e.g. stations, parking lots, etc.) known as intermediate points. Each component included in the residents' mobility structure contains characteristics specific to transport activities, such as waiting time at the stop, parking cost, etc.

Another of the discussed mobility components is the choice of the means of transport, which we can present in the form of:

$$ST = \{cp, kp, kd, bst, dst, wb, pst\} \tag{10}$$

where:

cp - travel time,
kp - the cost of travel,

kd - travel comfort (in this case the traveler can count on rest, eating a meal, comfortable seating),

bst - travel safety,

dst - availability of means of transport (we can include here extensive point infrastructure, e.g. bus and railway stations, passenger terminal, number of connections per day),

wb - luggage size,

pst - punctuality of the means of transport.

Another of the considered mobility elements is the base of characteristics of elements of the mobility structure defined in the form:

$$BM = \{ZCPM, ZCPT\} \tag{11}$$

where:

ZCPM – referred to as the set of characteristics described at mobility points,

ZCPT – referred to as the set of characteristics described on transport connections.

The last of the elements discussed is the organization of OP travels. The model assumes two variants of travel organization:

$$OP = \{1, 2\} \tag{12}$$

where:

$OP = 1$ – means a one-step variant,

$OP = 2$ – means the three-stage variant.

A one-stage journey is very rare, only if someone travels on foot. We can describe it in the form of:

$$OP1 = \{pp, pk\} \tag{13}$$

where:

pp – is the starting point of the trip,

pk – is the end point of the journey.

Most often, the three-stage journey consists of the following elements: walking, e.g. reaching the stop, public transport, walking to the destination. We can describe this kind of travel in the form of a vector:

$$\overrightarrow{OP2} = \{(pp, n1), (n1, n2), (n2, pk)\} \tag{14}$$

where:

n1, n2 – waypoint number.

Taking into account the mobility model of the inhabitants, presented on the formula describing the mobility model (1.1), the research on the mobility of urban residents was presented below.

3 Study on the Mobility of Polish Residents

3.1 Purpose and Scope of Research

The article aims to study the analysis of communication behavior of Polish residents. The results obtained may form the basis for determining the directions of their mobility. The survey was conducted using a survey among Polish residents in 2019.

3.2 Research Methodology

The research was conducted in the form of surveys. A pilot study was initially carried out, on the basis of which the question sheet was corrected. Then the survey was made available on the Internet to find out the opinions of Polish residents on the questions asked. The survey consisted of 15 closed questions that asked, among others about sex, age, place of residence, number of inhabitants and status on the labor market. The most important questions in the survey concerned the main and additional destination. To this end, the respondents were asked what they were like, how they got there, how far they were from their place of residence and how long the journey took. At the end of the study, each respondent had the opportunity to express an opinion on mobility.

Due to the correctness of the survey results, the survey was conducted on the Internet and was sent to various groups of recipients. If the survey was not fully completed, in this case it was not taken into account. The results of the survey are presented in charts and finally the appropriate conclusions are drawn.

3.3 Research Object

The subjects of the study were the inhabitants of Poland, broken down by gender, voivodship of residence, estimated number of inhabitants and their status on the labor market.

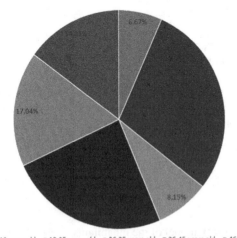

■ under 18 years old   ■ 18-25 years old   ■ 26-35 years old   ■ 36-45 years old   ■ 46-55 years old   ■ over 55 years old

Fig. 2. Age of respondents [own study]

51% were women and 49% men. A significant proportion of people were adults. 37% of them are young people between 18 and 35 years old. People between 36 and 55 years old constituted 41.5% and 14.81% over 55 years old. 6.67% of people declared they were under 18 years of age. The data is presented in Fig. 2.

The largest number of respondents lived in the Wielkopolskie Voivodship - 80%. The remaining 20% were residents of the following voivodships: Kujawsko-Pomorskie, Łódzkie, Mazowieckie, Opolskie, Pomorskie, Śląskie, Świętokrzyskie, and Zachodniopomorskie. This division of respondents is mainly related to the place of residence of the author of the publication (Fig. 3).

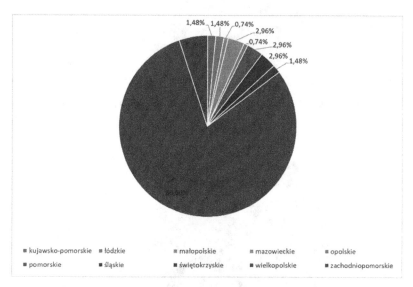

Fig. 3. Place of residence of the respondents [own study]

In the next question, the respondents defined their status on the labor market. Among the respondents, over 63% were working people and almost 21% were students. The remaining group were respectively: students - 8.15%, unemployed 3.7%, retirees and pensioners 2.22%. In addition, it was possible to enter your own answer. 1.48% chose this option. This group includes: persons on maternity leave and self-employed persons. The data is presented in the chart below (Fig. 4).

In the next question, the respondents had the opportunity to choose the estimated number of inhabitants of their town. On this basis, it can be concluded that in a town below 10 thous. the population is inhabited by over 31% of respondents, in the range of 10–100 thousand - 57%, and above 100,000 nearly 12% residents. Detailed data is presented in the chart below (Fig. 5).

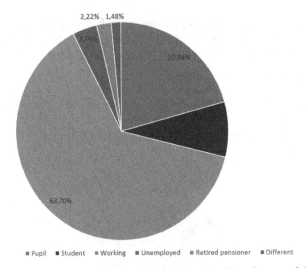

Fig. 4. Status on the labor market of the respondents [own study]

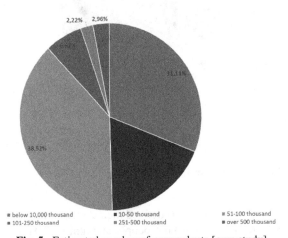

Fig. 5. Estimated number of respondents [own study]

3.4 Findings

The first of the substantive questions of the survey was: how do they get to the main and additional destination? When asked about the main destination, almost 60% of respondents answered that they mainly commute to work, this is confirmed by the age of the surveyed, about 30% commute to school and 8.15% for shopping. When asked about a different destination, 2.12% of respondents answered that they travel to meetings, to the university and to clients. As for the additional destination of the respondents, this is the majority of respondents (almost 76%), indicated shopping. There were also answers about the school (8.15%) and the workplace (9.63%). Almost 7% of the respondents indicated the answer "other", and included: mainly visits of parents, also visits of friends, a walk, tourist travels in the area, leisure, visit to a doctor, socializing. The percentage share of individual answers is presented in Fig. 6.

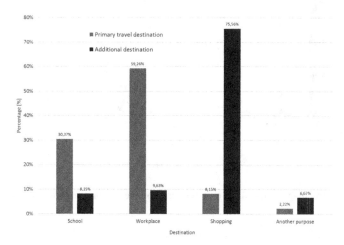

Fig. 6. Daily travel destinations of the respondents [own study]

Then the respondents were asked how they get to the main and additional destination? In response to this question, respondents stated that they mainly use from the car: 57% to the main and 65% to the additional goal. Less than 15% of respondents in both cases reach their destination using public transport, mainly a bus, sometimes a tram. Only 8% of respondents in the main way and 13% in the case of an additional way to reach their destination lead an active lifestyle and walk. As another way of reaching the destination, the respondents also indicated an airplane, trolleybus or motorcycle. The above results are mainly related to the basic activity of people such as the school or workplace as well as shopping. The results are presented in the Fig. 7.

The next question concerned the distance from the place of residence to the main and additional destination. Most of the respondents have from 1 to 5 km and there are over 37% and 44%. 6.67% and 8.15%, below 1 km, and 35.6% in the 6–20 km range, and over 38% of those surveyed. The furthest to the main destination, over 20 km, has over 20% of respondents and over 8% to the additional destination. It is mainly caused by commuting to work or school. The data are presented in the Fig. 8.

The next question was about the duration of the trip to the main and additional destination? In this case, more than 45% of respondents get to the main destination (usually a company or school) within 15 min. At the same time, nearly 58% of respondents get to an additional destination (usually a store).

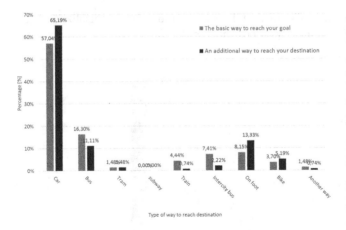

Fig. 7. Percentage of means of transport used by the respondents [own study]

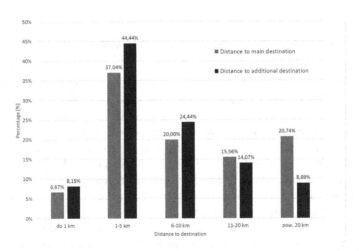

Fig. 8. Percentage of the distance from the place of residence to the main and additional purpose? [own study]

A small number of respondents have a goal of over 1 h. This is closely related to the previous question regarding the distance from the place of residence to the main and additional destination, and this is shown in the Fig. 9.

In the last question, the poll indicated their comments on mobility in their city. These comments include, among others

- Traffic jams during peak hours - 7.00–8.00 and 15.00–17.00. Departures of all buses from the estate almost at the same time and long breaks (about 30 min between subsequent courses).
- Prefer walking, and only for longer trips - by car, bus or train.

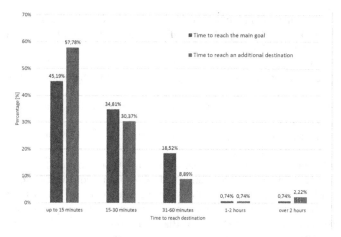

Fig. 9. Percentage of travel time of respondents to the main and additional purpose? [own study]

- Use of a bicycle or motorcycle for recreational purposes during the summer.
- Twice the travel time during peak hours.
- Cycling in your spare time.
- Moving only by car in everyday life.
- Using the car only to travel outside the city.
- Mobility in small towns based on owning a car due to the lack of public transport.

3.5 Discussion on the Results

Based on the data presented, it can be concluded that the respondents mainly use the car, but quite often they choose an active lifestyle: cycling or walking. In addition, it is confirmed that during rush hour access to the destination takes much more time, and public transport is not always correlated with working hours or lessons. The improvement on this condition is the improvement of the functioning of public transport as well as group travel, e.g. many employees to one workplace in one car.

4   Conclusion

Nowadays, many people moving out of town or to smaller cities and towns are forced to use cars because intercity public transport is poorly developed. Opinions on this subject confirm the results of surveys according to which more and more people use their own transport than public transport. The situation is different in big cities, where people come to the city by car and use Park & Ride parking lots, they change to public transport.

References

1. Central register of vehicles and drivers "The number of means of transport in Poland". Accessed Mau 1. 2019. http://www.cepik.gov.pl/statistics. Accessed 12 Dec 2019

2. Szołtysek, J.: Creating Mobility of City Dwellers. Wolters Kulwer, Warsaw (2011)
3. Załoga, E., Dudek, E.: Selected problems of European society mobility. In: Scientific Note-books of the University of Szczecin, Problems of Transport and Logistics from 9, Szczecin, pp. 99–109 (2009)
4. Flejterski, S., et al.: Contemporary Economics of Services. PWN Scientific Publisher, Warsaw (2008)
5. Menes, E.: Socio-economic aspects of the development of individual motorization in Poland. Commun. Rev. (2001)
6. Treaty on the Functioning of the European Union. Official Journal EN Official Journal of the European Union, C 326/49 of 26 October 2012
7. Kruszyna, M.: Traffic engineering and shaping mobility. Commun. Rev. **11-12**, 52–53 (2010)
8. Kruszyna, M.: Railway station as a mobility node. Communication Review **10**, 34–37 (2012)
9. Borys, T.: Measurement of sustainable transport development. In: Kiełczewski, D., Dobrzańska, B. (eds.) Ecological Problems of Sustainable Development, Wydawnictwo Wyższa Szkoła Ekonomiczna in Białystok, Białystok (2009)
10. Litman, T.: Developing indicators for comprehensive and sustainable transport planning. In: Transportation Research Record: Journal of the Transportation Research Board, Vol. 2017/2007, Transportation Research Board of the National Academics, Washington (2007)
11. Chamier-Gliszczyński, N.: Sustainable urban mobility as part of the transport plan Koszalin University of Technology, Logistics, April 2015
12. Banister, D.: The sustainable mobility paradigm. Transp. Policy. T. **15**(2), 73–80 (2008)
13. White Paper on Transport - Plan for creating a single European transport area - striving for a competitive and resource-efficient transport system. European Commission, Directorate-General for Mobility and Transport (2011)
14. European Parliament resolution of 23 April 2009 on an action plan for urban mobility 2008/2217 (INI) (2009)
15. Cervaro, R.: Paradigm shift: from automobility to accessibility planning (Working Paper No. 677). Berkeley CA (1996)
16. Komsta, H., Droździel, P., Opielak, M.: The role of urban public transport in creating mobility of residents. Logistics 1–2 (2019)
17. Kłos-Adamkiewicz, Z.: Mobility plan as a tool for implementing sustainable transport development in cities. Logistics 2/2014
18. Chamier-Gliszczyński, N.: A model of mobility of city users for the needs of transport activities. Urban and regional transport 06/2016

Telematics in Road Transport - General View

Transport System Telematics for Smart Cities Concept - A Case of Addis Smart Mobility Project

Frehaileab Admasu Gidebo[2](✉) and Janusz Szpytko[1](✉)

[1] AGH University of Science and Technology, Ave A. Mickiewicza 30, Krakow, Poland
szpytko@agh.edu.pl
[2] Addis Ababa Science and Technology University, Addis Ababa, Ethiopia
frehaileab.admasu@aastu.edu.et

Abstract. The mobility of people and goods from one place to another point is mounting from time to time in both developed and developing world. This is as result of rapid urbanization and lead to economic benefit in order to secure better income and ease of mobility access. Cities are indeed engines for new jobs and could be able to provide safer and proper movement of peoples and goods. Recently many of developing countries are taking in to consideration the agenda of smart cities and mobility concept and all urban mass transport must operate on low renewable and low emissions fuel, to promote access to sustainable urban transport system. However, many challenges poses the positive impact of cities such as traffic congestion, air pollution, environment degradation, unplanned transport infrastructure, lack of integration of transport system, nonexistence of environment friendly technologies and solutions, lack of government/policy makers commitment, rapid increasing number of motorized vehicles and absence of predictive maintenance mechanism and intelligent parking management systems. Hence, transport telematics is currently emerging technological solution as part of sustainable transport system and connects many of vehicle structures with remotely connected communication devices and is ensuring smart mobility. The subject of this paper is mainly aimed to examine applicability of the innovative management solution of transport telematics technology for smart cities mobility and its environment.

Keywords: Smart cities · Telematics · Mass transportation · Connected mobility · ICT

1 Introduction

The mobility of people and goods from one place to another point is mounting from time to time in both developed and developing world. This is as result of rapid urbanization and lead to economic benefit in order to secure better income and ease of mobility access. Cities are indeed engines for new jobs and could be able to provide safer and proper movement of peoples and goods. Recently many of developing countries are

© Springer Nature Switzerland AG 2020
J. Mikulski (Ed.): TST 2020, CCIS 1289, pp. 17–26, 2020.
https://doi.org/10.1007/978-3-030-59270-7_2

taking in to consideration the agenda of renewable energy and all urban mass transport must operate on low renewable and low emissions fuel, to promote access to sustainable urban transport system [1]. The most serious and recognized problems of urban mobility in recent years become traffic congestion, traffic accidents, and deterioration of the environment because of growing population, increasing urbanization, and increasing car ownership/private motorized vehicles [3]. Not only the mentioned challenges but also lack of proper management/coordination of urban transport network, absence of suitable technologies to overthrow problems, gap of practical knowledge and technical know-how are vulnerable issues of most cities particularly in developing countries [8].

In the other hand, such hurdles are pushing the users to look in to solutions in order to ensure ease and smart mobility by the help of intelligent information sharing system and real time based information for travellers. Moreover, it would be very important when passenger could able to make right decision in terms of choice of route selection that means start to end information, waiting and departure time based on correct, available and real time travelling information [2]. This indicates that information is critical decision making tool in the mobility of peoples and goods. Smart cities are results of having smart information, smart mobility, smart society and smart environment as well as smart system. Eco-driving is among the most important feature of smart city mobility with respect to reduction of fuel cost and giving advice to drivers for safer driving habits.

Obviously urban transport serves as veins to accelerate developments in industry, trade, education, health and other services in many ways. However, urban transport supply and effective management to meet the increasing trip frequency and mobility needs of the people and goods facing critical challenges. Hence, in order to maintain sustainable transport system and concept of smart city mobility principle; there must be existence of non-motorized zones, integration of public transport with bike lane and free walk ways, providing green technology or emission free cars, and implementing technological solutions related to smart cities concept and mobility [4]. Ensuring all the necessary modes of transport in the city has many positive impacts such as income generation, job creation, improving the wellbeing of the life and enhancing faster exchanges in terms of information, business, goods and communications.

Addis Ababa city has been launched the smart mobility project in order to align it with smart city concept mainly focusing to answer the city major mobility challenges. In this move, the project is expected to deploy ITS master plan and its architecture with respect to improvement of traffic management system and creation of integrated transport system with high quality and consistent operational goals. In addition to that, the project is anticipated to build traffic signals, car tracking systems, CCTV, ITS devices, road side sensors and others in main intersection corridors. In this research we tried to find the reasons why this project has been initiated and need assessed prior to implement the project. The following reasons with illustration have been identified as transport and mobility challenges in the city [13];

- **Traffic Congestion**: Despite the relatively low number of registered motor vehicles in Addis Ababa, even by Sub-Sahara African standard and the great success stories with th unprecedented expansion of the road and highway networks in the City in recent years, regular congestion has become a daily experience in the City. This congestion has resulted in a high frequency of traffic accidents, and high green house gas (GHG) emissions levels.

- **Pedestrian/Non-motorised facilities** e.g. walkways: Despite pedestrians constituting more than 55% of the trips generated in the city, there is still a lack of adequate and safe pedestrian facilities and inefficient traffic control and management systems resulting in poor safety conditions and frequent traffic accidents in the City.
- **Public Transport System**: Even though there has been a recent introduction of new public transport systems such as the Light Rail and bus systems such as Sheger and Anbessa, the public transport system remains largely informal. The system is characterised by inadequate supply to meet the growing demands, low quality and service delays due to congestion.
- **Traffic Management System**: Even with increased capacity of road networks, the capacity especially at junctions should be optimised with appropriate traffic management measures. The city still faces traffic management challenges, characterised by inadequately controlled junctions and inefficient enforcement measures and requires other traffic management interventions relating to parking management, signalization management, and road markings.

The city aimed to be benefited from this project as: 1) increasing the efficiency of use of highways- increasing road capacity, 2) improving road safety, 3) reduction in travel cost and time, 4) advance quality of environment through reduction in greenhouse gas emissions. By implementing this project in to the city; drivers-as direct users of the system, travellers, traffic system controllers and decision making officials are among the main frontline users/beneficiary of the system.

2 Objective of the Research

This research study is designed to examine the concept of smart city mobility with transport system telematics as an innovative technological solution. It is also aimed to introduce new approach in to the smart cities concept with integrated networking elements and systems.

3 Rationale of the Research

It is clearly known that transportation is critical factor in a day to day movement of peoples. Providing smooth flow of traffic system, free of accident and properly managed transport network systems as of reduction in pollution, accidents, and climate adverse impact. In the other hand, lack of e-ticketing system-integrated fair collection system, improper data exchanging platform has key consequences in to realization of the concept of smart cities We have listed here some of basic socio-economic problems as result of new roads construction or expansion projects in case of Addis Ababa city.

- Investing for new road construction is very expensive and time taking
- Abuse land use management
- Environment degradation
- Resettlement and right of way issues
- Exisitng utility collapse (Electric, Water and sewerage lines, Tele lines, etc.)

– Relocation of city residents

Using modern technologies in transport sector provides better management of the existing transport infrastructure. The faster growing in technological advancement and solutions in transport sectors is becoming preferred as an option regardless of investing in new road construction and expansion. Optimum decision making with relatively shorter period of time can be achieved by implementing transport system telematics (ITS) solutions and other tools.

4   Architecture of Addis Smart City Mobility Project

In order to workout with architecture of Addis smart mobility, the necessary criteria such as need assessment, functional and system requirements with respect users perspectives have been identified. As part of Intelligent Transport System (ITS) component, the main elements that make the architecture of city smart mobility are Vehicle Tracking System (VTS), Automated Fair Collection System (AFCS), CCTV Surveillance System and Passenger Information System (PIS). The Fig. 1 below is used to show the features of main and sub system of architecture of smart mobility in Addis.

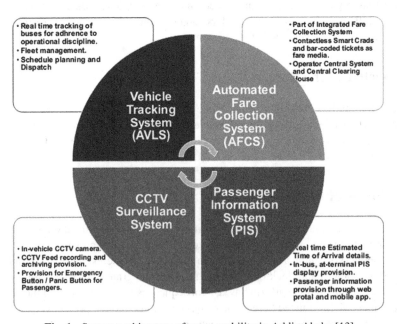

Fig. 1. System architecture of smart mobility in Addis Ababa [13]

According to above Fig. 2, this citywide architecture is fundamentally based on these functional systems and subsystem elements in order to bring the concept of smart city mobility. The system is used to describe the ITS components with respect to availability, reliability and maintainability. Each of the above system has comprised many components and is capable to integrate with each other with respect to exchanging data/information and undertake the tasks as per the functional requirements.

5 Development of Smart Cities Concept and Mobility

Cities and mobility is entirely connected each other. Newly advanced technologies are creating the platform for more connected cities and smart mobility where cities are changing in cutting-edge paradigm called digital cities. Nowadays, everything related with technology is used to call smart; smart phone, smart energy, smart city, smart technology, smart decision etc.

In the concept of smart city, the meaning of technology, future development, and application are based primarily on the finding of methods how to make life easier and it would be the ultimate goal of smart city. Naturally, users of the "smart cities" system are inhabitants of the city, and therefore, the basic concept should support their commercial activities (employment), public activities (education, security, access to health care) and leisure activities (housing, culture, sport) through services [12].

According to [11] research indicates that smart cities can be divided into six different components:

- **smart governance** using ICT infrastructure in order to enhance the efficiency and transparency of public sector organizations in the management of public resources
- **smart economy** employ ICT and related technologies to improve productivity and to enhance and fortify online transactions for the promotion of e-commerce
- **smart human/social capital** aims to improve the people awareness level and promote active public participation through the provision of enriched information
- **smart environment** reduce pollution and resolve other environmental issues with the ultimate goal of improving urban/city sustainability through the use of technology
- **smart living** improved quality of life (e.g., security, housing quality, social cohesion, etc.) through the implementation of advanced technologies
- **smart mobility** focus on the efficient transport of people, attempts to use advanced ICT to optimize logistics and transportation systems and provide efficient, safe, and environmentally friendly services for passengers and freight

In this context, the urban eco-system would become more easier and convenient place as result of connected city system with many of intelligent components. With a connected environment, vehicles, infrastructure, and passengers can exchange information, either through a peer-to-peer connectivity protocol or a centralized system via a 4G or more advanced telecommunication networks [11]. The Fig. 2 is used to illustrate simple basic concept of smart city

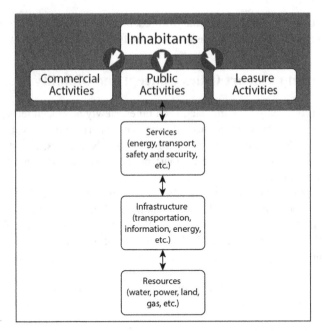

Fig. 2. The basic conceptual diagram of smart city [12]

6 Telematics for Smart Cities Mobility and Sustainable Environment

Application of telematics in to transport system has been widely used as result of its wide range functional performance and large number of system units. It has been widely introduced and implemented in modern systems of intelligent transport management and supervision and development of effective traffic control and maintenance systems [9]. In the other hand, the exchange of information-between vehicles to vehicle (V2V), and vehicle to infrastructure (V2I) and vehicle to passenger (V2P), in the cities could be critical component in transport system. Hence, telematics can facilitate this information exchange up on request or automatically. Therefore, telematics, which is a combination of solutions from areas such as transport, information technology and telecommunications, could serve as a response to the never-ending transport problems in urban areas [7].

Safety and environmental impact factors with respect to using various modes of vehicles in transport system can be seen as significant challenges in the cities. Reduction of greenhouse emission and optimal use of energy consumption in the cities are important parameters since the effects of health of urban community (noise, congestion, climate change, pollution) and severe traffic accidents could be minimized. Combination of new and existing traffic management as well as control of systems for the optimization of traffic flow on the highways are crucial features of traffic management system. Primary feature is the integration of traffic control subsystems (e.g. signalization, motorway and transit control systems) and the provision of dynamic checking in real time in a way that reflects the changing traffic conditions [6]. In the Fig. 3 below, we used to illustrate the advancement of telematics system as part of smart city concept.

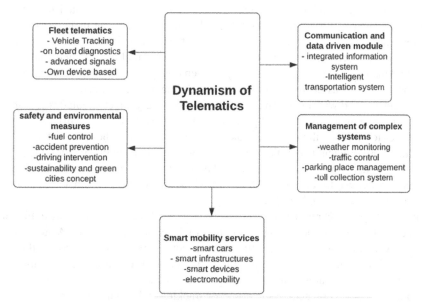

Fig. 3. The schematic diagram of dynamism of telematics system [own study]

Cities are experiencing with increasing number of motorized vehicles year by year. Each year, the carbon emission, air pollution, as well as accidents are increasing. The concept of being smart at smart cities would become under critical situation. Kos-Łabędowicz described that the concept of sustainable urban mobility is associated with objectives concerning optimisation of energy consumption and improvement of environmental indicators in urban areas [7].

The technological solutions are basically needed in order to tackle urban mobility problems and achieve the smart way of living. Collection of traffic data and information from relevant sources will produce positive effect in terms of decision making and data acquisition for users. In this regard, creating the means to use all the available resources in order to make smart mobility should be taken in to considerations. This implies that to ensure smart city mobility it is essential to make available all the means of transportation system in the cities with other integrated resources. Through discussion and awareness creation to all the stake holders in the cities are key step in the smart city and smart mobility concept. Telematics by itself can do nothing unless proper implementation and mechanism to avoid barriers in the cties well addressed. One connected technology solution that plays a significant role in the development of smart cities is vehicle telematics. Vehicle telematics is a tool used to monitor vehicle diagnostics and movements such as trip duration and length, location and CO2 emissions

7 Fleet Telematics Management for Urban Transport System

As we can see new devices and communication technologies are incredibly changing the trends of using the vehicles fleet management and exploitation mechanism. According to whitepaper of Vehco group, fleet (vehicles) management can include a range of functions, such as vehicle financing, vehicle maintenance, vehicle telematics (tracking and diagnostics), driver management, speed management, fuel management and health and safety management. Most importantly, implementing fleet management system has many benefits such as decreased costs for vehicle maintenance, decreased fuel costs, fewer accidents and with increasing productivity and safety. Fleet telematics can allow users to manage their own data and protect car theft as well as improve driver's behavior in order to optimize the decision making in every incident. The smarter the system works the more efficient use of fleet management would happen in the cities and urban transport system [4]. Vehicle telematics also helps to analyze and shape driving behavior and has been proven to reduce speeding, harsh braking and help eliminate preventable deaths caused by distracted driving.

Improving passenger transportation system at certain level in the cities has significant contribution in terms of increasing of quality of the services and access. A sustainable fleet management strategy is the one that aims to reduce environmental impacts through a combination of cleaner vehicles and fuels, fuel-efficient operation and driving systems. The simplified features in fleet management system can be seen in many aspects; for example, eco-driving, geo-fencing, vehicle tracking and fuel monitoring. Now days, many car insurance companies are also giving attention to implement telematics because of its dynamic features and system units. The insurer could give priority on the generated data during driving. At this trend, the fleet telematics has economic implication as result of avoiding unnecessary travel, changing the behavior of driver through ensuring safe driving system, minimizing costs related with congestion, maintenance and ensure productivity in day to day operation, and react to unforeseen events in real time situation.

Among many of fleet telematics features, vehicle tracking system is widely used and accepted by many users. Vehicle tracking system is used to track the location of vehicles in real time through the use of Global Positioning System (GPS) technology. This system can enables to establish a link between individual vehicles (buses) with the operations control center and provides a means to transport agencies to track the buses in real time. This system has also significant role in real-time monitoring of air quality transforming urban areas into smart Cities. Moreover, the concern and growth of using fleet management in transportation system is become rapidly increasing due a number of benefits. However, the level of using this system could be vary from users to users and as well as from country to country.

8 Availability and Reliability Problems of Transport System in Smart City

The disruptions of technologies in the smart cities are critical issues in terms of availability, reliability and maintainability. Smart cities are supposed to be packed with many of technological solution and systems. This has significant impact in any system which is used to undertake the certain task or system. Transport systems, energy systems, ICT and other integrated approaches must evolve systems availability and reliability. When the city population grows the demand for using energy, transportation and mainly ICT solutions could be increasing. The unexpected downing of the system and failure to satisfy the expected demand will cause a divide. Then, the concept of city with respect to all the necessary positive results cannot be achieved easily as stated goal and visions unless availability, reliability and maintainability issues has given prior attention.

Furthermore, there is huge gap between well-developed cities and developing cities in terms of knowledge, practical skill and implementation process. The systems provided might be weak, lacking to work properly, inefficient and most of time it is not user friendly. In order to ensure highest percentage availability of the system devices, there must exist predictive maintenance schedule and fully functional devices. Hence, the system components and devices must show up scalable and capable of delivering required high performance and availability [4]

There is also need for reliability of transportation systems to provide all the necessary and reliable information/data to the travellers. Transport system is highly spectacle for dynamism and changes. Travel times are also most likely dependent on time and space due the basic reasons such as [16];

- recurring congestion such as the rush hour period,
- operational treatments for unexpected disruptions (e.g., traffic signal preemption for emergency vehicles and highway railway at-grade crossings), and
- traffic control devices and different roadway characteristics - weather conditions, emergencies and accidents.

Many systems comprising in the smart city that can be integrated each other and the systems should have flexibility through which the required modifications, additions of new functionalities can be carried out smoothly. Providing error free system is extremely useful for urban citizens and quality, availability and reliability of transport services are becoming vital in promoting urban public transport services [10].

9   Conclusion

The concept of smart city is very wide which comprises various systems and functions. This research critically examined the smart city concept with respect to smart mobility. We have investigated that there is some of misconceptions in the implementation of smart cities. In order to make happen digital cities, there must be awareness in different level from ordinary citizen to government official. Transport system telematics is among the one digital solution in the smart city concept. Implementing transport system telematics and its use in the smart cities has been deeply studied. The connected mobility system is a feature of smart cities as result of availability of data/information, choice to make the possible routes, and safe and comfortable travel system. The systems and devices availability and reliability could be considered as critical issues of the smart cities. Environment, free of emission, congestion and smooth mobility creates novelty in urban transportation through implementing efficient, effective, environmentally friendly and safe solutions in people and goods transportation.

Acknowledgement. The work has been financially supported by the Polish Ministry of Science and Higher Education. The work has been also supported by the UNESCO AGH Chair for Science, Technology and Engineering Education.

References

1. AGENDA 2063: The Africa We Want-A Shared Strategic Framework for Inclusive Growth and Sustainable Development, September (2015)
2. CIVITAS 2010: Policy Advice notes-Innovative information systems for public transport, Austria (2010). www.civitas.eu
3. Gidebo, F.A., Szpytko, J.: How to implement telematics into the urban public transportation system in Addis Ababa, concept study. In: Mikulski, J. (ed.) TST 2019. CCIS, vol. 1049, pp. 302–318. Springer, Cham (2019). https://doi.org/10.1007/978-3-030-27547-1_22
4. Gidebo, F.A., Szpytko, J.: Reliablity assessment in Transport system, Addis Ababa case study. KONBiN J. **49**(4), 27–36 (2019)
5. ITS Report: Design and Supervision of the Installation of ITS/ICT Infrastructure and Systems for Anbessa Bus Operation, Addis Ababa, July (2019)
6. Kalašová, A., Krchová, Z.: Telematic Applications – Key to Improve the Road Safety, Archives of Transport System Telematics (2012)
7. Kos-Łabędowicz, J.: Telematics in sustainability of urban mobility. European perspective, Archives of Transport, System Telematics (2017)
8. Makino, H., et al.: Overview: solutions for urban traffic issues by ITS technologies. IATSS Res. **42**, 49–60 (2018)
9. Mikulski, J., Kedziora, K.: Current condition in the transport telematics. Inf. Commun. Technol. Serv. **8**(4), 84–89 (2010)
10. Mikulski, J.: The possibility of using telematics in urban transportation. In: Mikulski, J. (ed.) TST 2011. CCIS, vol. 239, pp. 54–69. Springer, Heidelberg (2011). https://doi.org/10.1007/978-3-642-24660-9_7
11. Sumalee, A., Ho, H.W.: Overview: smarter and more connected: Future intelligent transportation system. In: International Association of Traffic and Safety Sciences. Production and hosting by Elsevier Ltd. (2018)
12. Svítek, M.: Telematic approach into program of smart cities. Faculty of Transportation Science, Czech Technical University in Prague (2014)
13. TRANSIP: Transport Systems Improvement Project, Addis Smart Mobilty Project, Addis Ababa Ethiopia (2019)
14. Vehco Group (2018). https://www.vehcogroup.com/en/blog/whitepaper/5-trends-fleet-management-2018-and-onwards. Accessed 15 Jan 2020
15. https://ims.tech/opinion/smart-cities-telematics-technology/. Accessed 15 Jan 2020
16. Wu, Z.: Measuring reliability in dynamic and stochastic transportation networks, http://digitalcommons.unl.edu/civilengdiss/77. Accessed 15 Jan 2020

Autonomous Vehicles Within the ITS Systems

Elżbieta Grzejszczyk[(✉)]

European University in Warsaw, Modlińska 51, Warsaw, Poland
elzbieta.grzejszczyk@ewsie.edu.pl

Abstract. The aim of the article is to analyze and present individual areas of remote communication with a moving object, what a vehicle is. A network model of a vehicle will be shown along with typical solutions of on-board automation systems, i.e. ADAS systems. Next, the layered model of the Autosar on-board real-time operating system will be presented, with particular emphasis on the communication protocols responsible for V2X (Vehicle to Everything) and V2V (Vehicle to Vehicle) communication. A hardware layer based on the latest specialized SoC (System on Chip) controllers will be subjected to concise and selective analysis. When discussing the programming capabilities of embedded systems, their ability to communicate in wireless networks (including 5G) will be used on the example of enabling the terminal device (here: vehicle's Gateway/Ethernet) within the surveillance network (TCP/IP). Finally, the application launched that carries out remote communication with the vehicle will be presented as an example of supervision and control in ITS systems.

Keywords: Autonomus vehicles · A network model of a vehicle · ADAS systems · SoC in autonomus vehicles · Remote communication with the vehicle

1 Introduction

"The semi -automated systems (level 2) necessary for autonomus driving are already a reality, while systems for mass-production self-driving cars (level 3) are in development, representing a quantum leap in technology" [6].

2 The Development of Vehicle Autonomy

Automation of vehicle control processes and the need to handle many situations and events occurring while driving has led to the intensive development of many in-vehicle automation systems. Several stages of their development should be distinguished.

The First Control Systems in Vehicles
The first in-vehicle (on-board) controller, the Bosch Motronic four-bit microprocessor-based system (1979) that controlled the injection-ignition system in gasoline engines was implemented in the BMW 732i. The engine control unit (ECU) operation was based on an algorithm saved in the controller's memory. The following parameters, cyclically

© Springer Nature Switzerland AG 2020
J. Mikulski (Ed.): TST 2020, CCIS 1289, pp. 27–40, 2020.
https://doi.org/10.1007/978-3-030-59270-7_3

saved to the controller memory, constituted the algorithm input data: (1) vehicle speed, (2) accelerator pedal position, (3) throttle inlet position /deflection, (4) engine air temperature, (5) engine temperature, (6) position of the engine shaft and camshaft, (7) knock sensor reading, (8) amount of oxygen in the exhaust fumes. These data were/are the basis for calculations and selection of values for fuel injection control systems (fuel dose), inflow of appropriate air volume to engine cylinders as well as calculation of the ignition moment of the mixture. These drivers also had special diagnostic devices and a memory dedicated for errors.Even this brief description of one of the first algorithms controlling the operation of an internal combustion engine shows how important in in-vehicle systems is **the speed** of data transmission between individual systems (e.g. saving information collected from the accelerator pedal pressure sensor and the engine shaft position sensor has a direct impact on controlling its rotational speed). Hence, the next stage in the development of in-vehicle control systems was the introduction of high-speed digital data transmission buses (1980s/90s). The most popular bus used in the automotive industry was/is the CAN bus (Control Area Network), the standard announced by Bosch in 1986 (and in 1987 the first Intel CAN controller). The first implementation of the CAN standard took place in the mass-produced Mercedes-Benz S Model.

The First Communication Standards in the Area of In-vehicle Networks

The introduction of the OBDII (On-Board Diagnostic- set of standards issued by SAE/ISO (Society of Automotive Engineers/International Organization of Standarization), EPA (Environmental Protection Agency) CARB (California Air Resources Board), etc.) standard for automotive components for the American market in 1996 and the EOBD (European On-Board Diagnostic) standard in 2000 for the European market meant an important standardization activity. The introduced standards were aimed at ensuring sufficiently low /permitted level of car exhaust emissions as well as the passive and active safety of a motor vehicle. Diagnostic standardization has forced the development of systems that meet defined requirements (including a standard DLC connector with its own communication standard). All OBDII system procedures, in accordance with the recommendations of SAE (Society of Automotive Engineers), have been included in the relevant standardization documents. Thanks to them: - diagnostic system operating modes have been defined (J2190 standard), - the unambiguous error designation has been introduced (the so-called diagnostics trouble codes, DTC), - the transmission protocol between an on-board computer and a diagnostic reader has been defined (J1850), - the terminology determining the critical emission elements (J1930), - the connector (DLC) used in diagnostic data transmission has been defined (J1962), - the diagnostic information reader has been defined (J1979). The implementation of these standards was supported by the simultaneous development of advanced on-board microcontrollers and fast communication buses.

The Development of Driving Assistance Systems

DAS (Direct Adaptive Steering) Systems. Along with the development of on-board electronics, there was the development of DAS systems replacing mechanical systems with electronic systems. Examples of DAS systems commonly installed in modern cars are, among others, ABS systems (preventing the wheels from locking during sudden braking), ESP (systems stabilizing the car's track whilst cornering) or ASR (anti-skid system during sudden turning the steering wheel) and many more (for example: DAS: ABS – Anti-lock Breaking System, EFI – Electronic Fuel Injection, ASR – AccelerationSlip Regulation, ESP – Electronic Stability Program. DAS systems operating on the basis of reliable and fast networks (CAN, CAN FD, FlexRay) have confirmed their effectiveness in assisting the driver in steering a vehicle [11].

ADAS Systems (Advanced Driver Assistance Systems). The next stage in the development of systems ensuring the active and passive safety of motor vehicles is the development of advanced driver assistance systems while driving. These systems include the following: active cruise control, lane assist, automatic emergency braking, collision warning, vehicle blind spot monitoring, road sign recognition and parking assist. The implementation of these systems is possible thanks to the continuous analysis of the vehicle environment, viz. V2X (Vehicle to Everything) communication described later in the article. In researching the vehicle environment, a key role is played by specialist devices (long-range and short-range radars, lidars, 3D cameras) as well as by intelligent ultrasonic sensors, various acceleration sensors, steering wheel sensors, acoustic sensors, 3D imaging sensors and weather sensors related to, among others, slippery surface detection. These systems installed in /on the vehicle follow the vehicle surroundings in the area assigned to them on an ongoing (on-line) basis (Fig. 1).

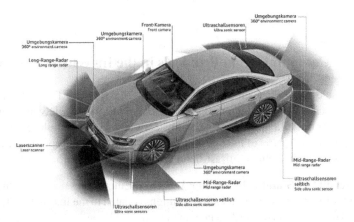

Fig. 1. Driver assistance systems (02/17/17 Technology, Audi A4) [20]

A sample list of devices and systems that track the surroundings of the AUDI A4 vehicle on a regular basis is shown in the following list: long and mid range radars, lidars, front and 360° cameras, different ultra sonic sensors [1]. The common feature of both DAS and ADAS systems is the use of predictive decision algorithms based on data received /collected from a network of intelligent sensors. An important role in the decision making executed by the control system is played by both rapid integration and analysis of the received data as well as the communication with any on-board subsystem responding to the result of this analysis. An example of the above action may be, for example, making a decision about sudden braking when an obstacle appears on the track. Another action may be to reduce the vehicle's own speed after detecting a vehicle approaching too fast from the opposite direction. The actions described above are implemented ultimately by the controlling subsystem, the so-called Body Domain, whose diagram is shown in Fig. 2. Attention is paid to the Head Unit module, which is the basis of the communication interface between the driver /user and the vehicle. The implementation part of the article is devoted to this aspect.

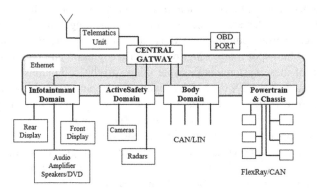

Fig. 2. Model of the Body Domain System [own study]

3   Selected Communication Protocols in the In-Vehicle Networks

Classic in-vehicle networks such as CAN, CAN FD, FlexRay or LIN are well known, software-supported and some of them (CAN, LIN, CAN FD) are widely used. A breakthrough in the control of a motor vehicle and its communication with the external environment was the introduction of the 802.11 Ethernet standard for on-board networks and communication with the vehicle infrastructure by means of cellular networks (2011).

The Ethernet 802.11 Standard in Motor Vehicles. Ethernet has become /is the source of many new software and communication solutions (related to the Internet, LTE cellular networks and the future 5G) described later in the article. The on-board network architecture based on the discussed standard is shown in Fig. 2. The network is managed from the central Gateway /Router. Attention is drawn to the Telematics module that provides the ability to remotely control and communicate with selected network components (vehicle components) and the Infotaintmant domain acting as a multimedia and graphic communication interface between the driver /user and the vehicle, the so-called HMI (Human Machine Interface). Other domains and networks interconnecting them are typical for currently installed solutions.

Communication Protocols in Wide Area Vehicle Networks. Controlling/semi-self-driving of a car in ITS systems requires programming of various new functions. The basis of many of them is communication with the vehicle's environment. The data collected by the in-vehicle system relate to road infrastructure (road signs read, information read ahead of traffic lights at intersections, etc.), data on other road participants (cars or pedestrians in the surrounding area) as well as information obtained from the cloud (map updates, information about traffic jams or traffic obstacles, information about free parking spaces etc.) [12].

The above-mentioned use cases of communication with the vehicle's environment have been divided into appropriate communication modules/fractions [8]. These fractions distinguish among the following data exchange cases: V2V (Vehicle-Vehicle), V2P (Vehicle-Pedestrian), V2I (Vehicle-Infrastructure), V2N (Vehicle-Network), V2D (Vehicle-Device) and V2G (Vehicle-Grid) for electric vehicles. All these modules form V2X (Vehicle to Everything) communication, which can generally be described as a system of data exchange between a vehicle and any entity affecting the vehicle (and vice versa).

The discussed V2X data exchange system uses two types of communication protocols: (1) based on the WLAN protocol (802.11p) and (2) on the Cellular V2X cell network protocol (previously LTE-V2X). V2X protocols and standards were the first to be defined for the V2V and V2I communication[1] (2012) based on the IEEE 802.11p WLAN standard, commonly known as DSRC (Dedicated Short-Range Communications). DSRC uses basic radio communication (5.9 GHz), does not require any communication infrastructure and the exchange of messages between vehicles is carried out in accordance with the principles of ad hoc Networks. In these networks, wirelessly connected vehicles (devices) can act as both a client and an access point (the first manufacturer of cars using DSRC technology was Japan (2016), and next General Motors (2017)) [14]. The second basic technology in V2X communication is the C-V2X (future-oriented in the 5G range) technology, in existing solutions based on cellular LTE (Long Time Evolution) technology. The specification of the standard was published by the 3GPP organization (3rd Generation PartnerShip Project, unites seven telecomunications standard development organizations) w 2016. The advantage of this standard over 802.11p is the ability to communicate in wide area networks V2N (Vehicle-Network) and not only V2V and V2I. The new C-V2X Technology is promoted by 5GAA (5G Automotive Association, 5GAA established by Audi AG, BMW Group, Daimler AG (automotive industry), Samsung, Ericsson, Huawei, Intel, Nokia, Qualcomm, Harman (SoC hardware and software)) and the association's goal is to develop the next generation of standards for end-to-end solution and transportation services (based on 5G cellular networks) in the automotive field. These works are carried out in cooperation with other standardizing organizations such as ETSI, 3GPP and SAE - Society of Automotive Engineers. Currently, C-V2X provides a migration path to systems and services based on 5G technology. The conducted research and comparative analyzes of both technologies (V2X and C-V2X) showed that LTE-V2X proves to have a better communication range and better packet transmission efficiency. It also allows better protection for other types of road users (e.g. pedestrians, cyclists). Summarizing, it should be stated that both technologies, i.e. 802.11p and C-V2X will probably coexist in autonomous vehicle servicing.

The ease of connecting to a motor vehicle seen as a WLAN node and establishing connections with other vehicles in motion is shown in Fig. 3 [9].

---

[1] IEEE 802.11p defines communication V2X in the 5,9 GHz frequency band (5,85–5,925 GHz); European Standard ETSI ITS-5G described IEEE 1609 regulation.

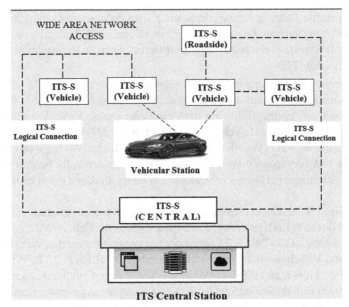

Fig. 3. Logical connection of the vehicular station with ITS environment [own study based on [9]]

"**Central ITS** – may play the role of a traffic operator, services provider or content provider (sometimes may require further connection via Internet); **Road side ITS** - provides applications from the road side; **Vehicle ITS** - provides ITS applications to vehicle drivers and/or passengers. It may require an interface for accessing in-vehicle data from the in-vehicle network or in-vehicle system" [9].

4 Automotive SoC (System on Chip)

Qualcomm (member of 5GAA), an American IT company, has recently been one of the leading producers of technologically advanced embedded SoC systems in the automotive field (based on the Snapdragon series /ARM architecture processors). The company deals with both satellite techniques and advanced ImoD (Interferometric Modulator Display - class of displays using the phenomenon of optical resonance) display technologies as well as with wireless communication. The Qualcomm 9150 C-V2X ASIC system, developed for the automotive market (Fig. 4), implements many complex functionalities necessary to monitor vehicle operation during its movement and, in the future, fully autonomous driving.

The Qualcomm 9150 aims to comprehensively integrate the applications necessary to support both ADAS systems, Infotainment services and cloud management mobile solutions. Some of its functionalities, described in /taken from the technical documentation of the system [17], are listed below:

– Optimized and comprehensive foundational function libraries for computer vision, sensor signal processing, and standard arithmetic libraries

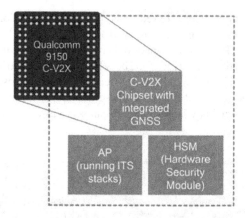

Fig. 4. The Qualcomm® 9150 C-V2X ASIC [own study]

- Safety frameworks from automotive industry leaders, including Adaptive AUTOSAR (Adaptive Autosar is the leading software for automotive on-board systems, discussed later)
- Communication C- V2X – Intelligently connecting the car to surroundings and cloud (V2V, V2I & V2P) - Global navigation satellite services (GNSS) time synchronization (Qualcomm software augments sensor data to improve accuracy, availability, reliability including absolute GPS time, position, and velocity) - Optimizing communications Automotive 4G/5G Platforms with integrated C-V2X technology, including simultaneous WWAN network communication - AI (Artificial Intelligence) tools for improving model efficiencies, as well as optimizing runtime on heterogeneous compute units
- Comprehensive autonomous driving stack for highway functions, such as perception and planning for highway driving functions

and many others described in detail in the technical documentation [17].

5   Software in Automotive Systems

The AUTOSAR consortium has been fostering the development of software standardization for the Automotive industry since 2003. Standardization work provides software tools to support a wide range of automotive applications such as diagnostics, multimedia, ADAS functions, the ECU Gateway framework and many more. The appearance of new instances of using a motor vehicle (in the area of autonomous cars) forced the development of a new programming platform, the so-called Autosar Adaptive Platform (The latest release: v.R4.0 Classic Platform and R18-10 Adaptive Platform; AUTOSAR 4.2-completion to Ethernet as in-vehicle cluster protocol (Ethernet Switch Driver, Ethernet Time Synchronization, SOME/IP) [4]. The platform implements new protocol stacks, mainly for V2X and Ethernet support (from ver. 4.2 on) [18].

The user's Application Layer referred to as SW-C (Software Component) uses the software of lower layers through the so-called RTE (Real Time Environment) interfaces and access points (PORTS) assigned to them, enabling communication with each other and with the outside world (Fig. 5). The VFB (Virtual Function Bus) inter-layer communication created in this way allows for free configuration /design of desired system functionalities, the so-called Services. These Services include typical automotive applications from all domains which should or can serve as a standard for application software.

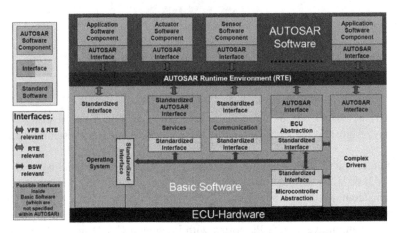

Fig. 5. Diagram of Interfaces facilitated by Autosar [5]

A diagram of how Adaptive Platform performs as a service-oriented system architecture is shown in Fig. 6.

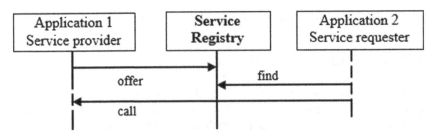

Fig. 6. Service - Oriented Communication [own study based on [19]]

6 Implementation of the Selected Interface of the Autosar Platform

Thanks to the appearance in cars of the latest generation of the screen visualizing both events around the car (e.g. Google maps) as well as events in the on-board system (e.g. fuel consumption, car speed, driving efficiency assessment) as well as presenting various audio/video media services (so-called Infotainment or on-board information and entertainment system; MMI in Audi or i-Drive in BMW), the next stage of driving automation has begun. One example is the vehicle's autonomous parking function (for example: Audi Q7 (2018) or BMW i3 (parks itself at the touch of a smartwach) [6]). The procedure is possible thanks to its comprehensive software. This software is stored in the on-board computer memory and ready to be run by the superior system at any time.

The service can be called either from the car's cockpit (from the Infotainment screen) or from an external mobile device (e.g. Audi smartphone interface), paired with the car using an appropriate communication protocol (Bluetooth, USB or TCP/IP).

The cooperation of devices is implemented by using one of the more popular interfaces of the Adaptive Autosar platform, i.e. the MirrorLink interface (802.11 CCC (IE) Number TS 103 544-18 [2019-10-09] – Car Connectivity Consortium used to advertise availability of MirrorLink support).

MirrorLink ®Ver.1.2 Interface. The interface enables audio/video communication between MirrorLink Server/mobile client device and the Automotive Head Unit/Infotainment car interface called MirrorLink Client [15, 16]. The cooperation diagram of the devices in presented in Fig. 7.

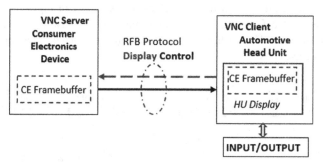

Fig. 7. Cooperation of devices, the car's one and client's for the needs of information exchange (**VNC** – Virtual Network Computing; **RFB** – Remote Framebuffer Protocol (a simple protocol for remote access to any short of framebuffer-based user interface)) [own study]

Setting Up Communication Between Devices

In order to exchange information between the server and the client a connection must be established. A connection session is depicted in diagram Fig. 8, while exchange of information during the session in Fig. 9

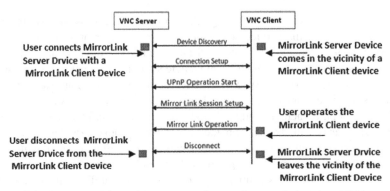

Fig. 8. MirrorLink session sequence diagram [own study based on [10]]

Communication between the devices, preceded by Connection Setup, is based on the UPnP (Universal Plug-and-Play) protocol. This protocol co-works with the TCP /IP and HTTP protocols and enables data transfer between the two devices under the control of one of them. After establishing the UPnP connection, the MirrorLink session is opened and the data /operations of the control application are transferred. After completing all operations, the connection is closed. The exchange of the Basic Meta Information between the client and the server during the session is shown in Fig. 9. The sequence diagram (written in UML language) shows the interactions between devices in order to call the right service. The exchange of information takes place via a common CDB (Common Data Base) bus.

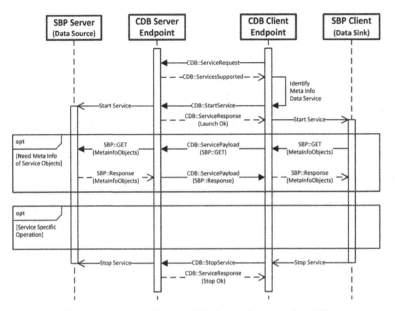

Fig. 9. Sequence diagram of basic service operation [10]

The Common Data Bus (CDB) is a low-bandwidth shared bus, which allows exchanging data between two CDB endpoints, residing in the MirrorLink Server and MirrorLink Client. The Common Data Bus is fully symmetrical, i.e. services can be provided on both endpoints independently from each other.

The endpoints are responsible for marshalling and de-marshalling of all the data from multiple applications passing through the common data bus. A CDB data sink subscribes to a service, provided from a data source service.

The MirrorLink Server has in its resources a list of applications ready to cooperate with Common Data Bus. The Mirror Link Client, by opening the TCP connection to The Mirror Link Server identifies this list of applications.

An example of communication between CDB Endpoints is as follows (Fig. 9):

- ServicesRequest: Requests the list of supported services
- ServicesSupported: Provides a list of supported data services
- StartService: Requests to start a specific service
- StopService: Requests to stop a specific service
- ServicePayload: Delivers service specific payload
- ServiceResponse: Responses to StartService, StopService, ServicePayload
- ByeBye: Terminates the Common Data Bus
- Ping: Message to check the connection
- PingResponse: Responds to a Ping message

7 Implementation of the TCP/IP Standard in the Remote Control of an in-Vehicle Low Power Actuating Device. Simulation [13]

Symbolic visualization of the control system of the low-power car actuating system (EDS10 engine) is shown in Fig. 10. The control is implemented using the TCP/IP network standard (on port 100). The control flow described by the UML sequence diagram shows Fig. 12.

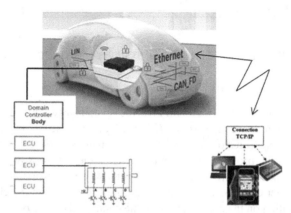

Fig. 10. Connected-mobility. Domain Controller Body connected with the EDS10 actuating system [7]

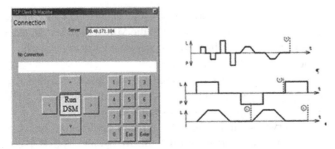

Fig. 11. Server interface in the remote control system - Server/Client mode (on the left) and selected characteristics of the EDS10 system control (on the right) [own study]

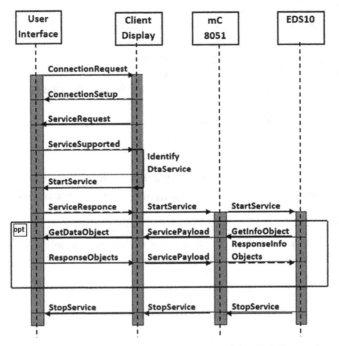

Fig. 12. Sequence diagram of the remote control (TCP/IP) of the EDS10 actuating system [own study]

Remote control of the EDS10 system involves several stages (Fig. 12). After establishing the connection between the server (Mobile Device /Smartphone /Tablet) and the domain client controller (mC8051), information is exchanged between the Server's interactive protocol and the program stored in the Client's memory (mC8051). During the data exchange, the server instructs the client to perform an appropriate control number (from 1 to 9) or other commands regarding sending feedback from the client, e.g. providing the information on the current speed of the controlled device or the current angle of the rotor. Feedback is displayed in the white field of the Server Interface (Fig. 11).

Completion of control /information exchange is initiated by the Server by issuing a Stop command, which the Client accepts by a StopOk response.

Physical implementation of the control is enabled by the server screen, as shown in Fig. 11, with examples of control characteristics. The system was programmed based on the mControler 8051 assembler, while the server interface was made in a high-level language (Visual Basic).

8 Conclusion

The above-described example of the MirrorLink interface sharing the Infotainment cockpit screen with an external mobile device (a smartphone) is an example of various latest solutions in the area of remote vehicle control and checking its status. Some of the features mentioned are: remote checking of the fuel tank level and/or oil level, closing/opening of the vehicle or remote programming of the parking heater. Other applications include sharing a destination programmed on a smartphone and sharing /transferring destination settings directly to the car navigation (service is available in the Audi MMI connect App based on Google Maps and the myAudi portal), assistance that the driver can use while driving. One of the flagship solutions in the discussed area of application is the myAudi App available for all models that have entered the market since mid-2014. The application connects a smartphone with the car and provides the Audi Connect integrated services in three areas: Vehicle, Navigation and Menu [15].

The basis for the development of autonomy in vehicle control is primarily (and still) the development of digital technologies supported by the development of highly advanced computational algorithms in the area of AI (Artificial Intelligence). The expected stage of development in the area of vehicle autonomy is the transformation of ADAS (Advanced Driver Assistance Systems) systems into AD (Autonomous Driving) systems preceded by intensive development of unique platforms for machine learning, computer vision, sensor fusion and smart connectivity.

References

1. Audi A4 – driver assistance system. https://www.audi-mediacenter.com/en/technology-lexicon-7180/driver-assistance-systems-7184. Accessed 10 Apr 2020
2. Audi Media Center. http://audi-mediacenter.pl. Accessed 10 Apr 2020
3. AUTOSAR Classic Platform. https://www.autosar.org/standards/classic-platform. Accessed 10 Apr 2020
4. AUTOSAR Adaptive Platform. https://www.autosar.org/standards/adaptive-platform. Accessed 10 Apr 2020
5. AUTOSAR interfaces. https://www.autosar.org/standards/application-interfaces, https://automotivetechis.files.wordpress.com/2013/03/autosar-interfaces.png?w=736. Accessed 10 Apr 2020
6. BMW i3 parks itself at the touch of a smartwatch. https://www.driving.co.uk/news/news-bmw-i3-parks-itself-at-the-touch-of-a-smartwatch, and Roads to Autonomus driving. https://www.bmw.com/en/innovation/the-development-of-self-driving-cars.html. Accessed 10 Apr 2020
7. BOSCH products and services. https://www.bosch.com/products-and-services/connected-mobility. Accessed 10 Apr 2020

8. ETSI - European Telecommunications Standards Institute. https://www.etsi.org/technologies/automotive-intelligent-transport. Accessed 10 Apr 2020

9. ETSI TS 102 894-1 V1.1.1]: Users and applications requirements; Part 1: Facility layer structure, functional requirements and specifications

10. ETSI TS 103 544-2 V1.3.1 (2019-10): Publicly Available Specification (PAS); Intelligent Transport Systems (ITS); MirrorLink®; Part 2: Virtual Network Computing (VNC) based Display and Control

11. Grzejszczyk, E.: Vehicle stability control and supervision based on CAN network. Part II. GSTF J. Eng. Technol. Singapore, **2**(4), 38-44 (2014)

12. Grzejszczyk, E.: GPRS network as a cloud's tool in EU-Wide real time traffic information services. In: Mikulski, J. (ed.) TST 2016. CCIS, vol. 640, pp. 59–71. Springer, Cham (2016). https://doi.org/10.1007/978-3-319-49646-7_6

13. Gryszpanowicz, B.: The implementation of Wide Area Network for remote communication with motor vehicle. MA thesis, Electrical Dept., /04 Warsaw University of Technology, Thessis Advisor: Grzejszczyk E

14. Jarkowski, J., Grzejszczyk, E., Wydro, K.: Vehicle collision protection systems using DSRC and 5G communication standards, ITS Polish Seminar "Science-Business, 1st Edition, Department. Transport, Warsaw University of Technology (2018)

15. Publicly Available Specification (PAS); Intelligent Transport Systems (ITS); MirrorLink®; Part 5: Common Data Bus (CDB); ETSI TS 103 544-5 V1.3.1 (2019–10)

16. Publicly Available Specification (PAS); Intelligent Transport Systems (ITS); MirrorLink®; Part 13: Core Architecture; (ETSI TS 103 544-13 V1.3.1 2019-10)

17. Qualcomm 9150 C-V2X ASIC: https://www.qualcomm.com/products/qualcomm-9150-c-v2x-chipset. Accessed 10 Apr 2020

18. Specification of TCP/IP Stack AUTOSAR CP Release 4.3.1.pdf. https://www.autosar.org/fileadmin/user_upload/standards/classic/4-3/AUTOSAR_SWS_TcpIp.pdf. Accessed 10 Apr 2020

19. Specification of Communication Management AUTOSAR AP R19-11/ 11.2019

20. Image No: A1711285, Copyright: AUDI AG, 02/17/17 Technology, Rights: Use for editorial purposes free of charge (2017)

Artificial Intelligence Applied in the Road Transport - A Scientific Literature-Based State-of-Art

Aleš Janota$^{(\boxtimes)}$ and Roman Michalík

University of Žilina, Univerzitná, 8215/1, Žilina, Slovakia
{ales.janota,roman.michalik}@feit.uniza.sk

Abstract. The paper presents a scientific literature-based analysis of artificial intelligence applications identified in the domain of road transport. The investigation period covered the years 2017–2019. The state-of-art was analyzed using the scientific literature sources indexed in the databases Web of Science, Scopus and IEEE and followed various aspects (mostly solved problems, participation of individual countries and institutions, funding, publishing houses, trends, etc.).

Keywords: Artificial intelligence · State-of-art · Road transport · Literature · Survey

1 Introduction

The track of artificial intelligence (AI) is quite long, starting at the Dartmouth conference in 1956. An abundance of definitions brings different understandings of what AI really is. According to The New Oxford American Dictionary (3rd ed.): AI is "the theory and development of computer systems able to perform tasks that normally require human intelligence, such as visual perception, speech recognition, decision making and translation between languages". However, many people are confused about the content of AI since it is associated with movies, it is a very broad topic and we use AI applications in our daily lives even without realizing it (in our smartphones, smart appliances, web-services, etc.), [1]. Disrespecting arguments of some philosophers and religious figures, that true intelligence can never be achieved by a mere machine [2], multiple scientific experiments aiming to achieve superhuman intelligence (here referred to as superintelligence) appears to be a major and most important topic for future of humans. Seemingly, several paths can lead us to superintelligence, which increases our chances that some of them will be successful: whole brain emulation; biological cognition; brain-computer interfaces; collective superintelligence; artificial intelligence [3]. Nowadays we face two technological megatrends - global interconnecting of the world (thanks to the Internet) and dynamic development of AI technologies. All of the above approaches have different eventual outcomes and will bring a lot of controversy, ethical objections, violations of currently applicable laws, serious medical complications or other even unsuspected problems. There is no consensus among scientists about the future development of AI, about

J. Mikulski (Ed.): TST 2020, CCIS 1289, pp. 41–53, 2020.
https://doi.org/10.1007/978-3-030-59270-7_4

future forms it will potentially take, timescales and potential impacts on human society. Some authors distinguish and discuss three forms of AI (sometimes called calibers [1]):

- ANI - Artificial Narrow Intelligence (or Weak AI): it specializes in one area only and does no other thing;
- AGI - Artificial General Intelligence (or Strong AI, or Human-Level AI): In this case, computers are as smart as humans are;
- ASI - Artificial Superintelligence: based on Nick Bostrom's definition, it is much smarter than the best human brains in practically every field, including scientific creativity, general wisdom and social skills."

Our civilization is a human civilization of machines – we use technology to improve our physical a psychical horizons. Machine can do things faster; however, there is nothing the machine can do and a human cannot. The machine still lacks common sense and we work over the ANI level; the other levels lie ahead of us. The controversial question "What will happen after we reach AGI?", has no answer yet. Some scientists refer to this aftermath as the Life 3.0. There are many visions – from optimistic (see e.g. the "Omega tale" in [4]) to absolute catastrophic ones. Ethical aspects are usually open and discussed within the context of safety issues of particular AI-based technologies. According to [4], there are three distinct thought streams (schools) represented by the following viewpoints:

- Techno-skeptics: "We shouldn't worry since human-level AGI won't happen in the foreseeable future (at least hundreds of years)";
- Digital utopians: "We shouldn't worry - it will happen but is virtually guaranteed to be a good thing (digital life is the natural and desirable next step in the cosmic evolution)";
- Members of the beneficial-AI movement: "Concern is warranted and useful, because AI-safety research and discussion now increases the chances of a good outcome (the goal should be to create not undirected intelligence, but beneficial intelligence)".

In academic circles we can meet 2 viewpoint streams – one group thinks that AI represents an existential threat to humanity but its contribution is higher than costs; another group appreciates benefits of AI technologies and concentrates on justice, responsibility and transparency. AI penetrates all areas of our lives and have increasing effect on many processes. Progress in AI creates new opportunities for transport domain and our mobility. Implementation of AI could enable drastically reducing (maybe even bringing to zero) traffic accidents and traffic fatalities. Road traffic with its unflattering accident statistics seems to be the most promising sector for applications. On the other side, finding safe behaviors for AI is a much more difficult problem than it may have initially seemed - to be safe, AI will likely need to be given as extremely precise and with complete definition of proper behavior, but it is very hard to do so [2]. In principle we could distinguish between two situations: AI is programmed to do something devastating (being abused), and AI is programmed to do something beneficial, but it develops and use a destructive method for achieving its goal (being too imperfect).

Within this context, this paper presents an analysis of the state-of-art of AI applied in the domain of road transport, performed on scientific literature indexed in world scientific databases Web of Science (WOS), Scopus and IEEE during the recent period 2017–2019. The authors' intention was to answer several principal questions such as "What mostly solved problems (using AI) could be identified?", "How individual countries are participating in the publication process?", "What is share between academia and industry?", "How funding of AI & transport research projects looks like?", "What publishing houses are involved mostly in documenting achievements?", "What trends could be seen?", etc.

2   AI Applications in Road Transport-Oriented Literature

From a methodological point of view, the baseline data were obtained by crawling the following three databases:

- "Web of Science with Conference proceedings" (apps.webofknowledge.com): the most powerful research engine, delivering our library with best-in-class publication and citation data for confident discovery, access and assessment. We used the option "All Databases"; and searched for the terms "artificial intelligence" & "road" & "transport" within the "Topic" settings;
- "Scopus" (www.scopus.com): a citation and abstract database of peer-reviewed literature that can be used by researchers to determine the impact of specific authors, articles/documents, and journals. We searched for the same terms "artificial intelligence" & "road" & "transport" within the "Article title, Abstract, Keywords" settings;
- "IEEE Xplore" (ieeexplore.ieee.org): a research database for discovery and access to journal articles, conference proceedings, technical standards, and related materials on computer science, electrical engineering and electronics, and allied fields. We again used and advanced search for the terms "artificial intelligence" & "road" & "transport" in "All Metadata" settings.

The search was performed separately for the individual years 2017, 2018 and 2019. After automatic processing the manual check had to be performed to exclude misclassified sources (e.g. papers addressing railway transport domain without any connection to road transport), several patents (the case of WOS database) and so. Other data processing details and problems are mentioned when presenting and discussing the final findings. Data were collected on 20th January 2020, which means that due to the gradual process of inserting papers into the databases some of datasets should be considered incomplete. Absolute numbers of found items are depicted in Fig. 1 (Note: WOS core collection was not separately considered since contained only 6, 4 and 10 papers for the years 2017 up to 2019, respectively).

2.1   Representation of Countries

Another follow-up aspect was the representation of the countries according to researchers' origin. Figure 2, 3 and 4 show percentages of participating countries. Only those countries are individually named that have percentage ≥ 5%. Total numbers of countries were (in the time order from 2017 to 2019) WOS: 20, 24, 20; in Scopus: 27, 22, 21; and in IEEE: 15* , 29 and 34 (*Note: some countries could not be identified).

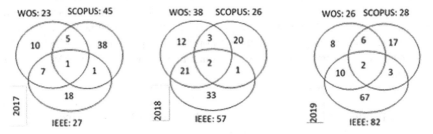

Fig. 1. Absolute numbers of papers obtained from indexed databases [own study]

Fig. 2. WoS: Countries' participations over the period 2017–2019 [own study]

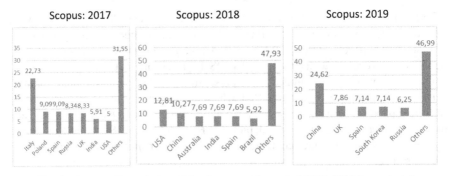

Fig. 3. Scopus: Countries' participations over the period 2017–2019 [own study]

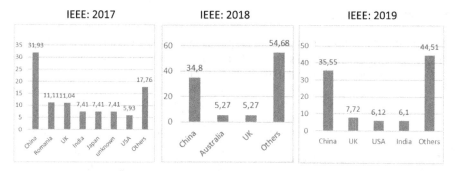

Fig. 4. IEEE: Countries' participations over the period 2017–2019 [own study]

2.2 Academia Versus Industry

The next graph (Fig. 5) shows how the academic sector (here called "Academia", covering universities, academies, government research institutions, etc.) and the "Industry" (private companies, industrial enterprises, etc.) contributed to individual databases. The given data are estimations only since sometimes it was not possible to distinguish between both sectors (e.g. both public and private universities considered together). Some affiliations could not be identified at all (here declared "Unknown").

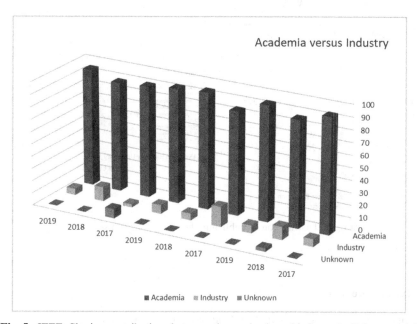

Fig. 5. IEEE: Sharing contributions between the academia and industry in % [own study]

2.3 Publishing Houses

The graph in Fig. 6 shows how individual publishing houses were represented in the analyzed sources. Those having share ≥ 5% are given separately, publishers with lower shares are presented together within the group of "Others".

Fig. 6. Distribution of publishing houses in % [own study]

2.4 Type of the Source

The graph in Fig. 7 shows proportions of "journals" and "proceedings papers" (including book chapters) analyzed for the given databases and calendar years.

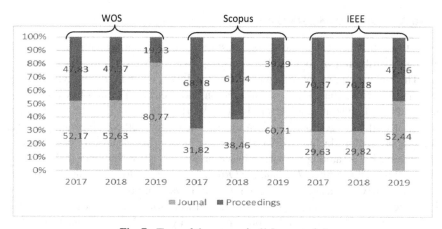

Fig. 7. Type of the source in % [own study]

2.5   Funding

The graph in Fig. 8 reflects analyzed data about identified funding – based on acknowledgment statements included in publications. In the case of multi-source funding it was practically impossible to find exact proportion, therefore arithmetic estimations were applied instead.

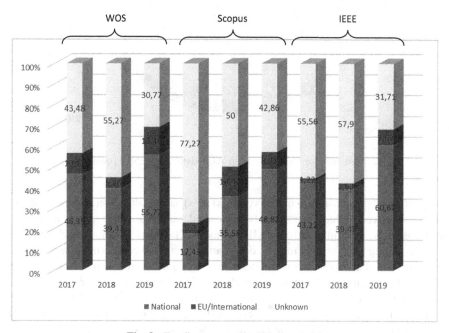

Fig. 8. Funding sources in % [own study]

2.6 An Analysis of WoS 2019 Data

The most attention has been paid to the latest data, i.e. the sources published in 2019. The rough distribution of topics addressed by papers indexed in WoS is depicted in Fig. 9. The highest number of solved problems (ca 35%) covered different types of prediction and identification tasks, e.g. formulation and prediction of taxi-based mobility using conditional generative adversarial network-driven learning [5]; automated identification of traffic congestion, based on machine learning methods (Neural Networks (NN), Support Vector Machine (SVM)) [6]; online monitoring strategy for bus routes on a collaborative basis (among the users), based on the k-Nearest Neighbor (k-NN) algorithm and 2 new algorithms [7]; dynamic Origin-Destination flows by transport modes using mobile network data [8]; predicting traffic flows using multi-layered perceptron and deep learning networks [9]; predicting bus traffic flows using NN [10]; identifying mode of transportation from the sound recorded by a user's smartphone using deep learning [11]; and others.

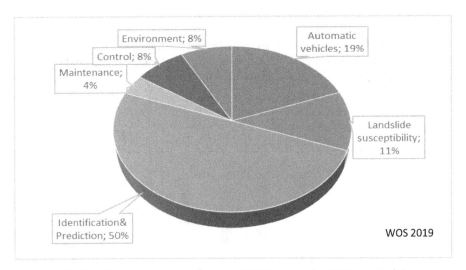

Fig. 9. AI-related topics addressed in WOS database in 2019 [own study]

The group of papers on Automated Vehicles (AVs) have dealt e.g. on a connection and correlation between vehicle (vertical) dynamics and the performance of vision systems with the use of deep learning and other ML methods [12]; a deep-learning-based approach for range finding [13]; or lane merge coordination using and comparing 9 various ML algorithms [14]. Papers dealing with landslide susceptibility used various conditioning factors as the inputs to ML methods to classify [15], map [16] and/or predict [17]. Environment-related papers dealt on models to estimate commuting emissions with the use of classification and regression trees (could be included in prediction tasks as well) [18] or optimize power of electrical vehicles in the context of smart cities [19]. Control tasks addressed adaptive traffic control and traffic signal timing strategies, supported with reinforcement learning [20] or realized using fuzzy rules [21]. Maintenance-oriented AI application was about simulation of the deterioration of the roads' network [22]. Ca 38% of analyzed papers assumed some kind of image processing (static or dynamic), practically all papers proposed some kind of a model. Almost all papers (ca 97%) utilize some kind of ML.

2.7 An Analysis of Scopus 2019 Data

Unlike the previously mentioned database, orientation of sources in the Scopus database seems to be much broader and more diverse. Rough distribution to identified thematic groups (obviously with fuzzy borders) is available in Fig. 10.

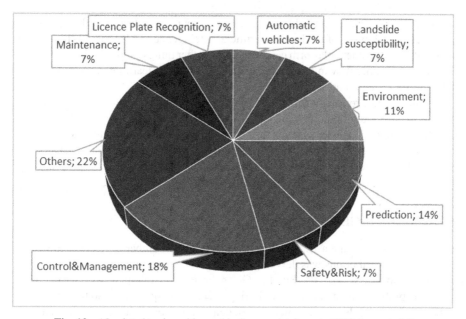

Fig. 10. AI-related topics addressed in Scopus database in 2019 [own study]

The largest group (Others, 22%) brings together sources of a very specific nature or hardly assignable to other followed. According to the nature of the output, 21% sources have a character of study and/or review, in the remaining number of sources (79%) the authors propose, use, test and/or evaluate some kind of a specific model, method, algorithm, etc.

To refer some of the sources assigned to the "Others" group (covering mostly studies and reviews) we'd mention at least the following papers: [23] considers a labelled network (describing a public transport system) controlled or owned by different agents; this approach makes possible to allocate the worth to those agents; [24] describes the main characteristics of traffic cooperative systems architecture and some of its applications; [25] tries to identify the form of a new digital economy in Russia, considering the territorial structure of the country and identifying signal delay in a telecommunication network as the most critical parameter for controlling future smart objects; [26] focuses on computerization (electronic processing) of documents in transport domain as a pre-requisite for the 4th industrial revolution; [27] introduces the basic concept of future Internet of Vehicles (as a technological application of IoT) and discusses its architecture and key technologies; [28] defines an intelligent pavement, including its architecture, major technologies, design and construction methods.

Another broad group contained in Fig. 10 includes topics addressing management, control (and partially also planning) tasks. As typical representatives, we could mention [29] dealing with traffic signal control at a single isolated intersection relying on super-vised learning (NN); [30] about the road traffic management system using ITS and NNs; or [31] using floating taxi data from Thessaloniki city to apply spatiotemporal dynamics identification techniques among urban road paths.

The group of "Prediction" (11%) contains e.g. sources about traffic flow forecast-ing suggesting adoption of explainable artificial intelligence (xAI) tools [32]; or about smart traffic management platform capable (among other things) of predicting the spatial propagation of traffic flow in specific urban segment or deep learning based traffic flow prediction for critical road segments [33].

An interesting group devoted to risk and safety issues (7%) investigates the risk structure of Semi-Autonomous Vehicles [34] or wants to improve safety and efficiency of the Underground Express Systems through a novel on-ramp metering strategy [35].

Other minor groups overlap completely or partially with the similar groups of the WOS database. Generally, unlike WOS sources (38%), proportion of articles dealing with or using image-based analysis is slightly smaller here, only 25%.

2.8   An Analysis of IEEE 2019 Data

Among the analyzed databases, this contained the highest number of items. The largest percentage of contributions was devoted to "monitoring, detection and analysis" of cer-tain road transport aspects (44%, Fig. 11). Given the diversity of topics, we have included here all the problems related to the monitoring of selected aspects of road transport (e.g. classification of vehicle types, vehicle logos, congestions, or license plate recognition); analysis of various transport related aspects (e.g. analysis of origin-destination flows, driver's route choice or brake intention, the influence of altitude change on driver's behavior), and detection/identification of specific characteristics or events (e.g. incidents, accidents, fatigue driving, pickpocketing gangs).

The second largest group (35%) was devoted to the issue of prediction – most often prediction of traffic flows, traffic speed, congestion, arrival times, customers' demands (for taxi, for free-floating bike sharing). Approximately 30% out of all solutions were based on some kind of static and/or dynamic image processing.

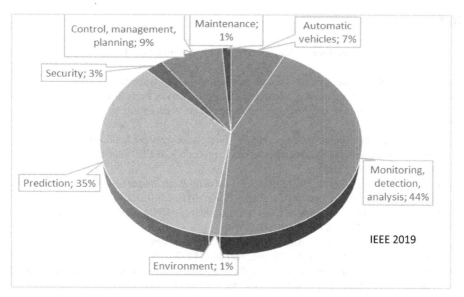

Fig. 11. AI-related topics addressed in IEEE database in 2019 [own study]

3 Conclusion

The aim of this paper was to study the impact and importance of artificial intelligence in the field of road transport in the last three years, with a special interest in the last year 2019. Following this goal, we conducted a systematic literature review of scientific articles (journals and conferences) related to artificial intelligence in road transport. Articles were taken from three popular databases "Web of Science", "Scopus" and "IEEE". The search was conducted separately for each year and each database and was followed by detailed expert review to avoid articles misclassification due to improperly defined key words (e.g. several found articles were unrelated or only marginally related to the road transport). This was followed by a categorization of articles according to several selected criteria, some of which having a sociological-like dimension. Special attention was paid to identification of prospective application areas (defined on the expertise approach), significantly based on keywords processing and detecting AI methods (e.g. machine learning, expert/knowledge systems, decision support systems, evolutionary techniques, static and/or moving image processing methods). The results of the analysis may be beneficial for researchers in academia or industry working in the road transport field.

Acknowledgment. This work has been supported by the Educational Grant Agency of the Slovak Republic KEGA, Project No. 014ŽU-4/2018 "Broadening the content in a field of study with respect to the current requirements of the industry as regards artificial intelligence methods and IT" (http://ui.kris.uniza.sk).

References

1. Urban, T.: The AI Revolution: Our Immortality or Extinction. Wait But Why, e-book, pp. 51 (2015)
2. Armstrong, S.: Smarter than us. The rise of machine intelligence, MIRI (2014)
3. Bostrom, N.: Superintelligence. Strategies. Oxford University Press, Paths, Dangers (2014)
4. Tegmark, M.: Life 3.0: being human in the age of artificial intelligence. Alfred A. Knopf (2017)
5. Yu, H., et al.: Taxi-based mobility demand formulation and prediction using conditional generative adversarial network-driven learning approaches. IEEE Trans. Intell. Transp. Syst. **20**(10), 3888–3899 (2019)
6. Li, Y., et al.: Direct generation of level of service maps from images using convolutional and long short-term memory networks. J. Intell. Transp. Syst. **23**(3), 300–308 (2019)
7. Sa, J., et al.: Online monitoring of buses information using KNN, ATR and DMC algorithms. IEEE Latin Am. Trans. **17**(4), 564–572 (2019)
8. Bachir, D., et al.: Inferring dynamic origin-destination flows by transport mode using mobile phone data. Transp. Res. Part C – Emerg. Technol. **101**, 254–275 (2019)
9. Pamula, T.: Impact of data loss for prediction of traffic flow on an urban road using neural networks. IEEE Trans. Intell. Transp. Syst. **20**(3), 1000–1009 (2019)
10. Liu, P.B.: Improved spatio-temporal residual networks for bus traffic flow prediction. Appl. Sci. Basel, **9**(4) (2019). Article Number 615
11. Wang, L., et al.: Sound-based transportation mode recognition with smartphones. In: IEEE International Conference on Acoustics, Speech and Signal Processing (ICASSP), IEEE, pp. 930–934 (2019)
12. Weber, Y., Kanarachos, S.: The correlation between vehicle vertical dynamics and deep learning-based visual target state estimation: a sensitivity study. Sensors, **19**(22) (2019). Article No. 4870
13. Yashrajsinh, P., et al.: DeepRange: deep-learning-based object detection and ranging in autonomous driving. IET Intelligent Transp. Syst. **13**(8), 1256–1264 (2019)
14. Sequeira, L., et al.: A lane merge coordination model for a V2X scenario. In: European Conference on Networks and Communications (EUCNC), IEEEE, pp. 198–203 (2019)
15. Chen, W., et al.: Novel hybrid artificial intelligence approach of bivariate statistical-methods-based kernel logistic regression classifier for landslide susceptibility modelling. Bull. Eng. Geol. Environ. **78**(6), 4397–4419 (2019)
16. Hong, H., Liu, J., A-Xing, Z.: Landslide susceptibility evaluating using artificial intelligence method in the Youfang district (China), Environ. Earth Sci. **78**(15) (2019). Article No. 488
17. Chen, W., et al.: Applying population-based evolutionary algorithms and a neuro-fuzzy system for modeling landslide susceptibility. CATENA **172**, 212–231 (2019)
18. Ahmad, S., et al.: Spatially contextualized analysis of energy use for commuting in India. Environ. Res. Lett. **14**(4) (2019). Article Number 045007
19. Aymen, F., Mahmoudi, Ch.: A novel energy optimization approach for electrical vehicles in a smart city. Energies **12**(5) (2019). Article No. 929
20. Aslani, M., et al.: Developing adaptive traffic signal control by actor-critic and direct exploration methods. In: Proceedings of the Institution of Civil Engineers - Transport, vol. 172, no. 5, pp. 289–298 (2019)
21. Thamilselvam, B., et al.: Coordinated intelligent traffic lights using Uppaal Stratego. In: 11th International Conference on Communication Systems & Networks (COMSNETS), IEEE, pp. 789–794 (2019)

22. Yacou, S., Ouali, M.S.: Using artificial intelligence for block maintenance of pavement segments with similar degradation profile. In: Annual Reliability and Maintainability Symposium (RAMS 2019) - R & M in the Second Machine Age - The Challenge of Cyber Physical Systems (2019)

23. Algaba, E., Fragnelli, V., Llorca, N., Sánchez-Soriano, J.: Labeled network allocation problems. An application to transport systems. In: Nguyen, N.T., Kowalczyk, R., Mercik, J., Motylska-Kuźma, A. (eds.) Transactions on Computational Collective Intelligence XXXIV. LNCS, vol. 11890, pp. 90–108. Springer, Heidelberg (2019). https://doi.org/10.1007/978-3-662-60555-4_7

24. Mandžuka, S.: Cooperative systems in traffic technology and transport. In: Karabegović, I. (ed.) NT 2018. LNNS, vol. 42, pp. 299–308. Springer, Cham (2019). https://doi.org/10.1007/978-3-319-90893-9_36

25. Blanutsa, V.I.: Territorial structure of the russian digital economy: preliminary delimitation of smart urban agglomerations and regions. Region. Res. Rus. **9**(4), 318–328 (2019)

26. Mxoli, A., et al.: A modernization of the South African licensing department's processes to improve service delivery. In: Proceedings of the European Conference on e-Government, ECEG, vol. 2019 - October, pp. 213–219 (2019)

27. Xu, Z., et al.: A review on intelligent road and its related key technologies. Zhongguo Gonglu Xuebao/China J. Highway Transp. **32**(8), 1–24 (2019)

28. Wang L., et al.: Development and prospect of intelligent pavement. Zhongguo Gonglu Xuebao/China J. Highway Transp. **32**(4), 50–72 (2019)

29. Kurmankhojayev, D., et al.: Road traffic demand estimation and traffic signal control. In: ACM International Conference Proceeding Series, 2 (2019)

30. Brzozowska, A., et al.: Analysis of the road traffic management system in the neural network development perspective. East.-Eur. J. Enterp. Technol. **2**(3–98), 16–24 (2019)

31. Myrovali, G., Karakasidis, T., Charakopoulos, A., Tzenos, P., Morfoulaki, M., Aifadopoulou, G.: Exploiting the knowledge of dynamics, correlations and causalities in the performance of different road paths for enhancing urban transport management. In: Freitas, P.S.A., Dargam, F., Moreno, J.M. (eds.) EmC-ICDSST 2019. LNBIP, vol. 348, pp. 28–40. Springer, Cham (2019). https://doi.org/10.1007/978-3-030-18819-1_3

32. Barredo-Arrieta, A., et al.: What lies beneath: a note on the explainability of black-box machine learning models for road traffic forecasting. In: 2019 IEEE Intelligent Transportation Systems Conference, ITSC 2019, 8916985, pp. 2232–2237 (2019)

33. Ryan, C., et al.: Semiautonomous vehicle risk analysis: a telematics-based anomaly detection approach. Risk Anal. **39**(5), 1125–1140 (2019)

34. Shao, M., et al.: Left-side on-ramp metering for improving safety and efficiency in underground expressway systems. Sustainability (Switzerland) **11**(12), 3247 (2019)

The Main Assumptions
for Functional-Operational Configuration
of Tasks in Transport Projects

Grzegorz Karoń[1(✉)] and Jerzy Mikulski[2]

[1] Silesian University of Technology, Krasińskiego 8, Katowice, Poland
grzegorz.karon@polsl.pl
[2] University of Technology, Rolna 43, Katowice, Poland
mikulski.jurek@gmail.com

Abstract. The paper presents main assumptions for functional-operational configuration of tasks in transport projects (FOCT). The assumptions include a variety of decision problems related to shaping transport systems, decisions of transport users, and traffic flows in urban transportation network. The following issues were characterized, i.e.: area of urban agglomerations and traffic zones, urban transportation systems, activity and transport needs of users of urban area, traffic control and management using ITS systems, mobility management using sustainable urban mobility plans, functional improvement of transport systems in the scope of transport services. The formal description of functional-operational configuration of tasks in transport projects (FOCT) was discussed.

Keywords: Transport systems · Intelligent transportation systems · Mobility management · Functional-operational configuration of tasks in transport projects

1 Introduction

The continuous growth of individual motorization and the related congestion of road and street in the cities and urban agglomerations results, among others, in unsatisfactory level of quality of life. One of the possibilities to improve the situation is the implementation of intelligent transport systems (*ITS*). Unfortunately, the complexity of urban agglomerations and urban transport systems as well as the complexity of their users' transport needs make it necessary to develop dedicated system solutions that shape the transport accessibility of urban space and the mobility of its users.

The analysis of the above-mentioned issues indicates that changes in socio-economic and transport relations resulting from the development of telecommunications technologies, mobile devices, wireless communications as well as new human activities and its requirements shaping transport needs as well as people's behavior and transport preferences are of significant importance. Modern transport systems are subject to constant technological and innovative changes in the field of transport, transport infrastructure and organization of transport and thus shape the behavior and preferences of users not

© Springer Nature Switzerland AG 2020
J. Mikulski (Ed.): TST 2020, CCIS 1289, pp. 54–70, 2020.
https://doi.org/10.1007/978-3-030-59270-7_5

only statically but also increasingly as dynamic transport needs – ad hoc, temporary transport needs.

It is worth emphasizing that both technological changes in transport systems that increase their usability, as well as changes in public communication and new forms of activity related to a specific place and time may be associated with the events referred to as black swan – unexpected and sudden events strongly affecting reality. An example of such events is the current global situation, known as the *COVID-19* coronavirus pandemic. This example shows how quickly and dramatically changed passenger transport needs and cargo transport needs as a result of reduced activity of people and stopping/slowing down socio-economic systems on national, European and global scales.

Contemporary trends in planning and development of urban agglomerations are moving towards smart cities. This is favored by development of information and communication technologies (*ICT*) and devices that enable the use of collected and processed data by many stakeholders. The mobile devices of transport system users should be mentioned here, among others smartphones with a *GPS* module and relevant applications, on-board devices of vehicles, e.g. passenger cars, public transport vehicles or goods vehicles, and stationary devices of technical transport infrastructure. The integration of these devices is currently shaped in the form of the Internet of Things (*IoT*) [1] and introduced to transport as a technology implementing intelligent transport systems and shaping the mobility of smart city users [2, 3]. In addition, a common global IT platform is envisaged to additionally include: Internet of People (*IoP*), Internet of Energy (*IoE*), Internet of Media (*IoM*) and Internet of Services (*IoS*) [1]. Potential threats to the functioning of smart cities, related to the complexity of processes to be controlled using digital technology, *ICT* is indicated. Therefore, actions are postulated to ensure backward compatibility of *ICT* technologies and parallel operation of analogue technologies constituting a kind of back-up in the event of failure of digital ICT systems [4].

2 Problems and Decisions in Designing of Functional-Operational Configuration of Tasks FOCT in Transport Projects

Problems and decisions in designing of *Functional-Operational Configuration of Tasks FOCT* in transport projects are presented in this chapter in the following scientific and research aspects [5]:

– area of urban agglomerations and traffic zones,
– urban transportation systems,
– activity and transport needs of users of urban area,
– determinants shaping transport systems and decisions of transport users.

2.1 Characteristics of Area of Urban Agglomerations and Traffic Zones

Urban agglomeration is described as *a type of city with decreasing population density, consisting of central districts and a set of settlement units*. It is emphasized that *the city's administrative boundaries are losing their significance from a transport point of view because the population living outside the city is still associated with downtown areas through work, study and other daily activities and must be transported to them.*

The central area of the city (agglomeration) – downtown, city – are compact districts with a high density of cultural, administrative, commercial, gastronomic and entertainment institutions. In the downtown, you can usually distinguish a small central zone – the center – characterized by a particularly high density of various types of services and a relatively small number of inhabitants. Around the center there is a downtown with significant multi-storey buildings and a smaller density of services than in the center. The peripheral districts surrounding the downtown include housing estates, industrial plants and railway areas. Outside the urbanized area extends the suburban area under the influence of the proper city, with lower population density and single-family housing, as well as forest and recreational and leisure areas.

As the service character of central districts increases, the population moves to peripheral districts, which causes depopulation of the center with the simultaneous inflow of various types of institutions. Urban agglomerations are usually monocentric, but there are also polycentric agglomerations, called conurbations, resulting from the expansion of neighboring human aggregates – urban agglomerations. Further transformation of the agglomeration, including on further concentration of the population, but on a much larger spatial scale, leads to the creation of a metropolis for which the neighborhood is not the surrounding region, but distant other metropolises. The metropolis is treated as an international city and its further spatial development leads to reaching the stage called megalopolis – one compact urban region, which in further expansion reaches the size of the megaregion called the endless city.

Considering the city space and its district system (center, downtown, peripheral districts), when organizing transport in the city center (central zone), it is strived to ensure that road surface traffic is limited or stopped at all, and the whole district is adapted to pedestrian traffic. In addition, in order to limit individual car transport, the city area is divided into the following zones - considering the center, through downtown towards the peripheral districts, the role of individual transport increases, while in the opposite direction, i.e. to the city center, the role of public transport increases [5]:

– zone 0 – priority for pedestrians,
– zone A (the largest concentration of travel destinations, limited area of roads and parking lots) – restriction of passenger car traffic but service by public transport,
– zone B (average concentration of travel destinations – multi-family housing, industrial and recreational areas) – cooperation of passenger car traffic and public transport,
– zone C (low concentration of travel destinations – extensive, dispersed buildings) – the advantage of passenger car traffic over public transport (public collective transport).

It is important that parking lots [6] can (should) be located on the edge of the central district, enabling visitors to leave cars within walking distance.

2.2 Characteristics of Urban Transportation Systems

Urban transport systems use urban means of transport and urban transport infrastructure. Means of public transport can be divided into: rail (metro, city rail, tram) and road (buses, trolley buses, passenger cars). Taking into account functional classification, the following means of transport are distinguished with some of them classified into two categories depending on whether they are used individually or in groups [5]:

– individual means of transport: bicycle, moped, motorcycle, taxi, car,
– group means of transport: microbus, taxi and passenger car used jointly by several passengers,
– collective means of transport: bus, trolleybus, tram, subway, city rail, regional rail.

The technical classification of urban transport means, taking into account the mode of transport and the type of energy used to propel vehicles, distinguishes [5]:

– ground means of transport using the streets and powered solely by internal combustion engines: bus, motor, motorcycle,
– ground means of transport using the streets and powered solely by electricity supplied from the outside: trolleybus,
– ground means of transport using the streets and powered by internal combustion and electric motors powered from the outside or from the battery: a trolleybus with an internal combustion engine, with a battery,
– ground means of transport using the track integrated with the street and driven solely by electricity, supplied from the outside: tram,
– ground means of transport using a separate track and driven solely by electricity supplied from the outside: urban rail, regional rail,
– underground means of transport using tunnels and powered solely by electricity: metro, premetro,
– ground means of transport using the streets and powered by human muscles: bicycle,
– aboveground means of transport using the track at altitude above the ground and powered solely by electricity supplied from the outside: suspended railway,
– water means of transport powered by internal combustion or electric engines: water tram.

The specificity of urban transport infrastructure results from its adaptation to service transport needs occurring within urban areas. It includes, among others [5]:

– roads and streets (for traffic and parking of vehicles and pedestrians, together with squares, parking bays, pedestrian walkways, bicycle paths) together with all equipment used to organize and control traffic (signs, signals, etc.); there are: urban expressways, accelerated main streets, main streets, collective streets, local streets, access streets,
– subway, rail and tram tracks,
– energy network with substations supplying the underground, railways, trams, trolley buses, electric buses,

- public transport stops, stations and interchanges,
- bus, tram and trolleybus depots,
- car parks.

Shaping mobility is associated with the concept of livable cities, functioning according to the so-called mobility rules [5, 7]:

- hierarchy of transport users (from the most important to the least important) – pedestrians, cyclists, public transport vehicles, moving cars, cars parked only in places where they do not bother those users,
- appropriate stratification of the street network – vehicle traffic on city streets is subordinated to pedestrians by significant vehicle speed restrictions and the dominant role of traffic lights in controlling traffic at intersections; whereas there are no restrictions for cars only on high-speed bus lines outside the urban development area,
- restrictive parking rules – parking cars is only possible with the consent of the owner of the area (city authorities, property owner) and allowed only in designated places and after paying the appropriate fee,
- parking fees – the amount of parking fee increases progressively when approaching the city center, and free parking applies to exceptions.

2.3 Characteristics of Activity and Transport Needs of Users of Urban Area

Activities are a set of characteristics of any human activity implemented in space and in objects with such characteristics that allow mapping the size of transport needs caused by these activities, i.e. the number of displacements carried out to and from the object at a given time, over a specified period of time per day.

People's needs related to transport are generated by activities in everyday life that can be defined as activities. The occurrence of transport needs is due to the fact that the places and times of different activities in many cases differ, so they require movement. Following the paths of people from place to place in time – in space-time – shows their life history, which can be described as a sequence of displacements – also called a displacement chain [8].

Telecommunications technologies (*ICT*) affect users' activities and displacements as follows [5]:

- mobile phones - reduction or elimination of space and time restrictions,
- internet services - freedom of time and space - at any time of the day and 24 h a day, 7 days a week,
- virtual space - specific activities can be carried out despite space-time barriers (distance, travel time etc.) [9, 10],
- the concept of extended time geography, which includes space-time presence - takes into account the relationship between physical presence and the remote presence of people, allows to distinguish four types of space-time presence [11]:

  - *PhSy* – physical-time synchronous presence – stay of people in the same place and at the same time (synchronized),

- *PhAs* – space-time physical asynchronous presence – people stay in the same place, but not at the same time (unsynchronized),
- *ReSy* – space-time remote synchronous presence of people in different places of stay and at the same time (synchronized tele),
- *ReAs* – space-time remote asynchronous presence – stay of people in different places and at different time (unsynchronized tele),

- types of interpersonal interactions – result from the relationship between the space-time physical presence *PhSy* and *PhAs* and remote *ReSy* and *ReAs*:

  - *CoEx-PhSy* – co-existence of individuals (people) in space-time – physical presence synchronously *PhSy* – contacts include face to face meeting,
  - *CoLoS-PhSy* – co-location in space of units (people) in space-time – asynchronous physical presence *PhSy* – contacts are e.g. a traditional note, notice board etc.,
  - *CoLoT-ReSy* – co-location in time of units (people) in space-time – presence of synchronous remote *ReSy* – contacts are e.g. teleconferences, instant messengers etc.,
  - *NoCoLo-ReAs* – no co-location (either co-location in either space or time) of units (people) in space-time – presence of remote asynchronous *ReAs* – contacts are e.g. e-mail, voicemail etc.

- the main types of space-time analysis rely on the search for [5]:

  - co-existence of *CoEx-PhSy*,
  - spatial co-location *CoLoS-PhSy*,
  - time co-location *CoLoT-ReSy*,
  - no time co-location *NoCoLo-ReAs*.

2.4 Characteristics of Determinants Shaping Transport Systems and Decisions of Transport Users

The systemic description of the functioning of transport in agglomeration areas requires a description of the elements and relationships that make up the spatial development structure in which there are transport needs related to the activities of people, and the structure of the transport system that handles transport needs by implementing transport processes. Therefore, the description of the functioning of transport can be distinguished, among others the following subsystems:

- land use subsystem,
- user activity subsystem,
- transport demand subsystem (transport needs, transport demand) [12],
- transport subsystem – subsystem of transport systems – modes of transport (supply of transport).

Functional conditions for shaping travelers' decisions, including activity, accessibility and mobility, including time, space, cost and mode of movement can be characterized by the following factors [5]:

– purpose (work, study – absolutely mandatory purposes; shopping, services – relatively obligatory purposes; entertainment, recreation, social contacts, etc. –optional purposes),
– usefulness of the destination (local small shop versus shopping center, services located in the city center versus location of services in the suburbs, outside the city),
– day of the week (working days, weekend days, days of religious and national ceremonies, non-working days),
– period of the day, time of day (peak hours, inter-peak hours, non-peak hours, night hours),
– seasonality (summer/winter holiday months, working months),
– user's characteristics shaping his transport behavior and preferences (e.g. level of income, ownership of the car and access to the car (driving license) ownership of the bicycle and access to the bicycle (bicycle rental), status of the person in the household, type of activity during the day, etc.),
– the transport utility of the points of initial and final displacement perceived by the user in terms of:

  – public collective transport, including:
  – walking time of arrival/departure to/from the start/end stop,
  – relations served by public transport lines at the start and end stops of the journey,
  – distribution of the number of courses per day (during peak, off-peak and night hours),

– number of alternative routes between start and end locations (dense street network with many alternative routes versus expressways with limited availability and thus a small number of long alternative routes),
– current travel times (depending on traffic conditions),
– risk of extending the travel time and being late due to the likelihood of various events on the routes [13–15] (congestion, collisions and road accidents, and persistent slowdowns at peak times caused by e.g. reduced road capacity due to work repair or unfavorable distribution of traffic flows),
– possibility of parking the car:

  – distance to the parking place,
  – parking location information,
  – availability of parking spaces – number of parking spaces, restrictions on access to parking spaces, amount of parking fee, entry authorization,

– bicycle transport – the type of parking spaces for bicycles (type of bicycle stands, their roofing and protection of the bikes against theft), bicycle rentals and other amenities,
– cost of travel (toll sections of roads and highways, parking fees, ticket price/fuel price).

3   Transport System Components that Shape Traffic Flows in Urban Transportation Network

Taking into account the complexity of the issues mentioned in the previous chapter and the possibility of applying systems engineering methods to transport projects, the following methodological assumptions were adopted [5]:

- shaping traffic flows in the transport network takes place at **different levels of mapping** transport demand and depending on the usefulness of transport systems,
- the shaping of traffic flows is significantly influenced by the specific **functional and operational configuration of tasks in the transport project** covering the following system components as groups of instruments [5]:

    - **traffic control and management** using ITS systems [16],
    - **mobility management** using sustainable urban mobility plans [17],
    - **functional improvement of transport systems** in the scope of **transport services** as the results of modernization and development of technical infrastructure and means of transport [18],

- the **simultaneous application** of the **three groups** of **tasks** in a specific *Functional-Operational Configuration of Tasks FOCT* allows synergy effects to be achieved – including operational synergy and functional synergy as a result of the following activities: optimal configuration of components (functions), their optimal integration, diversification and merger as well as the use of shared resources [5].

3.1   Characteristics of Traffic Control and Management Using ITS Systems

Dynamic traffic management and control in transport systems assumes monitoring, control and impact on: users' transport needs, their travels and traffic (traffic flows) in the entire transport system. From the users' point of view, monitoring, control and impact apply to all stages of displacement [19–21]. The goal is to provide users with the ability to make transport decisions [22–25] before the trip (pre-trip) and at every stage (en-route), including the choice of [5]:

- destination,
- period of the day,
- mode of traveling,
- network route,
- transport infrastructure components (lanes, parking lots etc.).

Dynamic strategies [26, 27] that are used to dynamically manage travel and traffic include, but are not limited to:

- impact on users' transport behavior to generate travel,
- dynamic control and management of network traffic flows, leading to optimization of the efficiency of transport systems and increasing the usability of transport modes,

- monitoring, analysis and prediction of traffic conditions.

Dynamic traffic management and control can be characterized by, among others as:

- use of data available on-line and determination of values in real time (calculated, estimated, forecast),
- sending data and providing useful information in real time to users and vehicles,
- matching activities to changes in the size of transport needs (number of trips and the number of travelers) and changes in the road traffic conditions,
- impact on transport needs through fee strategies and limitation/authorization of access to transport infrastructure,
- focusing on changing the transport behavior of travelers in the field of modal split and additionally focused on changes in demand, including:

  - travel start, duration or end time in relation to peak hours,
  - congestion of routes in the transport network – the use of traffic conditions prediction and earlier redirection of traffic flows to alternative routes, which will be less crowded at peak times,
  - location of targets with similar activities that can be identified as opportunities from the point of view of better transport accessibility (spatial, temporal, economic) at peak times,

- focusing on dynamic temporary shaping of transport behaviors - using on-line tools and strategies for dynamic demand management, and not only permanent change in transport behavior of travelers,
- use of vehicles – passenger cars – offered in the system of municipal transport systems (carsharing – vehicle rentals – so-called cars for minutes), and not only vehicles owned by private users (ridesharing, carpooling, vanpooling),
- the use of urban city and social networking sites for the presentation of city transport services, as well as for analyzing users' opinions regarding the possibilities of effective mobility or occurring transport problems,
- offering the possibility of comparing travel times for different modes of travel - displaying current (or estimated) travel times for different modes of travel in travel planners, on city and social networks, on variable message signs (VMS), in dynamic passenger information systems (DPI) in multimodal hubs/interchange centers [28],
- improving the quality of transport systems (efficiency, effectiveness, reliability, flexibility, attractiveness), and not only for reducing the movement of transport means.

3.2 Characteristics of Mobility Management Using Sustainable Urban Mobility Plans

The goal of mobility management is to increase the sustainability of urban mobility [29, 30] by:

- greater use of alternative modes for passenger cars, including public transport (including public transport), pedestrian and bicycle movements and a combination of means of transport, e.g. Park & Ride, Bike & Ride etc.,

- improving/increasing the accessibility of transport systems for users,
- increasing the integration and interoperability of transport systems, including existing infrastructure, to increase their functional efficiency,
- reducing traffic flows in the transport network by reducing the number of journeys, shortening the travel distance, reducing transport needs - in particular motorized journeys.

Mobility management instruments/activities can be divided into coercive instruments, forcing certain behaviors, often in the form of legal regulations, and non-coercive instruments, to which the user may or may not comply [31]. There is also a division into 'pull' activities, which have the form of incentives to use sustainable forms of displacement, and 'push' activities, aimed at limiting individual motor transport [32].

Mobility management is focused, among others for activities shaping the behavior and preferences of transport (communication) of travelers at the stage of making travel decisions with transport mode, i.e. even before travel (pre-trip decision). These are primarily the so-called soft activities within the organization of transport services, using: information, communication, organization and coordination. Soft actions have the nature of "incentives" related to alternative car modes (the term "incentives" is enclosed in quotation marks, because for users who prefer using a car, some of these actions may be perceived as impediments or even restrictions):

- entrance fees to the city center, paid parking zones, numerous traffic calming measures (speed bumps, harassment, etc.), traffic restricted areas – for passenger cars,
- a joint ticket, separate bus lanes, proper shaping of platforms and bays of public transport facilitating the exchange of passengers and joining the traffic, priority at intersections – for public transport vehicles,
- consistent and safe bicycle routes, secure parking lots for bicycles, city bike rentals,
- charging points (paid, free) of electric cars,
- purchase financing and participation in operating costs – for electric car users,
- electric car rentals, separate lanes, parking lots, parking spaces, preferential parking fees or lack of them – for electric vehicles,
- separate lanes, discounts for entering pay zones, parking discounts – for *HOV* (*High Occupancy Vehicles*) and for carpooling, vanpooling, carsharing.

Whereas the so-called hard activities related to the modernization and expansion of infrastructure and means of transport as well as formal and legal regulations are conditions that are obligatory for users and their behavior and transport preferences. In addition, the use of existing infrastructure and transport systems to manage mobility makes soft activities less expensive compared to hard activities.

Issues related to transport demand management - transport demand management - in the case of activities related to mobility management, require support from local authorities, public transport organizers and other interested entities and institutions (e.g. employers, carriers of passenger transport, carriers of cargo transport etc.).

In addition, complementary activities should include:

- awareness raising campaigns and events aimed at raising travelers' awareness of sustainable mobility and promoting alternative modes of mobility for passenger cars,
- training on cycling rules for children, adolescents and adults to increase road safety and the attractiveness of bicycle transport,
- eco-driving training courses that reduce fuel consumption and emissions of harmful substances into the environment and increase road safety.

3.3 Characteristics of Functional Improvement of Transport Systems in the Scope of Transport Services

Functional improvements of transport systems are currently activities using new organizational and technical solutions – activities using mobility management and the use of functionalities of intelligent transport systems *ITS* that allow better use of modes of passenger and cargo movement. However, as part of the approach presented in this paper, it was assumed that the functional improvements of transport systems are those that relate to transport services and are primarily the results of actions in the field of modernization and development of technical infrastructure of transport and means of transport. It is a set of all other activities except for activities in the field of intelligent transport systems and in the field of mobility management. Therefore, these are, inter alia, activities related to the construction and development of roads and streets in the city, changes in the scope of geometric solutions of intersections and road junctions as well as signs that increase their capacity, changes in the number of lanes and directions of traffic on roads and streets etc.

4   Functional-Operational Configuration of Tasks in Transport Project (FOCT) – The Main Assumptions

The main assumption of the *Functional-Operational Configuration of Tasks in Transport Project (FOCT)* is the application of system engineering and the V model. The justification for this approach results from the features of modern transport systems, which was summarized in the previous parts of this article. Modern transport systems are large-scale systems with specific features:

- a wide spectrum of various components of the socio-economic system, including transport, spatial development and users as well as various stakeholders, connected with each other by a set of complex functional, behavioral, information, management, steering, managing, etc. relations,
- multi-problem transport phenomena characterized by randomness, indeterminacy, structural instability, significant non-linearity, many categories of users and stakeholders, many interacting subsystems of the socio-economic system,
- high complexity of decision-making processes characterized by high indeterminacy resulting from the behavior and transport preferences of users and stakeholders, as well as from various traffic incidents related to disturbances in traffic flows, as well as unpredictable events of the type "black swan", the effects of which have a significant

impact on the surrounding reality; an example of such events is currently the "*COVID-19 pandemic*", the announcement of which has currently difficult to predict effects but significant effects in socio-economic systems, whereas in transport systems it can significantly change transport behavior and preferences as a result of changes in the activities of people associated with much larger and the rapid use of remote and virtual contacts for work, science, education, entertainment and remote purchasing and other services.

The listed relationships and issues can be mapped from a system perspective, and the use of systems engineering methods allow to prepare and implement a transport project appropriate to the problem diagnosed using models, methods and tools. In this project [5]:

– project stakeholders will be defined,
– the aspirations and requirements of the stakeholders as well as the main and detailed objectives of the project will be defined,
– appropriate system requirements will be determined, which will be the basis for the model of the analyzed or designed system in the appropriate functional-technical and organizational scope, divided into functions and sub-functions as well as systems, subsystems and components necessary for their implementation,
– appropriate actions/tasks will be prepared, the implementation of which will allow achieving the main and specific objectives with a specified level of efficiency and with a specific use of resources,
– selection of appropriate activities/tasks will be carried out analytically, using appropriate mathematical models implemented in the form of methods and tools,
– the choice of recommended variant will be made from several alternative variants, using appropriate analyzes and selection criteria,
– the design process of variants will take place iteratively, with properly planned verification and validation processes of the proposed solutions/variants,
– the course of design work will be properly documented, in particular in terms of meeting the requirements of the stakeholders by the relevant system requirements implemented by the functions and sub-functions in the subsystems and components of the proposed problem solution variant,
– the implementation of the transport project using systems engineering methods will allow to expect synergy effects – including operational synergy and functional synergy [33] resulting from the following activities: optimal configuration of components (functions), optimal integration, diversification and merger, and the use of shared resources.

System approach refers to both mapping the system in its existing state and mapping its condition in specific forecast horizons for specific socio-economic scenarios and in a specific urban area of analysis including its immediate and distant surroundings. In this approach, it is proposed to include the following sets of tasks, from which the *Functional-Operational Configuration of Tasks in Transport Project (FOCT)* will be determined as follows [5]:

– set of **Tasks** in the field of **Mobility Management** (mobility management as services) – **ToMM**,
– a set of **Tasks** in the field of traffic control and management using **Intelligent Transport Systems** (ITS services) – **ToITS**,
– a set of other **Tasks** in transport activities – related to improvement in the field of **Other Transport Services**, which include, among others with the modernization and development of infrastructure and means of transport (transport services) – **ToOTS**.

Individual tasks within each of these collections have been numbered accordingly. Therefore, **sets of task numbers** can be represented as:

$$\textbf{\textit{ToMM}} = \{0, 1, \ldots, to\_mm, \ldots, \overline{ToMM}\}, \tag{1}$$

$$\textbf{\textit{ToITS}} = \{0, 1, \ldots, to\_its, \ldots, \overline{ToITS}\}, \tag{2}$$

$$\textbf{\textit{ToOTS}} = \{0, 1, \ldots, to\_ots, \ldots, \overline{ToOTS}\}, \tag{3}$$

where:
$\overline{ToMM}, \overline{ToITS}, \overline{ToOTS}$ – numbers of tasks in sets respectively: **ToMM**, **ToITS**, **ToOTS**.

At the same time, it was assumed that $to\_mm = 0$, $to\_its = 0$, $to\_ots = 0$ means that no tasks from the specified sets are used.

Within the mentioned sets it is possible to indicate **partial task configurations**, which can be mapped specified **subsets**: **CToMM**, **CToITS**, **CToOTS** of the sets: **ToMM**, **ToITS**, **ToOTS**, respectively:

$$\textbf{\textit{CToMM}}(c\_mm) \subset \textbf{\textit{ToMM}}, \tag{4}$$

$$\textbf{\textit{CToITS}}(c\_its) \subset \textbf{\textit{ToITS}}, \tag{5}$$

$$\textbf{\textit{CToOTS}}(c\_ots) \subset \textbf{\textit{ToOTS}}, \tag{6}$$

$$\textbf{\textit{CToMM}} = \{\textbf{\textit{CToMM}}(c\_mm) : c\_mm \in \textbf{\textit{C\_MM}}\}, \tag{7}$$

$$\textbf{\textit{CToITS}} = \{\textbf{\textit{CToITS}}(c\_its) : c\_its \in \textbf{\textit{C\_ITS}}\} \tag{8}$$

$$\textbf{\textit{CToOTS}} = \{\textbf{\textit{CToOTS}}(c\_ots) : c\_ots \in \textbf{\textit{C\_OTS}}\} \tag{9}$$

where:
c_mm, c_its, c_ots – task configuration numbers,
C_MM, **C_ITS**, **C_OTS** – sets of configuration numbers.

For each subset of the task configurations: **CToMM**, **CToITS**, **CToOTS** the **characteristics** of these configurations are specified, including among others **characteristics** of **individual tasks** that are part of the configuration: **start date**, **duration**, end **date**, **priority** and **order** of tasks, **necessary resources** (time, personnel, financial, etc.).

The number of **functions describing these characteristics** for each group of tasks may be different because it depends on the complexity and type of tasks. Therefore, it was assumed that on sets: **CToMM**, **CToITS**, **CToOTS** mapping transforming elements of these sets into a set of real numbers is given as follows:

$$fctomm^{ifctomm} : \textbf{CToMM} \to \mathbb{R}, \ ifctomm = 1, \dots \overline{IFCToMM}, \tag{10}$$

$$fctoits^{ifctoits} : \textbf{CToITS} \to \mathbb{R}, \ ifctoits = 1, \dots \overline{IFCToITS}, \tag{11}$$

$$fctoots^{ifctoots} : \textbf{CToOTS} \to \mathbb{R}, \ ifctoots = 1, \dots \overline{IFCToOTS}, \tag{12}$$

where:

$\overline{IFCToMM}$, $\overline{IFCToITS}$, $\overline{IFCToITS}$ – numbers of elements in sets respectively: **IFCToMM**, **IFCToITS**, **IFCTo_OTS**; these sets contain numbers of various functions (with different interpretations) specified on the sets, respectively: **CToMM**, **CToITS**, **CToOTS**,

$$fctomm^{ifctomm}(\textbf{CToMM}(c\_mm)) \in \mathbb{R}, \ fctoits^{ifctoits}(\textbf{CToITS}(c\_its)) \in \mathbb{R},$$

$fctoots^{ifctoots}(\textbf{CToOTS}(c\_ots)) \in \mathbb{R}$ – should be interpreted as the function values of the following types, respectively: *ifctomm, ifctoits, ifctoots* for task configuration numbers, respectively: (c_mm), (c_its), (c_ots).

The values of functions specified for individual sets of task configurations can be presented in the form of the following matrices:

$$\textbf{FCToMM} = \left[\begin{array}{c} fctomm^{ifctomm}(\textbf{CToMM}(c\_mm)) : CToMM(c\_mm) \in CToMM, \\ c\_mm \in C\_MM, ifctomm = 1, \dots \overline{IFCToMM} \end{array} \right] \tag{13}$$

$$\textbf{FCToITS} = \left[\begin{array}{c} fctoits^{ifctoits}(\textbf{CToITS}(c\_its)) : CToITS(c\_its) \in CToITS, \\ c\_its \in C\_ITS, ifctoits = 1, \dots \overline{IFCToITS} \end{array} \right] \tag{14}$$

$$\textbf{FCToOTS} = \left[\begin{array}{c} fctoots^{ifctoots}(\textbf{CToOTS}(c\_ots)) : CToOTS(c\_ots) \in CToOTS, \\ c\_ots \in C\_OTS, ifctoots = 1, \dots \overline{IFCToOTS} \end{array} \right] \tag{15}$$

The set of all functions describing all characteristics for all analyzed task configurations can be written as **Functional-Operational Configuration of Tasks in Transport Project**:

$$\textbf{FOCT} = \textbf{FCToMM} \cup \textbf{FCToITS} \cup \textbf{FCToOTS} \tag{16}$$

By comparing individual configurations from the presented sets of tasks, it is possible to build various variants of task configuration. Therefore, variants of task configuration can be numbered and compiled as a set:

$$\textbf{VFOCT} = \{VFOCT(ivfoct) : ivfoct = 1, \dots, \overline{IVOCT}\}, \tag{17}$$

where:

ivfoct is the task configuration variant number, and $\overline{IVOCT}$ indicates the number of elements of the set **IVOCT**, that contains the numbers of different variants.

A single *ivfoct*-th task configuration variant can be presented as:

$$
\begin{aligned}
VFOCT(ivfoct) = (\textbf{\textit{CToMM}}(c\_mm), \textbf{\textit{CToITS}}(c\_its), \textbf{\textit{CToOTS}}(c\_ots)): \\
\textbf{\textit{CToMM}}(c\_mm) \in \textbf{\textit{CToMM}}, \textbf{\textit{CToITS}}(c\_its) \in \textbf{\textit{CToITS}}, \\
\textbf{\textit{CToOTS}}(c\_ots) \in \textbf{\textit{CToOTS}}, c\_mm \in \textbf{\textit{C\_MM}}, \\
c\_its \in \textbf{\textit{C\_ITS}}, c\_ots \in \textbf{\textit{C\_OTS}}, \\
ivfoct = 1, \ldots, \overline{IVOCT}
\end{aligned}
\tag{18}
$$

5   Conclusion

The *Functional-Operational Configuration of Tasks in Transport Project (FOCT)* can be in *n*-different variants **Vn** and each of this **FOCT-Vn** is subject to multi-criteria analysis and assessment in order to indicate the variant recommended **Vr** for implementation – **FOCT-Vr**. The results of implementing a specific **FOCT-Vn** are the subject of analyzes within distinguished fields of impact [34–38], including the following fields of transport impact:

– field of urban area – effects on stakeholders (including transport users), objects, activities,
– field of trip generation – effects on trip production and trip attraction in sources and destinations,
– field of spatial distribution – effects on origin-destination matrix,
– field of modal split – effects on modal origin-destination matrices,
– field of traffic flow assignment – effects on traffic flows in transportation network,
– field of transportation systems – effects on components of transport systems, including on: transport infrastructure, means of transport, organization and functioning of transport, personnel etc.

In addition to **the fields of transport** mentioned above, the results of implementing a specific **FOCT-Vn** affect the other fields, among which the basic ones are:

– field of institutional and legal,
– field of economic and financial,
– field of environmental and ecological,
– field of sensitivity and risk in the project.

References

1. Vermesan, O., Friess, P. (eds.): Internet of Things. Global Technological and Societal Trends. River Publishers, Aalborg (2011)

2. Wang, Y., Qi, H.: Research of Intelligent Transportation System Based on the Internet of Things Frame. Wireless Engineering and Technology, vol. 3, pp. 160–166. Scientific Research Publishing (2012)
3. Sethi, P., Sarangi, S.: Internet of things: architectures, protocols, and applications. J. Electr. Comput. Eng. **2017**, 1–26 (2017). Article ID 9324035
4. Ringenson, T., et al.: The limits of the smart sustainable city. In: LIMITS 2017, Santa Barbara, CA (2017)
5. Karoń, G.: Kształtowanie Ruchu w Miejskich Sieciach Transportowych z Wykorzystaniem Inżynierii Systemów. (In Polish: Traffic Shaping in the Urban Transport Network with the use of Systems Engineering); Wydawnictwo Politechniki Śląskiej, Gliwice, Poland (2019)
6. Young, W.: Parking and traffic control. In: Button K.J., Hensher D.A. (eds.) Handbook of Transport Systems and Traffic Control, pp. 375–385. Emerald Group Publishing Limited, Amsterdam (2009)
7. Vuchic, V.: Transportation for Livable Cities. Taylor & Francis, Routledge (2017)
8. Ellegård, K., Svedin, U.: Torsten Hagerstrands time-geography as the cradle of the activity approach in transport geography. J. Transp. Geogr. **23**, 17–25 (2012)
9. Janelle, D.G.: Impact of information technologies, In: Hanson S., Giuliano G. (eds.) The Geography of Urban Transportation, pp. 86–112. The Guilford Press, New York (2004)
10. Kwan, M.P.: GIS methods in time-geographic research: computation and geovisualization of human activity patterns. Geografiska Annaler B **86**, 267–280 (2004)
11. Shaw, S.L., Yu, H.: A GIS-based time-geographic approach of studying individual activities and interactions in a hybrid physical-virtual space. J. Transp. Geogr. **17**, 141–149 (2009)
12. Karoń, G.: Travel demand and transportation supply modelling for agglomeration without transportation model. In: Mikulski, J. (ed.) TST 2013. CCIS, vol. 395, pp. 284–293. Springer, Heidelberg (2013). https://doi.org/10.1007/978-3-642-41647-7_35
13. Karoń, G., Żochowska, R.: Modelling of expected traffic smoothness in urban transportation systems for ITS solutions. Arch. Transp. **33**(1), 33–45 (2015)
14. Karoń, G.: Modeling of traffic smoothness for railway track closures in the rail network. In: Sładkowski, A. (ed.) Rail Transport—Systems Approach. SSDC, vol. 87, pp. 319–359. Springer, Cham (2017). https://doi.org/10.1007/978-3-319-51502-1_8
15. Karoń, G., Żochowska, R.: Problems of quality of public transportation systems in smart cities—Smoothness and disruptions in urban traffic. In: Sładkowski, A. (ed.) Modelling of the Interaction of the Different Vehicles and Various Transport Modes. LNITI, pp. 383–414. Springer, Cham (2020). https://doi.org/10.1007/978-3-030-11512-8_9
16. Żochowska, R., Karoń, G.: ITS services packages as a tool for managing traffic congestion in cities. In: Sładkowski, A., Pamuła, W. (eds.) Intelligent Transportation Systems – Problems and Perspectives. SSDC, vol. 32, pp. 81–103. Springer, Cham (2016). https://doi.org/10.1007/978-3-319-19150-8_3
17. Karoń, G., et al.: Sustainable urban mobility planning (SUMP) at subregional area level with the use of transportation model. Arch. Transp. Syst. Telemat. **10**(2), 19–26 (2017)
18. Karoń, G., Mikulski, J.: Transportation systems modelling as planning, organisation and management for solutions created with ITS. In: Mikulski, J. (ed.) TST 2011. CCIS, vol. 239, pp. 277–290. Springer, Heidelberg (2011). https://doi.org/10.1007/978-3-642-24660-9_32
19. Schintler, L.: Traffic flow control. In: Button K.J., Hensher D.A. (eds.) Handbook of Transport Systems and Traffic Control, pp. 439–447. Emerald Group Publishing Limited, Amsterdam (2009)
20. Smith, M., Clegg, J., Yarrow, R.: Modeling traffic signal control. In: Button, K.J., Hensher, D.A. (eds.) Handbook of Transport Systems and Traffic Control, pp. 503–524. Emerald Group Publishing Limited, Amsterdam (2009)

21. Watson, R., Pitfield, D.: High-occupancy routes and truck lanes. In: Button, K.J., Hensher, D.A. (eds.) Handbook of Transport Systems and Traffic Control, pp. 413–423. Emerald Group Publishing Limited, Amsterdam (2009)

22. Bhat, C.R., Eluru, N., Copperman, R.B.: Flexible model structures for discrete choice analysis. In: Hensher, D.A., Button, K.J. (eds.) Handbook of Transport Modelling, pp. 75–101. Elsevier, Amsterdam (2008)

23. Bonsall, P.: Stimulating modal shift. In: Button, K.J., Hensher, D.A. (eds.) Handbook of Transport Systems and Traffic Control, pp. 613–633. Emerald Group Publishing Limited, Amsterdam (2009)

24. Koppelmann, F.S.: Closed form discrete choice models. In: Hensher, D.A., Button, K.J. (eds.) Handbook of Transport Modelling, pp. 257–275. Elsevier, Amsterdam (2008)

25. Nelson, D., Tarnoff, P.J.: Route guidance systems. In: Button, K.J., Hensher, D.A. (eds.) Handbook of Transport Systems and Traffic Control, pp. 489–501. Emerald Group Publishing Limited, Amsterdam (2009)

26. Mirshahi, M., et al.: Active Traffic Management: The Next Step in Congestion Management. Report FHWA-PL-07–012. Federal Highway Administration U.S. Department of Transportation American Association of State Highway and Transportation Officials (2007)

27. Karoń, G., Mikulski, J.: Functional configuration of ITS for urban agglomeration. In: Mikulski, J. (ed.) TST 2017. CCIS, vol. 715, pp. 55–69. Springer, Cham (2017). https://doi.org/10.1007/978-3-319-66251-0_5

28. Changeable Message Sign Operation and Messaging Handbook. Report FHWA-OP-03-070. Federal Highway Administration, US Department of Transportation (2004)

29. Jacyna, M., et al.: Simulation model of transport system of Poland as tool for developing sustainable transport. Arch. Transp. **31**(3), 23–35 (2014)

30. Nosal, K., Starowicz, W.: Evaluation of influence of mobility management instruments implemented in separated areas of the city on the changes in modal split. Arch. Transp. **35**(3), 41–52 (2015)

31. Marshall, S., Banister, D.: Travel reduction strategies: intentions and outcomes. Transp. Res. Part A **34**, 321–338 (2000)

32. Meyer, D.M.: Transport Planning Handbook. Wiley, Hoboken (2016)

33. Asnoff, I.: Synergy and capabilities. In: Campbell, A., Luchs, K.S. (eds.) Strategic Synergy. Butterworth – Heinemann Ltd., Oxford (1992)

34. Karoń, G., Janecki, R.: Development of various scenarios of ITS systems for urban area. In: Sierpiński, G. (ed.) Intelligent Transport Systems and Travel Behaviour. AISC, vol. 505, pp. 3–12. Springer, Cham (2017). https://doi.org/10.1007/978-3-319-43991-4_1

35. Karoń, G., Mikulski, J.: Forecasts for technical variants of ITS projects – example of Upper-Silesian conurbation. In: Mikulski, J. (ed.) TST 2013. CCIS, vol. 395, pp. 67–74. Springer, Heidelberg (2013). https://doi.org/10.1007/978-3-642-41647-7_9

36. Karoń, G., Mikulski, J.: Problems of ITS architecture development and ITS implementation in Upper-Silesian conurbation in Poland. In: Mikulski, J. (ed.) TST 2012. CCIS, vol. 329, pp. 183–198. Springer, Heidelberg (2012). https://doi.org/10.1007/978-3-642-34050-5_22

37. Karoń, G., Mikulski, J.: Problems of systems engineering for ITS in large agglomeration – Upper-Silesian agglomeration in Poland. In: Mikulski, J. (ed.) TST 2014. CCIS, vol. 471, pp. 242–251. Springer, Heidelberg (2014). https://doi.org/10.1007/978-3-662-45317-9_26

38. Karoń, G., Mikulski, J.: Selected problems of ITS project development – concept exploration and feasibility study. In: Mikulski, J. (ed.) TST 2017. CCIS, vol. 715, pp. 1–15. Springer, Cham (2017). https://doi.org/10.1007/978-3-319-66251-0_1

ITS and Systems Engineering – Methodical Aspects

Grzegorz Karoń[1](✉) and Jerzy Mikulski[2]

[1] Silesian University of Technology, Krasińskiego 8, Katowice, Poland
grzegorz.karon@polsl.pl
[2] University of Technology, Rolna 43, Katowice, Poland
mikulski.jurek@gmail.com

Abstract. The aim of this paper is to present the main methodological aspects related to the process of designing ITS systems for urban agglomerations. This paper presents, among others systems engineering in ITS design as an essential part of the system approach, possibilities of using the V model of systems engineering in ITS project and development, example of results of the application of systems engineering in the pre-project documentation of ITS are presented.

Keywords: Intelligent transportation systems · Systems engineering · V model

1 Introduction

The purpose of the paper is to present the main methodological aspects related to the process of designing ITS systems for urban agglomerations. The principles of applying the system approach, system engineering and in particular the V model are formulated in the following sections of the article and are the result of the authors' research work carried out in real conditions of designing the ITS system for urban agglomeration.

Despite the fact that selected issues of ITS systems design are well described in the scientific literature in the theoretical aspect [1–4] there are still relatively few scientific articles presenting engineering aspects, i.e. the problems of implementing theoretical issues while working on real ITS systems.

The authors of this paper had the opportunity to work as independent experts and thus could freely combine theoretical issues with engineering practice - freely, i.e. without any obligations to the contracting authority as well as to the contractor of ITS systems. As a result of such work, it was possible to verify and validate theoretical issues of system engineering based on the real conceptual and design process of ITS. The results and conclusions of these works were presented, among others in the following scientific studies:

– problems of use of transport model for assessment of ITS configuration [5–8],
– problems of concept exploration and feasibility study for ITS project development [9],

© Springer Nature Switzerland AG 2020
J. Mikulski (Ed.): TST 2020, CCIS 1289, pp. 71–84, 2020.
https://doi.org/10.1007/978-3-030-59270-7_6

- selected problems of use of systems engineering for ITS development [5],
- selected problems of functional configuration of ITS [5, 10–12],
- managing traffic congestion problems in aspects of use of ITS [5, 13].

The structure of this paper includes the following sections: Sect. 1 explains the purpose and scope of the issues presented in the paper, Sect. 2 presents systems engineering in ITS design as an essential part of the system approach, Sect. 3 characterizes the possibility of using the V model of systems engineering in ITS project and development, Sect. 4 exemplary results of the application of systems engineering in the pre-project documentation of ITS are presented. The paper ends with a summary and conclusions.

2 Systems Engineering in Project of ITS – as the Main Part of the System Approach

Systems engineering is defined as the science of creating complex systems to guarantee the most effective design, adaptation, testing and operation of all the subsystems that make them up. This term refers to complex systems in which components must be designed, manufactured and integrated to achieve the system's goal. Systems engineering during the concept and design phases enables the construction of the entire system taking into account the entire system life cycle including the following phases: concept, definition, design and development, manufacture and testing, installation and introduction, production, operation and maintenance, improvement and development, replacement and withdrawal from the use of [14].

The **system approach to design** is characterized primarily by the following **principles**:

- it is system thinking that includes a way of conceptualizing, analyzing and solving problems using concepts in the field of system theory, including system structure and conceptual process for developing solutions and their implementation,
- uses the main system components, which are: system efficiency goals and criteria, system resources, system elements along with functions, attributes and effectiveness measures, system interactions and system management,
- takes into account the interdependence of the parts making up the system and cause-effect relationships,
- it is focused on the overall picture and the final goal of the project, which means considering parts of the system only depending on their contribution to the whole system,
- allows, due to the holistic nature, to avoid considering problems too narrowly; system planning, i.e. creating its model, must therefore cover the following issues:

  - goals and efficiency criteria of the system,
  - environment and limitations of the system,
  - system resources,
  - system elements, their functions, attributes and efficiency measures,

    – interactions between individual elements of the system,
    – system management,

– in creating the plan of system, i.e. building its model, iterative procedure and feedback loop are used (interactions between: system goals and system plans, system goals and system requirements); the process includes system analysis phases (requirements and criteria related to each goal and alternative ways to achieve it) as well as system synthesis phases (integration of selected modes of action identified at the stage of system analysis and creation of a model, i.e. plan of system),
– it uses instruments in the form of system engineering covering the entire system and its life cycle (see Fig. 1), with the system life cycle being observed from at least two basic perspectives - the perspective of the (enterprise) and system engineering perspective.

Considering these principles, it can be assumed that the system approach to ITS system design will ensure the use of modern solutions, better use of existing solutions, integration of knowledge, techniques and transport technologies. Such principles and assumptions allow the integration of elements such as knowledge, techniques and technologies at all stages of the system life cycle.

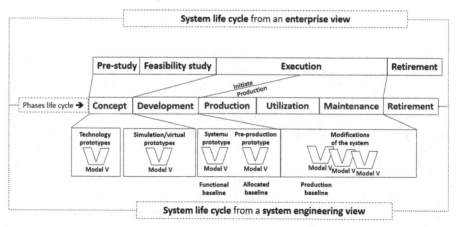

Fig. 1. System life cycle – enterprise view and system engineering view [own study based on [15]]

During the development of the ITS system concept, **systems engineering tools** – a field of applied research – defined as *"science dedicated to the creation of all complex systems to ensure the most effective design, adaptation, testing and operation of all the subsystems that make them"* were used [16]. Among others, the following aspects of this approach were used:

– a multidisciplinary design team that can be characterized as follows:

    – it is a team performing multifunctional, interdisciplinary, simultaneous work,

- it is a team that cooperates with the stakeholders of a system, with the main stakeholders being clients, end users and system developers,
- the creators in the team (system design and construction) cooperate with system users (system operation and maintenance) and system clients (those who finance the system and are its owners),
- the creators in the team define the following system issues through contacts with other stakeholders:

  - what needs/aspirations should the system meet,
  - formulate system requirements based on the needs/aspirations that define the usefulness of the system, i.e. what exactly the system should implement, i.e. what should be the result of a working system,
  - structure, elements and modularization of the created system, which will cover, in particular:

  - functional and physical structure of the system,
  - components and subsystems are created in such a way that they fulfill the functions necessary to achieve the objectives and meet the requirements of the system's customers,
  - one of the priorities is a specific way the system functions to meet stakeholder requirements.

- **system life cycle**, which means including all phases of this cycle in the creation of the system (see Fig. 1),
- **system life cycle** from an **enterprise view** – includes stages focused on management with decision making, including investment decisions on whether the system should go to the next stage (preliminary study, feasibility study, execution, retirement) or whether the system should be modified, canceled or retired, taking into account decision criteria regarding risk, costs, schedule, functionality etc.; the enterprise perspective applies not only to the system of interest, but also to its subsystems and elements that make up the structure of the system; subsystems and components may have a shorter lifetime than the system of interest in which they are embedded and may require modification during the lifetime of the system of interest,
- **system life cycle** from a **system engineering view** – systems engineering is used at the beginning of the cycle to develop technological or simulation (virtual) prototypes in the concept phase including pre-testing and feasibility studies; then, during the development phase, a system prototype and a pre-production prototype are developed; in the stages of implementation, use and maintenance, system engineering is used in modification (redesign) processes when unwanted and unexpected changes occur, for example due to design errors or failures or the need to take into account new requirements caused by changes in technology, competition or expected threats to system functionality.

The effect of the presented principles of preparing a conceptual design of an ITS system should be a real ITS system that meets current and future requirements, needs and aspirations of stakeholders. Therefore, ITS in the conceptual design is considered as a technical-human system in which the way of considering problems focuses on the whole issue (holistic approach) and not only on its individual elements. ITS is therefore a purposeful set of specific components and relationships between them, and is characterized by the following features and principles specific to systems:

– there are various interactions between system components and the entire system, as well as between individual system components; the form of these relationships is referred to as the structure of the system, e.g. hierarchical or network structure; a holistic perception of a given phenomenon or synergy effects is observed in this structure,
– systems have a dynamic character manifested in specific activities resulting from the objectives and tasks implemented by a given system,
– the set of system components is of particular interest to stakeholders because these components can be changed to suit newly formulated goals; it should be emphasized that among the system stakeholders there is a project team called the creating stakeholder,
– systems achieve their goals and tasks, so the creation of the system should begin with formulating its purpose,
– systems can be divided by distinguishing successively subsystems, which are systems in themselves, and distinguishing elements that are the smallest (elementary) parts of the system and its subsystems,
– systems, subsystems and system elements have specific attributes, expressing their states and qualitative or quantitative properties,
– systems have their boundary and environment; the environment consists of everything that affects the operation or results of the system and is beyond the control of system conceptualizers,
– each system has a specific structure composed of elements and subsystems connected by a network of mutual relations,
– systems, including their subsystems and system components, realize their goals and tasks by processing the input at the system input into the results during a given process, but it should be noted that:

  – input to the system:

    – it can take the form of tangible and intangible resources as well as the steps necessary for the system to work, produce results and achieve its objectives and tasks,
    – it should be possible to control and monitor,
    – it can be as a feedback in the system itself,

  – processes in the system:

- it is a set of activities that process input into results in the system,
- it has, among others the following desirable properties: it processes system tasks, effectively achieves the expected results, minimizes input consumption and harmful effects,

- system results:
    - these are the target results of the system's operation or the system's goals,
    - the results are varied: desirable results contribute to the achievement of goals, undesirable or harmful results hinder the achievement of goals and/or negatively affect the environment, neutral results - do not affect the achievement of goals.

- systems have limitations that hinder achievement of goals and implementation of tasks; systems may have conflicts between tasks of individual components of its structure, which negatively affects the functioning of the system; resolving a given conflict of this kind is achieved during system integration,
- the operation of all parts of the system must be coordinated and the system that implements its objectives and meets the requirements through coordinated work is referred to as the integrated system,
- systems can be open to their environment and in their creation must take into account the system environment; systems can also be closed, i.e. independent and autonomous, not requiring references to the environment.

3   Model V of Systems Engineering in ITS Project and Development

Systems engineering is based on general system theory and in connection with this theoretical basis, allows the use of many different system models. For the ITS system, a V model has been proposed (see Fig. 2) with specific phases:

- phase of defining and decomposing problems in terms of the system – this phase includes formulating the assumptions of the system, defining system requirements, developing a high-level project containing solutions in the field of subsystems, developing a detailed project that is the specification of the elements of the system, leading to its implementation; the phase of defining and decomposing is a descending analysis, which is a breakdown of the created system into components corresponding to specific systemic problems,
- integration phase of system components (system synthesis) – this phase involves connecting and coordinating individual system components (activities) that are combined into subsystems and form a constructed system (variants of system) assuming that the system meets defined requirements and meets the needs and requirements of stakeholders of this system,
- the evaluation phase of the results achieved by the system components and the entire system – is the phase of checking the system results, including verification and validation plans for subsequent levels of decomposition and integration phases; it is also an assessment of the proposed variants of system.

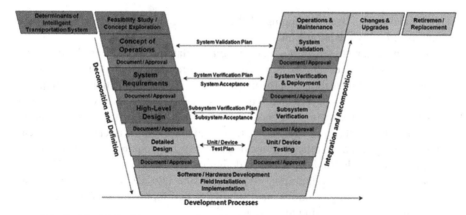

Fig. 2. Model V of Systems Engineering for ITS Design [own study based on [17]]

The main components, which are specific levels of Model V, can be synthetically characterized as follows:

- the level of **system assumptions** covers the following scope:
  - goals and tasks – defining the needs and requirements of system stakeholders; developing a basic verification plan (validation → functional utility) of the system at the final stage of implementation,
  - actions necessary to perform – identification of stakeholders related to the system; preparation of the system description from the point of view of its stakeholders, including their aspirations and requirements including efficiency, cost and time requirements; selection of key measures of system performance (its results),
  - results of actions taken – a document describing the essence of the system, including the needs and requirements of stakeholders, restrictions (scope of the system); a document that is a system validation plan that defines the approach that will be used to check the correctness of project implementation,

- the level of **system requirements** covers the following scope:
  - goals and tasks – mapping the needs, aspirations and requirements of stakeholders and current capabilities related to the construction of the system, by defining a set of system requirements to meet the needs and requirements of stakeholders,
  - actions necessary to perform – determining the system requirements in the iterative process including obtaining information, specifying requirements, analyzing and reviewing them; documentation, verification and management of requirements; developing ways to verify and accept the system,
  - results of actions taken – a document containing system, functional, efficiency and verification requirements; a document being a system verification and acceptance plan in relation to system requirements,

- the **high level design** covers the following scope:

- goals and tasks – it is a mapping of the system's functional requirements to the subsystem design requirements,
- actions necessary to perform – examining the relationship between the elements constituting the system and assigning system requirements to individual subsystems (construction of traceability matrix); grouping of identified functions and requirements takes place in accordance with the so-called system architecture, being a configuration of the main components of the system, enabling the implementation of system functions; each main subsystem should meet one or a set of basic system functions (requirements) listed in the document system requirements; determining the interface levels between systems; definition and selection of alternative solutions composed of configuration elements, taking into account the synthesis of components (existing solutions, new solutions); developing methods for verifying the subsystems constituting the system,
- results of actions taken - creation of a framework project of the system that meets all the requirements; developing a system architecture that allows you to assign all system requirements to major subsystems (configuration items); a document being a plan for the verification and acceptance of subsystems; a document that is a plan to integrate configuration elements,

- the level of **detailed design** covers the following scope:
  - goals and tasks – mapping the initial framework project (high-level project) into a project that is possible to implement,
  - actions necessary to perform – actions necessary to perform - designing a system composed of configured subsystems that contain appropriately selected components; a detailed design should be made for each component identified in the high-level design; developing a plan for checking (testing) the elements of a detailed system design; checking of individual components in terms of whether they meet the assigned requirements and are suitable for the intended purpose (testing of elements); preparation of the "prototype" system and preparation of project documentation,
  - results of actions taken – a detailed system project will be created that meets all the requirements; a document containing detailed design specifications at the component level,

- level of **integration along with verification and validation** covers the following scope:
  - goals and tasks – mapping the hierarchical integration of components, subsystems and the system; checking and verifying components, subsystems and the system in terms of meeting all system requirements; system validation in terms of its correct construction and its usefulness for stakeholders,
  - actions necessary to perform – it is the integration of system components in accordance with the prepared integration plan and high-level project requirements; creating an integration and verification environment that maps the system's functioning environment, which gives the opportunity to test system components in ex-ante

mode; testing the effects of each integration step for the functionality of the integrated subsystem; carrying out up-directed checks, verifications and validations according to developed plans,
- results of actions taken – confirmation of compliance of the implemented system with all requirements and restrictions; confirmation of the correct implementation of the system; this is included in the document that describes the activities that were performed along with the results (integration plan, integration tests, verification and validation plan, including procedures and results),

- the **level of development, construction and implementation** of the system covers the following scope:

  - goals and tasks – creating new or improving existing systems,
  - actions necessary to perform – final creation (construction) of the system and its testing; after conducting acceptance tests, the system is installed, implemented and becomes part of the user's environment; as part of development, the existing system is being improved,
  - results of actions taken – transformation of the conceptual design into a complete, material end product, which is the built system.

4   An Example of the Use of Systems Engineering in the Pre-project Documentation of ITS

The issues of the application of systems engineering methods and the V model characterized in the previous sections have been checked and specified during work on the ITS system project for the urban agglomeration. This section of the paper presents a synthetic selection of ITS system design problems identified during work on pre-design documentation and analysis of bidders' questions in an open tender and investor (municipal authorities) responses during the ITS contractor selection process.

Figure 3 presents problems at current status inventory stage, among others problems of TMC's location (traffic management centers), problems of using existing infrastructure, problems of using ICT networks (sharing existing or build dedicated), problems of transportation model in ITS development.

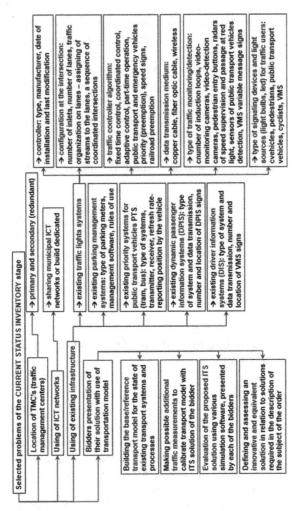

Fig. 3. Selected problems of the current status inventory stage [own study based on [17]]

Figure 4 presents problems at design and implementation stage, including problems of preparation of a complete project documentation, i.e. all necessary projects and studies ensuring the launch of the system together with the approval of all necessary arrangements, decisions and permits provided for this type of construction process. In addition, problems of workplace trainings of employees and users in a way that ensures the use and ongoing maintenance of ITS subsystems were indicated.

Figure 5 presents problems at maintenance stage, including problems of ensuring consistency of documentation for the ITS system, ensuring continuity of correct ITS system operation through periodic maintenance activities for devices and software.

Details of these problems are included in the authors' work [17].

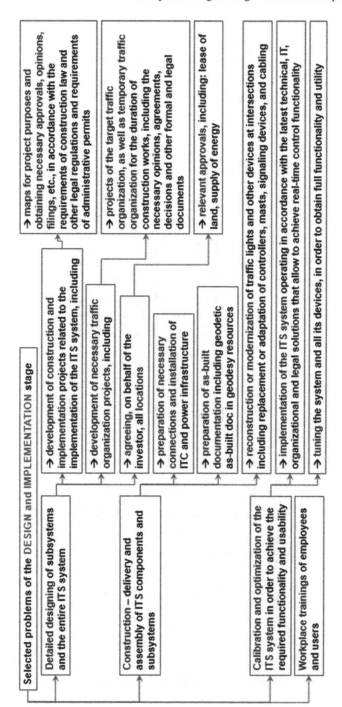

Fig. 4. Selected problems of the design and implementation [own study based on [17]]

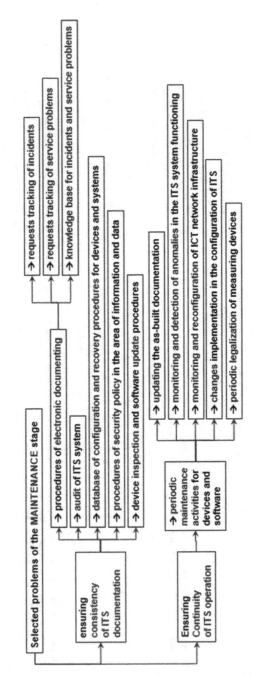

Fig. 5. Selected problems of the maintenance stage [own study based on [17]]

5   Conclusion

The design of intelligent transport systems has been carried out for many years around the world and in most cases the systems engineering methods are used in this process. However, the current significantly rapid growth of modern ICT technologies, including the Internet of Things, enables the design of very advanced ITS solutions, whose functions in the form of ITS services can be delivered to a much wider group of users and other stakeholders, not just to vehicle drivers and passengers of public transport.

Therefore, it is even more necessary to apply and at the same time modify and develop systems engineering methods throughout the entire ITS life cycle, because the systems engineering principles presented in this paper guarantee orderly, rational and innovative design of ITS solutions.

Such conclusions arise from practical engineering scientific papers discussed in this paper, because the multidisciplinary design team is the main factor through which modern innovative technical solutions are implemented, both throughout the entire ITS life cycle but above all at the concept and design stages ITS.

References

1. Architecture Development Team for Research and Innovation Technology Administration (RITA), National ITS Architecture. Service Packages. US Department of Transportation Washington D.C. (2012)
2. European Intelligent Transport System (ITS) Framework Architecture (E-FRAE). http://frame-online.eu/. Accessed 12 Feb 2017
3. National ITS Architecture 7.1. http://local.iteris.com/itsarch/. Accessed 12 Feb 2017
4. Systems Engineering Guidebook for Intelligent Transportation Systems. U.S. Department of Transportation, November 2009
5. Karoń, G.: Kształtowanie ruchu w miejskich sieciach transportowych z wykorzystaniem inżynierii systemów (eng. Traffic Shaping in the Urban Transport Network with the Use of Systems Engineering). Wydawnictwo Politechniki Śląskiej, Gliwice (2019)
6. Karoń, G., Mikulski, J.: Forecasts for technical variants of ITS projects – example of Upper-Silesian conurbation. In: Mikulski, J. (ed.) TST 2013. CCIS, vol. 395, pp. 67–74. Springer, Heidelberg (2013). https://doi.org/10.1007/978-3-642-41647-7_9
7. Karoń, G., Mikulski, J.: Problems of modelling of its services in transportation models. Arch. Transp. Syst. Telemat. 11(3), 30–34 (2018)
8. Karoń G., Mikulski, J.: Structure of transport model on strategic level of management for assessment of ITS configuration. J. KONES Powertrain Transp. 24(3), 119–126 (2017)
9. Karoń, G., Mikulski, J.: Selected problems of ITS project development – concept exploration and feasibility study. In: Mikulski, J. (ed.) TST 2017. CCIS, vol. 715, pp. 1–15. Springer, Cham (2017). https://doi.org/10.1007/978-3-319-66251-0_1
10. Karoń, G., Mikulski, J.: Functional configuration of ITS for urban agglomeration. In: Mikulski, J. (ed.) TST 2017. CCIS, vol. 715, pp. 55–69. Springer, Cham (2017). https://doi.org/10.1007/978-3-319-66251-0_5
11. Karoń, G., Mikulski, J.: Modelling of ITS service configuration and stakeholders aspirations. Arch. Transp. Syst. Telemat. 11(3), 24–29 (2018)
12. Karoń, G., Mikulski, J.: Problems of ITS architecture development and its implementation in Upper-Silesian conurbation in Poland. In: Mikulski, J. (ed.) TST 2012. CCIS, vol. 329, pp. 183–198. Springer, Heidelberg (2012). https://doi.org/10.1007/978-3-642-34050-5_22

13. Żochowska, R., Karoń, G.: ITS services packages as a tool for managing traffic congestion in cities. In: Sładkowski, A., Pamuła, W. (eds.) Intelligent Transportation Systems – Problems and Perspectives. SSDC, vol. 32, pp. 81–103. Springer, Cham (2016). https://doi.org/10.1007/978-3-319-19150-8_3

14. Janelle, D.G.: Time space convergence and urban transportation issues. In: Blong, C.K. (ed.): Systems Thinking and the Quality of Life, pp. 594–600. The Society for General Systems Research, Washington DC (1975)

15. Systems Engineering – Guide for ISO/IEC (System Life Cycle Processes). http://evmworld.org/wp-content/uploads/2017/05/Guide-to-Isoiec15288.pdf. Accessed 17 May 2020

16. Nicholas, J.M., Steyn, H.: Zarządzanie projektami. Zastosowanie w biznesie, inżynierii i nowoczesnych technologiach, Oficyna a Wolters Kluwer business, Warszawa (2012)

17. Karoń, G., Mikulski, J., Janecki, R.: Design and implementation of ITS systems in urban agglomerations – selected system problems. Arch. Syst. Telemat. **12**(1), 17–21 (2019)

Mobile App to Unloading Areas - Which Could We Learn with the Brazilian Experience?

Leise Kelli de Oliveira[1], Kinga Kijewska[2(✉)], Sérgio Antônio de Sena Rocha[3], Anete Andrade Gomes Cosentino Alvarez[3], and Odirley Rocha dos Santos[3]

[1] Universidade Federal de Minas Gerais, Belo Horizonte, Brazil
leise@etg.ufmg.br
[2] Maritime University of Szczecin, Wały Chrobrego 1-2, 70-500 Szczecin, Poland
k.kijewska@am.szczecin.pl
[3] Empresa de Transporte e Trânsito de Belo Horizonte, Belo Horizonte, Brazil
{sena,anete,Odirley}@pbh.gov.br

Abstract. Mobile apps are online services offered in smartphones, combining data, functionality and user interface to the customer. In urban freight transport, app-based services are increasingly focused on last-mile delivery. This paper presents a mobile app to unloading zones developed by Belo Horizonte municipality. The initial purpose of this app is identifying the unloading bays used by carriers. Since June 2019, the municipality launched the "rotativo digital" app. The first results show a progressive increase in the number of users of the application. In general, those who download the app, use it regularly. However, there is resistance in the download of the application by the drivers. In addition, the most used loading and unloading areas were identified. From the lessons learned, it is important to use technology to collect data on urban freight transport. Educational and inspection campaigns can encourage more users to use the application. Knowledge about the type of data and its benefits for urban planning can be vital to its success.

Keywords: Urban freight transport · App-based service · Mobile app · Unloading zones · Collection data

1 Introduction

Mobile devices, like smartphones, are increasing day by day and become indispensable in daily lives [1]. Today, a smartphone is part of modern life, reached penetration rates of 80% in developed countries and 82% in developing countries [2]. In Brazil, there are 220 million mobile phones in operation and 207.6 million inhabitants, more than one per inhabitant. On average, Brazilians have just over 70 applications installed and just over 30 used by browsers [3].

Digital apps are online services offered in smartphones, combining data, functionality and user interface to the customer. In transport, digital apps could represent the future of urban mobility with the offer of sharing rides, bikes, and cars. According [4], "apps

© Springer Nature Switzerland AG 2020
J. Mikulski (Ed.): TST 2020, CCIS 1289, pp. 85–94, 2020.
https://doi.org/10.1007/978-3-030-59270-7_7

are allowing commuters to compare the time, cost, convenience, carbon footprint and health benefits across all modes of public and private transport, broadening their range of choices and allowing for on-the-fly decision making that takes into account real-time conditions". There are apps to integrated fare management, incentives (ex.: discounts, travel vouchers), car-sharing, ride-sharing, bike-sharing, smart parking, telecommuting, real-time traffic management, personal travel assistant apps, between others. Gebresse-lassie & Sanchez (2018) presents some mobility apps identified in a literature review [5].

In urban freight transport, app-based services are also increasing, focused mainly on last-mile delivery. Iwan et al. (2014) relate some telematics solutions to urban freight transport as a traffic management system [6]. In this sense, this paper presents a panorama of digital apps for urban freight transport and an app developed to unloading zones in Belo Horizonte, Brazil by the municipality. In order to evidence the importance of digital app for unloading zones, some information's about these places are presented. Finally, the Rotativo Digital app, some results from the usage of this app, and lessons learned by the municipality are also reported. We hope this paper motivate other municipality to implement similar initiatives to improve the unloading operation on-street in the same way to collect data about this activity.

2 Digital Apps for Urban Freight Transport

The literature presents some mobile apps for urban freight transport and this section summarize them. In general, mobile apps provide instant deliveries, as UberRush, Amazon Prime Now, UberEats, Glovo, Cocolis (France), Ifood (Brazil), between others. As an example, in 2019 black Friday, Ifood performed 1.4 million of prepared food deliveries in 912 Brazilian cities [7].

DHL has a crowd shipping platform in Stockholm called MyWays, focused on the delivery of goods ordered online and delivered by city's residents along their daily routes with the chance to earn a little extra money [8]. Results indicate 'Stockholm's residents embrace the flexibility of MyWays and make use of their regular city travels for delivering parcels to fellow individuals' [8]. Bikemike was bike messenger software connecting restaurants, shops and bike messengers to provide bike delivery service in Brussels (Belgium). No current data was found on these platforms.

Considering other UFT activities, some scholars relate some apps initiatives. Comi et al. (2017) relate the DynaLOAD, a project which intends to develop a delivery system to booking unloading zones [9]. Results showed the importance of telematics applications to manage the unloading activities. Comi et al. (2018) share the components and results from the use of this tool in a limited area of Rome [10]. Authors relate that the Rome Municipality is evaluating the implementation of the tool due to the positive results obtained.

Oliveira et al. (2017) analyze the characteristics of a collaborative mobile application to support drivers to find the best routes, unloading zones [11]. Also, the app provides information about restrictive urban freight policies. The authors present the flow navigation of the app.

Kolbay et al. (2018) relate a parking management app which drives needs to use when are parked in parking spaces in Barcelona [12]. The authors analyzed some attributes from a dataset: Delivery Area ID, Plate Number, User ID, Vehicle Type, Activity Type, District ID, Neighborhood ID, Coordinate, Weekday, Date, Time. From the conclusion, we highlighted that people usually to bypass the use of new technology.

Kim et al. (2018) report a value stream mapping application to collect data about the delivery process [13]. This application was developed based on a real situation in the Central Business District of Seattle (US). Results showed the importance of standardization and reliability of the application.

In Brazil, digital apps for urban freight transport focused on last-mile delivery. Table 1 summarizes some apps available to download in Brazil. Most of them provide fast delivery of food, beverage and goods. Some restaurants also have their own digital app, like MacDonald's, Habib's, Pizza Hut. In this case, another platform connects the order to deliver.

Table 1. Example of digital apps for urban freight transport in Brazil [own study]

App	Purpose
Delivery much, Quero Delivery, Ifood, 99Food, UberEats, James, aiqfome, PedidosJa, Ragazzo, Bee, Zé Delivery	Instant delivery of food and beverage
Rappi, Glovo, Click Entregas Expressas, Shipp, Loggi, DTudo	Instant delivery of goods
Ultragaz	Instant delivery of gas stove
FarmaciaApp	Delivery of medicine
Giuliana Flores	Delivery of flowers

This brief review shows that there are few and limited applications for urban freight transport, mainly focused on last-mile delivery as reported by Morganti et al. (2016). In this sense, any initiative is important, since data can be obtained using digital applications, as reported by Kim et al. (2018) and Kolbay et al. (2018) [12, 13].

3   Unloading Zones in Belo Horizonte

In order to show the importance of the digital application developed by Belo Horizonte Municipality, this section presents an overview about unloading zones in Belo Horizonte, based on Oliveira (2014), Ramos et al. (2014), and Santos et al. (2017), all publication in Portuguese [14–16].

Initially, it is important to inform that the loading and unloading operation is defined by the Brazilian Traffic Code as the immobilization of the vehicle, for the time strictly necessary for the loading or unloading of animals or cargo (Law 9.503, September 23 1997). The same law considers the loading and unloading operation as transit "Transit is the use of roads by people, vehicles and animals, isolated or in groups, driven or not, for circulation purposes, stop, parking and loading or unloading operation". The regulation, inspection and enforcement are carried out by the local authorities responsible for the road.

Besides that, the National Urban Mobility Policy (Law 12,587 of January 3, 2012) contemplates cargo movement as an integral part of the national urban mobility system, and the unloading zones make up the urban mobility infrastructure.

Despite these laws, the unloading zones are the main problem related to urban freight transport in Brazilian cities [17, 18]. In particular, the main complaint from transporters and retailers is the lack of unloading zones in commercially dense regions.

Oliveira (2014) proposed a framework to collect information about urban deliveries operation. In a practical way, it is presented a diagnosis of unloading zones in the Central Area of Belo Horizonte. The results came from a parking occupancy survey in the 550 unloading zones in the central region (these zones offer 1147 parking spaces for loading or unloading operations). Also, an interview with 491 drivers in unloading operation was carried to obtain complementary data. In general, 49% of respondents declared parking the vehicle as soon as they arrive at the delivery destination. However, on average, a vehicle travels, on average, 9.5 min around the destination looking for a parking area. In

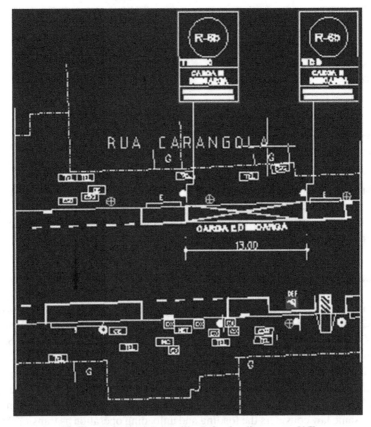

Fig. 1. A project of signalling of unloading zones [15]

general, 57.7% of unloading zones are occupied by cars. Cargo vehicles occupied 37.7% of the unloading zones. The average time for a cargo vehicle parked in an unloading zone is 66.2 min.

The result of Oliveira (2014) highlighted the irregular occupation of unloading zones by cars. Possible causes may be associated with poor and/or confused signalling, verified by Ramos et al. (2014), which observed that unloading zones when close to the on-street parking areas caused doubts in the car drivers, who often used the unloading zones to park passenger vehicles. This result was also corroborated by the number of fines and cars removed in unloading zones with parking payment: 46,178 cars received fine enforcement between July 2013 and May 2015 for irregular parking in unloading zones [16].

In order to reduce the illegal parking and improve the use of unloading zones, Ramos et al. (2014) proposed a project in which the vertical signalling is reinforced by horizontal signalling of the unloading zones in Belo Horizonte (Fig. 1). In order to prove the efficiency of this proposal, Santos et al. (2017) report a pilot test that compared the use of unloading zones before and after installing horizontal signage. A pilot test was carried out in the places with an elevated number of fines. Results indicated a reduction in the number of illegal parking (from 84 to 45 vehicles), and in the total parking time (from 15.5 h to 3.5 h) [16].

Santos et al. (2017) conclude that horizontal sign reinforces the vertical sign. However, it does not remove the illegal parking, being necessary enforcement for it. Between 2016–2020, all unloading zones close to parking areas in the Central Area of Belo Horizonte are receiving horizontal signalling, as showed in Fig. 2.

Fig. 2. Unloading zones with vertical and horizontal signalling [own study]

4   Rotativo Digital: A Mobile Application to Unloading Zones in Belo Horizonte

In 2018, rotativo digital app was launched in Belo Horizonte to parking vehicles on-street. The turnover in the on-street parking zones is a way to democratize parking spaces for vehicles. There are 23,631 on-street parking zones that transform into 106,079 parking opportunities in 876 blocks in Belo Horizonte. It is possible to parking a vehicle by 1, 2 or 5 h (depending on the desired parking area) using this app paying R$4.40 (Brazilian currency, ≈1 euro).

In October of 2018, the use of the app has been expanded to motorcycle courier. There are there are 2,656 parking slots (generating 36,387 parking opportunities per day to the motorcycle with a red plate, which are authorized to perform motorcycle courier service. In June of 2019 the usage of the app has been expanded to freight vehicles. Belo Horizonte has 2,942 unloading areas. Figure 3 presents the location of unloading zones to freight vehicles in the Central Area of Belo Horizonte. For motorcycle courier and freight vehicles, the parking is free of charge and the maximum parking time is 1 h.

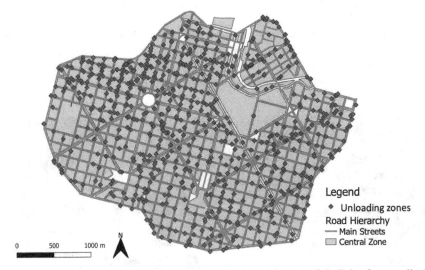

Fig. 3. Unloading zones in Central area of Belo Horizonte [own study] (Color figure online)

The use of rotativo digital for urban freight vehicles is increase day by day. Figure 4 shows the evolution of the number of usages in unloading zones. From July until October, the app was usage 116,752 times. However, there is still resistance from transportation companies in using the application. Same results were observed in Barcelona by Kolbay et al. (2018).

Initially, many transport companies understood that the city wanted to create mechanisms to reduce accessibility to commercial establishments. This point was discussed during III Forum of Urban Logistics, promoted by the Belo Horizonte Municipality. The criticisms indicated that the application intended to "harm the business". However,

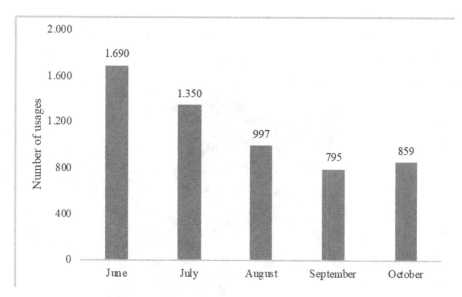

Fig. 4. The number of usages, by month [own study]

four months later, after the presentation of the first results, these same stakeholders understood the benefits of the app for society, creating a fairer use.

The main data obtained with the use of the app is the identification, in real-time, the places where the unloading zones were most used. In general, 59.7% of users informed the GPS location, being possible to identify the places where the deliveries operation was being carried. Figure 5 presents the unloading zones more usable in the Central Area of Belo Horizonte. It is possible to identify a cluster of areas with high utilization, the same area with the largest number of commercial establishments. In addition, it is in this region that there is the largest number of loading and unloading areas available.

Other results obtained by the app is the time in which the unloading operation occurs in the Central Area of Belo Horizonte. Figure 6 presents the percentage of usage during the working day. Deliveries occur mainly from 9 a.m. until 3 p.m.

Although this time is a little be late of rush time, in general, the freight vehicles are in congestion during rush time. This result could provide measures more effective to improve urban freight transport in Belo Horizonte.

4.1 Lessons Learned

Which could we learn with the Brazilian experience? The lessons learned from this experience are interesting. Firstly, Rotativo Digital allows us to collect data about the usage of unloading zones. Although it is not possible to identify the parking time (it is a limitation of the app), it is possible to identify the most used areas and hours in which areas are being used, initial information that may support public policies. In Brazil, there is no frequent data collection about urban freight, and this application can be a form of recurrent and systematic data collection.

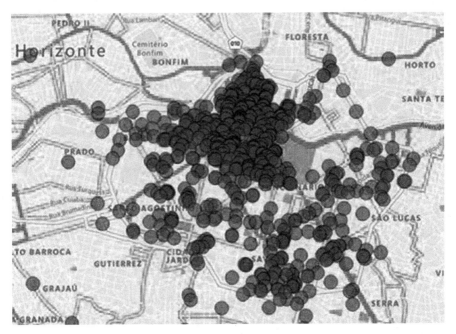

Fig. 5. Unloading zones usable with Rotativo digital app in a working day [own study]

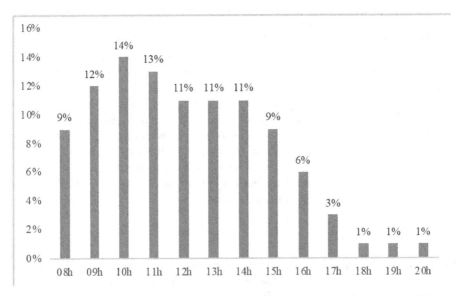

Fig. 6. Percentage of the utilization of app, in a working day, by the hour [own study]

In addition, some functionality can be incorporated into the application to ensure the principles in relation to usability, engagement, and procedure to improve data quality and assurance [19]. Still, the engagement of the usage of the app by drivers is one barrier which could be broken with awareness campaigns to show the importance of the usage of the app by all.

Finally, it is a digital application developed and managed by the municipality. Despite the limitation, it is one initiative positive which could support others and could be improved by all society. Any application can be improved. However, the limitations of Rotativo Digital do not detract from the initiative of the city hall, which has been positive and has become a way of acquiring preliminary data for future analyzes of urban freight transport in Belo Horizonte.

5   Conclusion

This paper presented a mobile application to unloading zones called Rotativo Digital, developed by Belo Horizonte municipality. Unloading zones was one of the first measures implemented in Belo Horizonte to improve urban freight transport. Despite that, unloading zones is one of the main problems related by carriers and retailers in Belo Horizonte, due to illegal parking. Some measures were implemented to reduce illegal parking and presented a reduction. However, a systematic and recurrent collection data in unloading zones is necessary to identify other problems and improve the efficiency of urban distribution.

In general, the suggestion to use a mobile application to urban freight transport is presented by researchers or from some companies. In this paper, the digital application Rotativo Digital, which was developed by the municipality of Belo Horizonte, initially focused on parking areas and extended to unloading zones. This app was launched in June of 2019 and had, until November, 116,752 usages. When the drivers use GPS, it is possible to identify unloading zones more requested. This information could support other measures by the municipality to improve the urban freight activities.

The increase in the number of users is a challenge for the city. Dissemination and awareness campaigns can achieve this goal. Finally, this initiative could inspire other municipalities, which could create partnerships with Universities to develop the digital application to them.

References

1. Bicen, H., Kocakoyun, S.: The evaluation of the most used mobile devices applications by students. Proc. - Soc. Behav. Sci. **89**, 756–760 (2013)
2. Deloitte: Global Mobile Consumer Trends. Report (2017)
3. PagBrasil: O Brasil é o 5° país que mais usa smartphone. Report (2019). https://www.pagbra sil.com/pt-br/insights/uso-smartphone-brasil/. Accessed 15 Jan 2020
4. Deloitte: Digital-Age Transportation: The Future of Urban Mobility. Report (2012)
5. Gebresselassie, M., Sanchez, T.W.: Smart tools for socially sustainable transport: a review of mobility apps. Urban Sci. **2**, 45 (2018)
6. Iwan, S., Małecki, K., Stalmach, D.: Utilization of mobile applications for the improvement of traffic management systems. In: Mikulski, J. (ed.) TST 2014. CCIS, vol. 471, pp. 48–58. Springer, Heidelberg (2014). https://doi.org/10.1007/978-3-662-45317-9_6
7. Ifood: Expansão do delivery de comida no Brasil. Report (2019)

8. DHL: DHL Crowd Sources Deliveries in Stockholm with MyWays. Press Release (2013)
9. Comi, A., et al.: DynaLOAD: a simulation framework for planning, managing and controlling urban delivery bays. Transp. Res. Proc. **22**, 335–344 (2017)
10. Comi, A., et al.: An advanced planner for urban freight delivering. Arch. Transp. **48**(4), 27–40 (2018)
11. Oliveira, L.K., et al.: Evaluate of collaborative transit system to urban goods delivery: an exploratory study in Belo Horizonte (Brazil). Transp. Res. Proc. **25**, 928–941 (2017)
12. Kolbay, B., Mrazovic, P., Larriba-Pey, J.L.: Analyzing last mile delivery operations in Barcelona's urban freight transport network. In: Longo, A., et al. (eds.) IISSC/CN4IoT - 2017. LNICST, vol. 189, pp. 13–22. Springer, Cham (2018). https://doi.org/10.1007/978-3-319-67636-4_2
13. Kim, H., Boyle, L.N., Goodchild, A.: A mobile application for collecting task time data for value stream mapping of the final 50 feet of urban goods delivery processes. In: Proceedings of the Human Factors and Ergonomics Society 2018 Annual Meeting, pp. 1808–1812 (2018)
14. Oliveira, L.K.: Diagnosis of loading and unloading spaces for urban freight distribution: a case study in Belo Horizonte. J. Transp. Lit. **8**(1), 178–209 (2014)
15. Ramos, C.M.F., Pena, C.A.L.M., Oliveira, L.K.: Proposal for the adequacy of the signalling of on-street unloading zones in the central area of Belo Horizonte. In: XVIII PANAM, Santander (Espanha) (2014)
16. Santos, O.R., et al.: Pilot test of the effectiveness of the implementation of horizontal signage in the loading and unloading areas: the case of Belo Horizonte. In: 21° Congresso Brasileiro de Transporte e Trânsito, São Paulo (2017)
17. Oliveira, L.K., et al.: An overview of problems and solutions for urban freight transport in Brazilian cities. Sustainability **10**(4), 1233 (2018)
18. Oliveira, L.K., et al.: Transport service provider perception of barriers and urban freight policies in Brazil. Sustainability **11**(24), 6890 (2019)
19. Sturm, U.: Defining principles for mobile apps and platforms development in citizen science. Res. Ideas Outcomes **3**, e21283 (2017)

Research of the Influence of Demand Factors on Suburban Bus Transport in Slovak Republic

Vladimír Konečný[✉] and Mária Brídziková

University of Žilina, Univerzitná 8215/1, Žilina, Slovakia
{vladimir.konecny,maria.bridzikova}@fpedas.uniza.sk

Abstract. Demand for transport services is determined by many factors each having a different impact on demand. The impact of individual factors on demand also depends on the group of passengers using services of suburban bus transport. The article deals with the identification of factors affecting the demand for suburban bus transport and research on the impact of individual factors. The most important factors of demand include the quality of transport services, fare price, incomes of the population and potential of demand in the form of population numbers and structure. Knowing the impact of factors is an important basis for the procurement of transport services and its scope, as well as for the competitiveness and sustainability of the system of suburban bus transport. The research is carried out under the conditions of the Slovak Republic, in a specific system of suburban bus transport.

Keywords: Demand · Factor · Transport service · Suburban bus transport · Sustainability

1 Introduction

Demand for transport is derived demand (secondary), that is, it results from the demand of companies and inhabitants for goods and services, closely related to the mobility of the population [1, 2]. Population aging is one of the major challenges that most countries faces and the situation is expected to intensify over the next decades. It is also necessary to take this issue into account in Slovakia [3]. The whole change in the population's demographic distribution also affects the demand for public passenger transport [4]. As the age structure of the population changes, the transport habits of the population also change, this has a significant impact on the future functioning of the public passenger transport system [5, 6]. Changing population structure in terms of the aging population also affects the need for barrier-free access in public passenger transport systems [7–9].

Demand for transport services is determined by many factors, each having a different impact on demand [10]. The article deals with the identification of factors affecting the demand for suburban bus transport and research into the impact of individual factors. Foreign surveys identify as the important factors of demand the quality of transport services, the price of fares, the incomes of the population and the potential of demand in the form of the number and structure of the population [11]. Given the availability of

© Springer Nature Switzerland AG 2020
J. Mikulski (Ed.): TST 2020, CCIS 1289, pp. 95–109, 2020.
https://doi.org/10.1007/978-3-030-59270-7_8

information, statistical data, we are researching the demand for suburban bus transport under the conditions of the Žilina self-governing region.

2 Data, Materials and Methods

2.1 Analysis of Individual Factors Resulting in Demand for Suburban Bus Transport

The demand for transport is influenced by several factors, whose change may increase or decrease the volume of realized transports. When choosing a mode of transport, passengers consider several factors that influence their choice. The behavior of passengers is determined by the social environment, economic development of the country, but also territory, transport infrastructure, and habits of inhabitants. The most important factors influencing the demand for suburban bus services:

Quality of Transport Services

The quality of services is also one of the important factors influencing the demand for public passenger transport. Blacome et al. (2004), Berson et al. (2003), Francis (2002), Lythgoe and Wardman (2002) and FitzRoy and Smith (1998) are only some who have pointed out the quality of services as the factor with the strongest impact on demand. Bresson et al. (2003) concluded that the quality of service is at least as important as travel, if not more.

One of the factors that increase the quality of services and influence the level of demand is the existence of an integrated transport system. Integration involves coordinating the level of provided services, coordinating routes and timetables. Therefore, the more the public passenger transport system is integrated, the higher the quality of services provided and the level of demand in the region [12, 13]. Subsequently, the preconditions are created to increase road safety [14, 15].

Fare Price

The effects of fare on public passenger transport demand are relatively easy to trace. In general, if prices rise, the demand for public passenger transport will decrease. Changing fares has the most direct and strong impact on demand [16]. Several studies investigate the impact of changes in fair prices on demand. Most of these studies more or less agree that changes in fares have a relatively significant impact on the demand for public passenger transport. Sensitivity when changing fares is higher if prices increase when prices decrease.

Suburban bus transport as one of the types of regular bus transport in Slovakia is subject to price regulation. Free pricing (price liberalization) is applied in the Slovak republic in regular long-distance bus transport and non-regular bus transport.

The price fares of suburban bus transport are currently set by the prices of the self-governing regions in the form of maximum fares for individual groups of passengers, luggage and animals.

Population Incomes
Equally important factor, which can be categorized into the demography category and significantly affects the demand for public transport are the incomes of the population [17]. The income of the population is closely related to the development of the economy. From the economic and statistical point of view, economic development is represented by the development and value of GDP. The level of population income varies considerably and may have a direct or indirect on the demand for suburban bus transport. Direct impact on demand is a situation when individual residents have more income, which can be used to use suburban public transport. This situation increases to passengers transported. On the contrary, the indirect impact on demand for suburban public transport means that, with increased incomes, residents will tend to buy cars, or this may result in increased demand for fuel if they already own a car. In this case, rising incomes of the population may result in a decrease in the number of people transported.

The Population
The most important demographic indicator in connection with the demand for bus transport is the number of inhabitants and their development in the given settlement unit. The region's population represents a potential demand for transport. The prerequisite of real demand is the very existence of the population and its sufficient number.

In general deal, different types of population have different travel requirements. Also, certain selected demographic groups, such as low-income inhabitants, inhabitants who do not car ownership, people with disabilities, pupils, students, undergraduates and retirees tend to make greater use of services suburban bus transport to a higher degree than the rest of the population. However, these selected demographic groups represent a minority of the total population.

3 Methods Used to Research Individual Factors Affecting the Demand for Suburban Bus Transport

In particular, methods of correlation and regression analysis, selected methods of time series theory (average growth rate) and methods of statistical analysis (average unit price) are used to research demand factors, identify their impact on demand of individual passenger groups.

Calculation of Unit Price of Fare in Suburban Bus Transport
Based on fiscal decentralization in Slovakia since 1.1.2005 is the fare in suburban bus transport regulated from the position of self-governing regions, exist differences in maximum fares between individual self-governing regions. There are also differences in providing travel discounts. The suburban bus tariff for individual self-governing regions is distant, exist tariff classes according to the distance in km, fares are set within tariff classes. Tariff rates are defined in the form of matrices, where the lines represent tariff

distances in km and columns represent the types of fare. To be able to compare different fares in different fares, it is necessary to define a suitable variable. This appears to be the average unit price in euros per km for a particular type of fare. The reason for calculating average unit prices in suburban bus transport for comparison, there are also different numbers of tariff classes and their different width in km. The average unit price is determined as an average value of fare determined for each tariff zone based on the relationship (1):

$$\bar{f_j} = \frac{\sum\limits_{i=1}^{n} \frac{TR_{ij}}{TR_{zavgi}}}{n} = \frac{\sum\limits_{i=1}^{n} \frac{TR_{ij}}{TR_{zvagi}}}{n} = \frac{\sum\limits_{i=1}^{n} \frac{TR_{ij}}{\frac{TD\min_i + TD\max_i}{2}}}{n} = \frac{\sum\limits_{i=1}^{n} \frac{2TR_{ij}}{\frac{TD_{nim\,i} + TD\max_i}{2}}}{n} \qquad (1)$$

f_j - is the average unit price of the "j" type of fare (average fare) in eur/pkm, [eur/pkm]
f_{ij} - is the average unit price (average fare) in the "i" tariff zone for the "j" type of fare v eur/pkm [eur/pkm]
TR_{ij} - is the tariff rate (tariff rate) in "i" tariff zone for the "j" type of fare in eur/p
n -is the number of tariff zones
$TZavg_i$ - is the arithmetic mean of the lower and upper limits of the "i" tariff zone [km]
$TDmin_i$ - is the lower limit of the i-th tariff zone [km]
$TDmax_i$ - it is the upper limit of the i-th tariff zone [km]

Average Growth Rate

It expresses the average time series growth coefficient from time series values from 1 to "n", it is average time series growth.

$$\bar{k_t} = \sqrt[n-1]{\frac{y_n}{y_1}} \qquad (2)$$

n – number of time series members,
y_1 – value of the 1st member of the time series,
y_n – value of the "nth" member of the time series.

Correlation Analysis

Correlation analysis examines the tightness of statistical dependence between quantitative variables. Correlation analysis, unlike regression, does not express causally – subsequent relationship. The variable Y does not depend on the variable X, but the two random variables X and Y change together. Regression analysis assumes that the variable Y is random and variable X is fixed. The correlation analysis tool is called the correlation coefficient (mark like "r"). Determines the degree of tightness (degree) of dependence. The correlation coefficient is a measure of the linear dependence of two variables and we can express it with the following relationship (3):

$$r_{xy} = \frac{n \cdot \sum\limits_{i=1}^{n} x_y \cdot y_i - \sum\limits_{i=1}^{n} x_i \cdot \sum\limits_{i=1}^{n} y_i}{\sqrt{\left[n \cdot x_i^2 - \left(\sum\limits_{i=1}^{n} x_i \right)^2 \right] \cdot \left[n \cdot \sum\limits_{i=1}^{n} y_i^2 - \left(\sum\limits_{i=1}^{n} y_i \right)^2 \right]}} \quad (3)$$

r – correlation value
n - number of associated values
x – value of the first variable
y – value of the second variable

Multi-criteria Regression Analysis

Multi-criteria regression analysis allows expressing the influence of several independent variables (X, P, Q, R, ...) on the monitored indicator (Y) simultaneously. The multi-criteria regression function should take into account all important variables that result from the dependent variable Y. Each of the independent variables considered must be causally related to the dependent variable. This dependence can be confirmed, for example, by calculating the correlation coefficients. The influence of independent variables on dependent variables is determined by the parameter values of the general multi-criteria regression model, which has the general form:

$$y_i = b_0 + b_1 \cdot x_{1i} + b_2 \cdot x_{2i} + b_3 \cdot x_{3i} + \ldots + b_k \cdot x_{ki} + e_i \quad (4)$$

and a specific model of multi-criteria linear regression function has the form:

$$y_i = b_0 + b_1 \cdot x_{1i} + b_2 \cdot x_{2i} + b_3 \cdot x_{3i} + \ldots + b_k \cdot x_{ki} \quad (5)$$

where is the estimate of y_i ($i = 1, 2, \ldots, n$).

The individual regression coefficients ($b_1, b_2, \ldots, b_n$) express the average change of the dependent variable Y, which is caused by the change of the respective independent variable. It is also important to reassess the inclusion of the coefficient b_0 in the proposed multi-criteria function, i.e. whether it logically makes sense if the independent variables X_1 to X_n reach 0, whether the dependent variable Y should be zero, or whether its value should be non-zero due to the possible non-zero coefficient b_0.

4   Result and Dissemination

4.1   Demand for Suburban Bus Transport in Žilina Self-governing Region

The number of passengers traveling by suburban bus transport has a decreasing character. Figure 1 shows the development, the number of passengers traveling for ordinary fare decreases, the demand for student fare decreases, but on the other hand the number of passengers traveling for other fares on increasing. This group of passengers (other fares) includes inhabitants aged 65–69 years, 70 years and over, as well as holders of license disabled person and person with reduced mobility.

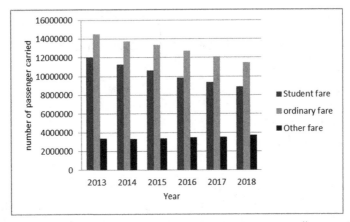

Fig. 1. Number of passengers transported by suburban bus transport in Žilina self-governing region by type of fare [own study based on 18]

Average annual coefficient of the development of people transported in the period 2013 to 2018 calculated according to the relationship (2) in the Žilina self-governing region is:

- For the demand of people transported for students'(special) fare is the coefficient of 0.941339, which means on average, demand fell by 5.9% annually,
- For the demand of people transported for ordinary fare is the coefficient of 0.954110, which means, on average, demand fell by 4.6% annually,
- for the demand of people transported for other fare is the coefficient of 1.0195377, which means, on average, demand increased by 2.0% annually,
- A total coefficient of 0.957572, which means, on average, demand fell by 4.2% annually.

4.2   Factors of Demand for Suburban Bus Transport in Žilina Self-governing Region

Within the Žilina self-governing region we investigated the impact of the most important factors on the demand for suburban bus transport. The Žilina self-governing region is a customer of transport services in suburban bus transport under the valid legislation, which means that it is a guarantor of transport services of its territory. Based on public service contracts concluded with selected transport companies, if finances the incurred loss from the ordered transport services.

Offer of Suburban Bus Transport in Žilina Self-governing Region

The offer connections expressed as the number of kilometers performed by suburban bus transport significantly determines the demand for suburban bus transport. Within the Žilina self-governing region for the period 2013–2018, the offer was stable, since 2014 it has been slightly growing, Fig. 2.

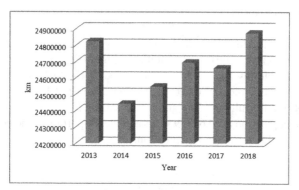

Fig. 2. Number of kilometers performed in the Žilina region in the period under review [own study based on 18]

Potential of Demand for Suburban Bus Transport – Inhabitants of Žilina Self-governing Region

Population aging is a social problem not only in Slovakia. It causes changes in the potential demand for specific groups of the population. The development is age-specific. In the context of examining the demand for bus transport, it is necessary to create and analyze such population groups that represent a real group of bus passengers concerning individual types of fare and performance, i.e. a group of pupils and students, a group of economically active (productive) inhabitants and a group of inhabitants of post-productive age (pensioners). In the Slovak Republic, there are also regional differences in the proportionality of the age groups of the population, at the regional level they are manifested in differences in the demand for regular bus transport.

The population in individual age groups is determined mainly by the birth rate and aging population over time. Demographic development and settlement structure of the territory are among the determinants of demand, which the carrier or the customer of services in the public interest cannot influence them, but they can respond to them by changing the offer of transport services and quality of transport services.

Individual passenger groups behave individually concerning the demand for suburban bus transport and their demand is determined to varying degrees by demand factors.

The potential of demand for suburban bus transport was analyzed by the population of the Žilina self-governing region, its structure and development are the years 2013–2018. To examine the potential of demand for services to suburban bus transport, the inhabitants of Žilina self-governing region were divided into groups according to the suburban bus tariff and individual types of fare (full, discounted, registered), the following age groups were designed and used:

– children from 0 to 5 years,
– pupils from 6 to 14 years,

- students from 15 to 19 years,
- students from 20 to 25 years,
- economically active population from 26 to 64 years,
- citizens from 65 to 69 years,
- citizens aged 70 and over.

The population of Žilina Region has not changed significantly year on year. In 2018 the Žilina Region had 691,286 inhabitants. Figure 3 shows the development of the population structure by age group for the period 2013–2018. The largest share is represented by an economically active population aged 26–64 years. This group of people is transported for full fare. The graph also shows that there is an increase in the proportion of the population aged 65–69 years and the proportion of the population aged 70 and over. This is due to an aging population.

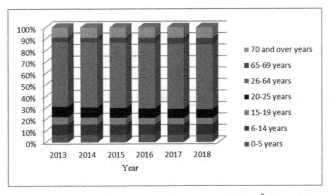

Fig. 3. Development of the population structure by age group in the Žilina self-governing region between 2013 and 2018 [own study based on 18]

Price of Fare in Suburban Bus Transport in Žilina Self-governing Region
The price for transport in suburban bus transport depends on the transport distance and type of fare, so the calculation is based on the average unit price (€/pkm) determined for each reference year. Based on the relationship (1) the average unit price for each type of fare was calculated. Within the Žilina self-governing region, the average unit price has not changed since 2012. Table 1 shows the value of the average unit price of ordinary fare and special fare in suburban bus transport in Žilina self-governing region.

Income of Population in the Žilina Self-governing Region – Monthly Wage and Old-Age Pension
Another important factor influencing the demand for suburban bus transport is the income of the population – we consider the average monthly nominal wage for economically active inhabitants and the average monthly old-age pension for retirees. Table 2 shows the development of wages and pensions for the period 2013–2018 in the Žilina self-governing region.

Table 1. The average unit price of fare in suburban bus transport for individual types of fare in Žilina self-governing region [own study]

Average unit price [€/pkm]			
Ordinary fare	Ordinary fare from traffic card	Special fare	Special fare from traffic card
0.0699	0.0666	0.0422	0.0381

Table 2. Development of population incomes in Žilina self-governing region in the monitored period [own study based on 19]

Year	2013	2014	2015	2016	2017	2018
Average monthly nominal wage [€/month]	839	877	920	690	1015	1084
Average monthly old-age pension [€/month]	359	368	375	380	389	402

The growth of the Slovak economy was influenced by the growth of the average monthly wage. With the disposable incomes of the population, demand for suburban bus transport could be expected to grow, but the opposite is true.

4.3 Correlation Analysis of Selected Factors of Demand for Suburban Bus Transport in Žilina Self-governing Region

We investigated the relationship of demand factors to the demand for suburban bus transport, using relationship (3).

Correlation of Demand and Income of Population
The relation between the demand for suburban bus transport (number of passengers transported in suburban bus transport) and population income (average monthly nominal wage, average monthly old-age pension) is also confirmed by the calculated correlation coefficients:

- The coefficient of correlation between the number of persons transported for ordinary fare and average monthly nominal wage in the Žilina self-governing region reached −0.9929, it is a strong indirect statistical dependence,
- The coefficient of correlation between the number of persons transported for other fare and average monthly old-age pension in the Žilina self-governing region reached 0.8863, it is a strong direct statistical dependence.

The growth of the average monthly nominal wage reduces the demand of the economically active population for suburban bus transport. Inhabitants are becoming more accessible passenger car and so in many cases individual cars transport substitute public passenger transport services.

On the other hand, the growth of old-age pensions stimulates demand for suburban bus transport, which is also influenced by the fact that pensioners are transported for other fares, which is several times lower than full fare in suburban bus transport.

Correlation of Demand and Number of Population

The coefficients of correlation between population numbers according to their age and number of selected groups of passengers reach different values, the results are shown in Table 3.

– Elementary school children pupils (0–12 years old) have a medium direct relationship,
– There is a strong direct relationship with secondary and tertiary pupils (age 16 to 25),
– Economically active persons (26 to 61 years of age) have a strong indirect relationship,
– There is a strong direct relationship with pensioners aged 70 and over.

Table 3. Correlation coefficient values between the number of population and transported persons by age group [own study]

Population by age	Number of passengers carried by age	Correlation coefficient
0–15 years	0–15 years	0.5323
16–25 years	16–25 years	0.9858
26–29 years	26–29 years	−0.9504
70 and over years	70 and over years	0.8539

For an economically active person, the strong indirect relationship between population and demand can be interpreted in such a way the demand is fundamentally influenced by other factors, in particular population income. The choice of relocation is determined by the availability of a particular mode of transport. The greatest potential for shifting from bus to individual car transport has the economically active population, followed by pensioners, the lowest potential is for pupils and students under 18 years of age.

4.4 Multi-criteria Regression Analysis

The MS Excel software was used for the design of the multi-criteria demand regression function, namely the "data analysis" tool and its multi-criteria regression function. This tool allows generating a function based on the past development of the monitored indicator (in our case the number of passengers carried) and the factors that determine it, whose variables are the determining factors. The input is, therefore, statistical sets (time series) of data from previous periods. The output of the model is an output set containing the coefficients of the multi-criteria regression function characterizing the observed phenomenon. For the proposed model is also determined coefficient of determination, the statistical suitability of the proposed multi-criteria model is also assessed.

Based on the identification of demand factors and statistical data for the period 2013 to 2018, three multi-criteria regression models of demand for passenger groups were compiled.

Multi-criteria Regression Model for the Demand for Pupils and Student Fare

The regression statistics of the model are shown in Table 4, the model considers three independent variables, the independent variables and the calculated coefficients of the independent variables are shown in Table 5.

Table 4. Regression statistic for the multi-criteria model for the demand for pupils and students fare [own study]

Regression statistics	
Multiple R	0.999931874
R Square	0.999863752
Adjusted R Square	0.666439857
Standard Error	171635.5361
Observations	6

Table 5. Variables and Coefficients for multi-criteria model for demand for pupils and student fare [own study]

Coefficients		
Intercept		0
X Variable 1	Inhabitants (6 to 19 years old) - persons	479.3990607
X Variable 2	Supply in PPT - km	−1.276152337
X Variable 3	Reduced fare - €/pkm	−206440362.3

The multi-criteria regression function for the demand for suburban bus transport for pupils and students fare in Žilina self-governing region has the form:

$$Y = 479.3990607X_1 - 1.276152337X_2 - 206440362.3X_3$$

Multi-criteria Regression Model for the Demand for Full Fare

The regression statistics of the model are shown in Table 6, the model considers four independent variables, the independent variables and the calculated coefficients of the independent variables are shown in Table 7.

The multi-criteria regression function for the demand for suburban bus transport for full-fare in Žilina self-governing region has the form:

$$Y = 36.47407986X_1 + 0.883197002X_2 - 214485150X_3 - 11462.44122X_4$$

Table 6. Regression statistics for the multi-criteria model for the demand for full-fare [own study]

Regression statistics	
Multiple R	0.999931874
R Square	0.999863752
Adjusted R Square	0.499926248
Standard Error	122467.2479
Observations	6

Table 7. Variables and Coefficients for the multi-criteria model for the demand for full-fare [own study]

Coefficients		
Intercept		0
X Variable 1	Inhabitants (20 to 64 years old) - persons	36.47407986
X Variable 2	Supply in PPT - km	0.883197002
X Variable 3	Full fare - €/pkm	−214485150
X Variable 4	Average monthly wage - €/month	−11462.44122

Multi-criteria Regression Model for the Demand for Other Fare

The regression statistics of the model are shown in Table 8, the model considers three independent variables, the independent variables and the calculated coefficients of the independent variables are shown in Table 9. The model has a reliability of 99.98%. The model does not include fare, as this group of passengers is transported for minimum (registration) fare.

Table 8. Regression statistic for the multi-criteria model for the demand for other fares [own study]

Regression statistics	
Multiple R	0.999869
R Square	0.999738
Adjusted R Square	0.66623
Standard Error	79288.09
Observations	6

Table 9. Variables and Coefficients for multi-criteria model for demand for other fares [own study]

Coefficients		
Intercept		0
X Variable 1	Inhabitants (65 and over year) - persons	20.57751
X Variable 2	Supply in PPT - km	0.070626
X Variable 3	Average monthly pension - €/pkm	−614.25

The multi-criteria regression function for the demand for suburban bus transport for other fares in Žilina self-governing region has the form:

$$Y = 20.57751X_1 + 0.070626X_2 - 614.25X_3$$

5 Conclusion

Bus transport is an important and irreplaceable transport system used by all age groups to satisfy transport requirements. The performances of regular bus transport had declined significantly in recent years. This decrease is caused not only by price changes and changes in the income of the population but also by the change in the population structure and the structure of population settlement. The population in specific settlement units represents a potential demand for regular bus services. Student and ordinary fare represent the largest share of the demand for suburban bus transport. In recent years, the proportionality of groups of passengers traveling with discounts and without discounts has also changed significantly. The number of passengers transported for ordinary fare is significantly reduced compared to other passengers. Passengers transported for ordinary fare in the past accounted for the largest share of demand and revenues from regular bus transport. It is assumed that the loss of revenues from ordinary fare will be solved in the future by rising fare prices for groups of passengers transported for the reduced fare. These rules need to be respected as they affect revenue, economic results of carrier and may put future additional pressure on increasing resources to finance suburban bus transport.

The demographic development and changes in population structure as well as the settlement structure influence both the quality parameters of the transport services of the territory and the quality parameters of the provided transport services in the area of suburban bus transport.

The proposed regression models can be used to estimate the demand of passenger groups in the future. Using this forecasting method is difficult to collect, analyze, and process available statistical data representative of past socio-economic phenomena. Application of the method also requires the calculation of the values of some demand determinants of specific groups of passengers on suburban bus transport (e.g. average fare price).

Acknowledgments. This paper has been developed under support of the project: MŠVVŠ SR VEGA No.1/0566/18 KONEČNÝ, V.: Research on the impact of supply and quality of transport services on the competitiveness and sustainability of demand for public transport.

References

1. Kral, P., Janoskova, K., Kliestik, T.: Key determinants of the public transport user's satisfaction. Administratie si Manag. Public **31**, 36–51 (2018)
2. Hansson, J., et al.: Preferences in regional public transport: a literature review. Eur. Transp. Res. Rev. **11**(1), 38 (2019). https://doi.org/10.1186/s12544-019-0374-4
3. Gnap, J., Konečný, V.: The impact of a demographic trend on the demand for scheduled bus transport in the Slovak Republic. Komunikacie **10**(2), 55–59 (2008)
4. Veternik, M., Gogola, M.: Examining of correlation between demographic development of population and their travel behavior. In: 12th International Scientific Conference of Young Scientists on Sustainable, Modern and Safe Transport, vol. 192, pp. 929–934 (2017)
5. Fatima, K., Moridpour, S.: Measuring public transport accessibility for elderly. In: 2018, 6th International Conference on Traffic and Logistic Engineering, ICTLE 2018, vol. 259 (2019)
6. Fatima, K., et al.: A case study of elderly public transport accessibility. In: 2018 Asia-Pacific Conference on Intelligent Medical (APCIM)/2018 7th International Conference on Transportation and Traffic Engineering, ICTTE 2018, pp. 253–257 (2018)
7. Starzynska, B., et al.: Requirements elicitation of passengers with reduced mobility for the design of high quality, accessible and inclusive public transport services. Manag. Prod. Eng. Rev. **6**(3), 70–76 (2015)
8. Ludici, A., Bertoli, L., Faccio, E.: The "invisible" needs of women with disabilities in transportation systems. Crime Prev. Commun. Saf. **19**(3–4), 264–275 (2017)
9. Bühler, C., Heck, H., Becker, J.: How to inform people with reduced mobility about public transport. In: Miesenberger, K., Klaus, J., Zagler, W., Karshmer, A. (eds.) ICCHP 2008. LNCS, vol. 5105, pp. 973–980. Springer, Heidelberg (2008). https://doi.org/10.1007/978-3-540-70540-6_146
10. Polat, C.: The demand determinants for urban public transport services: a review of the literature. J. Appl. Sci. **12**(12), 1211–1231 (2012)
11. Paulley, N., et al.: The demand for public transport: the effect of fares, quality of service, income and car ownship. Transp. Policy **13**(4), 295–306 (2006)
12. Poliak, M., et al.: Public transport integration. Commun. – Sci. Lett. Univ. Zilina **19**(2), 127–132 (2017)
13. Poliak, M., et al.: The competitiveness of public transport. J. Compet. **9**(3), 81–97 (2017)
14. Kalašová, A., Černický, L., Hamar, M.: A new approach to road safety in Slovakia. In: Mikulski, J. (ed.) TST 2012. CCIS, vol. 329, pp. 388–395. Springer, Heidelberg (2012). https://doi.org/10.1007/978-3-642-34050-5_44
15. Kalašová, A., Mikulski, J., Kubíková, S.: The impact of intelligent transport systems on an accident rate of the chosen part of road communication network in the Slovak Republic. In: Mikulski, J. (ed.) TST 2016. CCIS, vol. 640, pp. 47–58. Springer, Cham (2016). https://doi.org/10.1007/978-3-319-49646-7_5
16. Sharaby, N., Shiftan, Y.: The impact of fare integration on travel behavior and transit ridership. Transp. Policy **21**, 63–70 (2012)
17. Holmgren, J.: An analysis of the determinants of local public transport demand focusing the effects of income changes. Eur. Transp. Res. Rev. **5**(2), 101–107 (2013). https://doi.org/10.1007/s12544-013-0094-0

18. Report on suburban bus transport carried out in the framework of services in public interest in the territory of the Žilina self-governing region. https://www.zilinskazupa.sk/files/odbory/doprava/2018/dokumenty/6/sprava-primestskej-autobusovej-doprave-realizovanej-ramci-slu zieb-vo-verejnom-zaujme-uzemi-zsk.pdf. Accessed 7 Jan 2020
19. Statistical Office of the Slovak Republic. Žilina Region on figure, years 2014–2019. https://slovak.statistics.sk/. Accessed 7 Jan 2020

Analysis of the Carsharing System
in the Slovak Republic

Stanislav Kubaľák[✉], Ambróz Hájnik, and Kristián Čulík

University of Žilina, Univerzitná 8215/1, Žilina, Slovakia
{stanislav.kubalak,ambroz.hajnik,kristian.culik}@fpedas.uniza.sk

Abstract. The main aim of the paper is to define the carsharing as part of the sharing economy as well as to describe its task in the concept of sustainable development. Because most major cities solve problems with over dense traffic and lack of parking spaces, many European cities, therefore, prefer to invest in the development of urban public transport and new forms of mobility. The prospective concept is carsharing, i.e. sharing cars on a commercial basis. The article also analyzes the current situation of carsharing in foreign cities, where the system is most developed and also a detailed analysis of the current situation in the Slovak republic. In the final part of this paper, based on analyzed knowledge, complex studies, and Qsurveys, and the carsharing system is designed to be applied to the territory of Slovakia.

Keywords: Mobility · Carsharing · Vehicle · Slovak Republic

1 Introduction

Carsharing is one of the latest concepts based on the principle of a shared economy. It is the sharing of cars by several people for whom it is disadvantageous to have their own car because of the low frequency of its use. This means that several people bear the cost of ownership and operation of vehicles and increase their usability. Sharing is a comparable alternative to using a privately owned car and can be very beneficial for an irregular car user [18].

Carsharing is already well known in the world and enjoys great popularity, but in Slovakia, carsharing systems are only beginning to develop and develop slowly, as it is a novelty that is unknown to most of the population. Based on the results obtained from surveys, studies and gained knowledge from the functioning of these systems abroad, respectively in Slovakia, the following study suggested carsharing systems applicable in the territory of Slovakia.

Thanks to this service it is possible to reduce the number of cars in towns, also to reduce the number of constantly expanding car parks and to improve the quality of life.

© Springer Nature Switzerland AG 2020
J. Mikulski (Ed.): TST 2020, CCIS 1289, pp. 110–123, 2020.
https://doi.org/10.1007/978-3-030-59270-7_9

Foreign studies dealing marginally with this issue are:

- **Carsharing use by college students: The case of Milan and Rome:**
  The paper analyses carsharing use by college students in the Italian cities of Rome and Milan. The main finding is that college students use carsharing on an occasional basis and vary rarely their habitual transport choice. The students prefer the free-floating carsharing type over the station-based or roundtrip one. Carsharing substitutes mainly the private car and, to a lesser extent, public transport [13].

- **Location Suitable for the Implementation of Carsharing in the City of São Paulo:**
  This study aimed to analyze the relationship between carsharing and urban mobility in the context of smart cities. The results obtained shows which are the best places for the implementation of carsharing and its possible partnerships with several types of commercial establishments in the city of São Paulo [14].

- **The Impact of Carsharing on Car Ownership in German Cities:**
  Carsharing, currently growing strongly in Germany, is an important instrument for sustainable urban mobility. The present boom is mainly due to so-called "free-floating carsharing". The findings show that station-based and free-floating carsharing leads to a reduction of private cars but to different degrees [15].

2   Carsharing and Social Impact

The current trend of year-on-year growth in individual car transport and the increasing degree of automation is also bringing several negative impacts on the environment.

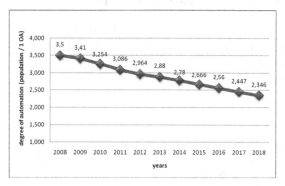

Fig. 1. Development of the degree of automation in the territory of Slovakia for the period 2008 to 2018 [own study based on 8]

Figure 1 shows the development of the degree of automation in Slovakia over the period 2008 to 2018. The growth of transport is also related to its sustainability and the company's attitude toward the quality of the environment [8].

The number of cars that reduce one carsharing vehicle can be determined by various surveys. Most often, these are user surveys where targeted questions are asked about how their car use costs have changed before and after carsharing starts. In Europe, the best results of the surveys are those that show that the interviewed family or the individual sells his own car or eventually ceases to consider buying a new car. On the other hand, the results of surveys from America show different values. This is due to the fact that in US households carsharing is often used as a substitute for a second or third car in the home. In Europe, car-sharing is primarily used by people who do not own their cars. Specific survey-based values can be seen in Table 1 [1, 2].

Table 1. Total of reduced cars due to carsharing [1, 2]

Carsharing reduces the number of cars		
Area	Europe	North America
Number of cars replaced by one shared vehicle	4%–10%	6%–23%
The percentage of users who sell a car when they connect to the system	15,6%–34%	11%–29%
The percentage of carsharing users who, after connecting to the system, avoided buying a new car	23%–26,2%	12%–68%

Table 1 is based on the study: Introduction Shared-Use Vehicle Services for Sustainable Transportation: Carsharing, Bikesharing, and Personal Vehicle Sharing across the Globe [1, 2]. As a result, after switching from own car to carsharing, drivers reduce passenger car use by 40–60% and the mileage of passenger cars is also decreasing, according to the study, by 30–45% compared to own vehicle ownership [4].

3   Carsharing Versus Vehicle Ownership

Regular car user is one who drives at least 15000 km per year [4]. When owning a new private car, people often underestimate the cost of car depreciation, which is the largest share of the total cost of owning or operating a car, according to the Dutch company LeasePlan car depreciation is up to 37% of all costs [22].

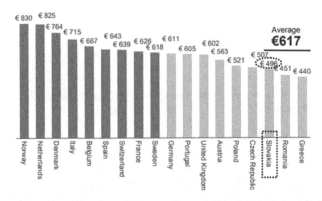

Fig. 2. Average monthly total cost of ownership of all fuel types [28]

From Fig. 2 is obvious that the average monthly cost of operating a new private car in Slovakia is € 496. This value is almost equal to the average of the selected countries. By comparison, all EU countries bordering the Slovak Republic, i.e. Hungary, the Czech Republic, Poland and even Austria, where the average wage level is significantly higher than in Slovakia, reach these costs at a lower level. This is mainly due to higher car insurance prices or higher fuel prices [22]

4   Analysis of Carsharing Systems in the Abroad

Many countries with highly developed car-sharing systems can be found in Europe, especially the developed Western European countries. In the following part of the study, I focus on a comprehensive analysis of the shared car system in European countries, which are Germany and Switzerland, and I also study analysis in Asia. These countries are among the most developed and in the future, they could either expand to other corners of the world or serve as examples for the development of car-sharing systems, e.g. also in the Slovak Republic.

Germany
In this country, the largest number of carsharing companies in the world operate, and the systems also use the largest population. The evolution of the number of car-sharing users between 2008 and 2019 can be seen in the trend graph (Fig. 3) [24].

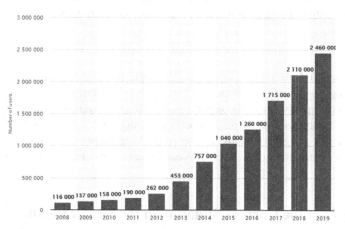

Fig. 3. Registered carsharing user in Germany 2008 to 2019 [28]

Figure 3 shows the number of registered cars sharing users in Germany from 2008 to 2019. In 2010, there were 158,000 registered carsharing users in Germany. From 2010 to 2019 this number steadily increased, leading to 2.46 million registered car sharing users in Germany in 2019. Due to the relatively large area of the country, there are hundreds of carsharing companies in Germany, which operate in smaller settlements and large conurbations [1, 24].

Despite a large number of companies, these carsharing operators are able to work together. A very important aspect of this cooperation is the fact that the local rail carrier DB (Deutsche Bahn) is also one of the carsharing operators. In practice, it is the integration of carsharing systems with rail transport, where the members of this group are acting on the market under their own name and, moreover, use the designation 'DB carsharing'. German railways provide these companies with 24-hour customer service (call-centre) for handling reservations, reporting accidents and other technical assistance [1, 23].

In addition to Deutsche Bahn, there is another carsharing coordinating body in Germany. That body is known as the 'Bundesverband CarSharing' ('the BCS'). The members of this association are the carsharing organizations themselves. The role of BCS is to promote the common interests of all car-sharing providers, e.g. changes in legislation. Among other things, it collects nationwide data on the number of users of carsharing, the number of vehicles and also participates in the promotion of carsharing [10, 12].

Switzerland

The success of the successful Swiss company Mobility consists in offering its services in more than 400 locations, of which only cities such as Bern, Basel, Zurich or Geneva have more than 100,000 inhabitants. Therefore, it also provides services in small municipalities with less than 20,000 inhabitants. The combination of several factors, such as cooperation with the Swiss Federal Railways (SBB), the rail carrier in the country and other public transport providers. Shared cars therefore often stand close to railway stations and passengers using train travel have preferential conditions for using carsharing [1, 23].

China

However, after 2015, the number of systems has started to increase rapidly and more than 40 carsharing organizations operate in China with approximately 40,000 shared cars. This increase is mainly due to the support of the Chinese government, which set targets in the city of Shanghai such as. reach 6,000 carsharing service points or 20,000 electric cars and 30,000 charging stations. It also offered carsharing companies free parking spaces and a contribution of EUR 5 180/year for each new electric car involved in the system.

5   Analysis of the Current Situation in the Slovak Republic

In contrast to the situation abroad, carsharing systems have been built in Slovakia in the last two years. Figure 4 shows cities that provide carsharing services within the Slovak Republic, namely Bratislava, Nitra and Kosice.

Fig. 4. Cities offering car sharing service system [own study]

5.1 Analysis of Companies Providing Carsharing Services

We currently have 4 different carsharing companies in Slovakia. A comprehensive analysis of individual companies is elaborated in the following part of the article.

– Carrivederci:
Carrivederci is the first and currently the only carsharing company of its kind in Slovakia. This carsharing company was founded in July 2017. It is a car-sharing system operated through an application on the website www.carrivederci.com, which operates on the principle of "P2P carsharing".

In this system, it is a direct sharing of the vehicle from the car owner to the candidate, where both parties are on the same level in the system. Currently, this carsharing works only in Bratislava, but is beginning to consider expansion to other large Slovak cities [6].

Carrivederci provides services solely to the lessor and lessee of a vehicle registered in the system under a rental agreement and charges a fee for the provision [6].

– UP! City:
Traffic Sharing Service "UP! City", which operates in Slovakia in Bratislava, was established in 2017. This system includes the sharing of Volkswagen e-up electric cars, electric scooters and bicycles, and is not required for a pure carsharing system. There is currently no application for booking a car and hence car rental works more on the principle of car rental using the lessor-lessee contractual relationship [9].

To use the system the candidate needs: a driving license, identity card and the conclusion of a lease. The car can be rented for the whole day or 5-hour. If the candidate wants to use the car for less than 5-hour, he is obliged to pay the amount for 5-hour of use [3].

– ShareCar:
ShareCar is the first direct carsharing company operating in Slovakia. It was founded in 2018 in Nitra. Currently, the system is used by 26 registered members who have access to 2 Suzuki vehicles. ShareCar is a tied carsharing system and the car must be parked in the car park from which it was taken [10].

– **Share'n go:**

Carsharing company Share'n go is the operator of the latest car sharing system in Slovakia. At the same time, it is the first Slovak carsharing using only electric cars, specifically electric cars of ZhiDou brand. Currently, there are 30 vehicles for sharing in Kosice. The Carsharing Share'n go system was launched in February 2019. Carsharing Share'n go is the only carsharing system in Slovakia that has a mobile app in addition to a functioning website. To unlock a car to share, you don't need a smart card, but only a smartphone that generates a QR code to open the car. The application also displays the location of parked cars in the city using GPS. Share'n go has the advantage that cars can be parked at the end of their sharing anywhere in the operating area, as it works on the principle of free -floating carsharing [11].

5.2 Comparison of Carsharing Services Companies

The following Table 2 lists all carsharing systems operating in Slovakia, their comparison with respect to the principle of operation, the way of equipping and the possibility of integration of private vehicles into the system. The table is based on the above described carsharing systems in Slovakia [5, 7].

Table 2. Comparison of carsharing systems operating in the Slovak Republic [own study]

System	City	Principle of system operation	Method of handling	Possibility to engage private cars
Carrivederi	Bratislava	station-based carsharing	App on the website	No
UP! City	Bratislava	free-floating carsharing	App on the website or directly on the smartphone (Android, iOS)	No
ShareCar	Nitra	station-based carsharing	Customer Center; the principle of functioning as a car rental	No
Share´n go	Kosice	P2P (peer to peer) carsharing	App on the website	Yes

6 Design of a Shared Car System for the Slovak Republic

Based on surveys carried out in Slovenia, it was found that the respondents addressed would engage in car-sharing systems as a user, i.e. share cars from carsharing companies. By elaborating knowledge on the functioning of carsharing systems abroad, in Slovakia and also taking into account the results of surveys, this subchapter of the study contains a proposal of a car sharing system that could be applicable in the territory of the Slovak Republic. Specifically, there are two different design options:

– Proposal 1 - a system of shared cars on the principle of free –floating carsharing.
– Proposal 2 - a system of shared cars on the principle of station – based carsharing.

6.1 Proposal 1 - A System of Shared Cars on the Principle of Free – Floating Carsharing

The first proposed alternative is a system operating on the whole territory of Slovakia, which operates on the principle of free-floating carsharing with a large number of shared vehicles, i.e. a large vehicle fleet of the operator is necessary for its operation.

This system allows a registered user to return or hand over the vehicle to a place other than that from which the vehicle was picked up. The vehicle should be parked anywhere within the operator's operating area. In order for this proposal No. 1 to be effective, the following needs to be ensured:

Territorial Scope of the System

Since carsharing on the Slovak market is currently not very developed, it would be appropriate to change this fact. Therefore, the first design alternative, following the example of Switzerland, is oriented to the whole territory of Slovakia and thus it is a nationwide carsharing.

Get Cars for the System

The basis of this system is to exploit the potential of a large number of car factories in Slovakia. Since 2016, Slovakia has been the leader in the number of cars produced per capita since 2016. In 2019, the number of vehicles produced was approximately 1 080 000 per year [16].

To ensure a large number of vehicles, it is necessary to cooperate with KIA Motors Slovakia, Volkswagen Slovakia, PSA Group Slovakia and Jaguar Land Rover [19–21].

Cooperation with the Government of the Slovak Republic

Another necessary element of the system is cooperation, or support from the Government of the Slovak Republic. One option is to provide direct financial assistance to the carsharing operator for the purchase of vehicles and carsharing systems (control units) needed to make the vehicles suitable for sharing. Another positive factor for the proposed carsharing system is that the Government of the Slovak Republic, namely the Ministry of Economy of the Slovak Republic, offers subsidies for electric vehicles of EUR 5000 and hybrid vehicles of EUR 3000, which can lead to preferential purchases of vehicles for sharing and it also implies a reduction of emissions in cities [17, 29].

To Obtain Parking Spaces for the System

The last prerequisite for the functioning of the system is the support of municipalities in settlements, or cooperation with local authorities. As the proposal is geared towards a large number of cars, the appropriate number of parking spaces is also required, so it is crucial that municipalities are willing to allow carsharing users to park in urban car parks without restrictions and to provide sufficient parking cards at discounted prices for cars [25].

Cooperation with Public Passenger Transport

For better promotion and functioning of the system also contributes or cooperation. cooperation with public passenger transport. And that:

- **public passenger transport - railway transport:** cooperation with public transport is mainly cooperation with the national railway carrier ZSSK. Users who would prove that they had arrived at their destination by train would then receive a discount on carsharing [26].
- **public passenger transport - bus transportation:** bus transportation (BT), especially suburban bus service, also offers space for cooperation. Carsharing as a public passenger support system can attract more BT passengers. As part of the cooperation, it is necessary for the company operating BT to allocate parking places for carsharing organizations at selected stops, or bus stations [32, 33].

Car Rental

For a more reliable operation of the first proposed system, it is preferable to use the smartphone application to unlock the vehicle to the client and then unlock the car using servers at the headquarters of the carsharing company. This tripping method should ensure a smoother operation of the system and also reduce the cost of producing smart cards, since a large number of car-sharing users are a prerequisite for a prosperous system with a large number of vehicles [27].

6.2   Proposal 2 - the System of Shared Cars on the Principle of Station-Based Car Sharing

The second proposal for the territory of Slovakia is a system operating based on tied carsharing. It is a system where cars are not shared by people. This structure is shared by vehicles owned by a third party carsharing operator. For this proposal No. 2 to be effective, the following needs to be ensured:

The Territorial Scope of the System

Unlike the first design alternative, the second focuses only on the territory of, for example, the city of Zilina with subsequent expansion into the entire region of the Zilina self-governing region. Since the city of Zilina has long been known for its poor traffic situation, a carsharing system could help reduce these problems, for example. reducing the number of cars [30].

Get cars for the System Because the KIA Motors Slovakia car plant is located near the city of Zilina, it would be advisable to obtain cars from this car manufacturer. For the proposal, it would be necessary to get or to buy 3 to 5 cars for the city of Zilina, ideally with electric or hybrid drive [19, 31].

To Obtain Parking Spaces for the System Because it is station-based carsharing, it is necessary to have a reserved parking space within the city serving as a carsharing station or a reserved parking zone in a selected paid car park, which is under the administration of Zilina and in the vehicle available parking card with unlimited time scope, or parking card with limited time validity with the possibility of extension. When setting up the system, it is necessary to agree and obtain from the local council of Zilina and also to sign a formal agreement (contract) [32].

Cooperation with Public Passenger Transport

As with the first proposal, there is also the possibility for cooperation with public passenger transport for the second alternative. This cooperation can be achieved especially in cooperation with the integrated transport system of the Zilina self-governing region, so that at the main station of the city of Zilina the carsharing vehicle will have its dedicated station, thus creating a support system of public passenger transport [34].

Car Rental

For the alternative of tied carsharing, it is preferable to use a method of taking over the vehicle using a smart card. The main reason for this is that the private cars involved do not have an integrated car-sharing system in the dashboard and therefore it is not possible to open these vehicles using a smartphone and servers. The only option is to mount the chip card reader control units on the vehicles. The advantage is also that cars of the carsharing operator do not need to be purchased with an integrated system, which means that the purchase price of vehicles will not be so high.

6.3 Specifics of the Proposed System no. 2

The second proposed alternative includes certain specifics compared to the functioning of the first proposal. These specifics are:

– **Private Car Integration:** Due to the low number of shared cars of the cash company, this proposal also includes the possibility of integrating privately owned cars.
– **Unlimited vehicle sharing time:** Another specific feature of the proposal is unlimited vehicle sharing time. The principle is that users can rent a car for example for 6 months and travel anywhere within the EU. The only condition is the subsequent return of the vehicle to the carsharing station predetermined by the operator located in Zilina.

7 Comparison and Evaluation of Proposalas

In this part of the article, the proposals are compared, described the main differences and then evaluated. The result of the evaluation is to determine which of the systems would be more suitable for operating in Slovakia.

7.1 Differences Between Proposals

Principle of Operation The main difference in the proposed systems is the principle of functioning since the first proposal is a free-floating system after use vehicles can be parked at any place in the operational area, which represents the whole territory of Slovakia. On the contrary, the second proposal is a station-based system where it is necessary to return the vehicle to the original location of the carsharing station after the vehicle has been used.

Territorial Coverage
In general, the first proposal provides more flexibility for people using the system when parking or parking. picking up the vehicle, but they have this flexibility exclusively in Slovakia. On the contrary, the second proposal requires the takeover and return of the vehicle to a predetermined location but allows the vehicle to be used outside the borders of Slovakia throughout the EU.

Investment
Another difference is that the first proposal requires large initial investment due to the need for a high number of vehicles (note that for regional cities alone, the number is more than 200 cars); 5 vehicles.

Integration of Private Vehicles
Since the first proposal offers a sufficient number of passenger cars, the integration of private cars does not offer a system. On the other hand, the second proposal offers the possibility of involving private cars in the system, thus improving the supply of services without increasing the initial investment. Private cars can, therefore, help to meet the demand for shared vehicles when the operator's cars are fully loaded.

Possibilities of Cooperation with Public Passenger Transport
As the first alternative envisages a nationwide scope, public passenger transport, in particular the ZSSK railway carrier, can also serve to support the system. Of course, the second alternative also offers the possibility of cooperation with public passenger transport, namely the integrated transport system of the Zilina self-governing region, where it can act as a support system [34].

Car rental Method
When designing as free-floating carsharing, it is sufficient to have a smartphone with the car, which can be used to open the vehicle using an application that communicates with servers located in the operator's headquarters and thus all that is necessary to have at the time of use is driver's license and smartphone.

On the other hand, for a design that works as a station-based carsharing, it is always necessary to carry a smart card with you without which the vehicles cannot be unlocked and thus the system cannot be used when the customer does not have the card with him.

7.2 Comparison of Proposals

The following Table 3 summarizes the main differences between the proposed alternatives mentioned above in the article.

Table 3. Comparison of design alternatives [own study]

Comparative characteristics	Proposal 1	Proposal 2
Kind of carsharing	Free –floating carsharing	Station- based carsharing
Territorial application	The whole territory of Slovakia	Zilina self - governing region
Number of vehicles	High	Low
Initial investment	High	Low
Private vehicle integration	no	yes
Acceptance of the vehicle	Use your smartphone	Using a smart card

7.3 Evaluation of Proposals

Of the presented proposals, **proposal no. 2** is more suitable for the territory of Slovakia, because Slovaks have little knowledge about car sharing systems and lack of experience with their use. Although good publicity and cooperation with the government could also be successful for **proposal no. 1**, the introduction of such a system would not be successful at present, because there are not enough potential customers in Slovakia. **Proposal no. 2** for the area of the city of Zilina and the Zilina self-governing region as a whole could bring several advantages that would improve the traffic situation in the city.

8 Conclusion

Almost all large cities are dealing with congested traffic problems and lack of parking spaces. Therefore, many European capitals prefer to invest in the development of public transport and new forms of mobility. A promising concept is carsharing, i.e. car sharing on a commercial basis. This article aimed to analyze the current situation of carsharing in selected foreign countries, where this system is the most developed and also a detailed analysis of the current situation in Slovakia. In the final part of this article, two different alternatives of the carsharing system are proposed, which could be applied to the territory of Slovakia, based on analyzed knowledge, complex studies and surveys. The proposed systems set up operate on different modes of operation, the first on the principle of free carsharing and the second on the principle of tied carsharing. In these different concepts, other differences such as e.g. ways of taking over the vehicle or value of initial investments.

The biggest advantage of the first proposal is the high flexibility of the system resulting from the large number of vehicles located throughout Slovakia, even in small municipalities with up to 5,000 inhabitants. On the contrary, the great advantage of the second alternative over the first is that the second option involves the integration of private vehicles into the system and the possibility of reserving the vehicle for an unlimited period, with the advantage of unrestricted movement within the EU. From the created proposals has greater potential for successful functioning in Slovakia, or in the territory of any self-governing region proposal no. 2.

References

1. Shaheen, A.S., Cohen, P.A.: Carsharing and Personal Vehicle Services: Worldwide Market Developments and Emerging Trends. Taylor & Francis. http://innovativemobility.org/wp-con tent/uploads/2015/07/Carsharing-and-Personal-Vehicle-Services.pdf. Accessed 7 Jan 2020
2. Shaheen, A.S.: Introduction Shared-Use Vehicle Services for Sustainable Transportation: Carsharing, Bikesharing, and Personal Vehicle Sharing across the Globe. Taylor & Francis. https://www.tandfonline.com/doi/full/10.1080/15568318.2012.660095. Accessed 7 Jan 2020
3. Loose, W.: The State of European Car-Sharing. https://ec.europa.eu/energy/intelligent/pro jects/sites/iee-projects/files/projects/documents/momo_car-sharing_the_state_of_european_ car_sharing_en.pdf. Accessed 7 Jan 2020
4. Loose, W.: The enviromental impacts of carsharing, IAPT, June (2009)
5. European Commission, 2011. White Paper - Roadmap to a Single European Transport Area - Creating a competitive and resource efficient transport system (2011)
6. Britton, E.: Carsharing 2000: Sustainable Transport's Missing Link. EcoLogica Ltd., Lancaster, 2000. pp. 317. http://innovativemobility.org/wp-content/uploads/2015/07/Carsharing-and-Personal-Vehicle-Services.pdf. Accessed 7 Jan 2020
7. Kalašová, A., Mikulski, J., Kubíková, S.: The impact of intelligent transport systems on an accident rate of the chosen part of road communication network in the slovak republic. In: Mikulski, J. (ed.) TST 2016. CCIS, vol. 640, pp. 47–58. Springer, Cham (2016). https://doi.org/10.1007/978-3-319-49646-7_5
8. https://www.mindop.sk/files/statistika_vud/reg_prev_ukazovatele.htm. Accessed 7 Jan 2020
9. http://www.upcity.sk/. Accessed 7 Jan 2020
10. https://www.sharecar.sk/. Accessed 7 Jan 2020
11. https://site.sharengo.sk/. Accessed 7 Jan 2020
12. http://www.carsharing.de/. Accessed 7 Jan 2020
13. Rotaris, L., Danielis, R., Maltese, I.: Carsharing use by college students: the case of Milan and Rome. Transportation Research Part A: Policy and Practice **120**, 239–251 (2019)
14. de O. Lage, M., et al.: Location Suitable for the Implementation of Carsharing in the City of São Paulo. Procedia Manufacturing, vol. 39, pp. 1962–1967 (2019)
15. Giesel, F., Nobis, C.: The impact of carsharing on car ownership in german cities. Transport. Res. Procedia **19**, 215–224 (2016)
16. https://automagazin.sk/2019/01/13/na-slovensku-sa-v-roku-2018-vyrobil-rekordny-pocet-aut/. Accessed 7 Jan 2020
17. https://www.mhsr.sk/press/mh-pokracuje-v-podpore-elektromobility-vlada-suhlasila-s-pla nom-jej-rozvoja. Accessed 7 Jan 2020
18. https://www.car4way.cz/. Accessed 7 Jan 2020
19. http://www.kia.sk/. Accessed 7 Jan 2020
20. http://www.psa-slovakia.sk/. Accessed 7 Jan 2020
21. https://www.landrover.sk/. Accessed 7 Jan 2020
22. https://www.leaseplan.com/sk-sk/. Accessed 7 Jan 2020
23. https://www.mobility.ch/en/. Accessed 7 Jan 2020
24. http://www.cambio-carsharing.com/. Accessed 7 Jan 2020
25. https://www.topspeed.sk/PODKLADY/2013/2013-cennik-Skoda-Octavia-3.pdf. Accessed 7 Jan 2020
26. https://www.skoda-diely.sk/online-obchod.html. Accessed 7 Jan 2020
27. https://www.auto.cz/vyplati-se-ojete-auto-vic-nez-nove-pocitejte-dobre-71707. Accessed 7 Jan 2020
28. https://www.statista.com. Accessed 7 Jan 2020

29. Berezny, R., Konecny, V.: The impact of the quality of transport services on passenger demand in the suburban bus transport. In: Bujnak, J., Guagliano, M. (eds.) 12th International Scientific Conference of Young Scientists on Sustainable, Modern and Safe Transport, Procedia Engineering, pp. 40–45, Amsterdam: Elsevier Science Bv (2017)
30. Culik, K., Harantova, V., Kalasova, A.: Traffic modelling of the circular junction in the city of zilina. Adv. Sci. Technol.-Res. J. **13**(4), 162–169 (2019)
31. Kapusta, J., Kalašová, A.: Motor vehicle safety technologies in relation to the accident rates. In: Mikulski, J. (ed.) TST 2015. CCIS, vol. 531, pp. 172–179. Springer, Cham (2015). https://doi.org/10.1007/978-3-319-24577-5_17
32. Konecny, V., Berezny, R., Bartonikova, M.: Research on the impact of quality on demand for bus transport. In: Stopka, O. (ed.) 18th International Scientific Conference-Logi 2017, MATEC Web of Conferences, Cedex A: E D P Sciences (2017)
33. Poliak, M.: The relationship with reasonable profit and risk in public passenger transport in the Slovakia. Ekonomicky Casopis **61**(2), 206–220 (2013)
34. Poliak, M., et al.: The competitiveness of public transport. J. Competitiveness **9**(3), 81–97 (2017)

Charging Stations for Electric Vehicles - Current Situation in Poland

Elżbieta Macioszek$^{(\boxtimes)}$ and Grzegorz Sierpiński

Silesian University of Technology, Akademicka 2A, Gliwice, Poland
{elzbieta.macioszek,grzegorz.sierpinski}@polsl.pl

Abstract. The forecasts of the Ministry of Energy regarding the development of the charging infrastructure for electric vehicles in Poland envisage that, over the next years, ca. 6,000 new normal power charging points (under 22 kW) and ca. 400 high power charging points (over 22 kW) will be built. There are also other very optimistic projections indicating a sharp increase in the number of electric vehicle charging points in Poland. This paper presents the characteristics of electric vehicle charging points and stations, websites allowing for electric vehicle charging stations to be searched for in Poland, as well as the current situation and problems related to the charging stations for electric vehicles in Poland.

Keywords: Electric vehicles · Plug-in hybrid electric vehicles · Battery electric vehicles · Charging stations · Electromobility

1 Introduction

An electric vehicle is a motor vehicle featuring a power transmission system containing at least one non-peripheral electric device functioning as an energy converter with an electrically charged energy storage unit which can be charged from an external source. Electric vehicles can be divided into:

- Plug-in electric vehicle (PEV) - a motor vehicle that can be recharged from an external source of electricity, such as wall outlets, and the electricity stored in the rechargeable battery packs drives or contributes to driving the wheels,
- Plug-in hybrid electric vehicle (PHEV) - a motor vehicle with a combustion-electric engine, featuring batteries that can be recharged from an external source of electricity,
- Battery electric vehicle (BEV) - a motor vehicle that only uses the energy accumulated in batteries for propulsion, where the batteries can be recharged from an external source of electricity or changed,
- Extended-range electric vehicle (EREV) - a motor (electric) vehicle with a built-in low-capacity engine unit. The latter can function as an external electric power generator when the vehicle's on-board batteries are discharged. Once it has switched on, the built-in engine functions as a typical power generator feeding the empty batteries.

© Springer Nature Switzerland AG 2020
J. Mikulski (Ed.): TST 2020, CCIS 1289, pp. 124–137, 2020.
https://doi.org/10.1007/978-3-030-59270-7_10

According to the Polish and European transport policies, assuming significant reduction in the emission of harmful exhaust gases produced by motor vehicles, the interest as well as the sales of battery electric vehicles (BEV) and plug-in hybrid vehicles (PHEV) with on-board battery units have been continuously increasing. Hence the growing need for more and more charging stations for electric vehicles. Nearly all major automotive corporations (including BMW, Daimler, General Motors, Fiat, Ford, Honda, Hyundai-Kia group, Jaguar, Mazda, Citroen, Opel, Renault-Nissan-Mitsubishi alliance, Subaru, Suzuki, Tesla, Toyota, Volkswagen, Audi, Porsche, Seat, Volvo) have announced an intent to significantly extend their offering of hybrid and fully electric vehicles over the next 10–15 years. The increasing demand for energy required to charge electric vehicles is beginning to pose a growing challenge to the power grid [1].

The main research areas currently addressed in this respect include the problems of maximising the efficiency of energy conversion systems, minimising the mass and volume of systems, as well as increasing the range of electric vehicles. The main barriers to the growth of both popularity and the number of BEV/PHEVs in Poland are claimed to be the lack of adequate vehicle battery charging infrastructure, high prices of such vehicles, and the lack of appropriate incentive programmes implemented on the national level.

According to the data provided by the Ministry of Energy [2], in 2019, there were ca. 1,400 public electric vehicle charging stations available in Poland. In terms of the development of the vehicle charging infrastructure, the Ministry of Energy plans to have 6,000 normal power and 400 fast charging points installed by the year 2020. Moreover, the Polish electromobility development plan [3] envisages that, in 2025, the power grid will be ready to deliver energy for one million electric vehicles and adapted to using these vehicles as the system regulating elements. However, the actual increase in the number of electric vehicles is considerably slower.

There are numerous studies in the literature of the subject, especially foreign, dedicated to the problems of electric vehicles and siting of electric vehicle charging stations [4–9]. For some time now, extensive scientific research in this field has also been conducted in Poland [e.g.: 10–20].

This article describes the characteristics of electric vehicle charging points and stations. It also discusses the available internet sites which make it possible to search for electric vehicle charging stations in Poland, as well as addresses the current problems related to the electric vehicle charging stations in Poland.

2 Charging Systems for Passenger Cars

A publicly accessible charging point is assumed to mean a point which provides access capabilities to users throughout the EU, without discrimination (under different conditions of authentication, operation and payment), including the plug, the power supply unit, and the parking space for cars (Fig. 1).

Such a charging point comprises a device which enables charging a single electric vehicle or replacing the battery of a single electric vehicle. On account of the time needed for charging and the voltage, these charging points can be divided into the following categories [21]:

Fig. 1. Electric vehicle charging infrastructure located near one of the Polish universities [own study]

- normal power charging points (also referred to as points enabling normal charging) - charging points with the power output lower than or equal to 22 kW, except for devices whose power outlet is lower than or equal to 3.7 kW which are installed in private households or whose primary purpose is not charging of electric vehicles, and which are not accessible to the public,
- high power charging points (also referred to as fast charging points) - charging points with the power outlet higher than 22 kW. These charging points can be further divided into such sub-categories:
- Chademo (CHArge de MOve) - trade name of a quick charging system for battery electric vehicles, delivering up to 62.5 kW of high voltage direct current via a special electrical connector. It is proposed as a global industry standard by an association of the same name,
- CCS (Combined Charging System) - charging system where the combo coupler is based on the Type 2 (VDE) AC charging connector, with full compatibility with the SAE specification for direct current charging, with additional pins to accommodate fast direct current charging at 200–450 V and up to 90 kW,
- Tesla SC (Tesla Super Charger) - proprietary direct current fast charging system comprising stations that provide up to 135 kW of power, giving the 85 kWh Model S some 270 km of range in about 30 min and full charge in 75 min,
- Type-2 AC (Type 2 AC Connector) - electric car charging system also known as Mennekes, where the connector is circular in shape, with a flattened top edge, capable of charging battery electric vehicles at 3–70 kW.

The term charging station refers to equipment comprising more than a single electric vehicle charging point. The number of units of the electric vehicle charging infrastructure publicly accessible in European countries and in Turkey over the years 2008–2019 has been presented in Fig. 2 in a breakdown into normal power and high power charging units. The data provided in Fig. 2 imply that the decided majority of publicly accessible electric vehicle charging stations in European countries and in Turkey are the normal power charging units. What can also be observed over the recent years is faster quantitative growth of the normal power charging infrastructure compared to the high power charging infrastructure.

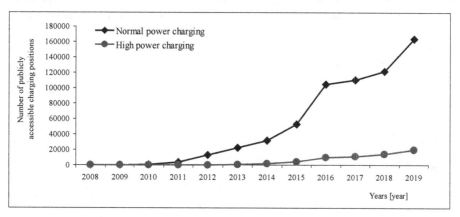

Fig. 2. Total electric vehicle charging infrastructure in European countries and in Turkey in 2008–2019 [own study based on [21]]

Figure 3, on the other hand, provides the number of publicly accessible charging units in European countries and in Turkey in a breakdown by the charging system type, including: normal power charging system, type 2AC system, ChaDeMo system, CCS system and Tesla SC.

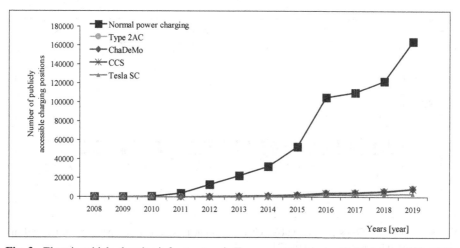

Fig. 3. Electric vehicle charging infrastructure in European countries and in Turkey in 2008–2019 according to the charging system type [own study based on [21]]

Figure 4 provides the number of publicly accessible charging units in Poland broken down according to the charging system type: normal power charging system, type 2AC system, ChaDeMo system, CCS system, and Tesla SC. The data provided in Fig. 3 and Fig. 4 imply that, in European countries as well as in Turkey and Poland, the normal power charging infrastructure prevails. The market share of the charging systems such as 2AC, ChaDeMo, CCS, and Tesla SC is considerably lower. However, one can observe evident growth of the electric vehicle charging infrastructure with every passing year.

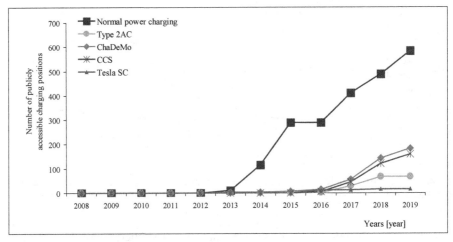

Fig. 4. Electric vehicle charging infrastructure in Poland in 2008–2019 according to the charging system type [own study based on [21]]

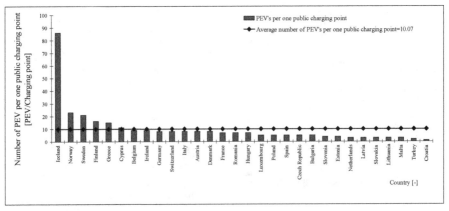

Fig. 5. Number of PEVs per one public charging point in selected European countries and in Turkey in 2019 [own study based on [21]]

Figure 5 provides the number of PEVs per one public charging point in European countries and in Turkey in 2019. The average number of PEVs per one public charging point equals to 10.07. It is in Iceland that the PEVs per public charging point ratio is the highest. It is the lowest, on the other hand, in countries such as Croatia, Turkey, Malta, Lithuania, Slovakia, Latvia, the Netherlands, and Estonia.

From the perspective of long-distance travelling, it is the number of public fast charging points installed near motorways that matters the most. Figure 6 shows the number of public fast charging points per 100 km of motorways in 2019. The ratio of fast charging points to 100 km of motorways is the highest in Norway (655), Iceland (227), and Estonia (131).

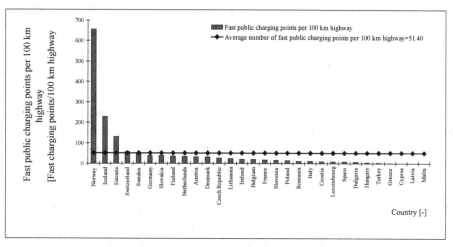

Fig. 6. Number of public fast charging points per 100 km of motorways in selected European countries and in Turkey in 2019 [own study based on [21]]

Having reviewed the methods of charging electric vehicles (PEV) currently used in practice, one can distinguish between:

- solar charging - enabled by photovoltaic panels installed on the vehicle roof. Toyota has been testing this solution, but the energy from full day's charging suffices only to travel up to 5 km;
- wireless (inductive) charging - wireless charging systems typically use inductive energy transfer, i.e. the principle of inductance or magnetic resonance, and they are currently in the test phase. This solution will not replace traditional charging, but may extend the vehicle running range, e.g. by enabling buses to be charged while at a stop;
- full battery pack replacement - mechanical replacement of the batteries used in a vehicle;
- pantograph charging - solution mainly found on buses, which consists in automatically connecting the vehicle's roof system with the charging station by means of an extendable pantograph;
- wired charging - the car must be connected to the charging device by means of a conductor.

The latter of the above solutions is currently the most popular, most advantageous, and most frequently used method of passenger car charging. However, this method also has many disadvantages, mainly including the need for the user to connect and disconnect the cable before and after each charging, which then translates into the electric shock hazard. It may also pose problems with connecting the cable to the vehicle (e.g. in the period of lower temperatures in winter, or in the absence of knowledge of how to operate the electric vehicle charging station), reduce the vehicle's visual quality (visible sockets), and involve the possibility of vandals damaging the docking station, etc. An extensive review of the potential solutions for charging electric vehicle batteries has been provided in papers [22–24].

3 Websites Dedicated to Searching for Electric Vehicle Charging Infrastructure

Although the number of electric vehicle charging points available in Poland is relatively low compared to some other European countries, dynamic development of the charging infrastructure dedicated to low-emission vehicles has been observed over the recent years. The network of charging points and stations in Poland is growing in density, but it is still difficult to establish exactly how many such stations are currently in service. As stipulated in the Act on Electromobility [25], the plan is to create a register of the alternative fuel infrastructure. Such records will be kept by the Office of Technical Inspection (UDT). However, the installation of electric vehicle charging points may be handled by various entities. The prerequisite for rendering such charging points or stations available to drivers is that they have been officially accepted by the Office of Technical Inspection.

For the purpose of the electric car charging process itself, alternating current (AC) can be provided by means of the car's on-board charger responsible for current transformation into direct current (DC), which then the battery stores. The second option is DC charging, where electric energy is delivered directly to the battery, in which case the entire charging process is much faster. Fast charging stations are based on DC charging. However, when an electric car is plugged into a home-base electrical outlet (also via a home charger), the electric car is charged with alternating current. The same applies to charging stations dedicated to commercial facilities such as office buildings, shopping centres, sports facilities, cinemas, museums, hotels, and public utility institutions.

Information about the electric vehicle charging infrastructure can be found using various maps published on websites, including Tesla [26], GreenWay [27], Auta Elektryczne [28], Galactico [29], Ecomoto [30], Obserwatorium Rynku Paliw Alternatywnych [31], Plugshare [32], on which users can add charging points they themselves have verified and share their opinions with other users. Some sites allow you to filter and display stations according to such criteria as e.g. the chosen charging power. These maps often differ in terms of the information they provide. Table 1 summarises the currently available maps providing information about the electric vehicle charging infrastructure locations.

The charging stations located along transit routes (motorways and expressways) are mainly dedicated to drivers travelling long distances. Charging stations are often installed at petrol stations because that is where auxiliary infrastructure, including exit slips, catering points, or sanitary facilities, is already available. Several companies have already started their operations at those sites, e.g. Orlen and Lotos. Charging points of this type feature fast chargers with 50 kW and 100 kW of capacity, making it possible to replenish the energy storage in a reasonable period of time (approx. 20–40 min). Complementing this system, slow chargers are predominantly installed next to shopping centres, public places, or office buildings. The electric car owners themselves use their own home-based stations, and insofar as possible, they make the most of the night

Table 1. Websites dedicated to searching for electric vehicle charging points and stations [own study]

No.	Website name	Source	Remarks about website
1.	MT My Tesla Interactive map of electric vehicle charging points in the territory of Poland	[26]	- information on the location (location name), - information on availability (e.g. 24/7), - information on the manufacturer, - information on the available charging options, - number of points on the map – 50 (status as of 15 October 2018)
2.	Auta Elektryczne	[28]	- information on the location (location name), - information on availability (e.g. 24/7), - information on the payment form (e.g. free, price list), - available facilities, - available services (e.g. nearby restaurants and shops), - information on the charger power (e.g. 120 kW)
3.	Obserwatorium Rynku Paliw Alternatywnych (alternative fuel market observatory)	[31]	- map covered by honorary patronage of the Ministry of Energy, - information on the location (location name), - number of charging points per station, - number of sockets, - type of sockets, - information on the manufacturer, - information on the operator, - opening hours, - phone number, - information on parking options (paid/free), - opening hours

(continued)

Table 1. (*continued*)

No.	Website name	Source	Remarks about website
4.	Greenway	[27]	- all-Poland network, - charging stations spaced at every 85–100 km, - stations located near main transport corridors (motorways and expressways), - 24/7 technical support (hotline and e-mail enquiry option), - paid service. Fees according to the operator's price list. Possible variants: direct current charging service at the charger's nominal power (DC), direct current charging service at the power reduced to 40 kW (DC), alternating current charging service (AC), - 200 charging stations, including 10 ultra-fast and 135 fast ones
5.	PlugShare	[32]	- information on the location (location name), - information on parking options (paid/free), - number of sockets, - facilities and services available (e.g. restaurants, shops), - type of sockets, - location photos, - information on the charger locations closest to the one being analysed
6.	Eco Moto. Electric cars and other vehicles	[30]	- information on the location (location name), - contact details
7.	Galactico	[29]	- information on the location (location name), - paid service, information on the charging station use fees
8.	Elektrowóz	[33]	- information on the location (location name), - phone number, - number of sockets, - information on payment methods
9.	Infor.Pl Moto	[34]	- information on the location (location name), - opening hours

(*continued*)

Table 1. (*continued*)

No.	Website name	Source	Remarks about website
10.	Wysokie napięcie	[35]	- information on the location (location name), - number of sockets, - facilities and services available (e.g. restaurants, shops), - information on the available sockets, - charging point description

electricity tariff, since it is currently the most convenient and cost-effective options for charging an electric vehicle in Poland.

4 Charging Stations for Electric Vehicles - Current Problems and Issues in Poland

Electric vehicles represent an important stage of progress towards mobility implemented in line with the principles of sustainable development. Investing in eco-friendly transport can undoubtedly bring a number of benefits, such as air quality improvement and reduction of negative health effects. In many cities in Europe and worldwide, the dense network of electric vehicle charging stations constitutes an integral part of the city infrastructure. In Poland, electric vehicles are not yet a popular means of transport (mainly due to their very high prices), and there is still much to be done and improved in terms of the charging infrastructure. The main problems and issues currently associated with the electric vehicle charging stations in Poland include the following:

- it is difficult to explicitly determine the exact number of charging points and stations for electric vehicles currently available in Poland. The existing sources of information frequently provide disparate data;
- there are no websites enabling vehicle owners to book a charging point in a specific location;
- there are no incentives, such as discounts and loyalty schemes for charging at a particular station, which is probably due to the absence of strong competition. Such schemes could cover, for instance, the total number of charging hours or the number of charging hours within a specific period of time, e.g. weekly, monthly, etc.;
- there are too few charging points next to many public venues, workplaces, multi-family buildings, housing estates, hotels, supermarkets, and numerous service points;
- there is clear shortage in terms of adequate marking as well as information for drivers concerning the locations of electric vehicle charging stations in urban areas;
- there are no detailed guidelines on the siting of electric vehicle charging stations;
- there is no single standard for the plug and socket design in the market of electric cars and charging stations. In practice, one can come across many different types of charging sockets. The lack of infrastructure standardisation forces vehicle owners to

look for a charging station featuring a plug that matches the socket on board their cars, or to have the right adapter in place. Such standards are set by vehicle manufacturers, and they are expected to become uniform in the future. There are currently two main DC standards in Europe: CCS and CHAdeMO, as well as the AC standard which comes in two types. CCS (combined charging system) is a system that enables charging with the power of up to 350 kW, while CHAdeMO - up to 50 kW. As for AC plugs and sockets, type 1 is typically to be found in households, while type 2 is used in slow charging stations. Tesla, on the other hand, uses the CHAdeMO adapter. Table 2 and Table 3 provide an overview of the types of plugs available in the market along with examples of corresponding sockets.

Table 2. Alternating current plugs and sockets [own study based on [36]]

AC plugs and sockets		
Type 1 – SAE J1772	Type 2 – IEC 62196 (also known as Mennekes)	Type 3 – EV Plug Alliance

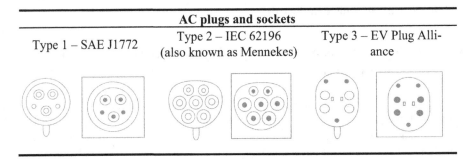

Table 3. Direct current plugs and sockets [own study based on [36]]

DC plugs and sockets	
CHAdeMO	CCS (Combined Charging System)

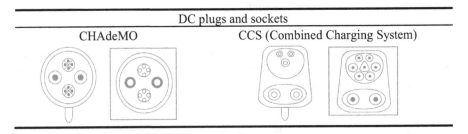

– according to the CDE group's report [36], ca. one million electric vehicles will have been put into service by 2024 in Poland, consuming 4 TWh of energy per annum. These vehicles will hugely encumber the power grid. With regard to the foregoing, the Polish electric power system will be forced to satisfy power demand multiple times higher than at the present;
– there are no requirements concerning the procedure of connecting charging stations to the power grid;
– in the years to come, one should expect gradual upgrading, extension, or construction of a completely new network, to which further new units of the charging infrastructure will be connected in successive stages;

- so far, there are no specific technical requirements as to the operating safety, repair and upgrading of charging stations in general, and no requirements as to the operating safety, repair and upgrading of the charging stations which constitute elements of the public road transport charging infrastructure;
- there are also no specific technical requirements concerning the conditions to be met by publicly accessible charging stations and charging points which constitute elements of the public road transport charging infrastructure, neither with regard to sockets, nor to vehicle service connectors;
- there are no specific requirements defining either the procedure or the time limits under which the Office of Technical Inspection should perform inspections of charging points; there are no specific requirements defining the types of the tests to be performed on the charging stations and charging points which constitute elements of the public road transport charging infrastructure, and neither are there any requirements concerning the documentation related to such tests;
- there are no specific facilities which would enable disabled persons to operate charging points;
- there are no safety requirements and guidelines for replacement and storage of batteries dedicated to electric and hybrid vehicles;
- there are no technical requirements concerning the safety of users operating electric vehicle charging points.

5 Conclusion

Over the recent years, one of the greatest challenges observed in the field of transport in Poland is the dynamic growth of the market of electric vehicles. The common drive towards the shift from conventional fuel-powered vehicles to electric vehicles is connected with the overall body of problems related to the technical infrastructure adaptation to the needs of electric vehicle users.

On account of the absence of well-developed electric vehicle charging infrastructure, it is currently very difficult to travel longer distances by this means of transport in Poland, which makes transfers between cities and provinces problematic. While planning their travels, electric car owners use a variety of applications and websites to match the route to the existing infrastructure of charging points or stations, and make sure that they can successfully use them. Another problem is that the relevant information provided by different sites is not consistent. In accordance with the objectives set forth in the Electromobility Development Plan for Poland [3], by the year 2025, ca. 1 million electric vehicles are expected to be in service in Poland, and this entails formation of a separate and numerous group of users for whom one of the factors determining their choice of the place of accommodation, service or entertainment will be the availability of the electric vehicle charging infrastructure. As discussed in the article, the current problems and issues observed in the sphere of the infrastructure of electric vehicle charging stations in Poland imply considerable deficiencies, both in terms of the relevant legal regulations, and the functional solutions themselves.

Acknowledgements. The present research has been financed from the means of the National Centre for Research and Development as a part of the international project within the scope of ERA-NET CoFund Electric Mobility Europe Programme "Electric travelling - platform to support the implementation of electromobility in Smart Cities based on ICT applications".

References

1. Biernat, K., Nita, K., Wójtowicz, S.: Architektura mikrosieci do inteligentnego ładowania pojazdów elektrycznych. Prace Instytutu Elektrotechniki **260**, 171–183 (2012)
2. Ministerstwo Energii: Krajowe ramy polityki rozwoju infrastruktury paliw alternatywnych. http://bip.me.gov.pl/files/upload/26450/Krajowe_ramy_polityki_final.pdf. Last accessed 20 Dec 2019
3. Ministerstwo Energii: Plan Rozwoju Elektromobilności w Polsce. http://bip.me.gov.pl/files/upload/26453/Plan%20Rozwoju%20%Elektromobilno%C5%9Bci.pdf. Last accessed 20 Dec 2019
4. Cao, Y., et al.: Electric vehicle charging recommendation and enabling ICT technologies: recent advances and future directions. IEEE Comsoc MMTC Communications **11**(2) 50 (2016), http://nrl.northumbria.ac.uk/33139/. Last accessed 20 Dec 2019
5. Mathur, A.K., Charan, T.S., Yemula, P.Y.: Optimal charging schedule for electric vehicles in parking lot with solar power generation. In: 2018 IEEE Innovative Smart Grid Technologies, pp. 611–615 (2018)
6. Ivanova, A., et al.: Coordinated charging of electric vehicles connected to a net-metered PV parking lot. In: 2017 IEEE PES Innovative Smart Grid Technologies Conference Europe, pp. 1–6 (2017)
7. Teja, S.C., Yemula, P.K.: Energy management of grid connected rooftop solar system with battery storage. Innovative Smart Grid Technologies-Asia (ISGT-Asia) 2016 IEEE, pp. 1195–1200 (2016)
8. Eisel, M., Schmidt, J., Kolbe, L.M.: Finding suitable locations for charging stations. In: Electric Vehicle Conference 2014 IEEE International, pp. 1–8 (2014)
9. Verzijlbergh, R.A., et al.: Network impacts and cost savings of controlled ev charging. IEEE Trans. Smart Grid **3**(3), 1203–1212 (2012)
10. Czyż, P., Cichowski, A.: Przegląd systemów ładowania elektrycznych osobowych pojazdów i koncepcja dwukierunkowej ładowarki pokładowej. Zeszyty Naukowe Wydziału Elektrotechniki i Automatyki Politechniki Gdańskiej **57**, 11–16 (2017)
11. Figura, R., Sadowski, S., Siroić, R.: Stacje szybkiego ładowania dla pojazdóa. elektrycznych. Autobusy. Efektywność transportu 6, pp. 839–842 (2018)
12. Paska, J., et al.: Autonomiczna stacja ładowania pojazdów elektrycznych. Zeszyty Naukowe Wydziału Elektrotechniki i Automatyki Politechniki Gdańskiej **42**, 171–174 (2015)
13. Jacyna, M., Merkisz, J.: Kształtowanie systemu transportowego z uwzględnieniem emisji zanieczyszczeń w rzeczywistych warunkach ruchu drogowego. Oficyna Wydawnicza Politechniki Warszawskiej, Warsaw (2014)
14. Jacyna, M., Merkisz, J.: Encouraging sustainable development of transport system with regard to the emission of harmful compounds of exhaust gases in real traffic conditions. In: Jacyna, M., Wasiak, M. (eds.) Simulation Model to Support Designing a Sustainable National Transport System. Index Copernicus, pp. 49–63 (2014)

15. Sierpiński, G., Staniek, M., Celiński, I.: Travel behavior profiling using a trip planner. Transportation Research Procedia 14C, pp. 1743–1752, Warsaw (2016)

16. Sierpiński, G., Staniek, M., Celiński, I.: New methods for pro-ecological travel behavior learning. In: 8th International Conference of Education, Research and Innovation (ICERI2015), 16–18 November 2015, Seville, Spain ICERI2015 Proceedings, Edited by: L. Gómez Chova, A. López Martínez, I. Candel Torres, Published by IATED Academy, pp. 6926–6933 (2015)

17. Sierpiński, G.: Distance and frequency of travels made with selected means of transport - a case study for the Upper Silesian conurbation (Poland). In: Sierpiński, G. (ed.) Intelligent Transport Systems and Travel Behaviour. AISC, vol. 505, pp. 75–85. Springer (2017)

18. Macioszek, E.: First and last mile delivery - problems and issues. In: Sierpiński, G. (ed.) Advanced Solutions of Transport Systems for Growing Mobility. AISC, vol. 631, pp. 147–154. Springer, Switzerland (2018)

19. Macioszek, E.: Electric vehicles - problems and issues. In: Sierpiński, G. (ed.) TSTP 2019. AISC, vol. 1091, pp. 169–183. Springer, Cham (2020). https://doi.org/10.1007/978-3-030-35543-2_14

20. Macioszek, E.: E-mobility infrastructure in the Górnośląsko - Zagłębiowska Metropolis, Poland, and potential for development. In: Proceedings of the 5th World Congress on New Technologies (NewTech 2019), Lisbon, Portugal, August 18–20, 2019. Paper No. ICERT 108, ICERT 108-1-ICERT 108-4

21. European Alternative Fuels Observatory. www.eafo.eu. Last accessed 20 Dec 2019

22. Sendek-Matysiak, E.: The condition of EV infrastructure in the world - analysis for years 2005-2016. In: Macioszek, E., Sierpiński, G. (eds.) Directions of Development of Transport Networks and Traffic Engineering. LNNS, vol. 51, pp. 55–65. Springer, Switzerland (2019)

23. Sendek-Matysiak, E., Szumska, E.: Infrastruktura ładowania jako jeden z elementów rozwoju elektromobilności w Polsce. Prace Naukowe Politechniki Warszawskiej. Seria Transport **121**, 329–340 (2018)

24. Zajkowski, K., Seroka, K.: Przegląd możliwych sposobów ładowania akumulatorów w pojazdach z napędem elektrycznym. Autobusy. Technika, Eksploatacja, Systemy Transportowe **7–8**, pp. 483–486 (2017)

25. Kancelaria, S.: Ustawa z dnia 11 stycznia 2018 r. o elektromobilności i paliwach alternatywnych. Dz.U.2018 poz. 317. http://prawo.sejm.gov.pl/isap.nsf/download.xsp/WDU201800 00317/T/D20180317L.pdf. Last accessed 20 Dec 2019

26. MT My Tesla. http://www.mytesla.com.pl/punkty-ladowania/. Last accessed 20 Dec 2019

27. Greenway. http://greenwaypolska.pl. Last accessed 20 Dec 2019

28. Auta elektryczne. http://www.autaelektryczne.pl/stacje-ladowania-aut-elektrycznych.html. Last accessed 20 Dec 2019

29. Galactico. http://www.galactico.pl.. Last accessed 20 Dec 2019

30. EcoMoto. http://www.ecomoto.info/punkty/nowe.html. Last accessed 20 Dec 2019

31. Obserwatorium Rynku Paliw Alternatywnych. http://www.orpa.pl/infrastruktura. Last accessed 20 Dec 2019

32. PlugShare. https://www.plugshare.com/. Last accessed 20 Dec 2019

33. Elektrowóz. http://elektrowoz.pl/ladowarki/. Last accessed 20 Dec 2019

34. Infor.Pl Moto. https://mojafirma.infor.pl/moto/eksploatacja-auta/uklad-elektryczny/269 9273,Punkty-ladowania-samochodow-elektrycznych-w-Polsce-lista-lokalizacji.html. Last accessed 20 Dec 2019

35. Wysokie napięcie. https://wysokienapiecie.pl/2465-nowa-mapa-ladowarek-samochodow-ele ktrycznych-w-polsce-ev-auta-baterie/. Last accessed 20 Dec 2019

36. Mroskowiak, M., et al.: Grupa CDE. Perspektywy rozwoju elektromobilności w Polsce. Raport 2018. https://www.teraz-srodowisko.pl/media/pdf/aktualnosci/4514-perspektywy-roz woju-elektromobilnosci-w-polsce-raport-2018.pdf. Last accessed 20 Dec 2019

Telematics Solutions for Traffic Management of Public Transport Vehicles

Dariusz Masłowski[✉]

Opole University of Technology, Prószkowska 76, Opole, Poland
d.maslowski@po.edu.pl

Abstract. Professional transport companies face various challenges on a daily basis, ranging from increasing passenger numbers, improving service quality to reducing operating and vehicle costs. In order to achieve the objectives of success in this field, it is necessary to implement effective system and implementation solutions for urban public transport management. The introduction of telematic solutions that can meet the high expectations of public transport users is nowadays becoming a compromise between the time of passengers' expectations and the economic possibilities of cities. The aim of this article is to present telematics solutions for the management of urban public transport. The following research methods were used to achieve the goal: generalizations, comparisons, analysis of literature and websites. Moreover, the paper presents an innovative method of urban public transport management using the PERT method.

Keywords: City logistics · Telematics · Optimization · PERT method

1 Introduction

Today's urban transport challenges are primarily about efficient, sustainable, green and economic transport. Solutions involving the implementation of new information and communication technologies are a very good tool for urban transport control and management [1]. The latest technologies allow for better management of vehicle traffic in urban areas and allow for processing and transmitting information to all traffic participants, i.e. drivers, passengers. One of the elements improving the functioning of public transport in cities is the implementation of implementations that significantly facilitate the movement of buses between key areas forming the space of urban agglomerations [2].

Often the purposefulness of urban travel forces its users to be unconventional in defining different destinations. A larger percentage of journeys are made in passenger vehicles, while excluding public transport. Two types of traffic factors can be mentioned in connection with urban travel [3]:

- the communicative behaviour of people travelling in the city (people's approach to travelling by different means of transport, where choices are based, among other things, on current possibilities, limitations and customs), [4–6],
- mobility of users (number of movements in terms of their demand) [7].

© Springer Nature Switzerland AG 2020
J. Mikulski (Ed.): TST 2020, CCIS 1289, pp. 138–151, 2020.
https://doi.org/10.1007/978-3-030-59270-7_11

Telematics solutions are tools to, among other things, motivate passengers to choose passenger transport services which have been booming in recent years. Also in the interest of the environment, it is a key factor in urban development, aimed at making full use of the infrastructure for telematics deployments.

The purpose of this publication is to present telematic solutions for the management and support of urban public transport in terms of passenger service. The paper presents companies that provide services that provide integrated solutions for urban public transport management. The following research methods were used to achieve the goal: generalisations, comparisons, analysis of literature and websites of companies providing urban passenger transport services, analysis of urban traffic. Moreover, the paper presents an innovative method of urban public transport management using the PERT method.

2   Public Transport by Bus in Terms of City Logistics

City logistics has recently become more and more popular. Growing opportunities for city management provide a wide range of solutions as part of research on the movement of people, goods and information. Based on a detailed literature review, the author defines urban logistics as: "all processes that improve and optimise the flow of people, goods and information in cities by managing them appropriately to meet the needs of their inhabitants, while taking into account environmental, safety and energy-saving aspects" [8–13].

Not always can such a defined concept be agreed upon. Because in the literature one can find the wrong translation of the expression city logistics or urban goods transport, where in the context it is understood in two ways [14]. Therefore, two different understandings of the term can be mentioned:

– urban logistics as management of (and only of) goods flows [15]
– city logistics managing all flows in the city [16, 17].

The contemporary tasks of city logistics include ensuring an appropriate distribution of specific, regular, so far uncoordinated and scattered transport streams running through the city [18].

Urban transport plays a significant role for the whole city, as it is the transport processes that are responsible for every task in the urban area. The following transport categories can be distinguished [17]:

– Car transport, including bus, trolleybus and individual transport,
– Rail transport, including: tram and rail,
– transmission including: waterworks, gasworks, sewage,
– and, in some cases, most often islands, water transport.

The creation of optimal production and spatial links, taking into account their costs, efficiency and range of services provided to individual entities, allows for economic and ecological development of the region. Therefore, such an important factor is the city's transport policy, which gives the possibility to choose a specific direction and method of development (transformation) of the existing transport system so that it is consistent with the adopted city development strategy.

The introduction of an effective transport policy in cities allows the introduction of various solutions to improve travel and life, so the following concepts can be distinguished in recent years [19]:

- clean city transport,
- sustainable transport (a concept that aims to minimise the use of environmentally harmful means of transport),
- the concept of dividing the city into 3 zones (A, B, C),
- Urban travel concepts (Bike&Ride, Park&Ride, Kiss&Ride)

Among the advantages of choosing public transport are the possibility to talk to other traffic participants, to perform other non-traffic-related activities, the possibility to observe the surroundings or the most important transport factor to reduce time and money [20]. As far as defects of the bus are concerned, it is primarily exposed to the congestion effect. Moreover, travellers have to adjust their time to the current timetable or, in some cases, long waiting times at bus stops, which may consequently discourage them from using such services. However, according to a study carried out by Sierpiński, it is the low ratings of urban public transport that may trigger the following changes shortening the travel time in relation to the car, closing the city centre to passenger car traffic, adjusting the timetable, introducing high fees for parking a car or for entering the centre, introduction of discounts/promotions for urban public transport passengers, punctuality during rush hour, more frequent courses, to increase the number of stops, fewer transfers [3].

Demonstration of such changes is needed for the development of urban transport, which is an indispensable element of the city by law.

Urban transport, often referred to differently as urban transport, can be defined as: regular, public collective transport carried out on behalf of a local government transport organizer - an organizational unit of a commune or intercommunal union or a commune and provincial government, or an intercommunal union and provincial government, which performs organizing tasks in relation to urban transport - exclusively within the area [21]: of one municipality, two or more municipalities, on the basis of intercommunal agreements.

Public collective transport according to the Act of 16 December 2010 [30] can be defined as a generally available regular passenger transport carried out at specific intervals and along a specific communication line, lines of communication or network [21].

By definition, for a transport operation to be considered public transport, it has to fulfil 3 main conditions:

- should be accessible to the public, i.e. accessible to any person observing the carrier's regulations,
- should be carried out regularly at specific intervals in the relevant timetables,

– should be carried out along a specific communication line, lines or network, i.e. on the route the traveller should have easy access to the stops.

The process of planning urban public transport vehicle traffic should be based on the calculation of the capacity for these services and the determination of the route. This mode of transport can be divided into 3 planning stages [22]:

– Grade I - determines the local line connections, by calculating the number of vehicles or the flow of goods from or to the city,
– Grade II - determines the average value of the goods stream to, from and within the transport area and determines the size and range of the route,
– Grade III - determines the additional capacity, using the daily variation statistics for the daily flows to, from and within the transport area.

The most common means of travel for residents, which occurs in almost every city, is the bus. Table 1 shows a comparison of the inland public transport modes used in the cities.

Table 1. Comparison of certain collective inland transport modes [own study]

Type of transport	Capacity	Advantages	Disadvantages
Rail transport			
Railway	Large	- long-distance transport - high flexibility in passenger transport volumes - average transit time - the longer the distance, the lower the cost - no possibility of congestion - The tracks represent a small area compared to roads - low impact of weather conditions	- limited transport infrastructure - few stops in 1 city - lack of adequate number of vehicles - expensive construction of railway traction
Tram	Average	- average transit time - high possibility to control the passages - The tracks represent a small area compared to roads - internal city transport - the design of new tramway lines takes into account the safety of traffic flows	- high implementation cost - Infrastructure constraints for the establishment of the crossing lines - potential congestion - difficult location of tram lines in road infrastructure - extended time compared to the railway crossing (stopping at stops, intersections)
Metro	Large	- the fastest time - no possibility of congestion - the most efficient means of transport - total contingency - very high frequency - no influence of weather conditions - no impact of city traffic	- very high implementation cost - unprofitable in medium-sized and small towns
Trackless transport			

(*continued*)

Table 1. (*continued*)

Type of transport	Capacity	Advantages	Disadvantages
Bus	Average	- the most popular mode of transport - possibility of transport to any place (highly developed infrastructure) - high flexibility in creating bus lines - high flexibility for change - relatively low introduction cost compared to other vehicles - possibility of separating lanes for crossings	- weather-dependent - causes environmental pollution - high vehicle maintenance costs - high traffic congestion, causing delays
Trolleybus	Average	- reducing urban pollution - low running costs - combining the advantages of bus and tram - the possibility of introduction in cities where buses are not enough and there is no possibility of spatial construction of rails	- the need to build traction - Infrastructure limitations, flow of communication lines - average cost of introduction - the possibility of delays - reduce the visual value of cities
car (TAXI, UBER)	Small	- possibility of transport to any place (highly developed infrastructure) - high availability - high flexibility for change	- weather-dependent - causes environmental pollution - high accident rates - high vehicle maintenance costs - high traffic congestion, causing delays - plans to restrict the driving of these vehicles in city centres

3   Telematics Solutions for Urban Public Transport Management

Telematics, due to its rapid development, is difficult to define, while, on the basis of the analysis of the literature, the author defines telematics as "solutions that function effectively in a given system, including the use of all tools and technologies that have been created as a result of the correlation of three aspects: telecommunications, computerization and information, while automating them" [23–27].

The process of planning, organising and managing public transport has become a problem for contemporary planners. IT solutions that support these processes come with help. Companies offering these solutions are constantly developing and looking for better and better solutions. However, it should be remembered that local systems should be the basic tool for the construction and construction of timetables, while maintaining system coherence.

According to the analysis of the Act, public transport organizers have to deal with many guidelines that improve the quality and effectiveness of services provided. Therefore, companies providing public transport support services, using advanced mathematical algorithms and computer software, have to continuously improve their products in order to become competitive in the markets. For the analysis of IT solutions in the article, examples of systems have been selected, such as:

– Tristar
– Elte GPS
– Trapeze
– DPK System

– Systra

The main focus of companies is on creating programs that optimize existing timetables while reducing operating costs. An important aspect is the planning interface. One of the most interesting planning solutions on the market is DPK System. It is this company that has selected software in its product range that fully adapts to the conditions in which it is implemented while maintaining its initial assumptions. Comprehensive optimization tools used to build timetables take into account complex interdependencies such as [28]:

– the overall passenger flow,
– frequency of vehicles of different lines on selected sections of transport and the need to change trains,
– the most efficient use of available rolling stock (regardless of the number of contractors),
– active saw-tooth diagram for line synchronization,
– intuitive graphical user interface, full view configuration, dockable windows, selection of view style, saving individual settings at the workstation.

In addition to companies providing public transport management support services, there are a number of solutions aimed at improving public transport journeys, so that passengers can travel their planned journey without obstacles (Table 2).

Table 2. Examples of solutions to improve urban public transport by voivodeship cities in Poland [own study]

No.	City	Telematics solution
1	Białystok	- Bialystok City Card (e-card) - Online payment application (SkyCash, MPay) - Applications supporting travel (JakDojade, mMPK, DHKM, BUSstok, Transportoid) - Application for checking departures in real time (Wirtualny Monitor, rozkładzik.pl, e-podróżnik.pl) - Tariff zone system (4 zone) - Traffic management system - Integrated Information Systemc ERP class, supporting company management - TSI (Transport Information Systems). This support includes financing, human resources management and budgeting.
2	Kielce	- Online payment application (SkyCash, moBILETm MPay) - Kielce City Card - Application for checking departures in real time: myBus online - Applications supporting travel (JakDojade) - Tariff zone system (2 zone) - Bus traffic isolation system - Bus pass

(*continued*)

Table 2. (*continued*)

No.	City	Telematics solution
3	Bydgoszcz	- T Interchange system - Agglomeration ticket for REGIO and interREGIO trains on the Bydgoszcz-Toruń route BiT City ticket - Tariff zone system (2 zone) - Bydgoszcz City Card (e-card) - Online payment application (SkyCash, Mint Mobile) - Purchase of a ticket in a vehicle with a proximity card - Passenger Portal - a website supporting travel management - Ticketing machine system - Intelligent Transport System for Urban Transport,
4	Gdańsk/Trójmiasto	- Applications supporting travel (JakDojade) - City Card (e-card) - Common ticket for public transport and SKM and PKM - Integrated Traffic Management System TRISTAR - Variable table of contents - Application for checking departures in real time - Bus traffic isolation system - Bus pass - Online payment application
5	Katowice	- Metropolitan Transport Authority Traffic Management Centre - Online payment application (SkyCash, moBILETm MPay) - Contactless payments on buses - Silesian Public Services Card (e-card) - Applications supporting travel (JakDojade) - Dynamic Passenger Information System - Passenger information boards - Bus traffic isolation system - Bus pass
6	Kraków	- Area-based Motion Control System (UTCS) - Coordination system in strings - Access control system for the calm zone and public transport lane surveillance - Public transport management system (TTSS) - Tariff zone system (2 zone) - Bus traffic isolation system - Bus pass - Online payment application (SkyCash, moBILET) - Applications supporting travel (JakDojade) - Krakow City Card - BUS TV - Television on bus
7	Lublin	- Traffic Control Centre (CSR) - Variable content tables - Intelligent Transport System (ITS) - Bus traffic isolation system - Bus pass - Traffic light controllers, integrated with video detection cameras - Tariff integration allowing for travelling by collective and regional transport in the area of Lublin - Extending the scope of the dynamic passenger information system to include regional and road transport - the passenger will be provided with information on the most convenient connection including regional transport in addition - Electronic Ticket Card - Applications supporting travel (JakDojade) - Dynamic passenger information system - Automatic toilets at bus stops - Over-standard shelters and information, inteligent posts - Application for checking departures in real time: myBus online
8	Łódź	- Bus traffic isolation system - Bus pass - Open Payment System - START-STOP payments - Stationary ticket machines

(*continued*)

Table 2. (*continued*)

No.	City	Telematics solution
9	Olsztyn	- Application for checking departures in real time: myBus online - Applications supporting travel (JakDojade) - Olsztyn City Card (OKM) - Variable content tables - Online payment application (MPay)
10	Opole	- Dynamic passenger information system (kiedy.przyjedzie) - Applications supporting travel (JakDojade, e-podróznik) - Opolanka City Card - Variable content tables - Intelligent Transport System (ITS) - Passenger portal for information flow - Ticketing system in buses and at bus stops - Online payment application (SkyCash) - Bus traffic isolation system - Bus pass
11	Poznań	- Variable content tables - Parking Parkuj i Jedź (Park&Ride) - Open Payment System - Application for checking departures in real time: „myMPK" - Bus traffic isolation system - Bus pass
12	Rzeszów	- Online payment application (SkyCash, CallPay, zbiletem.pl, GoPay, MPay) - Applications supporting travel (JakDojade, my bus) - Integrated Traffic and Public Transport Management System (IMSMSRiTP) with a dedicated ICT platform (PTITS) - Area Traffic Control System (SOSRD) - Traffic light control system - Public transport vehicle priority system - Public Transport Management System (PMS) - Passenger Information System (E-INFO) - Electronic Toll Collection System (E-BILET) - Rzeszów Intelligent Transport System - Bus traffic isolation system - Bus pass - WIM (Weight in Motion) Dynamic Vehicle Weighing System
13	Szczecin	- Mobile City Card Szczecin - Szczecin Agglomeration Charter - Applications supporting travel (JakDojade, take&drive, dedicated program for the city) - Variable content tables - Dynamic passenger information system
14	Warszawa	- Dynamic passenger information system - Applications supporting travel (JakDojade) - Warsaw City Card - Mazovian Charter - Variable content tables - Parking Parkuj i Jedź (P + R) - Zones Kiss&Ride (K + R) - Ticket purchase possible at ticket machines, online(www), via smartphone - Common Ticket ZTM-KM-WKD - Public transport management system Trapeze - Online payment application (SkyCash)
15	Wrocław	- Applications supporting travel (JakDojade) - URBANCARD - Wroclaw City Card - Stopover ticket machine system - iMPK mobile application - Dynamic Stopping Information (DIP) - Area based motion control (OSR) - Traffic conditions information subsystem (PERUCHU i INFO ITS) - Video surveillance system at selected intersections - TETRA communication system

(*continued*)

Table 2. (*continued*)

No.	City	Telematics solution
16	Zielona Góra	- Applications supporting travel (JakDojade, rozkladzik.pl, Transportoid) - Online payment application (SkyCash, zbiletem.pl, MoBILET, mPay) - Zielona Góra City Card - Variable content tables

The data were taken from the websites of individual companies. As a result, the solutions not mentioned in the above overview may be motivated by poor information to passengers about the opportunities in individual cities. It is proposed to develop a nationwide information tool for passengers making inter-city journeys in order to inform people coming to different cities in Poland.

4   Urban Public Transport Management Method

The PERT method (Program Evaluation and Review Technique, the second correct version is the name Program Evaluation Research Task), which is a probabilistic method of project planning and control, using network programming, used in project management [29].

However, it is possible to use the PERT method to manage and optimise the traffic of urban transport vehicles, where:

- optimistic time is the shortest possible travel time for a given road Sect. (5 = 50 km/h),
- pessimistic time is the longest possible time of driving a given road Sect. (5 = 1 km/h),
- realistic time is the real average travel time of a given section resulting from the research,
- AoA notation node is respectively A - number of a given road junction, B - earliest time of vehicle's entry to a given junction, C - latest time of vehicle's entry to a given junction, D - differences between the latest entry and the earliest bus's entry to a junction (driving delay),
- an arrow connecting it to the crossroads from junction to junction,
- the objective of the network solution is to define the optimal route of the bus line between specific points in the city, taking into account different dependencies and constraints
- the critical path is a designated public transport route.

The method of municipal public transport management has been described in detail in [31].

The current bus line no. 7 (Fig. 1) has been superimposed with a model using the PERT method, the aim of which is to optimize the current traffic of this vehicle (Fig. 2). After the analysis of places which may be sensitive for the route of this line, a solution could be proposed which would consist in calculating whether a given route could be modified so that it would move around the city in a shorter period of time, while at the same time passing through a shorter route.

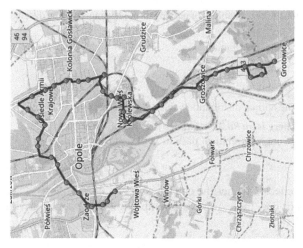

Fig. 1. Line 7 of municipal transport in Opole [own study based on [32]]

The basic step of the multi-criteria model is to determine the critical path that indicates the bus line with the most advantageous coverage of places that shape traffic in the city, while the longest travel time (Fig. 2). The critical path at critical points indicates the same solutions to current cases. The choice of a more favourable route must be based on certain assumptions. For this purpose, it is necessary to calculate the probability with which a given bus is able to drive on the planned new route of the bus line, marked by the critical path.

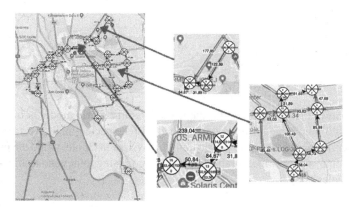

Fig. 2. Optimisation measures to reduce travel time [own study based on [32]]

The result of applying the PERT method to the infrastructure of the existing bus line is the answer in what time with what probability the bus will pass this route. Table 3 shows with what probability the indicated bus line will pass the route within 30 min.

The probability of this phenomenon is 80, 59%. which, according to the model criteria, meets these assumptions. Therefore, the last element for the assessment of the

Table 3. Calculation of the probability of passing through using a normal distribution [own study]

Normal distribution	
Check value (D)	30
Probability	0,85
The normal distribution value read from the tables	80,59%
There is an 80.23% chance that the bus will pass through the critical path in 1814 s, or 30 min	

model used is to check whether the calculated travel time is more favourable after the model is applied or not. Table 4 shows a comparison of the actual driving time with its modelled reflection.

Table 4. Bus journey time of bus no. 7 before the application of the PERT method, after the application and the journey time of the passenger car [own study]

	Average actual bus journey time before optimisation [min]	Average optimised bus journey time [min]	Passenger car time (14.10, Wednesday) [min]
Bus driving time (including stops)	55		
Number of stops	36		
Stopping time at bus stops	18		
The time of the bus ride itself	**37**	**30**	**28**

Table 4 shows that the indicated route using a multi-criteria model is on the same line by almost 3 min, which is a very good result. The expected final effects should be expected after designing the entire public transport system in Opole, while the presented results of the analysis show measurable benefits of optimising routes and traffic of public transport vehicles.

5 Conclusion

Management and organisation is an integral part of effective development. The application of new standards in static and dynamic transport systems is only possible if a sustainable alternative to public transport is offered to passengers.

The role of public transport in creating efficient city logistics is one of the most important issues. The way it is managed determines its functioning. Therefore, it is important to adapt existing market solutions to the functioning of the city. In the road network of cities there are many different types of means of transport with their advantages and disadvantages, but the most popular is the bus. Because it is the bus that exists in practically every city.

The way any telematics system works is based on the process of collecting, analysing and processing information at a given section in order to interpret current situations and decide on the application of appropriate control measures. Data on the volume and nature of traffic can be transmitted to the headquarters by means of modem-equipped detectors or cameras. This allows to count vehicles passing through a given section, speed and time, direction and type of vehicles.

However, in addition to the compact and integrated large telematics systems, there are a number of additional solutions that are compatible with these systems. The author presented an analysis of existing additional solutions functioning in Polish voivodeship cities. As a result, solutions not mentioned in the article, but functioning in the analyzed cities, may be the result of poor passenger information. Therefore, it is proposed to develop a nationwide information tool for passengers making intercity travels.

The key part of the article was to present an innovative tool for urban public transport management based on the PERT method. The tool is to be used not only to plan completely new timetables and transport routes, but most of all to optimize the existing routes in such a way as to make the crossing of the city as short as possible.

Therefore, the conclusion from the application of the tool is the possibility to optimize the existing transport solutions in cities, while estimating the exact time of the journey through the indicated bus line on the basis of conducting a normal distribution and calculating the probability of such traffic. The advantage of this method is first of all a great potential in developing the whole system of urban public transport management, which in the future may become an additional tool supporting the work of municipal transport companies.

References

1. Mikulski, J.: The possibility of using telematics in urban transportation. In: Mikulski, J. (ed.) TST 2011. CCIS, vol. 239, pp. 54–69. Springer, Heidelberg (2011). https://doi.org/10.1007/978-3-642-24660-9_7
2. Perzyński, T., Lewiński, A.: Telematyka transportu w komunikacji miejskiej. Prace naukowe Politechniki Warszawskiej, Transport, z. 113, 401–409 (2016)
3. Sierpiński, G.: Zachowania komunikacyjne osób podróżujących a wybór środka transportu w mieście, PNPW: Transport z. 84, pp. 93–106 (2012)
4. Lu, X., Pas, E.I.: Socio-demographics, activity participation and travel behavior, Transportation Research Part A 33, Elsevier, pp. 1–18 (1999)
5. McGuckin, N., Nakamoto, Y.: Trips, Chains, and Tours—Using an Operational Definition, The National Household Travel Survey Conference, 1–2 November (2004)
6. Zhang, M., et al.: Travel behavior analysis of the females in Beijing. J. Transport. Syst. Eng. Inf. Technol. 8(2), 19–26 (2008)
7. Rudnicki, A.: Zrównoważona mobilność a rozwój przestrzenny miasta. Czasopismo techniczne. Architektura Z. 3, 57–74 (2010)

8. Masłowski, D., Kulińska, E., Kulińska, K.: Application of routing methods in city logistics for sustainable road traffic. In: 3rd International Conference Green Cities 2018 – Green Logistics for Greener Cities, 13–14 September, Szczecin, Poland (2018)

9. Witkowski, K.: Aspekt logistyki miejskiej w gospodarowaniu infrastrukturą transportową miasta, Prace Instytutu Prawa i Administracji PWSZ w Sulechowie, "Studia Lubuskie", nr 3, PWSZ Sulechów, Sulechów, pp. 203 (2007)

10. Szymczak, M.: Logistyka miejska. In: Gołembska, E. (red.) Kompendium wiedzy o logistyce, PWE, Warszawa, pp. 311 (2013)

11. Szołtysek, J.: Logistyczne aspekty zarządzania przepływami osób i ładunków w miastach, Akademia Ekonomiczna w Katowicach, Katowice, p. 105 (2005)

12. Kiba-Janiak, M., Witkowski, J.: Modelowanie logistyki miejskiej Wydawnictwo PWE Warszawa, pp. 14 (2014)

13. Taniguchi, E., Thompson, R.G., Yamada, T.: City Logistics – Network modeling and intelliegent transport systems, "Pergamon", pp. 2 (2001)

14. Iwan, S.: Wdrażanie dobrych praktyk w obszarze transportu dostawczego w miastach, pp. 23–24. Wydawnictwo Naukowe Akademii Morskiej w Szczecinie, Szczecin (2012)

15. Taniguchi, E., Thompson, R.G., Yamada, T.: Modelling city logistics. In: City Logistics I, Taniguchi, E., Thompson, R.G. (ed.) Institute of Systems Science Research, Kyoto, pp. 4 (1999)

16. Rzeczyński, B.: Logistyka miejska. Propedeutyka, pierwszy polski wykład, Instytut Inżynierii Zarządzania, Politechnika Poznańska, Poznań (2007)

17. Tundys, B.: Logistyka miejska. Koncepcje, systemy, rozwiązania, Difin, Warszawa (2008)

18. Witkowski, K., Saniuk, S.: Logistyka miejska a jakość życia mieszkańców Zielonej Góry - wstęp do badań. Prace Naukowe Uniwersytetu Ekonomicznego we Wrocławiu, Nr 234, 171–181 (2011)

19. Jackiewicz, J., Czech, P., Barcik, J.: Polityka transportowa na przykładzie aglomeracji Śląskiej, ZNPŚ: Transport z.69, pp. 53–62 (2010)

20. Zwerts, E., et al.: How children view their travel behaviour: a case study from Flanders (Belgium), J. Transport Geography 18, Elsevier, pp. 702–710 (2010)

21. Kołodziejski, H., Wyszomirski, O. (eds.) Transport miejski. Ekonomika i organizacja, Uniwersytet Gdański, Gdańsk (2007)

22. Topolski, M.: Planowanie optymalnej trasy przejazdu transportu samochodowego z wykorzystaniem miękkich metod obliczeniowych, "Autobusy", nr 6, pp. 1174–1179 (2016)

23. Weintrit, A., Neumann, T.: Safety of Marine Transport, Introduction. In: Weintrit, A., Neumann, T. (eds.) Safety of Marine Transport, pp. 9–10. CRC Press-Taylor & Francis Group, USA (2015)

24. Szpytko, J., Kocerba, A., Tekielak, M.: Telematic based transport device tracking and supervision system. IFAC Proceedings Volumes 39, 99–104 (2006)

25. Kiba-Janiak, M., Tronina, P.: Wpływ systemów telematycznych na usprawnienie międzynarodowych łańcuchów dostaw, ZNPŚ: Organizacja i Zarządzanie, z. 103, pp. 80 (2017)

26. Iwan, S., Małecki, K., Korczak, J.: Impact of Telematics on Efficiency of Urban Freight Transport. In: Mikulski, J. (ed.) TST 2013. CCIS, vol. 395, pp. 50–57. Springer, Heidelberg (2013). https://doi.org/10.1007/978-3-642-41647-7_7

27. Mikulski, J.: Telematyka – przyszłość transportu i logistyki. Logistyka, nr 2, 36–37 (2010)

28. Masłowski, D., et al.: Analiza rozwiązań informatycznych wykorzystywanych w procesie planowania przejazdów komunikacji miejskiej. Autobusy 6, 1467–1473 (2017)

29. Brandenburg, H.: Zarządzanie Projektami. Wydawnictwo Akademii Ekonomicznej w Katowicach, Katowice (2002)

30. Dz.U. 2011 nr 5 poz. 13 z późn. zm

31. Masłowski, D.: Wielokryterialny model sterowania pojazdami miejskiej komunikacji zbiorowej. Case study na podstawie miasta Opola. PhD thesis. Politechnika Opolska, Opole (2019)
32. Google.maps. Accessed 11 Dec 2019

Smart City Design Based on an Ontological Knowledge System

Pavel Přibyl[1], Ondřej Přibyl[1(✉)], Miroslav Svítek[1], and Aleš Janota[2]

[1] Czech Technical University in Prague, Konviktská 20, Prague, Czech Republic
pribylo@fd.cvut.cz
[2] University of Žilina, Univerzitna 8215/1, Žilina, Slovak Republic

Abstract. Smart city has several definitions. Typically, it is an alliance of subsystems that have following objectives: improvement of quality of life of citizens, better use of limited resources and best use of existing infrastructure. Transportation as one of the most important subsystems shall be thus understood as one player working together with energy management, economy, eGovernment, and others. Synergy is the key to successful implementation. In order to be able to aim at the joint objective function and any synergy, the different subsystems must "understand" each other. Ontology has been acknowledged to be the most common tool to do that. To prepare an ontology for a domain (for example transportation) is a complicated task. In order to do that in a city, where there are several subsystems with complex behaviour is even more challenging. It is very difficult if not impossible to get experts from different fields to prepare a common ontology. In this paper we address the issue of Smart City Design and propose a pragmatic method to prepare an ontological knowledge system using the knowledge of various expert groups. A new concept, so call a knowledge matrix, is defined and used to enable cooperation of experts from different fields. We believe this can further help in implementation of any smart city projects. In order to demonstrate the approach, transportation domain is used as an example for the ontology design. The approach will be further validated within two case studies that are also introduced within this paper: Smart Evropská street in Prague and within a project Smart City – Smart Region – Smart Community, where a transport behavioristic model is being developed based on the ontology described within this paper.

Keywords: Smart cities · Ontology · System design · UML

1 Introduction

The term smart city (SC) has many different definitions. In the last years, there is a clear shift from a technology-oriented definitions (e.g. "Smart city as one that has digital technology embedded across all city functions" [1] or "A smart city is a place where the traditional networks and services are made more efficient with the use of digital and telecommunication technologies, for the benefit of its inhabitants and businesses" [2]) to more people-oriented ones ("Smart city is a process rather than a static outcome, in which increased citizen engagement, hard infrastructure, social capital and

© Springer Nature Switzerland AG 2020
J. Mikulski (Ed.): TST 2020, CCIS 1289, pp. 152–164, 2020.
https://doi.org/10.1007/978-3-030-59270-7_12

digital technologies make cities more livable, resilient and better able to respond to challenges" [3]). For the purpose of this paper, we adopt a definition by EU, which states that "Smart Cities should provide a significant improvement of citizens' quality of life, an increased competitiveness of Europe's industry and innovative SMEs together with a strong contribution to sustainability and the EU's 20/20/20 energy and climate targets" [4]. We perceive a Smart City as a pragmatic alliance of subsystems which stream to the global target function to ensure quality of life for city residents [5]. It is not possible to "buy a smart city". It is a continuous process [3] aiming at the targets mentioned above.

A city clearly covers different domains, such as transportation, energy, environment, health care, safety, buildings, but also government and citizens [5]. We can see that the domains are spatially distributed, they cover technology as well as humans, they are all dynamic and non-linear, strongly connected, etc. This all leads to the fact, that a city is a complex system. According to the definition [6], complexity is "a property of an open system that consists of a large number of diverse, partially autonomous, richly interconnected components, often called Agents, has no centralised control, and whose behaviour emerges from the intricate interaction of agents and is therefore uncertain without being random."

A city is created by complex technological systems composed by many parts. The hardware components are heterogeneous, usually delivered by variety of suppliers even from different countries. The components haven't information about global process in the real time. They work effectively in their own environment according to implemented algorithms.

At the same time, in order to achieve the objectives of smart cities (such as minimising the use of resources – i.e. sustainability), we cannot address the partial city domains individually.

It is necessary to find a common platform to ensure that all sub-subsystems and devices will understand each other and converge to the global target function. This is only possible if all information about each entity is available to anyone who designs, operates and manages SC. Typically, so called ontology or domain ontology can be used to do that [7]. But an ontology needs to be prepared by an expert (or rather a group of experts). Clearly, there is no one, who can be considered an expert in all various domains of smart cities. And how to get experts and even decision makers from different domains to understand each other? Each domain contains several technical and organizational documents. They are often linked even to other fields. They have often hundreds of pages. There are national as well as international documents, which make the information content even larger. This is certainly a challenge that has not been successfully addressed yet.

In this paper, we propose a solution that was successfully used in the field of transportation, particularly applied by the Road Tunnel Operation Committee D.5 of PIARC (Permanent International Association of Road Congresses) in the 2007. It is a process that leads to an ontology, but it is pragmatic in a way that different experts can participate on the final solution. The structure of the knowledge system has been developed as a road tunnels domain ontology. The knowledge system covers 39 technical documents with a volume of around 2000 pages. The original name for this knowledge system is

"Road tunnel Manual RTM". Please note that the Czech Highway Directorate is also using a similar ontological approach to unify the quality of the "Design Documentation of the road tunnels technological systems".

Therefore, and this is why it is necessary to find a common platform to ensure that all sub-subsystems and devices will converge to the global target function. This is only possible if all knowledge about each entity is available to anyone who designs, operates and manages SC. In connection with the SC, a number of technical and organizational documents are issued. They are often hundreds of pages. Information contained therein is required to mediate to end users.

The methodology section of this paper describes the particular terms and processes commonly used to create an ontology. We add new steps that make it usable. In the discussion, the process is demonstrated on a real world example.

2   Ontology as an Instrument for Smart City Design

The original term "ontology" comes from the metaphysics and philosophical sciences; according to Aristotle it systematically examined the existence of being [8]. There are many definitions of what is ontology that changed and evolved over the years, see their review e.g. in [9]. The concept of ontology later spread to other areas of science, including Artificial Intelligence [10] and Computer Science [11], with a slightly different meaning - an ontology as a formal explicit specification of a shared conceptualization.

In the 70s, two main directions in the field of information technologies describing surrounding world and processes in it were established. The first branch crystalized in object oriented modelling using classes and the Unified Modeling Language (UML®) [12] as a tool. The second one describes the same objective reality in a form of ontology [13] using concepts and taxonomy of their arrangement.

Nowadays ontologies are the subject of increasing research interests in many domains, e.g. in the field of geography, computer technology, transportation, etc. [7]. In order to be able to aim at the joint objective function and any synergy, the different subsystems must "understand" each other. Ontology has been acknowledged to be the most common tool to do that. To prepare an ontology for a domain (for example transportation) is a complicated task. In order to do that in a city, where there are several subsystems with complex behaviour is even more challenging. It is very difficult if not impossible to get experts from different fields to prepare a common ontology. Various definitions of smart cities emphasize importance of interoperability between involved systems. It is influenced and depends on the ability to share and exchange data across different tools and platforms [14]. Ontology seems to be one way of overcoming interoperability problems; it is a basic building block for the Semantic Web (usually in the form of the RDF (Resource Description Framework) Schema or OWL (Ontology Web Language) [15, 16] advocates the use of semantic Web technologies for better data interoperability and integration in smart city applications - they discuss existence of several ontology catalogs and using four of them (particularly READY4SmartCities; Linked Open Vocabulary - LOV; OpenSensingCity - OSC; and LOV4IoT). They also demonstrate how to use them to design and develop smart city applications. Ontology helps semantic systems to represent formally the concepts, objects, properties and relationship between them. The model of the world created in this way makes it possible to derive machine-processed knowledge and evaluate it [17, 18] applies an approach that uses ontology and reasoning techniques based on the NIST Framework for Cyber-Physical Systems and shows how reasoning can be used to analyze and validate the trustworthiness of elements of Smart Cities. In [19] Qamar et al. study four smart city applications particularly Smart Parking, Smart Garbage Control, Smart Streetlight and Smart Complaint management. They use semantic web technologies to share and merge data of different systems and propose their Smart City Services Ontology. Semantic models are also used by [20] who exploit the concept of semantic Web for designing a new smart city ontology that is considered as a system of systems, and [21], describing a semantic modelling framework to annotate streaming sensor data. [22] uses an intermediate part (called the activity model) as a transition layer in the process of building smart city ontology. Thus their approach is understandable even by non-computer scientists. [23] examines how the ontologies of a sample of smart city applications adapt the ontology (with a special attention paid to the energy and transport domains). [24] aims to explore ontology-based approaches for particular smart city mobility application - an ontology-based Smart Bike Sharing System. [25] presents an ontology as the foundation for the proposed collaborative navigation (supposing collaboration of drivers, autonomous cars, and pedestrians), which is an important feature of smart cities. [26] defines an ontology-based modelling approach to build adaptation services, using a methodology for context awareness driven by 4 dimensions (Environment, Device, User, and Services) and applied to the smart phone I-parking case study. [27] chooses an efficient way to handle a wide range of non-emergency events in a smart city and develop an ontology (so called Open 311 Ontology) to classify them in an organized manner, based on a semantic model of the city. [28] develops an indoor space ontology model for finding the indoor lost property; from technological point of view they use data from the Bluetooth Low Energy (BLE) devices. [29] presents an ontology for a smart parking in a university campus. [30] describes the ontology-driven approach that allows access and visualization of energy-related information for various value added services. Many of the existing Internet of Things (IoT) deployments create isolated islands designed to fit different devices, data, platforms, and applications. Therefore, there is a trend in data management to define, standardize and make use of standardised ontologies which is supported by increasing industry adoption of semantic technologies. [31] provides a general review of standardized ontologies. Km4City Ontology presented by [32] combines Linked Open Data, street graph data and selected Public Administration services. The fact that different people create different ontologies using different methods, often in the same domain, causes some heterogeneity. To solve this problem, ontology matching systems are developed [33]. A special challenge is processing of uncertain information; therefore some research has also focused on extending ontologies and Semantic Web technologies to handle uncertain information where one of promising approaches leads to fuzzy ontologies [34].

This paper describes creation methodology of the text-oriented knowledge system covering field of a Smart City based on domain ontology. The basic draft of ontology can be developed as a UML model of SC´s technical and operational systems, which is close to human perception. The ontology is available on web sites in a form of electronic encyclopedia and it contains the links to the relevant text units. Unlike strictly ontologically oriented and thus rigid knowledge systems, this solution, based on a web-ontology is sufficiently flexible. To process new information (a new term) means to add term on the website and to add appropriate link to the text document.

3   Practical Creation of Ontological Model

3.1   Ontology Design Methodology

The purpose of the Smart City Knowledge Management system is to provide to all kinds of users (experts or non-experts), in fast and user-friendly way, the relevant information about smart city. The goal of the search is to find relevant information which is hidden in several published documents. Figure 1 depicts how a city knowledge system is being built and maintained according to our proposal.

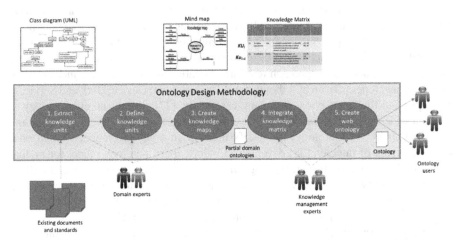

Fig. 1. The work flow and basic steps of proposed methodology [own study]

As an initial step, the actual technical and organizational documents assembling corporative experiences about technological and organizational subsystems and partial domains are collected. Also, for each domain, appropriate Domain's experts are designated.

Ontology Design Methodology (ODM) includes the following steps:

- Searching for knowledge units/concepts (KU): Based on the existing knowhow and existing documents, knowledge units (KU) are extracted. The knowledge unit is basically a term (noun) important for each domain. Each KU has a unique name (terms).
- Defining KUs: A textual description (alternatively using other means of description, for example selected UML diagrams) is provided for each knowledge unit.

- Creating Knowledge Maps for each domain: They are a visual representation of terms and links among them. Up to this step, we are dealing with particular domains separately and domain experts are responsible for each knowledge map. Typically, a min mapping tool can be used to visualize the knowledge maps.
- Creating Knowledge Matrix: In order to integrate the knowledge from partial domains into a system view, the KUs are integrated into a knowledge matrix (KM). The first column of KM carries unique title of the KU. The last column shows the link to the relevant text section (T-KU). Let us suppose, that first hundred rows in the KM is reserved for domain traffic, next hundred for street lighting, etc. This process is relatively time-consuming and complex, and may not be omitted. Each relevant document must be examined and the terms and T-KUs have to be found. The knowledge unit provides an overview of all elements in the different domains. This is the level used to find and define interactions (associations) among KUs from different domains. The knowledge matrix is the first version of the system ontology.
- Creating web-based ontology: In order to provide users with an easy to understand view on the ontology, a web-based ontology shall be created. Here, all terms collected by domain experts are provided together with hyperlinks among them.

There are three major actors (https://www.omg.org/spec/UML/About-UML/) defined in the process.

Domain experts connect people with expert knowledge for partial subsystems (domains), for example, transportation, energy management and others. Their first task is to collect all relevant documents and extract and define KUs.

Knowledge management experts typically consists of a smaller group, created by 1–3 experts, who do not need detailed knowledge of the partial domains, but are efficient in the principles of creating a knowledge system. The activity consists in connecting through all the terms by hyperlinks with KU, searching for the KUs and gradually recording the appropriate terms in the knowledge management including their associations with others terms in the knowledge matrix (KM).

Ontology users are typically municipality representatives or experts searching for a joint knowledge in the field of smart cities. They shall within this process not only use the resulting product (web-based ontology), but also provide feedback and help to finalize the product.

3.2 Example Application to City Road Tunnels

The methodology presented in the paper has been developed and applied in practice by the Road Tunnel Operation Committee D.5 of PIARC (Permanent International Association of Road Congresses) in the 2007. The structure of the knowledge system has been done as road tunnels domain ontology. The knowledge system covers 39 technical documents with a volume of around 2000 pages. The original name for this knowledge system is "Road tunnel Manual" (RTM). RTM disseminated information on tunnels between 2007 and 2019. At the world PIARC congress in Abu Dhabi, October 2019 PIARC decided to update the RTM and the address (https://www.piarc.org/en/) will be soon active. Note that the Czech Highway Directorate is also using a similar ontological approach to unify the quality of the "Design Documentation of the road tunnels technological systems" [35].

On the address http://tunely.unas.cz by clicking on, let say "Tunel kategorie TA - S ventilací" (Tunnel Category TA – With ventilation), you are opening the 1st level of ontology with main branches and main technological systems as it is shown in Fig. 2. The items of the second level are also displayed. It is possible to navigate among different levels.

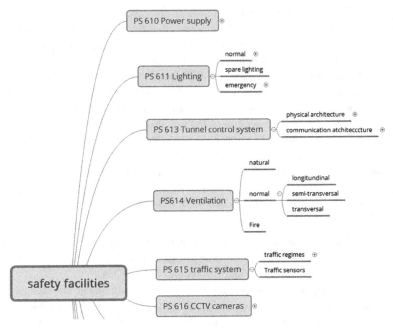

Fig. 2. An example of the knowledge maps for an ontological tree as a part of road tunnel documentation [own study]

4   Extension to Smart Cities

Smart City Management uses a variety of sensors, starting with physical detectors, cameras, and ending with satellite pictures (weather prediction, city temperature maps, emission maps). It should be noted that even a vehicle or a mobile phone in this concept becomes an intelligent sensor providing important data. The public lighting infrastructure can accommodate sensors to ensure the availability of telecommunication services throughout the city.

The basic principle of creating a new ontology for the Smart City is an incremental approach. It should start from the basic generic components of the city (streets, roads, buildings, citizens, etc.), subsequently injecting more complicated cases. In the final step, different ontology layers can be created (more specific ontologies: energy, ecology, transport, security, etc.). But when creating the new ontology there is a need to design and consider the "primary data source", rather than collecting knowledge from existing ontologies.

Very simplified example of city ontology is depicted in Fig. 3. A more detailed analysis of street lighting technology in the figure shows that the lighting is controlled by pedestrian sensors and darkness sensor. The street lighting is switched on if it is night and the pedestrians are identified. The designer can also see requirements on road surface brightness or uniformity of illumination - both values will be found by link to appropriate standard.

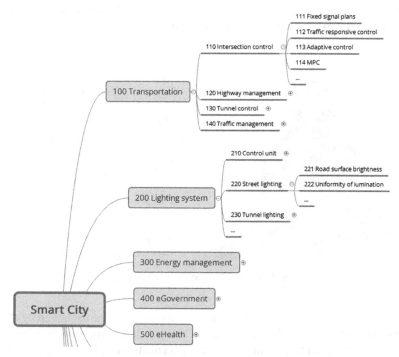

Fig. 3. Example - selected extract of smart city ontology [own study]

5   Case Studies

5.1   Smart Evropská Street

A number of metropolises that are developing their "smart city" concept have, over time, built so-called living laboratories, or parts of cities designed for the development and testing of new technologies. It is not just about testing the functionality of technologies, but rather about monitoring the impact of smart solutions on the behaviour of the population in the area, examining how different groups of people accept these solutions, how to adjust them to increase their impact, etc. Living Labs is a rather new research area and phenomena that introduces new ways of managing innovation processes [36]. Prague so far conceived living laboratory does not have its own territory.

The Smart City Prague Testbed was inspired by a project conducted in Berlin – "DIGINET PS". It consists of a 2.3-mile-long corridor from Ernst-Reuter-Platz to Zum Brandenburger Tor in the heart of Berlin. The location is presented as the entire Evropská street that spans from Vítězné náměstí in Dejvice to Václav Havel Airport Prague.

Smart City Prague Testbed conceived in this way would not only be a "smart street", but would also include the surrounding area around Evropská street, where a number of development projects are planned. During the partial negotiations, a request was made to make this concept part of the Czech Presidency of the EU in 2022 and was accompanied by the slogan "Smart European - Gateway to Europe".

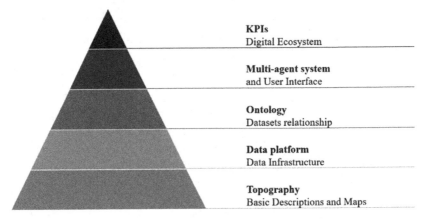

Fig. 4. Hierarchy of system layers [35]

When describing a system structure, one should first determine the hierarchy of each layer. Such hierarchy is described as a pyramid in Fig. 4. It is visible that ontology (level 3) is very important part that connects available data platform with multi-agent systems. For the sake of illustration, we show the concept of Prague's digital polygon in Fig. 5. For applications of artificial intelligence algorithms what should be the main task of the testbed it is first necessary to create the ontology in accordance with the result of this paper.

The project aims to create a virtual traffic model of Evropská Street and to verify in practice the functioning of the modeling framework for in-depth analysis of traffic behavior in real time and for different urban traffic management scenarios. The proposed set of components will be able to receive data from available sensors (traffic detectors, cameras, cooperative vehicles and other IoT elements of the transport system), consolidate this data into a single ontology structure so that it can be used as input values of traffic simulation. The result will be a virtual transport system, modeling traffic in the area and using the same data and control algorithms as those we use on the real street (virtual digital twin). On this model, it will be possible to test alternative scenarios in virtual environment, including their evaluation. The most advantageous solution from the point of view of predefined parameters will then be implemented in real traffic management.

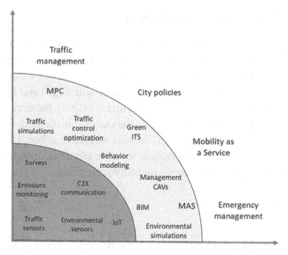

Fig. 5. Vision of the digital polygon Prague [own study]

The traffic model will be automatically calibrated to the current data and will still be ready to verify alternative scenarios. It will also become the basis for the development and testing of more advanced methods of traffic management, including the integration of cooperative and autonomous systems.

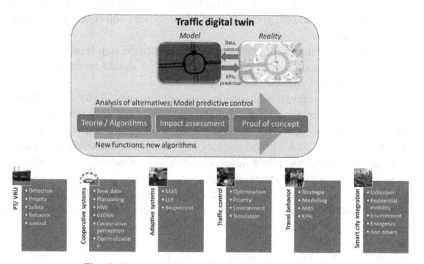

Fig. 6. Structure of the traffic digital twin [own study]

5.2 Behavioral Modeling in Ústí nad Labem

This principle will be further applied in the city Ústí nad Labem (Czech Republic), where within the project Smart City – Smart Region – Smart Community (http://smart-mateq. cz/projekty/projekty-smart/smart-iti/), a model of travel behavior based on multi-agent systems will be developed and validated in accordance with Fig. 4 and Fig. 6. The behavior of the agents will be based on knowledge of current activity patterns of citizens in the region. Compared to other simulation models, the use of this methodology (particularly the use of ontologies) allows the agents to interact with each other. The system will be opened to new agents. It will also be possible to move from the transportation field and add ontologies for example of residential mobility (urbanism).

6 Conclusion

It is clear that the concept of smart cities is an interdisciplinary issue that presents a new way of managing the city with the help of available knowledge and technologies that were unimaginable until recently. In this concept, it is possible to use models of different situations that can occur in the city, analyse them and ensure implementation of the most optimal response with respect to given criteria.

Due to this quality, the Smart City is a new vision of a city as a digital platform and eco-system of smart services, where agents of infrastructure components, people, things and other entities can directly negotiate with each other on resource demand principals [35] providing the best solution possible. It creates a smart environment making possible self-organization of individuals, group and the whole system objectives in a sustainable or, if needed, resilient way.

The approach presented in the paper is the first practical step how the knowledge system can be created and how the necessary knowledge should be shared within the alliance of heterogeneous subsystems.

In general, the interconnection of subcomponents brings new, unanticipated benefits. Only future development will show their full importance for the sustainable development of urban agglomerations. Generally, technology can be bought, but the smart city system not – it is built for years, taking into account the specifics of the territory, its history, cultural traditions, economic possibilities, etc. It is by no means a quick short-time project but a long- activity for several decades.

Having regard to above remarks, the interconnected sub-systems will have an impact on all the processes of the economy, so we are talking about Society 4.0 or Thinking 4.0. This is actually the (fourth) revolution, not just an evolution.

Acknowledgement. This paper was supported by the project "Smart City – Smart Region – Smart Community" (CZ.02.1.01/0.0/0.0/17_048/0007435) financed by the Operational Programme Research, Development and Education of the Czech Ministry of Education, Youth and Sports, supported by EU funds.

References

1. Smart Cities Council "Smart city as one that has digital technology embedded across all city functions". http://smartcitiescouncil.com/smart-cities-information-center/definitions-and-overviews. Accessed 07 Jan 2020
2. European commission "A smart city is a place where the traditional networks and services are made more efficient with the use of digital and telecommunication technologies, for the benefit of its inhabitants and businesses". https://ec.europa.eu/digital-agenda/en/smart-cities. Accessed 07 Jan 2020
3. Department for Business, Innovation and Skills "Smart city is a process rather than a static outcome, in which increased citizen engagement, hard infrastructure, social capital and digital technologies make cities more liveable, resilient and better able to respond to challenges". https://www.gov.uk/government/organisations/department-for-business-innovation-skills. Accessed 07 Jan 2020
4. European Innovation Partnership on Smart Cities and Communities, Operational Implementation Plan: First Public Draft (2013). http://ec.europa.eu/eip/smartcities/files/operational-implementation-plan-oip-v2_en.pdf. Accessed 07 Jan 2020
5. Přibyl, O., Svítek, M.: System-oriented approach to smart cities. In: Proceedings of the IEEE First International Smart Cities Conference (ISC2) (2015)
6. Rzevski, G., Skobelev, P.: Managing Complexity. WIT Press, New Forest, Boston (2014)
7. Abberley, L., et al.: Modelling road congestion using ontologies for big data analytics in smart cities. In: 2017 International Smart Cities Conference (ISC2), Wuxi, pp. 1–6 (2017)
8. Corazon, R.: Theory and history of ontology. https://www.ontology.co/. Accessed 14 May 2020]
9. Gómez-Pérez, A., Fernández-López, M., Corcho, O.: Ontological Engineering with Examples from the Areas of Knowledge Management, e-Commerce and the Semantic Web. In: Wu, X., Jain, L. (Series eds.) Advanced Information and Knowledge Processing. Springer (2004). https://doi.org/10.1007/b97353
10. Russel, S., Norvig, P.: Artificial Intelligence: A Modern Approach. Prentice-Hall, Englewood Cliffs (1995)
11. Gruber, T.R.: A translation approach to portable ontology specifications. Knowl. Acquisition 5, 199–220 (1993)
12. The OMG® Specifications Catalogue. https://www.omg.org/spec/. Accessed 7 Jan 2020
13. Mahmoodi, S.A., Mirzaie, K., Mahmoudi, S.M.: A new algorithm to extract hidden rules of gastric cancer data based on ontology. SpringerPlus 5, 312 (2016). https://doi.org/10.1186/s40064-016-1943-9
14. Bergvall-Kareborn, B., Hoist, M., Stahlbrost, A.: Concept design with a living lab approach. In: 2009 42nd Hawaii International Conference on System Sciences, Big Island, HI, pp. 1–10 (2009)
15. Forbes, David E., Wongthongtham, P., Terblanche, C., Pakdeetrakulwong, U.: Ontology Engineering Applications in Healthcare and Workforce Management Systems. SSDC, vol. 123. Springer, Cham (2018). https://doi.org/10.1007/978-3-319-65012-8
16. Gyrard, A., Zimmermann, A., Sheth, A.: Building IoT-based applications for smart cities: how can ontology catalogs help? IEEE Internet Things J. 5(5), 3978–3990 (2018)
17. Lourdusamy, R., John, A.: A review on metrics for ontology evaluation. In: 2018 2nd International Conference on Inventive Systems and Control (ICISC), Coimbatore, pp. 1415–1421 (2018)
18. Burns, M., et al.: Reasoning about smart city. In: 2018 IEEE International Conference on Smart Computing (SMARTCOMP), Taormina, Sicily, Italy, pp. 381–386 (2018)

19. Qamar, T., et al.: Smart city services ontology (SCSO): semantic modeling of smart city applications. In: 2019 Seventh International Conference on Digital Information Processing and Communications (ICDIPC), Trabzon, Turkey, pp. 52–56 (2019)
20. Abid, T., et al.: Towards a smart city ontology. In: 2016 IEEE/ACS 13th International Conference of Computer Systems and Applications (AICCSA), Agadir, pp. 1–6 (2016)
21. Barnaghi, P., et al.: A linked-data model for semantic sensor streams. In: 2013 IEEE International Conference on Green Computing and Communications and IEEE Internet of Things and IEEE Cyber, Physical and Social Computing, Beijing, pp. 468–475 (2013)
22. Chung, T.L., Xu, B., Zhang, P., Tan, Y., Zhu, P., Wubulihasimu, A.: Constructing city ontology from expert for smart city management. In: Kim, W., Ding, Y., Kim, H.-G. (eds.) JIST 2013. LNCS, vol. 8388, pp. 187–194. Springer, Cham (2014). https://doi.org/10.1007/978-3-319-06826-8_15
23. Komninos, N., et al.: Smart city ontologies: improving the effectiveness of smart city applications. J. Smart Cities 1(1), 31–46 (2016)
24. Patel, A.S. et al.: Ontology-Based multi-agent smart bike sharing system (SBSS). In: 2018 IEEE International Conference on Smart Computing (SMARTCOMP), Taormina, pp. 417–422 (2018)
25. Syzdykbayev, M., Hajari, H., Karimi, H.A.: An ontology for collaborative navigation among autonomous cars, drivers, and pedestrians in smart cities. In: 2019 4th International Conference on Smart and Sustainable Technologies (SpliTech), Split, Croatia, pp. 1–6 (2019)
26. Ghannem, A., et al.: An adaptive I-parking application: an ontology-based approach. In: 2016 Future Technologies Conference (FTC), San Francisco, CA, pp. 777–785 (2016)
27. Rani, M.S., et al.: Ontology-based classification and analysis of non-emergency smart-city events. In: 2016 International Conference on Computational Techniques in Information and Communication Technologies (ICCTICT), New Delhi, pp. 509–514 (2016)
28. Khruahong, S., et al.: Develop an indoor space ontology for finding lost properties for location-based service of smart city. In: 2018 18th International Symposium on Communications and Information Technologies (ISCIT), Bangkok, pp. 54–59 (2018)
29. Nagowah, S.D., Sta, H.B., Gobin-Rahimbux, B.A.: An ontology for an IoT-enabled smart parking in a university campus. In: 2019 IEEE International Smart Cities Conference (ISC2), Casablanca, Morocco, pp. 474–479 (2019)
30. Brizzi, P., et al.: Towards an ontology driven approach for systems interoperability and energy management in the smart city. In: 2016 International Multidisciplinary Conference on Computer and Energy Science (SpliTech), Split, pp. 1–7 (2016)
31. Li, W., et al.: Review of standard ontologies for the web of things. In: 2019 Global IoT Summit (GIoTS), Aarhus, Denmark, pp. 1–6 (2019)
32. Bellini, P., et al.: Km4City ontology building vs data harvesting and cleaning for smart-city services. J. Vis. Lang. Comput. 25(6), 827–839 (2014)
33. Babalou, S., Kargar, M.J., Davarpanah, S.H.: Large-scale ontology matching: a review of the literature. In: 2016 Second International Conference on Web Research (ICWR), Tehran, pp. 158–165 (2016)
34. Cross, V.V.: Fuzzy ontologies: the state of the art. In: 2014 IEEE Conference on Norbert Wiener in the 21st Century (21CW), Boston, MA, pp. 1–8 (2014)
35. Svítek, M., et al.: Smart city 5.0 testbed in Prague. In: Proceedings of Smart Cities Symposium Prague (SCSP) (2020)
36. Villanueva-Rosales, N., et al.: Semantic-enhanced living labs for better interoperability of smart cities solutions. In: 2016 IEEE International Smart Cities Conference (ISC2), Trento, pp. 1–2 (2016)

Equalising the Levels of Electromobility Implementation in Cities

Grzegorz Sierpiński[✉] and Elżbieta Macioszek

Silesian University of Technology, Akademicka 2A, Gliwice, Poland
{grzegorz.sierpinski,elzbieta.macioszek}@polsl.pl

Abstract. Launching activities oriented towards electromobility development in urban areas is a difficult process, which is mainly due to the existence of barriers of infrastructural and social nature. This article provides a discussion concerning different levels of electromobility development and highlights the main efforts undertaken for the sake of identification of potential sites for vehicle charging stations. The research of transport accessibility was conducted in two cities characterised by diverse levels of maturity of electromobility implementation (The Hague and Budapest). The authors have proposed a method intended for acquisition of data concerning the real-life needs of the travelling population, assumed to function as a means of decision making support for local authorities with regard to installation of charging infrastructure. The method relies on the use of modern technologies, including a multimodal travel planner developed under the international project entitled Electric Travelling, implemented within the framework of the ERANET CoFund Electric Mobility Europe programme.

Keywords: Electromobility · Charging stations · Data and mobility · Sustainable transport system · Environment-friendly mobility · Travel planning · ICT solutions

1 Introduction

Implementing electromobility in cities is one of the action aimed at reducing the negative environmental impact of transport, which also means reducing external costs of transport ([1–6], inter alia). The specificity of cities, or the actions undertaken on the national level are only some of the most crucial factors affecting the speed of implementations related to the policy of incentives and restrictions ([7–9], inter alia). Introducing every new mode of travelling requires specific actions to be performed in the spheres of information, education, organisation, law, and infrastructure ([10–16], inter alia). The current habits of the travelling population should become transformed in order to trigger a change to the modal split of traffic in favour of more eco-friendly travelling, which includes electric cars.

Studies of transport behaviour patterns as well as of distribution of traffic streams in cities (performed in the micro and macro scale) have proven useful in supporting the evaluation of the actions undertaken by local authorities for purposes of sustainable

© Springer Nature Switzerland AG 2020
J. Mikulski (Ed.): TST 2020, CCIS 1289, pp. 165–176, 2020.
https://doi.org/10.1007/978-3-030-59270-7_13

transport development, both with regard to the modal split of traffic, and the development of public transport ([17–27], inter alia). Given the fundamental assumptions on which the principles of sustainable development are based [28], one should also pay close attention to the problem of technological development, as it entails increasingly easy access to information transfer and data acquisition methods ([29–34], inter alia). Among the means of information transfer associated with the new ways of travelling, one should mention travel planners ([35–38], inter alia). They make it possible to share information on the optimum travel route using desktop computers as well as mobile devices. The solution proposed in this article is to use a travel planner to collect data on the real-life needs of the travelling population. This could translate into specific support provided directly to the travelling population as well as to bodies in charge of the city and its transport system. The information acquired in such a manner can significantly improve the process of decision making with regard to siting of vehicle charging stations, with the promotion of electric cars in mind. The advantages of the tool discussed in the paper include its territorial universality and lack of additional costs.

2   Levels of Implementation of Electromobility

For drivers, the fact that charging stations have emerged in cities is a clear signal that changes are inevitable. It may also be a prelude to actions aimed at allocation of green zones – to be entered only by eco-friendly vehicles. The maturity level of electromobility development within the given area can be analysed by taking numerous aspects into consideration. The indicators thereof may include the share of electric cars in the modal split of traffic, the set of incentives provided on the national or local level, the existing infrastructure of charging stations, or the total time of occupancy and the energy consumption for purposes of these stations. And since this article pertains to regions, and not entire countries, the analyses it contains focus on the accessibility of charging stations, as well as on their types and siting. The fact that charging stations have come into being, and the increase in their number (assuming their optimum siting) both constitute forms of encouragement for the travelling population [39].

Analysing the development of electromobility in light of the foregoing, one can distinguish between the following three levels of maturity of a city:

- high level – characterised by a well-developed and dense network of charging stations, involving dynamic responding to changes in terms of emerging new traffic generators (areas which attract traffic),
- moderate levels – applicable to cities with a network of charging stations in place, yet characterised by insufficient density, inappropriate siting, or insufficient power capacity against the actual demand,
- low level – means cities with a negligible number of charging stations, where proper promotion of electromobility is virtually out of question.

In order to determine characteristics of the above three levels of maturity, three areas were chosen under the international project entitled "Electric travelling – platform to support the implementation of electromobility in Smart Cities based on ICT applications" implemented within the framework of the ERA-NET CoFund Electric Mobility Europe programme [40]. These areas corresponded to the following cities: The Hague (The Netherlands), Budapest (Hungary), and Sosnowiec (Poland). The infrastructure-related data used in the relevant analyses were of open source nature. The GIS environment was used for purposes of the accessibility analysis (Fig. 1 and 2). Thanks to this technology, it is generally easier to perform spatial analyses. The walking distances to be covered in order to reach charging stations were assumed at 500, 1,000 and 2,000 m, respectively.

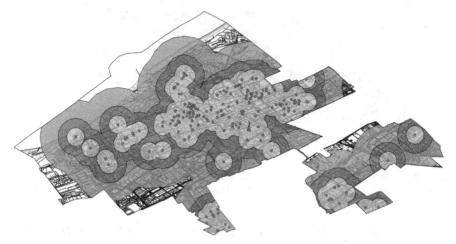

Fig. 1. Analysis of accessibility of charging stations in the territory of The Hague using the QuantumGIS tool (for the distances of 500, 1,000 and 2,000 m) [own study based on [41–44]]

Numerous Dutch cities feature a dense network of charging stations. As many as ca. 2,100 charging points have been installed in The Hague to date [45], and the city authorities are inclined to double this number within the next 4 years [46]. Figure 1 clearly shows the high accessibility of charging stations. In the first stage of electromobility implementation, the charging stations were sited according to the actual needs. The next stage involved installation of charging stations in the direct vicinity of tourist attractions and shopping centres, as well as in other locations where they would be clearly visible. By that means, the local authorities strived to change the perception of the charging infrastructure, which had been considered as one of the barriers to purchasing an electric car. In 2019, the number of fast charging stations per 100 km of motorways in the Netherlands came to 35, while the total number of charging points all around the country exceeded 50,000 [47].

The spatial analysis of the charging infrastructure available in Budapest (Fig. 2) implies its high accessibility, yet only within the city centre. The number of local charging stations exceeds 220, and they come with nearly 500 parking places dedicated to charging [44]. The 2019 ratio of fast charging stations in Hungary was 7 per 100 km of motorways, and the total number of charging points exceeded 690 countrywide [47].

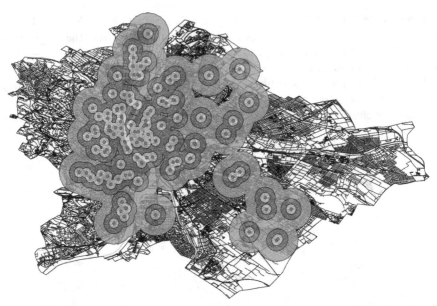

Fig. 2. Analysis of accessibility of charging stations in the territory of Budapest using the QuantumGIS tool (for the distances of 500, 1,000 and 2,000 m) [own study based on [41–44]]

What could be observed in Poland is some progress in the development of the vehicle charging infrastructure. As of the end of 2019, the total number of charging stations came to 1,011, including 288 direct current stations [48]. The current level of maturity of the charging infrastructure in the city of Sosnowiec should be considered very low. In light of the national strategic regulations, including the act on electromobility and alternative fuels (2018) [49], large Polish cities are obliged to commission a specific number of charging stations by the end of the year 2020. Under the National Policy Framework for Alternative Fuel Infrastructure [50, 51], Sosnowiec is assumed to have installed 123 normal charging points and 6 high-power charging points as at the end of 2020.

3   Possible First Steps and ETPlanner Support

What proves to be particularly important for cities of low level of electromobility development maturity is the optimised siting of the first charging stations. It is intended to initiate building trust towards travelling by means of electric cars. This is precisely why locations of charging stations should correspond to the actual needs of the travelling population, which can maximise the effect of the implementation in favour of electromobility promotion.

Support for local authorities, especially at this stage, may considerably accelerate the deployment of electromobility in the city. Keeping track of the solutions introduced in cities with mature electromobility and making the most of their experiences can help in limiting the mistakes typically made in the initial implementation steps.

One of the first actions performed on this path is the siting of charging stations depending on their types. Bearing in mind the breakdown into fast and slow charging stations, one can establish their specific applications, and consequently also the potential locations:

– fast (high-power) charging stations are primarily sited next to main roads of higher classes (Fig. 3). This provides for the needs of the transit traffic. The stations are mainly installed within 60–100 km away from one another, in motorway services areas [52, 53] (longer distances are applied in the USA, i.e. up to 160 km [54]). The time required to be spent at the station is still incomparably longer than that of traditional refuelling, but in a foreseeable future, some car models should enable battery charging up to 80% in 15–20 min;
– charging stations enabling vehicle battery charging in 3–5 h are typically installed next to traffic generators, in business/industry areas, etc. Where this is the case, the stopover time is usually used for some other activities as well (work, education, shopping, entertainment, etc.), which means that the electric car can be left at the station for a longer period of time (not wasting time for waiting).

The prospecting for appropriate locations for charging stations is typically limited to a rather small territory in the vicinity of main roads, which is due to the specifics of those who use them [55]. Therefore, it is not a complicated process. What poses far more problems is the siting of the first charging stations in other areas. In this case, in line with the principles of sustainable development [28], one should rely on real-life needs. Among the available solutions, one can choose questionnaire surveys to determine the real-life needs of the travelling population. These, however, are rather expensive, and the knowledge they provide requires updating whenever the transport system is subject to alteration or new investments are implemented. Where this is the case, solutions based on modern technologies seem far more efficient. One of the ways to acquire the necessary data is to use a logged-on SIM card in the GSM system, and transfer between base stations. Unfortunately, on account of the personal data protection requirement and other legal regulations, mobile network operators do not render such data available.

Fig. 3. Road network with the main roads of higher classes marked in the territory of the selected city (Sosnowiec) [own study based on [41]]

A different solution was proposed under the Electric Travelling project. A travel planner developed as a part of the project (ETPlanner, Fig. 4) was provided with a module intended to record data concerning the queries submitted by users (feedback channel [56]). As a means to encourage the travelling population to make use of this tool, ETPlanner enables route optimisation for a travelling mode chosen among 12 available options:

– new travelling modes, e.g. bike sharing or car sharing,
– traditional travelling modes, e.g. walking, bicycle, collective transport, motorcycle, or passenger car,
– multimodal travelling modes based on the use of systems such as Bike&Ride and Park&Ride.

The planner is particularly intended to support owners of electric cars in overcoming the barrier related to the need for independent en route planning of the charging operation. And since one of the project's main assumptions is to provide information transfer

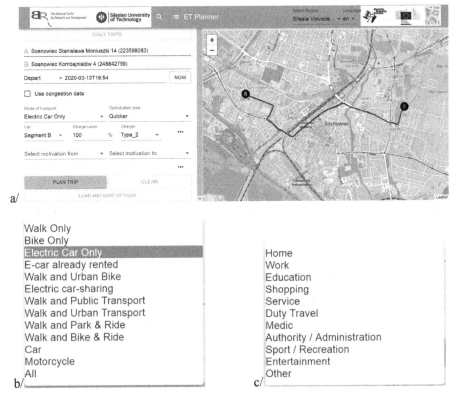

Fig. 4. ETPlanner's user interface: a/basic view; b/travelling mode selection; c/travelling motivation selection [own study]

and promotion of electromobility, the planner users receive information about the environmental impact related to such travelling. This means that it is possible to compare different travelling modes in this respect. It was assumed that a query submitted to the travel planner corresponds to a real-life travel-related need. Such a query is stored in the database with filtering and analysing features to be used afterwards. The method in question makes it possible to obtain various information, including:

- planned date and time of the travel start or completion,
- location of travel start and completion (using geographical data of both locations),
- selected travelling mode (although one can also choose "all"),
- additional parameters of the specific travelling mode, e.g. maximum acceptable walking or cycling distance, parameters of the vehicle in use, etc.,
- criterion according to which an optimum route is to be established (four criteria are available: time, distance, cost, and environmental impact, and in each case the algorithm is intended to return a result with the lowest value of the pre-set criterion),
- travelling motivations, corresponding to the purpose for which or the destination to which the given person intends to travel. These include: home, work, education, shopping, service, business trip, health-related travel, official business, sports and recreation, entertainment, etc.

Most typically, with the help of the travel planner one intends to determine how and in what time one can reach a specific destination using the preferred travelling mode. The database also makes it possible to establish the actual needs concerning diverse means of transport within the area subject to analysis.

Stating the motivation is not obligatory, although having implemented ETPlanner, the city can force users to define these parameters on the system administrator level. Acquiring the information on the travelling motivation is valuable, since it enables selection of the locations where vehicle users may stop for longer (e.g. at work or home).

Assuming that the tool in question was used on a broader scale in the chosen area, or if travel planners were standardised and furnished with similar data logging modules, one could obtain information that makes it possible to identify, among other factors:

- places related to the *home* motivation. Having superimposed the identified needs on a map of the settlement structure (Fig. 5), one can identify areas with multi-family buildings (housing and tower block estates). Such buildings often lack private garages, hence the need for charging of electric cars at dedicated parking spots next to the house (while there is no need for fast charging). The solutions implemented in such countries as, for instance, the Netherlands combine charging stations and street lamps into units of transport infrastructure;
- the *work* (sometimes also *education*) motivation (with regard to travelling by passenger car) provides information about the need for longer parking at the given place. The cyclic nature of parking motivated by these factors would make it profitable to install charging stations at the locations in question (thus encouraging one to switch to another means of transport). Also in this case, charging time is not that important, which means that fast charging stations are not necessary;

Fig. 5. Identification of residential buildings (green colour) in the settlement structure of the chosen city (Sosnowiec) using QuantumGIS [own study based on [41]] (Color figure online)

– other motivations, where it is important to determine the time spent at the given location. Since the IP address of the query origin is also recorded in the database, it is possible that queries could be linked in chains of planned transfers, and when combined with the information about the time of travel start/completion, this may help in identification of such connections.

At the location planning stage, charging stations may also be linked with access to the car sharing service ([57, 58], inter alia). Where this is the case, the fleet of municipal electric vehicles may provide additional encouragement toward becoming familiar with the new travelling mode and speed up the observed increase in the sale of electric cars [59].

4   Conclusion

No change in the behaviour patterns of the travelling population is easy and quick. It requires adequate approach and well-thought-out actions. For this reason, it is so important to prepare an appropriate strategy of handling changes over the incoming years. Electromobility can be implemented by overcoming the barriers which exist in the sphere of transport infrastructure, as well as those of social and economic nature.

The authors of the article have placed the emphasis on the problem of support for the decisions made by local authorities while taking initial steps towards electromobility, namely when installing the first charging stations in the city. Relying on the experiences of cities on a high maturity level in this respect makes it possible to establish the first and fundamental breakdown of charging stations according to their purpose. The second of the methods proposed in the article, namely the use of a travel planner to identify the needs of the travelling population, makes it possible to reduce the costs of data acquisition, while it can be applied multiple times and enables recording of the changes in behaviour patterns and needs in time.

Further research planned to be conducted will comprise implementation of the ETSys support system designed for local authorities (including the ETPlanner tool) in the aforementioned cities, and acquisition of research material exceeding the pilot studies discussed in this paper.

Acknowledgements. The present research has been financed from the means of the National Centre for Research and Development as a part of the international project within the scope of ERA-NET CoFund Electric Mobility Europe Programme "Electric travelling - platform to support the implementation of electromobility in Smart Cities based on ICT applications".

References

1. Communication From The Commission To The European Parliament, The Council, The European Economic And Social Committee And The Committee Of The Regions: Clean Power for Transport: A European alternative fuels strategy, COM(2013). 17
2. White Paper on the Future of Europe, Reflections and scenarios for the EU27 by 2025, COM(2017) 2025
3. White Paper: Roadmap to a Single European Transport Area – Towards a competitive and resource efficient transport system. COM(2011) 144
4. Maibach, M., et al.: Handbook on Estimation of External Costs in the Transport Sector. Internalisation Measures and Policies for All external Cost of Transport (IMPACT). Delft (2008)
5. Becker, U.J., Becker, T., Gerlach, J.: The true costs of automobility: external costs of cars overview on existing estimates in EU-27. Dresden (2012)
6. Korzhenevych, A., et al.: Update of the handbook on external costs of transport. Final Report. Ricardo-AEA/R/ ED57769, Oxford, Didcot (2014)
7. Meyer, M.D.: Demand management as an element of transportation policy: using carrots and sticks to influence travel behavior. Transp. Res. Part A **33**, 575–599 (1999)
8. Banister, D.: The sustainable mobility paradigm. Transp. Policy **15**, 73–80 (2008)
9. Sierpiński, G.: Model of incentives for changes of the modal split of traffic towards electric personal cars. In: Mikulski, J. (ed.) TST 2014. CCIS, vol. 471, pp. 450–460. Springer, Heidelberg (2014). https://doi.org/10.1007/978-3-662-45317-9_48
10. Mikulski, J.: Telematic technologies in transportation. In: Janecki, R., Sierpiński, G. (ed.): Contemporary transportation systems. Selected theoretical and practical problems. New Culture of mobility, pp. 131–143. Publishing House of the Silesian University of Technology. Monograph no. 324. Gliwice (2011)
11. Szymczak, M., Sienkiewicz-Małyjurek, K.: Information in the city traffic management system. the analysis of the use of information sources and the assessment in terms of their usefulness for city routes users. LogForum **7**(2), 37–50 (2011)
12. van der Zwaan, B., Keppo, I., Johnsson, F.: How to decarbonizes the transport sector? Energy Policy **61**, 562–573 (2013)
13. Szołtysek, J.: Ekonomia współdzielenia a logistyka miasta – rozważania o związkach. Gospodarka Materiałowa i Logistyka **11**, 2–9 (2016)
14. Taniguchi, E.: Concepts of city logistics for sustainable and liveable cities. Procedia Soc. Behav. Sci. **151**, 310–317 (2014)
15. Santos, G.: Road transport and CO2 emissions: what are the challenges? Transp. Policy **59**, 71–74 (2017)
16. Stanley, J.: Land use/transport integration: starting at the right place. Res. Transp. Econ. **48**, 381–388 (2014)

17. Cárdenas, O., Valencia, A., Montt, C.: Congestion minimization through sustainable traffic management: a micro-simulation approach. LogForum **14**(1), 21–31 (2018)
18. Dembińska, I., Jedliński, M., Marzantowicz, Ł.: Logistic support for a rescue operation in the aspect of minimizing the ecological footprint as an environmental requirement within sustainable development on the example of a natural disaster. LogForum **14**(3), 355–370 (2018)
19. Małecki, K.: The importance of automatic traffic lights time algorithms to reduce the negative impact of transport on the urban environment. Transp. Res. Procedia **16**, 329–342 (2016)
20. Macioszek, E.: The comparison of models for follow-up headway at roundabouts. In: Macioszek, E., Sierpiński, G. (eds.) TSTP 2017. LNNS, vol. 21, pp. 16–26. Springer, Cham (2018). https://doi.org/10.1007/978-3-319-64084-6_2
21. Macioszek, E.: Analysis of significance of differences between psychotechnical parameters for drivers at the entries to one-lane and turbo roundabouts in Poland. In: Sierpiński, G. (ed.) Intelligent Transport Systems and Travel Behaviour. AISC, vol. 505, pp. 149–161. Springer, Cham (2017). https://doi.org/10.1007/978-3-319-43991-4_13
22. Galińska, B.: Intelligent decision making in transport. evaluation of transportation modes (types of vehicles) based on multiple criteria methodology. In: Sierpiński, G. (ed.) TSTP 2018. AISC, vol. 844, pp. 161–172. Springer, Cham (2019). https://doi.org/10.1007/978-3-319-99477-2_15
23. Pijoan, A., et al.: Transport choice modeling for the evaluation of new transport policies. Sustainability **10**, 1230 (2018)
24. Kijewska, K., Iwan, S., Małecki, K.: Applying multi-criteria analysis of electrically powered vehicles implementation in urban freight transport. Procedia Comput. Sci. **159**, 1558–1567 (2019)
25. Grzelec, K., Birr, K.: Development of trolleybus public transport in Gdynia as part of a sustainable mobility strategy. Sci. J. Silesian Univ. Technol. Ser. Transp. **92**, 53–63 (2016)
26. Krawiec, S., et al.: Urban public transport with the use of electric buses – development tendencies. Transp. Probl. **11**(4), 127–137 (2016)
27. Lejda, K., et al.: The future of public transport in light of solutions for sustainable transport development. Sci. J. Silesian Univ. Technol. Ser. Transp. **95**, 97–108 (2017)
28. Our Common Future. Report of the World Commission on Environment and Development (1987)
29. Iwan, S., Małecki, K.: Data flows in an integrated urban freight transport telematic system. In: Mikulski, J. (ed.) TST 2012. CCIS, vol. 329, pp. 79–86. Springer, Heidelberg (2012). https://doi.org/10.1007/978-3-642-34050-5_10
30. Karoń, G., Mikulski, J.: Problems of systems engineering for ITS in large agglomeration – upper-silesian agglomeration in Poland. In: Mikulski, J. (ed.) TST 2014. CCIS, vol. 471, pp. 242–251. Springer, Heidelberg (2014). https://doi.org/10.1007/978-3-662-45317-9_26
31. Karoń, G., Mikulski, J.: Forecasts for Technical Variants of ITS Projects – Example of Upper-Silesian Conurbation. In: Mikulski, J. (ed.) TST 2013. CCIS, vol. 395, pp. 67–74. Springer, Heidelberg (2013). https://doi.org/10.1007/978-3-642-41647-7_9
32. Jacyna, M., et al.: Selected aspects of the model of proecological transport system. J. KONES Powertrain Transp. **20**, 193–202 (2013)
33. Macioszek, E.: First and last mile delivery – problems and issues. In: Sierpiński, G. (ed.) TSTP 2017. AISC, vol. 631, pp. 147–154. Springer, Cham (2018). https://doi.org/10.1007/978-3-319-62316-0_12
34. Kauf, S.: City logistics - a strategic element of sustainable urban development. Transp. Res. Procedia **16**, 158–164 (2016)

35. Celiński, I., Sierpiński, G., Staniek, M.: Sustainable development of the transport system through rationalization of transport tasks using a specialised travel planner. In: Dell'Acqua, G., Wegman, F. (eds.) Transport Infrastructure and Systems, pp. 1071–1079. CRC Press, Taylor & Francis Group, London (2017)
36. Esztergár-Kiss, D., Csiszár, C.: Evaluation of multimodal journey planners and definition of service levels. Int. J. Intell. Transp. Syst. Res. **13**, 154–165 (2015). https://doi.org/10.1007/s13177-014-0093-0
37. Lewczuk, K., et al.: Vehicle routing in urban area – environmental and technological determinants. WIT Trans. Built Environ. **130**, 373–384 (2013)
38. Borkowski, P.: Towards an optimal multimodal travel planner—lessons from the European experience. In: Sierpiński, G. (ed.) Intelligent Transport Systems and Travel Behaviour. AISC, vol. 505, pp. 163–174. Springer, Cham (2017). https://doi.org/10.1007/978-3-319-43991-4_14
39. Sierpiński, G.: Using ICT applications to support sustainable development and tackle the barriers related to extensive introduction of electric cars into transport systems – a case study based on the green travelling planner tool. In: Suchanek, M. (ed.) New Research Trends in Transport Sustainability and Innovation: TranSopot 2017 Conference. Springer Proceedings in Business and Economics, pp. 62–72. Springer (2018). https://doi.org/10.1007/978-3-319-74461-2_6
40. Electric travelling - platform to support the implementation of electromobility in Smart Cities based on ICT applications – Project proposal under EMEurope programme (2016)
41. OpenStreetMap service. https://www.openstreetmap.org/. Accessed 20 Jan 2020
42. Overpass service. http://overpass-turbo.eu/. Accessed 20 Jan 2020
43. EV-Charging Stations in Europe. https://ev-charging.com/. Accessed 20 Jan 2020
44. PlugShare - EV Charging Station Map. https://www.plugshare.com/. Accessed 20Jan 2020
45. The Hague Online website. The Hague leading in charging points for electric cars. https://www.thehagueonline.com/news/2019/08/29/the-hague-leading-in-charging-points-for-electric-cars. Accessed 20 Jan 2020
46. Vision on the charging infrastructure for electric transport looking ahead to 2035. The Ministry of Economic Affairs, The Hague (2017)
47. European Alternative Fuels Observatory. https://www.eafo.eu/. Accessed 20 Jan 2020
48. Licznik elektromobilności. Polskie Stowarzyszenie Paliw Alternatywnych (PSPA) oraz Polski Związek Przemysłu Motoryzacyjnego (PZPM). http://pspa.com.pl/. Accessed 20 Jan 2020
49. Ustawa z dnia 11 stycznia 2018 r. o elektromobilności i paliwach alternatywnych – Dz. U. 2018 poz. 317 [in Polish: Act of 11 January 2018 on electromobility and alternative fuels – Dz. U. (Journal of Laws) 2019, item 317]
50. Ministry of Energy. National Policy Framework for Alternative Fuel Infrastructure, Warsaw (2017)
51. Ministry of Energy. Electromobility Development Plan in Poland. Energy for the Future, Warsaw (2018)
52. Jochema, P., Szimba, E., Reuter-Oppermann, M.: How many fast-charging stations do we need along European highways? Transp. Res. Part D **73**, 120–129 (2019)
53. Csonka, B., Csiszár, C.: Determination of charging infrastructure location for electric vehicles. Transp. Res. Procedia **27**, 768–775 (2017)
54. He, Y., Kockelman, K.M., Perrine, K.A.: Optimal locations of U.S. fast charging stations for long-distance trip completion by battery electric vehicles. J. Cleaner Prod. **214**, 452–461 (2019)
55. Csiszár, C., et al.: Urban public charging station locating method for electric vehicles based on land use approach. J. Transp. Geogr. **74**, 173–180 (2019)

56. Sierpiński, G., Staniek, M., Macioszek, E., Standardisation of travel planners and use of a return channel. In: Proceedings of the 2nd World Congress on Civil, Structural, and Environmental Engineering, Barcelona, Paper No. ICTE 121 (2017)
57. Ocicka, B., Wieteska, G.: Sharing economy in logistics and supply chain management. LogForum **13**(2), 183–193 (2017)
58. Sierpiński, G., Turoń, K., Pypno, C.: Urban transport integration using automated garages in park and ride and car-sharing systems – preliminary study for the upper silesian conurbation. In: Sierpiński, G. (ed.) TSTP 2018. AISC, vol. 844, pp. 218–228. Springer, Cham (2019). https://doi.org/10.1007/978-3-319-99477-2_20
59. Global EV Outlook 2019. Scaling-up the transition to electric mobility. International Energy Agency (2019)

Pedestrian Safety in Smart Cities
– The Challenges and Solutions

Katarzyna Sosik[(✉)] and Stanisław Iwan

Maritime University of Szczecin, H. Pobożnego 11, Szczecin, Poland
{k.sosik,s.iwan}@am.szczecin.pl

Abstract. The increase in the level of urbanisation is associated with the dynamics of changes taking place in the world. The literature on the subject described the contemporary structure of society as an information society or a knowledge society. Common access to information resources and participation in their acquisition affects the use of knowledge resources in industrial systems. The development of the information society determines the availability of ICT solutions. In the era of the information society, changes in expectations towards the urban transport system have become significant. The complexity of transport processes has made it necessary to use telematics systems to enable effective management. The main purpose of telematics solutions in road transport is to eliminate transport congestion. The European Union and the member states are taking action to solve transport problems. Due to the information revolution and globalisation, special attention is paid to ensuring safety for road users. Prevention of transport and industrial disasters was set as the goal of the transport system development. The effect of the aforementioned activities is interest in the Smart Cities concept. In recent years, much attention has been devoted to ensuring safety for road users, including the use of Smart City tools. In particular, innovations created for the needs of road vehicle users are noticed. Designing, producing and implementing technology supporting the safety of vulnerable road users, including pedestrians, is becoming a problem. Many European cities create original propositions of good practices in this area. The article reviews the existing solutions of Intelligent Transport Systems in the field of Smart City supporting pedestrian safety.

Keywords: Smart City · Intelligent Transport System · Safety of pedestrian

1 Introduction

As a result of the fast-progressing urbanisation, the urban population has been growing, production becomes ever more complex, and road traffic intensifies. All these factors lead to changes taking place in urban areas, which have an impact on the natural environment and the changing climate, life quality of the residents and safety of all city users. Determinants of urbanisation effects include: population growth, transport congestion, noise, degradation of the natural environment, traffic incidents and related safety issues, amount of waste, problems with providing accommodation and employment, and

© Springer Nature Switzerland AG 2020
J. Mikulski (Ed.): TST 2020, CCIS 1289, pp. 177–189, 2020.
https://doi.org/10.1007/978-3-030-59270-7_14

other. All these aspects have become a constraint to cities' sustainable development and improving the life quality of its citizens.

In view of the dynamic urban growth, the concept of Smart City has been gaining popularity in many countries all over the world, as a response to the various challenges posed to city administrators. Changes regarding the social aspects result first and foremost from transformations of social structures, better access to information, continuous enhancement of qualifications and development. Currently, the society is referred to as a knowledge society or information society. The progress observed over the past decades will further increase as a result of the migration of people from rural areas to city, as forecast by the United Nations. The current situation forces cities to search for ways to cope with the challenges they are exposed to. The Smart City concept regards many areas of city functioning, one of them is transport. The fact that people need to travel to various places mainly leads to increasing the road traffic in urban transport systems [1–3]. Therefore, it is necessary to pay attention to the negative effects of this process, such as transport congestion, noise, degradation of the natural environment, traffic incidents and their consequences. Searching for solutions aimed at mitigating the occurrence of the above mentioned problems becomes a priority in developing strategic goals for cities. The challenges are addressed by transport telematics solutions and their combinations, referred to as Intelligent Transport Systems [4]. Over the recent years, there has been a heightened interest in and deployment of systems to support urban road transport, however, they are predicated on bringing benefits in the context of road traffic and the vehicle users' comfort, while still not enough attention is paid to implementing technologies that facilitate the traffic and safety of unprotected participants of the road traffic, such as pedestrians. They constitute an important group among all participants of road traffic, due to the potential consequences of traffic accidents involving them.

2   From City Development to Smart City

According to the publications of the United Nations, the world has been undergoing intensive urbanisation over the past decades/years. In 1950, 20% of the world population lived in cities, whereas in 2018 the percentage rose to 55%. The global urbanisation rate masks differences in the development of individual processes across the countries all over the world. However, according to the estimations made by the UN, 68% of the world population will be living in cities by 2050 [5]. Cities all over the world evolve as a result of the globalisation processes which make it possible to notice the multidimensional progress. Growth of cities is connected with emergence of opportunities and barriers affecting their actual functioning. Due to identifying the constraints of the processes affecting urban growth, it is possible to eliminate them beforehand or mitigate their effects. One of the solutions applied is making use of good practices. There may be barriers resulting from various sources that play an integral role in city development, and these are economic, social, environmental, spatial, and infrastructural factors, also those connected with institutional conditions. Notwithstanding the barriers that constrain the city growth, the processes taking place within their structure are determined by the changing needs of their residents [6].

The needs of the society are met via supplying them with any required goods and services in a possible manner. The processes taking place within the social and economic context of cities pose a challenge to their administrators, which determines the use of Information and Communications Technology (ICT). The possibility of using ICT added to the significance of possessing information and its further use. Transforming data into information and then into knowledge, and skills to use it via applying ICT systems, have contributed to development of many industries and to increasing their competitiveness on the market, as well as it made it possible for the society to access the public life and the digital culture, which consequently shaped a new type of a society: an information society or a knowledge society. The changes are also connected with the development of a knowledge-based economy, which is manifested by a greater number of people employed in the information processing sector compared to the industry sector. The challenges posed by the fast developing world economy and the society forced the cities to introduce changes in their management [7]. Based on ICT systems and making use of the possibilities offered by them, the Smart City concept was developed, which makes it possible to better satisfy the society's needs and to improve the life quality of the city residents [8]. Moreover, the Smart City solutions enable to mitigate the negative effects of urbanisation while increasing the safety, protecting the natural environment and ensuring an appropriate quality of life for city dwellers [3, 9].

3 Dimensions of Smart City

Over the recent years, there has been a heightened interest in the concept of Smart City and in promoting cities as Smart Cities. The concept is a response to the fast changing challenges connected with sustainability and measures taken in that respect. Smart City is a multi-faceted idea, referring to issues from various areas, such as multiple aspects of the philosophical, economic, political, and sociological nature, as well as those from the fields of management and technology. According to the literature on the subject, it is a problem to formulate a consistent definition to nail down the concept. The reason for this might be the lack of a consistent definition of a city, which is of fundamental significance in the context of explaining the analysed concept [1, 10]. The issue of specifying the meaning of Smart City was addressed not only by enterprises, researchers, self-governments and others, but also by standardising institutions such as ISO – International Organisation for Standardising, BSI – British Standards Institution, PAS – Publicly Available Specification, and other [10, 11]. Due to the vast extent and general approach to the issue, it is possible to enumerate some common aspects which were considered in any individual definitions (Fig. 1).

First and foremost, the fundamental role in implementing the idea of Smart City is played by Big Data. Large datasets used in urban calculations consist in acquisition, integration and analysis of heterogeneous data derived from diverse sources in the urban space. Combining urban big data makes it possible to obtain valuable input for developing and implementing the best solutions in cities and urban systems functioning. They are used mainly for the purpose of solving major problems in a given city. Collecting, converting, analysing and exploring Urban Big Data is possible thanks to the tools such as the Internet of Things, cloud computing and AI technologies [3, 13]. Another key aspect covers the areas to which implementation of smart systems pertains. The relevant academic literature enumerates many areas, and the most often recurring ones include [12, 14–16]:

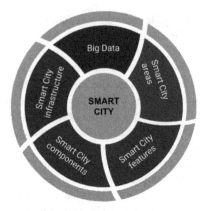

Fig. 1. The specified common aspects in the structure of the Smart City concept [12, 13]

- Smart Society/Smart People – this area is characterised by people who are constantly striving to acquire new knowledge and to share it, to raise their qualifications and education level, additionally, it is a creative society which is open to changes and to international cultures;
- Smart Governance – it focuses on transparency in management, administration functioning, services provided to citizens and taking care of their democratic rights;
- Smart Living – it covers any aspects that directly pertain to the society's life quality which depends on access to cultural, education, accommodation, healthcare, social welfare facilities as well as on safety;
- Smart Environment – it refers to city administration pursuant to the principles of sustainability in order to constrain the degradation of the natural environment, and providing the society with a liveable environment, good for spending one's free time;
- Smart Mobility/Smart Transport – specified in the context of sustainable, innovative and safe urban transport systems;
- Smart Economy – it is determined by innovativeness and entrepreneurship of business entities and the public, flexibility of the labour market, market integration in terms of the area of operation, as well as economic competitiveness of relevant entities.

Another aspect on which the development of the Smart City concept focuses includes the features pursued by cities in their development, such as [12]:

- Sustainability – it presents a concept of meeting the needs of the public on the same level of well-being as the subsequent generations, and of adjusting to the constraints regarding natural environment protection, resulting from the negative environmental impacts of the society's activities;
- Quality of life – it is measurable in terms of material and non-material well-being of the society;
- Urbanisation – it is determined by the development and availability of technologies and infrastructures in terms of management and the economy level;
- Smartness – it makes it possible to achieve the set goals by using one's resources;

- Competitiveness – it makes it possible to continuously source new knowledge, improve one's qualifications and education level and pursue self-development;
- Safety – due to the multidimensionality of the meaning of safety and ensuring it in a city, first and foremost efforts are taken to implement innovative solutions to support the processes taking place within a city, which at the same time are capable of disturbing some aspects of the residents' safety.

Components of a Smart City are its elements such as: buildings, infrastructure, technology, transport, energy, healthcare, administration, education and social capital. In the context of building a smart city, an important role is played not only by physical elements, but also the electric and digital ones, which include road networks, traffic light system management, waste management systems, digital libraries and other [12].

To develop a coherent and at the same time complete Smart City concept, it is necessary to employ a holistic approach that enables to see the big picture of the issue. In the literature on the subject it is possible to notice that the Smart City concept as such is abandoned in favour of the Smart Sustainable City concept. One of the reasons for this was the fact that cities pursued to be called a Smart City via implementing innovative solutions in that respect, which not necessarily facilitated the cities' development in accordance with the sustainability principles [18].

4 Opportunities and Measures for a Smart City in the Context of Pedestrians' Safety

One of the fundamental components of the Smart City concept is Smart Transport/Mobility. It is particularly important for city residents due to the need or desire to move around the city and due to the increased demand of city users for transport of goods, products, resources, components or waste. The most often used type of transport in urban transport systems is road transport [19]. Along with the technological progress, there are more and more vehicles in urban transport systems, which contributes to the occurrence and exacerbation of problems observed in cities functioning [2]. One of the factors affecting evaluation of the quality of urban transport systems is safety. The scale of traffic accidents and the number of related casualties force city administrators to take steps in order to mitigate this problem via upgrading and expanding urban transport systems, also by way of implementing transport telematics technologies.

The number of road accidents involving unprotected traffic participants is still high. It is particularly important in the context of consequences of such traffic accidents. Occurrence of traffic incidents involving this group of urban transport system users varies depending on weather conditions and daylight length. As per the data gathered by the European Union, available for 2018 [20]:

- Sunday is the day of the week on which the greatest number of traffic incident fatalities is observed (compared to any other week day),
- in terms of time of day, the number of fatalities is similar from Monday through Thursday,
- traffic accidents involving fatalities take place in the afternoon,

– the highest number of traffic accident fatalities is observed in early morning hours on Saturdays and Sundays.

There are numerous initiatives with regard to increasing the road traffic safety, including the European Mobility Week. The campaign is aimed at enhancing the awareness of the risks faced by road traffic participants. Regardless of the number and impact range of any campaigns, the number of traffic accidents is nowadays considerable. However, in the context of providing safety, particularly important are telematics technologies which fit the Smart City concept.

One of the solutions aimed at improving the safety of unprotected participants of road traffic is application of LED Strip Crossing (Fig. 2).

Fig. 2. LED Stripe Crossing [21]

This system is still a prototype and the technology is still being improved by the company in order to facilitate the implementation in the UK. This solutions is based on a camera system to detect pedestrians and a system of LED strips to alert vehicle drivers. This crossing is equipped with a camera integrated with LED strips on both sides of the crossing, which illuminate with red light upon detecting any approaching pedestrians. When the pedestrians have crossed the street safely, the red light will start flashing, and when the pedestrians are completely gone, it will be a sign for the drives that they can continue along [21].

Another solution aimed at improving the pedestrian safety is the Smart Pedestrian Crossing – LED panels (Fig. 3). The system is implemented by many different companies in the world, whose products have been used on a global scale. They have a vast range of clients in the world, including cities such as Lisbon in Portugal, Barcelona and Fuengirola in Spain, Santa Fe in Mexico. The task of this smart crossing is to detect a pedestrian that is about to cross the road – then LED panels turn on automatically via the sensors that send the signal within the integrated system. These LED pedestrian crossing signs also light up at the same time, as a result, the vehicles should stop [22].

Another concept is Eco and Safe Pedestrian Crossing (Fig. 4). This solution was developed by a designer from Kyongpook National University in South Korea. This concept is based on a solar energy system. The generated energy will power the LED panels installed on the ground and operate turning on and off the traffic lights for pedestrians [23]. An impediment to implementation of this type of solution may be the legal

Fig. 3. Smart pedestrian crossing – LED panels [22] (Color figure online)

regulations in the countries which have introduced strictly specified regulations with regard to markings used in road traffic.

Fig. 4. Eco and Safe Pedestrian Crossing [23]

Another measure is Pedestrian Crossings with built-in LED System in concrete slabs (Fig. 5). The creator of the idea is the Australian company LCT Light & Concrete Technology. The patented StoneLight technology has found many application possibilities, also in traffic management systems. Thanks to the use of long slabs with LED backlight, it is possible to incorporate them in pedestrian crossings. This solution has found a wide range of applications due to its energy efficiency and the development of lightweight concrete slabs. Implementation of the solution becomes a problem due to existing legal regulations in various countries regarding the marking of pedestrian crossings and the use of signs [24].

The Signalised Pedestrian Crossings, also known as Pavement Traffic Lights or LED Pavement Warning Light (Fig. 6). In 2017, the Netherlands was one of the first countries to implement this solution, which took place on the sidewalks at pedestrian crossings near three schools in the city of Bodegraven. Another of the cities selected for installation

Fig. 5. Pedestrian Crossings with built-in LED System in concrete slabs [24]

was the German city of Augsburg. Currently, this system is used on a global scale. This system can use illuminated longitudinal strips or point elements. The solution is aimed at pedestrians who are using their phones and are at risk at crossing points. The on pavement lighting systems at pedestrian crossings are installed in pavements outside the vehicle traffic zone. This system is based on a control module compatible with each traffic light controller. The colour displayed on the LED strips corresponds to the colour of the traffic light at the pedestrian crossing.

Fig. 6. The Signalised Pedestrian Crossings [25] (Color figure online)

Pedestrian safety solutions include the Smart Pedestrian Crossing System (Fig. 7). One of the proposing companies is Ellumin. This system consists of three components: activation equipment, warning equipment and the cloud warning platform. The activation equipment comprises infrared sensing bollards detecting a pedestrian located between them. The system is activated by touching by a pedestrian or the intelligent pedestrian system using a camera to detect pedestrians in the selected area of operation.

Warning equipment, however, may consist of Fully or Edge Lit Sign, Embedded Road Stud-Urban Type and Pedestrian Fill Light System. Depending on the phase of its activation, each of these systems works as an early warning for drivers by using different LED lights. This system allows for early warning of drivers that pedestrians

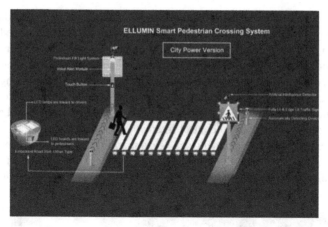

Fig. 7. The Smart Pedestrian Crossing System [26]

are approaching to the crosswalk. The warning platform in the cloud allows for remote solving of any emerging problems and managing the traffic [26].

Other solution is Sustainable Road Elements for Speed Reduction (Fig. 8). This solution is in the design phase, financed by the Centre for the Development of Industrial Technology of the Spanish Ministry of Science, Innovation and Universities, it will last from 2018 to 2021. This project intends to develop new sustainable components to reduce the speed of cars at pedestrian crossings. These elements have three main functions: power generation, safe signalling of pedestrian crossings and connection of pedestrian crossings with the environment. Generation of electricity will be possible thanks to the use of reliable materials and a customised design that must withstand passing vehicles [27].

Fig. 8. Sustainable Road Elements for Speed Reduction [27]

Another innovative solution is Stigmergic Adaptive Responsive Learning (Fig. 9), also known as The Starling Crossing or Starling CV. In 2017, this system as a prototype was implemented in the south of London (Great Britain). Further work is underway to implement the system in other locations. The system was designed by the London-based company called Umbrellium. This system uses a neural network and computer vision system to observe and classify moving objects in real time on busy roads as well as roadside areas. By calculating trajectories, determining the location of hidden pedestrians or cyclists, e.g. behind the high sides of vehicles and determining the future speed of objects, this system can detect, predict and respond to changing conditions in the area of intersections, pavements and roads. The system can be installed at any road junction or crossing. It is used to control interactive surfaces of roads and pavements and to light the curb side, or road markings. Road markings and lighting can be adapted to different usages for different times of day or different conditions (e.g. street markets or events) and respond in different ways depending on the current usage [28–30].

Fig. 9. Stigmergic Adaptive Responsive Learning [28]

Another measure is the Traffic Light Virtual Wall (Fig. 10). This solution is being developed by Chinese designers as they think the traditional traffic lights are small and not highly visible to everyone, as some of them are shadowed by signs etc. This concept differs from the previous solutions using virtual walls due to the display of pedestrian tracking image. The system is a holographic Virtual Wall, forcing the "reckless" drivers to stop at a red light. The principle is based on a laser projector that projects the images of moving pedestrians visible only to the drivers in front of them. In the night-time the hologram should be much brighter [31].

The SafeWalk – Stereovision Video Sensor is the next solution used in urban transport system, otherwise called FLIR Intelligent Transportation Systems by its producer. SafeWalk integrates 3D stereovision technology and intelligent detection of pedestrian presence on the sidewalks. The main applications are detection of pedestrians waiting to cross the road, detection of approaching pedestrians intending to cross the road. SafeWalk was created to improve pedestrian behaviour and safety at traffic lights. By detecting any waiting pedestrians by way of dynamic traffic light management, this intelligent sensor increases the traffic capacity for both pedestrians and drivers. This ground sensor moves in the designated zone and is designed to display the detection zone adjacent to the pole on which it is mounted [32].

Fig. 10. Traffic Light Virtual Wall [31] (Color figure online)

The above mentioned examples of solutions implemented pursuant to the Smart City concept are aimed at improving the safety of all participants of road traffic, and in particular the safety of unprotected participants of road traffic, including pedestrians. They constitute an important aspect in cities' pursuit of sustainability via measures taken by city administrators in order to implement technologies that make it possible to mitigate the effects of the observed transport issues. The overview of the development strategies of some European cities and of the European Union has shown a need for taking up measures that strive in particular to mitigate any road incidents, also those involving pedestrians. Some of the described solutions are still being tested, which has an effect on the cities' response to the changing requirements of their citizens and setting new levels of a Smart City. Additionally, the solutions in that respect open up an environment for developing the potential of entrepreneurs and researchers [1].

5   Conclusion

The purpose of this article is to present some Smart City solutions aimed at improving the safety of unprotected participants of road traffic, including pedestrians who experience the greatest harm as a result of road accidents. The described solutions include those that have been used on a global scale only recently, as well as the ones which are an innovative initiative and are still in the testing phase. The major contribution of this article is presenting the latest solutions that may serve as a basis for good practices implementation. Overall, this research study may contribute to expanding the knowledge body via taking note of good practices across various metropolises, which are based on intelligent solutions. The solutions are aimed at drawing attention to the possibility of taking measures to mitigate transport issues and to increase competitiveness among cities in the context of Smart City solutions. The challenges and solutions presented by the authors may constitute the basis for considering, using, and testing them in other cities that strive to grow in accordance with the Smart City concept, paying special attention to the safety of unprotected participants of road traffic, including pedestrians.

References

1. Albino, V., Berardi, U., Dangelico, R.M.: Smart city: definitions, dimensions, performance, and initiatives. J. Urban Technol. **22**(1), 3–21 (2015)
2. Xie, F., Naumann, S., Czogalla, O.: Speed control system for pedestrians crossing signaled intersections time optimally. IFAC-PapersOnLine **51**(34), 139–144 (2019)
3. Pan, Y., et al.: Urban big data and the development of city intelligence. Engineering **2**(2), 171–178 (2016)
4. Iwan, S.: Wdrażanie dobrych praktyk w obszarze transportu dostawczego w miastach, Wyd. Naukowe Akademii Morskiej, Szczecin, p. 109 (2013)
5. United Nation. Press Release of the World Urbanization Prospects 2018 (2018). https://population.un.org/. Accessed 20 Oct 2019
6. Stawacz, D.: Współczesne dylematy zarządzania rozwojem miast, pp. 8–21 (2016)
7. Karpov, A.O.: The problem of separating the notions of "knowledge" and "information" in the knowledge society and its education. Proc.-Soc. Behav. Sci, **237**, 804–810 (2017)
8. Nautiyal, L., et.al.: Cybersecurity system: an essential pillar of smart cities. In: Mahmood, Z. (ed.) Smart Cities Development and Governance Frameworks, p. 34 (2018)
9. Małecki, K., Iwan, S., Kijewska, K.: Influence of Intelligent Transportation Systems on reduction of the environmental negative impact of urban freight transport based on Szczecin example. Proc. – Soc. Behav. Sci. **151**, 215–229 (2014)
10. Gotlib, D., Olszewski, R.: Smart City, Informacja przestrzenna w zarządzaniu Inteligentnym Miastem. PWN, pp. 9–13 (2016)
11. Bronk, K.: Inteligentne miasta (Smart Cites) na progu technologii 5G, Instytut Łączności, Państwowy Instytut Badawczy (2017)
12. Mohanty, S.P., Choppali, U., Kougianos, E.: Everything you wanted to know about smart cities: the internet of things is the backbone. IEEE Consum. Electron. Mag. **5**(3), 60–70 (2016)
13. Liu, J., et al.: Urban big data fusion based on deep learning: an overview. Inf. Fusion **53**, 123–133 (2020)
14. Giffinger, R., et al.: Smart Cities: Ranking of European Medium-sized Cities, Final Report, Centre of Regional Science (2007)
15. Patel, Y., Doshi, N.: Social implications of smart cities. Proc. Comput. Sci. **155**, 692–697 (2019)
16. Stephanedes, P.E., et al.: Challenges, risks and opportunities for connected vehicle services in smart cities and communities. IFAC-PapersOnLine **51**(34), 139–144 (2019)
17. Bibri, S.E., Krogstie, J.: Smart Sustainable Cities of the Future: An Extensive Interdisciplinary Literature. The Untapped Potential of Big Data Analytics and Context–Aware Computing for Advancing Sustainability, pp. 183–212 (2017)
18. Akande, A., et al.: The Lisbon ranking for smart sustainable cities in Europe. Sustain. Cities Soc. **44**, 475–487 (2019)
19. Sosik, K., Turzeniecka, M., Iwan, S.: Difficulties affecting distribution process in a city - a forwarder perspective. Transp. Res. Proc. **39**, 480–487 (2019)
20. European Commission: Road safety in the European Union. Trends, statistics and main challenges (2018). https://ec.europa.eu/. Accessed 11 Mar 2020
21. https://www.thesun.co.uk/motors/5708869/this-is-what-pedestrian-crossings-will-look-like-in-the-future-with-light-up-strips-on-the-road/. Accessed 21 Nov 2019
22. https://www.stepvial.com/en/solutions. Accessed 21 Nov 2019
23. https://ifworlddesignguide.com/entry/88280-eco-safe-cross?fbclid=IwAR3-6MpS2EPJh9jHs9vkEV3-IpVyIOlGnc1EIpTZs_yS4SaqjYwJgo7N9lM. Accessed 21 Nov 2019
24. https://www.transformative-technologies.com/lighting-systems.html. Accessed 21 Nov 2019

25. https://smartcitystreets.com/pedestrian-safety/. Accessed 21 Nov 2019

26. https://www.ellumin.com/project/non-light-control-area-intelligent-pedestrian-system%ef%bc%88urban-type%ef%bc%89/. Accessed 21 Nov 2019

27. https://projects.leitat.org/sustainable-road-elements-for-speed-reduction/. Accessed 21 Nov 2019

28. https://www.borntoengineer.com/starling-crossing-lights-way-pedestrian-safety.   Accessed 21 Nov 2019

29. https://www.citymetric.com/horizons/here-are-four-futuristic-new-designs-pedestrian-crossings-4309. Accessed 21 Nov 2019

30. https://umbrellium.co.uk/products/starling-cv/. Accessed 21 Nov 2019

31. https://www.tweaktown.com/news/35489/could-this-laser-hologram-concept-be-the-stoplight-of-the-future-/index.html. Accessed 21 Nov 2019

32. https://www.flir.co.uk/. Accessed 21 Nov 2019

The Telematics Concept for Integrated Management of Road Transport Risks

Janusz Szpytko[1(✉)] and Weam Nasan Agha[1,2(✉)]

[1] AGH University of Science and Technology, Ave A. Mickiewicza 30, Krakow, Poland
szpytko@agh.edu.pl
[2] University of Aleppo, Aleppo, Syria
weam.agha@alepuniv.edu.sy

Abstract. The number of road traffic accidents has been on the rise worldwide with severe impacts. Road transport risk management has been one of the most important issues in the transport systems during the last several years. Where new technical solutions have been developed towards ensuring road and driver safety. The paper is focused on the telematics concept for the integrated management of road transport risks. Firstly, all the potential risks and transport engineering problems were identified. A new comprehensive framework for managing transport risks was developed on the basis of information and communications technology (telematics, ICT). This framework contains advanced strategies and processes for successful transport risk management using telematics. The paper presents the efficiency of the proposed framework in improving road safety, preventing avoidable accidents and reducing the probability of critical accidents.

Keywords: Risk · Risk management · Telematics · Road transport

1 Introduction

Road traffic accidents are one of man-made disasters. Where road accidents are the leading cause of death and injuries around the world. The World Health Organisation launched the global status report on road safety which reaffirmed that injuries due to road traffic crashes are a significant and major global health and development problem. Where the number of deaths on the world's roads remains unacceptably high, with an estimated 1.35 million people dying each year. However, the rate of death relative to the size of the world's population has remained constant [1], Fig. 1.

More than half of all road traffic deaths are among vulnerable road users: pedestrians, cyclists and motorcyclists. It is also reported that middle- and high-income countries have more progress in reducing the number of road traffic deaths than low-income countries. However, the progress to realise Sustainable Development Goal (SDG) target 3.6 – which calls for a 50% reduction in the number of road traffic deaths by 2020 – remains far from sufficient [1].

© Springer Nature Switzerland AG 2020
J. Mikulski (Ed.): TST 2020, CCIS 1289, pp. 190–213, 2020.
https://doi.org/10.1007/978-3-030-59270-7_15

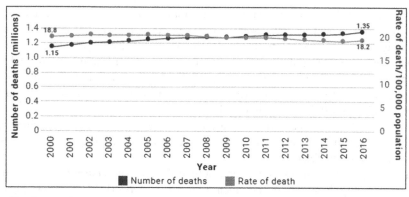

Fig. 1. Number and rate of road traffic death per 100 000 population: 2000–2016 [1]

Several studies have found that there are many problems and risks leading to the occurrence of road accidents such as poor infrastructure, drunkenness, negligence of drivers and riders, unqualified drivers, lack of road safety education and road traffic signs, etc. [2].

Ensuring road safety is one of the major concerns around the world. Road safety aims to reduce the harm (deaths, injuries, and property damage) resulting from accidents. It has been reported that harm from road-traffic accidents is greater than other transportation modes (air, sea, space, etc.) [3].

All above, there is an urgent need to adopt integrated safety management systems, where integral safety management is based on integral risk management to reduce the number of accident and their serious consequences [4]. The road safety management includes risk management to be more effective, where more practical and advanced tools and technologies are adopted towards identifying & assessing road risks and developing & implementing effective and appropriate mitigations strategies for those risks [5].

Recently, there has been a shift from accident prevention to injury prevention, which means a new paradigm in transport safety and change of attitude, from "an accident is a random event that cannot be foreseen" to "an event causing human injury can be foreseen". If it can be foreseen, it can be averted, if it does happen though, its impact can be mitigated [6].

In this paper, we will present an overview of the integrated safety management system in road transportation and identify the key road crash risks based on the content analysis of related research materials. Where Transport risk management plays a crucial role in transport systems towards ensuring road and drivers safety, preventing avoidable accidents and reducing the probability of critical accidents.

Transportation sector has witnessed a significant advance in the application of advanced sensor, computer, electronics and communications technologies. These applications are known as Transport Telematics/Intelligent Transportation Systems (ITS) and considered as one of the most important innovations towards improving the management, maintenance, monitoring, control and safety of transportation [7].

It is reported that all Organisation for Economic Co-operation and Development (OECD) member countries have been involved in developing or deploying Telematics/Intelligent Transport Systems (ITS) to some extent. It is estimated that safety technologies can potentially reduce the total number of road crash injuries and fatalities by approximately 40% and save as many as 47 000 lives per year in OECD countries. Also, the cost savings related to a 40% reduction in injuries and fatalities would be approximately USD 194 billion annually [8].

Several studies have been done in the use of telematics data for ensuring road safety and reliability. However, these studies are scattered on different methods and technologies of using Telematics [9].

In this paper, we will investigate and outline the current perspective of literature review concerning the ability of intelligent transport systems (ITS) to address the key crash risks and how telematics helps to improve safety in road transportation. In addition, A new comprehensive framework for ensuring road safety and managing the key crash risks will be developed on the basis of information and communications technology (telematics, ICT).

This paper is organized as follows: Sect. 2 introduces the research target, then the used research methodology to meet the research objectives is clarified in Sect. 3. Section 4 presents an overview of the integrated safety management system in road transportation. Also, this section introduces an extensive review of integrated risk management in road transportation through investigating the key risks leading to the occurrence of road accidents. Section 5 presents the concept of Telematics and how Telematics helps to manage the key risks and improve the safety in road transportation. Section 6 presents the proposed framework for the integrated management of road crash risks using Telematics. Finally, the conclusion is presented in Sect. 7.

2 Research Target

This paper is focused on the Telematics Concept for the Integrated Risk Management in Road Transportation. The main target is broken down into three sub-objectives as follows:

- Investigating & Defining the key risks leading to the occurrence of road accidents;
- Investigating & Outling the role of telematics in managing risks and improving road safety;
- Developing a new comprehensive framework for the integrated management of road crash risks on the basis of information and communications technology (telematics, ICT).

3 Research Methodology

An exploratory mixed approach has been used to meet the target of this research, this methodology is divided into two main stages:

The first stage is qualitative in nature where an exploratory content analysis of related research materials has been conducted towards identifying the key crash risks in road transportation and the crucial role of telematics in managing risks and improving the safety in road transportation.

While the second stage is Framework Design where data and results from the previous stage will be adopted to develop the proposed framework for improving road safety and achieving successful integrated management of the key road crash risks.

4 Integrated Safety Management System

In 1995, the Department of Energy's (DOE) nuclear facilities adopted the concept of Integrated Safety Management System as a new approach towards integrating work and safety, enhancing safety awareness, upgrading formality of operations, and improving safety performance. The implementation of effective integrated safety management systems has been extended to several sectors. However, this implementation varies from sector to another [10].

In this section, we go through the concept of the integrated safety management system in road transportation sector. After that, we present an exploratory review of integrated risk management in road transportation through investigating the key risks leading to the occurrence of road accidents.

4.1 Integrated Safety Management System in Road Transportation

The integrated safety management system in road transportation is a subsystem of the surface transportation system and is defined as "an organizational structure that is supported by resources and defined in terms of leadership; mission and vision statements; and processes equipped with tools for managing the attributes of road, driver, and vehicle" [11].

This system aims to achieve the highest level of safety for existing and future transportation networks, all road users, and supporting systems (enforcement, emergency services, and so forth) by integrating the work of disciplines and agencies involved in highway safety within a jurisdiction. These disciplines include the planning, design, construction, operation, and maintenance of the roadway infrastructure; injury prevention & control; the design and manufacture of vehicles; and those disciplines involved in controlling and modifying road user behaviour (education, enforcement, and department of motor vehicles) [11].

Two key components are needed in order to achieve the mission of integrated safety management system: The first is an organizational structure that will allow for the integration of the agencies involved in highway safety. The second is a formal management process that will direct activities of these agencies in a successful and effective manner to meet the highest levels of safety [11].

The formal management process includes integral risk management as one of its basic components, where safety management system requires a structured risk management system to be more effective. We go through the concept of integrated risk management and investigate the key road crash risks in the following section.

4.2 Integrated Risk Management in Road Transportation

Integrated risk management is one of the major concerns around the world, where there has been more and more attention in all types of enterprises and organizations to the identification and management of the potential risks.

The concept of risk is defined as "an effect of uncertainty on objectives (such as financial, health and safety, and environmental goals)". Risk is often expressed in terms of a combination of the associated likelihood of occurrence and the consequences of an event (including changes in circumstances) [12].

In the scope of road transportation, a risk factor in is defined as "any factor that, under otherwise equal conditions, increases the probability of injuries in accidents or aggravates the severity of injuries" [13].

Risk management process is defined as "systematic application of management policies, procedures and practices to the activities of communicating, consulting, establishing the context, and identifying, analysing, evaluating, treating, monitoring and reviewing risk" [12].

The main purpose of integrated risk management is to minimise the number of risks and their consequences and to take advantage of the capacities and opportunities. Also, the basic tool for delivering a safety policy and its objectives is risk management [14].

Integrated risk management in road transportation offers a basis for the integrated view of the necessary practices and processes towards identifying and assessing all the types of risks relevant to accident occurrence and adopting advanced strategies and technologies for managing those risks. All above, Integrated risk management plays a crucial role towards improving road safety, preventing avoidable accidents and reducing the probability of critical accident.

World Health Organization (WHO) reported that improving road safety involves two key processes, the first is identifying the risk factors that contribute to crashes and injuries, while the second is managing those risks through identifying the interventions that reduce the risks associated with those factors [15].

A risk cannot be managed unless it is first identified and assessed. Therefore, the first important step towards improving road safety and eliminating the causes of the road accidents is identifying and assessing the relevant risks factors.

Risk assessment in road transportation has been the subject of numerous research and scientific publications around the world for many years [16].

In this paper, we identify the key risks in road transportation leading to the occurrence of road accidents based on the content analysis of the related research materials as stated in the following.

Altogether (15) research materials, during the period (2003–2019), were reviewed to identify the key risks leading to the occurrence of road accidents. Through the qualitative content analysis of these research materials, fifteen (15) key risks in road transportation have been extracted.

Risks can be generally categorized in several ways according to its nature, impact, or source. In this paper, these (15 Risks) were classified according to its source within three categories:

- Road Users-related risks (7 risks);
- Vehicle-related risks (2 risks);
- Road Environment-related risks (6 risks), Table 1.

Table 1. The key road crash risks [own study based on [2, 8, 15, 17–28]]

	Code	Risk name	References
Road users	UR01	Inappropriate or excessive speed	[8, 15, 17, 18, 21–24, 27, 28]
	UR02	Lack of using helmets and seat-belts	[15, 18, 21, 24]
	UR03	Lack of vulnerable users' awareness	[22, 27]
	UR04	Drink-Driving	[2, 8, 15, 18, 20, 22, 24, 28]
	UR05	Lack of driver skills and inexperience	[2, 17, 20, 22–24, 28]
	UR06	Distraction (using mobile phones, kids, etc.)	[15, 22, 24, 26, 28]
	UR07	Driver fatigue/drowsiness	[8, 15, 20, 22, 23, 27, 28]
Vehicle	VR01	Insufficient vehicle equipment	[15, 24]
	VR02	Lack of vehicle maintenance	[15, 22–24]
Road environment	ER01	Increase in traffic flow	[15, 22]
	ER02	Defects in road design, layout and maintenance	[15, 19, 22, 23, 25, 27, 28]
	ER03	Defects in roadside objects	[15, 19]
	ER04	Inadequate visibility	[15, 22, 23, 27]
	ER05	Weather conditions	[17, 19, 22, 24, 28]
	ER06	Lack of road traffic signs	[2, 15, 19, 22, 27]

After identifying the key risks leading to the occurrence of road accidents, the next step is managing those risks towards improving road safety, preventing avoidable accidents and reducing the probability of critical accident. The integrated management of road crash risks will be achieved by adopting advanced technologies as stated in the following section.

5   Telematics/Intelligent Transport Systems (ITS)

In the recent years, there has been a rapid and significant development of advanced technologies in road transportation, where more attention has been paid to the development of Intelligent Transport Systems (ITS) that can improve the safety and efficiency of road transportation while improving user comfort and convenience [8].

In this section, we go through the concept of telematics/Intelligent Transport Systems (ITS). After that, we present an extensive review of the role of telematics/Intelligent Transport Systems (ITS) in managing the key road crash risks and improving the safety in road transportation.

5.1 The Concept of Telematics/Intelligent Transport Systems (ITS)

The term "information society" was introduced to the literature in the seventies of the previous century. The development of infrastructure and new telematic technologies is considered as one of the important elements and stages in the implementation of the concept of information society [29].

The etymology of telematics is from the Greek "tele" ('far away', especially in relation to the process of producing) and "Matos" (a derivative of the Greek machinari). As combined, the term "telematics" describes the process of long-distance transmission of computer-based information [29].

Currently, the term telematics is defined as "telecommunication, information and information technology and automatic control solutions adapted to the needs of management and operation of systems and physical processes". Telematics systems use different hardware, software and applications such as communications systems, databases, navigation systems, monitoring and data transmission equipment. Telematics is used in a broad range of equipment and database regarding various aspects such as medicine, building, finance, library, transport, etc [29].

The term transport telematics began to be applied on a larger scale since the early nineties in Europe. The transport telematics regards the maximum utilization of information technology in transport and the introduction of the term intelligent transport management systems (ITS) [29].

Intelligent Transport Systems (ITS) are defined generally as "the application of advanced telecommunications, computing, and sensor technologies to improve the safety, efficiency and sustainability of the transportation system" [7].

Intelligent Transport Systems (ITS) apply information and communication technologies to every transport mode (road, rail, air, water) and provide services which can be used by both passenger and freight transport. Intelligent Transport Systems (ITS) play a crucial role in improving the mobility of people and freights in terms of safety, efficiency, sustainability and comfort [30].

Intelligent Transport Systems (ITS) are multisystem structures that involve integration of four fundamental subsystems: (1) Infrastructure subsystem; (2) Vehicular subsystem; (3) Users subsystem; (4) Communications subsystem. These subsystems combine tasks of management, control, information collection and actuation systems, and have to be perfectly related and synchronized to meet the objectives of the whole system [30]. Figure 2 illustrates the Intelligent Transport Systems Conceptual Model.

The application of telematics concepts in the area of transport offers several intelligent services to traffic users; among many others, the following can be mentioned:

- Automatic traffic management systems [30, 31];
- Public transport information services [30, 31];
- Traveler information systems [30, 31];
- Fleet management and location systems [31];
- Emergency management [30];
- Electronic payment systems [30];
- Cooperative vehicular systems [30, 31].

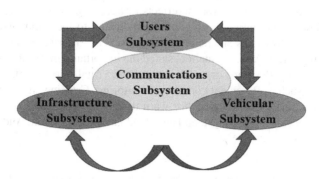

Fig. 2 Intelligent Transport Systems Conceptual Model [own study based on [30]]

Moreover, Intelligent Transport Systems (ITS) are being identified as a domain of high potential to solve many problems facing the transportation sector such as, traffic congestion, safety, transport efficiency and environmental conservation [31].

5.2 The Role of Telematics in Road Transportation

In the recent years, the world has witnessed unprecedented advancements in information and communications technology (Telematics, ICT) [32].

Telematics/Intelligent Transport System (ITS) has become the cornerstone of transport and attracts several researchers from the academia, where a broad range of technologies and applications have been developed towards increasing the efficiency and reliability of transportation systems, improving the safety and reducing the environmental impacts.

In this paper, an exploratory review was conducted towards investigating the role of telematics in road transportation, especially in managing the key road crash risks and improving the road safety.

Altogether (18) research materials, during the period (1998–2018), were reviewed to identify how telematics helps in improving the road safety. In the following, we present this review and show the evolution of the concerns according to the year of publication of the works.

Suen et al., in their work, indicated to the crucial role of Intelligent Transportation Systems (ITS) in enhancing vehicle safety for elderly and less able road users where elderly drivers, pedestrians and transit users have high average accident rates per year.

An extensive review of the potential of ITS to improve the safety of elderly and less able road users was made. For car drivers, the authors examined the potential of two classes of ITS system, Advanced Vehicle Control and Safety Systems (AVCSS) and Advanced Traveller Information Systems (ATIS) to provide services that make driving easier, less stressful and safer. Where (AVCSS) can provide information specifically to avoid collisions, improve visibility at night, assist with the longitudinal and lateral control of the vehicle and assist with speed control, and (ATIS) can provide information on traffic conditions, provide specialized weather forecasts and guide the driver to a selected destination. The authors discussed how (ITS) equipment has the ability to solve safety problems and compensate for the effects of age-related impairments in drivers as stated in Table 2. Furthermore, the authors indicated to the importance of smart cards in avoiding further risks and helping transit users by ensuring better information before and during travel. Also, the authors stated the importance of better road-crossing facilities in helping pedestrians especially who have visual impairments by utilizing (ITS) equipment such as Pavement condition monitoring; Crossing signals that extend crossing time for slow pedestrians and/or warn drivers of pedestrians on crosswalks; Hand-held fall detector/Mayday system; Hand-held navigation system; Audible signals at cross walks [33].

Table 2. Car drivers impairments, safety problems and ITS equipment [33]

Impairments	Problems	ITS equipment
Increased reaction time. Difficulty dividing attention between tasks	Difficulty driving in unfamiliar or congested areas	Navigation/route guidance Traffic information, VMS
Deteriorating vision, particularly at night	Difficulty seeing pedestrians and other objects at night, reading	Night vision enhancement In-vehicle signs
Difficulty judging speed and distance	Failure to perceive conflicting vehicles. Accidents at junctions	Collision warning. Automated lane changing
Difficulty perceiving and analysing situations	Failure to comply with yield signs, traffic signals and rail crossings. Slow to appreciate hazards	In-vehicle signs and warnings Intelligent cruise control
More prone to fatigue	Get tired on long journeys	Intelligent cruise control Automated lane following
Difficulty turning head, reduced peripheral vision	Failure to notice obstacles while manoeuvring. Merging and lane changes	Blind spot/obstacle detection. Automated lane changing and merging
Some impairments vary in severity from day to day. Tiredness	Concern over fitness to drive	Driver condition monitoring

The National Highway Traffic Safety Administration established The Vehicle Safety Communications (VSC) project in 2002 where seven automotive manufacturers—BMW, DaimlerChrysler, Ford, GM, Nissan, Toyota, and VW—formed the VSC Consortium (VSCC) to participate in this project in partnership with the U.S. Department of Transportation (USDOT). This project aims to evaluate the potential benefits and deployment feasibility of communication-based vehicle safety applications, perform some Dedicated Short-Range Communications (DSRC) vehicle testing and develop the (DSRC) standards towards meeting the needs of vehicle safety applications. The (VSCC) participants identified More than (75) communications-based vehicle application scenarios which have been analysed resulting a comprehensive list included (34) safety and (11) non-safety application scenario descriptions. The (VSCC) participants divided Safety-Related Application into five main Categories: Intersection Collision Avoidance (ICA), Public Safety, Sign Extension, Vehicle Diagnostics and Maintenance, and Information from Other Vehicles. Furthermore, the (VSCC) participants performed a set of analysis categories by which the potential safety benefits of application scenarios could be compared and ranked. The results were subset of eight representative near- and mid-term safety applications identified as high priority for further research and will be used as a basis for establishing preliminary communication requirements, Table 3 [34].

Table 3. Vehicle safety applications with greatest benefits in near and mid-term [34]

Near-term		Mid-term	
Safety application	Communication type	Safety application	Communication type
Traffic signal violation warning	Infrastructure-to-vehicle Point-to-multipoint	Pre-crash sensing	Vehicle-to-vehicle Point-to-multipoint
Curve speed warning	Infrastructure-to-vehicle Point-to-multipoint	Cooperative forward collision warning	Vehicle-to-vehicle Point-to-multipoint
Emergency electronic brake lights	Vehicle-to-vehicle Point-to-multipoint	Left turn assistant	Vehicle-to-infrastructure Infrastructure-to-vehicle Point-to-multipoint
		Lane change warning	Vehicle-to-vehicle Point-to-multipoint
		Stop sign movement assistance	Vehicle-to-infrastructure Infrastructure-to-vehicle Point-to-multipoint

The Federal Highway Administration (FHWA) sponsored The International Technology Scanning Program during the period 2004–2005. The main aim of this program is investigating the existing intelligent transportation systems (ITS) applications deployed in other countries that could be effective in mitigating safety problems in the United States. The scanning team visited three countries Japan, Germany and France because of existing and emerging applications of ITS strategies in these countries. The scanning team presented some examples of the observed ITS applications and technologies such as Overhead signs with static and changeable messages; Various European Union (EU) initiatives, including eSafety, INVENT, and PReVENT; The eCall system; Image processing; Electronic toll collection; Various initiatives involving digital mapping took static and dynamic information about the roadway and its geometric; Speed management and control; Video incident detection; Optimizing system, Various driver assistance initiatives such as adaptive cruise control, lane keeping, and assisted braking. Also, the scanning team presented recommendations with an eye toward the four main elements: the driver, the vehicle, the environment, and policy in order to achieve in substantive improvements in highway safety [35].

Jarašūniene and Jakubauskas, in their work, confirmed the importance of the Intelligent Vehicle Safety Systems (IVSS), vehicle-based or infrastructure-related systems, in increasing road safety and efficiency. The authors presented some types of vehicle-based systems such as Adaptive Brake Lights, Adaptive Head Lights, Alcohol (inter) Lock, Automatic Headlight Activation, Blind Spot Monitoring, Driver Condition Monitoring, Lane Departure Warning, Lane Keeping Assistant, Obstacles & Collision Warning, Run flat Indicator/Tire Pressure Monitoring System, Vision Enhancement and Dynamic Control Systems. Also, they presented some types of infrastructure-related systems such as E-Call, Event Data Recorder, Extended Environment Information, High Quality Congestion/Traffic Information, Infrastructure Based Warning Systems, Inter Vehicle Hazard Warning, Traffic Sign Recognition & Alert and Dynamic Traffic Management. Furthermore, the authors discussed aims, nature and examples of IVSS during pre-crash, accident-time, and post-crash, as well as passive and active safety applications where passive safety applications help people stay alive and uninjured in a crash, while active safety applications help drivers to avoid accidents, Table 4. In addition, the authors analysed the usefulness of IVSS systems from the drivers' point of view. The results showed that majority of drivers would like to have IVSS in their car especially (E-Call), Anti-Lock Braking System (ABS) and Electronic Stability Program (ESP). Finally, Possible solutions to deploying ITS in Lithuania were introduced with more emphasis on enhancement of traffic safety and improvement of road information infrastructure, traffic conditions on roads and streets [36].

Spyropoulou et al., in their work, confirmed the vital role of Intelligent Transport Systems (ITS) in improving road safety. The authors adopted more 'humanistic' and 'safety-related' approach by defining firstly the risk factors that contribute to road accidents and then proposing potential ITS-solutions. The authors classified the risk factors within three main categories: the human, the road environment and the vehicle. Then the authors proposed the potential Intelligent transport system solutions, pre-crash systems, for managing each risk factor within only two categories human and road environment. Examples of such systems include alco-lock, intelligent speed adaptation (ISA), intelligent cruise control (ICC), longitudinal vehicle control (forward collision warning), lateral vehicle control (lane keeping and lane departure warning), intersection, pedestrian or obstacle warning, driver monitoring systems, vision enhancement system (VES) and enhanced navigation systems. Furthermore, the authors introduced a structured evaluation, included the potential capabilities and shortcomings, of the suggested ITS-solutions

Table 4. Active and passive safety systems [36]

	Aims of IVSS	Nature of IVSS	Examples of IVSS
Active safety	To inform	Foresighted driving systems	Digital map-based systems
	To support	Warning and assistance systems	Lane, distance, and speed warning
	To intervene	Pre-crash systems and reversible protection systems	Brake assistance, active control of a vehicle
Accident			
Passive safety	Aid in minor accidents	Soft-level systems	Airbags, crashworthiness,
	Aid in severe accidents	Hard-level systems	Intelligent restraint systems
	Post-crash aid	Rescue systems	eCall

through three types of analysis: The first is based on previous research studies; the second used SWOT analysis; while the third is Delphi study. Finally, the authors indicated to the importance of employing the proposed ITS considering the anticipated shortcomings and ways of overcoming them towards successful ITS implementation [28].

Malik and Rakotonirainy, in their work, indicated to the importance of Intelligent Transport systems (ITS) in managing the major risks in crashes such as driver inattention, inexperience, poor judgment and/or fatigue etc. The authors presented an overview of ITS where many technologies such as Telematic and/or Advance Driver assistance systems have been adopted for improving road safety. The authors pointed out the vital role of Driver's driving competencies in improving road safety and avoiding any possible collision. Therefore, the authors discussed the necessity for developing and evaluating (ITS) that assess driving competencies and improve training and education of drivers. The authors designed an Intelligent Driver Training System (DTS) that mainly consists of two main modules (i.e. Data Acquisition Module and Maneuver Identification Module). The proposed system would integrate the vehicle dynamics, driver behaviour and road/traffic information where the required data would be fused from multiple cameras and sensors over time and evaluate the competency of the driver. Finally, the authors presented a description of preliminary implementation and evaluation criteria used for the proposed system [37].

Chen et al., in their work, indicated to the vital role of Intelligent Transport systems (ITS) in improving road safety where there has been an urgent need towards mitigating traffic accidents by adoption of vehicular communication networks. The authors reviewed and classified broadcast protocols for vehicular communication networks where broadcasting plays a crucial role in increasing the reliability and efficiency of disseminating safety messages to all nearby vehicles such as look-ahead emergency warnings and information about unsafe driving conditions. Furthermore, the authors discussed network design considerations and presented vehicular safety applications where, time-sensitive, safety-critical applications are so necessary in vehicular communication networks towards achieving the future road safety vision. Finally, the authors emphasized on the importance of traffic flow dynamics, along with improvements in the communication stack in designing reliable, efficient, and scalable broadcast methods for vehicular communication networks [38].

Chen and Qu, in their work, found out the problems and the insufficiency in the exiting transport systems and the necessity to develop ITS technologies in Chinese road safety management. Where the authors focused on three types of ITS technologies towards improving road traffic safety as the following: technology which directly influences driving behaviour, technology which indirectly influences driving behaviours and information system after a crash, Table 5. In addition, the authors developed policy suggestions and promotion strategy with national situation to solve related issues and ensure substantial progress achieved for ITS technology as well as comprehensively guarantee road traffic safety sustainable development [39].

Table 5. ITS technologies towards improving road traffic safety [39]

Target	Potential ITS technology	ITS technologies
Application of ITS to improve road safety	Technology which directly influences driving behaviour	1. GPS 2. Flashing warning lamp 3. Speed display boards 4. Variable message sign
	Technology which indirectly influences driving behaviours	5. On-board video monitoring device 6. Whole distance monitoring device 7. Speeding capture device
	Information system after a crash	8. Tachographs

Khorasani et al., in their work, emphasized the importance of Intelligent Transport Systems (ITS) in improving the road safety situation for all types of road-users. The authors presented firstly the identification of ITS and its benefits. then, they stated how ITS can influence on all the key macroscopic variables of the road safety problem, i.e. exposure, risk, and the severity of accident. In addition, the authors discussed several ITS technologies in-vehicle systems for enhancing road safety such as advanced driver assistance system, intelligent speed adaptation, driver monitoring system, collision warning and avoidance system, lane keeping and lane-change warning system, visibility enhancing system, seat belt reminder system. Furthermore, the authors presented one case study of South Africa ITS implementation. The results showed the importance of ITS in enhancing quality and standards of road safety parameters and the urgent need for implementing ITS especially in developing countries [40].

Jiménez et al., in their work, indicated to the significant advances in information technologies and its crucial role in developing wide range of complex road safety applications. The authors developed an integrated Advanced Driver Assistance System (ADAS) for inter-urban environments, mainly single-carriageways roads, towards solving their special problems and improving both safety and efficiency. This system is based on cooperative systems to enhance multisensory perception and communication between vehicles (V2V) and with the infrastructure(V2I) and provide the additional information in order to promote actions involving several vehicles. The authors used artificial vision and 3D-laser scanner, and wireless communications modules. Where many applications have been developed such as adaptive cruise control with consumption optimization; overtaking assistance system; assistance system in intersections with speed control during manoeuvres, and collision avoidance system. this system analyses especially complex critical manoeuvres and detects further risks that may arise on the road, alerting the driver of these situations. Moreover, the system has the ability to take control of the vehicle automatically, if the driver does not react in a proper way, both on speed control or steering manoeuvres to improve safety and/or efficiency. Finally, this system has been implemented on a passenger car and several tests have been performed in specific scenarios on a test track with satisfactory results [41].

Bagheri et al., in their work, proposed energy-efficient adaptive multimode (AMM) approach to enable development of cloud-based pedestrian road-safety systems and improve road safety particularly in obstructed visibility and bad weather conditions. The authors developed road safety mobile app using energy-efficient methods and non-dedicated existing technologies namely smartphones, cellular network and cloud. This app frequently sends vehicle and pedestrian geolocation data (beacons) to cloud servers where threat analysis is performed using cloud and alerts are sent to road users who are in risky situation. The authors employed adaptive multi-mode (AMM) approach to reduce power consumption using beacon rate control while it keeps the data freshness required for collision prediction timely vehicle-to-pedestrian. Also, AMM has several advantages such as enabling running wireless-based pedestrian road safety systems with mainstream smartphones, increasing smartphone state-of-charge (SOC) after pedestrian's mobility and extends the total battery lifetime. In addition, the results showed the feasibility of running such road-safety systems on conventional cellular networks and cloud providers [42].

Pauer, in own work, analysed the safety aspects of Intelligent Transportation Systems (ITS) and explored the opportunities for development. The author classified ITS within (10) constructed groups and presented some examples, Table 6. Moreover, the author assessed these ITS categories (based on experts' opinions) using multi-criteria analyses, KIPA-analysis and cluster analysis. The results illustrated the order of preference (ranking) of the identified ITS-groups where the following have the highest ranking and are highly recommended: in-vehicle active road safety systems; systems facilitated to comply with the Highway Code rules; forewarning systems; as well as systems supporting the rescue operations. Finally, the author investigated medium and long-term development opportunities, primary and secondary functions of ITS solutions towards efficient utilization of development potentials of ITS systems [43].

Table 6. ITS-groups and examples [43]

Notation	ITS-groups	Examples
1	Intervention systems based on the condition of drivers	Fatigue Monitoring Systems, Alcolock
2	Systems facilitate to comply with the rules of the roads	Overspeed Warning Systems, Speed Measuring and Displaying Signs, Intelligent Cameras
3	Personalized, real-time, continuous traffic behaviour monitoring and supporting systems	Fleet Management Systems, VEMOCO, Smart Phone Applications
4	Dangerous traffic situation forewarning systems	Variable Message Signs, Meteorological Systems
5	Systems supporting rescue operations	eCall System
6	Integrated electronic driving license and registration system	Smart Card Systems (e.g. Gemalto, Netherlands)
7	Traffic management systems	SITRAFFIC Scala, VEKTOR
8	Systems to create safety characteristics of road infrastructure	ROADMASTER-G, KARESZ, Hazard Maps, Road Accident Databases
9	In-vehicle active safety systems	ACC, City Safety, ESP, ASR, BSW, FCW, LDW
10	Compulsory, road safety supporting in-vehicle systems	Digital Tachograph

Jutila et al., in their work, indicated to the vital role of Cooperative intelligent transportation system (C-ITS) in improving the safety of vulnerable road users (VRUs) as well as the safety of vehicles through communications between vehicles and infrastructure. The Authors discussed the applicability of ITS-G5 (IEEE 802.11p), the main technology for vehicle-to-vehicle time-critical communications, for VRU applications. ITS-G5 is the most performant technology, allowing low latency and rather long detection range. The authors assessed and optimised the performance of ITS-G5 for time-critical safety conflict scenarios between vehicles and vulnerable road users (VRUs). They studied the range for different VRU antenna transmission levels, various non-line-of-sight (NLOS) scenarios in urban environments and line-of-sight (LOS) simulations have been tested to support C-ITS message prioritisation and scalability with different amounts of vehicles. The results showed that when the transmission medium is congested, the V2VRU communication benefits from adaptive flow prioritisation to guarantee critical C-ITS message transmissions [44].

Kirushanth and Kabaso, in their work, emphasized the vital role of using telematics for road safety and the necessity for finding the best possible ways of using telematics data for safe driving. The authors made a review with the aim of finding the use of telematics data in detecting driving behavior, road anomalies, and the effects of feedback on driving behavior. Also, the authors identified how best telematic data can be accessed, compiled and used to make the best driver feedback techniques. They discussed summary of the used techniques such as data collection devices, sensors, features, algorithms, etc. Finally, the authors found that few studies concerned with implementing algorithms on smartphones to detect real-time activities. In addition, there are more need on studies concerned with presenting effective feedback techniques [9].

Guerrero-Ibáñez et al., in their work, indicated to the vital role of sensors in the development of a broad range of Intelligent Transportation Systems (ITS) applications towards enhancing traffic safety and driver assistance. The authors presented classification of safety sensors used in a vehicle and in road. Examples of such sensors include micro-mechanical oscillators, speed sensors, cameras, radars and laser beams, inertial sensors, ultrasonic sensors, proximity sensors, night vision sensors, haptic, etc. As well as the authors presented some example of ITS safety applications such as lane keeping aid, adaptive cruise control, blind spot information, intersection collision warning, road hazard warning, driver alert control system and surround view monitoring. Furthermore, the authors discussed how sensor technology can be integrated with the transportation infrastructure to achieve a sustainable Intelligent Transportation System (ITS). Also, they discussed how user applications and ITS applications can benefit from sensor technologies deployed in ITS components. In addition, a case study scenario was presented to show how sensing technologies can be integrated with information and communication technologies to improve the transportation systems. Finally, the authors discussed the potential challenges of this integration and the possible ways for addressing these challenges and ensuring operational and cooperative ITS environment [45].

Perzyński and Lewiński, in their work, discussed the necessity for introducing new transport telematics solutions towards improving road safety. The Authors proposed a new system, as an element of the urban ITS infrastructure, based on V2V (Vehicle to Vehicle) technology. The proposed system is based on the use of location data from the satellite (GPS) and data received from another vehicle via short range radio transmission module with a range up to 1 km. This system could have wider application to inform about the upcoming privileged vehicle and reduce the number of road collisions, especially in places where there are visibility restrictions. The authors also tested the proposed system through Markov processes. Where Mathematical analysis allowed to estimate characteristic safety-related coefficients. The results showed the essential role of using dedicated or additional telematics solutions in transport [46].

Govindarajulu and Ezhumalai, in their work, indicated to the importance of Internet of Things (IoT) products towards a vision of the "Intelligent Transport System (ITS)", providing more safety and comfortable driving for road users. The authors propose an intelligent transport system using internet of things in the vehicle to prevent the road accidents and avoids the damage of the vehicle. Where they designed the required framework of intelligent transport system based on a novel cluster head selection technique for the distribution of road hazard warning (RHW) messages. This framework includes: PIC microcontroller, Power supply and Ultrasonic Sensor. Where the ultrasonic sensor is used to detect the speed breakers in the road, the people who are crossing the road and the curvature of the road. All this information is passed to the vehicle user through the PIC microcontroller towards improving the road safety and preventing accidents [47].

Lu et al., in their work, emphasized the importance of Cooperative Intelligent Transport Systems (C-ITS) in increasing road safety, traffic efficiency, energy efficiency and comfort. The authors presented the history and the state of the art of C-ITS. Where C-ITS has been developed more than one decade and are based on Information and Communication Technologies (ICT) that are combined in different ways to create standalone in-vehicle systems and cooperative systems (V2X). Also, the authors stated C-ITS services which were launched in Phase I & II of the C-ITS Platform by the European Commission. Examples of safety C-ITS services include In-vehicle speed limits including dynamic speed limits, Emergency electronic braking light, Road works warning, Weather conditions, if linked to dynamic in-vehicle speed limits, Intersection safety, Vulnerable road user protection etc., Furthermore, the authors conducted C-ITS survey based on the defined services and use-cases. The results showed the importance and the potential of the C-ITS services as well as the necessity for well-structured business models towards ensuring sustainable large-scale service implementations. In addition, the authors investigated the potential challenges and innovation actions for sustainable C-ITS deployment [48].

All above, this review has emphasized the vital role of Telematics/Intelligent Transport Systems (ITS) in providing solutions to the traffic safety problems, managing the potential risks leading to the occurrence of accidents, improving road safety and increasing road efficiency.

It is worth noting that the Information and Communications Technology (Telematics, ICT) is growing at immense rate. Where a broad range of ITS applications and technologies are being developed for preventing avoidable accidents, reducing the probability of critical accident and achieving continuous improvement in road safety performance of road users, vehicles and road environment.

However, here the following question arises: " What are the highly recommended ITS applications and technologies for managing each risk of the key risks leading to the occurrence of accidents?".

In the following section, we will answer this important question through developing a new comprehensive framework for the integrated management of road crash risks on the basis of information and communications technology (telematics, ICT).

6 The Proposed Framework

A new comprehensive framework is developed based on the content analysis of the previous related research materials. The main aim of the proposed framework is improving road safety and managing the key risks leading to the occurrence of road accidents through adopting the Information and Communications Technology (Telematics, ICT).

In this paper, the (15) key risks leading to the occurrence of road accidents have been identified and classified within three categories: Road Users-related risks (7 risks); Vehicle-related risks (2 risks); Road Environment-related risks (6 risks). The proposed framework demonstrates the potential existing and emerging intelligent transport system (ITS) applications and technologies that are highly recommended for managing each risk of the key road crash risks and improving road safety.

The structure of the proposed framework consists of three sub-frameworks:

– Road Users-related sub-framework
– Vehicles-related sub-framework
– Road Environment-related sub-framework

6.1   The Road Users-Related Sub-framework

The proposed road users-related sub-framework aims to provide more safety and comfortable environment for all road users (drivers, cyclists and pedestrians). It is clear noting that the road users are highly vulnerable to death and injuries. However, the road users are causing many problems and considered as one of the main sources of risks that leading to the occurrence of serious road accidents.

Therefore, there is an urgent need to develop a comprehensive sub-framework that states all the potential risks caused by road users and describes the potential existing and emerging ITS applications and technologies that would reduce the probability of each risk and managing it successfully.

The proposed road users-related sub-framework is built on the basis of the extensive content analysis of the related research materials to investigate the highly recommended ITS applications and technologies that would act as targeted countermeasures for managing each risk of the (7) key risks related to road users.

Figure 3 illustrates the proposed road users related sub-framework where the highly recommended ITS applications have been selected for managing (UR01 To UR03 risks) and improving the safety of road users.

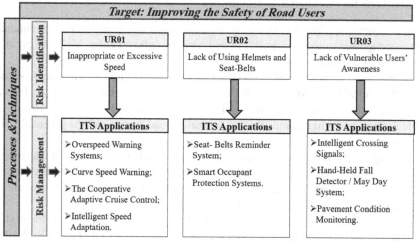

Fig. 3. The proposed road users sub-framework for managing (UR01 to UR03 risks) [own study]

Also, Fig. 4 illustrates the proposed road users related sub-framework for managing (UR04 to UR07 risks). Although (UR05, UR06 & UR07) were identified as separate risk factors, the targeted ITS applications for monitoring driver behavior and providing the required warnings are the same towards the integral management of these risks and improving the safety of road users.

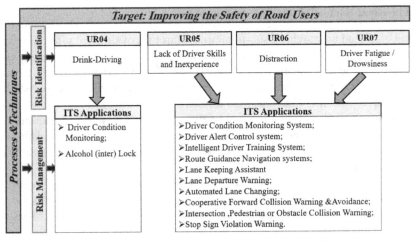

Fig. 4. The proposed road users sub-framework for managing (UR04 to UR07 risks) [own study]

6.2   The Vehicles - Related Sub-framework

Vehicular communications are considered the basis of cooperative systems that enhance communication between vehicles (V2V) and with the infrastructure (V2I) and provide the necessary information towards making vehicular transportation safer.

The proposed vehicles-related sub-framework aims to improve the safety performance of vehicles. It is worth noting that the vehicles have been the concentrate of many safety improvements including several ITS applications aiming to give assistance in vehicle control, perform dynamic driving operations and manage all the potential risks leading to the occurrence of serious accidents.

The proposed vehicles-related sub-framework is built on the basis of the extensive content analysis of the related research materials to investigate the highly recommended ITS applications and technologies that would act as targeted countermeasures for managing each risk of the (2) key risks related to vehicles.

Figure 5 illustrates the proposed vehicles related sub-framework where the highly recommended ITS applications have been selected for managing (VR01 and VR02 risks) and improving the safety of vehicles.

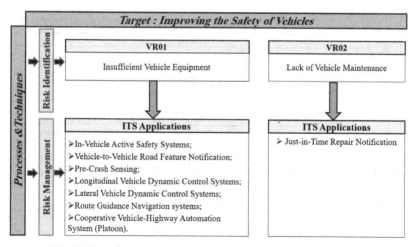

Fig. 5. The proposed vehicles-related sub-framework [own study]

6.3 The Road Environment - Related Sub-framework

The proposed road environment-related sub-framework aims to provide more safety and efficient environment for road and its infrastructure elements. Where the road environment and its infrastructure elements are more susceptible to many risks leading to the occurrence of serious road accidents.

Therefore, there is an urgent need to develop a comprehensive sub-framework that states all the potential risks related to road environment and describes the potential existing and emerging ITS applications and technologies that would reduce the probability of each risk and managing it successfully.

The proposed road environment-related sub-framework is built on the basis of the extensive content analysis of the related research materials to investigate the highly recommended ITS applications and technologies that would act as targeted countermeasures for managing each risk of the (6) key risks related to road environment and its infrastructure elements.

The proposed road environment-related sub-framework is illustrated in Figs. 6 and 7 where the highly recommended ITS applications have been selected for improving the safety of road environment and managing (ER01 to ER03 risks) and (ER04 to ER06 risks) respectively.

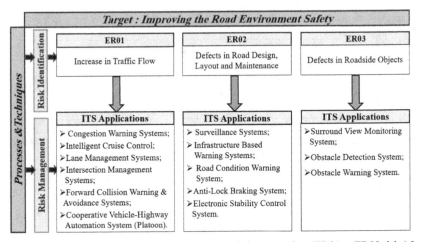

Fig. 6. The proposed road environment sub-framework for managing (ER01 to ER03 risks) [own study]

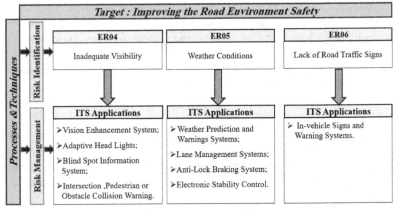

Fig. 7. The proposed road environment sub-framework for managing (ER04 to ER06 risks) [own study]

7 Conclusion

Integrated safety management is considered as one of the most important issues in road transportation planning processes. Integrated safety management depends on integrated risk management to manage all the potential road crash risks towards reducing the number of crashes, fatalities and injuries.

The integration of information and communications technology (telematics, ICT) into transportation sector is considered as one of the significant achievements for ensuring safe, reliable and efficient transportation. Where Telematics/Intelligent Transport

Systems (ITS) plays a vital role in providing solutions to the traffic safety problems, managing the potential risks leading to the occurrence of accidents, improving road safety and increasing road efficiency.

In this paper, a new comprehensive framework for the integrated management of road crash risks is developed based on an exploratory content analysis of the research materials regarding the information and communications technology (telematics, ICT).

The proposed framework includes three sub-frameworks: Road Users-related sub-framework, Vehicles-related sub-framework, and Road Environment-related sub-framework.

Firstly, all the key risks leading to the occurrence of accidents were identified within these proposed sub-frameworks: (7) seven key risks in Road Users-related sub-framework, (2) two key risks in Vehicles-related sub-framework, (6) six key risks in Road Environment-related sub-framework.

After that, the highly recommended ITS applications and technologies have been investigated for managing each risk of the key risks leading to the occurrence of accidents in these proposed sub-frameworks.

Moreover, the proposed framework, including three sub-frameworks, helps in achieving substantial improvements in road safety performance through shifting the safety concept from minimizing the consequences of crashes to utilizing ITS applications and technologies in managing all the key risks leading to the occurrence of accidents towards reducing the probability of serious accidents and preventing avoidable accidents.

In addition, there is an urgent need to promote the accelerated development in ITS equipment and further integrate all the most promising ITS applications in these sub-frameworks towards the sustainable employment of these ITS applications and continuous improvement in the safety performance of road users, vehicles and road environment.

Acknowledgement. The work has been financially supported by the Polish Ministry of Science and Higher Education. The work has been also supported by the UNESCO AGH Chair for Science, Technology and Engineering Education.

References

1. World Health Organisation: Global status report on road safety 2018: summary, Geneva, Switzerland, p. 20 (2018)
2. Haulle, E., Kisiri, M.: The impact of road accidents to the community of Iringa municipality: challenges in reducing risks. Int. Multidiscip. J. Soc. Sci. **5**(3), 253–280 (2016)
3. Dolinskaja A.W., Slobodkina A.W.: Safety Road, Collection of texts, exercises and test assignments in English for students of the specialty OWD. VolgGASU - Volgograd State University of Architecture and Civil Engineering, Volgograd, p. 37 (2011)
4. Kertis, T., Procházková, D.: Description of safety management systems in transportation. J. Environ. Prot. Saf. Educ. Manage. **5**(9), 13 (2017)
5. Jamroz, K., Smolarek, L.: Road safety management tools for country strategic level. In: 16th Road Safety on Four Continents Conference, Beijing, China, p. 12 (2013)
6. Żukowskaa, J., Mikusovab, M., Michalskia, L.: Integrated safety systems – the approach toward sustainable transport. Arch. Integr. Saf. Syst. **10**(2), 44–48 (2017)

7. Williams, B.: Intelligent Transportation Systems, Sustainable Built Environment, vol. II, p. 409. Eolss Publishers Co. Ltd., Oxford (2009)
8. Organisation for Economic Co-operation and Development (OECD): Road Safety: Impact of New Technologies, France, p. 99 (2003)
9. Kirushanth, S., Kabaso, B.: Telematics and road safety. In: 2nd International Conference on Telematics and Future Generation Networks (TAFGEN), pp. 103–108 (2018)
10. Matthews, R.B., DiNunno, J.J.: Integrated safety management: the foundation for a successful safety culture. Defence Nuclear Facilities Safety Board/Technical Report, United States, p. 44 (2005)
11. Transportation Research Board Executive Committee: National Cooperative Highway Research Program (NCHRP) Report 501: Integrated Safety Management Process, Washington, p. 156 (2003)
12. International Organization for Standardization (ISO) Guide 73:2009: Risk management vocabulary, Geneva, Switzerland (2009)
13. Hermans, E., et al.: Benchmarking road safety: lessons to learn from a data envelopment analysis. Accid. Anal. Prev. **41**(1), 174–182 (2009)
14. Jamroz, K., et al.: Trans-risk – an integrated method for risk management in transport. J. KONBiN **1**(13), 209–220 (2010)
15. World Health Organisation: Road traffic injury prevention training manual, Geneva, Switzerland, p. 126 (2006)
16. Tubis, A.: Risk assessment in road transport – strategic and business approach. J. KONBiN **45**(1), 305–324 (2018)
17. Demmel, S., Rakotonirainy, A., Gruyer, D.: Crash risk assessment with cooperative systems. In: Proceedings of 2009 Australasian Road Safety Research, Policing and Education Conference, pp. 1–7 (2009)
18. Chisholm, D., Naci, H.: Road traffic injury prevention: an assessment of risk exposure and intervention cost-effectiveness in different world regions. World Health Organisation, Department of Health Systems Financing, p. 59 (2008)
19. Hill, F., et al.: Case studies and best-practice guidelines for risk management on road networks. NZ Transport Agency Research Report 415, New Zealand, p. 118 (2010)
20. Peck, R.C., et al.: The relationship between blood alcohol concentration (BAC), age, and crash risk. J. Saf. Res. **39**, 311–319 (2008)
21. Sakhapov, R., Nikolaeva, R.: Traffic safety system management. Transp. Res. Procedia **36**, 676–681 (2018)
22. Rolison, J.J., et al.: What are the factors that contribute to road accidents? An assessment of law enforcement views, ordinary drivers' opinions, and road accident records. Accid. Anal. Prev. **115**, 11–24 (2018)
23. Cafiso, S., Di Graziano, A., Pappalardo, G.: Road safety issues for bus transport management. Procedia Soc. Behav. Sci. **48**, 2251–2261 (2012)
24. EU-OSHA – European Agency for Safety and Health at Work: Managing Risks to Drivers in Road Transport, p. 214. Publications Office of the European Union, Luxembourg (2011)
25. Noland, R.B., Oh, L.: The effect of infrastructure and demographic change on traffic-related fatalities and crashes: a case study of illinois county-level data. Accid. Anal. Prev. **36**(4), 525–532 (2004)
26. Neyens, D.M., Boyle, L.N.: The influence of driver distraction on the severity of injuries sustained by teenage drivers and their passengers. Accid. Anal. Prev. **40**, 254–259 (2007)
27. Haque, R., et al.: Identification of factors in road accidents of Pabna-Sirajgonj highway. Int. J. Eng. Manage. Res. **9**(5), 159–166 (2019)
28. Spyropoulou, I., et al.: Risk factors and intelligent transport system answers - possible opportunities and shortcomings. In: Proceedings of the 11th World Conference on Transportation Research, Berkeley, USA, p. 40 (2007)

29. Mikulski, J.: Introduction of telematics for transport. In: ELEKTRO 2012 Engineering, pp. 336-340 (2012)
30. Perallos, A., et al.: Intelligent Transport Systems Technologies and Applications, p. 468. Wiley, Chichester (2016)
31. Figueiredo, L., et al.: Towards the development of intelligent transportation systems. In: IEEE Intelligent Transportation Systems Conference Proceedings, Oakland, CA, USA (2001)
32. Nasan Agha, W., Szpytko, J.: The intelligent transport system concept for post - disaster infrastructure under reconstruction. In: Mikulski, J. (ed.) TST 2019. CCIS, vol. 1049, pp. 250–272. Springer, Cham (2019). https://doi.org/10.1007/978-3-030-27547-1_19
33. Suen, S., et al.: Application of intelligent transportation systems to enhance vehicle safety for elderly and less able travellers. In: Transportation Development Centre, Paper Number 9% S2-O-03, pp. 386-394 (1998)
34. National Highway Traffic Safety Administration: Vehicle Safety Communications Project Task 3 Final Report. Identify Intelligent Vehicle Safety Applications Enabled by DSRC, VSC Consortium: Report No. DOT HS 809 859, Washington, p. 1291 (2005)
35. Federal Highway Administration - U.S. Department of Transportation: Safety Applications of Intelligent Transportation Systems in Europe and Japan, Report No. FHWA-PL-06-001, Washington, p. 52 (2006)
36. Jarašūniene, A., Jakubauskas, G.: Improvement of road safety using passive and active intelligent vehicle safety systems. Transport 22(4), 284–289 (2007)
37. Malik, H., Rakotonirainy, A.: The need of intelligent driver training systems for road safety. In: 19th International Conference on Systems Engineering, pp. 183–188 (2008)
38. Chen, R., Jin, W.-L., Regan, A.: Broadcasting safety information in vehicular networks: issues and approaches. IEEE Netw. 24(1), 20–25 (2010)
39. Chen, X., Qu, D.: Application of intelligent transport systems to improve road traffic safety in China. In: International Conference on Multimedia Technology. Computer Science, pp. 979–982 (2011)
40. Khorasani, G., et al.: Evaluation of intelligent transport system in road safety. Int. J. Chem. Environ. Biol. Sci. (IJCEBS) 1(1), 110–118 (2013)
41. Jiménez, F., et al.: Advanced driver assistance system for road environments to improve safety and efficiency. Transp. Res. Procedia 14, 2245–2254 (2016)
42. Bagheri, M., Siekkinen, M., Nurminen, J.K.: Cloud-based pedestrian road-safety with situation-adaptive energy-efficient communication. IEEE Intell. Transp. Syst. Mag. 8(3), 45–62 (2016)
43. Pauer, G.: Development potentials and strategic objectives of intelligent transport systems improving road safety. Transp. Telecommun. J. 18(1), 15–24 (2017)
44. Jutila, M., et al.: ITS-G5 performance improvement and evaluation for vulnerable road user safety services. IET Intell. Transp. Syst. 11(3), 126–133 (2017)
45. Guerrero-Ibáñez, J., Zeadally, S., Contreras-Castillo, J.: Sensor technologies for intelligent transportation systems. Sensors 18(4), 24 (2018)
46. Perzyński, T., Lewiński, A.: The influence of new telematics solutions on the improvement the driving safety in road transport. In: Mikulski, J. (ed.) TST 2018. CCIS, vol. 897, pp. 101–114. Springer, Cham (2018). https://doi.org/10.1007/978-3-319-97955-7_7
47. Govindarajulu, P., Ezhumalai, P.: In-vehicle intelligent transport system for preventing road accidents using internet of things. Int. J. Appl. Eng. Res. 13(8), 5661–5664 (2018)
48. Lu, M., et al.: C-ITS (cooperative intelligent transport systems) deployment in Europe: challenges and key findings. In: 25th ITS World Congress, Copenhagen, Denmark, p. 10 (2018)

Telematics in Road Transport - Details in Applications

Transport Management Online Games as the Example of Knowledge Sharing Among Drivers

Anna Dewalska-Opitek[✉] and Katarzyna Bilińska–Reformat

University of Economics, 1 Maja 50, 40-287 Katowice, Poland
{anna.dewalska-opitek,katarzyna.bilinska-
reformat}@ue.katowice.pl

Abstract. The article examines the transport management games as a way to increase the knowledge of drivers. The intellectual value (information, knowledge, innovation) is created by games providers, to satisfy target markets. The global, innovative firms have been using new tools to create relations based on knowledge-sharing, because global customers are more exacting, and they take decisions more knowingly. The aims of the paper are to show the preferences of drivers related to using different transport management games and to identify the process of knowledge sharing among drivers through transport games. It has been assumed that knowledge sharing among drivers through the transport management games enables creating satisfaction of game users (drivers). This study partially has an overview character. A critical analysis of the literature reports of research companies, as well as Internet sources is used in the study. Documentary methods are applied, and the results of qualitative research based on case study research are presented. Findings of this study indicate that using games can lead to successful increasing of drivers' knowledge

Keywords: Knowledge sharing · PC transport games · Drivers as customers

1 Introduction

Knowledge sharing among drivers is the scientific problem undertaken in the proposed paper. Economic and social development is conditioned by knowledge sharing. In many cases it is difficult to assess what kind of knowledge, or at what pace it will undergo diffusion, what the result of this diffusion will be and when it will occur. The authors verify phenomena associated with knowledge sharing among drivers on the example of gaming sector.

The article examines the transport management games as a way to increase the knowledge of drivers. The intellectual value (information, knowledge, innovation) is created by games providers, to satisfy target markets. The global, innovative firms have been using new tools to create relations based on knowledge-changing, because global customers are more exacting and they take decisions more knowingly.

© Springer Nature Switzerland AG 2020
J. Mikulski (Ed.): TST 2020, CCIS 1289, pp. 217–230, 2020.
https://doi.org/10.1007/978-3-030-59270-7_16

The aims of the paper are to show the preferences of drivers related to using different transport management games, to identify the process of knowledge sharing among drivers through transport games as well as main motives enhancing the game players' inclination.

In the paper the following assumption has been made: knowledge sharing among drivers through the transport management games enables creating satisfaction of game users (drivers).

Transport management games are helpful in sharing knowledge among drivers. This study partially has an overview character. A critical analysis of the literature on the subject of knowledge sharing among transport management games drivers based on books and journals, reports of research companies, as well as Internet sources is used in the study. Documentary methods are applied, and the results of qualitative research based on case study research are presented.

Importance of the paper will concern filling in the gap associated with the lack of generalised explanations related to knowledge sharing among drivers by the use of PC games, which is very important tool for increasing drivers competences. From an academic point of view, the research examines some relevant questions in the field of knowledge sharing among drivers by the use of pc games Among them, it is showing the role of gaming in developing a drivers knowledge. From a managerial perspective, the presented study brings several contributions to marketing professionals, especially gives examples how to develop drivers knowledge by gaming. Findings of this study indicate that using games can lead to successful increasing of drivers knowledge.

2 Knowledge Sharing – Literature Review

Knowledge is interpreted as information and as assets. In the first approach, knowledge is treated as information[1]. that can be processed and applied to make reasonable economic decisions [2, 3]. In the other approach that is emphasised in the project [12, 30], knowledge constitutes economic good that can be a private property and, as a commodity, it can be the object of market turnover [19]. According to this view, every company operates on the grounds of possessed knowledge (knowledge assets) - "a company as knowledge repository". Knowledge belongs to resources that contribute to establishment and strengthening of competitive advantage. As OECD observes, knowledge is particularly difficult to calculate and assess. The sphere of knowledge storage and knowledge flow, its distribution and relationships between knowledge formation and condition of economy are still practically unexplored [26].

The notion of knowledge-based economy is broadly defined by P. Drucker, who defines it as "economic order in which knowledge, and not labour, resources or capital, is the key resource; social order in which knowledge-based social inequality is the major challenge; and the system in which the government can be perceived as the entity that has to solve social and economic problems". Similarly clear emphasis of knowledge significance together with stressing its importance for the theory of management can be

---

[1] Data make the material to be processed, for example to be codified [24]; There are no data per se, but they are constructed by perception. Data converted into information must have specific significance and are dependent on determined system of situational context [28].

found in A.K. Koźminiski's work, who directly writes that "knowledge-based economy is economy in which a lot of enterprises operate in the way that they base their competitive advantage on knowledge" [18].

Knowledge diffusion (knowledge transfer, knowledge sharing) is the key element of the process of knowledge management in an organisation/network. It consists in its dissemination within or outside the organisation. Knowledge transfer is a complex process because it concerns (1) knowledge found in human resources of an organisation as well as tools, tasks and their relationships [1], and (2) a large part of knowledge in an organisation is implicit or difficult to articulate [22]. Argote and Ingram defined knowledge transfer as "a process in which one entity (e.g. a group, a department, and a section) is influenced by experiences of others [1].

While many would look at gaming usage numbers as a measurement of wasted time, intrepid businesses are applying this trend strategically to improve business outcomes. Just as marketers and educators use gamification to create contests, generate excitement, and increase usage, knowledge managers can do the same for knowledge sharing. By integrating gaming elements like leaderboards, collaboration, reward points, or achievement badges into your knowledge sharing strategy, you increase the likelihood of not only users participating in knowledge sharing, but also enjoying the experience of doing so [31].

As noted by Trees, gamification is not a silver bullet to solve all KMS issues in a company. It is only a tool that can, but does not necessarily have to, help accomplish company's KMS goals [27].

3 Transport Management Online Games as a Emerging Trend in Gamification

Online games are video games that are either partially or primarily played through the Internet or any other computer network available. Online games are ubiquitous on modern gaming platforms, including PCs, consoles and mobile devices, and span many genres, including first-person shooters, strategy games and massively multiplayer online role-playing games [11]

Studies of online games allow noticing a variability of games, many games can be considered to be more than one genre. The most popular types of online games are [16].

1. Massively Multiplayer Online (MMO) – players play against people from all over the world.
2. Simulations – involve taking control of real-world vehicles, including trucks, tanks, ships, and aircraft; players may learn how to control these vehicles, and use simulation games to train professional skills.
3. Adventure – usually single player games, generally starts with a back story of a character, and let the player know what his/her mission is.
4. Real-Time Strategy (RTS) – require building up an inventory of items, armies, etc.; played in real time allow many player to interact at the same time.
5. Puzzle – brain games, with no action involved.
6. Action – fast-paced games, requiring excellent reflexes to fight with enemies.

7. Stealth Shooter – war games or spy-based games where a player uses stealth to defeat enemies.
8. Combat – fighting games.
9. First Person Shooters (FPS) – a player takes the role of a soldier and shoots at the enemies.
10. Sports – allow to play real-world sports like football, baseball, basketball, and more.
11. Role-Playing (RPG) – a player gets to act out the part of the main character, be the hero, etc., and makes decisions that go along with the games' story lines. Many of these games have narrative guides.
12. Educational – games may enhance the learning process and develop specific competences of players.

In 2019, the global games market generated revenues of $152.1 billion, a +9.6% year-on-year increase. A regional differentiation may be observed in terms of market value (see Fig. 1)

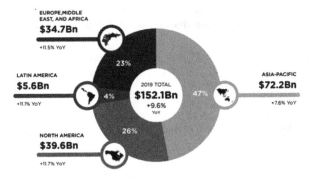

Fig. 1. Global games market value per region in 2019 [11]

The global online gaming market is expected to witness substantial growth in future. It is estimated that by 2022, the global games market will grow to $196.0 billion with a compound annual growth rate (CAGR 2018–2022) of +9.0%. Owing to the licensing freeze that heavily impacted China, Asia-Pacific is no longer the fastest-growing region. Driven by improving infrastructure and an increased appetite for games and esports, Latin America is now the fastest growing games market in the world (based on the four regions illustrated on the right), boasting a CAGR of +10.4%.

This may be attributed to increasing number of users taking up online gaming as an entertainment tool. Furthermore, increasing consumer awareness towards interactive entertainment systems is also expected to drive the market demand. Availability of high-speed internet connectivity, efficient hardware compatibility, sophisticated gaming techniques and increased consumer disposable income are some of the key factors driving the market. Technological advancements across the online gaming industry are expected to favourably impact market growth over the forecast period.

As far as transport games sector is concerned, it may be noticed, that it is much differentiated, offering the opportunity of simulation for any mean of transport, i.e.

trucks, buses and coaches, railway transport, even aviation (e.g. Euro Track Simulator 2, Ultimate Bus Driving- 3D Driver Simulator, Railway Empire, Airport Simulator, or strictly business simulation games, like Open TTD and Transport tycoon among others, allowing gamers to develop their management skill by running virtual transport companies.

Consumer engagement with games has changed dramatically over the past 10 years. Now more multi-dimensional and fragmented than ever, gamers aren't just playing games; watching esports and game video content is an equally important part of entertainment. Hardware and peripheral ownership is, in many cases, another vital component for many game enthusiasts. But there are also others, who are more interested in paying just for redemption keys. These new dimensions of gaming demand a new segmentation that captures all its unique, passionate fans [11]. The consumer segments of gamers are presented in Table 1.

Table 1. Game players' segments [11]

No	Customer segment	Market share	Description
1.	Popcorn gamers	13%	Do not play many games but love watching game video content/esports. This persona, therefore, is easier to reach through mediums like Twitch and YouTube than with in-game advertising
2.	Cloud gamers	19%	Enjoy high-quality game experiences, preferably free-to-play or discounted titles, but only spend on hardware when necessary. The imminent cloud gaming platforms from Microsoft (xCloud), Google (Stadia), or others (G2A), which do not require the consumer to buy expensive hardware, are a potential game changer for this group
3.	Basket viewers	6%	Watch game video content or esports but rarely play games. Many consumers in this persona are lapsed gamers who once enjoyed playing games, but due to work and/or family commitments no longer have time to play
4.	Ultimate gamers	13%	Live and breathe games across all spectrums of the market (playing, owning, and viewing). In addition, these consumers are likely to have an interest in computers, electronics, and gadgets, and enjoy watching movies in their spare time
5.	The conventional players	4%	Watching others play is of little interest to Conventional Players; still, they revel in staying up to date with the latest game releases and developments. Nothing will get in the way of this persona fulfilling their gaming needs, so owning the newest hardware and peripherals also a key part of their engagement

(*continued*)

Table 1. (*continued*)

No	Customer segment	Market share	Description
6.	All-round enthusiasts	9%	Avid gamers, playing for many hours each week. They enjoy a holistic gaming experience, combining playing games, viewing game content, and owning dedicated game hardware. They are typically full-time workers, so paying for the newest titles and hardware is no issue
7.	Time fillers	27%	Consumers who play games, typically on mobile, to pass the time. They rarely spend more than a few hours gaming each week and don't see gaming as a major part of their lives
8.	Hardware enthusiasts	9%	Casual about gaming and don't play many games each week. When they do play games, however, hardware is vital for their experience. They simply cannot turn a blind eye to the newest gaming gear and peripherals, so they spend big on these products. And their love of computers, electronics, and gadgets extends beyond games

The gamers use various devices to play games, like PC, consoles, mobile devices. Mobile gaming (smartphone and tablet), remained the largest segment in 2019, growing +10.2% year on year to $68.5 billion—45% of the global games market. Of this, $54.9 billion came from smartphone games (Fig. 2). It is predicted, that Mobile gaming will generate revenues of $95.4 billion in 2022 and account for almost half of the entire games market [11].

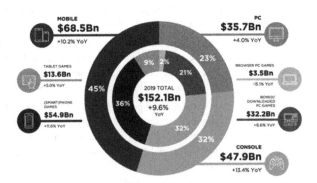

Fig. 2. Global games market per device in 2019 [11]

Another interesting trend may be noticed, i.e. platforms with innovative gaming models, a global digital marketplace offering games by the use of redemption keys. Platforms like G2A.com, do not purchase or sell any digital products themselves, they act as intermediaries by connecting the buyer to the seller. Such business model is the example of supporting knowledge sharing among gamers and game producers.

4   Incentives to Share Knowledge Among Drivers

Various theories of motivation have been proposed to explain consumer behaviour with respect to knowledge sharing and gaming, and previous research has identified a variety of motives for these behaviours. It shall be stated that knowledge sharing requires consumers investing their resources or a sacrifice on customers' part (such as time and effort) which is sometimes described by as commitment or supportive behaviour [29]. Since the behaviour is voluntary, it should be driven by specific motives. A question may therefore arise: what may be the antecedents of customer value co-creation? Addressing this question requires the consideration of related concepts and theories relevant to the subject matter.

According to Fowler (2013), theory of motivation may bring the answer to the question, with special regard to intrinsic and extrinsic motivations. The intrinsic motivation refers to doing something because it is inherently interesting, enjoyable or in accordance with customer's values or attitudes [8].

Elster (2006) pointed at altruism motivation. Studies on human altruistic behaviours have shown that extra role behaviour can make the person sharing knowledge feel happy and satisfied. Once people do a good thing, they will do more to obtain inner happiness [5]. The extrinsic motivation however, refers to doing something because it leads to a separable outcome, for instance may be appreciated and rewarded by a reference group or a company [25].

Fernandes and Remelhe (2016) proposed a model, in which they point at four specific motives as drivers for customer involvement in the co-creation process, which may be adopted to knowledge, i.e.: intrinsic motives (such as joy, curiosity, new experience), financial motives (such as expected monetary compensation or other rewards e.g. special offers, prices), knowledge motives (improvement of skills, self-development) and social motives (the sense of belonging, the sense of community, communication), which may be referred to as orientation towards Maslow's social and self-esteem needs [7].

Knowledge sharing as a voluntary activity, may also be explained by the social exchange theory in general, and the principle of reciprocity in particular. The core tenants of this framework are voluntary actions of an unspecified nature that extend beyond basic role obligations and suggest a personal commitment to others [4]. By sharing knowledge, customers expect to be appreciated and helped in future – not necessarily by the same beneficiaries, but they will become the recipients of support when needed [6].

A conceptual model of motives enhancing the online players inclination to engage in knowledge sharing among game players was proposed by D.M. Koo, S.H. Lee, H.S. Chang (2007). It is presented in Table 2.

The presented motives of concentration, enjoyment, and escape were derived from the concept of flow. This flow concept is defined by Csikszentmihalyi (1990) as the state in which people are so intensely involved in an activity that nothing else seems to matter; the experience itself is so enjoyable that people will do it even at great cost, for the sheer sake of doing it. Epistemic curiosity is the extent to which the activity of playing an online game is perceived to provide learning experiences about new things, strategies, and trends about online game-playing [20]. In this respect, Griffiths et al. (2004) demonstrate that online game players crave new information about: team-building skills, learning and

Table 2. Motives for online gamers to share knowledge with others [17]

Construct	Operationalization	Sources
Perceived enjoyment	The extent to which the activity of participating in an online game is perceived to be pleasurable, exciting, enjoyable, fun, and happy	Moon and Kim (2001); Ghani and Deshpandes (1994); Chou and Ting (2003)
Concentration	The extent to which online game playing is perceived to be a state of losing consciousness of time elapsed, self-consciousness, and being isolated from environmental cues	Ghani et al. (1991), Moon and Kim (2001), Webster et al. (1993), Koufaris (2002); Chou and Ting (2003)
Escape	The extent to which online game playing is perceived to be a relief of boredom and an escape from routine	Bloch et al. (1994); Wood et al. (2004)
Curiosity	The extent to which the activity of playing an online game is perceived to be learning experiences about new things, strategies, and trends about online game playing	Moon and Kim (2001); Griffiths et al. (2004); Bloch et al. (1994)
Social affiliation	The extent to which the activity of playing an online game is perceived to be enjoyment of talking to and socializing with other online game players	Griffiths et al. (2004); Rohm and Swaminathan (2004); Bloch et al. (1994)

thinking, upgrading their skills, developing strategies for the game, and also enhancing problem-solving skills.

Social affiliation is defined as the extent to which the activity of playing an online game provides enjoyment as a result of socializing with other online game players Social collaboration among members is important in achieving complex goals and advancing in the game [21]. According to Griffiths et al. (2004) online games have a social dimension through the formation of online communities [13].

In the context of the present study of online games, the above mentioned motives might be the salient motivating factors in playing these games. In the present study, these factors are referred to as experiential motives.

5   Research Methodology

For accomplishment of scientific goals of the paper the qualitative method of data gathering was used in the form of focus group interviews. The research was exploratory in nature, conducted in order to determine the nature of the problem, and was not intended to provide conclusive evidence, but to have a better understanding of the problem [15]. The research was conducted in February 2020 on Polish game users, nevertheless the games are available globally.

The focus group was composed of 12 participants - transport online game players. Respondents were invited to participate in the interview via snowball sampling. The selection criterion was being experienced in online game playing.

Subjects of the research were mainly men, aged 25–34, with higher educational level, with professions connected to transportation services. Table 3 illustrates the sample characteristics.

Table 3. Focus groups' sample characteristics (N = 12) [own study]

Specification	Sample (in %)
1. Gender	
a. Male	91,7
b. Female	8,3
2. Age	
a. 18–24 years	41,7
b. 25–34 years	58,3
c. 35– 44 years	–
d. 45–55 years	–
e. 56 years and more	–
3. Education	
a. Primary and junior high school	–
b. Vocational	41,7
c. Secondary	58,3
d. Higher	
4. Professional activity	
a. Connected to transportation	66,7
b. Not connected to transportation	33,3
c. Not employed at the moment	–

Research was conducted on a small and unrepresentative sample. However, the research in question allowed becoming familiar with game players' opinions and attitudes towards the process of knowledge sharing. Although the study lacks stochastic confirmation, the focus group interview provides a qualitative method of data collection and thus does not require statistical confirmation.

According to Poovey (1995) "[…] there are limits to what the rationalized knowledge epitomized by statistics can do" [23]. Qualitative research can draw the strong attention in detail, the competency to encirclement both verbal and non-verbal behaviour, to penetrate fronts, reveal denotations and find the delicacy and difficulties [10]. Focus groups have found applications in previous research concerning computer games. In 2011, Guo and Barnes investigated factors influencing purchase behaviour in virtual worlds [14]. Guo and Barnes decided to apply semi-structured interview format to allow participants comfortably express their beliefs, opinions and experiences. They also prepared a discussion guide which consisted of several sections, from introduction questions, questions exploring the goal of the study, to the summary of the interview [14].

In present study on knowledge sharing activities in transport games, the authors also employed semi-structured focus group interview and divided the discussion into four parts. In the introduction study subjects were asked general questions on how long they had played and what kind of computer games they had played. Then, players were asked about their experience in playing transportation games. Further questions were focused on individual motives for sharing knowledge with others. The discussion ended with summaries.

6 Research Findings

All of the researched subjects were familiar with game online transport game Euro Truck Simulator 2. Asked about other transport simulation games the played, respondent mentioned Simutrans, SimCity 4: Rush Hours or Bus Driver Simulator. They also declared playing other online games, nevertheless they were not the subject matter of interest in the study. All focus participants stated they had been playing online games for a long time: "for ages", "a half of my life", or even "all my life", "since I was a teenager". Respondents were asked why they had decided to join virtual worlds. They were most frequently motivated by interest in the topic of the game, but also pointed at "enjoyment from playing", "quality of the game", "feeling of reality", and "interaction with others".

After the introduction part, participants were asked about their experiences with transport online game, and Euro Truck Simulator 2. Respondents explained that: "the game gives you the chance to become a real truck driver", "you never know whether it can be something you like, so you may try it. You stay at home and you visit many places".

The interviewed game players also mentioned the reality of the game: "All the landmarks and precisely mapped territories create great experience, making you feel as if you were driving the trucks in real life". The reality is also provided to the players by having an individually created truck - the gamers may not only choose from a vide variety of car brands but also by the customization options.

Euro Truck Simulator 2 is not only about driving - the economy in game allows the players to create and grow their own transportation companies. As the respondents stated: "You start as a low-skilled, truckles lorry driver, forced to take work from established companies. Slowly (or rapidly if you go to a bank) you amass the funds to buy your first truck and rent your first yard. Then the fun really begins. Contract negotiations, truck renting, skill upgrading, driver hiring". The longer a gamer plays, the better experience gains, and it is reflected in the game: "As you work you gain valuable experience. The more distance you cover, the more experience you gain. Eventually, this earns you skill points which you can assign here to highlight your trucking skills".

The subjects of the study were also inquired about knowledge sharing. They declared using various forums to exchange information about the game, give hints and tips to the less advanced drivers or to report defects or problems with the game. Sometimes other users are much better ("quicker", "very professional") in problem solving, than the game producer. The players pointed at etrucks.pl, forum.scssoft.com or ets2world.com.

The researched subjects were also asked who can benefit from sharing knowledge. In response they pointed at other gamers, who can use knowledge or experience, and companies as well. They can game producers or game providers. One of the respondent mentioned: "It is about a business model. If you are looking for a relatively cheap game, you can choose G2A. It is a company offering game key codes to such platforms as Steam, Origin, *Uplay*, PlayStation Network and Xbox. You recommend it to other players and you share knowledge".

Another interesting thread that appeared in the discussion was game modding as a form of knowledge sharing. Mods are game modifications that allow game users enjoy better usability of the game. They are created by the players and made public legally (game producers allow other players to use them) or illegally (game producers ban this kind of practice). Asked about their attitudes toward mods, the researched subjects declared they liked them, use them, but they do not create them. The respondents are eager to use mods, because: They all declared they often use them, when they are available because "they extend the game, make it more diversified", "same of the add-ons are like a new game, so they make a huge difference", "they sometimes add new topics and plots to the old game", "sometimes the add-ons offer corrections for some game errors" or even "significantly prolong the game's life span, giving it a revival, making the game back in fashion again, more up-to-dated".

Due to mods, players may introduce real brands into the virtual worlds. The studied subjects stated that: "generally there are restaurants or other firms with fictitious names in the game, however, modifications released by game fans add real names"; "there is a lot of real life brands in the game, like Lidl, Biedronka"; "As modification, for example, I saw McDonalds restaurants, KFC, Pizza Hut. Yes, and Starbucks"; "there are also petrol stations, usually on highways"; "Orlen, Shell, BP or Lotos". Euro Truck Simulator 2 players perceive branded add-ons as elements making the game more attractive.

The studied game users were asked about their motives to share knowledge with other players. They presented a wide range of specific motives, but they can be grouped into three main categories, i.e.:

- perceived enjoyment – "it is fun", "If I figure it out how to make it – you know, how to be better, how to gain something, I am so excited, I want to share it with others",
- concentration – "when I play, I am so focused on the game, I do not realize the time that has elapsed", "I want to play fluently so to say, so I get information from others, but also share my experience with them later on",
- engagement and social affiliation – "I usually put the recommendations from other players into practice", "I joined a few game communities, we discuss various modes and options and how they enrich the players' experience", "I like that others take my opinions into considerations", "you can help yourself and others to experience greater fun by playing a game with mods",
- altruistic attitude - "I share my knowledge, because I can",
- reciprocity – "I can do something for other players. Maybe, if need any information, I can be helped as well",

– epistemic curiosity – "it is a learning experience", "you can learn something new using tools shared by others, and then when you become better, more fluent and proficient, you can help others".

Nevertheless, there were also contrary attitudes towards knowledge sharing. Some participants declared they are not much interested in sharing their knowledge, stating that "If I know how to do something, how to achieve a higher level in the game, why shall I let everyone know it? I had to figure it out by myself, others can too. Otherwise there is no fun" and "It is like in real life – you run your business, you never tell others what they can do to be as good as you are". Asked about reasons for not willing to share their knowledge, they declared "I was never really appreciated for helping others or telling them what to do". This statement allows noticing that there are not only incentives, but also barriers to knowledge sharing activities among online game players.

7   Conclusion

Literature studies, as well as results of conducted research, allow noticing that knowledge sharing is a process in which one entity (a person, a group of people, game players for example) is influenced by experiences of others. Knowledge sharing activity was referred to game market, which has been a constantly growing market in terms of value and number of customers for decades. The transport simulation games were taken as an research area, as they play an important role in gaming industry, allowing not only enjoy a game but also develop gamers' knowledge and skills, as well as create a successful knowledge sharing environment.

The major objectives of this study were to identify the process of knowledge sharing among online truck drivers through transport games as well as main motives enhancing the game players' inclination. Several conclusions can be drawn. First, online game players are eager to share their knowledge, and there are various motives. The main motives for knowledge sharing are: perceived enjoyment, the opportunity to concentrate on a game that is fun to play, and also engagement and social affiliation and epistemic curiosity. The motives that resulted from the study, were consistent with motives identified by Koo et al. (2007), but may also be referred to other motivational theories: altruism and reciprocity [4, 5].

Second, there are not only incentives, but barriers to share knowledge among game players. They were not a subject matter of the study, nevertheless, they are worth noticing.

On a managerial level, the current study provides useful information, how to create an experience which motivates participants to engage in knowledge sharing among members of virtual communities. By enhancing the motivators previously mentioned, firms can stimulate consumers' engagement. Also brand placement may become an important tool of communication with online communities [7].

Another important issue regarding the problem of knowledge sharing among drivers by the use of computer games is connected with the business model of games providers. Giving drivers access to transport computer games makes also games providers more attractive self for drivers and transport companies and can be important source of their competitive advantage. Introducing PC transport games by the games providers enhances close cooperation between them and transport companies as well as gives opportunity to share knowledge among drivers. That be the trigger for development of innovative programs regarding making drivers skills better.

The study findings are constrained by several limitations. A lack of quantitative evaluation prevents generalisability beyond theory. Further, the study did not use multiple samples of consumers such as those engaged and not engaged in the full range of co-creation activities. The new insights offered by this study suggest that empirical work is needed to extend our understanding of the consumer's motivation to participate (or not) in knowledge sharing. It indicates the possible future research areas.

References

1. Argote, L., Ingram, P.: Knowledge transfer: a basis for competitive advantage in firms. Organ. Behav. Hum. Decis. Process. **82**, 150–169 (2000)
2. Beckman, T.A: Methodology for knowledge management. In: International Association of Science and Technology for Development AI and Soft Computing Conference, Banff, Canada (1997)
3. Brdulak, J.J.: Knowledge management and the process of product innovation. Establishment of product competitive advantage. SGH [Warsaw School of Economics], Warsaw, p. 13 (2005)
4. Blau, P.M.: Exchange and Power in Social Life, pp. 215–224. Wiley, New York (1964)
5. Elster, J.: Altruistic behaviour and altruistic motivations. In: Kolm, S.C., Ythier, J.M. (eds.) Handbook of the Economics of Giving, Altruism and Reciprocity, pp. 57–63. Elsevier, Amsterdam (2006)
6. Falk, A., Fischbacher, U.: A theory of reciprocity. Games Econ. Behav. **54**, 293–315 (2006)
7. Fernandes, T., Remelhe, P.: How to engage customers in co-creation: customers motivation for collaborative innovations. J. Strateg. Manag. **24**(3–4), 311–326 (2016)
8. Fowler, J.G.: Customer citizenship behaviour: an expanded theoretical understanding. Int. J. Bus. Soc. Sci. **4**(5), 1–8 (2013)
9. G2A now provides electronics, hoping to become a "one-stop shop" for gaming. PCGamesN. Accessed 10 Mar 2020
10. Gephardt, R.: What is qualitative research and why is it important? Acad. Manag. J. **7**, 454–462 (2004)
11. Global Game Market Report (2019)
12. Grayson Jr., C.J., O'Dell, C.S.: Mining your hidden resources. Across the Board **35**, 23–28 (1998)
13. Griffiths, M.D., Davies, M.N.O., Chappell, D.: Online computer gaming: a comparison of adolescent and adult gamers. J. Adolesc. **27**, 87–96 (2004)
14. Guo, Y., Barnes, S.: Purchase behaviour in virtual words: an empirical investigation in Second Life. Inf. Manage. **48**(7), 303–312 (2011)
15. Henson, R.K., Roberts, J.K.: Use of exploratory factor analysis in published research common errors and some comment on improved practice. Educ. Psychol. Measur. **66**(3), 393–416 (2006)
16. Hurst, J.: Types of computer games every gamer should know about, February 2015. https://thoughtcatalog.com/jane-hurst/2015/02/12-types-of-computer-games-every-gamer-should-know-about/. Accessed 12 Mar 2020
17. Koo, D.M., Lee, S.H., Chang, H.S.: Experimental motives for playing online game. J. Convergence Inf. Technol. **2**, 37–48 (2007)

18. Koźmiński, A.K.: Jak zbudować gospodarkę opartą na wiedzy? Żelazny, R., Gospodarka oparta na wiedzy w Polsce – diagnoza stanu według Knowledge Assessment Methodology 2006. [in:] Okoń-Horodyńska, E.: Unia Europejska w kontekście strategii lizbońskiej oraz gospodarki i społeczeństwa wiedzy w Polsce, Warsaw, p. 247 (2006)
19. Łobesko, S.: Systemy Informacyjne w Zarządzaniu Wiedzą i Innowacją w Przedsiębiorstwie. SGH, Warsaw, p. 33 (2004)
20. Moon, J.W., Kim, Y.G.: Extending the TAM for a world-wide-web context. Inf. Manage. **38**(4), 217–230 (2001)
21. Ng, B.D., Wiemer-Hastings, P.: Addiction to the internet and online gaming. Cyberpsychol. Behav. **8**(2), 110–113 (2005)
22. Nonaka, I., Takeuchi, H.: The Knowledge-Creating Company. Oxford University Press, New York (1995)
23. Poovey, M.: Making a Social Body. The University of Chicago Press, Chicago (1995)
24. Rehauser, J., Krecmar, H.: Wissensmanagement im Unternehment, pp.1–40. de Gruyter, Berlin (1996)
25. Ryan, R.M., Deci, E.L.: Self-determination theory and the facilitation of intrinsic motivation, social development, and well-being. Am. Psychol. **55**(1), 68–78 (2000)
26. The Knowledge-Based Economy, p. 7. OECD, Paris (1996). www.oecd.org. Accessed 12 Mar 2020
27. Trees, L.: Gamification in Knowledge Management. APQC Overview. http://www.apqc.org/knowledge-base/documents/gamification-knowledge-management-apqc-overview Gamification in knowledge management systems (2013). https://www.researchgate.net/publication/283003527_Gamification_in_knowledge_management_systems. Accessed 13 Apr 2020
28. Willke, H.: Systemisches Wissensmanagement. Lucius & Lucius, Stuttgart (1998)
29. Tung, V.W.S., Chen, P.J., Schuckert, M.: Managing customer citizenship behaviour: the moderating roles of employee responsiveness and organizational reassurance. Tour. Manage. **59**, 23–35 (2017)
30. Zack, M.H.: Developing a knowledge strategy. Calif. Manage. Rev. **41**, 125–145 (1999)
31. https://bloomfire.com/blog/gamification-improves-knowledge-sharing/. Accessed 12 Mar 2020

Customers' Value Co-creation in Automotive Sector – the Case Studies of BMW Co-creation Lab and Volkswagen's People's Car Project in China

Anna Dewalska-Opitek[✉]

University of Economics, 1 Maja 50, Katowice, Poland
a.dewalska-opitek@ue.katowice.pl

Abstract. The paper analyses the concept of value co-creation, which has become an emerging market trend in the automotive industry. It contributes the existing studies on value co-creation by analysing the impact of customer engagement in collaborative innovation process on enterprises. The main purposes of the paper are presenting the co-creation concept and identifying the co-creation incentives from both customers' and companies' perspective based on literature review. The theoretical deliberation is followed by empirical cognition based on case studies examples of BMW Group Co-Creation Lab and Volkswagen's People's Car Project in China.

Keywords: Customers' value co-creation · Automotive sector

1 Introduction

Contemporary market is a dynamic and an increasingly complex environment, where traditional roles of customers and producers are partly reversed and complemented. Customers are no longer a "passive audience", they become "active co-creators" [26]. Customers engage in several behaviours that strengthen their relationship with the product or company, but also with other customers, which go beyond traditional customer loyalty measures [14]. This particular behaviour is called customer value co-creation [5] and is a subject matter of interest presented in the paper.

A focus was put on automotive industry. Car producing firms must contend with more complex projects, intertwined consumer markets, greater competition and the trend towards instant, and constant, customer feedback. Traditional approaches to business – solo, private innovation and simple, linear supply chains – cannot adequately address these challenges. So automotive businesses are turning to collaboration, bringing new partners into their ecosystems that all benefit from working collectively towards a common goal. This collaborative creation is a dynamic way not only to successfully navigate the new business conditions, but also to solve society's biggest challenges in terms of automotive solutions.

© Springer Nature Switzerland AG 2020
J. Mikulski (Ed.): TST 2020, CCIS 1289, pp. 231–245, 2020.
https://doi.org/10.1007/978-3-030-59270-7_17

The main purposes of the paper are presenting the co-creation concept and identifying the co-creation incentives from both customers' and companies' perspective based on literature review. The theoretical deliberation is followed by empirical cognition based on case studies examples of BMW Group Co-Creation Lab and Volkswagen's People's Car Project in China.

2   Customers' Value Co-creation as a Form Collaborative Innovation

The term "customer value co-creation" was first used by Kambil, Ginsberg and Bloch (1996) to emphasize the role of customers in business strategy. It was than popularised and disseminated by Prahalad and Ramaswamy (2004), who conceptualised value co-creation as the "co-creation of personalised experiences with the customers". Instead of focusing only on the offering, organisations should emphasise on experiences at the multiple points of exchange as the basis of value co-creation [1].

Today, various perspectives have been considered by authors to study value co-creation, i.e.: management perspective, marketing perspective, service logic and service dominant logic, design logic, or innovation and new product development perspective [1]. Different perspectives are represented by numerous definitions of value co-creation. Chosen definitions synthesised from various authors are presented in Table 1.

Table 1. Definitions of vale co-creation [1, 9]

Authors	Value co-creation definition
1	2
Fernades & Remelhe (2016)	"[…] is considered as an important manifestation of customer engagement behaviour toward a brand or a firm, resulting from motivational drivers"
Roser et al. (2013)	"[…] an interactive, creative and social process between stakeholders that is initiated by the firm at different stages of the value creation process"
Ind & Coates (2013)	"[…] as a process that provides an opportunity for on-going interaction, where the organization is willing to share its world with external stakeholders and can generate in return the insight that can be derived from their engagement"
Gronroos (2012)	"[…] is a joint collaborative activity by parties involved in direct interactions, aiming to contribute to the value that emerges for one or both parties"
Xie et al. (2008)	"[…]is an activity undertaken by the consumer that result in the production of products they eventually consume and that become their consumption experiences"
Zwick et al. (2008)	"[…] as a set of organizational strategies and discursive procedures aimed at reconfiguring social relations of production, works through the freedom of the consumer subject with the objective of encouraging and capturing the know-how of this creative common"
Wikstrom (1996)	"[…] is company-consumer interaction (social exchange) and adaptation, for the purpose of attaining added value"

Consumer value co-creation may be therefore concluded as collaborative work between a consumer and a firm in an innovation process, whereby the consumer and supplier engage (to different degrees) in the activity of co-ideation, co-design, co-development and co-creation of new products or services [26].

According to Roberts et al. (2013), value co-creation is a specific form of user contribution whereby 'active' (as opposed to "passive") consumers participate with the firm and voluntarily contribute input (be that knowledge, informed opinions, experience or resources) into an innovation process, whose outcome is better and more market-focused innovation [29].

Literature studies allow to indicate a noticeable difference between two similar terms, that nonetheless are not synonymous. These are: co-creation and co-production. According to Payne et al. (2008) "co-creation" presents the service-dominant (S-D) logic, according to which acting together, supplier and customer have the opportunity to create value. The term "co-production" is tainted with connotations of goods-dominant (G-D) logic, where there is a transfer of some activities to customers (for example IKEA involving customers in transportation and assembly of flat pack furniture) [25].

Tommasetti et al. (2017) in their value co-creation conceptual framework present that co-production is a constituent of a value co-creation behaviour, together with cerebral activities, cooperation, information research and collation, co-learning and connection [34]. While co-production refers to customers' participation in the realisation of value proposition, the co-creation is defined as the customers' creation of value-in-use. It means that value for the user is created or emerges during usage, which is a process of which the customer as user is in charge [13]. As Vargo and Akaka (2009) observe, there can be no value without the customer incorporating the firm offering into his or her life [36]. Hence, value is created by the user, and moreover, also experienced by the user, who also uniquely determines what value is created [5, 37].

Agrawal and Rahman (2015) present an opinion, that customers may play even more differentiated roles in the value co-creation process, which they call "customer-mix in value co-creation" [1] (see Fig. 1).

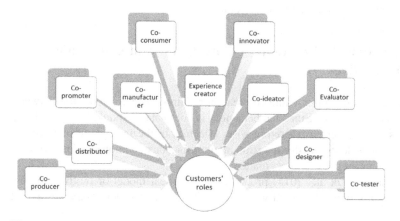

Fig. 1. The classification of customers' roles in the value co-creation [own study]

Customers today are demanding a more dominant role in customisation of the firm's offerings. They are actively helping companies to improve their value propositions and serve their customers better.

Co-production is deemed to be the earliest form of co-creation. It may be defined as customer participation in production and the delivery of services within the boundaries defined by the organisation. Customers as co-producers are enhancing productivity, reducing costs, improving quality and acting as partial employees. They also get involved in the distribution process, which may help companies by relieving them of extra responsibilities and help transfer benefits to customers in the form of reduced prices. It may also be noticed that customers are becoming more vocal in propagating the experiences of goods and services they consumed. Word of mouth of customers may strongly influence the behaviour of other customers. Those, who are strongly engage in the promotion process are called evangelists. Customers create content, such as news, ideas, blogs and are willing to share the content amongst the masses, with firms acting as facilitators. Customers then play they extra roles as co-manufacturers. A natural consequence is the co-consumption. It is defined as experience sharing amongst customers and other companies' stakeholders, and can help many companies, brands, customers and online communities in selecting the best offer in the market. Customers not only share but co-create experience by developing customising companies' offerings. By presenting their opinions and feedback, they are called innovators, and by generating ideas for companies they co-ideators. These roles are reflected in the concepts of "collective intelligence" [6], "wisdom of crowds" [33] and "crowdsourcing innovation" [15], pointing to the fact, that customers may bring large scale innovations and creativity to companies. Customers as co-designers help to customize products to better fit a standard and meet the needs of the target market. Once a good or a service is created, customers may become co-evaluators and co-testers before products are launched in the market [1].

The classification of customers' roles presents eleven most popular and common roles. Although they are all distinct aspects, they are interrelated and all play an important role for both companies and their customers.

3   Incentives to Co-create – Customers' and Companies' Perspectives

It should be noticed that value co-creation requires close collaboration between companies and customers. Since the behaviour is voluntary, it should be driven by specific motives. A question may therefore arise: what may be the antecedents of customer value co-creation? Addressing this question requires the consideration of related concepts and theories relevant to the subject matter.

Garcia Haro et al. (2014) proposed a theoretical model of motives to co-create, indicating not only situational variables of the consumers, but companies as well (see Fig. 2).

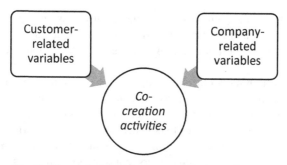

Fig. 2. Theoretical model of co-creation incentives [10]

Literature studies allow identifying various theories explaining customer-related variables. Fernandes and Remelhe (2016) pointed at four specific motives as drivers for customer involvement in the co-creation process, i.e.: intrinsic motives (such as joy, curiosity, escapism, passion or desire for better product, as well as personal development capability and skills development), financial motives (such as expected monetary compensation or other rewards e.g. special offers, prices), knowledge motives (improvement of skills, self-development) and social motives (the sense of belonging, the sense of community, communication, are helping others, building ties to the community or reciprocity), which may be referred to as orientation towards Maslow's social and self-esteem needs [9].

Elster (2006) pointed at altruism motivation. Studies on human altruistic behaviours have shown that extra role behaviour can make the value co-creator feel happy and satisfied. Once people do a good thing, they will do more to obtain inner happiness [7].

Value co-creation as a voluntary activity, may also be explained by the social exchange theory in general, and the principle of reciprocity in particular. The core tenants of this framework are voluntary actions of an unspecified nature that extend beyond basic role obligations and suggest a personal commitment to others [3, 24]. By value co-creation, customers expect to be appreciated and helped in future – not necessarily by the same beneficiaries, but they will become the recipients of support when needed [8].

As far as company-related variables are concerned, there are four main elements influencing the co-creation tendency of customers, i.e.:

- technology (ICT),
- social media,
- activity sector,
- corporate culture.

Information and communication technologies (ICT) now represent one of the most important elements for product innovation, enabling customers to be more active, better informed, more aware at a global level, and more willing to use virtual environments to interact with companies to obtain new products and services [31]. In addition, ICT allows companies to communicate with different customers quickly and smoothly, by eliminating the barriers of space and time, such that it supports an effective transfer of knowledge [12]. When the company establishes connections with customers, ICT can stimulate collaboration and the transfer and use of knowledge among members [32], which makes the construction of virtual working groups throughout the world possible [28].

The open innovation model has been supported by the emergence of social media. Currently, many social media applications (e.g., blogs, open collaborative projects, social networking sites, content communities, virtual worlds, games) enable individual consumers, communities, and businesses to connect and exchange information [19]. These social media also enable companies to interact in real time and more frequently with users, which accordingly increases customers' participation [30]. This provision should lead to a dynamic environment, marked by creative and social partnerships between the company and its customers in a new product development context [18].

Quick and unpredictable changes in the environment make innovation a key element for achieving competitiveness and success in markets [21]. Organizations rely on innovations to adapt to changes in their internal and external environments, though the external factors mean that outcomes of these innovation processes differ for each organization, depending on its industry sector [35]. According to Hitachi Social Innovations Report "Co-creating the future" (2018), automotive sector is the dominant one in implementing a collaborative approach to innovation [4].

To facilitate external collaborations, an organization needs a culture of internal collaboration [21] and innovation [11, 22], because such a culture determines if the organization can support the development of innovations, exceed customers' expectations, and gain a competitive advantage.

The companies' inclination to co-create may be stronger when they identify to what extend they can benefit from customers' engagement in innovation. Kennedy and Guzman (2016) have identified several benefits for companies engaging customers in value co-creation process [20]. The main advantages are:

– **Increased return on investment**

Sharing power and co-creating with consumers helps firms to grow sales and profit in the long term. Research participants stated that engaging with consumers enabled them to stay relevant, increase sales and insights, as well as reducing churn, and gaining a higher shareholder value.

– **Improved customer insight**

Engaging with consumers helps firms to better understand their consumer needs and validate learnings from formal market research. Managers have also found that keeping lines of communication open with consumers impacted sales, and that this sort of informal research could help to drive concept development.

– **Expanded intellectual resources**

Engaging with consumers increases the intellectual property of a firm and aids its competitive position in the marketplace. Marketers who participated in the research commented that co-creation enables firms to make sure that they are both providing the right content and evolving the product to the market's needs.

– Alignment with mission statement

An organizational culture built around the importance of the consumer is a prime factor in co-creation with consumers. The researchers note that by embracing co-creation, many firms are simply delivering against a key part of their mission statement to work closely with customers or put the customer first.

– Better quality of service

Co-creation enables firms to enhance the service that they provide. For many firms, personal interaction with customers is a core part of the services they provide, and therefore essential to providing a better brand experience.

– Stronger brand

Co-creation helps to enable the alignment of brand perception and brand identity, increasing the value of the brand. Research participants noted that engaging with consumers enables brands to create better, more relevant content, which builds equity and improves ROI. One participant commented that consumers are an extension of the brand – without them, a brand loses relevance and market position.

– Increased brand loyalty

The more communication a consumer has with a brand, the more loyal they will be to that brand. Marketers who participated in the study noted that engagement keeps brands fresh, connected, and relevant. In order to create long-term relationships with customers, engagement is simply key.

– Greater brand awareness

Co-creation leads to increased brand awareness, especially when a brand is attempting to change their image or move into new markets. Research participants noted that brands have an advantage if they are top of mind for consumers, helping them to feel confident in the choices they make.

– Improved differentiation

Co-creation is a way that brands can differentiate themselves from competitors. Marketing managers noted that the closer relationship with consumers that is enabled by co-creation helps brands to garner a competitive position.

– **Enhanced brand experience**

Brand experience is enhanced by co-creation. Research participants noted that co-creation with consumers leads to better experiences, in turn leading to greater customer satisfaction, more referrals and word-of-mouth, new customer acquisition and repeat business.

It is argued that customer value co-creation is solely a positive process. There are some limitations, that must be taken into consideration regardless the above-mentioned positive impact. The main internal barriers to co-creation are [4]:

- Concerns over intellectual property
- Concerns over privacy and data security.
- A culture that does not encourage sharing and collaboration around ideas.

The barriers to co-create share one common theme, i.e. lack of mutual trust between companies and customers. According to Hitachi Report, there are other potential limitations, like time, effort and money involved in launching co-creation projects as the biggest external barriers to co-create, despite the potential pay-off that may come through embracing co-creation.

4 Automotive Sector Companies' Inclination to Co-create

Today, products and services must be tailored to suit individual needs. Innovation can no longer happen in hermetically sealed environments: it must be pursued hand in hand with key stakeholders - customers. For most, this requires a significant shift of mindset. Companies must learn to be more open, to share ideas at an early stage, to adopt the right technologies that can help the process, and to build a culture that encourages collaboration.

For nearly two decades, the automotive sector has exploited the potential of co-creation to generate innovation both in its product ranges and its engagement with consumers and stakeholders. The sector's successful track record is reflected in our survey's findings, which show that over four-fifths of automotive firms (83%) agree that co-creation has transformed their approach to innovation, compared with 57% for all industries. The most significant benefit has been how car makers now collaborate with consumers to source and test designs and explore emerging-market opportunities.

It may be noticed, that automotive is the top sector in implementing a collaborative approach to innovation (See Fig. 3). This is perhaps unsurprising given that the cost of designing and manufacturing a new vehicle is so prohibitive, which puts the onus on manufacturers to give their products the best possible chance when they're released onto the market.

The automotive sector is in the middle of a radical shift, as several transformative factors converge. Connected cars are becoming increasingly commonplace, and a driverless future for the automobile approaches.

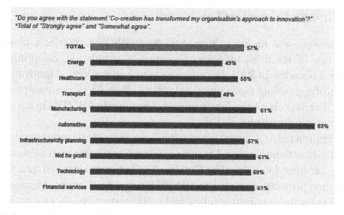

Fig. 3. Opinions of surveyed 554 senior executives across a range of sectors in Europe [4]

The biggest fear for carmakers is that the public will stop viewing cars as a desirable product and begin to see them as a service. It's this desire to continue creating relevant and attractive products that is spurring the automotive sector towards co-creation. Crucially, automotive companies are no longer relying on simplistic market research or focus groups when testing the potential of new products. Instead, automotive companies are sourcing consumer feedback at the design stage to ensure that their products meet or exceed market expectation, while gaining a competitive edge over rivals. This plugs consumers into the design process from inception through to potential completion, giving them a very real and vested interest in the finished product. The auto sector aims to boost trust, transparency and innovation efficiency and it has subsequently led to closer relationships with customers.

While more work still needs to be done within the auto sector – perhaps surprisingly, only 67% of surveyed automotive firms believe they have the right culture for co-creation – the success of its existing collaborative projects offer proof that co-creation can benefit all [4].

5 Practical Examples of Collaborative Innovativeness of Automotive Companies - Case Studies of BMW, Volkswagen and Toyota

While automotive companies develop products and technologies to meet the market demand, co-creation method can provide outlets to engage customers (as well as other stakeholders) and use their innovativeness, create in-depth customer experience and gain a competitive advantage. How can automotive companies integrate customers within co-creation process that results in enhanced innovativeness? Examples of BMW and Volkswagen prove that collaborative innovativeness may bring mutual benefits: for customers and companies.

5.1 BMW Group's Co-creation Lab

German automobile and motorcycle manufacturer BMW Group is a pioneer in co-creation and one of the most innovative companies worldwide, engaging customers to innovate for 2 decades. In 2001 the company launched the Virtual Innovation Agency, an online platform enabling consumers and other stakeholders to submit their ideas to the company. The success of the firm's initiative encouraged BMW Group to introduce the BMW Group Co-Creation Lab [2].

The Co-Creation Lab is a virtual meeting place for individuals interested in car related topics, eager to share their ideas and opinions on tomorrow's automotive world with one of the leading car manufacturers. The Co-Creation Lab was launched as a platform for future co-creation projects soon after the BMW Group Idea Contest. Members can then share their ideas for the automotive future and collaborate with other users and the team of the BMW Group [16].

The BMW Group organized an Idea Contest "Tomorrow's Urban Mobility Services". The company was seeking new ideas for mobility services in urban areas. In total 497 customers submitted around 300 innovative ideas which were evaluated and commented by over 1000 experts worldwide. The final decision about the winning projects was made by the jury, representing the Strategy and Innovative Mobility Services and Customer Foresight of BMW Group. There were 3 innovative ideas wining the contest. The first innovative concept was PMUP ("Pick me up please"). It is a mobility-system for pedestrians. So called "trip cards" installed in cell phones as well as in car computers enable the communication between driver and pedestrian. The second and third winning ideas were: the invention of a "park-sharing-programme" and a concept that receives available parking spaces via GPS signals.

The lab also hosts innovation competitions such as the BMW Group Interior Design Contest that challenged the crowd to come up with innovative ideas to personalise the interior of cars. In framing and scoping the open innovation contest BMW asked participants to think of how their car could fit their individual needs in every imaginable situation such as business trips, school runs and traffic jams. There were three categories of ideas:

- Function and convenience – individualized features and services that make handling easier and/or provide extra comfort;
- Style and design – focusing on style aesthetics to give the interior an individual touch;
- Experience – participants were asked to consider the car as part of the home to come up with ideas for elements that may be missing from the vehicle's interior.

The contest winners were chosen by a panel of experts drawn from BMW and different fields of automotive transportation. The overall winning idea was the 'Colour Matching Camera' - a camera is mounted in the car's interior that detects the colours of the clothes the occupant/s is/are wearing and then hidden LED lighting will adjust lighting to match the colour of those outfits. In second place was 'BMW Fluid'. Here the colour of the interior changes according to the emotions of the people travelling in the car. Fragrance and ambient lighting would change accordingly, offering people a new experience every time they drive. And in third place was 'Customizable Clip-On Interior Panels'. The interior is enhanced by adding fabricated/moulded panels with colours and graphics that suit the owner's tastes. The panels can be for the dashboard, front and rear speaker sections, centre console and kick panel amongst other interior locations. There were no cash prizes on offer, but the winners were invited to BMW in Munich, Germany to present their idea to developers at the company's Research and Innovation Centre.

BMW's adoption of open innovation provides the company with numerous benefits. These include forming long-term and deeper relationships with users; access to a wider and more diverse pool of ideas, observations and perspectives (a very cost-effective form of market research); and the ability to leverage external brain power to create more user-centric products and services [23].

5.2 Volkswagen's People's Car Project in China

Volkswagen is one of the first international automobile manufacturers to have noticed the market potential of China. Chinese automotive market has been the world's fastest growing market for cars. Despite the decline in 2018, China remains the growth market for the automotive industry. A look at the country's passenger-car density makes this clear. Only around 134 of every 1,000 inhabitants own a car. That figure was 864 for the US, and 553 for Germany in 2017. At the same time, China is becoming a pioneer in developing new drivetrain technologies as well as autonomous driving and digital mobility solutions. China has made a crucial contribution to the world's leading mobility technologies and products. Volkswagen is therefore determined to develop technologies and mobility strategies with its partners in the Chinese automotive sector and in the tech industry – "in China, for China and for global markets" [27].

Today Volkswagen faces increased competition. To tackle this challenge, they decided to change their business model. Instead of building cars for the people, the company began building cars with the people. Volkswagen introduced a project called: 'The People's Car Project' (PCP), a long-term co-creation platform that re-invents how cars are ideated, designed, and built. Volkswagen provided customers with tools to create and share car ideas. An online system allowed the fans to vote for the most original ones.

As the result of the People's Car Project, there were 119,000 ideas submitted from the 33 million visits to the project's site, during 11 months. The best ideas were picked and made into concepts of future automotive solutions.

The first concept was the PCP Music car, covered in OLEDs that changed colours with the music playing inside the car. It's "a means of self-expression and a fashion statement for young drivers," according to the Project (Fig. 4).

Fig. 4. The PCP Music car [17]

Another concept chosen by Volkswagen was the Hover Car, which hovers on an electromagnetic road network. Although the car and the electromagnetic network were both imaginary, but the idea of a surface-skimming hover car was innovative (Fig. 5).

Fig. 5. The Hover Car [38]

The third concept was the Smart Key, a smart-key that features a high-res touch screen that displays fuel level, climate conditions, and the car's security status, as well as the real-time monitoring of the driver's car via satellite imagery.

Though the PCP was originally planned to run just one year, the high level of quality submissions and popular demand have prompted Volkswagen to extend it indefinitely. New ideas in the areas of design, personalization, connectivity, and environmental impact were explored. Volkswagen designers together with millions of fans in China helped us to upgrade current cars and shape future ones. "We are no longer just building cars for, but also with customers and at the same time initiating a national dialog which gives us a deep insight into the design preferences, needs and requirements of Chinese customers," said Volkswagen Director of Marketing Luca de Meo. In a long-term context the findings of the 'People's Car Project' will influence Volkswagen's product strategy. The design of Volkswagen models will, however, be a combination of customers' opinions and brand tradition. Due to the project, Volkswagen rose to the number 1 car brand on Chinese social media in 10 weeks.

6 Conclusion

It may be noticed that customers' co-creation has been developing as a new paradigm in the management literature, allowing companies and customers to create value through interaction. This article has studied value co-creation activities as an important business strategy, necessary to support innovation processes and the achievement of competitive advantages in the automotive sector.

The co-creation process has transformed the traditional functions of a company, in which the producer and the consumer had different roles. Today, the consumer also serves as a co-producer, co-distributor, co-promoter, co-manufacturer, co-innovator, co-ideator, co-designer and co-tester. Both customers and companies combine their efforts to develop new products and services together.

Making customers involved in the car designing and problem solving process allow automotive companies to achieve significant benefits: financial (by reducing costs of innovations), technological (by having access to innovative ideas and solutions), and marketing (by building stronger market relationships, increasing brand loyalty, and by gaining competitive advantages).

The studied examples of BMW Group Co-Creation lab and Volkswagen's People's Car Project showed clearly the advantages of engaging customers in the co-creation process. A general notice may be presented, that co-creation is emerging as a mainstream method of collaboration and idea generation in the automotive industry.

The paper contributes to the existing studies on customer value co-creation by presenting the topic from companies' perspective, identifying the drivers for value co-creation enhancing both customers and producers. Also, some limitations are worth addressing. Firstly, only two case studies - the most spectacular – were chosen and presented in the paper. Secondly, they both focused on the advantages of the customer engagement in co-creation process. Although, they seem predominant over potential disadvantages, nevertheless, they should be taken into consideration. This leaves place for a future study.

References

1. Agrawal, A.K., Rahman, Z.: Roles and resource contributions of customers in value co-creation. Int. Strat. Manag. Rev. **3**, 144–160 (2015)
2. Augsdörfer, P., et al.: Discontinous innovation. Ser. Technol. Manag. **22**, 192–199 (2013)
3. Blau, P.M.: Exchange and power in social life, pp. 215–224. John Wiley, New York (1964)
4. Co-creating the Future, Hitachi Social Innovation Report 2018, [electronic source]. https://social-innovation.hitachi/en-eu/about/whitepaper. Accessed 6–8 Mar 2020
5. Dewalska-Opitek, A., Mitręga, M.: Appreciate me and I will be your good soldier. Expl. Antecedents Consum. Citizen. Eng. Manag. Prod. Serv. **11**(3), 48–59 (2019)
6. Ebner, W., Leimeister, J.M., Kromar, H.: Community engineering for innovations: the ideas competition as a method to nurture a virtual community for innovations. R&D Manag. **39**(4), 342–356 (2009)

7. Elster, J.: Altruistic behaviour and altruistic motivations. In: Handbook on the Economics of Giving, Reciprocity and Altruism, pp. 57–63. Elsevier

8. Falk, A., Fischbacher, U.: A theory of reciprocity, games and economic. Behaviour **54**, 293–315 (2006)

9. Fernandes, T., Remelhe, P.: How to engage customers in co-creation: customers motivation for collaborative innovations. J. Strat. Manag. **24**(3–4), 311–326 (2016)

10. Garcia Haro, M.A., Martinez Ruiz, M.P., Martinez Cañas, R.: The effects of value co-creation process on the consumemer and the company. Expert J. Mark. **2**, 68–81 (2014)

11. Griffin, A.: The effect of project and process characteristics on product development cycle time. J. Mark. Res. **34**(1), 24–35 (1997)

12. Grönroos, C.: Creating a relationship dialogue: communication, interaction and value. Mark. Rev. **1**(1), 5–14 (2000)

13. Grönroos, Ch.: Value co-creation in service logic: a critical analysis. Mark. Theory **11**(3), 271–301 (2011)

14. Gummerus, J., et al.: Customer engagement in a Facebook brand community. Manag. Res. Rev. **35**, 857–877 (2012)

15. Howe, J.: Crowdsourcing: how the power of the crowd is driving the future of business. Random House (2008)

16. https://www.press.bmwgroup.com [date of access: 6–8.03.2020]

17. Ireson, N.: Volkswagen gets China's take on the People's Car of the future, 2013, [electronic source] https://www.motorauthority.com/news/. Accessed 6–8 Mar 2020

18. Kang, M., Young, J.: Repurchase loyalty for customer social co-creation e-marketplaces. J. Fashion Marketing and Management **18**(4), 452–464 (2014)

19. Kaplan, A., Haenlein, M.: Users of the world, unite! The challenges and opportunities of social media. Bus. Horizons **53**(1), 59–68 (2010)

20. Kennedy, E., Guzman, F.: Co-creation of brand identities: consumer and industry influence and motivations. J. Consum. Markng **33**(5), 313–323 (2016)

21. Lee, S., Olson, D., Trimi, S.: Co-innovation: convergenomics, collaboration, and co-creation for organizational values. Manag. Dec. **50**(5), 817–831 (2012)

22. Menor, L., Roth, A.: New service development competence in retail banking: construct development and measurement validation. J. Oper. Manag. **25**(4), 825–846 (2007)

23. Open innovation fuels BMW ideation process, [electronic source] https://www.ideaconnection.com/. Accessed 6–8 Mar 2020

24. Patterson, P.G., Smith, T.: A cross-cultural study of switching barriers and propensity to stay with service providers. J. Retail. **79**(2), 107–120 (2003)

25. Payne, A.F., Storbacka, K., Frow, P.: Managing the co-creation of value. J. Acad. Mark. Sci. **36**, 83–96 (2008)

26. Prahalad, C.K., Ramaswamy, V.: Co-creation experience: the next practice in value creation. J. Interact. Mark. **18**(3), 5–14 (2004)

27. Powerhouse of the mobility of tomorrow, [electronic source]. https://www.volkswagenag.com/. Accessed 6–8 Mar 2020

28. Roberts, J.: From know-how to show-how? Questioning the role of information and communication technologies in knowledge transfer. Technol. Anal. Strat. Manag. **12**(4), 429–443 (2000)

29. Roberts, D., Huges, M., Kertbo, K.: Exploring consumers' motivations to engage in innovation through co-creation activities. Eur. J. Mark. **48**(1/2), 147–169 (2013)

30. Sawhney, M., Verona, G., Prandelli, M.: Collaborating to create: the internet as a platform for customer engagement in product innovation. J. Interact. Mark. **19**(4), 4–17 (2005)

31. Seppä, M., Tanev, S.: The future of co-creation. Open Sour. Bus. Res. 6–12 (2011)

32. Smith, P., Blanck, E.: Leading dispersed teams. J. Product Innovat. Manag. **19**, 294–304 (2002)

33. Surowiecki, J.: The Wisdom of Crowds. Anchor, New York (2004)
34. Tommasetti, A., Troisi, O., Vesci, M.: Measuring customer value co-creation behaviour. J. Serv. Theory Pract. **27**(5), 930–950 (2017)
35. Van de Ven, A.: Central problems in the management of innovation. Manag. Sci. **32**(5), 590–607 (1986)
36. Vargo, S.L., Akaka, M.A.: Service-dominant logic as a foundation for service science: clarifications. Serv. Sci. **1**(1), 32–41 (2009)
37. Vargo, S.L., Lusch, R.F.: Evolving to a new dominant logic for marketing. J. Mark. **68**(1), 1–17 (2004)
38. Yew, Ch.: People's car Project by Volkswagen, 2015, [electronic source]. https://www.chr isyew.com/. Accessed 6–8 Mar 2020

Preferences for the Demand for Telematics Services on the Rail Freight Transport Market

Janusz Figura[✉]

University of Economics in Katowice, 1 Maja 50, Katowice, Poland
janusz.figura@ue.katowice.pl

Abstract. Preferences for the demand for telematics services on the rail freight transport market are an important element of modern economic processes. Telematics services not only ensure the development of safety or efficiency in the use of mobility of various rail vehicles, but also improve the implementation of specific preferences on the demand side of the rail freight transport market. Preferences for the demand for rail freight transport services still constitute a significant research gap that needs to be filled. The purpose of the study is to identify the preferences of demand for telematics services on the rail freight transport market among a deliberately selected group of entities performing logistics operations. The author of the study, based on direct and secondary research, will attempt to determine the structure as well as the dynamics of preference for demand for telematics services on the rail freight transport market.

Keywords: Telematics · Demand · Rail market · Freight transport

1 Introduction

The dynamics of development of telematics services in Poland is characterized by a significant level of evolution on the rail freight market [3]. The importance of telematics services on the rail freight transport market is conditioned, in particular, by demand preferences, which allows the competitiveness of operators providing transport to increase, as well as shapes the level of competitiveness [1]. Preferences for the demand for telematics services on the rail freight transport market are currently a key element not only of technological and technical development conditions, but also significantly affect the relationships of many economic aspects of the economy [6].

The purpose of the study is to identify the preferences of demand for telematics services on the rail freight transport market among a deliberately selected group of entities performing logistics operations. The author of the study, based on direct and secondary research, will attempt to determine the structure as well as the dynamics of preference for demand for telematics services on the rail freight transport market.

2 Forecasts of Demand on the Freight Transport Market as an Element of Global Trade

Trade is a main determinant of freight demand. Current estimates show global trade growing slightly stronger than GDP, but on a downward path. The OECD ENV Linkages

© Springer Nature Switzerland AG 2020
J. Mikulski (Ed.): TST 2020, CCIS 1289, pp. 246–258, 2020.
https://doi.org/10.1007/978-3-030-59270-7_18

model projects 3.4% annual growth through 2030 and 3.2% through 2050 - Table 1. Global merchandise trade volumes are expected to grow at gradually descending growth rates from 2017 onwards, reaching 3.7% in 2019. The figures for merchandise trade growth reflect the risks of going protectionism that will not only reduce trade flows, but diminish the exchange of information and new technologies - with important impacts on productivity and long-term growth [9]; Growth in trade will be impacted by the trend of global value chains becoming more consolidated. Trade in emerging economies is also likely to be affected by market disturbances such as rising interest rates in developed economies [9]. Nevertheless, exports and imports will grow faster in emerging economies than developed economies. The compound annual growth rate of imports for developing and emerging economies will be 60% higher than that of developed economies for imports and nearly three-quarters higher for exports by 2050 [9].

Table 1. World merchandise trade [9]

Percentage change over previous year						
	2016	2017	2018*	2019*	2015–2030*	2015–2050*
World	1.8	4.7	3.9	3.7	3.4	3.2
Exports						
Developed economies	1.1	3.4	3.5	3.3	2.7	2.3
Developing and emerging economies	2.5	5.3	4.6	4.5	4.2	4.0
North America	0.6	4.2	5.0	3.6	3.5	2.8
South and Central America	2.0	3.3	2.8	2.6	3.1	3.4
Europe	1.2	3.5	2.9	3.2	2.2	2.0
Asia	2.3	6.7	5.5	4.9	4.2	3.8
Other regions	3.4	0.2	2.6	3.6	3.6	4.2
Imports						
Developed economies	2.1	3.0	3.2	3.0	2.7	2.5
Developing and emerging economies	1.6	8.1	4.8	4.5	4.3	4.0
North America	0.0	4.0	4.3	3.6	2.8	2.9
South and Central America	−6.7	4.0	3.6	4.0	4.3	3.9
Europe	3.3	2.5	3.1	3.0	2.4	2.1
Asia	3.5	9.8	5.7	4.9	4.2	3.9
Other regions	−1.7	3.5	0.5	1.4	3.6	3.7

Notes: *Figures for 2018 onwards are projections. Figures for 2015–2030 and 2015–2050 are based on the OECD ENV linkages model

According to the OECD forecast from 2019, the most dynamic growth until 2050 will be noted by air transport, whose annual growth rate will be about 5.5%, while the lowest level of growth will be recorded by rail transport 2.5% per annum [4]. The growth dynamics of the other branches of transport are presented in Table 2.

Table 2. Projected growth rates of freight transport demand [4]

Current demand pathway, global compound annual growth rate in percentages		
	2015–2030	2015–2050
Freight transport demand	3.1	3.4
Rail	2.7	2.5
Road	3.5	3.2
Inland waterways	3.4	3.8
Aviation	5.5	4.5
Sea	3.0	3.6

Maritime shipping covers most of the movement of goods over long distances. This will continue to be the case in the coming years. The current demand pathway projects that maritime freight transport will grow at a compound annual growth rate of 3.6% through 2050 Table 1. This will lead to a near tripling of maritime trade volumes by 2050. The economic value of freight flows in the North Pacific and Indian Oceans will increase nearly four-fold between 2015 and 2050. Approximately one third of all maritime freight movements in 2050 will take place in these two regions Fig. 1. The North Atlantic Ocean will remain the third-busiest maritime corridor, with 15% of maritime freight movements in 2050, equalling 38 trillion tonne-kilometres. A recent trend, particularly strong in China, is the relocation of factories inland. This may impact mode choice for Eurasian freight flows if these relocations significantly increase the time and cost of maritime shipments relative to inland modes. Seaborne trade volumes grew 4% in 2017, the fastest rate since 2012, An estimated 10.7 billion tonnes were transported by sea that year. In terms of tonne-kilometres, global shipping activity amounted to over 58 trillion in 2017, an in crease of 5% on 2016. An estimated 752 million twenty-foot equivalent units (TEUs) were shipped through container ports. The size of the global ship fleet also grew +3.3% in 2017, but the growth in capacity was surpassed by increased freight volumes. UNCTAD projects that maritime freight volumes will continue expand through 2023, although this could change depending on the development of international trade agreements [4].

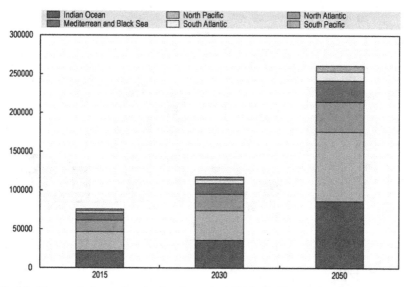

Fig. 1. Maritime trade demand projections by region, 2015–50 (Current demand pathway, billion tonne-kilometres) [5]

Over the past few years, road freight traffic levels have been growing across the globe, albeit at a more modest rate in the European Union Fig. 2. Surface freight volumes showed signs of recovery from the global economic downturn as early as 2011, but this trend is not uniform across modes and regions. China and India saw the fastest growth in road tonne-kilometres since 2016, with increases of 9.3% and 9.4% in 2017 respectively. China alone transported 6.7 trillion tonne-kilometres of road freight in 2017, nearly 700 billion tonne-kilometres more than the total freight traffic of OECD countries. Global rail freight volumes have declined in recent years, but for many countries 2017 marked a slight reversal in this trend. Rail tonne-kilometres in China grew by 13.3% on the previous year, returning nearly to their 2014 level. Russia also saw a notable increase of 6.4% in rail tonne-kilometres in 2017. Rail freight in India (+5.5%) and the United States (+5.2%) also grew significantly. Recent declines in rail traffic Fig. 2, are not likely to represent a strong long-term modal switch between road and rail, due to the fact that the compound annual growth rates of road and rail freight demand through 2050. Inland waterway freight traffic in China is projected to remain well above that of any other country or even any other continent, with strong growth rates through 2017. The volume of inland waterway freight in China was estimated at 4.4 trillion tonne-kilometres in 2017, a 10.9% increase from 2016 (Fig. 2) [5].

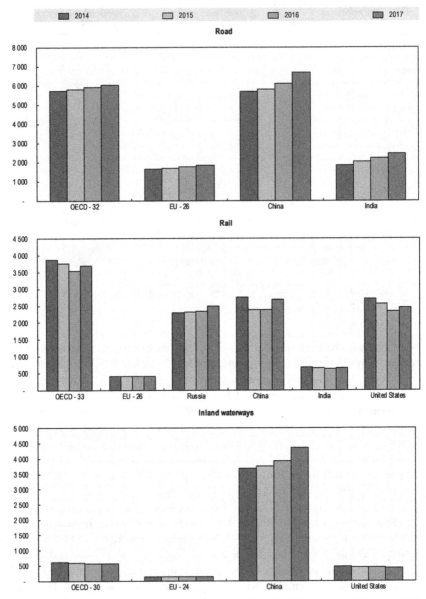

Fig. 2. Surface freight traffic by transport mode, 2014–17 (billion tonne-kilometres) [5]

3 The Rail Freight Market in Poland

The dynamic development of the rail freight market in Poland is growing at a rate of 3.5 - 4.5% per year 2000–2019 – Table 3. The increase in transport weight in rail freight in this period fluctuated between a minimum level of 166.9 million tonnes in 2001 and a maximum of 293.9 million tonnes in 2007. The average mass of freight transported by rail in Poland was 241.32 million tons. The trend was different considering the volume of rail transport work, the minimum level of which fell in 2009, i.e. 43601 million tkm, and the maximum in 2018, i.e. 59 642 million tkm. The average volume of transport work in the analyzed period amounted to 51,402.32 million tkm. The maximum transport distance in the years 2000–2019 in rail transport in Poland was 290.7 km and fell in 2000, while the minimum transport distance was 179.5 km and fell in 2009. The average transport distance in the analyzed period was 216.36 km – Table 3.

Table 3. Dynamics of freight transport by rail in the years 2000–2019 in Poland [8]

Year	Mass (in millions of tons)	Transport work (in million tkm)	Average transport distance (in km)
2000	187,3	54 448	290,7
2001	166,9	47 913	287,1
2002	222,9	47 756	214,2
2003	241,5	49 392	204,5
2004	283	52 053	183,9
2005	269,4	49 664	184,4
2006	290,3	53 291	183,6
2007	293,9	53 923	183,5
2008	276,3	51 570	186,6
2009	242,9	43 601	179,5
2010	235,5	48 842	207,4
2011	249,3	53 974	216,5
2012	231,3	49 063	212,1
2013	233,2	50 870	218,1
2014	228,9	50 098	218,9
2015	224,8	50 605	225,1
2016	222,2	50 620	227,8
2017	239,9	54 829	228,6
2018	250,3	59 642	238,3
2019	236,4	55 893	236,4

In 2018 licensed carriers carried international freight. Nearly 82.4 million tons were transported and transport performance of 26.5 billion tkm was carried out. The transported mass of cargo in international relations compared to 2017 increased by almost 8.1 million tons, and the transport work performed by more than 3.2 billion tkm. Analyzing the results in international transport it can be seen that from 2016 the mass of goods transported in import and transit increased dynamically. In the same period, export performance decreased. Intra-country transport was the least susceptible to changes mainly due to the very high demand for aggregates from infrastructure investments on the road and modernization of railway lines. In addition, significant demand could be seen generated by the Polish energy industry (Fig. 3).

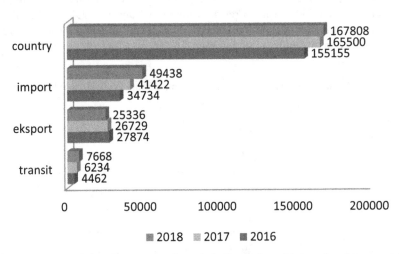

Fig. 3. Transport work in rail transport of goods in domestic and international transport in the years 2016–2018 in Poland (in thousand tone) [10]

In international transport, the largest volume of goods - 49.4 million tons - was transported in import, at the same time carrying out transport work at the level of 13.8 billion tkm. Compared to 2017, there was an increase in transported mass by 19.4% and transport performance by 19%. In export, the transported mass amounted to 25.3 million tons, and transport performance - 8 billion tkm. Compared to the year before, the volume of transported mass in exports fell by 5.2% with a simultaneous increase in transport performance by 2.1%. Nearly 7.7 million tons of goods were transported in transit through Poland, and transport performance amounted to 4.6 billion tkm. There was an increase in transported mass by 23% with a simultaneous increase in transport performance by 21.4%. For comparison, more goods were transported within the country by 1.4% (over 2.3 million tons) than a year ago and work was performed by 5.2% (over 1.6 billion tkm) – Fig. 3.

An important issue in the transport of goods by rail in Poland is the increase in the share of rail transport on the transport market compared to road transport, which in 2018 amounted to 4.1%, while in the volume of transport work 8.4 by leveling with road transport Table 4 and 5.

Table 4. Transport by rail and road in 2017 and 2018 in Poland (in thousand tonnes) [own study based on [8]]

	2017	2018	2017 = 100	% market in 2018
Altogether	2053244	2191889	6,8	
Trail	239501	249260	4,1	11,3
Truck	1747266	1873022	7,2	85,4

Table 5. Transport by rail and road in 2017 and 2018 in Poland (in million tkm) [own study based on [8]]

	2017	2018	2017 = 100	% market in 2018
Altogether	434932	467193	7,4	
Trail	54797	59388	8,4	12,7
Truck	348559	377778	8,4	80,6

The dynamics of changes on the Polish freight transport market - Tables 4 and 5, indicates a significant intensification of entities providing rail transport, which suggests that the structure of demand for transport services is also changing. Rail transport in Poland is gradually regaining the transport market by competing with road freight transport.

4 Methodology of Researching the Preferences of Demand for Telematics Services on the Rail Freight Transport Market in Poland

The research (article presents only selected results of the research on the preferences of demand for telematics services on the rail freight market in Poland) on identifying the preferences for the demand for telematics services on the rail freight transport market in Poland was conducted from May 2018 to February 2020 on a deliberately selected sample of 264 logistics service clients using rail ball freight services. The data for analysis were collected using empirical research based on a questionnaire tool. In questions regarding the intensity factors of the examined feature, a five-point Likert scale was used, where 1 was min. intensity 5 max. intensity of the examined feature. Identification of preferences for the demand for telematics services on the rail freight market concerned the following categories (preference categories for the demand for telematics services on the rail freight market have been determined by the expert method):

– pricing policy preferences for telematics services,
– flexibility preferences for telematics services,
– preferences regarding the complementarity of expenditure on telematics services,

– telematics services interoperability preferences,
– telematics service structure preferences.

The price policy preferences of telematics services in the group of examined operators focused on:

– price optimization,
– cost price calculation,
– stiffening the price level,

Preferences of flexibility of telematics services is a category that allows you to get an answer to the client's non-standard needs in the field of telematics services, including the ability to change the level and structure of quality of telematics services that were determined for the purposes of the study by:

– smooth implementation of telematics services,
– speed of telematics service implementation,
– effectiveness of the telematics service.

Preferences regarding the complementarity of expenditure on telematics services constitute a category that allows to obtain a response in terms of mixed demand elasticity, i.e. the degree of sensitivity to changes in its determinants, i.e. factors determining the size of the customer's own demand and thus the elasticity of own (individual) demand. Determining the level of elasticity of own demand for telematics services was determined based on the following ranges in the annual structure of expenses from the customer's basket:

– to 1%;
– 1,1%–2,5%;
– 2,6%–5,0%;
– 5,1%–10%;
– above 10%

Telematics services interoperability preferences is a category that provides the opportunity for technical and technological relationships in building international supply chains. The degree of preference for the needs of the study was determined by a five-point Likert scale of 1 min. 5 max. Telematics service structure preferences are a category that has been defined as the level of user usability from the consumption of a given telematics service. The degree of preference for the needs of the study was determined by a five-point Likert scale of 1 min. 5 max.

Telematics service structure preferences are a category that has been defined as the level of user usability from the consumption of a given telematics service. The degree of preference for the needs of the study was determined by a five-point Likert scale of 1 min. 5 max.

5 Results of Demand Preferences Research for Telematics Services on the Rail Freight Transport Market in Poland

The results of the research on the preferences of demand for telematics services on the rail freight transport market in Poland indicate a diverse picture of the preferences studied.

In the category of categories related to price policy, stiffening the price level 46% gained dominance, followed by cost price calculation 29% and price optimization 25% (Fig. 4).

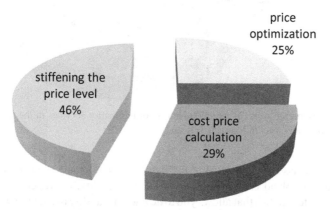

Fig. 4. The price policy preferences of telematics services in the group surveyed of clients logistics operators in Poland [own study]

Another category of demand preferences for telematics services on the rail freight transport market in Poland concerned the issue of preference flexibility. Research results show similar trends in preferences with a slight predominance of 38% effectiveness of telematics services (Fig. 5).

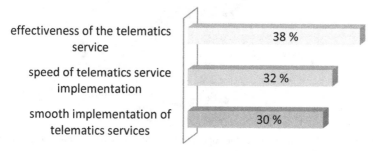

Fig. 5. Flexibility preferences for telematics services in the surveyed group of clients logistics operators in Poland [own study]

Research results regarding the criterion of complementarity of expenditure on telematics services on the market of rail freight transport services in Poland indicate a clear asymmetry of intensity towards complementarity of 62% of expenditure in the range of 1.1–2.5% of the company's annual budget. The remaining results regarding the complementarity criterion are presented in Fig. 6.

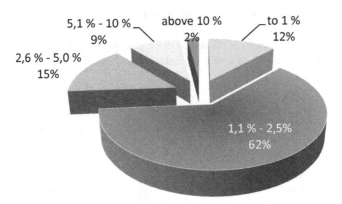

Fig. 6. Flexibility preferences for complementarity of telematics services in the surveyed group of clients logistics operators in Poland [own study]

An important issue in researching the demand for telematics services on the rail freight market in Poland is also the issue of interoperability. Interoperability is one of the key issues of telematics that allows you to develop the ability of a telematics service to or its components to exchange and use with other services and entities. Interoperability is a kind of window to the world of telematics. The test results clearly indicate the need for interoperability development, which is demonstrated by the maximum intensity value of 69% and high 21% - Fig. 7. Other research results regarding the interoperability criterion are presented in Fig. 7.

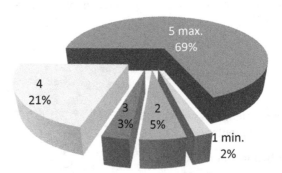

Fig. 7. Flexibility telematics services interoperability preferences in the surveyed group of clients logistics operators in Poland [own study]

The last of the criteria regarding the preference for demand for telematics services on the rail freight transport market was the issue of preference structure. The structure of preferences concerns the issue to what extent the current structure of telematics services is sufficient for their users. The research results indicate that the current structure of telematics services should be strongly developed 81% of the maximum level of the examined feature - Fig. 8. Other research results on the structure of telematics services are presented in Fig. 8.

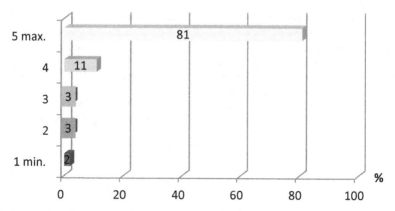

Fig. 8. Flexibility telematics service structure preferences in the surveyed group of clients logistics operators in Poland [own study]

6 Conclusion

The issue of demand preferences for telematics services on the rail freight market is a diverse issue that has been addressed from the perspective of five categories: pricing policy preferences for telematics services, flexibility preferences for telematics services, preferences regarding the complementarity of expenditure on telematics services, telematics services interoperability preferences, telematics service structure preferences. The most diverse categories were related to complementarity, interoperability and the structure of telematics services. The price categories for flexibility were less diverse. In the study, not only issues related to the level of intensity of asymmetry of category data were important, but also factors that reflected selected categories, such as price policy, or flexibility - the effectiveness, liquidity and efficiency of telematics services.

Generally, it can be concluded from the research that demand preferences are a multifaceted and diverse issue that requires further in-depth and expanded research, particularly in the field of interoperability and structure.

References

1. Figura, J.: Taksonomia w polityce logistycznej państwa, Prace Naukowe, Wydawnictwo Uniwersytetu Ekonomicznego w Katowicach, Katowice (2013)
2. ITF Transport Outlook 2019. How transport demand will change by 2050. OECD (2019)

3. Jabłoński, A.: A human factor and rail transport safety - a comparative criterion of selected assessment methods. Archives of Transport System Telematics, Polskie Stowarzyszenie Telematyki Transportu, pp. 20–26 (2018)
4. oecd-ilibrary.org/sites/transp_outlook-en-2019-en/1/2/1/index. Accessed 02 Marc 2020
5. oecd-ilibrary.org/transport/itf-transport-outlook-2019_transp_outlook-en-2019-en. Accessed 02 Mar 2020
6. Rokita, J.: Myślenie systemowe w zarządzaniu organizacjami. Wydawnictwo UE w Katowicach, Katowice (2011)
7. utk.gov.pl/pl/raporty-i-analizy/analizy-i-monitoring/statystyka-przewozow-to/15773,Dane-podstawowe.html [date of access: 02.03.2020]
8. WTO: WTO downgrades outlook for global trade as risks accumulate (2019). http://www.wto.org/english/news_e/pres18_e/pr822_e.htm. Accessed 6 Jan 2019
9. Zwiększenie roli kolei w równoważeniu transportu towarów w Polsce. Wyzwania, propozycje, dobre praktyki, Wersja zaktualizowana, Urząd Transportu Kolejowego, Warszawa (2019)

Analysis and Proposed Solutions for Parking in Rajecké Teplice

Alica Kalašová[(✉)], Ambróz Hájnik, Stanislav Kubaľák, and Veronika Harantová

University of Žilina, Univerzitná, 8215/1, Žilina, Slovakia
{alica.kalasova,ambroz.hajnik,stanislav.kubalak,
veronika.harantova}@fpedas.uniza.sk

Abstract. The article is focused on parking in the spa town of Rajecké Teplice. Spa towns are attractive in terms of transport and attract traffic. The most frequently used mode of transport is the individual automobile transport. The increasing number of visitors of Rajecké Teplice is also causing an increase in the number of cars and parking demand. A common problem for cities is the lack of space and land ownership to build new parking spaces. The result is parking on the streets, public space and green areas, which harms the environment and retrench the traffic flow and other participants of transport. A survey of the number of parking vehicles, the average length of parking and the purpose of parking was carried out in the town. The inhabitants of the town also expressed their opinion on the situation with parking in the questionnaire. The outputs of this questionnaire are given in the article. Based on the results of the survey and a questionnaire, solutions were proposed to improve the parking in the spa town of Rajecké Teplice.

Keywords: Parking · Traffic survey · Questionnaire · Rajecké teplice

1 Introduction

Rajecké Teplice (R.T.) is located in northwestern Slovakia in the district of Žilina. It is a spa town and is one of the smallest towns in Slovakia. R.T. is an important traffic node of valley of Rajec. Before building the bypass, all vehicles were passing through the town centre. The bypass significantly reduced the proportion of transit traffic passing through the town centre. Nevertheless, a certain proportion of transit traffic still passes through the town centre.

There are several private parking lots in the town, which are owned by spas, various hotels, restaurants and so on. Few parking spaces are owned by the city. Only parking places around the square are charged. A parking ticket can be purchased from the parking ticket machine. Inhabitants with permanent residence in the town have the opportunity to purchase a resident parking card. An important parking lot is located on both sides of the road I/64. This parking lot is important now and also for the future because its location is outskirts. At present, it is owned by the Slovak Road Administration, but soon, it should be owned by the city. A part of Osloboditeľov street near the swimming pool is one of the most problematic places in terms of parking. Another problem with parking

© Springer Nature Switzerland AG 2020
J. Mikulski (Ed.): TST 2020, CCIS 1289, pp. 259–271, 2020.
https://doi.org/10.1007/978-3-030-59270-7_19

is on Rudolf Súlovský Street, in parking spaces around the square, near the church and its surroundings during church services on Sundays and church holidays. The biggest problems with parking are during the summer [1, 10, 11].

2   Parking Analysis

The issue of parking in Rajecké Teplice was analyzed in two ways. The first way was to do a parking questionnaire in R.T. The questionnaire consisted of two parts. The Respondent Data Collection Part and the second part, which included questions about parking in R.T. At the end of the questionnaire, respondents had the opportunity to comment on parking in the city.

The second way of parking analysis in R.T. was a survey of the number of parking vehicles, the average length of parking and the purpose of parking. This survey was conducted at selected locations and parking lots. Individual places and parking lots were chosen based on knowledge about parking problems, or those parking lots that are widely used. Prior to the survey, a meeting was held with the mayor of the town, who was informed about the survey and the places included in the survey. The mayor of the town proposed to include in the survey R. Súlovský street too [7, 20].

2.1   The Survey of the Number of Parked Vehicles, the Average Length of Parking and the Purpose of Parking

Fig. 1. Marked locations included in the survey [own processing based on [19]]

Parking areas and places included in the survey (Fig. 1):

- parking places around the square,
- parking lot behind the municipal office,
- parking lot by the church,
- parking lot near the bus station and railway station,
- Rudolf Súľovský street
- gravel parking lot near the pond,
- parking lot by the pond,
- Osloboditeľov street,
- road by the swimming pool to the bridge before the Jozef Gabčík street,
- parking lots near road I/64.

The survey was conducted on Tuesday (14.8.2018) and Sunday (19.8.2018) to compare the average day of the week with the weekend. The time of realization was divided into two parts. The first part took place from 8:00 am to 12:00 am. The second part took place from 14:30 to 19:30.

The number of vehicles parked was checked every 15 min. The number plates of vehicles parked was recorded. The evaluation of the survey revealed the percentage shares of vehicles from the district of Žilina (ZA), other districts of the Slovak Republic and vehicles from abroad. The average length of parking was calculated based on the total number of parked vehicles during the realization of the survey and the amount of time each vehicle spent on the parking lot (also includes the inappropriately parked vehicles outside the parking lot). During the survey, the purpose of parking was determined by asking the driver a question. The results of the survey are divided into 3 groups:

1. group – Parking lots with the marked parking spots

This group includes the following parking lots:

- parking spaces around the square,
- parking lot by the church,
- parking lot by the pond.

There are 88 parking spaces in these parking lots. Parking spaces around the square are charged. Parking on parking lots by the church and by the pond are free of charge. The results of the survey of the number of parked vehicles are listed in Fig. 2. The occupancy of parking places in these parking lots was higher on Sunday. On Tuesday, the highest occupancy was 64.8% (57 vehicles) from 17:45 to 18:00. On Sunday, the highest occupancy was 126.1% (111 vehicles) from 10:15 to 10:30 a.m. The occupancy of parking spaces was over 100% from 9:30 a.m. to 10:30 a.m. The vehicles were parked inappropriately and restricted other traffic participants. The main reason for the high occupancy at this time was church service in the church. There are only 23 parking spaces in the parking lot by the church. There are often inappropriate parked vehicles on the streets and sidewalks during church services on Sundays and church holidays. The parking lot is also limited by a traffic sign allowing parking only at times of the church services. Despite the traffic sign, several vehicles are parked here throughout the day, as a result of the lack of parking spaces in the city [8, 9].

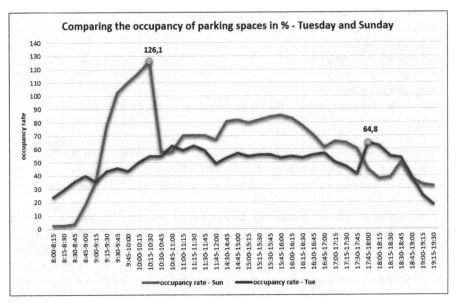

Fig. 2. Comparing the occupancy of parking spaces in % - Tuesday and Sunday [own study]

On Tuesday the average parking time was 1 h and 55 min. On Sunday the average parking time was shorter - 1 h and 30 min (Fig. 3).

On Tuesday, drivers most often mentioned the option "recreation" (48) and "other" (58) as the purpose of parking. The option "other" - the most frequently mentioned reasons were - services (34) and church service (19). On Sunday, drivers most often mentioned "recreation" (131) and "other" (130) as the reason for parking. The most common reason for parking was "church service" (119) in the option "other".

2. group – Parking lots where parking spots are not marked

This group includes the following parking lots and locations:

- parking lot behind the municipal office,
- parking lot near the bus station and railway station,
- gravel parking lot near the pond,
- parking lots near road I/64.

There are no marked parking spaces and parking is not charged at these locations. Parking is possible for a smaller number of vehicles because of inappropriate parking. The following figure shows the course of the number of parked vehicles on Tuesday and Sunday (Fig. 4).

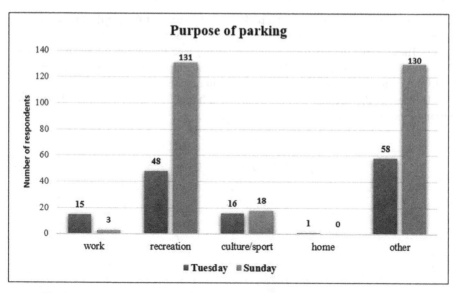

Fig. 3. The survey of the purpose of parking - Tuesday and Sunday [own study]

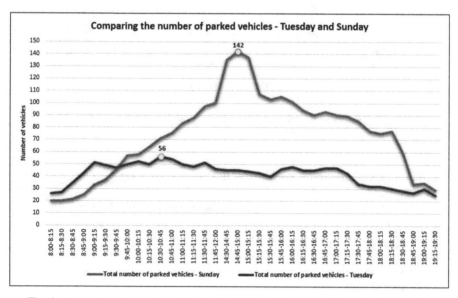

Fig. 4. Comparing the number of parked vehicles on Tuesday and Sunday [own study]

The results of the survey show that on Sunday (approximately from 9:45 am) there was a larger number of parked vehicles. On Sunday, the largest number recorded was 142 parked vehicles (between 14:45 to 15:00). On Tuesday, the largest number of parked vehicles was 56 vehicles (between 10:30 am to 10:45 am). During both days, the vehicles were parked inappropriately and the parking areas were not fully utilized. In addition, other traffic participants (pedestrians, cyclists) were restricted at the pond.

On Tuesday, the drivers most frequently mentioned the option of "recreation" (70) and "other" (52) - stop/pause (33), services (6), dinner (4), etc. On Sunday, recreation (186) and culture/sport (27) were the most common reasons.

On Tuesday the average parking time was 2 h and 34 min. On Sunday the average parking time was longer - 2 h and 47 min (Fig. 5).

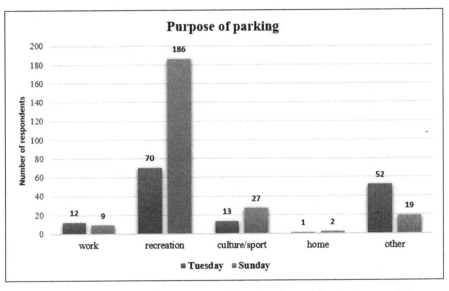

Fig. 5. The survey of the purpose of parking - Tuesday and Sunday [own study]

3. group – Places and areas, on which is not allowed parking

This group includes places where parking is inappropriate and restricts the traffic participants. It is parking on the streets and on grassy areas. This includes the following places:

– Rudolf Súľovský street,
– Osloboditeľov street,
– road by the swimming pool to the bridge before the Jozef Gabčík street.

Parking in these places causes significant problems and restricts traffic especially during the summer season. There are no marked parking spaces and parking is not prohibited or charged at these locations. Figure 6 shows the number of parked vehicles on Tuesdays and Sundays. On Sunday, the number of parked vehicles was significantly higher. The highest number of parked vehicles was recorded between 14:30 and 14:45– 223 vehicles. On Tuesday, the largest number of parked vehicles was recorded at 2 intervals - from 16:30 to 16:45 and from 17:00 to 17:15–56 vehicles. The weather on Tuesday was not favourable and the results were not as we expected. The number of parked vehicles is also large during weekdays and traffic in these places is severely limited (Fig. 7).

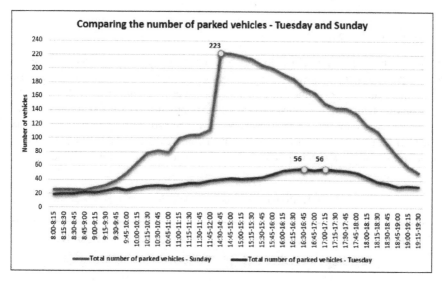

Fig. 6. Comparing the number of parked vehicles on Tuesday and Sunday [own study]

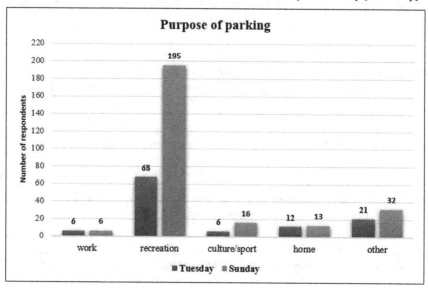

Fig. 7. The survey of the purpose of parking - Tuesday and Sunday [own study]

The results of the survey of the purpose of parking again brought the results, when drivers most frequently mentioned the option of "recreation" on Tuesdays and Sundays.

The second most common option was 'other'. In this option drivers most often mentioned as a reason for parking - a restaurant. There are several restaurants on and near the Rudolf Súĺovský street which attract traffic but do not have enough parking spaces. On Tuesday, the average parking time was 2 h and 50 min. On Sunday, the average parking time was longer - 3 h and 43 min.

2.2 Questionnaire Survey

The aim of the questionnaire was to find out how the visitors and residents of the town perceive parking in R.T. The questionnaire focused primarily on the residents of the town. A minimum sample size of the questionnaire had to be calculated before the realization of the survey. This sample size was based on the population of Rajecké Teplice (3 017). The result was a sample of 245 responses. We have received 249 responses from residents of the town and 43 responses from people who are not residents of this town. A sufficient number of responses was achieved only from the residents of the town (Table 1).

Table 1. Results of the questionnaire [own study]

Do you think parking in Rajecké Teplice is a problem to be solved?	
yes	no
217 (87%)	32 (13%)
Did you not find a free parking spot and had to park improperly outside the parking lot?	
yes	no
179 (76%)	57 (24%)
Did you get constrained by improperly standing vehicles? (You were in the position of a pedestrian, cyclist, driver of a motor vehicle, ...)	
yes	no
206 (83%)	43 (17%)
Do you think it is necessary to regulate parking in Rajecké Teplice?	
yes	no
216 (87%)	33 (13%)
Would you accept a solution in the form of charged parking to improve the current situation?	
yes	no
120 (48%)	129 (52%)
Do you think it is necessary to build new parking spaces, even if this should be at the expense of green areas?	
yes	no
128 (51%)	121 (49%)

3 Proposals for Improving the Current Situation

The proposals for the new organization of parking are based on the results of the surveys that have been carried out. Problem with parking in R.T. is evident and needs to be addressed. Below are the individual proposals for improving the current situation.

3.1 Parking Regulation

Parking regulation is one of the most important and easiest ways to improve parking. It is necessary to regulate parking especially in places that have been a problem for a long time and have not been addressed in any way. Parking regulation is suggested in 3 ways [5, 6].

1. Charging for parking - not only on the square but also on the streets. These are the most problematic streets - Osloboditeľov street, Rudolf Súľovský street, Lúčna street and Školská street. Currently, parking is only available at the square (€ 0.30 per half hour). The following table shows the parking rates I propose for parking areas near the square (zone RT1) and on the mentioned streets (zone RT2) (Table 2).

Table 2. Proposed price list of parking [own study]

Parking time	Fee
Parking areas near the square – RT1	
1. half an hour	1,00 €
Each additional half an hour	1,00 €
Parking on the streets – RT2	
1. hour	1,50 €
Each additional hour	1,50 €

Parking fees can be paid via mobile app, SMS, cash or bank card. We suggest paying the parking fee via SMS to the number 2200 and in the specified form of SMS. Several cities in Slovakia are using this phone number. SMS is designed as follows:

– RT(space)RT1/RT2(space)number plate

In the middle of the SMS is the name of the zone where the vehicle will be parked. The system recognizes the zone and determines the appropriate parking fee.

2. No parking - in certain places, streets. It is important to ensure smooth traffic on the streets without constraints created by improperly parked vehicles. Parking regulation using a parking ban is also possible in combination with charging for parking at the designated parking spots located on the street. It is necessary for municipal police to

levy fine for improperly parking vehicles. Without the intervention of the municipal police, the problem with inappropriate parking will be repeated.

3. Marking of parking spaces – several parking areas have no marked parking spaces, therefore it was designed to be marked according to the relevant standard STN 73 6056, which lists the dimensions of parking spots for parking - perpendicular, parallel and angle. At present there is unsuitable parking, where the parking spaces are not used sufficiently. Drivers, who were involved in parking research required for marking parking spots [3, 4].

3.2 Parking Cards

Just a resident parking card for residents of the town is available. The price of this card is 10 € and is valid for 1 year from the date of purchase. We propose to establish resident and abonent parking cards (Table 3).

Table 3. Proposed price list of parking cards [own study]

Number of vehicles	Fee
Resident parking card	
1. vehicle	20 €/year
2. vehicle	60 €/year
Each additional vehicle	180 €/year
Abonent parking card	
1. vehicle	50 €/year
2. vehicle	150 €/year
Each additional vehicle	450 €/year

In the event of loss, theft or damage to the card, you will be required to pay a 5 € fee to issue a new card. The parking card will only be valid for the vehicle whose vehicle registration plate is on the parking card. The parking card will be available at the municipal police in the municipal office building.

3.3 Parking App

Currently, in R.T. is not possible to use any mobile app for parking. Longer search times for a free parking spot increase fuel consumption and emissions. Considering that R.T. is a spa town, it is necessary to improve air quality and not conversely. A parking app can help to reduce emissions thanks to a shorter search time for the free parking spot. Before driving, the driver can view free parking spaces and start navigating to that location [12, 13, 15].

We propose to create a parking app for the town or to cooperate with an existing company that has a functioning parking application (e.g. ParkDots, Parkio, Parkopedia).

In this proposal, it would be appropriate for the town to cooperate with organizations operating in the town that have available parking spaces for visitors. These are especially hotels, pensions and SPA Aphrodite Rajecké Teplice (SPA RT). Sensors would be installed in parking spots to provide real-time information about the availability of these parking spots. Thanks to that the driver will see where he can to park the vehicle and start navigating to that location. The app will be able to notify the driver before the end of the validity of parking. The driver will receive this warning 10 min before the end of the paid parking period. The driver will be able to extend the parking time [2, 16, 18].

3.4 Parking House

Several respondents stated in a questionnaire survey that it would be necessary to build a parking house. Another important reason to build a parking house is the smaller ground area required. The town does not own enough land plot to build a parking house. For this reason, it is necessary to cooperate with entrepreneurs who own several large land plots where a parking house could be built [17].

The parking house is designed to be built in 2 locations (Fig. 8). The parking house with the number "1" is designed near the bus station and railway station, but also near the church. Here SPA RT plans to build a parking house. The parking house can solve the problem of improper parking on road I/64 and the surrounding streets during church service. Also, this parking house will have the potential for use in the P + R (park and ride) system. The location of the parking house is on the outskirts of the town [14, 21].

The parking house with the number "2" is designed near the swimming pool, where is currently a building used as a warehouse for SPA RT. SPA RT is planning to build here parking spaces on the ground level soon and then in the future, there is the possibility

Fig. 8. Proposal for the location of parking houses [own processing based on [19]]

to build a parking house. Parking house would improve the situation with parking in the most problematic part of the town - Osloboditeľov street. From an architectural point of view, both parking houses should be designed to minimize interference with the surrounding environment.

4 Conclusion

Problems with parking occur all over the world. Solutions are often costly but need to be applied. It is important to change people's thinking in order to increase the demand for public transport or other alternatives (cycling and walking).

The town of Rajecké Teplice has problems with parking for a long time. It was necessary to carry out traffic surveys to solve this problem. These were surveys of the number of parked vehicles, the average length of parking time and the purpose of parking. Later, a questionnaire survey about parking was carried out. By carrying out surveys have achieved one of the stated objectives - analysis of the current situation.

The proposals are another objective that has been achieved. The proposals include solutions to regulate parking, which is a necessary means of improving the current situation with parking. Problems with parking will not improve without parking regulation. In addition to parking regulation, other solutions to the problem with parking are also proposed. Through these proposals, it is possible to achieve a better situation compared to the current situation. Some proposals require a change in people´s thinking, as already mentioned. We believe that the realization of the proposals can solve the problems related to parking in Rajecké Teplice.

References

1. Surovy, D., Surovy, R.: Mobility and parking. In: Urbanita, vol. 30 (2017)
2. Kadlec, R.: Sygic zabudoval službu Parkopedia do svojej najnovšej aplikácie Car Navigation. Pomôže s nájdením a rezerváciou parkovacieho miesta. In TouchIT (2017)
3. ČSN 73 6056 – "Odstavné a parkovací plochy silničných vozidel" (1987)
4. STN 73 6110 – "Projektovanie miestnych komunikácií" (2004)
5. TP 09/2006 – "Použitie, kvalita a systém hodnotenia dopravných a parkovacích zariadení", p. 48 December 2006. https://www.ssc.sk/files/documents/technicke-predpisy/tp/tp_023.pdf. Accessed 15 Dec 2019
6. Kalasova, A., Faith, P., Palo, J.: Dopravné inžinierstvo I, Zilina: EDIS, p. 194 (2006)
7. Kalasova, A., et al.: Smart City - Model of Sustainable Development of Cities, 2018 Xi International Science-Technical Conference Automotive Safety, p. 5 (2018)
8. Culik, K., Kalasova, A., Kubikova, S.: Simulation as an instrument for research of driver-vehicle interaction. In: Stopka, O. (ed.) 18th International Scientific Conference-Logi 2017, MATEC Web of Conferences Cedex A: E D P Sciences (2017)
9. Culik, K., Harantova, V., Kalasova, A.: Traffic modelling of the circular junction in the city of Zilina. Adv. Sci. Technol.-Res. J. 13(4), 162–169 (2019)
10. Poliak, M., Konecny, V.: Factors determining the electronic tolling scope of road network. Ekonomicky Casopis 56(7), 712–731 (2008)
11. Berezny, R., Konecny, V.: The impact of the quality of transport services on passenger demand in the suburban bus transport. In: Bujnak, J., Guagliano, M. (eds.) 12th International Scientific Conference of Young Scientists on Sustainable, Modern and Safe Transport, Procedia Engineering, pp. 40–45. Elsevier Science Bv, Amsterdam (2017)

12. Konecny, V., Petro, F.: Calculation of selected emissions from transport services in road public transport. In: Stopka, O. (ed.) 18th International Scientific Conference-Logi 2017, MATEC Web of Conferences. E D P Sciences, Cedex A (2017)
13. Poliak, M.: The relationship with reasonable profit and risk in public passenger transport in the slovakia. Ekonomicky Casopis **61**(2), 206–220 (2013)
14. Poliak, M., Poliaková, A.: Relation of social legislation in road transport on driver's work quality. In: Mikulski, J. (ed.) TST 2015. CCIS, vol. 531, pp. 300–310. Springer, Cham (2015). https://doi.org/10.1007/978-3-319-24577-5_30
15. https://www.minv.sk/?statisticke-ukazovatele-sluzby-dopravnej-policie.Accessed 15 Dec 2019
16. https://www.parkopedia.com. Accessed 15 Dec 2019
17. https://www.parkhaus-bad-hersfeld.de. Accessed 15 Dec 2019
18. https://www.parkme.com. Accessed 15 Dec 2019
19. https://mapa-mapy.info.sk/. Accessed 15 Dec 2019

Assessment of Possibilities to Distinguish Vehicles on the Basis of Wheel Load Characteristics

Aleksander Konior[1]([⊠]), Paweł Piwowarczyk[1], Tomasz Konior[1], and Artur Ryguła[2]

[1] APM PRO sp. z o.o. ul., Barska 70, 43-300 Bielsko-Biała, Poland
{aleksander.konior,pawel.piwowarczyk,tomasz.konior}@apm.pl
[2] University of Bielsko-Biala, Willowa 2, 43-309 Bielsko-Biała, Poland
arygula@ath.eu

Abstract. In the article, selected analyses of data recorded by the test station of the intelligent Weigh In Motion system (iWIM) are presented. The station has been equipped with a dedicated system for recording signals from strain gauge sensors. The measurements were aimed at assessing the possibility of determining the type of vehicles based on knowledge of only the axle load profile of individual wheels. The test sample consisted only of light vehicles, i.e. with a permissible weight below 3.5t.

Keywords: Weigh in motion · Vehicle classification · Axle load

1 Introduction

Weigh In Motion (WIM) stations are an important component of intelligent transport systems (ITS). Currently, in Poland and many other European countries, WIM systems are used for pre-selection purposes and allow to indicate vehicles whose gross mass or axle loads have been exceeded with a high probability. WIM systems have been in use for many years and their functions and technological solutions have been confirmed both analytically and experimentally. Current solutions for WIM stations are based on proven technologies, but still do not provide a level of measurement reliability that would allow for their fully effective use as an automatic enforcement systems. Many companies and institutions work on increasing measurement precision by using e.g. fibre optic sensors [1, 2] or environmental conditions monitoring [3, 4]. The ongoing work aims at the widespread use of WIM systems for automatic law enforcement purposes, in particular in countries that already have this legal possibility, e.g. the Czech Republic. Also in Poland, since 2017 work has been carried out to create the basis for an administrative system for dynamic measurement of the vehicle parameters [5], which will ultimately enable the process of direct enforcement.

Currently, in existing WIM systems, the only criterion for assessing accuracy is the measurement class according to COST 323 specification [6]. This class determines the required accuracy of measurement of the gross vehicle weight, axle loads, vehicle

© Springer Nature Switzerland AG 2020
J. Mikulski (Ed.): TST 2020, CCIS 1289, pp. 272–284, 2020.
https://doi.org/10.1007/978-3-030-59270-7_20

speed and vehicle length. However, these parameters are only verified during the station calibration procedure, which is typically carried out once a year. Thus, this process does not allow to assess the accuracy and stability of measurements in the period between calibrations, and the auto-calibration procedures used in some solutions are based solely on corrections of weighting factors determined from statistical data sets [7, 8]. What is important, in the process of weighing vehicles in motion, there are a number of dynamic factors related to the vehicle's body vibrations, acceleration, braking, weather conditions, pavement parameters etc.

The analyses presented in this paper are part of the above-mentioned research and development project, the basic element of which is the development of a device for recording signals from, among others, strain gauges sensors. In the context of the above, APM PRO is working on the project of iWIM [9], an intelligent vehicle Weigh In Motion system which, thanks to the application of precise data recording and processing devices, additional sensors and algorithms for evaluation of measurement reliability, will allow to increase the efficiency of the system operation and improve the law enforcement process.

2   Research Area and Devices

The analyses were carried out with data gathered using the ITS test site located at the University of Bielsko-Biała (Fig. 1). The test site is equipped, among other things, with variable message sign, pre-selection scales, a set of weather measuring equipment, CCTV and ANPR cameras and loop systems to classify vehicles according to 8 + 1 standard. A detailed description of the training ground is presented in the paper [10].

Fig. 1. Vehicles Weigh in Motion system at the ITS campus, University of Bielsko-Biała [own study]

In the context of the conducted research, strain gauges for measuring the pressure of individual wheels are an important element of the system. The sensors are mounted in the road pavement perpendicularly to the direction of movement – one sensor each for the left and right lane side (Fig. 2). The distance between the sensors is 2 m.

Fig. 2. Strain-gauge sensors on the ITS test site [own study]

Intercomp sensors with the following parameters have been used on the test site [11]:

– length 1.5 m,
– width 70 mm,
– linearity <0.1 ± %FSO,
– hysteresis <0.2 ± %FSO,
– temperature coefficient of sensitivity 0.002 (0.0036) ± % of Load/°F (°C).

Importantly, as part of the project work (iWIM), data recording and processing circuits based on FPGA technology with built-in digital signal processor were developed. The developed amplifier has been tested for electrical parameters particularly for linearity of signal gain from strain gauges sensors. Figure 3 shows the results of the measurement used for testing the linearity of the amplifier (at Fig. 3 marked with the number 1). The input signal varies in the voltage range from −19.6 mV to +19.6 mV (in 0.2 mV steps). The output signal of the amplifier was sampled from an analog-to-digital converter with a frequency of 300 kS/s. Samples of the measured signal averaged 60,000 times for each given input voltage.

Obtained gain linearity parameters in the band up to 50 kHz (Fig. 4) do not exceed 3 bits, of course after decimation of measurements.

Fig. 3. Process of testing the gain ad linearity of amplifier [own study]

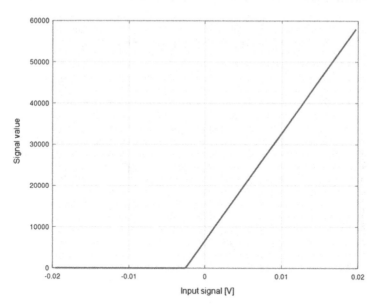

Fig. 4. The relation between input signal and output signal value of amplifier [own study]

Next, the recording device in combination with a strain gauge sensor has been tested in the laboratory (Fig. 5) on the test bench.

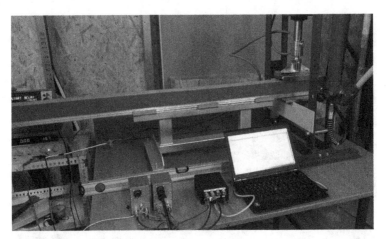

Fig. 5. Test stand of the device for recording signals from strain gauge sensors [own study]

On the test stand, among other things, the linearity of the sensor and correctness of the system operation was tested by generating pressure on the strain gauge beam at defined measuring points (point 5 to 150). The results are shown in Fig. 6.

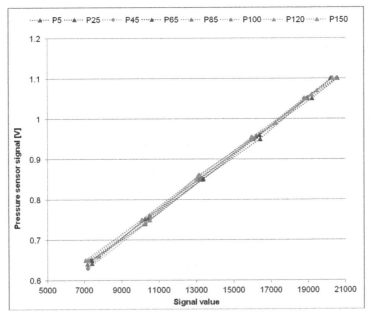

Fig. 6. The relation between pressure force and signal level from strain gauge sensor [own study]

Finally the system was mounted in the control cabinet of the ITS test site and connected to the pavement-mounted strain gauge sensors. An example of the waveform from strain gauge signals recorded for a passenger vehicle is shown in Fig. 7 – blue shows the signal from the sensor recording the pressures of the left side of the vehicle, while red shows the signal for the wheels on the right. The sampling rate after decimation is 3125 Hz.

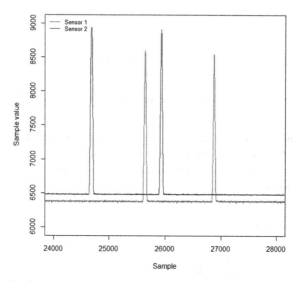

Fig. 7. Example of the signal from strain gauge sensors [own study] (Color figure online)

3   Data Analysis

Within the framework of the research, multiple test runs were conducted with three vehicles:

- SUV (length 4888 mm, wheelbase 2890 mm),
- Station wagon SW (length 4650 mm, wheelbase 2700 mm),
- LCV (length 8223 mm, wheelbase 4750 mm).

A total of 22 runs at different speeds were recorded. The speed distribution by vehicle type is shown in Fig. 8.

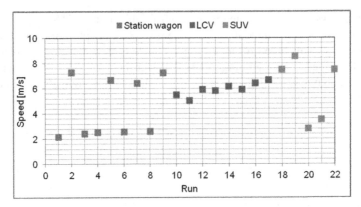

Fig. 8. Speed distribution during the test runs [own study]

For further analysis, it was decided to select only the data recorded for the vehicle's front left wheel. This is due to the fact that this pressure should, in principle, be the size with the least variation regarding the other vehicle wheels. The recorded signal waveforms are shown in Fig. 9.

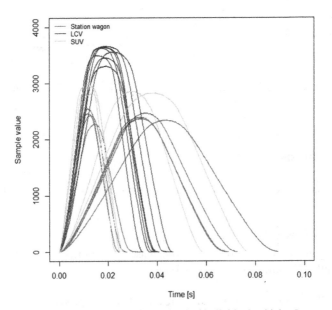

Fig. 9. Signal paths for the front right wheel of individual vehicles [own study]

The curve presented in Fig. 9 shown a possibility of assessment of the vehicle type, in particular in terms of the maximum value of the signal recorded. The shape of the recorded signals is influenced by, among other things, vehicle speed, which is an important parameter in the process of determining the wheel load [12]. Figures 10 and 11 shows the influence of the speed on selected parameters characterizing particular waveforms.

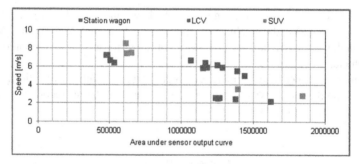

Fig. 10. Relation of the vehicle speed and the area under the signal value [own study]

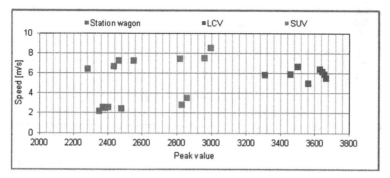

Fig. 11. Relation of the vehicle speed and the signal peak value [own study]

As can be seen, the speed has significantly affected the area under the curve, while no significant change in the maximum value was noted.

In the next step, it was examined how the recording time of the tyre-sensor contact in the function of speed changed (Fig. 12).

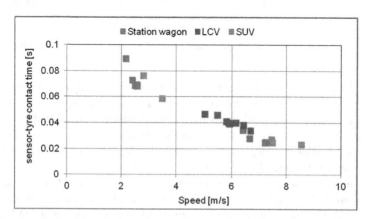

Fig. 12. The relation between the sensor-tyre contact time and speed of vehicle [own study]

As expected, the data presented in the graph shows an almost linear relationship of the sensor-tyre contact and the vehicle speed for each of the analysed vehicles. As could be anticipated, sensor-tyre contact time does not allow for a clear identification of the type of vehicle.

It was then examined whether there is a potential relationship between the maximum signal value and the sensor-tyre contact time and the area under the recorded wheel load signal curve (Fig. 13 and 14).

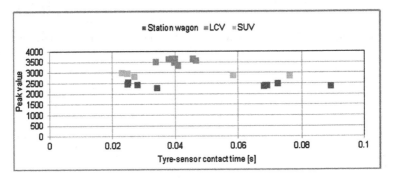

Fig. 13. The relation between the peak value and tyre-sensor contact [own study]

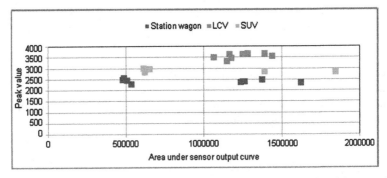

Fig. 14. The relation between the peak value and the area under the signal [own study]

Again, there were no significant correlations between the analysed quantities. Interestingly, a relation between the peak signal value and the coefficient of skewness was observed (Fig. 15). For the recorded waveforms, the symmetry of the signal also changes as the peak value of signal increases – the coefficient of skewness decreases. For LCVs and SUVs, left side asymmetry was noted, while for the lightest SW (Station Wagon) these values oscillated around zero (symmetrical distribution).

Suggesting the idea of using a single sensor to determine vehicle parameters presented in the work [13], in a further step of the analysis, an attempt was made to determine the vehicle speed based on the previously presented relation between speed S and the sensor-tyre contact time t_r (Fig. 12). For this purpose, it was assumed that this relation

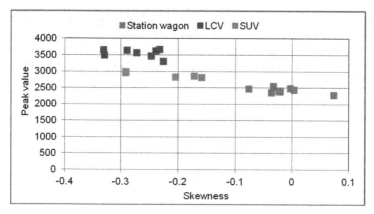

Fig. 15. Dependence of the peak signal value and the coefficient of skewness [own study]

is in the form of a polynomial:

$$S(t_r) = 778\,t_r^2 - 181.4\,t_r + 11.72 \tag{1}$$

The correlation coefficient R^2 of the measured speed and estimated with formula 1 was 0.97. A relation of the measured speed and estimation error (relative difference between estimated and measured speed) was shown in Fig. 16.

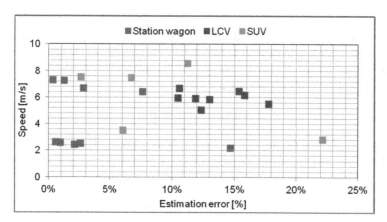

Fig. 16. Dependence of speed and estimation error [own study]

The resulting speed estimation error was between 1 and over 20%. The analysis of the presented dependencies also indicates a reduction in the error rate as the speed increases.

The next step was to determine the wheelbase W as multiplication of speed S and time between peak value for left front and left rear tyre. For this purpose, for the variant $W1$ the estimated speed value was used, while for the variant $W2$ the measured speed was used. The obtained results are shown in Fig. 17. When determining the distance using an estimated speed value, the spread of the values is so large that it makes it impossible to distinguish between an SUV and SW vehicles – it is mainly due to the speed estimation error. For the values determined using the speed calculated from the difference of signals on the two sensors, this spread is much smaller and the average error in measuring the wheelbase does not exceed 3%.

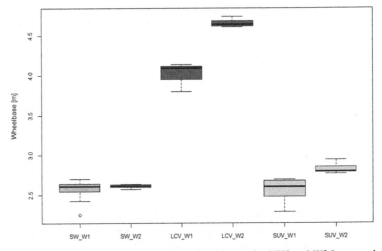

Fig. 17. Box plot of the wheelbase determined by method *W1* and *W2* [own study]

In the last stage of the presented analyses, the front left wheel load of the vehicle was estimated according to method 1 and method 2 presented in [14]. The first of these methods is based on determining the weight as a computation of the maximum value of the signal x_i and the calibration factor a:

$$WL1 = a \cdot Max \, x_i \tag{2}$$

The second method requires knowledge of the area under the curve of the recorded signal A, the width of the *sensor L*, the speed of the vehicle S and the calibration factor b.

$$WL2 = (A \cdot b \cdot S)/L \tag{3}$$

For both methods *WL1* and *WL2*, the calibration factors $(a$ and $b)$ was determined based on the previously known wheel load of the SUV. Significantly for method *WL2*, the value has been determined for the vehicle speed option estimated from relation (1) – method *WL2a* and the known speed determined from different signals for the two strain gauges (method *WL2B*). The result of the analyses is shown in Fig. 18. As can be seen, the smallest value scatter was obtained for method *WL1* using the maximum signal value. In the case of an SUV, this spread was less than 6% of the wheel weight. For the other two methods *WL1* and *WL2*, a spread of 14% and 12% respectively was obtained for the same SUV vehicle.

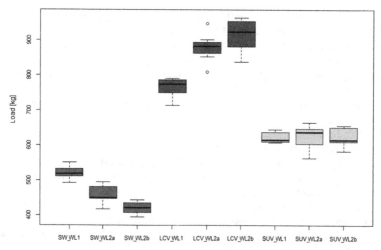

Fig. 18. Box plot of wheel load values determined by method *WL1*, *WL2a*, and *WL2b* [own study]

4   Conclusion

The analysis presented in the article is a part of research and development work on intelligent Weigh in Motion system (iWIM). On the one hand, the aim of the analysis was to indicate the differences in the values observed for selected vehicles with the laden mass below 3.5 tonnes - the obtained results shows that even using data from one sensor there is a possibility of determining the type of vehicles (e.g. SUV, SW, LCV). On the other hand, the aim was also conducting the test of the device operation, which was created within the R&D project.

The scope of the presented analysis was significantly limited by the permissible speed at the installation site (speed limit 30 km/h). The next steps are to build a dedicated test station on a selected section of the national road. Importantly, the recorded data will be supplemented with information from the additional strain gauge and polymer sensors. Ultimately, the system is also intended to enable assessment of the impact of external factors such as dynamics of vehicle movement, meteorological conditions, surface condition, road foundation temperature etc. on the vehicle weighing process.

References

1. Cross.#Optiwim. https://www.cross-traffic.com/en/optiwim/. Accessed 31 May 2020
2. Grakovski, A., Pilipovecs, A.: Weigh-in-motion by fibre-optic sensors: problem of measurement errors compensation for longitudinal oscillations of a truck. In: Kabashkin, I., Yatskiv, I., Prentkovskis, O. (eds.) RelStat 2017. LNNS, vol. 36, pp. 371–380. Springer, Cham (2018). https://doi.org/10.1007/978-3-319-74454-4_36
3. Traffic Data Systems. Weigh In Motion (WIM). https://www.traffic-data-systems.net/en/weigh-in-motion-wim.html. Accessed 31 May 2020
4. Chatterjee, I., Liao, C., Davis, G.A.: A statistical process control approach using cumulative sum control chart analysis for traffic data quality verification and sensor calibration for weigh-in-motion systems. J. Intell. Transp. Syst. **21**(2), 111–122 (2017)

5. GUM. GUM participates in the eMIM project. https://www.gum.gov.pl/pl/aktualnosci/155 4,GUM-uczestnikiem-projektu-eMIM.html. Accessed 31 May 2020

6. Jacob, B., O'Brien, E., Jehaes, S.: COST 323 Weigh-in-Motion of Road Vehicles (1999). http://www.is-wim.org/doc/wim_eu_specs_cost323.pdf. Accessed 01 Jan 2019

7. Rys, D.: Investigation of weigh-in-motion measurement accuracy on the basis of steering axle load spectra. Sensors **19**, 3272 (2019)

8. Burnos, P.: Autokalibracja systemów WIM, a korekta temperaturowa wyników ważenia. PAK **53**, 546–549 (2007)

9. APM PRO: Inteligentny system ważenia pojazdów. https://apm.pl/inteligentny-system-waz enia-pojazdow/. Accessed 31 May 2020

10. Loga, W., Ryguła, A., Maczyński, A.: Using ITS testing ground to measure selected vehicle parameters. In: Mikulski, J. (ed.) TST 2018. CCIS, vol. 897, pp. 70–84. Springer, Cham (2018). https://doi.org/10.1007/978-3-319-97955-7_5

11. Intercomp. Strip Sensors. https://www.intercompcompany.com/its-enforcement-scales/in ground-weigh-in-motion/strip-sensors. Accessed 31 May 2020

12. Kistler. Planning manual, Planning of a WIM station, Type 9195E, 002-300E-07.04 (200-348e) (2004)

13. Samer, R., et al.: Classification and speed estimation of vehicles via tire detection using single-element piezoelectric sensor. J. Adv. Transp. **50**, 1366–1385 (2016)

14. Taek, M.K.: Signal processing of piezoelectric Weight-in-Motion systems (2007)

Advantages and Disadvantages of Intermodal Freight Transportation

Jaroslava Kubáňová[✉], Zuzana Otáhalová, and Šimon Senko

University of Zilina, Univerzitna 8215/1, Zilina, Slovak Republic
{jaroslava.kubanova,zuzana.otahalova,
simon.senko}@fpedas.uniza.sk

Abstract. Intermodal transport is a relatively new mode of transport that has developed on the basis of existing basic modes of transport. In the historical context, therefore, traffic law defining the basic frameworks and necessary regulations for intermodal transport has also evolved under the law of the basic modes of transport and in the wider economy in general. Intermodal transport therefore does not have its own legislation in the form of special laws. At most it has its own notice as implementing rules, but they refer to the laws of the basic types of transport. The intermodal terminal only participates in the transport of basic intermodal freight unit translation services and their short-term storage, as basic services of a transition point between different types of transport networks. Intermodal terminals also include other additional services such as technical inspections, maintenance, cleaning or long-term storage of empty intermodal loading units. These services can already be provided by multiple subjects, which is a guarantee of a competitive environment. At the same time, the risk of damage to the goods during handling increases. Advantages and disadvantages of using intermodal transport from the perspective of carriers are described in the article.

Keywords: Terminal · Risk · Transport · Infrastructure · Incoterms 2020

1 Introduction

A characteristic feature of increasing the dynamics of the world economy in recent years is the process of globalization, i.e. world division of trade and is the result of activities of countries, members of OECD, which since 2000 also include the Slovak Republic. The streamlining of international trade in goods and services creates conditions for wider involvement of Slovakia in the international trade division, but strictly requires the creation of conditions for the provision of transport services in logistic transport chains at a significantly higher quality level than previously.

One of the basic condition for the effective exchange of goods is the establishment of transport hub, where are concentrated and distribution of goods for the purpose of effective transport between manufacturers, retailers and consumers within the logistic transport chain. These hubs, which also use the technical term logistics centres, will, in the future, create the core points of the intermodal transport network and the communication framework for goods and information flows in Europe and the world, according

© Springer Nature Switzerland AG 2020
J. Mikulski (Ed.): TST 2020, CCIS 1289, pp. 285–295, 2020.
https://doi.org/10.1007/978-3-030-59270-7_21

to EU transport policy [11]. Around these centres that arise in important communication hubs, suitable conditions are created for the construction of industrial parks and consumer agglomerations. An important part of these hubs are intermodal transport terminals, where the modal shift takes place and transport between them is provided by direct intermodal trains with high quality of transport.

Despite limited financial support for infrastructure, intermodal transport has been a dynamically developing, environmentally friendly transport sector in Slovakia since 1995, with the growth of transported goods. See Fig. 1. Further development of intermodal transport is slowed down mainly by unsatisfactory infrastructure of container transhipments in Slovakia. Therefore, it is necessary to create conditions for its support by accelerated completion of intermodal transport infrastructure and mainly terminals, given the expected rapid development of the Slovak economy [7].

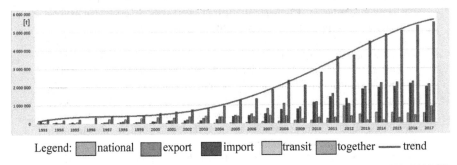

Legend: ☐ national ■ export ■ import ☐ transit ■ together —— trend

Fig. 1. An amount of transported goods by intermodal transport in SR in years 1993–2017 [7]

A key target of European transport policy is to achieve a 60% reduction in greenhouse gas (GHG) emissions from transport by 2050 compared to 1990 levels. One of the strategies to achieve this is to shift 30% of transport over distances of 300 km and longer from road to transport modes with lower CO_2 emissions, including shifting containers and other ITUs from road to rail and inland waterways [5] (Fig. 2).

Combined transport as part of intermodal transport is a sophisticated transport system based on the transport of cargo in one and the same cargo unit, which alternates different means of transport on different transport routes from consignor to consignee, "door to door". Intermodal transport uses all means of transport of basic types of transport such as road, rail, inland waterway or sea.

In general, intermodal terminals are very expensive devices that are built from long-term investment resources, usually with the participation of public funds and a return on the order of decades [15]. These investments usually exceed the financial capacity of individual carriers, operators or shippers of intermodal transport.

It is therefore a natural interest to achieve the use of intermodal transport terminals by several intermodal transport operators, whether or not they are competing, in order to achieve a better distribution of investments and their return. However, this creates a kind of natural monopoly and the potential for competition, which must be protected under European Union rules.

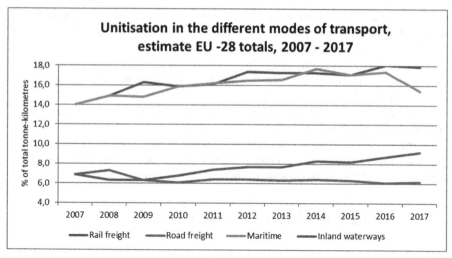

Fig. 2. Unitisation in the different modes of transport, estimate EU 28 totals in years 2007–2017 [3]

Entities operating in the intermodal/combined transport chain:

Carrier: since combined transport is characterized by a combination of several types of transport, it is logical that carriers may also alternate. The more carriers involved in the transport of goods, the more is the risk that something will happen to the goods.

Shipper (Consignor/Consignee): an important part of the transport chain, which also contributes to the possibility of risk occurrence. Whether it is a bad choice of carrier or bad transport scheduling, there may be a risk.

Freight forwarder: if there is a freight forwarder in the transport chain, it can be said, that against the shipper bears the risks of the same as if he himself were a transport operator.

Storekeeper: during the combined transport of goods it is possible that the goods will be stored during the journey in a warehouse, mostly in the terminal. During storage may result in the loss of goods, stolen goods or damaged during handling.

2   Advantages of Using Intermodal Transport

Intermodal freight transport provides the flexibility to choose how will be goods transported. In addition, the shipper has the opportunity to be creative in finding the most efficient way to move goods. In general, this process involves at least two modes of transport. The more effectively it is planned, the more money can be saved. Intermodal transport offers the advantage of a relatively low cost compared to other methods [4].

Intermodal freight transportation reduces truck driver capacity requirements over long distances.

IT led to an increase in shipping capability of utilizing the space.

Standardization of containers has permitted equipment to be designed anywhere in the world to support intermodal transportation. The containerized freight can be moved intact to customers virtually anywhere in the globe where containerships, container ports and inland transportation capable of handling containers exist. Standardization makes possible reduced handling, costs and transit time [12].

Intermodal provides more transportations options to shippers. Single modes may be too slow or too expensive for the shipper, however the combination of modes provides more options.

Intermodal can reduce highway congestion. A single intermodal train can replace 200 trucks on the highway using one-fourth the fuel [18].

Shippers have found intermodal to be an effective means to increase the sustainability of their supply chains. As sustainable supply chains increase in importance, more shippers will be attracted to this added benefit of intermodal transportation [10].

3   Disadvantages of Using Intermodal Transport

Speed
Although intermodal transportation offers the benefit of relatively low costs compared to other methods, it obtains this by sacrificing speed; any time cargo is transferred to a comparatively slower means of travel, for example trains, which operate on fixed rails that may not offer as direct route as the roads a truck uses, it slows down. The reason being is intermodal shipments are typically truck, plus a day. When an intermodal shipment requires two railroads to be utilized, a shipper can expect the shipment to be truck plus 2 to 3 days. To operate at peak efficiency, intermodal transportation must also reduce the amount of time spent waiting in depots for a new carrier to arrive or for cargo to be unloaded [13].

Lack of Reliability
Because of its reliance on more than one mode of transit, intermodal transportation is also subject to lower overall reliability; as the chain of different modes grows, the possibility of any link in the chain breaking down also increases. This is particularly problematic when one of the modes of transport is rail; railroads are more susceptible to delays introduced by bad weather or equipment failure. For this reason, as well as concerns over speed, shippers that require reliable, high-speed transportation are less likely to consider intermodal systems [17].

Intermodal Operation
Many intermodal terminals face logistical challenges. Congestion and inefficiency are still one of the main challenges posed by intermodal terminal operation.

Delivery Frequency
Delivery frequency will be directly affected by the level of service provided by the least frequent mode. In an ocean carrier provides twice a week service, then an intermodal network cannot provide greater frequency - unless, large shipments are transported, staged at an intermediate location and then delivered in more frequent but smaller shipments.

Intermodal transportation is not designed for small frequent shipments; JIT deliveries on a multiple delivery per day schedule may not be well suited for intermodal [9].

High Infrastructure Cost

Intermodal freight transportation also suffers from comparatively high infrastructure costs. Containerization has lowered the cost and difficulty of transporting goods by standardizing their form; shippers can easily move the same container from a ship to a train to a truck. Handling these containers, however, requires that shippers have the heavy-duty cranes and equipment necessary to manipulate large containers; this infrastructure may not exist in all places, particularly in developing countries.

Restricted or Prohibited Products

Not every commodity can be shipped via intermodal. There are products that can be either restricted or prohibited. Prohibited products are items that, without exception, are not allowed to travel via the rail or road infrastructure. Restricted products are products that have rules and regulations that a carriers needs to follow for the shipment to move legally via mode of transportation [1].

Damage

Whenever cargo has to be shuffled around, carriers risk the possibility of damage as the freight is transferred from one method of transportation to another. Fortunately, this danger can be mitigated, but doing so generally involves over packing by adding more bracing and protective material than would normally be deemed sufficient. The reason blocking and bracing is so important is because intermodal containers experience what is harmonic vibration [8]. The vibration has the ability to move the contents of a shipment both horizontally and vertically in the container. This added weight and expense partially counteracts the advantages intermodal transportation has in terms of energy efficiency and cost.

Risk of damage or theft of cargo during intermodal transportation can be:

- mechanical cargo damage,
- theft of cargo,
- theft of semi-trailer,
- fraudulent pickup,
- loss of cargo,
- delay in transport.

In the next figures we can see the global cargo theft trends in 2019 compared to 2018 (Figs. 3 and 4).

International transport and logistics insurer TT club and supply chain intelligence firm BSI released data for 2019 showing that 87% of cargo thefts targeted trucks in 2019, up from 84% in 2018, dwarfing theft from all other modalities, including warehouses and trains. What's more, 60% of truck incidents occurred while the vehicles were in transit, in rest areas, or at an unsecured parking location. There is an average of eight cargo theft incidents per day from unsecure truck parking worldwide [2, 16].

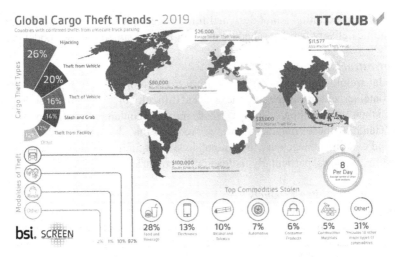

Fig. 3. Global cargo theft trends in 2019 [16]

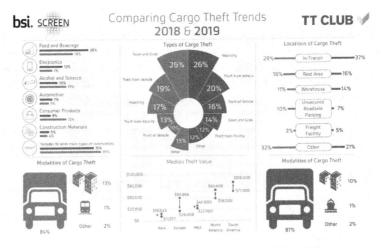

Fig. 4. Comparing cargo theft trends 2018 and 2019 [16]

The risks associated with the carriage of goods are classified in the group of commercial risks in international trade.

These risks may:

- Limited to the control of goods being transported (it can be accurately quantified and estimated).
- Extend to consequential damages if the goods are not in the right place at the right time (it is difficult to quantified and estimate).

Three levels of transport risk management:

- **transfer of risk** (transport and forwarding insurance),
- **risk reduction** (selection of suitable transport, suitable and safe packing and labelling of goods, national requirements for packing of goods can be found in the International Chamber of Commerce - ICC),
- **getting rid of the risk by transferring it to business partners** - it depends in the valid conditions governing liability:

  - *carrier for the goods in each international transport contract,*
  - *freight forwarder for goods under the forwarding contracts usually national.*

If the shipper does not want to rely on the limited liability of the carrier or freight forwarder, there is the possibility of using internationally recognized rules Incoterms 2020. However, this should be duly stated in the sales-purchase contract.

At that time, he will know exactly whether the responsibility for the goods to the buyer or to the seller. However, this should be right stated in the sales contract.

Incoterms rules were designed to reduce lack of misunderstanding and support communication between parties involved in shipping procedures and processes. It goes without doubts that the terms have become a communication tool between the parties [14].

Incoterms are terms that state the responsibilities of the shipper and buyer involved in an international or domestic shipment.

For example, in a door-to-door shipment, the cargo must be picked up by a truck, brought to a warehouse, consolidated, brought to a port, loaded onto a vessel, transported overseas by said vessel, and have everything repeated on the foreign side. While in transit, the costs associated with delivery and insurance can be very high. Thus, it is quite rare that any one side of the party should pay for all of it. This is where incoterms come in.

Incoterms state who is responsible to pay for and insure the cargo in each stage of its transit from point A to point B. If your incoterms state you are responsible until the goods are unloaded at their overseas port, then you are liable to pay for the insurance and/or any accidental loss or damages that occur between their pickup and unloading at the foreign port. Respectively, any damages or accidental loss that occurs after they have departed from the foreign port inland are the responsibility of the other party in the incoterm agreement [1].

The most recent version of the clauses dates from 1.1.2020. However, unlike amendments to laws, a new edition does not automatically mean that the previous versions will be lost. The legal binding effect is in the hands of the contracting parties, which can choose between themselves any choice, even an older version of the clauses (of course, it can be expected that the current version will be most adapted to the latest requirements and developments in the field). For this reason, the sales contracts always state the year of Incoterms, as agreed by the parties.

Incoterms are divided into 4 categories; in the first three groups (E, F, C) the obligations pass from the seller to the buyer when the goods are dispatched and are thus more demanding for the buyer. In the case of the fourth group (D), the obligations pass from the seller to the buyer only when the goods are delivered. And from the point of view of the necessity to fulfill the obligations, they place higher demands on the seller. In Fig. 5 we can see the increasing risk and cost from the perspective of the seller [6].

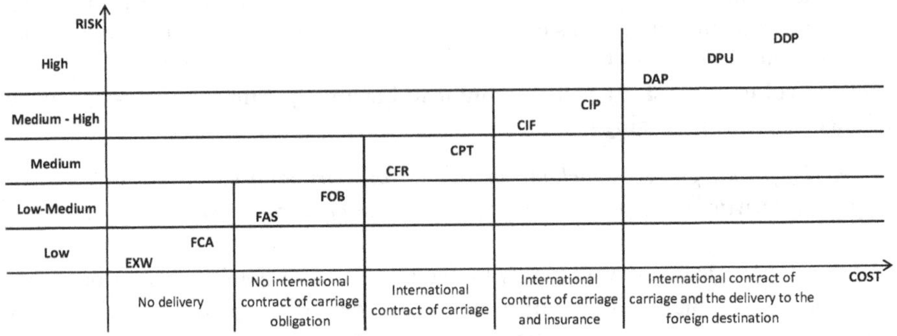

RISK	No delivery	No international contract of carriage obligation	International contract of carriage	International contract of carriage and insurance	International contract of carriage and the delivery to the foreign destination → COST
High					DAP DPU DDP
Medium - High				CIF CIP	
Medium			CFR CPT		
Low-Medium		FAS FOB			
Low	EXW FCA				

Fig. 5. Incoterms 2020 risk bands from seller's side [own study]

EXW means that the buyer is at risk when the goods are delivered to their final destination. The seller either does not load the goods on the collection vehicles or does not equip it for export, or if the seller loads the goods, he does so at the buyer's risk and expense. So EXW provides the lowest cost and risk option to the seller.

FCA means that the seller delivers the goods, cleared for export, at the named place (possibly including the seller's own premises). The goods can be delivered to a carrier nominated by the buyer, or to another party nominated by the buyer. If the delivery takes place in the premises of the seller or in another place under the control of the seller, the seller is responsible for loading the goods on the buyer's carrier. However, if the delivery takes place elsewhere, the seller shall be deemed to have delivered the goods after the shipment has arrived at the designated place; the buyer is responsible for unloading the goods and loading them on their own carrier. What is new in this rule is that the parties can agree that the buyer – at their own cost and risk – will instruct the carrier to issue a transport document to the seller, stating that the goods have been loaded on-board [1, 6].

The context of this provision is the letter of credit, and the firmly entrenched habit of banks who issue letters of credit to call for an on-board bill of lading – evidence that the goods are loaded on board a ship. This document may be called for, even where the carrier has taken charge of the goods by loading onto a truck at the seller's inland depot.

FAS and **FOB** have been banded in the low-medium risk category, reflecting the marginal increase in cost and risk faced the seller under these terms. Under FAS the seller completes the delivery by placing the goods alongside the ship nominated by the buyer at the named port of shipment. This means that the buyer has to bear all costs and risks of loss of or damage to the goods from that moment [6, 14].

Therefore, FOB contract requires a seller to deliver goods on board a vessel that is to be designated by the buyer in a manner customary at the particular port. In this case, the seller must also arrange for export clearance. On the other hand, the buyer pays cost of marine freight transportation, bill of lading fees, insurance, unloading and transportation cost from the arrival port to destination.

CFR and **CPT** are categorized as medium risks, because the seller must enter into a contract of international carriage and pay for the freight charges to the agreed destination. It should be noted that even though the seller is obligated to pay for transport costs, the risk in transit over the consignment transfers as per the FOB or FCA points, as the carriage of goods is conducted at the buyer's risk. Entering into a contract of carriage exposes the exporter to additional risks and causes additional pressure on cash flows as, typically, the buyer is extended payment terms, but the carrier demands immediate payment on lodgment of consignments in the exporting country. CFR should only be used for non-containerized sea freight and inland waterway transport; for all other modes of transport it should be replaced with CPT [6].

CIF and **CIP** consignments are categorized in the medium-high risk band, reflecting the seller's obligation to provide insurance to the buyer. The seller must provide insurance for the duration of the journey against risks covered at least by the minimum standard set of clauses – Institute Cargo Clauses. Here is change from Incoterms 2010 where the minimum was ICC C, or any similar set of clauses, unless specifically agreed by both parties [14]. In 2020 CIP requires the seller to insure the goods for 110% of the contract value under ICC A - All Risks insurance. The seller must also turn over documents necessary, to obtain the goods from the carrier or to assert claim against an insurer to the buyer. The documents include (as a minimum) the invoice, the insurance policy, and the bill of lading. These three documents represent the cost, insurance, and freight of CIF. The seller's obligation ends when the documents are handed over to the buyer. Then, the buyer has to pay at the agreed price [6, 16].

The high risk band comprises **DAP**, **DPU** and **DDP**, because the exporter retains the risks in transit until the goods reach the agreed destination in the country of import. Purchasing on these terms is comparatively more expensive because the seller incurs greater costs and risks. The most important consideration for DDP terms is that the seller is responsible for clearing the goods through customs in the buyer's country, including both paying the duties and taxes, and obtaining the necessary authorizations and registrations from the authorities in that country. Unless the rules and regulations in the buyer's country are very well understood, DDP terms can be a very big risk both in terms of delays and in unforeseen extra costs and should be used with caution [14].

Traders and bankers are facing problems with the proper application of Incoterms 2020. For Traders problem is the right choice of delivery conditions associated with transport modes, while they do not realize fully the risks that these decisions bring. Maritime containers are the biggest challenge and considerable efforts need to be made to support the correct selection of the appropriate Incoterms 2020 based on specific circumstances.

4   Conclusion

Contrary to popular belief, intermodal does not provide significant cost benefits over over-the-road trucking. While there are short-term fuel expense reductions, the total costs associated with building and maintaining railroad infrastructure counterbalances any periodic savings. Railroads generally do not work directly with shippers. Instead, they work with intermodal motor carriers who then sell their services to the shippers. It is vital for shippers to select an intermodal motor carrier who has sufficient experience in dealing with railroad operations. For example, weight restrictions, loading procedures, beneficial owner requirements, and document handling are areas that must be dealt with in intermodal transport. As mentioned in above Incoterms have been in use for several decades and eventually, were taken for granted by the people involved in international trade transactions. Incoterms in theory and Incoterms in practice are two different things. It is one of the reasons why Incoterms users misinterpret and make mistakes when selecting a delivery term to be used. And the right understanding and use of incoterms rules is a step towards risk reduction in intermodal transport. If parties become aware of what and until when they are responsible for the goods being transported, they can also anticipate the aforementioned risks of intermodal transport. For a better refer of the impact of risks, it would be appropriate to point to a specific case study.

Acknowledgment. This paper was developed under the support of project: MSVVS SR - VEGA No. 1/0245/20 Poliak, M.: Identification of the impact of a change in transport related legislation on the competitiveness of carriers and carriage safety.

References

1. Bergami, R.: Managing Incoterms 2010 risks: tension with trade and banking practices, Australia, vol. 6, no. 3 (2013). file:///C:/Users/KCMD/Downloads/Managing_Incoterms_2010_risks_tension_with_trade_a%20(1).pdf. Accessed 15 Jan 2020
2. Caban, J., et al.: Safety of maritime transport in the Baltic Sea. In: LOGI, vol. 134 (2017)
3. Eurostat (2017). https://ec.europa.eu/eurostat/statistics-explained/index.php/Freight_transpor ted_in_containers_-_statistics_on_unitisation. Accessed 15 Jan 2020
4. Gnap, J.: Modelling of transport and transport process in road Freight transport, 1st edn. University in Zilina. 2013120 (2013). ISBN 978-80-554-0744-9
5. Chłopek, Z., Strzałkowska, K.: Risks posed by particulate matter to the human health and environment near transport routes. In: The Archives of Automotive Engineering – Archiwum Motoryzacji, vol. 63, no. 1 (2014)
6. ICC Publication: Incoterms (2020). 723E. ISBN 978-92-842-0510-3
7. Intermodal promotion centre: Výkony kombinovanej dopravy v SR. http://www.intermodal.sk/vykony-kombinovanej-dopravy-v-slovenskej-republike/27s. Accessed 15 Jan 2020
8. Kalasova, A., Kupculjakova, J.: The future in the telematics applications as support for increased safety. Transp. Probl. 7(1), 103–109 (2012)
9. Kalašová, A., Faith, P., Mikulski, J.: Telematics applications, an important basis for improving the road safety. In: Mikulski, J. (ed.) TST 2015. CCIS, vol. 531, pp. 292–299. Springer, Cham (2015). https://doi.org/10.1007/978-3-319-24577-5_29
10. Konečný, V., Šimková, I., Komačková, L.: The accident rate of tourists in Slovakia. LOGI – Sci. J. Transp. Logist. 6(1), 160–171 (2015)
11. Kubasakova, I., Jagelcak, J.: Load distribution in general purpose maritime container and the analysis of load distribution on extendable semitrailer container chassis carrying different types of containers. Naše more = Our sea: znanstveno-stručni časopis za more i pomorstvo 61(5–6), 106–116 (2014)
12. Poliak, M.: The relationship with reasonable profit and risk in public passenger transport in the Slovakia. Ekonomicky casopis 61(2), 206–220 (2013)

13. Poliak, M., Poliaková, A.: Relation of social legislation in road transport on driver's work quality. In: Mikulski, J. (ed.) TST 2015. CCIS, vol. 531, pp. 300–310. Springer, Cham (2015). https://doi.org/10.1007/978-3-319-24577-5_30

14. Seredyuk, V.: Incoterms in practice: hidden risks (2017). https://www.theseus.fi/bitstream/handle/10024/135838/Seredyuk_Victoria.pdf?sequence=2. Accessed 15 Jan 2020

15. Intermodal promotion centre: Dobudovanie základnej infraštruktúry intermodálnnej dopravy v SR. http://www.intermodal.sk/dobudovanie-infrastruktury-kombinovanej-dopravy-ref/603s. Accessed 15 Jan 2020

16. BSI and TT Club: Cargo Theft Report (2020). https://www.ttclub.com/fileadmin/uploads/tt-club/Documents/TT_and_BSI_annual_theft_report/BSI___TT_Club_Report_2020.pdf. Accessed 15 Jan 2020

17. Kubasakova, I., Jagelcak, J.: Logistics system just-in-time and its implementation within the company. In: Communications: Scientific Letters of the University of Žilina, vol. 18, no. 2, pp. 109–112 (2016)

18. Marušinec, P.: Nediskriminačný prístup k infraštruktúre kombinovanej dopravy (2010). http://www.intermodal.sk/nediskriminacny-pristup-k-infarstrukture/482s. Accessed 15 Jan 2020

Simulation of Goods Transport

Iveta Kubasakova[✉] and Simon Senko

University of Žilina, Univerzitná 8215/1, Žilina, Slovakia
{iveta.kubasakova,simon.senko}@fpedas.uniza.sk

Abstract. At present the Slovak and abroad enterprises try to adapt to the new modern trends in distribution logistics processes and their technologies. However some companies have the problems with their implementation to the existing distribution logistics systems. That is why in the paper the computer simulation is used for selected logistics technologies in distribution process. It is based on the representation of real model of distribution process by its simulation model describing only those properties of real system of which we are interested in the terms of integration of selected logistics technologies. On the base of existing logistics technologies with using the simulation of existing distribution process it is possible to choose the right one. The paper is concerned about the use of computer simulation for selected logistics technologies in the distribution process for example Just in Time, Just in Sequence or their combinations. The results of computer simulation can be re-applied to the real distribution process in the form of improvements of its properties. The aim of paper is to point out the possibilities of using the computer simulation for selected logistics technologies in terms of distribution process in company.

Keywords: Transport process · Just in Time technology · Just in Sequence technology · Simulation

1 Introduction

In the area of transport and logistics, there is a great increase in competition, not only within individual types of transport but also between types of transport with each other. Businesses and logistics operators are thus becoming more flexible and more competitive by using several types of transport and logistics services. Transport in the company affects the speed, reliability of product delivery, but last but not least, timely and quality delivery of products, which increases the added value for the customer and thus the level of customer service.

Simulating the JIT and JIS logistics technology model in the distribution process can solve the problem. It is an analysis and identification of possible problem areas in the distribution process in any company providing transportation of goods and services on the road network.

By simulating the JIT and JIS logistics technology model in the distribution process, a solution can also be found in the case of designing and implementing a new logistics technology into the distribution process, or logistics technology (JIT, JIS) in any enterprise.

© Springer Nature Switzerland AG 2020
J. Mikulski (Ed.): TST 2020, CCIS 1289, pp. 296–305, 2020.
https://doi.org/10.1007/978-3-030-59270-7_22

Introducing JIT technology into an existing distribution system in an enterprise should benefit the enterprise from:

- spatial allocation of production sites or consumption sites (up to 50–70 km),
- shipping costs must be reduced as a result of the reduction of stock in the warehouse, and ultimately of the entire stock holding in the enterprise,
- traffic routes between production and place of consumption should be clear of traffic without collision points such as traffic accidents, traffic jams, …
- JIT orders must be precisely timed and these delivery intervals must be adhered to in order to fully eliminate inventory in stock over time.

The JIS technology has been known and used for several years in the world. The way JIS orders have become tried, proven and increasingly widespread. At present, parts that have not been considered in this way are also sequenced. For example, components with a small number of variations or sequencing over long distances between the supplier and the customer (there are no exceptions or distances exceeding 800 km, as is the case with Volkswagen Slovakia a. S.) [1].

Sequence pulses define the order in which the individual modules need to be delivered and are usually sent to the supplier a few days before the final assembly of the car. When sending them, it is necessary to respect the time needed to manufacture the ordered items and to deliver the shipment [2, 3].

In both the automotive industry and in subcontractors, the proportion of such types of goods transport increases from year to year. (approx. 70% in 2010). Aimtec implements JIS in Audi AG, BMW, SAAB and Man. The information necessary for the reaction is the vehicle type, product group, part number, assembly line, and part number ordered by assembly point six days prior to assembly. This information is sent continuously [4, 5] (Table 1).

Table 1. The resulting numbers of vehicles served by simulating JIT and JIS technology in the distribution process [own study]

Transport service	JIT model	JIS model
Day	Average	Average
Monday	21 141,16	45 990,00
Tuesday	4 661,57	17 472,00
Wednesday	1 020,83	4 356,00
Thursday	1 661,22	6 516,00
Friday	14 628,21	36 822,00

Figure 1 shows the number of vehicles served in the JIT and JIS models. It can be seen that during the 1000 replication simulation, which ran 24 h a day, 365 days a year, more vehicles served in the JIS technology were in the distribution process. It can be stated that these differences are considerable. This implies that the precise timing of JIS transport is much more positive for the organization, optimization, and management of transport than on-demand transport by JIT technology. In this case, it is a faster turnover of vehicles in the distribution process. It is a safer transport method and also more economically advantageous for the company, as the company has regular customers with regular requirements. The resulting numbers of vehicles served by simulating JIT and JIS technology in the distribution process.

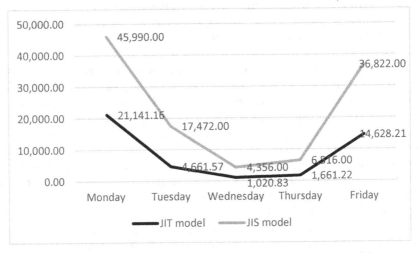

Fig. 1. Number of vehicles served in JIT and JIS models [own study]

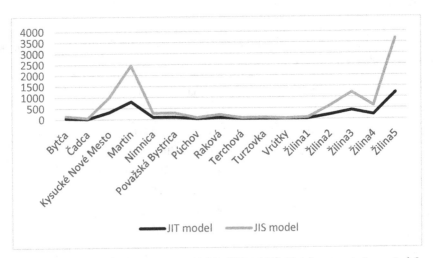

Fig. 2. The number of vehicles served in the JIT and JIS models per route [own study]

In Fig. 2 is the operation of vehicles on individual routes within the JIT and JIS models. Here you can see the direction of transport to the customer, which is important information for the company in terms of potential optimization of the distribution process.

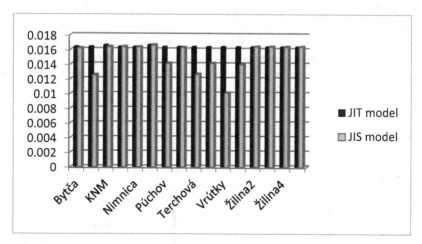

Fig. 3. Average loading time of vehicles in JIT and JIS models (hours) [own study]

In Fig. 3 shows the average loading time in hours in the JIT and JIS models in the distribution process. The simulation shows that the average loading times in both models are comparable with the exception of several transport routes namely Čadca, Púchov, Terchová, Turzovka, Vrútky and Žilina 1. It follows that the kind of logistic technology

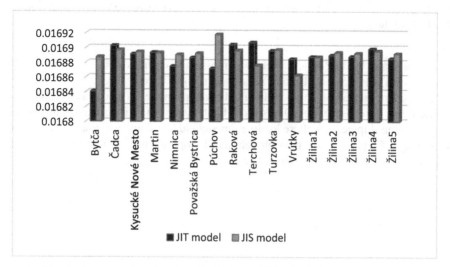

Fig. 4. Average unloading time of vehicles in JIT and JIS (hours) [own study]

JIS has a positive effect on shortening the average loading time delivery of goods in the aforementioned cities.

Similar data on average landing times can be seen in the following figure. It can also be stated that the chosen type of logistic technology has a positive effect on the average landing time in the JIS model compared to the JIT model.

In the following Fig. 4 and Fig. 5 it is possible to see more detailed statistical outputs from the simulation of the JIT and JIS model, namely the maximum and minimum average of the number of vehicles that have passed the individual routes. Based on these results, it can be stated that the company focuses mainly on customers operating in Žilina, Martin, KNM and therefore it is possible to adapt other possible orders by distribution on given transport routes (Fig. 6).

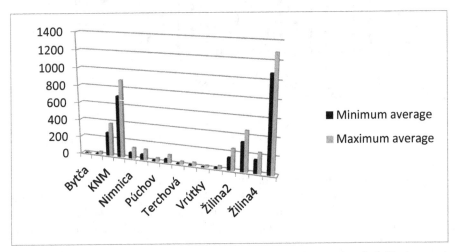

Fig. 5. Minimum and maximum average number of vehicles transported on individual routes in the JIT [own study]

The average loading time of vehicles transported on individual routes in the JIT model (hours) and JIS model (hours) is shown in Figs. 7 and 8.

For better comparison and possible modifications in the JIT and JIS models, it can be stated that the chosen type of logistics technology has a positive effect on the loading time for some shipments, i. these loading times could be minimized. Each model needs to be analyzed separately and possible solutions for optimization of individual processes within the distribution process should be found (Fig. 9).

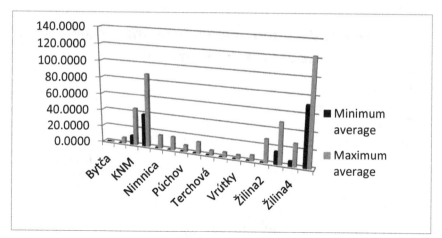

Fig. 6. Average loading time of vehicles transported on individual routes in the JIT model (hours) [own study]

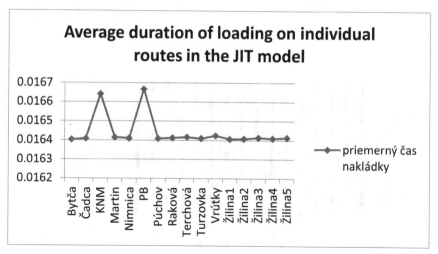

Fig. 7. Minimum and maximum average number of vehicles transported on individual routes in the JIT [own study]

Figures 10 and 11 represent output data on the number of vehicles that have been served in the minimum or the maximum possible number in JIT and JIS model in the distribution process.

In conclusion, choosing the right logistics technology in the distribution process can bring several benefits to the business. The possible benefits of simulating logistics technologies in the distribution process need to be divided based on the usability of the type of information.

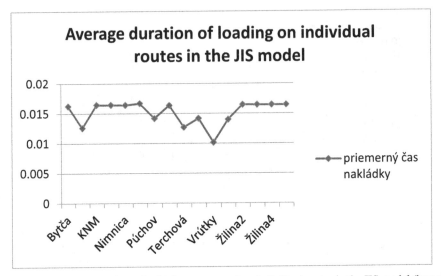

Fig. 8. Average loading time of vehicles transported on individual routes in the JIS model (hours) [own study]

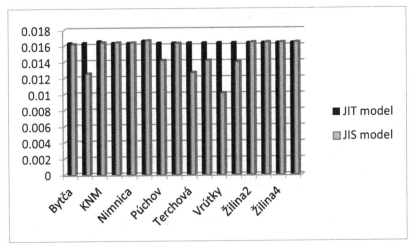

Fig. 9. Average loading time in the JIT and JIS models [own study]

Customer benefits:

– information on delivery of goods in time to the customer,
– presentation of company results,
– Possibility of acquiring a new customer by good advertising in the form of simulation of achieved business results.

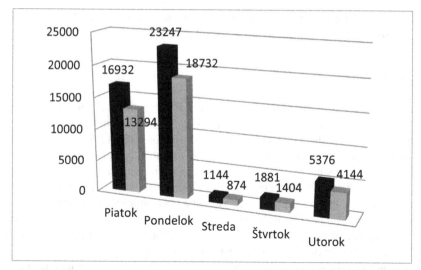

Fig. 10. Minimum and maximum average number of vehicles in JIT model [own study]

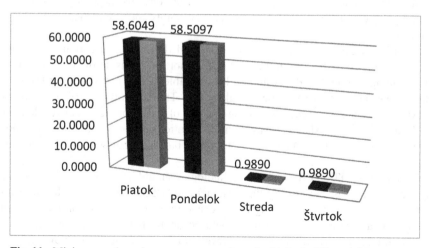

Fig. 11. Minimum and maximum average number of vehicles in JIS model [own study]

Business benefits:

– use of rolling stock,
– searching for possible reserves in logistics technologies in the distribution process,
– possibilities of comparing the application of logistics technologies,
– information on the possibilities of the distribution process failure, bottlenecks.

Logistics technologies and their simulations are beneficial not only for businesses and customers, but also for the theory, where it is possible to simulate results based on real facts and deduce other consequences. This information can be helpful in addressing other distribution processes and their individual parts [6, 7].

2 Conclusion

The paper is devoted to the problems of JIT and JIS logistics technologies. The comparison of these logistics technologies is based on the simulation of JIT and JIS in the distribution process of the company. At present, the use of JIT and JIS logistics technologies in the automotive, electronics and, to a large extent, subcontracting companies are largely used. The benefits of JIT technology are in shortening inventory replenishment times, timing of shipments, better customer service, increased mutual trust between supplier and customer. In the automotive industry, the JIS technology has started to be used to a greater extent as it is a precisely timed delivery of goods to the customer in a precise order and number of products. This technology is adapted to the requirements of the manufacturers, mostly two-hour and four-hour delivery intervals.

Computer simulation is one of the most accurate analytical methods used to simulate production systems, warehouse service systems, handling problems, etc. Simulation of logistics technologies is beneficial not only for distribution logistics processes but also for theory, where we can draw conclusions about the usability and cost of these technologies in companies [8].

By simulating the logistics technologies JIT and JIS in the distribution process, it is possible to point out changes in the time of transport of goods, at the time of loading and unloading of goods at the customer. It is possible to find bottlenecks of transport, i. days when the number of traffic is high or low. The JIS in the distribution process removes this problem by precisely setting the time of arrival of the vehicle for loading, usually at 4 h intervals. Also, this way of the distribution process in the company is more convenient for organizing not only the distribution, but also loading, unloading, size and utilization of the fleet [9].

Simulation of JIT and JIS logistics technologies should bring positive feedback not only for the company, but also for the customer and last but not least for the company, especially due to the precise timing of the exact number of vehicles on the transport network. In rare cases, JIT shipments would occur. In this way, the management of freight traffic on the road network could prevent traffic accidents, congestions ...

References

1. Gnap, J., Kubanova, J.: Selected options for modelling of transport processes particularly in relation to intermodal transport. In: LOGI 2017, vol. 134 (2017)
2. Hanšút, L., Dávid, A., Gašparík, J.: The critical path method as the method for evaluation and identification of the optimal container trade route between Asia and Slovakia. In: Business Logistics in Modern Management: Proceedings, Faculty of Economics in Osijek, Osijek, pp. 29–42 (2017)
3. Culik, K., Harantova, V., Kalasova, A.: Traffic modelling of the circular junction in the city of Zilina. Adv. Sci. Technol.-Res. J. 13(4), 162–169 (2019)

4. Kubanova, J., Poliakova, B.: Truck driver scheduling of the rest period as an essential element of safe transport. In: 20th International Scientific Conference on Transport Means, pp. 22–26 (2016)
5. Kubíková, S., Kalašová, A., Černický, Ľ.: Microscopic simulation of optimal use of communication network. In: Mikulski, J. (ed.) TST 2014. CCIS, vol. 471, pp. 414–423. Springer, Heidelberg (2014). https://doi.org/10.1007/978-3-662-45317-9_44
6. Piala, P., Galieriková, A., Dávid, A.: Global transportation of foodstuffs. In: Communications: Scientific Letters of the University of Zilina, vol. 19, no. 2, pp. 116–119. EDIS – EDIS - Publishing House of the University of Žilina (2017)
7. Poliak, M., Poliaková, A.: Relation of social legislation in road transport on driver's work quality. In: Mikulski, J. (ed.) TST 2015. CCIS, vol. 531, pp. 300–310. Springer, Cham (2015). https://doi.org/10.1007/978-3-319-24577-5_30
8. Poliak, M., et al.: The impact of the transport route on the cost of the transfer (2018)
9. Stopka, O., Cerna, L., Zitricky, V.: Methodology for measuring the customer satisfaction with logistics services. NASE MORE **63**(3), 189–194 (2016)

Variability Characteristics of Pavement Temperature and Road Conditions on Submontane Areas

Wiktoria Loga-Księska[✉] and Justyna Sordyl

University of Bielsko-Biala, Willowa 2, 43-309 Bielsko-Biala, Poland
{wloga,jsordyl}@ath.eu

Abstract. A significant number of road traffic accidents can be directly attributed to danger caused by unfavorable weather conditions. Road weather information system (RWIS) can provide a highly targeted information customized to area specificity. Well-build and developed system that provides real time high quality information, not only is a crucial element of ensuring safety and efficient travel for road users but also can be a great support in decision making process of road authorities. Up-to-date information about road conditions seems to be particularly important in the mountainous and submontane areas, where meteorological factors can change relatively rapidly. The paper presents the results of field tests on the pavement temperature performance in the submontane area in the city of Bielsko-Biala. Presented measurements were performed using a mobile road weather information sensor, installed on the vehicle. The test runs were pursued in variable weather conditions both by day and by night. Authors analysed the repeatability of measured indications and factors affecting fluctuations of pavement temperature.

Keywords: RWIS · Mobile weather sensor · Pavement temperature · Road surface temperature

1 Introduction

The road meteorological environment is a very complex issue. One of the crucial elements of effective traffic and road infrastructure management is the knowledge about atmospheric conditions and the ability to processes its influence on local areas. The required level of detail is usually much more precise than the scale regularly considered in operational frameworks. Weather conditions on the road are influenced by the local environment, including natural terrain, the lay of land, built structures, as well as land cover. Hazardous road conditions as fog or a slippery surface can develop due to abnormal or unique area conditions, even when the weather forecast predict clear skies. The example of such case scenario is the pavement temperature which will be colder at night in open areas rather than in the areas protected by nearby trees. These issues require accurate and real-time meteorological data in order to effectively and dynamically support the roadway operation decision systems [1, 2].

© Springer Nature Switzerland AG 2020
J. Mikulski (Ed.): TST 2020, CCIS 1289, pp. 306–319, 2020.
https://doi.org/10.1007/978-3-030-59270-7_23

Moreover, mentioned decision support system should be also based on peculiar weather and pavement conditions forecast that is tailored to the road authority's needs. Perfectly integrated decision support system is an effective foundation for reducing the costs of e.g. snow and ice control. Preventive decision making based on continuous weather conditions supervision is far more efficient than a delayed reaction triggered by the presence hazardous event on the road [3].

The study presents pavement temperature variability analysis based on measurements performed on a 4- km section of Bielsko-Biala district road no. 4405S. The road section is a part of the route linking Bielsko-Biała city to popular touristic resort Międzybrodzie Bialskie, situated in mountainous terrain above the lake. The test road section runs along forest covered Przegibek Pass, reaches the height of 721 m above sea level (elevation gain 250 m) and is characterised by sinuous alignment. As the effect of specific mountainous area local road surface temperature variabilities may be expected. In the study authors analysed the data obtained from advanced mobile road weather sensor MARWIS. The device provides the data determining pavement conditions based on both pavement and dew point temperature measurement, surface water film height, calculated road friction, icing percentage etc. As a part of analysis 10 test runs were performed. Measurements on a tested road section where carried out in both directions and in various winter weather conditions, including both daytime and nighttime drives. A majority of test runs were performed within 1 °C to 3 °C air temperature range, so potentially unfavorable weather conditions as the temperatures were approaching 0 °C. The results of presented analysis enable to identify the hazardous points of the route where the temperature variability is the highest [4].

2   The Impact of Meteorological Conditions on Traffic Safety

In many studies exploring the subject of meteorological condition impact on road safety, it is commonly believed that it may have an influence on road users in various aspects such as [2]:

- decision whether to travel or not,
- choice of transport mode,
- visibility of the road, as well as other road users (e.g. sunlight reflections by the wet road surface),
- available traction (e.g. ability to brake or control the vehicle),
- behavioral changes (e.g. more cautious driving).

The meteorological conditions impact on the road safety is particularly relevant when road surface temperature fluctuates around 0 °C. In this case the rapidity of thermal alteration seems be the key issue. Therefore the awareness of a current thermal conditions should be considered with due regard to location of areas where temperature variability is particularly significant. The location of hazardous areas can be essential information for road infrastructure operators. The knowledge could support decision making while placing traffic signs, variable message signs and road weather stations. Moreover, in the wintertime it would reinforce road maintenance authorities to take more efficient actions with particular emphasis on critical road sections [4].

2.1 Managing the Road Meteorological Environment in Submontane Terrain

The distinction between hill roads and those in the plains needs to be undertaken in detail for better Road weather information system (RWIS) management. The main factor distinguishing mountains from plains is the topography. While plains road are usually characterised by rectilinear alignment, the mountain roads besides land inclination typically are sinuous as these are leading through ridge-valley topography. The mentioned sinuosity of the road increases when the terrain is inclining and may lead to hazardous phenomena such as:

– limiting visibility across the curves and therefore increased probability of the driver being surprised by approaching vehicle or a road obstruction,
– speed unsuitable for the prevailing road conditions as the vehicle may not be able to maintain the grip.

The sinuosity of the roads in the submountain terrain is considered as a major factor responsible for road accidents and it is assumed that accident proneness of the mountain roads increases in direct proportion to the level of roads sinuosity [5].

The current and reliable information about local road conditions can enable the authorities to manage the road infrastructure as well as to develop efficient and flexible areal driver's information system. As the result of implementing roadway operation decision support systems the following aspects may be improved [5]:

– Awareness – the information regarding critical road sections identified as prone to high risk of accidents, addressed for drivers, policy makers and authorities responsible for managing and ensuring safety regulations along the road.
– Structural measures and future road alignments planning – suitable investment planning based on identified high accident risk prone road sections.
– Regulations – introducing valid traffic regulations e.g. dynamical speed limiting.
– Monitoring – strict and continuous area monitoring that is adhered to local terrain characteristic, including mobile monitoring established in hazardous zones and road network "weak spots".

All the above may support drivers correct behaviour on the road. Numerous studies have shown that human factor can straighten the efficiency of the transport process by 25–30% as it reduces the number of traffic accidents 2–3 times [6].

3   Measuring Device Used in the Study

The information about pavement temperature may be obtained from sensors mounted in the pavement as well as non-invasive ones. Non-intrusive measurement methods are rapidly gaining popularity as they do not violate the pavement structure. Modern sensing devices not only specify road surface temperature and dew point but also are able to determine the presence of chemical agents or de-icing substance. As the vast majority of road sensors are limited to data obtained from precisely determined location, mobile method of measurement are becoming the highly helpful tool. Mobile sensors not only monitor selected routes or areas but also create thermal pavement characteristics. Detail thermal characteristic exposes hazardous road sections or "weak spots" and support a process of selecting stationary measuring points for RWIS devices [4].

For measurement purposes authors used MARWIS mobile road weather sensor. It was created to detect road condition by providing information about:

- road surface temperature,
- dew point temperature,
- relative humidity of the air above the road surface,
- water film height,
- ice percentage,
- friction – describing tyre to road adhesion within a range of 0.1 to 1.0,
- surface condition – the sensor distinguishes between 8 surface conditions (dry, damp, wet, snow-/ice-covered, chemical wet, black ice, critically wet),
- pavement temperature measurement is carried out in the range from −40 to 70 °C with a resolution of 0.1 °C, accuracy of ±0.8 °C.

MARWIS sensor should be mounted on vehicle's roof or other vertical surface such as back door (Fig. 1). During the measurement sensing device cooperates with a MARWIS App installed on a mobile device. It enables to generate additional geolocation data through GPS system.

Fig. 1. MARWIS sensor mounted on the vehicle [own study]

4 Previous Studies

Before the exact road tests authors referred to previous research team studies exploring sensor's measurement suitability for obtaining thermal pavement characteristics. In the first stage research team examined fluctuations of the MARWIS sensor readings in the stationary measurement conditions. Most significant conclusions that can be drawn from the results of stationary test are as follows [7]:

- based on small values of standard deviation, authors concluded good stability of road surface temperature measurements,
- the accuracy of the measurement declared by the manufacturer was not exceed as the amplitude of indications changed less than 0.5 °C.

In the next step the test runs were performed using the customized route which enabled appropriate indications repeatability analysis, as well as speed impact relevance. Main conclusions drawn from the second study are as follows [8]:

- the results and analyses of the test runs performed on customized route indicate a high repeatability of the pavement temperature registered by the MARWIS sensor,
- in order to determine speed impact relevance on the measurement three test runs were performed. Test drives were carried out at vehicle's speed of 30, 45 and 60 km/h and did not result in a significant impact on the accuracy of road surface temperature measurement.

Obtained temperature variability has not been greater than discrepancy during the stationary tests (Fig. 2).

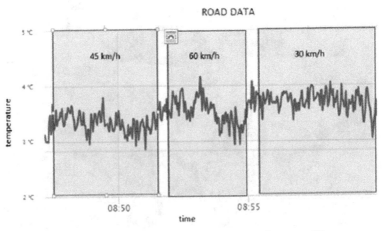

Fig. 2. Speed impact analysis on sensor performance [8]

The latest research team study examined the pavement thermal analysis of the highly trafficked east Bielsko-Biala bypass, it enabled to effectively obtain thermal characteristics map of the selected 6.25-km route. The analysis indicated critical (due to significant gradients of road surface temperature) road network points (Fig. 3). High gradients of the road surface temperature occurred regardless of the weather as far more important issue than the ambient temperature seemed to be the sun exposition of the road. More detailed information about research team previous work in this field is given in [4, 7, 8].

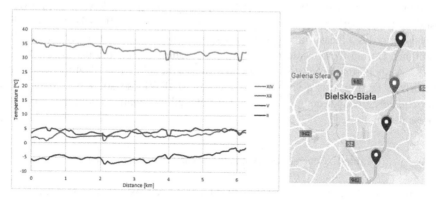

Fig. 3. Critical road network points [4]

5 The Analysis of Pavement Temperature and Road Conditions Variability on Selected Test Section

The field tests drives analysed in this study had been performed on two-lane road which is Bielsko-Biala's district road no. 4405S linking the city to popular touristic resort Międzybrodzie Bialskie. Due to the fact that the route is situated in mountainous terrain, it is characterised by sinuous alignment. For analysis proposes 4–km test section partly covered with forest was selected (Fig. 4).

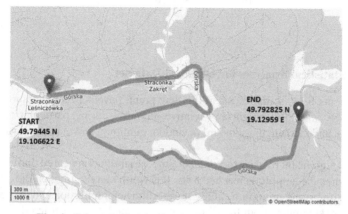

Fig. 4. Selected 4-km test section [own study based on [9]]

Mentioned test section runs along Przegibek Pass and in the highest point reaches 721 m above sea level while the elevation gain amounts to 250 m. In the wintertime usage of snow chains is suggested by road signs but it is not obligatory by polish law and as it is a commonly used shortcut handling local traffic between neighbouring districts, drivers usually do not obey the recommendation.

Authors accomplished 10 test drives (comprising both up and down the hill drives). Test drives were performed over the course of a month (07.02.2020–08.03.2020). For analysis purposes 3 measuring days were selected due to differences in general weather conditions. During the considered days air temperatures fell within the range of 3 °C ÷ 1 °C. Authors run the tests in various hour ranges including both daytime and night-time drives. During tests a vehicle handling the MARWIS sensor was moving at an approximately steady speed of 30 km/h. The detailed information about the test drives is presented in Table 1.

Table 1. General weather conditions characterisics [own study]

Measuring day no.	Date	Drive no.	Start time	Approximate air temperature	General weather conditions
1	07.02.2020	1	12:15:00 pm	2 °C	Partly cloudy
		2	13:00:00 pm	2.5 °C	
2	27.02.2020	3	15:15:00 pm	3 °C	Partly cloudy, small snowfall
		4	15:40:00 pm	2.5 °C	
		5	16:00:00 pm	3 °C	
		6	16:20:00 pm	2 °C	
		7	16:50:00 pm	1.5 °C	
3	08.03.2020	8	18:05:00 pm	2 °C	Overcast, after sunset
		9	18:30:00 pm	1.5 °C	
		10	18:50:00 pm	1 °C	

5.1 Basic Statistical Analyses for Obtained Data Set

Table 2 presents basic statistics regarding dew point, pavement temperature, friction, ice percentage, waterfilm height and relative humidity during particular test drives. Besides mean and median, the standard deviation, minimum and maximum values were calculated.

The most significant road surface temperature variabilities appeared during 2nd measuring day when the amplitude reached 5 °C. It is worth mentioning that the differences between maximum and minimum values of waterfilm height, friction and ice percentage on the road are significant both for 1st measuring day and 2nd measuring day.

Table 2. Data basic statistics [own study]

	Measuring day no.	Dew point [°C]	Surface temperature [°C]	Friction [%]	Ice percentage [%]	Waterfilm height [mL]	Relative humidity [%]
max	1	−0.29	3.33	82.00	100.00	58.00	94.91
min		−2.86	−1.27	11.00	0.00	0.17	72.92
mean		−1.79	0.66	75.01	10.51	5.81	83.77
median		−1.79	0.64	80.00	0.00	3.12	84.65
sd		0.60	0.83	14.03	27.75	7.55	3.82
max	2	0.70	4.15	82.00	100.00	17.42	95.61
min		−3.88	−0.86	54.00	0.00	0.19	69.57
mean		−1.45	1.33	79.80	0.82	4.05	81.87
median		−1.20	1.27	80.00	0.00	3.60	82.66
sd		1.06	0.85	2.20	7.89	2.54	4.65
max	3	−0.54	2.25	82.00	30.14	9.05	92.03
min		−2.48	−1.07	78.00	0.00	0.00	73.50
mean		−1.72	0.88	81.95	0.11	0.15	82.91
median		−1.80	0.91	82.00	0.00	0.00	83.45
sd		0.44	0.50	0.36	1.83	0.76	3.68

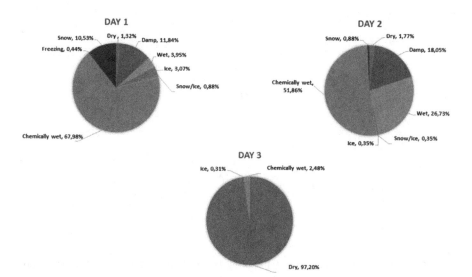

Fig. 5. Road condition status [own study]

Figure 5 presents the percentage of road condition status occurring on the road surface during the measuring day.

Most diverse road condition status has been noted during 1st measuring day, the sensor recognised 8 out of 9 available statuses. Similar diversity of road conditions can be observed during the 2nd testing day as the sensor identified 7 different statuses. During the 3rd day of measurement road condition has been relatively stable, for more than 97% of test drive duration road surface remained dry.

5.2 Thermal Characteristic of Test Route

On the next step of the study authors analyse variability of pavement temperature indications per each measuring day. To simplify the analysis test rides were divided into uphill and downhill drives. Due to high similarity of obtained results for both traffic directions in the following section only uphill drives are presented. On Fig. 6 and Fig. 7 road surface temperature variations during uphill rides per each measuring day are shown.

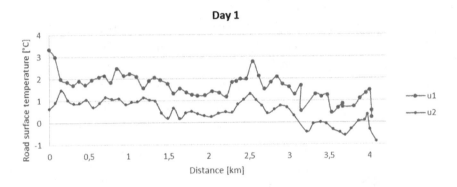

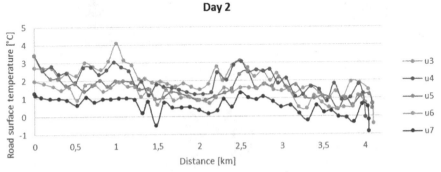

Fig. 6. Road surface temperature variations during 1st and 2nd day of measurement [own study]

Noticeable down shift of consecutive measurement series was a result of general air temperature drop during the test drives. It should be pointed out that successive drives were performed in relatively short time intervals (about 20 min) as shown in

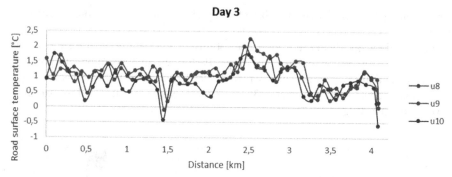

Fig. 7. Road surface temperature variations during 3rd day of measurement [own study]

Table 1. It indicates that high dynamic of local road surface temperature variability and rapid responsiveness to changes in meteorological conditions. This process seems to be particularly dangerous phenomenon especially in submontane areas.

Distribution analysis of pavement temperature as a function of the distance indicates corresponding local peaks and drops implying the presence of hazardous spots. To verify whether mentioned "weak spots" are the result of specific weather conditions during selected day or are a permanent phenomenon, authors compared test drives amongst measuring days. To present repeatability of indications in test route authors selected one uphill and one downhill drive representing each measuring day (Fig. 8). Moreover

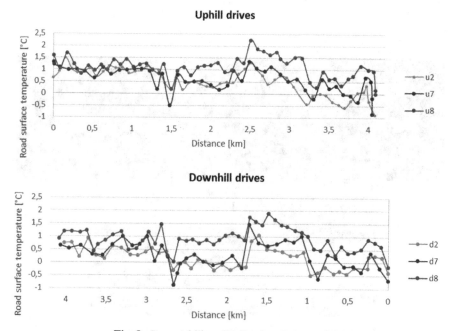

Fig. 8. Repeatability of indications [own study]

correlation analysis was performed based on previously mentioned representative test drives.

Presented results clearly indicates repeatability in distribution of road surface temperature in a form of local peaks and drops. Performed analysis allows to precisely identify potentially hazardous spots where reduced friction and dangerous road conditions may occur. Authors selected 3 presumed "weak spots" demanding particular driver's attention (Fig. 9):

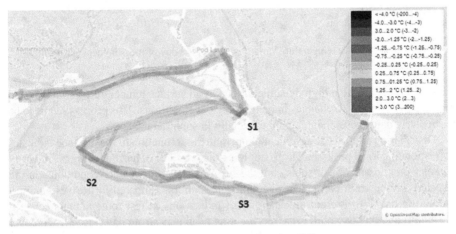

Fig. 9. Hazardous spots location [10]

Fig. 10. Hazardous spots S1, S2, S3 [own study based on [11]]

- S1 – located about 1.5 km of uphill route and 2.7 km downhill route. It is nearly 360° serpentine situated on the northern hillside with a nearby mountain stream and limited sun exposure (Fig. 10).
- S2 – located about 2.5 km of uphill route and 1.7 km downhill route. It is a section characterized by rectilinear alignment on southern and well insolated hillside (Fig. 10).
- S3 – located about 3.25 km of uphill route and 0.9 km downhill route. It is a constantly overshadowed short road section running along the precipice on the northern hillside (Fig. 10).

As the last element of the study authors performed correlation analysis between altitude, surface temperature and dew point changes (Table 3).

Table 3. Altitude correlation analysis [own study]

Drive no.	Temperature	Dew point
2	−0.81	−0.91
7	−0.53	−0.98
8	−0.26	−0.86

Correlation coefficient between altitude and dew point was significantly high for all test drives showing strong negative relationship. On the other hand correlation between altitude and surface temperature was characterized by changeability regarding selected test drives. Therefore, the drop of pavement temperature associated with the attitude is not a permanent phenomenon and is relatively sensitive on local meteorological conditions. As can be noted in Table 2 and Fig. 5 drive no. 2 which showed the greatest indications variability is characterized by the strongest surface temperature negative correlation. On the other hand test drive no.8 with the most stabile meteorological conditions demonstrated weak negative linear relationship.

6   Conclusion

Accurate information about area-related meteorological characteristic is notably important element of traffic organization and winter road maintenance planning. Mountain and submontane areas are particularly vulnerable to rapid and unpredictable changes of local road conditions. Mountain routes are great challenge to drivers due to steep inclines, precipices and sinuosity. Potentially hazardous spots prone to rapid road conditions changes are additional factors influencing traffic safety. Awareness of local meteorological environment supports decision making process regarding road maintenance and signposting. It is also a crucial informative element for drivers. Thermal road maps may be also a useful tool for appropriate placement of RWIS sensors.

In the study authors analysed selected submontane route with regard to distribution of road surface temperature variability. In the first step 3 exemplary measuring days have been selected. Test drives were performed under various weather conditions and during different times of a day. The basic statistics have been calculated for each measuring day. More detailed analyses of road surface temperature variability have been characterized by high repeatability of indications and revealed significant sensitivity to general temperature changes in short time intervals. The process has been identified as particularly dangerous especially in montane and submontane areas.

Authors attempted to establish whether the local pavement temperature peaks and drops were related to temporary weather conditions or occurred as a permanent phenomenon. In order to determine the dependence of indications on specific meteorological environment authors performed comparative analyses amongst measuring days. The comparison enabled to identify "weak spots" (S1, S2, S3) appearing on the route regardless of selected measuring day. Spots marked as S1 and S3 were characterised by rapid temperature drops while S2 was classified as a spot where surface temperature increased. Both situations are potentially dangerous – the first one while air temperature fluctuates around 0 °C and local freezing or lying snow may occur. The second one while the negative air temperature maintains, may cause local snowmelt, lying glazed ice or high water film leading to reduced friction.

The significant difference between measurement sections situated in northern hillside and southern hillside has been noted. As can be seen in presented thermal mapping analysis surface temperature of road sections with a northern exposure was notably lower than the south exposed ones. Another factor affecting local pavement temperature variabilities is the side road areas afforestation density as the level of insolation is also relevant. Moreover, volatility of correlation strength between surface temperature and altitude determined by temporary weather conditions may also have a significant impact on traffic safety especially in mountain and submontane areas.

In the future authors plan to extend the range of research to analyse also the additional meteorological factors such as relative humidity and dew point. Moreover optical measurements such as sky view factor (SVF) will be performed for comprehensive evaluation of insolation and immediate surroundings impact on local road weather conditions.

References

1. Strategic Highway Research Program National Research Council Washington: Road Weather Information Systems Volume 2: Implementation Guide. DC 1993. http://onlinepubs.trb.org/onlinepubs/shrp/shrp-h-351.pdf. Accessed 30 May 2020
2. Bijleveld, F., Churchill, T.: The influence of weather conditions on road safety. Report documentation no.: R-2009-9 [electronic source]: SWOV Institute for Road Safety Research, The Netherlands (2009). https://www.swov.nl/sites/default/files/publicaties/rapport/r-2009-09.pdf. Accessed 30 May 2020
3. Wood, W.H., et al.: Daily temperature records from a mesonet in the foothills of the Canadian Rocky Mountains, 2005–2010. In: Earth System Science Data 10 [electronic source], pp. 595–607 (2018). https://www.earth-syst-sci-data.net/10/595/2018/essd-10-595-2018.pdf. Accessed 30 May 2020
4. Loga, W., et al.: Thermal analysis of pavement for the east Bielsko-Biala bypass. Arch. Transp. Syst. Telematics 12(3), 8–14 (2019)
5. Rautela, P., Pant, S.: Delineating road accident risk along mountain roads. Disaster Prev. Manag. 16(3), 334–343 (2007)

6. Batrakova, A., Gredasova, O.: Influence of road conditions on traffic safety. Procedia Eng. **134**, 196–204 (2016)

7. Brzozowski, K., Maczyński, A., Ryguła, A.: Wstępna ocena powtarzalności wskazań mobilnego czujnika warunków drogowych. In: Autobusy. Technika, Eksploatacja, Systemy Transportowe, nr 6, pp. 368–374 (2018)

8. Maczyński, A., Brzozowski, K., Ryguła, A.: Repeatability of the road surface temperature indications using a mobile sensor in the context of a road weather information system. In: Transport Means: Proceedings of the 22th International Scientific Conference, Part 2, pp. 844–848 (2018)

9. OpenStreetMap. Accessed 30 May 2020

10. ViewMondo MARWIS App. Accessed 30 May 2020

11. GoogleMaps. Accessed 30 May 2020

The Possibilities of Applying Telematics Measures to Solve Problems Related to Construction Site Deliveries in Urban Areas, Based on the Example of West Pomerania

Oleksandra Osypchuk$^{(\boxtimes)}$ and Stanisław Iwan

Maritime University of Szczecin, Pobożnego 11, Szczecin, Poland
{o.osypchuk,s.iwan}@am.szczecin.pl

Abstract. The intensification of urbanisation and suburbanisation processes result in the increased number of construction projects, which affects the amount of freight transport for their needs. Construction site deliveries in modern cities present a complex problem in terms of spatial (e.g. infrastructural limits, construction site peculiarities) and organisational factors (e.g. local road regulations). More and more construction companies are using telematics measures in their construction supply chains to get over these obstacles. Solutions in the field of construction site deliveries deserve special attention. The research carried out for the purposes of this article allowed to identify problems in the field of construction site deliveries in urban areas and determine the possibilities of solving them by means of telematics measures. The purpose of the article is to present the possibilities and barriers of implementing these measures in the area of construction projects in the West Pomeranian region.

Keywords: Urban freight transport (UFT) · Telematics measures · Construction site deliveries · Construction supply chains

1 Introduction

Europe is the third most urbanised region in the world. The United Nations forecast that the urban population will increase up to 80% in 2050 [1]. Such forecasts constitute a serious challenge for both city authorities and residents, in particular with regard to mobility, environmental protection and general life comfort. Therefore, the significance of cities as the places of economic exchange has been on the rise. It is cities that combine commercial functions with services that are indispensable for the society functioning. Development of those functions contributes to increasing the intensity of material and non-material exchange, which leads to increasing the volumes of urban freight transport [2]. On the other hand, the life quality of residents in contemporary cities requires providing an attractive, safe and sustainable environment, which in turn seems to be a hard task due to the intensifying transport processes taking place within the cities [3].

© Springer Nature Switzerland AG 2020
J. Mikulski (Ed.): TST 2020, CCIS 1289, pp. 320–332, 2020.
https://doi.org/10.1007/978-3-030-59270-7_24

Creating an environment where city residents will be able to have their needs fulfilled is also connected with i.a. implementation of construction projects. The construction industry is one of the five sectors (in addition to retail, courier and post, waste and HoReCa) which constitute a source of future challenges in the area of urban freight transport [4]. Development of the construction industry and the increasing number of implemented construction projects contribute to increased flows of building supplies. Naturally, such development perspectives pose a difficult task for both city authorities and enterprises, especially in terms of planning and completion of deliveries [5].

UFT plays a major part in the functioning of contemporary cities, however, it also brings along some negative impacts. These include [4, 6, 7]:

- transport congestion – freight traffic within city areas leads to an increased number of vehicles in general, still, the bigger issue seems to be parking them, as in view of their dimensions freight vehicles may contribute to decreasing the road traffic capacity;
- deteriorated air quality – freight vehicles are often powered with diesel engines, which results in solid particles emissions that exert a negative impact on human health and the natural environment;
- greenhouse gas (GHG) emissions – UFT considerably contributes to increased emissions of greenhouse gases;
- noise emissions – noise pollution is a serious problem which affects residents' health and life comfort, and freight vehicles are one of the sources of traffic noise;
- decreased road traffic safety – due to their dimensions, freight vehicles are particularly dangerous in case of a serious accident.

The European transport policy regarding UFT assumes that such transport must be efficient in both economic and environmental terms so as to be able to reduce emissions and general costs for both enterprises and consumers [7]. There are documents provided to help implement the assumptions, such as e.g. The White Paper (2011), Study on Urban Freight Transport (2012), "The Europe 2020 Strategy: A strategy for smart, sustainable and inclusive growth" and others, which present i.a. measures aimed at providing sustainable transport. The particularly important are the initiatives focused on [4, 8]:

- Dissemination of knowledge about implementation of low emission vehicles;
- Intelligent traffic management;
- Intelligent Transport Systems;
- Measures aimed at noise reduction via i.a. night deliveries, installation of noise barriers;
- Minimising the number of freight movements;
- Developing and propagating good practices in the area of UFT.

The volume and intensity of urban distribution connected with construction site deliveries is a problem not only to the residents – the whole construction supply chains face challenges. However, following the general recommendations of the EU with regard to UFT and implementation of telematics solutions may be the way to solve the problems, achieve a better competitive position and meet the requirements of both customers and city authorities.

2 Construction Site Deliveries

Due to the specific nature of the construction industry, logistics plays a major role in it. It is not possible to develop a fixed logistics system to be used by a company, as each construction project is unique in its nature in terms of e.g. specificity of applied construction materials, the location, or deadlines. Depending on the adopted policy, construction companies may flexibly adjust their existing logistics system to any individual projects or adopt a separate logistic system for a given project, involving all the subcontractors [9].

In each of the presented points of view, logistics in the construction industry covers: procurement of resources and building materials, on-site transport, loading/unloading and storage of materials, final distribution of finished products to the final recipient, after-sales service, returns and complaints [10]. Procurement of resources and building materials is a prerequisite for implementation of construction works. However, due to the significance and risk connected with untimely or inappropriate procurement, the planning and delivery of the supplies may be a considerable challenge.

Enterprises that carry out construction projects strive to rationally plan the logistic activities predominantly in order to reduce the project costs. Most often this is possible via reducing the stock levels of supplies, which in turn decreases the frozen capital level and solves the problem of limited storage space on construction sites [9]. However, providing the supplies by means of the Just-In-Time method bears an increased risk of delays. Additionally, procurement planning for construction projects is also hindered by the specific nature of the distributed products, including the volume to weight ratio, the value to weight ratio, and the specific features of construction materials. These characteristics determine the choice of the means of transport, the manner of transshipment and storage [10].

When developing a logistics system in the construction industry, enterprises are required to make a considerable number of strategic decisions that are decisive for the timeliness, costs and implementation of the whole construction project [11]. Such decisions must take into account many aspects, among which the most important are [10, 11]:

– the spatial aspect – the location of the construction site, the source of materials and resources, distribution centres. The process of construction site delivery in cities is to a large extent complicated. The difficulties are most often connected with transport restrictions within given areas. In such situations, delivery planning must be done in cooperation with the road administrator. The cooperation consists in planning the routes, scheduling, closing some selected road sections and detouring the traffic;
– necessary transport operations in the supply chain;
– the adopted storage system – the size of storage space, the planned stock levels;
– the transshipment system applied in the supply chain;

- interaction between the various logistic activities in the supply chain (e.g. decreasing the stock levels contributes to lowering the storage costs, but on the other hand leads to increasing the number of freight transport trips necessary to meet the procurement needs, which results in increased costs);
- interaction between the links within the supply chain, i.e. the construction company, suppliers, intermediaries and the final recipients.

Additionally, when planning any construction project implementation, it is necessary to select an appropriate form of procurement. The academic literature on the subject discusses four ways to organise the process. This can take the form of centralised or dispersed procurement, which is carried out by logistic organisational units, or mixed models [12]. In the case of centralised procurement, construction supplies are provided by the general contractor, which often makes it possible to consolidate the deliveries and lower the transport costs. When the dispersed procurement is chosen, the individual subcontractors provide the supplies on their own account. In the case of large construction projects, procurement may be provided by specially established logistic organisational units, the purpose of such units is nothing but providing deliveries for the purposes of the project implementation. Mixed models combine any selected elements of the aforementioned models.

All the above mentioned factors that affect decision-making in the area of delivery planning and completion of construction site deliveries are critical points and they may indicate any problematic areas that may show in the course of construction project implementation. However, application of selected telematics solutions may reduce the risk of occurrence of such problems.

3 Methodology

For the purposes of this article, the relevant academic literature was reviewed, and the PAPI (Paper-and-Pencil Interview) method was applied in relation to selected construction projects being implemented in the West Pomeranian Voivodeship in the years 2018–2020. The research study involved 14 sites which met the specified criteria. As the construction sector is a project-based industry [13], various construction projects require separate planning of the procurement logistics. In order to standardise the research sample, the following major eligibility factors were adopted: kind of structure, project size, kind of works, location.

In view of the above, the first criterion stipulated that the structure must fall within the scope of Sect. 1 of the Polish classification of types of building structures (based on the European Classification of Types of Construction, CC), i.e. only residential buildings (single-family residential buildings, buildings with two residential units, multi-unit buildings, public accommodation buildings) and non-residential (offices, hotels and tourist accommodation, commercial and service outlets, transport and communication facilities, industrial and storage buildings, public cultural facilities, educational facilities, hospitals, physical culture facilities, and other).

The structure must also meet the size criterion. The research study included structures with an area exceeding 1000 m². Implementation of any smaller construction projects is connected with smaller volumes of procurement transport, which in turn means a less complicated logistics system.

Additionally, due to the specific nature of individual construction works and related construction site deliveries, the study included works related to erection of buildings and specialist construction works (as per the Polish Classification of Goods and Services, section F, parts 41 and 43, respectively).

All the construction projects qualified to be included in the study were carried out in the centres of selected cities in the West Pomeranian Voivodeship. The construction projects covered by the study were implemented either by a single contractor or involved subcontractors.

4   Problems Related to Construction Site Deliveries in Urban Areas

For the purposes of this article, a review of the literature on the subject was carried out, which showed that issues related to construction site deliveries are coincident with the problems encountered by other enterprises operating on the market.

The research studies conducted under the SULPs (Sustainable Urban Logistics Plans) made it possible to specify the problems encountered in the course of loading and unloading, which are: difficult access to the place of loading, safety during loading and unloading operations, delivery time, loading/unloading time, lack of delivery coordinator, lack of appropriate equipment for loading/unloading [14]. These problems are particularly important in cities, as loading or unloading in inappropriate places (e.g. in the street) and at unfavourable times significantly contributes to increasing the transport congestion and risk levels.

As a result of measures taken by city authorities to reduce CO_2 emissions or counteract noise pollution and traffic congestion, enterprises often encounter freight traffic restrictions or banning freight vehicles from city centres. This is one of the soft measures which have a positive impact on residents' life quality, but on the other hand such local constraints hinder procurement planning and construction site deliveries related to construction project implementation [15].

Road traffic accidents are also an issue in construction site deliveries, particularly in view of the consequences related to timeliness, delivery quality and related costs. However, it should be noted that over the past decade the number of accidents involving freight vehicles has been dropping. In 2016, drivers of freight vehicles with carrying capacity exceeding 3.5 tonnes contributed to merely 2.7% traffic accidents in Poland, whereas drivers of freight vehicles with up to 3.5 tonne carrying capacity – to 3,8% accidents [16].

Other issues are related to the area of procurement organisation and management. Such problems include: inappropriate deliveries in terms of quantity/quality, planning hindrances (e.g. problems with communication between the supply chain participants), inappropriate frequency of deliveries, delays and other.

All the above mentioned problems contribute to increased negative impacts of UFT related to construction site deliveries on the natural environment, quality of life of city residents, and the total logistics costs borne by enterprises [17, 18].

Based on the literature review as well as the PAPI interviews held with the enterprises engaged in the construction projects, the most frequent problems related to construction site deliveries were identified. Additionally, all the identified problems were categorised (Table 1).

Table 1 Problems connected with construction site deliveries [own study based on 5, 14, 16, 17, 19]

Category	Problem
Infrastructural	Limited access to the place of loading/unloading
	Lack of appropriate place for unloading
	Entry restrictions for freight vehicles
Safety	Traffic accidents
	Safety during loading/unloading operations
	Thefts
Organisational	Unloading/loading time
	Hindrances in delivery planning
	Frequency of deliveries
	Delivery delays
	Delivery time
	Inappropriate deliveries in terms of quantity/quality
Technical/technological	Damage to cargo in transport
	Damage to cargo during loading/unloading operations
	Lack of appropriate equipment for loading/unloading

The identified problems may cause financial losses, delays in project completion, and even lead to bankruptcy. In further parts of this article, the frequency of occurrence of the particular issues is analysed, with regard to construction projects carried out in the West Pomeranian Voivodeship.

5 Potential of Telematics Measures to Solve the Problems

As per the EU policy regarding UFT, city authorities tend to promote and implement soft (organisational) and hard measures in order to reduce negative effects of delivery processes. The soft measures implemented by cities include: time windows for deliveries, access restrictions, early/night deliveries, alternative delivery systems, strategic planning (local freight transport plans), and other. Hard measures that are implemented by local authorities most often refer to infrastructural, technical and telematics solutions. These include: traffic control systems, parking systems, vehicle classification and weigh-in-motion systems, road safety management systems such as variable message signs, and other [6, 15, 20].

In addition to solutions implemented by local authorities on a top-down basis, there are also solutions implemented by individual enterprises. Such solutions are deployed in order to solve problems encountered in the course of providing supplies and to streamline the processes. In the case of enterprises, soft measures consist only in implementing solutions in the area of management. Nevertheless, there should be more focus on telematics solutions. However, it should also be noted that they are more costly to implement.

Table 2 shows the results of the literature review and the PAPI interviews held with the enterprises which were carrying out their construction projects; it also identifies telematics solutions that are implementable in enterprises and capable of supporting construction site deliveries.

Table 2 Telematics solutions that support construction site deliveries [own study based on 6, 21–24]

Purpose of the implemented solution	Telematics solution
Supporting the construction procurement planning	BIM (Building Information Modelling)
	RFID (Radio Frequency Identification)
	ERP systems
Supporting transport of construction supplies	Programs for mapping and visualisation
	Traffic management and control systems
	Systems for automated vehicle access control
	Commercial fleet and freight management systems
	Solutions to support the drivers' work

The enumerated solutions may generally be classified as telematics solutions:

- implemented within the means of transport – e.g. Wireless Communications Systems, Longitudinal Assistance Systems and Lateral Assistance Systems, systems for automated vehicle access control, automated toll collection [21, 22];
- supporting the fleet management – e.g. measures for traffic monitoring, providing information about current traffic situation, accidents, road works, the estimated time of travel, programs for mapping and visualisation [23];
- supporting the delivery planning – solutions to support the process of identifying the need for resources (e.g. BIM, ERP), applying RFID for the purposes of gathering and use of information in construction supply chains, commercial fleet and freight management systems [24–26]

6 Characteristics of the Research Sample

The West Pomeranian Voivodeship is located in the north-west of Poland. It is inhabited by more than 1.7 million people [27]. Within its territory, there are three cities with *poviat* (second level of local government administration in Poland) rights: Szczecin, Koszalin, Świnoujście. Szczecin is located on the Oder River and is the capital city of the West Pomerania region. It is the seventh biggest city in Poland, with a population exceeding 400,000.

The West Pomeranian Voivodeship is a fast growing region. According to the regional development strategies with the 2030 time horizon, there will be an increased number of construction projects [27]. As the road transport is the dominating transport mode within the cities in the region, this may cause exacerbation of UFT problems, particularly in the historic centres [28].

Contractors engaged in construction projects being implemented in the West Pomeranian Voivodeship were interviewed about the kind of structure they were constructing. The sample included only four kinds of structures: residential with two and more units, hotels and tourist accommodation, office buildings, and commercial and service outlets.

All the construction projects were broken down into small, medium, and large in terms of space. Buildings with floor areas of up to 999 m² were classified as small and were not eligible to be included in the survey. The structures identified as eligible for the purpose of the research study included 9 medium structures (i.e. with a floor area from 1,000 to 9,999 m²), and 5 large ones (above 10,000 m²).

In accordance with the assumed criteria, the study included construction projects involving works related to erection of buildings, and specialist construction works. Among the 14 construction projects, specialist construction works were carried out on 10 sites, erection works were being done in 1 case, and the remaining 3 construction projects involved both the works related to erection of buildings and specialist construction works.

7 Research Results Regarding Problems Related to Construction Site Deliveries and the Use of Telematics Solutions

During the interviews, the selected projects were examined with regard to subcontractors, the form of procurement, number of suppliers, average number of deliveries per day, delivery hours and place of unloading. Next, the study identified problems occurring on individual construction sites.

As for the number of subcontractors identified on the individual sites, 7 construction projects employed up to 9 subcontractors, 3 projects engaged from 10 to 19 subcontractors, while 4 projects involved more than 20 subcontractors.

The construction projects were carried out using centralised (6 sites), dispersed (4 sites) and mixed (4 sites) procurement. The research study showed correlations between the number of subcontractors, the selected form of procurement and the project size. In the case of large projects, the most frequently selected procurement form was mixed procurement, and the number of subcontractors ranged from 15 to 40. Additionally, the analysis of the results showed that the number of subcontractors was not directly correlated with the project size and the number of subcontractors. It seems that in order to confirm such interdependencies it is necessary to take into account other parameters such as e.g. project implementation time or availability of indispensable materials.

In the case of 13 projects covered by the study, deliveries were made by 1 to 9 suppliers. One of the projects involved deliveries made by more than 20 suppliers. Additionally, the survey included a question about the average number of construction site deliveries per day. 13 construction sites received up to 9 deliveries per day, and one project even more than 19.

The survey showed that the deliveries were most often made between 7:00 am and 5:00 pm (in the case of 11 projects covered by the study), in the remaining cases the deliveries took place on a flexible time basis. It should be stressed that there were no time restrictions for large goods vehicles to enter the city or any time windows required near the construction sites. In the case of 12 projects, the supplies were unloaded directly on the construction site, which is rather rare in densely-built areas. This kind of unloading makes it possible to avoid a great number of problems related to the existing infrastructure. In the case of the remaining construction projects, the goods were unloaded in the street. Such situations contribute to compromised safety and transport congestion.

The survey showed that the identified problems actually occurred on the individual construction sites rather seldom, however, the respondents stressed that such occurrences had a considerable impact on the timeliness of the construction project completion and the logistics costs. Table 3 presents the individual results.

Table 3. Problems encountered during deliveries made for the analysed construction projects [own study]

Category	Problem	Number of projects coping with the problem
Infrastructural	Entry restrictions for freight vehicles	1
Safety	Traffic accidents	1
Organisational	Hindrances in delivery planning	1
	Frequency of deliveries	1
	Delivery delays	4
	Inappropriate deliveries in terms of quantity/quality	1
Technical/technological	Damage to cargo in transport	1

The most frequently occurring problem was delivery delays (on 4 construction sites). There were also problems connected with access restrictions for freight vehicles (no access for heavy goods vehicles in specific streets), road accidents, delivery frequency, hindrances in delivery planning (ineffective communication in the supply chain), damage to cargo and inappropriate quality of deliveries. The other identified problems were not encountered.

The survey also showed that none of the construction projects applied telematics solutions in order to decrease the risk of encountering the problems. The identified reason for this was lack of knowledge about such solutions as well as the cost of purchasing and implementing them.

8 Possibilities of Applying Telematics Solutions to Streamline Delivery Processes for the Studied Construction Projects

A small interest in telematics solutions among construction companies may constitute a big problem in the future, as the construction industry growth and increased number of large construction projects will naturally contribute to hindrances in planning and completion of construction site deliveries. Additionally, these processes are complicated by the intensified actions taken in contemporary cities to counteract transport congestion, noise pollution and CO_2 emissions.

The analysis of the relevant academic literature and of the survey results made it possible to develop a model that contributes to decreasing the risk of encountering problems when delivering construction supplies for the construction projects in question. The model assumes that the applied form of procurement is centralised procurement, as it was most often seen in the surveyed projects.

For the purposes of the model development, we identified the entities involved in the procurement, as well as basic processes necessary to deliver the supplies. These entities most often included: subcontractors, supply department of the construction site (or other unit/employee responsible for supplies), suppliers. The basic processes necessary for providing the supplies include: calculating the materials and components needed, materials demand analysis, preparation of orders and delivery schedules, placing orders, completing the orders, transport to the construction site. All the processes are connected with continuous exchange of information between the participants.

In order to maximally reduce the risk of encountering problems in the course of delivering any construction supplies, it is recommended to implement telematics solutions not only in enterprises that carry out construction projects, but also in all the links of the supply chain. This comprehensive approach will make it possible to achieve the synergy effect in applying the solutions. Additionally, particular attention should be paid to measures focused on streamlining the communication between the participants.

Figure 1 presents the model showing the possibilities of applying telematics solutions in order to reduce the risk of encountering problems when transporting construction supplies. The model assumes that 3 kinds of telematics solutions should be applied to support each of the basic processes in each of the links. Building Information Modelling (BIM) is suggested to be used for the purposes of precise specifying the demand for supplies. The obtained information is provided to the supply department of the construction site, where the demand for materials is analysed by means of ERP systems, schedules for orders and deliveries are prepared, and orders are placed with suppliers. The use of an ERP system makes it possible to ensure an efficient flow of information regarding availability of materials and delivery terms and conditions. Suppliers make use of ERP systems in the course of order handling. Transport was supported by telematics solutions that enabled the traffic monitoring, providing information about current traffic situation, accidents, road works, the estimated time of travel, programs for mapping and visualisation. Making use of the solutions enable continuous monitoring of the process and precise scheduling of deliveries.

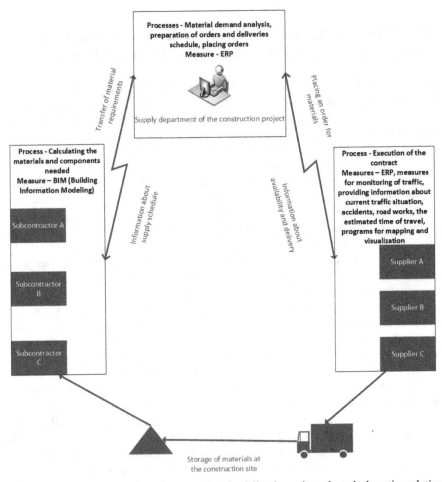

Fig. 1. Planning and completion of construction site deliveries, using selected telematics solutions [own study]

Application of the model will enable better delivery planning and scheduling, which will contribute to reducing the risk of encountering problems in the course of providing construction supplies.

9   Conclusion

Contemporary cities encounter a large number of challenges related to urbanisation, globalisation and intensification of the process of material and non-material exchange.

Meeting those challenges and city growth would not be possible without completion of construction projects. However, implementation of construction projects encounters a wide range of difficulties due to the complexity of the processes involved. One of them is the problem of organising, planning, completing and monitoring of logistics processes, particularly in the case of construction projects implemented within cities.

The survey carried out for the purposes of this article made it possible to identify problems that occur in the course of construction site deliveries. Additionally, telematics solutions were indicated, which help to reduce the risk of encountering problems and support the logistics processes in construction projects. Still, the survey that engaged some selected construction projects being carried out in the West Pomeranian Voivodeship showed that procurement-related problems were not that common, and telematics solutions were not at all applied. The most often encountered problem turned out to be delays. It seems reasonable to continue the research in order to identify the reasons for this problem and to develop a strategy to counteract it.

The fact that in the case of the surveyed construction projects there were no telematics solutions in place, seems to be a source of potential problems in the future. Due to the construction industry growth and increased numbers of big construction projects, construction site delivery planning and completion will be just impossible without applying telematics solutions. The research study made it possible to develop a model for planning and delivering construction supplies, using telematics solutions to reduce the related risks.

The reasons why telematics solutions are not used are mainly the lack of knowledge about the functionalities of the solutions, as well as costs. Therefore, dissemination of knowledge about such solutions seems to be an important goal for both local authorities and UFT-related projects.

References

1. www.un.org. Accessed 15 Feb 2020
2. Ambrosini, C., Routhier, J.-L.: Objectives, methods and results of surveys carried out in the field of urban freight transport. Int. Comparison. Transp. Rev. **24**(1), 57–77 (2004)
3. Witkowski, J., Kiba-Janiak, M.: Correlation between city logistics and quality of life as an assumption for referential model. Procedia. Social Behav. Sci. **39**, 568–581 (2012)
4. MDS Transmodal Limited: DG MOVE European Commission: Study on Urban Freight Transport. Final report (2012). https://ec.europa.eu/transport/sites/transport/files/themes/urban/studies/doc/2012-04-urban-freight-transport.pdf
5. Foltyński, M.: Sustainable urban logistics plan – current situation of the city of Poznań. Transp. Res. Procedia **39**, 42–53 (2019)
6. Kaszubowski, D.: Evaluation of urban freight transport management measures. LogForum **8**(3), 217–229 (2012)
7. Nowakowska-Grunt, J., Strzelczyk, M.: The current situation and the directions of changes in road freight transport in the European Union. Transp. Res. Procedia **39**, 350–359 (2019)
8. The White Papers (2011)
9. Sobotka, A., Czarnigowska, A.: Analysis of supply system models for planning construction project logistic. J. Civil Eng. Manag. **XI**(1), 73–82 (2005)
10. Brown, M.: The challenge of construction logistics. In: Lundesjo, G. (ed.) Supply Chain Management and Logistics in Construction, pp. 9–23. Kogan Page, London (2015)

11. Jaśkowski, P., Sobotka, A., Czarnigowska, A.: Decision model for planning material supply channels in construction. Autom. Constr. **90**, 235–242 (2018)
12. Sobotka, A.: Logistyka przedsiębiorstw i przedsięwzięć budowlanych. Kraków: Wydawnictwo AGH (2010)
13. Vrijhoef, R., Koskela, L.: A critical review of construction as a project-based industry: identifying paths towards a projectindependent approach to construction. In: Proceedings CIB Combining Forces. June, Helsinki. Forthcoming, pp. 13–24 (2005)
14. Ambrosino, G., Liberato, A., Pettinelli, I.: Sustainable Urban Logistics Plans (SULP) Guidelines (2015)
15. Kijewska, K., Johansen, B.G.: Comparative analysis of activities for more environmental friendly urban freight transport systems in Norway and Poland. Procedia-Soc. Behav. Sci. **151**, 142–157 (2014)
16. Bąk, I., Cheba, K., Szczecińska, B.: The statistical analysis of road traffic in cities of Poland. Transp. Res. Procedia **39**, 14–23 (2019)
17. Bardi, A., et al.: Impact mitigation of urban construction: logistics solutions and strategies in Europe, no. 93. EasyChair (2018)
18. Berden, M., et al.: Governance models for sustainable urban construction logistics: barriers for collaboration (2019)
19. Janné, M.: Construction Logistics Solutions in Urban Areas, vol. 1806. Linköping University Electronic Press (2018)
20. Karatsoli, M., Karakikes, I., Nathanail, E.: Urban traffic management utilizing soft measures: a case study of Volos City. In: Nathanail, Eftihia G., Karakikes, Ioannis D. (eds.) CSUM 2018. AISC, vol. 879, pp. 655–662. Springer, Cham (2019). https://doi.org/10.1007/978-3-030-02305-8_79
21. Taniguchi, E., Shimamoto, H.: Intelligent transportation system based dynamic vehicle routing and scheduling with variable travel times. Transp. Res. Part C: Emerg. Technol. **12**(3–4), 235–250 (2004)
22. Barth, M.J., Wu, G., Boriboonsomsin, K.: Intelligent transportation systems and greenhouse gas reductions. Current Sustainable/Renewable Energy Reports **2**(3), 90–97 (2015). https://doi.org/10.1007/s40518-015-0032-y
23. Oskarbski, J., Kaszubowski, D.: Potential for ITS/ICT solutions in urban freight management. Transportation Research Procedia **16**, 433–448 (2016)
24. Galkin, A., et al.: Improving the safety of urban freight deliveries by organization of the transportation process considering driver's state. Transp. Res. Procedia **39**, 54–63 (2019)
25. Wang, L.C., Lin, Y.C., Lin, P.H.: Dynamic mobile RFID-based supply chain control and management system in construction. Adv. Eng. Inform. **21**(4), 377–390 (2007)
26. Hardin, B., McCool, D.: BIM and Construction Management: Proven Tools, Methods, and Workflows. Wiley (2015)
27. Wydział Zarządzania Strategicznego, Urząd Marszałkowski Województwa Zachodniopomorskiego. Strategia Rozwoju Województwa Zachodniopomorskiego do roku 2030 (2017)
28. Kijewska, K., Torbacki, W., Iwan, S.: Application of AHP and DEMATEL methods in choosing and analysing the measures for the distribution of goods in Szczecin Region. Sustainability **10**(7), 2365 (2018)

Regulations and Forms of Business in Road Freight Transport Regulated in Legislation of Slovak Republic

Miloš Poliak[✉], Adela Poliaková, and Zuzana Otáhalová

University of Žilina, Univerzitná 1, Žilina, Slovak Republic
{milos.poliak,adela.poliakova,zuzana.otahalova}@fpedas.uniza.sk

Abstract. The problem of driver's business in road freight transport is regulated by several regulations in the Slovak legal order. An entrepreneur in the field of transport can use any of the legal forms offered by Slovak legislation. The transporter most often chooses between a business in the form of a trade or in the form of a limited liability company. In choosing the legal form, one specific aspect of freight transport must be taken into account in addition to the normal factors applicable to these legal forms, irrespective of the subject of business. During operation of a transport company, high-value goods are often transported, which entails considerable risks. In this article we will deal with the legal aspect of road freight transport, either in the form of a company, self-employed person or employee, as well as its legal impact on the performance of the road freight driver. We will focus only on the most appropriate form of company in this area, which is a limited liability company. We identify the current legal situation in the Slovak Republic and the possibilities of detours the law in the field of road freight transport.

Keywords: Transporter · Trade · Limited liability company

1 Introduction

The theme of the common transport policy is one of the most dynamically developing areas of European Union policy. The European Union aims to legally solve transport as one of the pillars of its common economic policies. The common transport policy is constantly changing and the EU is therefore constantly updating its objectives. The barriers to market access, unnecessary differences in technical and administrative standards and distortions of competition within EU countries have gradually been removed.

EU law currently unifies the conditions of market access for business in road freight transport. Despite these rules, transporters operating across the EU do not have fully harmonized market operating conditions for international road freight transport. Even in recent years, new restrictions have been introduced in the EU; for example, in the form of a minimum wage demonstration, which contributes to the distortion of the EU unified market in the field of transport. For this reason, it is important for transporters not only to know their respective national and EU legislation, but also to know the national rules of

© Springer Nature Switzerland AG 2020
J. Mikulski (Ed.): TST 2020, CCIS 1289, pp. 333–342, 2020.
https://doi.org/10.1007/978-3-030-59270-7_25

the countries in which they wish to carry out the transport operations. The competitive environment in international road freight transport is distorted by national regulations affecting the competitiveness of transporters. However, in addition to these constraints, the system of subcontracting and the existence of transporters, traders, are significantly distorting within the EU. Therefore, the aim of this contribution is to describe the existing situation, on the basis of which it is proposed on the basis of its own research, to propose measures to restore the common market.

2 The Market Approach Analysis

In road freight transport, access to the EU market has been gradually deregulated since 1985. According to the ECJ resolution, the requirements of freedom to provide services include the elimination of any discrimination against the service provider on the basis of his nationality or the fact that he is established in a country other than where the service is provided. In 1996, Council Directive No. 96/26 /EC was accepted.

Because the Directive recognizes the possibility of different approaches to its implementation between Member States, Council Directive No. 96/26/EC has not achieved the required harmonization of market access. The Directive is compulsory because of result to be achieved by each Member State, leaving the choice of forms and means to the national authorities [1]. The regulation of market access through the Directive has created different requirements in the EU for those who have considered entering the road freight transport market. Explanatory Memorandum to Directive (EC) No. 1071/2009 states that the implementation of Council Directive No. 96/26/EC has not been ensured uniformly by Member States. Fragmented implementation caused distortions of competition and market transparency. There is also a risk of employing low-skilled drivers or insufficient compliance with road safety and social security requirements [2–4]. A disadvantage of the Directive is also fact that the Directive produces binding effects only after it has been implemented in national law and the acceptation period has expired [5]. If the Directive is not implemented or is implemented incorrectly, it will create rights and obligations for the individual vis-à-vis the State only if the conditions for direct effect are met [6].

The Directive has several major advantages over the Directive. At first sight, and in accordance with Article 288 of the Treaty on the Functioning of the European Union, a Directive which has been adopted and published is almost immediately binding for all Member States without the need of transposition into internal national law of each Member State [5]. The advantage of using the Regulation to create the same rights and obligations that are uniformly applied and almost immediately binding in all Member States without delay or risk of different approaches that individual implementation of the Directives might cause, is clearly important for harmonizing market access, protection of personal data and financial services [7, 8].

In 2009, Directive (EC) No. 1071/2009 and 1072/2009, which regulate market access in road freight transport uniformly, were accepted. The regulations are effective from 4 December 2012. The regulations clearly define the way of access to the road haulage profession by defining the professional knowledge that a road freight transport operator must master. Given the primacy of EU law, the provisions of Directive (EC) No.

1071/2009 and No. 1072/2009 take precedence over conflicting national law since 4th December 2012 [9]. The primacy of EU law is reflected in the case of Leonesio (which is linked to the implementation of the Directive), where a court has laid a Member State under a duty of loyal cooperation, in the frame of Article 10 of the EC Treaty, to take all necessary measures of general or specific nature to ensure compliance with The Treaty of Establishment of the European Community or measures taken by the Community institutions. Since 4th December 2012, all entrepreneurs must demonstrate the same knowledge as defined in Annex 1 to Directive (EC) No. 1071/2009 (Table 1) [10, 11, 20].

Table 1. A list of subjects defined to meet the requirement of professional competence in road transport [own study]

Subjects' structure
A. CIVIL LAW
B. BUSINESS LAW
C. SOCIAL LAW
D. TAX LAW
E. BUSINESS AND FINANCIAL MANAGEMENT
F. MARKET APPROACH
G. TECHNICAL STANDARDS AND TECHNICAL ASPECTS OF OPERATION
H. ROAD SAFETY

The Directive requires Member States to adopt implementing national rules that regulate the technical procedures for market access according to national conditions in a country. On the basis of that analysis, it is possible to claim that conditions have been harmonized in terms of market access. Transporter meeting the conditions of market access under Directive (EC) No. 1071/2009 may apply for a Community license under which international road freight transport within the EU Member States can be carried out without restrictions. Cabotage operations may also be carried out under certain conditions [9, 12, 19].

The very approach to road transport business is unified across the EU, but the fact of unifying market access without harmonizing tax and social conditions has produced a number of undesirable effects in road transport business.

2.1 Own Research

Recently, many single-person transport companies have been registered without additional employees, either operating their own or a foreign truck. In fact, the creation of small structures makes it very easy to circumvent the restrictions that are set by national tax and social legislation. In general, illegal 'self-employed' workers are being used to that extent that this situation has become characteristic for the road freight sector in the context of strong competition in the EU. Subcontracting of transport services subsequently causes a spiral decreasing in prices in the sector. By delegation of social area responsibility to self-employed workers the requirements of Regulation (EC) No. 561/2006 are often circumvented, those regulate maximum driving times and minimum rest periods for drivers. By transferring responsibility from large companies to small transporters – self-employed people, the effectiveness of controls is reduced because, while checking in a company in great enterprises, it is possible to check multiple drivers at a single inspection by one controller, in small companies only one driver is controlled during a control. Given that EU regulations set a minimum number of drivers' working hours, which inspectors are obliged to check, there is a situation where inspectors are motivated to inspect business of larger companies [13].

The problem of employment of road freight transport drivers is very complex. It is necessary to differentiate whether the driver is a self-employed person who is also a road transport operator or whether the driver perform the activity of a driver for a trade involving the driving of an extraneous motor vehicle. Two surveys were carried out on this issue. The first survey was aimed at all EU countries, finding out whether there was **a trade for the profession of road freight transport driver in that country and therefore was not keeper of a Community license**. The survey was conducted electronically via email communication and ran from September to December 2018 (Fig. 1).

Within this time period, individual institutions of all EU countries were addressed, of which 11 countries responded (Table 2). The survey found that it is not possible to carry out the work of a driver on a base of trade in Slovakia as well as in most EU countries. The driver may only be a self-employed person who provide a transport service in his own name (that is, he shall submit an invoice for the transport service in his own name) and also have a Community license and a certified copy of the Community vehicle license as regulated in Directive (EC) No 1072/2009. In relation to the asked question, three states, namely Estonia, Slovenia and Poland, stated that a road freight transport driver (driving a vehicle over 3.5 t) can work for a trade respectively without holding a Community license at the same time.

An example of a statement by a representative of the Road and Rail Transport Department of the Ministry of Economic Affairs and Communications of the Republic of

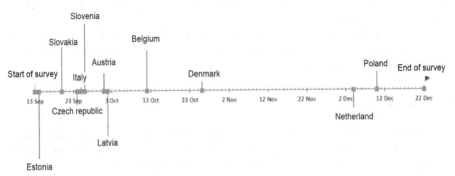

Fig. 1. A schedule for the provision of EU country data in the realized survey [own study]

Table 2. Survey results aimed on drivers employment in frame of EU countries [own study]

Country	Work of road freight transport driver for a trade
Slovakia	✗
Czech republic	✗
Poland	✓
Austria	✗
Estonia	✓
Latvia	✗
Denmark	✗
Netherland	✗
Belgium	✗
Italy	*Non-defined trade as individual form of business*
Slovenia	✓

Estonia: ... *'According to Estonian legislation, when the consignment note designates a self-employed driver as a transporter (road transport operator), it is a clear signal that this self-employed driver must have a Community license. **However, if the self-employed driver offers the transport company his/her workforce (such as hiring the workforce), this activity (management) does not require that person (driver) to have a Community license.'***

Subsequently, job portals advertising the job offers for a road freight transport driver were also examined in those countries, and in many cases it was the trade form that was listed as the type of employment without the need to hold a Community license. In addition to the countries that stated in the survey that this form of employment is possible for driver's work, it has been found that even in countries where the work of a road freight transport driver is legally prohibited, it is often possible to find such a job offer (Fig. 2).

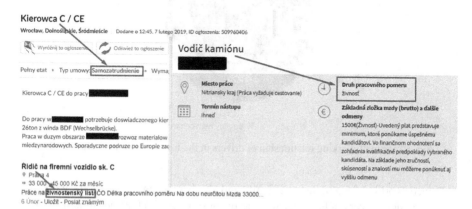

Fig. 2. An example of job portals in Poland and Slovakia advertising the work of a driver for a trade without requiring a Community license [own study]

The second survey was conducted in the Slovak Republic via Google questionnaire. The questionnaire was intended for road freight transport drivers and was published in the discussion forum at www.profivodic.sk, it was also distributed via social networks and added to groups of which road freight transport drivers are members. The questionnaire contains 3 questions. The first question is aimed at determining the form of the working relationship, where the answer could be an employment contract or a trade. The amount of remuneration for the driving performance is dealt by the second question, where we asked the drivers for their gross monthly remuneration in €. The last question we wanted to find out what benefits an analysed form of working relationship brings to the driver from his perspective. The survey was carried out in order to find out information about the possibility of employing drivers in road freight transport. The aim was to find out whether it is possible to carry out the work of the driver only on the basis of an employment contract or whether there is a possibility to perform this profession on the basis of trade. Furthermore, we wanted to find out whether the trade is also used in practice. The results of the questionnaire were subsequently processed and show that up to 11% of the responded drivers perform the profession of driver for a trade, 89% of the drivers work under contract. The percentages are shown in the following graph (Fig. 3).

The amount of remuneration for the performed work is quite different, which can be seen in the following figure. In particular, there is a significant difference between drivers who work for a trade, where their remuneration is considerably higher than for drivers working under an employment contract. The largest group of drivers receive remuneration for the work done in range from € 500 to € 1,000 of gross wage (Fig. 4). There are no drivers working on the trade within this range. The average gross monthly remuneration for drivers working under employment contract is € 1,027.4 [14, 18].

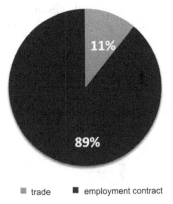

■ trade   ■ employment contract

Fig. 3. Form of working relationship of drivers in the frame of survey [own study]

Drivers working for a trade have significantly higher remuneration for the work they do, where such drivers achieve an income of more than € 3,000 per month in gross wage. The average wage of such drivers is € 2,222.2. The difference is caused mainly by the fact that driver-self-employer is the driver of lower costs for transporter [15–17].

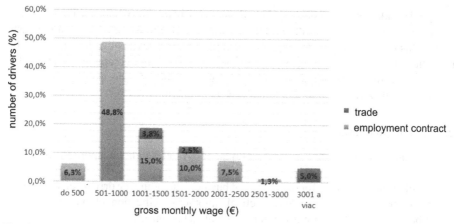

Fig. 4. Comparison of remuneration of drivers working for employment contracts and for trade [own study]

The form of work performed for the transporter or company depends mainly on the type of performed work. In most cases, the transporter therefore has two options:

- to employ an employee (in employment)
- to use the services of a self-employed person, who will execute them on demand.

Under the Labour Code, the work of an employee (dependent work) may only be performed in an employment relationship. The Labour Code expressly forbids any dependent commercial or civil relationship to replace dependent work. However, in practice, it is also possible to find cases where dependent work, especially employment, is replaced by work on a trade. This is an illegal activity and in case of proving, the employer and the trader are subject to a penalty and other sanctions. Dependent work is often replaced by work for a trade due to savings on employer's contributions, as **an employee is still the costliest way of work provision for an employer compared to the situation when the work is provided by a trader.**

In certain circumstances, however, the situation is more advantageous to both parties, both the 'employer' and the 'trader', but the law regulations prohibit such cooperation (cooperation containing signs of dependent work). If the service providing (it means work provision) is ordered by the transporter from the trader, he issues an invoice for the work performance. The transporter does not pay insurance for it and does not withhold income tax. He does not send notices, statements or other documents to insurance companies. The trader shall pay the invoiced amount in the contractually agreed amount. However, the transporter should pay close attention to the contractual terms of cooperation, as in the case of complaints about services delivered by the trader, the terms and conditions agreed in the contract are important. A trade person is also significantly less protected than an employee. If he gets an accident at work, the company for which he provides services is not responsible for him because he is not an employee. A trade person is not eligible to obtain meal vouchers, to have leave to visit a doctor and if he does not agree on a paid holiday with the company, he will not get paid in case of holiday. The employer must ensure the employee with a job and work aids. He must train him and regularly train at his own expense. It is subject to various administrative obligations towards the tax office, the Social Insurance Agency or the health insurance company. As a trade for the driver profession is prohibited in the Slovak Republic, it is necessary to cancel all old trades that were issued to individual drivers in previous years.

2.2 Recommendation

Suggested recommendations on the employment of road freight transport drivers:

- Cancellation of the trade for the subject of business including the driving of an extraneous (not owned) motor vehicle respectively another specification allowing to perform the profession of driver for trade in individual EU countries.
- Transposition of Directive 2002/15/EC of the European Parliament and of the Council on the organization of the working time of people performing mobile road transport activities, where, among other things, also the definitions of mobile employee and self-employment active driver in all EU states are defined in the same way - that is, the road transport driver can only be legally in each EU country like:
- a mobile employee employed by a transporter; or
- a self-employed driver, but the authorization to perform the occupation of road transport operator and the Community license must be in his name, i.e. the driver is also a road transport operator in same time.
- The proposal aim is to create more suitable conditions for business in road freight transport and to take measures towards prevention of illegal way of business.

3 Conclusion

The operation of a transport company requires a number of documents and permits. The transporter must respect not only national legislation but also European Union legislation, which is in preferred position in relation to national legislation.

Pursuant to Act no. 56/2012 Coll. on road transport, it is necessary to meet the specific conditions for obtaining a license and subsequently a license for the operation of road freight transport with vehicle weight over 3.5 tons. The operation of road freight transport is a business whose object is the provision of transport services to the public for remuneration by road motor vehicles which are type-approved for this purpose. Every entrepreneur who is an applicant for a license for the operation of road freight transport must be registered in the Commercial Register of the Slovak Republic, even if he is doing business as a natural person - self-employed.

In the case of absence of such entry in the Commercial Register of the Slovak Republic, the entrepreneur would be exposed to the risk of unauthorized business. An entrepreneur may only perform the activity which is registered as the subject of his business.

An entrepreneur in the field of transport can use any of the legal forms offered by Slovak legislation. The most common choice is between a business in the form of **a trade or a limited liability company**.

In the whole bureaucratic process of administrative proceedings, representation by another person is also possible, according to § 17 par. 4 of Act no. 71/1967 on Administrative Procedure (Administrative Procedure Code), as amended.

Finally, it is necessary to add that, even though it is illegal to perform the profession of driver for "free trade" in our conditions, in practice we can encounter this. The negative phenomenon of this form of business is that in many cases drivers will formally change into entrepreneurs in this way, despite the fact that the essential characteristics of business have not been fulfilled.

Acknowledgement. This paper has been developed under support of project: VEGA No. 1/0245/20 Poliak: Identification of the impact of a change in transport related legislation on the competitiveness of carriers and carriage safety and VEGA No. 1/0566/18 Konečný: Research on the impact of supply and quality of transport services on the competitiveness and sustainability of demand for public transport

References

1. Poliak, M.: Zmena podmienok podnikania v cestnej doprave. In: Doprava a logistika: odborný mesačník vydavateľstva Ecopress. Roč. 5, č. 4, pp. 29–31 (2010)
2. Poliak, M., et al.: Defining the influence of the support of bus service on road safety. Commun. Sci. Lett. Univ. Žilina **18**(2), 83–87 (2016)
3. Kalašová, A., Černický, L., Hamar, M.: A new approach to road safety in Slovakia. In: Mikulski, J. (ed.) TST 2012. CCIS, vol. 329, pp. 388–395. Springer, Heidelberg (2012). https://doi.org/10.1007/978-3-642-34050-5_44
4. Kalasova, A., Kubíková, S.: The interaction of safety and intelligent transport systems in road transport. In: Young researches seminar 2015 [electronic source]: 17–19 June, Sapienza - Universita di Roma. - [S.l.: S.n.], - CD-ROM, pp. 3–13 (2015)
5. Rotondo, E.: The legal effect of EU regulations. Comput. Law Secur. Rev. **29**, 437–445 (2013)
6. Scully, R.: Becoming Europeans? Attitudes, Behaviour, and Socialization in the European Parliament. Oxford University Press, Oxford (2005)
7. Blendon, R., et al.: Bridging the gap between the public' and economists' views of the economy. J. Econ. Perspect. **11**, 105–118 (1997)
8. Zodrow, G.: Tax competition and tax coordination in the European Union. Int. Tax Public Finan. **10**, 651–671 (2003)
9. Poliak, M.: Podnikanie v zasielateľstve a v cestnej doprave. 1. vyd. Žilinská univerzita v Žiline (2011)
10. Gnap, J., Poliak, M., Kováčiková, E.: Odborná spôsobilosť vedúceho dopravy a pre-vádzkovateľa cestnej nákladnej dopravy. 5. preprac. vyd. - Žilina: Žilinská univerzita (2017)
11. Sánchez-López, C., Aceytuno, M.T., de Paz-Báñez, M.A.: Inequality and globalisation: analysis of European countries. Econ. Sociol. **12**(4) (2019)
12. Poliak, M., et al.: The impact of the CMR protocol on carrier competitiveness [electronic] [Vplyv protokolu CMR na konkurencieschopnosť dopravcu]. In: Journal of competitiveness [print, electronic]: the scientific periodical published by the Faculty of Management and Economics of Tomas Bata University in Zlín. - ISSN 1804-171X. - Roč. 11, č. 4, pp. 132–143. https://www.cjournal.cz/files/305.pdf (2019)
13. Poliak, M., et al.: Driver salary identification by hypothesis testing. Transp. Commun. Sci. J. **5**(2), 25–29 (2017)

14. Poliaková, A.: Zvyšovanie nezdaniteľnej časti základu dane v kontexte s ekonomickým vývojom na Slovensku, Increasing the non-taxable part of the tax base in context of economic development in Slovakia. In: Rozvoj Euroregiónu Beskydy XIII: diagnostika spoločensko - ekonomických podmienok 15 rokov po vstupe do EÚ: stratégia - digitálna spoločnosť - bezpečnosť: zborník príspevkov. - 1. vyd. - Žilina: Žilinská univerzita v Žiline, pp. 165–174 (2019)

15. Graessley, S., et al.: Consumer attitudes and behaviors in the technology-driven sharing economy: motivations for participating in collaborative consumption. J. Self-Governance and Manag. Econ. **7**(1), 25–30 (2019)

16. Bartosova, V., Kral, P.: A methodological framework of financial analysis results objectification in the Slovak Republic. In: 3rd International Conference on Business and Economics 2016, (BE-ci), Malaysia, European Proceedings of Social and Behavioural Sciences, 17, pp. 189–197 (2016)

17. Poliak, M., et al.: The impact of the transport route on the cost of the transfer. In: Automotive safety 2018 [electronic] - 1. vyd. - New York: Institute of Electrical and Electronics Engineers. ISBN 978-1-5386-4578-9, pp. 1–6 (2018)

18. Poliak, M., et al.: The competitiveness of public transport [Konkurencieschopnosť hromadnej dopravy]. In: Journal of Competitiveness: The scientific periodical published by Tomas Bata University in Zlin, vol. 9(3), pp. 81–97 (2017)

19. Poliak, M., Šimurková, P.: Systém vzdelávania v súvislosti so získaním odbornej spôsobilosti na prevádzkovanie podniku cestnej dopravy. In: Logistika - ekonomika – prax, pp. 101–109 (2016)

20. Nariadenie (ES) č. 1071/2009, ktorým sa ustanovujú spoločné pravidlá týkajúce sa podmienok, ktoré je potrebné dodržiavať pri výkone povolania prevádzkovateľa cestnej dopravy. Dostupné: http://eur-lex.europa.eu/legal-content/SK/ALL/?uri=celex:32009R1071. Accessed 15 Jan 2020

Economic Consequences of Road Accidents for TSL Companies

Teresa Gądek-Hawlena[⊠]

University of Economics in Katowice, 1 Maja 50, Katowice, Poland
gadek@ue.katowice.pl

Abstract. Road accidents are a socio-economic problem for the entirety of society; the consequences of which, although different in nature for different groups of subjects, always involve bearing certain costs. Given the economic operators, the negative consequences of road accidents are of particular importance to the TSL sector. For the operators in this sector road accidents may, in certain situations, prevent the running of gainful activities or cause it to reduce significantly by the destruction of vehicles or by eliminating the driver that is licensed to carry dangerous goods. Despite many actions being taken to improve road safety, including the application of modern solutions in heavy goods vehicles to better vehicle safety, the administration of legislative changes, or the improvement of road infrastructure, the scale of the phenomenon that is road accidents, and the costs associated with them are still high. In the article with a theoretical background that is funded on the basis of an in-depth analysis of the literature on the subject, I will identify the factors important for the TSL sector companies that influence the costs of road accidents and attempt to estimate the cost of a liability insurance and its changes depending on the time of the accident-free driving on selected examples.

Keywords: Cost · Road accidents · Companies

1 Introduction

Road accidents are most often defined as incidents occurring in road traffic that are caused by a non-intentional breach of safety rules in the congestion, and that result in the death of one of the participants, or an injury leading to an infraction of organ function or a health disorder lasting more than 7 days [1]. From a systemic perspective, it is assumed that road accidents are affected by three factors: a person, a vehicle, and the road. In the case of the vehicles used by the TSL sector companies, the factors influencing the number and structure of accidents depend on their type [2]. The main ones are: poor visibility for the driver, a not entirely correct liaison of the vehicle safety system with the driver's actions, or vehicle failures such as technical malfunctions and tire explosions. The mentioned factors are not the only ones, but both accident statistics and car manufacturers' data deem them essential.

At the same time, an analysis of the mode of transport itself is not sufficient enough to illustrate the causes of a road accident. The driver's behaviour should also be examined.

J. Mikulski (Ed.): TST 2020, CCIS 1289, pp. 343–353, 2020.
https://doi.org/10.1007/978-3-030-59270-7_26

In the case of the human factor, the many elements taken into account are, among others: age, gender, the type of a driving license or the driving period [3, 4].

The results of many studies show that more than a half of long-distance drivers fell asleep behind the wheel at some point. The peak levels of fatigue-related accidents are often 10 times higher at night than during the day. The studies on the working hours and work habits of professional drivers held in France [5] showed that the risk of fatigue accidents increased when people drove at night, their working day was extended, or when their work was irregular [6]. The variables such as the drivers' age, years of experience in driving a truck, the level of education, and marital status also prove to be important for causing a road accident among professional drivers, as indicated by studies [7]. Among the important hazards present in the workplace of the truck driver, the hazards shown in Table 1 are indicated.

Table 1 presents several risks that have a significant impact on road transport safety, such as accidents and collisions, stress, falling asleep while driving, and digestive diseases. These risks are mainly caused by physical, psychosocial, ergonomic and work organisation factors to which they belong: irregular lifestyles, excessive working hours, driving against traffic regulations, excessive workload, time pressure, changing and

Table 1. Hazards occurring at the workplace of the driver of a heavy goods vehicle [8]

Risk of road accident	Cause	The effect
A collision, road accident	Fatigue or exhaustion of the driver's body, drowsiness, stressors, night work, insufficient lighting, poor visibility, dazzling effect of another vehicle's lights and headlamps, visual acuity disorder, speed not adapted to road conditions, driving not in accordance with traffic regulations road, potential risks from others traffic participants, high volume of traffic of a roadside, long-distance driving, driver's driving time exceeded, missing or too short breaks, bad weather, a faulty vehicle, dispersion by physiological factors (hunger, thirst)	Bruises, internal and external injuries, limb fractures, spinal injuries, concussion, loss of health, disability, death
Driver sleep while driving	Long-lasting driving, fatigue and exhaustion, poor visibility, too high temperature air in the cabin, inadequate ventilation in the cabin, driver's driving time exceeded, no or too short breaks, night work, eyestrain, limited concentration	Traffic collision or accident, including fatal accident, bruises, injuries internal and external, limb fractures, spinal injuries, brain concussion, disability
Gastrointestinal diseases	Irregular nutrition, stress, bad eating habits, consumption of large quantities of caffeine drinks, limited possibilities of preparing and eating valuable meals, poisoning, unfavourable food storage conditions	Stomach ulcers, liver problems, constipation
Stress	Excessive duties, time pressure, traffic obstructions, constant telephone and satellite control by superiors	Depression, sleepiness, somatic symptoms, exhaustion, aggression, mental illness, heart aches, dizziness, stomach problems

unfavourable weather conditions, faulty vehicle, insufficient lighting, sleepiness and night work. These risks are characterised by numerous material and human losses, such as the death or disability of road users, numerous injuries and illnesses, and damage to the vehicle fleet and the road surface [8]. In addition to personnel costs, accidents involving lorries also result in high costs for many businesses, throughout the entire supply chain [9].

In the light of the above, the article makes an attempt to identify the costs of road accidents that affect the company's losses and tries to indicate the selected costs related to road accidents that are relevant for economic operators, including primarily those from the TSL sector. Taking into account the factors influencing the costs of road accidents and their changes, the research part of the article uses statistical data of the Main Headquarters, National Security Council and selected entities of the TSL sector.

2 Literature Background

The identification of costs of road accidents and the methods of their determination was subjected to a multilateral analysis which resulted in the appearance of numerous studies addressing the matters mentioned above [10–15]. There are also many systematic road accident costs. The most general classification refers to dividing the road accident costs into internal [16] (private) ones that are compensated as a part of the insurance coverage. The amount of these costs depends, to a large extent, on the insurance system adopted in a given country and on liability regulations [11, 12]. The second cost group within this classification are the costs of road accidents caused by individual road users and borne by the whole society called external costs [12, 17, 18]. However, these divisions are not the only ones. In the case of the costs borne by the TSL companies, there are many studies that illustrate them in more detail. In *Volvo Truck Safety Report 2017* [2], they are divided into three groups: soft cost, indirect costs and direct costs (Table 2).

Table 2. The division of road accident costs [2]

Type of cost	Division	Distinction
Soft costs	Damage to reputation and image	–
Indirect costs (unrecovered hard cost)	Fleet cost	Vehicle downtime for repair and vehicle recovery Driver rec3overy or resignation/fatality injured Legal investigation Goods damaged Daily business routine disruption Delay in delivery Insurance cost Accident site cleaning
Direct costs (recovered hard cost)	Insurance claims	Driver health recovery Vehicle repair costs Vehicle downtime (repair)

This division can be expanded upon by the taxonomy of costs [19, 20]. The detailed cost model of a road accident is presented in Table 3.

Table 3 shows a detailed cost structure of road accidents. As can be seen, the loss that occurred during a road accident consists of two components - material (economic) and

Table 3. Accident cost model [own study based on [20]]

Cost factor	Components	Selected variables
Vehicle damage	cost of towing to the place of repair	− distance − time − the type of machinery used
	repair cost	− spare parts cost − labour cost
	cost of idle time of vehicle	− opportunity cost
Cargo loss or damage	cost of lost part of cargo	− the cost of defaulting on the contract, − cost depending on the relationship between the trading partners
	non-fulfilment of the production plan	
	interaptions in enterprises' production process	
Damage to road infrastructure	labour cost	− specialists' cost
	cost of materials and equipments which are necessary for repair	− material cost − cost of equipment operation time
	costs related to temporary immobilization of the road section	− congestion − cost of additional signalling devices
Losses at accident place	delays in commuting, delivering goods, delays, waste of fuel and etc.	− the cost of being late to work / school / to college − the cost of not delivering the goods on time
Expenses for conducting an accident investigation	expenses for intervention of road police, emergency, fire brigade and etc.	− costs according to the tariff − fine
	expenses for work-time insurance brokers, experts and surveyors which conduct the insurance investigation	− costs according to the tariff − costs of private experts − expenditure on preparing insurance documentation
	cost of legal proceedings	− costs according to the tariff − representative's cost
Losses related to the loss of human life or health	death	− the cost of hospitalization − morgue expenses − funeral costs − costs related to hiring a new employee and training − cost of work-time lost of relatives and colleagues − payment of compensations and pensions to relatives − insurance compensations − loss of part of national income
	injuries causing disability	− the cost of transport to the hospital − the cost of hospitalization

(continued)

Table 3. (*continued*)

	– costs related to the temporary employment of a new employee and his training – insurance compensations – loss of part of national income – expenses for treatment in hospital (clinic) – expenses related to sanatorium treatment – expenses related to special home care, – expenses for food and medicines – cost of work-time lost of relatives – payment of compensations and pensions – payment for sick-leaf certificate – expenses for obtaining new profession and – transfer to another less paid position
slight injuries	– insurance compensations – payment for sick-leaf certificate

social. The economic component consists of direct and indirect losses. Direct losses are those related to damaged road infrastructure, damaged vehicles, and damaged goods, expenditures on accident investigation, pensions, sickness allowances, treatments of injured, and funerals. Indirect losses include the temporary, partial, or total exclusion of members of the public from production, as well as losses related to the occurrence of traffic disruptions during the accident and the removal of its effects. Although the costs of road accidents are rather detailed, most of them are difficult to determine because they depend on many variables and thus make it difficult to be clearly estimated. The only group of costs connected with a road accident are the costs which can be most easily estimated using the various and commonly available tariffs, such as, among others, mandates or selected costs of expert opinions, while the costs that cannot be practically estimated are the costs of persons indirectly involved in the road accident (the costs resulting from congestion).

3   Costs of Road Accidents in Poland

The costs of road accidents in Poland are very high. Annually, the Polish state loses PLN 55.6 billion on road accidents. This amount is higher than the state budget expenditure on many ministries, including national defence (35 billion PLN), higher education (25.3 billion PLN) or the environment (23 billion PLN) [data for 2018; 21]. The costs of fatalities have the largest share in the costs of road accidents (Table 4).

Table 4. Costs of road accidents in Poland in 2014–2018 with a forecast until 2023 [22–24]

Cost category	Unit costs in PLN in 2014	Unit costs in PLN in 2015	Unit costs in PLN in 2018	Unit costs in PLN in 2023
Unit cost of fatalities	1 913 909	2 052 516	2 393 125	2 330 572
Unit cost of the seriously injured victim	2 291 214	2 323 299	3 309 300	3 224 14
Unit cost of slightly injured victim	27 107	26 860	48 165	46 926
Unit cost of material losses in a road accident	20 029	22 653	15 385	–
Unit cost of the road accident	993 934	1 018 160	1 420 191	-bd

According to the data presented in Table 2, the annual costs of road accidents are expected to fall below 56 billion to PLN 55.2 billion by 2023, with road safety stabilised. However, this is not a very large decrease. In 2018, the largest cost, representing as much as 58% of all road incidents, are losses in domestic production due to employee's death or indisposition to work. Another group are material losses (21%) followed by administrative and operational costs - 17%. The last group of costs are costs of intangible losses and medical costs [24].

In turn, material losses are the second most direct result of traffic events after injuries. There are three types of material losses: losses in vehicles participating in the event, losses in road infrastructure in the place where the road event took place, other losses related to the destruction of e.g. cubature infrastructure, i.e. buildings. In 2018, 787,770 vehicles participated in road events and it was about 9% more than in 2015 (then 720,201 vehicles). Based on the data from the KNF report, the average loss per vehicle was determined and then calculations were made according to the statistics of the number of vehicles in relation to regions. It was finally estimated that in 2018 the value of material losses of collisions and road accidents amounted to PLN 12.1 billion, which is a record-breaking 36% more than in 2015 (then PLN 8.9 billion). These losses are very important from the point of view of TSL sector operators [24].

4 Selected Effects of the Road Incident on Transport Undertakings

For companies in the TSL sector, the costs related to the means of transport or the cargo itself are crucial in a road accident. In the case of cargo, the costs resulting from a road accident may include: costs of failure to meet the service delivery deadline, costs of damage or destruction of the cargo. These costs vary and depend on the contracts and mutual relations between the principal and the transport company. In turn, the costs related to a means of transport that has been damaged in a road accident may cover several groups of them. Taking into account each of the elements presented in Table 3, it can be seen that these costs will be different. They will be influenced by many factors.

Using publicly available data and information from transport companies, an attempt was made to determine the cost of towing a truck. First, the number of road incidents was determined.

On the basis of the police report [25], it results that the total number of road accidents was 31 674 and collisions 436 414, which gives a total of 468 688 road events.

In order to determine the number of heavy goods vehicles involved in the road event, the methodology adopted in the article Selected costs of road collisions for road haulage companies [26]. The number of truck and bus incidents shall be determined according to the formula:

Number of truck and bus road incidents = ([Total number of road incidents in 2018] × 3%)/(100%)

Where 3% is the average share of HGV drivers involved in a traffic incident. This figure was determined on the basis of data from the National Road Safety Programme for the years 2013–2020 [27]. Thus, the number of road incidents of passenger cars and buses is 140 661. The unit cost of towing a vehicle is 4.5 PLN/km (shown cost includes only the towing of the vehicle without additional charges) [It's the cost of the tow. Determined from company data]. The structure of towing costs for transport companies depending on the length of the route is shown in Table 5.

Table 5. Total cost of towing lorries in 2018 [own study]

Distance [km]	Cost of towing trucks in 2018 in PLN
1	56 244
5	281 220
10	562 440
15	843 660
20	1 124 880
25	1 406 100
30	1 687 320
35	1 968 540
40	2 249 760
45	2 249 760
50	2 812 200

As can be seen from the above, the cost of towing heavy goods vehicles, which is one of the lowest costs arising from a road accident for the fleet of vehicles involved in the traffic incident, gives a significant amount. For a distance of 50 km, the amount of 28 122 200 allows the purchase of 122 commercial vehicles.

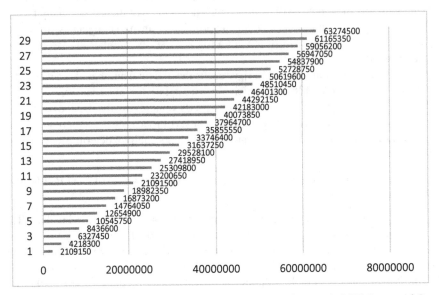

Fig. 1. Total cost of immobilization of vehicles due to road events in 2018 [own study]

There is another cost involved in towing the vehicle to the repair site. This is the cost of immobilizing the vehicle. Compared to the cost of towing it is much higher and amounts to 150 PLN/day (Amount adopted on the basis of information obtained from 5 transport companies (the given amount was averaged)). The cost of vehicle parking is shown in Fig. 1.

As can be seen from Fig. 2, the costs of parking trucks are very high. One day the trucks are stopped for more than 2 000 000 PLN. How big is the amount of money for stopping trucks requiring repairs? You can check how many new vans and trucks can be bought for this amount. This relationship is illustrated in Fig. 2.

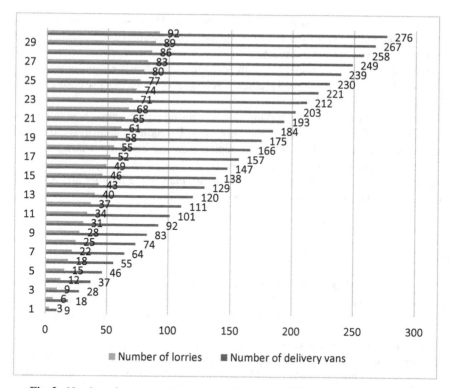

Fig. 2. Number of commercially viable vehicles available for purchase [own study]

As you can see, the cost of stopping the trucks for 30 is an amount allowing for the purchase of 276 vans and 92 trucks. At the same time, this cost is not one, as repairing a car involves the cost of spare parts or workshop work. Therefore, the cost presented is not the only one. So the cost presented is not the only one. Personnel and other costs are not included. As well as the cost related to the insurance of the vehicle, which covers part of the costs related to the road accident. On the other hand, road accidents increase insurance premiums.

5 Conclusion

On the basis of the carried out studies, several conclusions and generalizations can be identified:

– It is practically impossible to examine the factors influencing road accidents individually. A road accident is affected by several factors at once - where one of which can be considered the main one - and the problems associated with road accidents caused by professional vehicles and drivers show some specificities,
– The costs of road accidents are classified in different ways, but none of the classifications is able to capture all the costs of a road accident in detail,

– The costs of road accidents in Poland are very high. The costs of fatalities have the largest share in their structure. The forecast until 2023 assumes a decrease in the costs of road accidents, but not too much,
– In addition to the costs associated with accident victims, material costs are also an important part of the cost of road accidents. A large proportion of these costs are borne by the transport undertakings,
– A cost analysis of towing and parking vehicles during repairs shows how large these amounts are. These costs are not the only ones. Extending the analysis to include additional costs such as loss of a car or replacement car could show how much loss companies incur as a result of road accidents.
– An important issue in the research would be to analyse the liability and autocasco insurance paid by transport companies at several levels.

References

1. http://brd.org.pl/2,148,Kolizja_czy_wypadek_drogowy.htm. Last accessed 20 Jan 2020
2. Volvo Truckt Safety Report 2017. https://www.volvogroup.com/content/dam/volvo/volvo-group/markets/global/en-en/about-us/traffic-safety/Safety-report-2017.pdf. Last accessed 20 Jan 2020
3. Naevestad, T.O., Philips, R.O., Elvebakk, B.: Traffic accidents triggered by drivers at work – a survey andanalysis of contributing factors. Transport. Res. Part F34, 94–107 (2015)
4. Ebeli, L., Forciniti, C., Mazzulla, G.: Factors influencing accident severity: an analysis by road accident type. Transport Res. Procedia 47, 449–456 (2020)
5. National Transportation Safety Board, Evaluation of U.S. Department of Transportation Efforts in the 1990s to Address Operator Fatigue, Waszyngton 1999. Last accessed 20 Jan 2020
6. WHO, World Report on Road Traffic Injury Prevention, red. In: Peden, M., Scurfield, R., Sleet, D. (eds.) Genewa, pp. 84 (2004)
7. Meholizadek, M., Shariat-Mohaymany, A., Nordfjaern, T.: Accident involvement among Iranian lorry drivers: Direct and indirect effects of background variables and aberrant driving behaviour. Transport Res. Part F58, 39–55 (2018)
8. Wojdyło, D., Wierzba, A., Madejski, R.: Road transport safety as regards the work of the lorry driver. Logistyka 3, 6773 (2014)
9. Gądek-Hawlena, T.: Partnership for Improving Road Safety in Poland, Presscom, p. 69 (2019)
10. Gul, E.: Economic Evaluation of Road Traffic Safety Measures, "MPRA Paper" no. 48350 (2013)
11. OECD, Economic Evaluation of Road Traffic Safety Measures, Paryż, pp. 22–34 (2001)
12. Maśniak, D.: Cross-border protection system for road accident victims. Legal and Financial Studies, Warsaw, pp. 96 (2010)
13. Rizzi, L.I., de Dios Ortúzar, J.: Estimating the Willingness-to-Pay for Road Safety Improvements, "Transport Reviews" vol. 26(4), pp. 471–485 (2006)
14. Costs and fees in transport. In: Bąk, M. (ed.) Gdańsk (2009)
15. Moyer, J.D., et al.: Cost analysis of global road traffic death prevention: Forecasts to 2050. Dev. Policy Rev. 35, 743–757 (2017)
16. The European Parliament. Directorate-General for Internal Policies, Calculating External Costs in the Transport Sector, Brussels (2009)

17. Petruccelli, U.: Assessment of external costs for transport project evaluation: guidelines in some european countries, "Environmental Impact Assessment Review", vol. 54, pp. 434–757 (2015)
18. Fridstrøm, L.: A Framework for Assessing the Marginal External Accident Cost of Road Use and its Implications for Insurance Ratemaking, "Discussion Paper", no. 22 (2001)
19. Partheeban, P., Arunbabu, E., Hemamalini, R.R.: Road accident cost prediction model using systems dynamics approach. Transport **23**(1), 59–66 (2008)
20. Kapskij, D., Samoilovich, T.: The theoretical basis for an economic evaluation of road accident losses. Transport **24**(3), 200–204 (2009)
21. mapawydatków.pl. Last accessed 20 Jan 2020
22. KRBRD, Willingness to pay" (WTP) – study on the readiness of the public to participate in the active shaping of road traffic safety and the execution of the valuation of the costs of accidents and collisions on the road network in Poland at the end of 2014 including correlation with WTP test results, Warszawa (2015)
23. KRBRD, Valuation of the costs of accidents and collisions on the road network in Poland at the end of 2015, with a distinction made between the average social and economic costs of accidents on the trans-European transport network, KRBRD, Warszawa listopad (2016)
24. KRBRD, Valuation of costs of accidents and road collisions on the road network in Poland at the end of 2018, with separation of average social and economic costs of accidents on the trans-European transport network, KRBRD, Warszawa (2019)
25. Komenda, G.: Policji, Road accidents in Poland in 2019, Warszawa, s. 7 (2019)
26. Kozłowski, R., Adamek, R., Palczewska, A.: Selected collision costs for road transport companies thing, Studia Ekonomiczne. Zeszyty Naukowe Uniwersytetu Ekonomicznego w Katowicach, nr 306 (2016)
27. KRBRD, National Road Safety Programme for the years 2013–2020, Warszawa (2013)

On a Certain Approach Towards the U-Turn of a Motor Vehicle Maneuver

Jarosław Zalewski[✉]

Warsaw University of Technology, Plac Politechniki 1, Warsaw, Poland
j.zalewski@ans.pw.edu.pl

Abstract. The article presents the results obtained through several simulations of the so-called a u-turn maneuver of a motor vehicle's model in various traffic conditions, i.e. both flat and uneven as well as dry or icy road surface. The initial speed adopted for the maneuver is 100 km/h on the 5th gear as if the vehicle had to perform a sudden change of direction without the ability to reduce its speed. Randomly occurring irregularities of the road surface have been adopted as an additional disturbance affecting the safety of the vehicle's motion. The whole maneuver lasted about 8 s and consisted of two parts: a right turn and a left turn, while the radius obtained during the simulations changed along with the change of the traffic conditions. The simulations have been performed in the MSC Adams/Car software. Along with the random disturbances adopted for the most cases considered in this paper, the suspension of the vehicle's model has been adopted as fully non-linear. Such approach led to certain conclusions relevant for considering the extreme cases in road traffic.

Keywords: Fish hook maneuver · Road irregularities · Motor vehicle dynamics

1 Introduction

Research on motor vehicles' dynamics are mainly related to performing the different maneuvers in various traffic conditions. The most important issue seems to be able to relate the conducted research to different areas of knowledge. Such attitude is essential due to the unavoidable fact that different technologies can be used in order to obtain the same goal.

As for the telematics of transport, the scope of research presented in this paper can be related to the road vehicle safety form the point of view of the means of transport and their technical supply base, but at the same time using the information technology. Although these are mainly used to ease the study on transport safety it is obvious that telematics may as well combine automatics and telecommunication technology to interact with the previously mentioned problems. To sum up, the conditions of motor vehicles' motion are one of the main problems included in the wide scope of research, but in this paper only a small piece of it has been considered.

When considering safety and dynamics of motor vehicles some important issues, concerning dynamics and safety of motor vehicles' motion have so far been analysed

© Springer Nature Switzerland AG 2020
J. Mikulski (Ed.): TST 2020, CCIS 1289, pp. 354–367, 2020.
https://doi.org/10.1007/978-3-030-59270-7_27

over the years, for example a problem of wheel – road contact during the vehicles' motion (e.g. [1, 2, 8]) along with the normal reactions of the road on the wheels (e.g. [5, 10]), as well as the problem of road irregularities' influence on performing of the specified maneuvers (e.g. [3, 6, 7]).

In this paper the issue of a u-turn maneuver performed by the vehicle model (Fig. 1) has been considered in various and selected traffic conditions.

The selected vehicle model, laden as discussed in the following chapter, performed the selected maneuver in a simulation which has been conducted in the MSC Adams/Car, with its conditions described in chapter 3. Such research seem necessary and it seems possible to conduct them in case of real vehicle, e.g. with the properly prepared unmanned aerial vehicle as, for example, in [9] enabling the observation of a vehicle's response to the disturbances from above.

Fig. 1. Full vehicle model used in simulations [12]

2   General Assumptions for the Vehicle Model

The vehicle's model, which has been selected to perform the considered u-turn maneuver, had its mass increased from 995 kg to 1150 kg by adding a mass of a driver ($m_1 = 65$ kg) and a passenger ($m_2 = 65$ kg) along with a baggage ($m_B = 25$ kg). Locations of the loading masses in relation to the 'origo' point [4] have been presented in Figs. 2 and 3. The initial coordinates of the center of mass of a vehicle's body were:

$x_C = 1.5$ m, $y_C = 0$, $z_C = 0.45$ m

and after loading the vehicle with the additional masses:

$x_C = 1.489$ m, $y_C = 0$, $z_C = 0.452$ m.

The vehicle model used in the simulations has been previously described, among others, in [4, 10, 11]. As a basis of research the modified fish hook maneuver in Adams/Car has been adopted in order to examine the behavior of the selected vehicle's model while in motion during a so-called u-turn. The initial speed of the vehicle has been adopted at 100 km/h with the gearbox set to the fifth gear.

Moreover, the modifications of the adopted maneuver considered dividing it into two parts. At first the vehicle has performed the right, then the left turn, which will be described in Chapter 3.

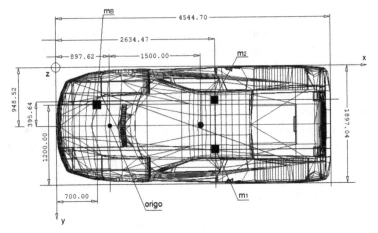

Fig. 2. Location of the loading masses in a plan view [5]

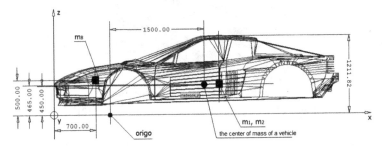

Fig. 3. Location of the loading masses in a left-side view [5]

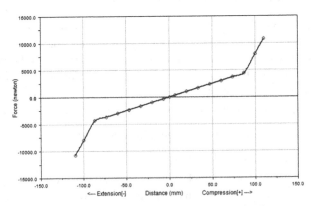

Fig. 4. The spring characteristics (force versus compression) for the presented case [12]

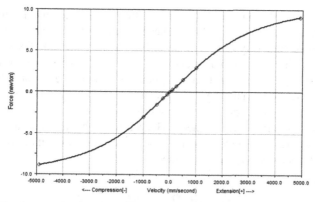

Fig. 5. The damper characteristics (force versus velocity) for the presented case [12]

Other assumptions have been adopted as in some previous works by the author, such as [4] and [11]. This means that the non-linear characteristics of the elastic – damping elements in vehicle's suspension have been adopted (Figs. 4 and 5), quasi-stiff vehicle's body, FTIRE model of the used tires, etc. Of course, the road irregularities occurring on an uneven road have been considered in many works so far (e.g. [3, 7]), so some information about their influence on performance of the adopted maneuver will be presented in further part of this paper.

3 Description of the Simulation of a U-Turn Maneuver

Simulation of a u-turn, modified fish-hook like maneuver has been prepared for various traffic configurations for the vehicle's model presented in Fig. 1 and laden according to Figs. 2 and 3. In Table 1 all the adopted configurations of the traffic conditions have been presented, from the most comfortable to the most extreme ones.

Table 1. The traffic configurations adopted for the u-turn maneuver [own study]

No of configuration	Road conditions	Road irregularities, profile similarity
configuration 1	flat, dry road	–
configuration 2	flat, icy road	–
configuration 3	uneven, dry road	intensity $= 0.3$, corrl $= 0.8$
configuration 4	uneven, dry road	intensity $= 0.9$, corrl $= 0.8$
configuration 5	uneven, icy road	intensity $= 0.3$, corrl $= 0.8$
configuration 6	uneven, icy road	intensity $= 0.9$, corrl $= 0.8$

In the traffic conditions such elements a flat or a randomly uneven road have been included, as well as both dry ($\mu = 1$) and icy ($\mu = 0.3$) surface, almost similar road profiles for the left and right wheels (*corr* = 0.8 in Table 1) and the maximum amplitudes of road irregularities in a randomly uneven profile (the parameter specifying this condition is called 'intensity' and is equal to 0.3 for the lower and 0.9 for the higher irregularities, which can be as high as about 0.1 m. From Table 1 it can be noticed that the configuration 1 means the motion of a vehicle's model on a dry and flat road (the traffic conditions related to a motorway on a sunny day) while the configuration 6 means the motion on a road with a rather poor condition surface, icy and the almost different road profiles for the left and right wheels. Hence, the problem has been analyzed as a comparison of the vehicle's motion in the least and the most difficult exemplary traffic conditions for the same maneuver performed.

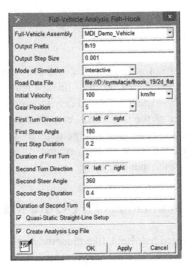

Fig. 6. The main settings for the considered u-turn simulation [12]

Simulations according to all of the 6 configurations have been prepared for the modified fish-hook maneuver, for which the settings have been presented in Fig. 6. According to them, the vehicle's model from Fig. 1 at first turns right with the angle of the steering wheel rotated 180° clockwise and then, after 2 s, it turns left with the steering wheel being rotated 360° counterclockwise, which lasted 4 s. In Fig. 6 also the initial speed and gear setting have been presented. As for the 'First Step Duration' and 'Second Step Duration' also presented in Fig. 6, their task is to specify what time it takes to turn the steering wheel at the adopted angle. According to Fig. 6 the first turn of the steering wheel by 180° lasted 0.2 s, while the second turn (counterclockwise) by 360° lasted 0.4 s.

4   Discussion on the Selected Results

Simulation of the u-turn maneuver has been conducted according to Fig. 6 for all of the adopted configurations presented in Table 1. For each configuration a set of results has been obtained, on the basis of which the selected problems of vehicle dynamics in the aspect of traffic safety and collision mitigation have been analyzed.

The first important aspect is the lateral displacement versus the covered distance, which has been presented in Figs. 7, 8 and 9. Starting with the motion on the least harsh conditions (Fig. 7) it can be observed that the lateral displacement for the icy and flat road (configuration 2) presents a deformed non-developed u-turn maneuver when comparing with the motion along the dry and flat road. However, the radius which the vehicle needed to perform the maneuver on a dry road was about 25 m which seems too much in terms of the typical road width, but enough when omitting the sudden obstacle as the slight break of the trajectory (configuration 1) at the 50th m of the covered distance can indicate at which road section the second turn of the steering wheel occurred.

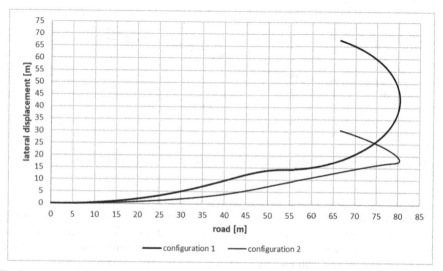

Fig. 7. Lateral displacement versus the covered distance for the configurations 1 and 2 [own study]

Let this trajectory, obtained for the configuration 1, be the reference to the rest of the results obtained after having performed the considered maneuver. If so, the motion on a flat and icy road can be considered as dangerous because the vehicle's model in this case did not omit the obstacle and performed the u-turn with much smaller radius, which can mean that the vehicle had to drift when turning around.

Trajectories presented in Figs. 8 and 9 present the same tendency as the curve for the configuration 2 from Fig. 7. However, in some cases performing the turn has not been so rapid and looks like the vehicle did not have to drift while turning around, while in others it did. In Fig. 8 both trajectories (configuration 3 and 4) mark the motion of the vehicle's model on a dry and uneven road. In both cases the vehicle's model had to move along the randomly uneven surface with the coefficient of similarity between the road profiles for the left and the right wheels (*corrl*) equal to 0.8. The only difference is that, although both curves marked an arc with the radius about the same as in case of configuration 1, it is clear that they reached 5 m further along the road axis. Also in case of the motion along the road with greater intensity of irregularities (configuration 4) the moment of omitting the obstacle was between 55th and 60th m.

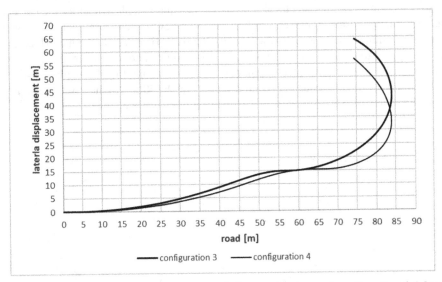

Fig. 8. Lateral displacement versus the covered distance for the configurations 3 and 4 [own study]

As for the last set of trajectories it seems that the motion along the randomly uneven road with the icy surface has caused the vehicle's model to drift. In case of the lower amplitudes of irregularities the turning maneuver does not resemble moving along the arc (configuration 5) and, although the vehicle has omitted the hypothetic obstacle at the 50th m, the second rotation of the steering wheel did not cause the vehicle to perform a full turn and at about 85th m it drifted suddenly to change the direction of motion. Meanwhile for the configuration 6 the higher amplitudes of the irregularities (intensity = 0.9) caused the vehicle to drift even after the first rotation of the steering wheel and then remain at the straight line course until the 85th m, when the vehicle suddenly changed its direction of motion as if the handbrake was used. In this case the omitting of the hypothetic obstacle at the 50th m was impossible.

In cases presented in Figs. 8 and 9 (configurations 3 to 6) the vehicle needed 5 m more distance on the abscissa axis (covered distance) to complete the maneuver in comparison of the motion on the flat road (configurations 1 and 2).

The next selected factor observed during the presented cases of the u-turn maneuver are the changes in the angular velocity related to the vertical axis of the vehicle passing through its center of mass. On the basis of the obtained results (Figs. 10 to 12) it can be observed, that drifting phenomena occurred mainly during the vehicle's motion along the randomly uneven road. In Fig. 10 the course of the angular velocity runs quite smoothly both for the dry (configuration 1) and the icy road (configuration 2). The maximum

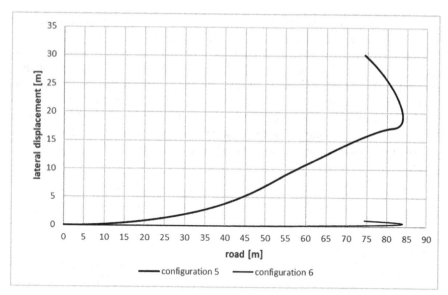

Fig. 9. Lateral displacement versus the covered distance for the configurations 5 and 6 [own study]

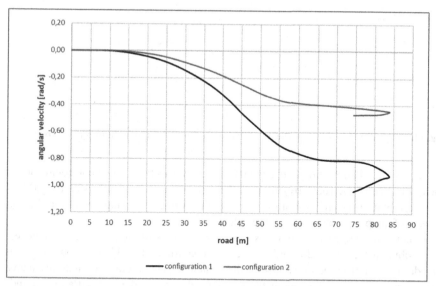

Fig. 10. Angular velocity versus the covered distance for the configurations 1 and 2 [own study]

values of this velocity were up to 1 rad/s for the dry surface and about 0.42 rad/s for the icy one.

However, at certain circumstances (here, the randomly occurring irregularities with the road profile almost similar for the left and the right wheels) the angular velocity changed more rapidly. In Fig. 11 it can be observed that the maximum values of the angular velocity for the dry road with lower amplitudes of the road irregularities (configuration 3) amounted to about 1.7 rad/s, whereas for the higher amplitudes (configuration 4) it reached up to 1.3 rad/s. This means that the worse road condition without the additional weather circumstances (dry road) partially prevented the vehicle from drifting allowing it at the same time to perform the narrower u-turn maneuver.

All of the presented values are absolute, so the minuses in Figs. 10 to 12 do not play any role.

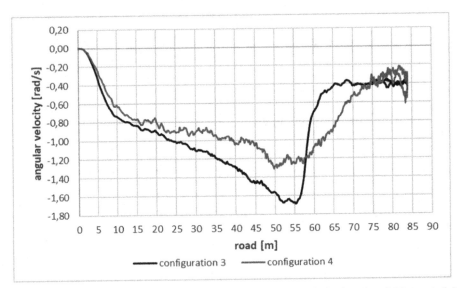

Fig. 11. Angular velocity versus the covered distance for the configurations 3 and 4 [own study]

On the other hand, taking into account the trajectories from Fig. 8 one could consider such influence of the road irregularities dangerous, because at the speed of 100 km/h such narrow u-turn as in case of the configuration 4 might be dangerous from the point of view of the possible rollover of the vehicle.

Relating to the possible vehicle's drift in some parts of the performed maneuver it seems obvious that the additional por weather conditions (Fig. 12, icy road) may cause the additional, unforeseen response of the vehicle moving along the randomly uneven road. Considering the changes of the angular velocity for the configurations 5 and 6 some certain decrease in the value of the considered velocity it may be noticed as if the icy road surface prevented the influence of the irregularities related to the yawing effect but may have increased drifting and not being able by the vehicle to remain at the desired course.

For the lower amplitudes of the irregularities (configuration 5) the maximum value of the angular velocity was up to 0.8 rad/s, while for the higher amplitudes (configuration 6) it was up to about 0.55 rad/s.

When comparing the values of angular velocity for configuration 5 and 6 (Fig. 12) with the shapes of trajectories in Fig. 9 it can be observed that the vehicle did not perform the full u-turn maneuver and did not indicate the significant yawing motions, but was not able to maintain the course set for the configurations 1 and 2 and slid along the road with the irregularities rather disturbing than helping regain the primary direction of motion in order to perform the turning around safely.

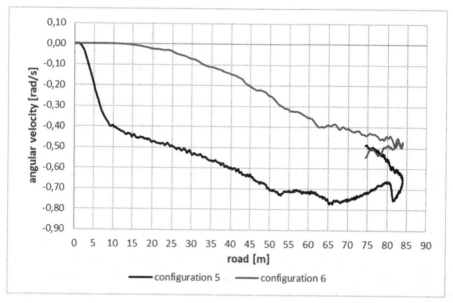

Fig. 12. Angular velocity versus the covered distance for the configurations 5 and 6 [own study]

As for the lateral acceleration similar observations can be made for each of the configurations. In Fig. 13 the changes in lateral acceleration for the configurations 1 and 2 were not turbulent and the maximum amplitude for the configuration 1 was about 1 m/s^2. For the 50th m its value changed which indicate the change in direction of motion (the second rotation of the steering wheel). As for the configuration 2 the icy road surface has caused that the maximum value of the lateral acceleration was about 0.25 m/s^2 which means that the vehicle slid forward through the entire covered distance rather than drifted.

Relating to the results presented in Fig. 14 the most rapid change of the lateral acceleration occurred for both of the configurations (3 and 4) between the 55th and the 60th m which corresponds to the previous considerations (Figs. 8 and 11) indicating the 55th m as the point at which the crucial changes in the motion of the presented vehicle's model occurred, especially from the point of view of the traffic safety. Of course, the amplitudes of the lateral acceleration was greater than in case of motion along the flat road, where for the configuration 3 they amounted up to 20 m/s^2 and in case of the configuration 4 – to about 12 m/s^2. It also provides the observation that the random irregularities may have caused the vehicle to drift or perform more turbulent lateral

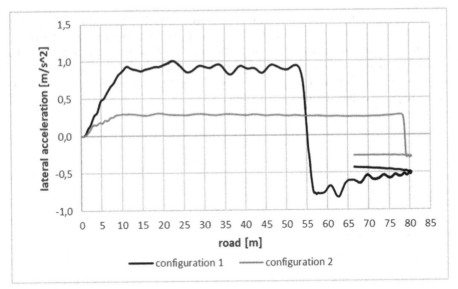

Fig. 13. Lateral acceleration versus the covered distance for the configurations 1 and 2 [own study]

motion during the performance of the considered u-turn maneuver. Here in Fig. 14 the changes in the acceleration are more turbulent than in case of the motion along a flat road (Fig. 13). To support this considerations Fig. 11 can be taken into account as the lateral velocities presented there had also the greatest values of all considered in this paper.

From the results of the lateral acceleration presented in Fig. 15 for the two remaining configurations (5 and 6) some interesting additional observations can be made. First, the amplitudes of acceleration in both cases (configuration 5 and 6) are not as great as in the two previous cases (3 and 4) which means that the icy surface may ease the effect the random irregularities may have on the vehicle. The maximum amplitude of the lateral acceleration in case of the configuration 5 was about 6 m/s^2, whereas for the configuration 6 it amounted to about 12 m/s^2. It is necessary to remember that the 'intensity' parameter specifying the amplitudes of road irregularities for the configuration 6 was assumed at 0.9.

The more interesting aspect however, is the shape of both curves in Fig. 15 presenting the changes in the lateral acceleration. The curve obtained for the configuration 5 indicates that there have been no turning around of the vehicle until about the 80th m, which is consistent with the results of the lateral displacement presented in Fig. 9. In case of the configuration 6 there have been no turning around until the 80th m as well and the increase of the amplitude at the end of the covered distance shows that the vehicle's models rather drifted and made the 180° turn around at the short distance of only few meters.

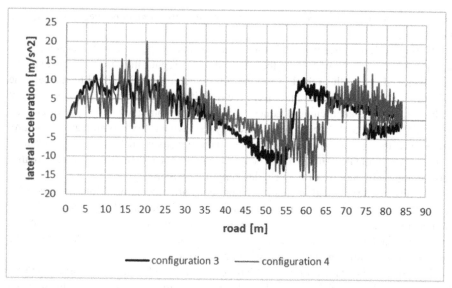

Fig. 14. Lateral acceleration versus the covered distance for the configurations 3 and 4 [own study]

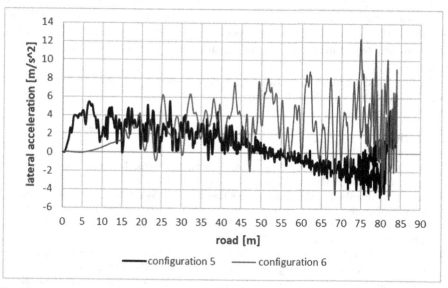

Fig. 15. Lateral acceleration versus the covered distance for the configurations 5 and 6 [own study]

5 Conclusion

It seems that such maneuver as the u-turn is rare in common road traffic, but in the extreme situations like omitting the obstacle some interesting phenomena depending on the traffic conditions may occur, especially in case of the contact between the road and the wheels.

The icy road can cause changes in the distance needed to perform a specific maneuver, but in some cases they may reduce the effect of road irregularities acting as the external disturbance affecting the vehicle's motion. Of course it would be hard to recreate the conditions adopted for the simulations in the real life. The most important aspect is that in the software the coefficient of adhesion is uniform along the whole area of contact between the road and the wheel, while in reality it does have more complicated structure. However, if the vehicle's model can perform any maneuver, such as the one presented in this papers while the whole road is covered, e.g. with ice, then it seems that in reality performing similar course of the vehicles should be possible.

The discussed rapid and interesting phenomena are especially visible when considering the lateral accelerations, not only as the feature affecting the possible safety of the performed maneuver, but also the riding comfort of the passengers. Nevertheless, the changes in the discussed acceleration have been more rapid and turbulent, when the vehicle has been moving on the road with irregularities.

The presented considerations can be used not only as the qualitative assessment of the behavior of a vehicle's model, but also a quantitative assessment of the selected maintenance features of motor vehicles, such as e.g. stability. It can also be useful to support the necessary decisions when road infrastructure needs modernization.

It seems ridiculous to consider performing such maneuvers as the attempt to asses the vehicle's response to disturbances of its motion, but in difficult traffic conditions and with sudden and unexpected occurrences that may affect the fluency of the motion on various sections of the roads, considering any dangerous situations seem, in a way, necessary.

Further considerations, concerning such extreme maneuvers, will contain different speeds and unbalanced vehicle loading.

References

1. Alatorre, V.A., Victorino, A., Charara, A.: Estimation of Wheel-Ground Contact Normal Forces: Experimental Data Validation, IFAC-PapersOnLine, vol. 50, Issue 1, Elsevier (2017)
2. Genta, G., Morello, L.: The Automotive Chassis, vol. 2, System Design, Second Edition, Springer, Heidelberg (2009). https://doi.org/10.1007/978-1-4020-8676-2
3. Haigemoser, A., et al.: Road and track irregularities: measurement, assessment and simulation, Vehicle Syst. Dyn. 53(7), 26–29 (2015)
4. Kisilowski, J., Zalewski, J.: Analysis of the stochastic technical stability of engineering structures on example of moving car. J. Theor. Appl. Mech. 54(4), 23 (2016)
5. Kisilowski, J., Zalewski, J.: Selected Aspects of Motor Vehicle Dynamics on the Example of a Power-Off Straight Line Maneuver, Archives of Transport, vol. 50, no. 2 (2019)
6. Kortis, J., Daniel, L., Duratny, M.: The Simulation of The Influence of Surface Irregularities in Road Pavements on The Response of The Bridge to Moving Vehicle, Procedia Engineering, vol. 199, Elsevier (2017)
7. Levulytė, L., Žuraulis, V., Sokolovskij, E.: The research of dynamic characteristics of a vehicle driving over road roughness, Maintenance Reliab. 16(4), 26–29 (2014)
8. Pytka, J., et al.: A portable wheel tester for tyre-road friction and rolling resistance determination, IOP Conference Series: Materials Science and Engineering, vol. 148 (2016)

9. Setlak, L., Kowalik, R.: Study of the motion dynamics of camera fastening platform for the object of the unmanned aerial vehicle, Proceedings – Mathematics and Computers in Science and Engineering, MACISE 2019, Article number 8944688, pp. 10–15 (2019)
10. Zalewski, J.: The impact of road conditions on the normal reaction forces on the wheels of a motor vehicle performing a straightforward braking maneuver. In: Mikulski, J. (ed.) Tools of Transport Telematics, Springer Verlag, Berlin Heidelberg, CCIS 531 (2015)
11. Zalewski, J.: The influence of road conditions on the stability of a laden vehicle mathematical model, realising a single lane change maneuver. In: Mikulski, J. (ed.) Telematics - Support for Transport, Springer Verlag, Berlin Heidelberg, CCIS 471 (2014)
12. MSC Adams/Car

Telematics in Rail and Marine Transport

Multi-criteria Assessment of Search and Rescue Units for SAR Action at Sea

Marzena Malyszko[✉]

Maritime University of Szczecin, Wały Chrobrego 1-2, Szczecin, Poland
m.malyszko@am.szczecin.pl

Abstract. Choice and selection of search and rescue units (SRU) is one of the steps in planning SAR actions at sea. Proper selection increases the effectiveness of actions. The paper presents the method of selection of SRU on the basis of their technical and operational parameters using Multi-Criteria Decision Analysis (MCDA). The results of the analysis based on computational experiments will be presented in the paper. The scenarios, a set of decision variants, a coherent family of criteria and decision-maker preference modelling were defined for the experiment. The method allows to determine the craft that best meets the expectations of the decision maker for a given type of task. Modelling of the SAR action is an important part of improving the response potential of rescue services to accidents. When planning an action, there is a need to make decisions quickly. Analysis is complicated when many factors need to be studied. Therefore, finding the right solution can be difficult. The developed method can be applied to decision support systems (DSS) for coordination centres and ship during action planning and conducting.

Keywords: Search and rescue · SAR action · SRU · Effectiveness · WIG craft · DSS · Decision support systems · MCDA · Promethee

1 Introduction

Conducting the SAR (Search and Rescue) action requires collecting and processing a lot of information, analyzing the situation, planning, coordinating activities, completing information and modifying the action plan on an ongoing basis.

The action coordinator significantly influences the result of conducted actions through the process of planning (preparing) the operation. Proper selection of elements in this process can increase the effectiveness of the action. One of the important elements, which requires making decisions at the planning stage, is the problem of selection and choice of Search and Rescue Units (SRU) for a given type of action [4].

The characteristics of a SRU have a large impact on the degree to which it can be useful for a particular task. The selection should be based on its technical and operational parameters and capabilities. The SAR action is modelled through the SRU selection phase [1, 2].

Many recommendations for SRU suitability analysis are included in the IAMSAR (International Aeronautical and Maritime Search and Rescue) Manual. However, there

© Springer Nature Switzerland AG 2020
J. Mikulski (Ed.): TST 2020, CCIS 1289, pp. 371–386, 2020.
https://doi.org/10.1007/978-3-030-59270-7_28

is no unequivocal way or method to determine the comprehensive theoretical suitability of SRU for SAR actions taking into account its all search and rescue properties. SRU selection is to be done by the coordinator based on own experience and assessment of the suitability of the craft.

The problem and difficulty in selecting SRU is the simultaneous consideration of many criteria and analysis of various factors. Moreover, when planning and coordinating the action, the coordinator is burdened with great responsibility for the decisions taken, as his way of conducting the action determines the possibility of saving human life [4, 5].

Due to various ways of moving, different equipment and technical and operational parameters, each type of vehicle (airborne, waterborne) is predisposed to perform specific tasks. Therefore, each vehicle has operational limitations too. There is no universal unit, so the rescue fleet (SAR services) should be diversified and adapted to the needs of a given SAR system.

The analytical way of solving the problem will support the coordinator in a complex decision-making process both during the selection of units for a given action and during the completion of the rescue fleet in a SAR system.

2   SRU Selection

When selecting a SRU for a task the coordinator must take into account many factors - technical and operational parameters. The most important of these include, among others [3]:

- determining how fast he available SRU can reach the site;
- how quickly it can carry out its search;
- which of SRUs will be able to operate safely in the area at all times;
- how long they will be able to stay in the area of the incident;
- whether they require additional fuel supply (or is it any another need to interrupt the action);
- with what precision they can carry out the search (following the search patterns);
- whether the detection equipment is available and the height of the observer's elevation is sufficient for an effective search;
- what are the capabilities of SRU to recovery survivors from the water;
- to what degree SRU will be able to provide medical assistance?

These and other questions posed by the coordinator lead to the identification of the assessment criteria necessary to select the units that will be most favored for the rescue task.

3   Proposed Method of Assessment

The author suggests that SRU should be assessed by analysing their usefulness based on their search and rescue capabilities. Suitability will be determined by means of many criteria (multi-criteria evaluation). The analysis will consist in examining the degree to which the unit meets expectations (simultaneously) in all criteria. The greater this degree, the better the unit will be in the eyes of the decision-maker.

Expectations for crafts performance will be determined by modelling the preferences of the decision-maker. This stage was carried out using expert studies. The experts shall express their opinion by indicating the value of the criterion when assessing craft.

The assessment will be carried out for a closed group of rescue crafts, which will be compared with each other. The final result (numerical values) will be presented in the form of a SRU ranking, ordered from this unit, which meets the preferences of the decision-maker (coordinator) to the greatest degree.

The available units for the coordinator in the SAR system will constitute a set of tested alternatives (decision options), between which the comparison will be made.

An important element of the proposed method are action profiles. Each event (accident) happens in a unique way, therefore the nature of each SAR action will be different. However, probable (imaginable) event scenarios can be categorized, for example, in terms of the type of object in danger. On the basis of the post-accident reports from actions carried out by rescue services, the most common types of search and rescue actions were identified by author.

The type of incident determines the range of assistance required and therefore the coordinator's preferences and expectations towards SRU too. The author suggests to distinguish action profiles and to define preferences for each action profile. The action profile will represent a typical sequence of the action taking into account the relation between the type of danger and the type of required assistance. The developed profiles include:

- Profile 1 (P1) - action "a single survivor" – search and rescue a single person from water;
- Profile 2 (P2) - action "mass evacuation" – search and rescue of many people, after passenger ship accident;
- Profile 3 (P3) - 'patrol - explaining' action.

Each action profile will require the establishment of appropriate preferences (expectations) for criteria. In order to determine these preferences, modelling of the decision-maker's preferences has been carried out by means of expert studies with the participation of rescue and maritime transport specialists.

In order to carry out the mathematical analysis, it is possible to use MCDA (Multiple Criteria Decision Analysis). The result of such research is to create a ranking of alternatives (SRU) from best to worst [6]. For the person coordinating the SAR action, such an ordering may make easier the process of selecting the unit that best meets the preferences for all criteria at the same time. This will be possible by comparing it to other vehicles in the surveyed group.

The following stages were formed in the proposed by author method:

- Stage. 1. Diagnosis of a decision problem:

  - definition of the decision-maker;
  - definition of the action profile;

- Stage 2: Definition of the set of alternatives (available SRU);

– Stage 3: Definition of a coherent family of criteria including the establishment of a system for evaluating each criteria;
– Stage 4: Modelling of the decision-maker's preferences (identification of the coordinator's expectations);
– Stage 5: Conducting a computational experiment (method choice and testing);
– Stage 6: Summary:

  – performance analysis;
  – sensitivity analysis of the results;
  – conclusions.

Stage 1 concerns the collection of data. The most important data include the determination of: the type of object in danger and its location, the type of assistance required and hydrometeorological conditions. Information on the location of the incident determines the coordinator of the action (decision maker) according to limit of Search and Rescue Region (SRR) and of SAR system.

Stage 2 consists in establishing a set of alternatives (decision options), i.e. available SRU. The defined set consists in obtaining information on the parameters of units. The craft must meet the basic condition of being ready (e.g. technically efficient, acceptable risk of use).

The foundation of the assessment in the multi-criteria decision analysis is to determine the appropriate set of criteria, called coherent family of criteria (Stage 3). The criteria represent the properties desired by the decision maker, which should be characterised by SRU.

Stage 4 involves identifying the expectations of the decision-maker in terms of preferences for SRU and criteria. Preferences are expressed in terms of the weighting of the criteria and sensitivity to changes in the criteria.

Stage 5 involves selecting appropriate calculation methods and implementing the actual information processing (testing). After the method has been chosen, the data obtained in stages 1–4 is to be implemented and an adequate calculation algorithm is to be performed.

Stage 6 includes the analysis of results and sensitivity of the results, which allows to determine the reliability of the result. The obtained results make it possible to create a ranking of alternatives (SRU ranking from best to worst). Conclusions formulated on the basis of the results make it possible to answer the basic questions posed in the study: which units are most suitable for a given type of task.

The proposed assessment method will be applied to decision-making problems concerning the stage of planning and coordinating SAR actions at sea. The developed method can be used for the following decision-making situations:

– During the selection of units for a given rescue task (selection of the best SRU).
– To assess the level of applicability of individual units in a given SAR system (comparison to other craft or group of crafts).
– When completing the fleet for newly created SAR systems or modifying the fleet of existing SAR systems.

4 Multi-criteria Decision Analysis

The MCDA is based on mathematical methods and tools allowing for comparison of available solutions of the problem, taking into account different, also contradictory criteria. There are two basic streams of methods for solving multi-criteria problems [6]:

– based on the outranking relation (e.g. Promethee II method);
– based on multiatribute utility theory (e.g. Analytic Hierarchy Process - AHP method).

In this paper the Promethee II method was use. The main assumptions of the method are:

1. Determination of deviations based on pairwise comparisons

$$d_j(a, b) = g_j(a) - g_j(b) \tag{1}$$

where,

d_j (a,b) – denotes the difference between the evaluations of a and b on each criterion

2. Applications of the preference functions

$$P_j(a, b) = F_j\big[d_j(a, b)\big] \quad j = 1, \ldots, k \tag{2}$$

where,

P_j (a,b) denotes the preference of alternative (a) with regard to alternative (b) on each criterion, as a function of d_j (a,b).

3. Calculation of an overall or global preference index

$$\forall a, b \in A, \quad \pi(a, b) = \sum_{j=1}^{k} P_j(a, b)w_j \tag{3}$$

where,

π(a,b) of (a) over (b) (from 0 to 1) is defined as the weighted sum p(a,b) of for each criterion, and w_j is the weight associated with the expressing the decision maker's preferences as the relative importance of the j-th criterion

4. Calculation of outranking flows (the PROMETHEE I partial ranking)

$$\varphi^+(a) = \frac{1}{n-1} \sum_{x \in A} \pi(a, x) \tag{4}$$

$$\varphi^-(a) = \frac{1}{n-1} \sum_{x \in A} \pi(x, a) \tag{5}$$

where,

$\varphi^+(a)$ and $\varphi^-(a)$ – denote the positive outranking flow and negative outranking flow for each alternative, respectively.

5. Calculation of net outranking flow (The PROMETHEE II complete ranking)

$$\varphi(a) = \varphi^+(a) - \varphi^-(a) \tag{6}$$

where

$\varphi(a)$ – denotes the net outranking flow for each alternative.

Based on net preferences, a ranking of decision-making options (alternatives) is established. If $\varphi(a) > \varphi(b)$ means that decision option (a) is better, more preferred than option (b).

5 Family of Criteria

The assessment will be carried out according to a defined set of criteria. A cohesive family of criteria is a set of criteria that meet the following requirements: exhaustiveness of the assessment (contemplating all possible aspects of the problem under consideration), consistency of assessment (based on proper determination of global decision preferences by the criterion) and the uniqueness of the criteria ranges. In the developed method 9 criteria have been defined to examine both the availability of SRU and its search and rescue properties. These criteria set include: estimated time of arrival, seaworthiness, draught, speed of search, range, detection capability, technical recovery of survivors, transport capacity of survivors and medical equipment.

Some of these criteria are quantitative in nature. They are measurable and expressed in units. Other criteria are of a qualitative nature and are expressed in descriptive terms.

Some MCDA methods allow analysis to be carried out even if the criteria are expressed in non-comparable units. However, some methods require a uniform way of expressing criteria evaluations. A quality scale of 1 to 5 points has been prepared for all the developed set of criteria. As an example the characteristics of criterion C1 (ETA) is described below.

Estimated time of arrival (t_a) is the period of time required for the unit to move from the location its currently staying to the reference point or area, taking into account aspects that may prolong the arrival. The formula below shall be used to determine the arrival time:

$$t_a = t_g + t_t \tag{7}$$

where,

t_a – estimated time of arrival

t_g – readiness time

t_t – minimal transfer time

The criterion is minimised. The model prefers units that shorten the response time of rescue services and thus speed up the time to find the object. The faster SRU can reach a designated place the higher it is classified. The criterion can be evaluated in two ways: quantitatively and qualitatively. The quantitative scale is determined by the numerical scale of hours. Whereas the qualitative scale will be created by normalizing the value to five levels with defined boundaries. The ranges are given ratings from 5 to 1 (Table 1). The limits of the intervals are calculated using the difference in arrival time between the fastest and slowest unit.

$$\Delta t = t_{a.max} - t_{a.min} \tag{8}$$

where,

$t_{a.max}$ – the highest value of the arrival time of the tested set of alternatives

$t_{a.min}$ – the lowest value of the arrival time of the tested set of alternatives

Table 1. Methodology of assessment of criterion C1 [own study]

Criterion C1	
ETA	Grade
$t_a \leq t_{a.min} + 0,2 * \Delta t$	5
$t_{a.min} + 0,2 * \Delta t < t_a \leq t_{a.min} + 0,4 * \Delta t$	4
$t_{a.min} + 0,4 * \Delta t < t_a \leq t_{a.min} + 0,6 * \Delta t$	3
$t_{a.min} + 0,6 * \Delta t < t_a \leq t_{a.min} + 0,8 * \Delta t$	2
$t_a > t_{a.min} + 0,8 * \Delta t$	1

A similar system of evaluation was applied for the other criteria.

6 Expert Studies

The research consisted in collecting and processing information provided by the respondents on the requirements for vehicles participating in SAR actions. The responders' point of views are subjective and the results of the research are qualitative. Modelling the preferences of decision-makers is one of the stages of the developed multi-criteria method of assessment of SRU vehicles. The results of expert research are used to conduct computational experiments. Expert study was conducted by means of questionnaires and interviews.

The research group consisted of a total of 107 persons with maritime education at management level, with experience on ships on the positions of captain, chief engineer, chief mate or watch officer and currently working on ships or in Rescue Coordination Centre (RCC).

Questionnaires are a method of indirect measurement, consisting of written or electronic answers to questions by the respondent. The questionnaires were conducted individually. The questionnaires were monothematic and anonymous. They had closed questions with an answer scale and open questions. In the questionnaires, the respondents expressed their opinion about the weight of criteria.

The expert interview consisted of interviews with specialists, which addressed topics related to the nature and complexity of rescue operations, requirements for ships and expectations of craft capacity. The interviews also gathered information about the sensitivity of decision makers to changes in the value of the criteria.

Weight of the Criteria

The respondents expressed their opinion on the impact of a particular craft's ability (criteria) on the possibility of achieving search and rescue success, taking into account the specificity of each action profile (P1–P3). The weight of each criterion was assessed on a seven-grade scale (from 0 to 6 points). Where 0 meant a small impact of a given parameter and 6 meant a large impact. The data are shown in Table 2.

For profile P1 the highest average assessment (over 5, 0 points) received criterion C1, C4, C6 and C7. The least relevant is criterion C8. According to the experts, the most important thing is to quickly and precisely search and high recovery capabilities in this type of action.

Table 2. Weight of the criteria assessed by the respondents [own study]

Criterion		Decision makers						Average		
		Coordinators			Crews					
		P 1	P 2	P 3	P 1	P 2	P 3	P 1	P 2	P 3
C 1	ETA	6,00	5,00	5,00	5,82	5,82	5,20	5,91	5,41	5,10
C 2	Seaworthiness	3,00	3,67	3,67	3,02	3,56	3,36	3,01	3,61	3,51
C 3	Draught	2,33	2,33	3,33	2,12	2,13	3,26	2,23	2,23	3,30
C 4	Search speed	5,67	5,67	5,67	5,99	5,17	5,66	5,83	5,42	5,66
C 5	Range	3,67	3,00	5,00	3,61	3,19	4,83	3,64	3,10	4,92
C 6	Detection capability	5,00	3,33	6,00	5,10	3,11	5,78	5,05	3,22	5,89
C 7	Technical recovery of survivors	5,67	6,00	3,00	6,15	5,88	2,08	5,91	5,94	2,54
C 8	Transport capacity of survivors	0,33	5,00	1,00	0,95	5,35	1,35	0,64	5,17	1,17
C 9	Medical equipment	3,33	3,67	1,67	2,89	4,09	1,53	3,11	3,88	1,60

Sensitivity to changes of the criteria

The research was conducted in the form of an interview. The equivalence (q), preference (p) and non-comparability (v) thresholds were used (Table 3).

The equivalence threshold is the maximum difference between the assessments of the two alternatives at which one of them cannot yet be found to be better (in terms of a given criterion). Preference threshold means the minimum difference between the assessments of the two alternatives, beyond which the decision-maker considers one of them to be better (in terms of a given criterion). Non-comparability threshold (veto) means a minimum difference between the assessments of the two alternatives to a criterion, above which the assessed alternative cannot be considered as generally better (in terms of a given criterion). When assessing the thresholds, respondents had the values (assessments) of individual alternatives for each criterion.

For example for C1 is expressed in hours, and in profile 1 the threshold equivalence is set on 0,1 h, the preference threshold is set on 0,75 h.

Table 3. Sensitivity of respondents to changes in the value of criteria [own study]

Average values

Criterion	P1			P2			P3		
	q	p	v	q	p	v	q	p	v
C 1	0,1	0,75	1,6	0,1	0,75	1,6	0,1	0,75	1,6
C 2	0,0	3,0	6,0	0,0	3,0	6,0	0,0	3,0	6,0
C 3	1,0	3,0	5,0	0,0	3,0	5,0	0,0	3,0	5,0
C 4	4,0	70,0	162,0	4,0	70,0	162,0	4,0	70,0	162
C 5	20,0	5900	5900	0,0	2500	5900	0,0	5900	5900
C 6	0,0	3,0	5,0	1,0	3,0	5,0	1,0	3,0	5,0
C 7	0,0	3,0	5,0	0,0	3,0	5,0	1,0	4,0	5,0
C 8	271,0	271,0	272,0	20,0	75,0	272,0	20,0	272,0	272
C 9	1,0	3,0	5,0	1,0	3,0	5,0	1,0	4,0	5,0

The above obtained information made it possible to confirm the relationship resulting from the type of action and the decision-maker's preferences for SRU search and rescue capabilities, allowed to verify the family of criteria and provided detailed information on preferences.

The obtained data were implemented into the applied calculation algorithms and allowed to obtain final answer: how to optimally select SRU for a given SAR action.

7   Experiment

Three scenarios were developed for the experiments. Elements of the scenario include: area of the incident, hydrometeorological conditions, available SRU and relation type of hazard - type of assistance required. The first three elements are common to all scenarios, while the last element represents P1–P3 action profiles.

7.1   Diagnosis of the Situation in SAR Action

Region of the Incident
The Pomeranian Bay was assumed to be he area of the event in the discussed scenarios. This area is included in the Polish search and rescue region. The following coordinates are used as a reference for rescue operations: $\varphi = 54°06'03"$ N $\lambda = 014°$ $17'06"$E.

Hydrometeorological conditions
The same conditions were adopted for all three scenarios:

- Wind - NW direction, force 3 °B
- Current - SW direction, speed 0.5 w
- Seasea 2
- Visibility - 20 Mm
- Cloud cover - 1000 m
- Air temperature - (+) 20 °C
- Water temperature - (+)15 °C

Determining the Decision-maker
According to the rules of defining the decision maker, the coordinator of the action is the Maritime Rescue Sub-Centre in Świnoujście in all three scenarios. An officer on duty is appointed to undertake organizational and coordination activities.

Determining the Action Profile
As an example one of the scenarios is discussed below. This is the first scenario based on the P1 profile. The following chronology of events has been adopted: accident involving one person; one crew member was found missing on the ship; the ship was searched, the crew member was not found; the crew member is suspected fallen overboard.

7.2   Defining a Set of Alternatives

All alternatives (SRU) meet the conditions of availability, which means that:

- they are ready for action - efficient, waiting for a call;
- at an acceptable distance from the site of the event - reasonable arrival time;
- the risk of use is acceptable - hydrometeorological conditions allow for operation, there are no other known phenomena and aspects that put rescuers and the unit at risk.

For the purpose of the experiment, 13 vehicles were selected in this paper (Table 4). Eleven of them belong to the Polish SAR service. They are waterborne and airborne crafts: 5 ships, 2 minor surface units, 2 helicopters, 2 airplanes. This selection of units allows to create a spectrum of the fleet. Thanks to this, the analysis will also indicate the rescue properties of a group of (similar) units.

The set also includes two WIG (Wing-in-ground) effect crafts. WIG crafts are not used in Poland currently, but the study will indicate their theoretical effectiveness in comparison with other units. It may be helpful in decisions concerning the completion of the fleet for a given SAR system.

Waterborne units and WIG craft were considered from the location of the port of Świnoujście, which is a nearby rescue base. In the real situation units would be sent from this base. Air borne units were considered from the theirs original airports in Darlowo, Cewice or Gdynia.

Table 4. SRU list [own study]

No	SRU
A 1	Rescue vessel SAR-1500
A 2	Rescue vessel SAR-3000
A 3	Multi-purpose rescue vessel m/s Kapitan Poinc
A 4	ORP Heweliusz
A 5	SG-312 typ SKS-40
A 6	Scooter Rescue Runner
A 7	Rescue Boat RIB Gemini Waverider 600
A 8	Rescue helicopter W-3WARM Anakonda
A 9	Rescue helicopter Mi-14 PŁ/R
A 10	Airplane An-28E
A 11	Airplane M-20 Mewa
A 12	Rescue WIG Craft Aron-7
A 13	Multi-purpose Search and Rescue WIG Craft ES-108

7.3 Definition of a Family of Criteria and Assessment Methods

Nine criteria have been defined for the method developed. An individual evaluation system has been developed for each criterion. As an example Criterion C1 is presented below.

According to the C1 assessment methodology, the readiness time and transfer time of each SRU were analyzed for calculated limits. (Table 5, Table 6). Criterion C1 is minimized.

Table 5. Evaluation indicators for criterion C1 [own study]

Data	ETA [h] Quantitative assessment C1	Qualitative assessment C1
• $t_{a.max} = 1,75\,h$	$t_a \leq 0,64$	5
• $t_{a.min} = 0,36\,h$	$0,64 < t_a \leq 0,92$	4
• $\Delta t = 1,39\,h$	$0,92 < t_a \leq 1,20$	3
• $20\% * \Delta t = 0,28$	$1,20 < t_a \leq 1,48$	2
	$t_a > 1,48$	1

7.4 Modelling of Decision-Maker Preferences

In this study three preference models have been developed, corresponding to the coordinator priorities for the three types of action. Preferences were expressed through the weighting of particular criterion in the created family of criteria and sensitivity to changes

Table 6. Evaluation of alternatives in criterion C1 [own study]

Alternative	Sub-criterion t_g	Sub-criterion t_t			Quantitative assessment C1	Qualitative assessment C1
No	Time of readiness [h]	Distance [Mm]	Speed [w]	Time [h]		
A1	0,25	10,8	25	0,43	0,68	4
A2	0,25	10,8	21	0,51	0,76	4
A3	0,25	10,8	11	0,98	1,23	2
A4	0,5	10,8	11	0,98	1,23	2
A5	0,5	10,8	15	0,72	0,97	3
A6	0,15	10,8	33	0,33	0,48	5
A7	0,15	10,8	33	0,33	0,48	5
A8	0,25	77,8	108	0,72	0,97	3
A9	0,5	77,8	108	0,72	0,97	3
A10	0,5	125,3	162	0,77	1,27	2
A11	0,5	153,9	123	1,25	1,75	1
A12	0,25	10,8	81	0,13	0,38	5
A13	0,25	10,8	100	0,11	0,36	5

in the value of the criterion. The results of the research are presented in part 6 of this article.

7.5 Testing (Realization of a Calculation Experiment)

On the basis of the analysis of multi-criteria methods, it was decided to choose Promethee II method (relation of outranking). For the purpose of conducting the computer simulation the software *Visual Promehtee* in Academic version was used.

The final ranking will be interpreted according to the purpose of the study, for the selection of units for SAR actions through:

- selecting the unit which obtained first position in the ranking; or
- designing a group of units which have obtained places equal to or greater than the 'reference unit'.

The term 'reference unit' is applied to the vehicle that is (has been) suitable for this type of task. In these tests, the rescue vessel SAR-1500 (A1) is considered to be the reference unit.

7.6 Results

As an example the results for Scenario 1 are shown. The flow table (Table 7) contains the final ranking by net flow $\varphi(a)$. The following order of decision options was obtained: A8; A9; A2; A13; A12; A10; A1; A3; A5; A4; A7; A6; A11.

The helicopters (Anaconda and Mi-14) are the highest on the list, while the M-20 the lowest. The SAR-1500 is in seventh position. Knowing that it is able to satisfactorily perform search and rescue tasks, it can be assumed that the alternatives that ranked above it (on positions 1–6) constitute an optimal set of vehicles for the task. Both WIG vehicles are in this group.

Table 7. Net flow table (final ranking) [own study on Visual Promethee Software]

No	SRU (Alternative)		$\varphi(a)$
1	Anakonda	A8	0,2078
2	Mi-14	A9	0,1902
3	SAR-3000	A2	0,0653
4	ES-108	A13	0,0391
5	Aron-7	A12	-0,0102
6	An-28E	A10	-0,0137
7	SAR-1500	A1	-0,0159
8	Kapitan Poinc	A3	-0,0443
9	SG-312	A5	-0,0618
10	ORP Heweliusz	A4	-0,0623
11	RIB	A7	-0,0729
12	Rescue Runner	A6	-0,0910
13	M-20	A11	-0,1304

It is possible to present the results in graphic form (Fig. 1). In addition to the numerical values, the alternatives could be distinguished by colour. In the figure below, the craft type was color-coded as follows: violet – aircraft, blue – waterborne units, orange - WIG craft. This way of presentation enables a quick assessment of the value distance of individual options.

The application also allows to present data in the form of a network (Fig. 2). The alternatives are distributed vertically by net flow values $\varphi(a)$ and with use of the partial rankings $\varphi^+(a)$ and $\varphi^-(a)$ affecting the horizontal distribution. Alternatives located closer to the left edge of the network are characterized by lower values of $\varphi^-(a)$. For example, the A10 alternative (aircraft An-28), despite its high overall performance, is at the extreme right of the graph, informing the decision maker that the unit had a high negative performance on several criteria and was worse than the others. By making a deeper examination by means of a single-criteria assessment it can be concluded that the weak points are the categories relating to rescue properties.

Using the reference unit, in this case A1, it is possible to easily mark on the network an area containing units equally favourable and better than A1 (green rectangle).

Summarizing all available forms of presentation of results, the action coordinator can proceed in several ways by selecting the most suitable unit for SAR actions with the participation of one survivor (action profile P1). The selection of SRU may consist of:

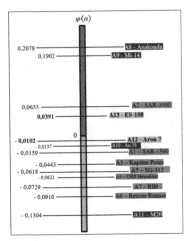

Fig. 1. Results for final ranking, graphic [own study on Visual Promethee Software] (Color figure online)

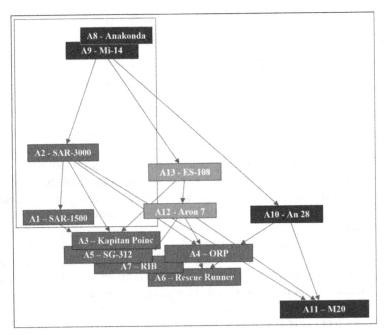

Fig. 2. Decision Network [own study on Visual Promethee Software]

- selection the craft located on first position in the ranking (A8) - this unit meets all preferences to the greatest extent;
- determine the suboptimal group consisting of crafts which have been ranked from one to seven (A8, A9, A2, A13, A12, A10, A1) - these units have a high potential effectiveness equal to or greater than the SAR-1500 ("reference craft");

– determine the optimal group consisting of vehicles which are in the upper left-hand quarter of the network (A8, A9, A2, A1) - in addition to their high potential effectiveness, these units also have good results in all or almost all criteria.

Both WIGs were found to be quite good for this type of task. They were higher in the ranking than the reference unit, which means that they would be equally likely to perform these operations. When estimating the need for resources for the rescue fleet, the method developed can support the decision-maker.

8 Conclusion

The research carried out has shown that multi-criteria analysis is applicable in the decision-making processes concerning the selection of units for SAR action. This approach to the assessment of rescue units improves the SAR action effectiveness.

It has been shown that the research problem was solved by building a coherent family of criteria, which takes into account the technical and operational parameters of SRU. The set of criteria takes into account capabilities, which are not equally required to carry out a given type of SAR action. This degree is expressed by the importance of a given criterion.

In order to create a preference model for the decision maker, expert study was conducted. The expert opinion made it possible to determine the degree to which a given criterion affects the effectiveness of SRU. Final ranking presented in different forms allows to perform deeper analysis.

The result of the analysis provides support for the person deciding on the most favorable SRU for a given SAR task. By optimizing the process of selecting units, it is possible to improve the effectiveness of actions and the efficiency of the SAR system. The developed method leads to:

– 1) determining the search and rescue capabilities of individual units in the fleet;
– 2) determining the unit or group of units that best meet the preferences of the coordinator in a given SAR action.

For the developed method of unit assessment, it is noted that the following work can be continued:

– testing with other methods of MCDA;
– development of the family of criteria, for example by specifying their subcriteria;
– modifications of the model to adapt it to the needs of assessment of non-rescue (civilian) ships recruited for search and rescue at sea;
– development of a computer program to support the decision-making process of the SAR action coordinator;

The developed method could be used in decision support systems (DSS) for search and rescue at sea both for the assessment of individual SRU in a given SAR action, as well as for the analysis of the performance of the entire SAR system in a given region.

References

1. Burciu, Z.: Bezpieczeństwo w transporcie morskim i zarządzanie w akcji ratowniczej, Wydawnictwo Akademii Morskiej w Gdyni (2011)
2. Burciu, Z.: Niezawodność akcji ratowniczej w transporcie morskim, Oficyna Wydawnicza Politechniki Warszawskiej (2012)
3. Bugajski, G., Małyszko, M, Wielgosz, M.: Analysis of the parameters influencing the suitability of a surface unit for search and rescue operations at sea, Zeszyty Naukowe Akademii Morskiej w Szczecinie, nr 53 (2018)
4. IMO/ICAO, International Areonautical and Maritime Search and Resce Manual, vol. I, London (2019)
5. IMO/ICAO, International Areonautical and Maritime Search and Resce Manual, vol. II, London (2019)
6. Roy, B.: Wielokryterialne wspomaganie decyzji. WNT, Warszawa (1990)

Influence of the Diagnostics and Recovery on Safety Integrity of Safety Function

Karol Rástočný[✉]

University of Žilina, Univerzitná 8215/1, Žilina, Slovak Republic
`karol.rastocny@uniza.sk`

Abstract. Early detection of these failures and subsequent negation of their effects can have a significant influence on the safety integrity level of the safety function and thus also on the elimination of risks related to the controlled process. Properly applied diagnostic mechanisms in combination with recovery mechanisms can increase not only the safety but also the availability of the safety-related system. In this paper, the impact of diagnosis and recovery on the safety integrity of the safety function is presented on a dual architecture based on composite fail-safety with fail-safe comparison. A Markov Chain method is used to model a hazardous failure of a safety function. Incorrect implementation of technical and operational parameters of the model results leads to incorrect results of the safety analysis.

Keywords: Diagnostics · Safety · Recovery · Availability · Safety integrity

1 Introduction

The standard [1] defines four Safety Integrity Levels (SIL 1 to SIL 4), distinguishing between the Systematic Failure Integrity (SFI) and the Random Failure Integrity (RFI).

The required safety integrity level is achieved by applying the prescribed design and organizational measures to prevent systematic failures. It is considered that this part of the safety integrity cannot be quantified.

The RFI can be quantified and expresses the random failures influence on the safety integrity of Safety Function (SF).

According to [1] is a Railway Signalling System (RSS) considered a safety-related system, which operates in continuous mode of operation (resp. high demand mode of operation). The SF, which RSS implements, keeps the Equipment Under Control (EUC) in the safe state, as part of normal operation. The acronym EUC means equipment (signal, point, ...) or controlled part of the railway process. Quantitative part of the safety integrity (the random failure integrity) is expressed as the Tolerable Hazard Rate (*THR*) - in the new edition of EN 50129 [2], the Tolerable Functional Failure Rate is considered ($TTFF_H$).

In general, in an Electronic Railway Signalling System (E-RSS) are implemented the measures to deal with failure (its negation), which are applied after the failure detection.

© Springer Nature Switzerland AG 2020
J. Mikulski (Ed.): TST 2020, CCIS 1289, pp. 387–401, 2020.
https://doi.org/10.1007/978-3-030-59270-7_29

Detection and negation of failures has a key importance in providing the required SIL for the SF implemented by the E-RSS.

From a safety point of view, it is important to detect failures that can cause, either alone or in combination with other failures, hazardous failure of the SF. Diagnostics influence on the RFI can be successfully modelled using different methods, for example using methods based on Continuous-Time Markov Chain (CTMC). CTMC can be used individually or in combination with Discrete-Time Markov Chain (DTMC). Since it is a system with electronic elements, whose failures occurrence follows the exponential distribution law [1], so in this paper the homogeneous MCs are considered.

In practice, it is possible to meet with different forms of diagnostics and with different ways of their application. In this paper it is considered:

– diagnostics test;
– proof test;
– combination of diagnostics test and proof test.

The diagnostics test is generally performed during operation of E-RSS (on-line diagnostics). This may be self-diagnostics applied to a single-channel structure or discrepancy (comparative) diagnostics, characterized in that the diagnostic result is based on detecting differences between signals from two or more objects performing the same function.

The proof test is generally performed when E-RSS is down (off-line diagnostics). The proof test may be performed as a result of the planned activity (for example, a failure analysis may result in a requirement to perform the proof test periodically) or proof test can be performed when the E-RSS is down for other reasons. Proof test can be perfect or imperfect. A perfect proof test is characterized (in comparison with an imperfect proof test) by allowing all hazardous fault to be detected. After the elimination of all detected fault, the E-RSS is considered "as good-as-new".

Specific diagnostics methods for chosen parts of a system can be found in [3–6].

If the SF is performed in the continuous mode of operation, resp. in the high demand mode of operation, the observed property is not only the RFI of the SF, but also the availability with which this SF is performed. The process from failure to system recovery

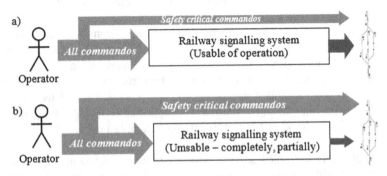

Fig. 1. Influence of the availability on the EUC safety [own study]

also has a significant impact on availability. In principle, the relationship between the availability and safety of the SF in shown in Fig. 1.

If the E-RSS is in operational state, the activity of service staff (activity related to keeping the EUC in the safe state) is fully performed by the E-RSS – it is so called "primary" safety. If the E-RSS is in incapable-operation state, resp. in partly operational state and the operation cannot be interrupted, the responsibility for activity related to keeping the EUC in the safe state is taken over (partly or fully) by service staff – it is so called "secondary" safety. Because the probability of person's mistake related to the keeping the EUC in the safe state is significantly greater than the hazardous failure probability of the E-RSS, it is desirable to minimize the time of the E-RSS incapable-operation state. Eventually, it is possible to claim that the E-RSS availability contributes to ensuring the safe state for the EUC.

The paper is dedicated to analysis of diagnostics and availability influence on the RFI of the SF and by its content complements the information published in [6, 7].

2 Theoretical Part

The standard [1] requires to realize the RFI assessment not for system, but individually for each SF. For clarity of the paper, in its next part it is assumed, that E-RSS: performs only one SF and therefore the hazardous failure of the E-RSS can be identified with the hazardous failure of the SF;

- is implemented from n mutually independent and identical units, which are connected so, that the E-RSS performs the SF safely, if at least one its unit is functional (structure 1 oo n);
- passes into the safe state and terminates its operation after the failure detection;
- works in continuous mode of operation.

These assumptions (simplifications) do not prevent application of the considerations stated in the paper to the more complex E-RSSs that perform more SFs.

Let the random failures occurrence of the E-RSS units follows the exponential distribution law and let it be valid, that

$$\lambda_1 = \lambda_2 = \ldots = \lambda_n = \lambda, \tag{1}$$

where λ_i is the random failures rate of i-th unit and $i = 1, 2, \ldots, n$.

In general, it is valid, that $\lambda_H \leq \lambda$. In the paper it is considered, that $\lambda_H = \lambda$. From a safety point of view, it is an acceptable assumption (pessimistic approach).

2.1 On-line Diagnostics

The on-line diagnostics is characterized by the fact, that operation of mechanisms of the failures detection and negation is continuous in time. It is an effort to detect the failure in the shortest possible time after its occurrence and activate the negation mechanism of its impact in the shortest time after the failure detection. To the on-line diagnostics influence on safety integrity of the SF are dedicated for example [8, 9].

Influence of the continuous-time operation of the failures detection and negation mechanisms on the RFI of the SF during the E-RSS operation can be modelled using homogeneous CTMC.

Model in Fig. 2 shows transition of the E-RSS from failure-free state **1** (neither unit has a random failure) into hazardous state **H** (each unit has at least one random failure).

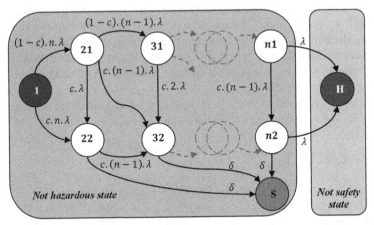

Fig. 2. CTMC for the E-RSS performing the SF with structure 1 oo n and the failures detection and negation mechanisms operating continuously in time [own study]

Let the E-RSS is in state **1** (Fig. 2). If the first undetectable random failure occurs, the E-RSS will pass from state **1** into state **21**. If another undetectable random failure occurs in unit, which already has undetectable random failure, the E-RSS state will not change. If detectable random failure occurs in unit, which already has undetectable random failure, the E-RSS will pass from state **21** into state **22**. The E-RSS can pass from state **21** into state **31** if undetectable random failure occurs in next unit of the E-RSS or into state **32** if detectable random failure occurs in next unit of the E-RSS. Similar considerations can also be applied to transitions between other model states. The rate of transitions between model states (states **1**, **21**, …, **n1**, **n2**, **H**) depends on the failures rate of units of the E-RSS (1) and on the diagnostic coverage coefficient ($c \in 0, 1$).

From states **22** to **n2** the E-RSS can pass into permanent safe state **S** due to the activation of negation mechanisms. In case of pessimistic assumption, the transition rate into state **S** can be calculated as inverted value of sum of the failure detection time T_d and the failure negation time T_n, i.e.

$$\delta = \frac{1}{T_d + T_n}. \tag{2}$$

Realistically it is possible to consider also with mean value of T_d.

States **H**, **S** are absorption states and the E-RSS can leave these states only after execution of prescribed organizational measures. After re-commissioning the E-RSS into operation is the E-RSS considered "as good as new" (the E-RSS is in state **1**).

Model in Fig. 2 can be described by the transition rate matrix. Based on this matrix and the initial probability vector (3) it is possible to calculate the probabilities for each model state in time $t > 0$.

$$\overrightarrow{P(t = 0)} = \{p_1(t = 0), \dots, p_H(t = 0), p_S(t = 0)\}, \tag{3}$$

where $p_i(t = 0)$ is probability of state i in time $t = 0$, while $i = 1, 21, 22, \dots, n1, n2, D, S$.

2.2 Off-line Diagnostics (Proof Test)

In case, that the E-RSS does not dispose with the on-line diagnostics, resp. the on-line diagnostics is insufficient regarding to required SIL, so for the random failures detection is necessary to use also the off-line diagnostics. The failures detection and negation mechanism of the off-line diagnostics is applied during regular (cyclically repetitive) preventive maintenance, when the E-RSS is in down state.

Problematic of the proof test diagnostic coverage and its influence on RFI of the SF can be found e.g. in [9–11]. Different approaches to realization of proof tests are described e.g. in [12]. Because the random failures occurrence is continuous in time, the random failures influence on the RFI between two neighbouring proof tests can be modelled using CTMC. Performing of the proof test is carried out in discreet time, therefore the proof test influence on the RFI of the SF can be modelled using DTMC.

Based on assumption of homogeneous MCs, the transition rate matrix $\mathbb{A}_{2n+1\times 2n+1}$ (matrix belonging to CTMC) and the transition probability matrix $\mathbb{P}_{2n+1\times 2n+1}$ (matrix belonging to DTMC) are the same in all operation cycles. Based on the initial probability vector at the beginning of m-th operation cycle $\overrightarrow{P^{(m)}\left(t^{(m)} = 0\right)}$ and matrix $\mathbb{A}_{n+1\times n+1}$ it is possible to calculate elements of the probability vector in time $t^{(m)} = T_o$, i.e. $\overrightarrow{P^{(m)}\left(t^{(m)} = T_o\right)}$. The initial probability vector for next operation cycle is

$$\overrightarrow{P^{(m+1)}\left(t^{(m+1)} = 0\right)} = \overrightarrow{P^{(m)}\left(t^{(m)} = T_o\right)}.\mathbb{P}, \tag{4}$$

where $m = 1, 2, \dots$ is the number of operation cycle of the E-RSS, $\mathbb{P}$ is the transition probability matrix for DTMC and T_o is the system operating time between two neighbouring proof tests.

Influence of the proof test and subsequent recovery of the E-RSS down state on the hazardous failure of the SF can be described by DTMC in Fig. 3 and the transition probability matrix (5).

In terms of the influence on the RFI of the SF, duration time of the proof test can be considered irrelevant, because in this time is the E-RSS out of operation. Therefore, in terms of modelling the RFI of the SF, duration time of the proof test can be considered zero ($T_{proof} = 0$).

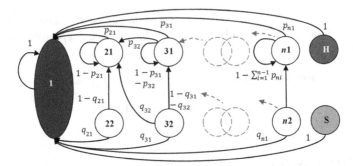

Fig. 3. DTMC for the E-RSS performing the SF with structure 1 oo n [own study]

The transition probability matrix describing the DTMC in Fig. 3:

$$\mathbb{P}_{(2n+1)\times(2n+1)} = \begin{pmatrix} 1 & 0 & 0 & \cdots & 0 & 0 & 0 \\ p_{21} & 1-p_{21} & 0 & \cdots & 0 & 0 & 0 \\ q_{21} & 1-p_{21} & 0 & \cdots & 0 & 0 & 0 \\ p_{31} & p_{32} & 1-p_{31}-p_{32} & \cdots & 0 & 0 & 0 \\ \cdots & \cdots & \cdots & \ddots & \cdots & & \\ 1 & 0 & 0 & \cdots & 0 & 0 & 0 \\ 1 & 0 & 0 & \cdots & 0 & 0 & 0 \end{pmatrix}. \tag{5}$$

If the proof test is perfect, then $p_{ij} = 1$ and $q_{ij} = 1$; if the proof test is imperfect, then $p_{ij} < 1$ or $q_{ij} < 1$ for $i = 2, \ldots, n$ and $j = 1, 2$.

The transition from state **H** into state **1** represents a specific case of recovery, when a hazardous state of the E-RSS has been recorded (theoretically it cannot be excluded; it is a probabilistic approach to the safety integrity assessment). In general, it is necessary to determine the cause of the hazardous state occurrence, what often leads to changes in the E-RSS and accordingly to range of changes is needed to apply all procedures and measures within each life cycle phase, as for a new system. In such a case, the recovery has some specific characteristics, for example also because of that these changes have to be approved by independent authority.

2.3 Availability

Basic availability indicators include the instantaneous availability function $A(t)$ and the asymptotic availability factor A.

$$A = \lim_{t \to \infty} A(t). \tag{6}$$

In practice, a simplified relation is often used for calculation of the asymptotic availability factor:

$$A = \frac{MUT}{MUT + MDT}, \tag{7}$$

where MUT is the mean up time and *MDT* is the mean down time.

In general, it is necessary to distinguish between the inherent availability of the system A_I (generally stated by the system manufacturer), whose value is determined based on ideal maintenance conditions ($MDT = MRT$) and the operational availability of the system A_O, whose value is determined based on real maintenance conditions ($MDT = MTTR$). Then

$$A_O = \frac{MUT}{MUT + MTTR},\tag{8}$$

$$A_I = \frac{MUT}{MUT + MRT},\tag{9}$$

where *MTTR* is the mean time to recovery and *MRT* is the mean repair time.

If during the useful lifetime of the E-RSS the preventive maintenance is not considered, it can be assumed, that $MUT = MTBF$, where *MTBF* is the mean operational time between failures.

If assumed, that during the repair all failures are removed, then the CTMC in Fig. 4 can be used for calculation probability of the usable state **US** under assumption, that the E-RSS is in state **1** after recovery (although this recovery is not shown in Fig. 4).

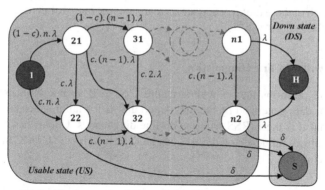

Fig. 4. CTMC describing only the transition of the E-RSS, which performs the SF, from available state (up state) into unavailable state (down state) [own study]

Transition from the down state into the usable state due to the recovery is shown in Fig. 5, where μ is the recovery rate and it is valid, that

$$\mu = \frac{1}{MTTR}.\tag{10}$$

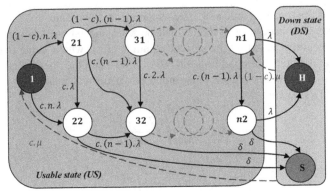

Fig. 5. CTMC describing also the recovery process of the E-RSS, which performs the SF [own study]

3 Experimental Part

In practice are very common the E-RSS with dual structure based on composite fail-safety. We assume, that the E-RSS consists of two hardware identical and physically independent units – unit A and unit B, which control the EUC, for example point machine or light. Let both of these units participate on realization of one SF. Let the random failure rate $\lambda_A = \lambda_B = \lambda = 10^{-5}$ h^{-1}.

3.1 E-RSS with On-line Diagnostics

Let the E-RSS performs the SF with structure 1 oo 2. If such E-RSS uses a mutual comparison of data generated by the unit A and unit B for failures detection, it can be concluded, that it is the E-RSS with the on-line diagnostics. Under these assumption, the random failures influence on the RFI can be described by the CTMC in Fig. 6 (it is reduced model in Fig. 2).

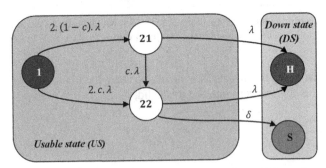

Fig. 6. CTMC for dual-channel system with on-line diagnostics, which performs the SF [own study]

Model in Fig. 6 can be described by the transition rate matrix (11) and the differential equation system (12).

$$
\mathbb{A} = \begin{pmatrix}
-2\lambda & 2\lambda.(1-c) & 2\lambda.c & 0 & 0 \\
0 & -\lambda.(1+c) & \lambda.c & 0 & \lambda \\
0 & 0 & -\lambda - \delta & \delta & \lambda \\
0 & 0 & 0 & 0 & 0 \\
0 & 0 & 0 & 0 & 0
\end{pmatrix}.
\tag{11}
$$

$$
\acute{p}_1(t) = -2\lambda.p_1(t)
$$

$$
\acute{p}_{21}(t) = 2\lambda.(1-c).p_1(t) - \lambda.(1+c).p_{21}(t)
$$

$$
\acute{p}_{22}(t) = 2\lambda.c.p_1(t) + \lambda.c.p_{21}(t) - (\lambda+\delta).p_{22}(t)
\tag{12}
$$

$$
\acute{p}_s(t) = \delta.p_{22}(t)
$$

$$
\acute{p}_H(t) = \lambda.p_{21}(t) + \lambda.p_{22}(t).
$$

If the E-RSS is in time $t = 0$ in failure-free state (state **1**), then the initial probability distribution $\overrightarrow{P_0(t = 0)} = \{1, 0, 0, 0, 0\}$ and the probability of hazardous state **H**

$$
p_H(t) = e^{-2\lambda.t} - 1 + \frac{2\delta}{(\lambda.c - \delta).(1+c)}\left(e^{-\lambda.(1+c).t} - 1\right)
$$

$$
- \frac{2\lambda^2.c}{(\lambda.c - \delta).(\lambda + \delta)}\left(e^{-(\lambda+\delta).t} - 1\right).
\tag{13}
$$

If $c = 1$, then

$$
p_H(t) = \frac{e^{-2\lambda.t}\lambda.\left(\delta - \delta.e^{2\lambda.t} + \lambda + \lambda.e^{2t.\lambda} - 2\lambda.e^{-(\delta-\lambda).t}\right)}{(\lambda + \delta)(\lambda - \delta)}.
\tag{14}
$$

If $c = 0$, then also $\delta = 0$ and

$$
p_H(t) = 1 + e^{-2\lambda.t} - 2e^{-\lambda.t}.
\tag{15}
$$

Influence of the failures detection and negation mechanisms parameters (failure detection and negation time and diagnostic coverage) on the RFI of the E-RSS can be seen in Fig. 7 and Fig. 8. If the E-RSS works in continuous mode of operation, then for specifying the RFI level is indicative the SF hazardous failure rate $\lambda_H(t)$.

For calculation of the availability of the E-RSS with dual structure can be used CTMC shown in Fig. 9.

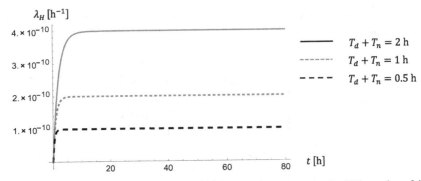

Fig. 7. Influence of the failures detection and negation mechanisms on the SF hazardous failure rate; $\lambda_A = \lambda_B = \lambda = 10^{-5}\text{h}^{-1}$; $c = 1$ [own study]

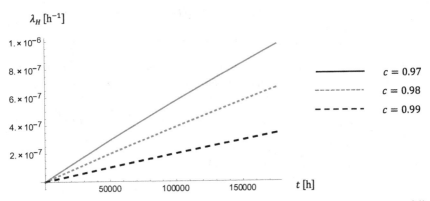

Fig. 8. Influence of the failures detection and negation mechanisms on the SF hazardous failure rate; $\lambda_A = \lambda_B = \lambda = 10^{-5}\text{h}^{-1}$; $(T_d + T_n) = 2$ h [own study]

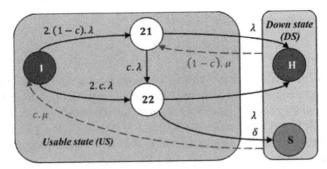

Fig. 9. CTMC for dual-channel system with on-line diagnostics and recovery [own study]

Calculated values of availability are graphically presented in Fig. 10 and Fig. 11.

The instantaneous availability of the E-RSS is given by the state **US** occurrence probability and the asymptotic availability factor is calculated according to (6).

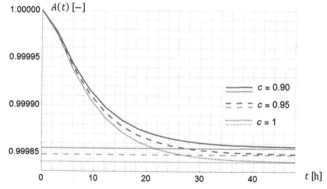

Fig. 10. Instantaneous availability function and asymptotic availability factor for the E-RSS – influence of the c, if $MTTR = 8$ h and $(T_d + T_n) = 2$ h; $\lambda_A = \lambda_B = \lambda = 10^{-5}$ h^{-1} [own study]

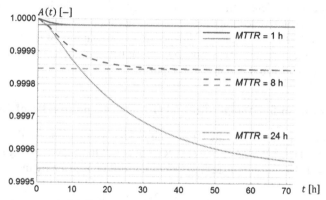

Fig. 11. Instantaneous availability function and asymptotic availability factor for the E-RSS – influence of the $MTTR$, if $c = 0,95$ and $(T_d + T_n) = 2$ h; $\lambda_A = \lambda_B = \lambda = 10^{-5}$ h^{-1} [own study]

Influence of the recovery rate on the hazardous failure probability of the E-RSS $(p_H(t))$ is shown in Fig. 12.

Figure 12 shows that with improving of the recovery process quality is possible to achieve lower hazardous failure probability of the E-RSS. In case that only the recovery from state **S** would be considered (it depends on the way of system operation), so paradoxically, the recovery would have a negative influence on the hazardous failure probability of the E-RSS (primary safety). However, it should be noted, that the availability has positive influence on the secondary safety.

The results analysis (Fig. 7, Fig. 8, Fig. 10, Fig. 11 and Fig. 12) shows, that:

– the increasing recovery rate has positive influence on the availability of the SF – expected result;

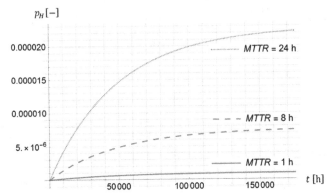

Fig. 12. Function of the hazardous failure probability for the E-RSS – influence of the *MTTR*, if $c = 0,95$ and $(T_d + T_n) = 2$ h [own study]

– quality of the failure detection and negation mechanism (the higher diagnostic coverage, the lower failure detection time, the lower negation time) has positive influence on the RFI of the SF, but negative influence on the availability of the SF; in practice, therefore, a certain compromise must be chosen between these opposing properties in order to meet the requirements of the specification.

3.2   E-RSS with On-line Diagnostics and Off-line Diagnostics (Proof Test)

Influence of random failures on the RFI of the E-RSS with the on-line diagnostics can be described by the CTMC in Fig. 6. If E-RSS does not have on-line diagnostics, then $c = 0$ and $\delta = 0$. The hazardous failure rate of the E-RSS is given by the equation

$$\lambda_H(0 \leq t < T_o) = \frac{2\lambda e^{-\lambda t} - 2\lambda.e^{-2\lambda t}}{2e^{-\lambda t} - e^{-2\lambda t}}. \tag{16}$$

Influence of the proof test on the RFI can be described by the DTMC in Fig. 13 (it is reduced model in Fig. 3) and by the transition probability matrix (5).

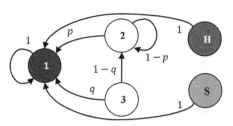

Fig. 13. DTMC for dual-channel system, which performs the SF [own study]

$$\mathbb{P} = \begin{pmatrix} 1 & 0 & 0\,0\,0 \\ p & 1-p & 0\,0\,0 \\ q & 1-q & 0\,0\,0 \\ 1 & 0 & 0\,0\,0 \\ 1 & 0 & 0\,0\,0 \end{pmatrix}, \tag{17}$$

where q and p are the transition probabilities corresponding to the diagnostic coverage coefficient of the proof test.

If the proof test executed during preventive maintenance is perfect, so all random failures of the E-RSS are detected and the E-RSS after removing all identified failures is considered "as good as new". Influence of the perfect proof test on the RFI can be described by the DTMC in Fig. 13 and by the transition probability matrix (17) (provided that $p = 1$ and $q = 1$). Influence of the perfect proof test and consequent recovery on the RFI of the E-RSS can be seen in and Fig. 14. This figure (Fig. 14) show, that the hazardous failure probability and also the hazardous failure rate of the SF are the same in all operation cycles of the E-RSS. Therefore realization of the RFI assessment is sufficient only for $t = \langle 0, T_O \rangle$.

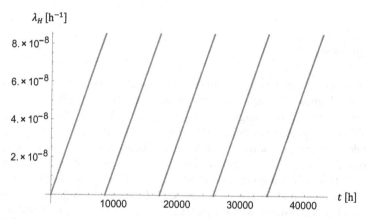

Fig. 14. Influence of the perfect proof test on the SF hazardous failure rate; $\lambda_A = \lambda_B = \lambda = 10^{-5}\ \mathrm{h}^{-1}$; $T_O = 8760$ h (about 1 year); $c = 0,95$; $p = 1$; $q = 1$ [own study]

If the proof test executed during preventive maintenance is imperfect, so not all random failures of the E-RSS are detected. Even after removing all identified failures, the E-RSS cannot be considered "as good as new", what is reflected by the gradual increase of the hazardous failure probability value, resp. the hazardous failure rate of the E-RSS. Influence of imperfect proof test on the RFI of the E-RSS can be described by the DTMC in Fig. 13 and by the transition probability matrix (17) (provided that $p < 1$ or $q < 0$). Even if the transition probability matrix (17) is the same in each operation cycle, the initial probability vector (3) changes at the beginning of each new operation cycle. As a result, probability values of states DTMC and also the hazardous failure rate values of the E-RSS changes at the end of each operation cycle. This fact can be seen in graphs in Fig. 15. In this case, it is necessary to realize the RFI assessment during entire useful life of the E-RSS.

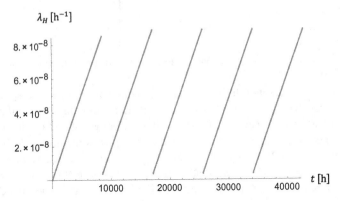

Fig. 15. Influence of the imperfect proof test on the SF hazardous failure rate; $\lambda_A = \lambda_B = \lambda = 10^{-5}$ h^{-1}; $T_O = 8760$ h (about 1 year); $c = 0,95$; $p = 0,95$; $q = 0,99$ [own study]

4 Conclusion

In general, it can be concluded, that diagnostic properties (in case of the on-line diagnostics – the diagnostic coverage and the failure detection time; in case of the proof test – the time between two neighbouring proof tests and the quality of the proof test execution) have a significant influence on the RFI of the SF.

More detailed analysis of results published in the paper shows, that if the operation interval between two neighbouring proof tests is significantly smaller than the useful life of the E-RSS, which implements the SF (21), so influence of the proof test on the RFI of the SF can be modelled by using only CTMC (without a significant influence on accuracy of obtained results), which significantly reduces the computational difficulty.

The paper provides information about the forms of diagnostics and recovery that are most commonly found in practice. In practice, however, the E-RSSs of different architectures can have several differently operating failures detection mechanisms and also various forms of system recovery (for example, system recovery without interruption of operation).

Acknowledgement. This work has been supported by the Educational Grant Agency of the Slovak Republic (KEGA) Number 008ŽU-4/2019: Modernization and expansion of educational possibilities in the field of safe controlling of industrial processes using the safety PLC.

References

1. EN 50129: Railway application. Communication, signalling and processing systems. Safety-related electronic systems for signalling (2003)
2. Fpr EN 50129: Railway application. Communication, signalling and processing systems. Safety-related electronic systems for signalling (2018)
3. Silveira, E.G., Paula, H.R., Rocha, S.A., Pereira, C.S.: Hybrid fault diagnosis algorithms for transmission lines. Electr. Eng. **100**(3), 1689–1699 (2017). https://doi.org/10.1007/s00202-017-0647-7
4. Martínez-Morales, J.D., Palacios-Hernández, E.R., Campos-Delgado, D.U.: Multiple-fault diagnosis in induction motors through support vector machine classification at variable operating conditions. Electr. Eng. **100**(1), 59–73 (2016). https://doi.org/10.1007/s00202-016-0487-x
5. Jimenez, G., Munoz, A., Duarte-Mermoud, M.: Fault detection in induction motors using Hilbert and Wavelet transforms. Electr. Eng. **89**(3), 205–220 (2007). https://doi.org/10.1007/s00202-005-0339-6
6. Rástočný, K., Ždánsky, P.: Modelling of the diagnostics influence on safety integrity of safety function. In: Conference Proceedings [Electronic], Elektro, pp. 1–6 (2018)
7. Rástočný, K., Bubeníková, E.: Safety and availability – basic attributes of safety-related electronic systems for railway signalling. In: Mikulski, J. (ed.) TST 2019. CCIS, vol. 1049, pp. 69–82. Springer, Cham (2019). https://doi.org/10.1007/978-3-030-27547-1_6
8. Ustoglu, I., et al.: Effects of varying diagnostic coverage on functional safety. In: International Symposium on Fundamentals of Electrical Engineering (ISFEE), Romania (2014)
9. Rástočný, K., et al.: Modelling of diagnostics influence on control system safety. Comput. Inform. **37**(2), 457–475 (2018)
10. Bukowski, J.V., Van Buerden, I.: Impact of proof test effectiveness on safety instrumented system performance. In: 55th Annual Reliability & Maintainability Symposium, Ft Worth, TX, Book Series: Reliability and Maintainability Symposium, pp. 157–163 (2009)
11. Rástočný, K.: Quantitative assessment of the diagnostics effect on the hardware safety integrity of the safety-related electronic system operating in low demand mode of operation. Adv. Electr. Electron. Eng. **17**(2), 211–219 (2019). http://advances.utc.sk/index.php/AEEE/article/view/3230/488488574
12. Liu, Y, Raus, M.: Proof-testing strategies induced by dangerous detected failures of safety-instrumented systems. In: Conference Proceedings, PSAM12, Honolulu, HI, Reliability Engineering & System Safety, pp. 366–372 (2016)

A Critical Analysis of the IMO Description of Maritime Services in the Context of e-Navigation

Adam Weintrit[1] and Paweł Zalewski[2]([⊠])

[1] Gdynia Maritime University, Morska 81-87, Gdynia, Poland
a.weintrit@wn.umg.edu.pl
[2] Maritime University of Szczecin, Wały Chrobrego 1-2, Szczecin, Poland
p.zalewski@am.szczecin.pl

Abstract. Initial description of Maritime Services has lately been proposed by International Maritime Organization (IMO). Its potential impact on initially identified most popular maritime services has been discussed in the article. Several issues that should be considered during organizational and technical implementation of the circular provisions and follow-up familiarization of navigators with the affected services have been identified. The authors present results of their critical analysis of the IMO initial description of Maritime Services Portfolio in the context of e-Navigation. They present the outcome of an informal meeting of the maritime states representatives and international organizations acting as domain coordinating bodies for the further development of descriptions of Maritime Services, held at IALA Headquarters, in October 2019 and the findings of the IMO NSCR Sub-Committee 7th session, held in IMO Headquarters in January 2020. The aim of the paper is to share information about current and future developments related to the initial descriptions of Maritime Services in the context of e-Navigation (MSC.1/Circ.1610) and explore opportunities for better collaboration amongst domain coordinating bodies, in particular in connection to future work on services harmonization.

Keywords: e-Navigation · Maritime services · Safety at sea · IMO

1 Background

The IMO Maritime Safety Committee (MSC) at its 101st session, having considered the outcome of the 6th session of Sub-Committee on Navigation, Communications and Search and Rescue (NCSR), adopted resolution MSC.467(101) on Guidance on the definition and harmonization of the format and structure of Maritime Services in the context of e-Navigation [6] and approved MSC.1/Circ.1610 on Initial descriptions of Maritime Services in the context of e-Navigation [5].

The MSC also agreed to include in the biennial agenda of the NCSR for 2020–2021 an output for the Consideration of descriptions of Maritime Services in the context of e-Navigation, with a target completion year of 2021.

© Springer Nature Switzerland AG 2020
J. Mikulski (Ed.): TST 2020, CCIS 1289, pp. 402–414, 2020.
https://doi.org/10.1007/978-3-030-59270-7_30

2 Introduction

Modern shipping relies on a large amount of data and information to safely navigate from berth to berth. A very important set of information is promulgated as maritime safety information (MSI). MSI includes navigational warnings, meteorological information and other urgent safety-related information. In addition to being safety-relevant, marine information services are used for optimizing voyage routes, which can include the best passage through ice, a security-risk area or avoiding the known path of marine mammals. Route optimization may also include taking advantage of favourable winds and currents and engine loads may be adjusted accordingly. To assess the dynamic effects mentioned above, the ship's bridge team needs up-to-date information for the ship's planned operation. The information flow also comprises ship-to-shore communications, in particular prior to entering the coastal waters, as ships are usually requested to provide details of their voyage, cargo, crew and passengers on board, advising on the next port of call and other information. Shore-to-ship, ship-to-ship, ship-to-shore and shore-to-shore information exchange enable new services and technologies to improve safety and efficiency of shipping. All those marine information services, referred to as Maritime Services, are being considered to be transitioned from conventional transmission methods to the contemporary digital technologies.

An informal meeting of representatives from the following maritime states and international organizations: Norway and Singapore, IMO (International Maritime Organization), WMO (World Meteorological Organization), IHO (International Hydrographic Organization), IALA (International Association of Marine Aids to Navigation and Lighthouse Authorities), IMPA (International Maritime Pilots' Association) and IMHA (International Maritime Health Association), acting as domain coordinating bodies for the further development of descriptions of Maritime Services (MSs) in the context of e-Navigation, was held at IALA Headquarters in October 2019. The aim of the meeting was to:

- share information about current and future developments related to the initial descriptions of Maritime Services in the context of e-Navigation (MSC.1/Circ.1610) [5];
- explore opportunities for better collaboration amongst domain coordinating bodies, in particular, in connection to future work on harmonization; and
- discuss expected work at NCSR 7 and future sessions.

Afterwards, in January 2020, NCSR 7 was held in London where information on the outcome of this informal meeting was considered and further actions were recommended to the stakeholders and MSC.

3 Maritime Services Portfolio

An Maritime Services Portfolio (MSP) in the context of e-Navigation can be defined as a set of operational MSs and associated technical services provided in a unified, digital format. Hence, an MSP may also be construed as a set of "products" provided by a stakeholder in a given sea area, waterway, or port as appropriate. Such marine information has been termed "maritime services" (MSs). MSs as digitally transmitted data and information displayed in a harmonized way on a ship's bridge or shore-based facilities broadcasting and receiving marine information have been envisaged as part of e-navigation.

3.1 MSP Definition

Before the work on the development on the definition and harmonization of the formats and structures of MSPs commenced, the IMO Secretariat considered that a clear understanding of MSPs is indispensable. A definition of MSP can be found in [11, 15], that is, an MSP defines and describes a set of operational and technical services and levels of services provided by a stakeholder in a given sea area, waterway, or port as appropriate.

The e-Navigation Strategy Implementation Plan (SIP) [5, 6] identified 16 MSs for use in MSP, including the type of service provided, as well as the associated responsible service provider. It is evident that the services vary significantly, ranging from, for example, vessel traffic service (VTS) information to a ship, medical information and instructions provided by doctors to the ship's crew responsible for medical care to ice navigation, route information, search and rescue coordinates and many more. The sets of data, instructions, and information are very different in nature and could take numerical values, geographical coordinates, medical terminology, courses to steer, waypoint coordinates, communication channels, and many more. Nevertheless the SIP requires that all Maritime Services are IHO S-100 conformant as a baseline.

As outlined in previous sections of this paper, MSs are considered to form a framework for the electronic provision of information in a harmonized way between the shore and ships. It is therefore necessary to harmonize the format, structure, and communication channels used to exchange [12–14]. It is also argued that a lack of coordination in the provision of information related to MSs among organizations responsible for their provision may lead to duplication of efforts, development of regional solutions, use of different communication systems, and the provision of superfluous or noninteroperable information. IMO acknowledges that the content of MSs will be developed by different international organizations, and thus coordination among these organizations is a priority to ensure harmonization of scope, format, structure, display on board, and communication systems used to transmit information electronically. While the work on contents of MSs is currently undertaken by the IALA, the IMO Secretariat considers that the voluntary body HGDM (IMO/IHO Harmonization Group on Data Modelling) should be tasked to work on the harmonization as outlined above. This interpretation concurs that a "general guidance" should be developed but should not define the detailed content of a particular MS or aim at harmonizing the service itself. This should be the responsibility of relevant data and service providers [15].

3.2 Responsible Service Providers

In each country, there are authorities responsible for providing information services. Table 1 below offers examples of authorities responsible in each case, which can be different between countries. Responsible authorities may require service providers to deliver operational services.

Table 1. Maritime services with responsible service providers [16, 17]

Service No	Identified services	Identified responsible service provider
MS 1	VTS information service (**INS**)	VTS authority
MS 2	Navigational assistance service (**NAS**)	VTS authority
MS 3	Traffic organization service (**TOS**)	VTS authority
MS 4	Port support service (**PSS**)	Local port/harbour authority
MS 5	Maritime safety information (**MSI**) service	National competent authority
MS 6	Pilotage service	Pilotage authority/pilot organization
MS 7	Tug service	National competent authority; local port/harbour authority; private tug service company
MS 8	Vessel shore reporting	National competent authority and appointed service providers
MS 9	Telemedical assistance service (**TMAS**)	National health organization/dedicated health organization
MS 10	Maritime assistance service (**MAS**)	Coastal/port authority/organization
MS 11	Nautical chart service	National hydrographic authority/organization
MS 12	Nautical publications service	National hydrographic authority/organization
MS 13	Ice navigation service	National competent authority organization
MS 14	Meteorological information service	National meteorological authority public institutions
MS 15	Real-time hydrographic and environmental information service	National hydrographic and meteorological authorities
MS 16	Search and rescue (**SAR**) service	SAR authorities

The following six sea areas have been preliminarily identified for the delivery of MSs:

- port areas and approaches;
- coastal waters and confined or restricted areas;
- open sea and open areas;
- areas with offshore and/or infrastructure developments;
- polar areas;
- other remote areas.

4 Work on the Descriptions of Maritime Services

As part of the improved provision of services to vessels through e-Navigation, maritime services have been identified as the means of providing electronic information in a harmonized way in e-Navigation strategy implementation plan [4]. They were assigned to e-nav solution 5: improved communication of VTS service portfolio (not limited to VTS stations) and the development of the MSs and MSP was subjected to task T17: further development of the MSP to refine services and responsibilities ahead of implementing transition arrangements. In order to progress the harmonized development of MS descriptions further, overarching coordination meetings to share experiences and reporting progress within the relevant domain coordinating bodies were arranged in 2019 and 2020. The main conclusions from these meetings (as mentioned in the introduction) are presented in the following subsections.

4.1 MS 1 (INS), MS 2 (NAS) and MS 3 (TOS)

IALA has worked on developments related to MSs 1, 2 and 3. The work in IALA has been organized basically under four Committees: the AtoN Requirements and Management (ARM) Committee; the Engineering and Sustainability (ENG) Committee; the e-Navigation, Information Services and Communications (ENAV) Committee; and the Vessel Traffic Services (VTS) Committee.

Among the most relevant developments, work has been in progress on Maritime Resource Names (MRN), S-200 and technical details for a connectivity platform for e-avigation. IALA also considers merging MSs 1, 2 and 3 into one, in line with the proposed revision of resolution A.857(20) on Guidelines for Vessel Traffic Services [10]. Furthermore, two new MSs are under development by its Committees, one for Marine Aids to Navigation (AtoN) and one for Position, Navigation and Timing (PNT) services. No further work on the revision of MSs 1, 2 and 3 has been conducted.

IALA advises that a Joint IHO/IALA workshop on IHO S-100/S-200 product specification development and portrayal should be organized in June 2020 in Norway. This event should be a good opportunity to harmonize and open feedback channels between both organizations, but in contemporary COVID-19 pandemic times its effects will be limited if it is led remotely. IALA also advises that one of the present challenges is the lack of experts to contribute to the drafting of product specifications and descriptions of technical services. This is also a common problem identified by other domain coordinating bodies.

4.2 MS 4 (PSS)

Norway has worked on an updated draft description of MS 4 considered by a Correspondence Group established by IMO FAL (the Facilitation Committee) 43 due to report to FAL 44 in April 2020 (FAL 43/20, paragraph 7.23) [2]. A better coordination is required in terms of the work being undertaken by the NCSR Sub-Committee and the FAL Committee.

4.3 MS 5 (MSI)

IHO has worked on the following IHO S-100 Product Specifications to support the delivery of MSs:

- S-122 Ed. 1.0.0 – Marine Protected Areas;
- S-123 Ed. 1.0.0 – Marine Radio Services;
- S-101 Ed. 1.0.0 – ENC;
- S-111 Ed. 1.0.0 – Surface Currents;
- S-102 Ed. 2.0.0 – Bathymetric Surface;
- S-127 Ed. 1.0.0 – Marine Traffic Management; and
- S-129 Edition 1.0.0 – Under Keel Clearance Management Information.

They are in an advanced stage of development

WMO has been concerned how to provide MSI through different GMDSS recognized mobile satellite service providers. That work has been undertaken through its own committees.

No further work on the description of MS 5 has been conducted, but further updates are required to reflect changes regarding new GMDSS recognized mobile satellite service providers. Especially the term "Technical Services" needs to be defined to allow for a common understanding that would assist in providing such information in the various MSs descriptions (Fig. 1).

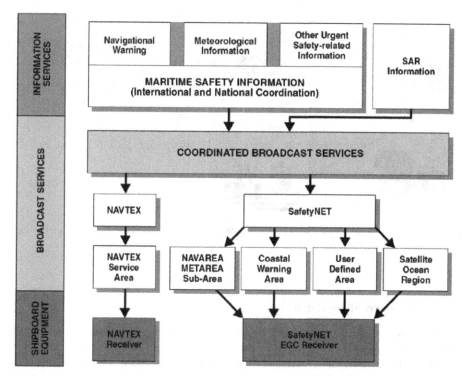

Fig. 1. The maritime safety information service of the Global Maritime Distress and Safety System based on IHO S-53 [own study]

4.4   MS 6 (Pilotage Service)

IMPA indicates that it is satisfied with the level of description provided so far, and that no further work is required but expresses its concern that trying to harmonize pilot booking services through the MS, as was being discussed in the FAL Correspondence Group, might not be consistent with pilotage services around the world. The FAL Correspondence Group should consider a revision of MS 6 as an attempt to further develop the MS in cooperation with IMPA.

4.5   MS 7 (Tug Service)

The FAL Correspondence Group considers a revision of MS 7. The intention is to clarify what kind of information is available and how it could be harmonized.

The main challenge is the missing link to technical services (the relation between technical specifications and operational services) (Fig. 2).

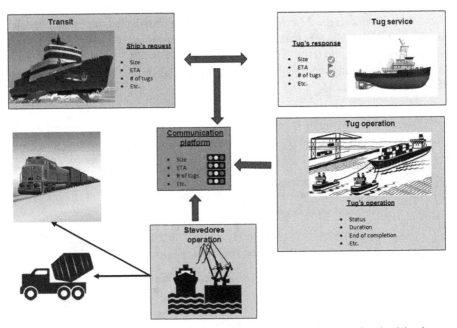

Fig. 2. Example of an electronic communication platform for all actors involved in the tug operations [own study]

4.6   MS 8 (Vessel Shore Reporting)

MS 8 has been divided into two parts: Vessel shore reporting (FAL requirements) and Ship reporting systems (SOLAS requirements).

The FAL Correspondence Group considers a revision of MS 8. There are parts that will require further elaboration, and this should be done progressively. There is a need of interested stakeholders contribution to the further development of MS 8, in particular, on relevant technical services (Fig. 3).

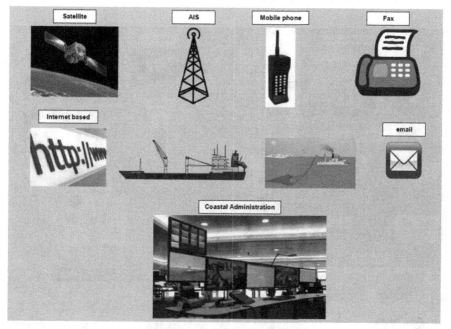

Fig. 3. Example of current communication systems used to report maritime information [own study]

4.7 MS 9 (TMAS)

The initial description of MS 9 has been prepared by Norway. IMHA conducts the work based on the outcomes of a recent workshop taking into account inputs from medical experts on tele-medical assistance. The goal is to derive ideas for the future from what is done today and what can be done to improve the current situation. A correspondence group, with involvement of other groups, such as technical experts, MRCCs and TMAS, might be established to progress this work. IMHA has listed some desiderata and some challenges as well in a document produced for a regional IMO workshop on e-Navigation held in Busan, Republic of Korea in September 2019. For example, life video connection and simultaneous monitoring of various physical parameters are on the list, but life streaming of data has consequences on technical services.

IMHA advises that harmonization among TMAS is needed. Technical experts should get involved to refine and specify needs in terms of technical specifications. Expertise from other domain coordinating bodies should be beneficial to interact or collaborate with other maritime services, so that some data needed to be produced only once for several services. Among the main challenges, privacy and ethical aspects regarding medical data are very important.

4.8   MS 10 (Mas)

Further work on the description of MS 10 is required. SAR experts should get involved in the further development of the description of this MS (Fig. 4).

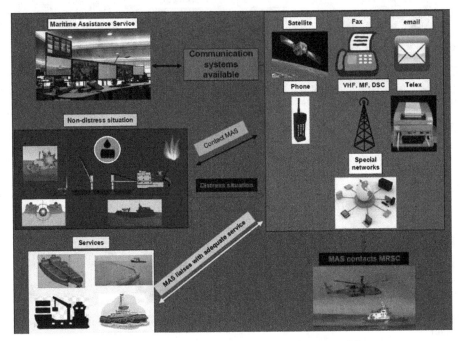

Fig. 4. Some functions provided by MAS [own study]

4.9   MS 11 (Nautical Chart Service), MS 12 (Nautical Publications Service) and MS 15 (Real-Time Hydrographic and Environmental Information Services)

IHO indicates that the descriptions of MSs 11, 12 and 15 could not be further developed at this stage and that present work is focused on the development of technical specifications and the harmonized display of information.

4.10   MS 13 (Ice Navigation Service) and MS 14 (Meteorological Information Service)

WMO conducts no further work on the descriptions of MSs 13 and 14 and further work on standardization is conducted in collaboration with IHO.

4.11   MS 16 (Search and Rescue (SAR) Service)

The revision of MS 16 is in progress by Norway and Singapore. Contributions from SAR experts are important to progress this work (Fig. 5).

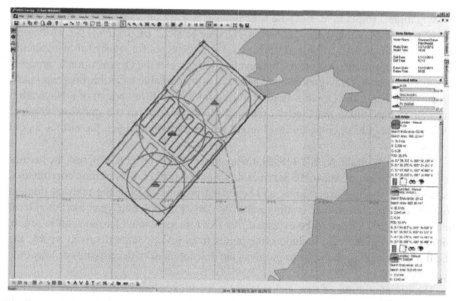

Fig. 5. Example of common sharing of digital search and rescue information based on contemporary ECDIS [own study]

5   Opportunities for Better Collaboration Amongst Domain Coordinating Bodies

One of the main issues highlighted so far is the need to harmonize the information exchanged through different MSs and how the information could be shared between different stakeholders. The use of the IHO registry is considered to be important for the further development of product specifications. The technical services of some MSs have been clearly defined (e.g. ECDIS) but means of communication need further consideration. The need to address interoperability between different MSs exists. The issues related to security, authentication and secure transmission of information could be addressed as a common technical service. Further consideration should be given to the way of describing MSs in general, to ensure consistency with the work being conducted under different domain coordinating bodies. A clear distinction should be made between the harmonization of existing information and data, and the development of new technical services. The domain coordinating bodies should ensure that the descriptions of technical services are not specific/ proprietary to any particular technology or service provider.

6   Consideration of Descriptions of Maritime Services in the Context of e-Navigation

The importance of IMO to continue to lead the work on the further development of Maritime Service descriptions is invaluable as the need to provide more certainty and directions for the implementation of changes to Maritime Services in the context of e-Navigation is imperative. Because time flows and work on solutions is tedious, the e-Navigation strategy implementation plan – Update 1 (MSC.1/Circ.1595) [4], addressing timelines for implementation and transitional arrangements for legacy services, should be updated once more. Despite a long-standing initiative of the Organization to progress the work related to e-Navigation, there had been no remarkable or visible progress made. On the other hand, the Organization's contribution in the development of e-Navigation had helped harmonize the digital exchange of information in the maritime domain. Although impact at operational level might not be experienced yet, the efforts should continue.

Accordingly, at the NCSR 7 [8, 9] it was agreed that in order to progress the harmonized development of Maritime Services descriptions further, overarching coordination meetings for sharing experiences and reporting progress within the relevant domain coordinating bodies should continue and the target completion year for the current output being 2021, need to be extended. An IMO intersessional harmonization group, with a scope which could include some inputs from FAL, could effectively enable the Organization leading the work to progress the development of descriptions of Maritime Services.

The dissemination of new technologies is very expected by prospective maritime users but until now only Singapore has developed a video to promote better understanding of Maritime Services in the context of e-Navigation (https://www.youtube.com/watch?v=WenDzWY-tXc).

7 Conclusion

The road to finalization of MSs descriptions will take some time. A critical analysis of the current IMO descriptions of MSs in the context of e-Navigation leads to the following conclusions:

- IMO requires a "general guidance" to be developed that should not define the detailed content of a particular MS or aim at harmonizing the service itself. This responsibility is relegated on service providers which pose a risk of very lengthy consultation procedure.
- The IHO S-100 framework standard specifies the method for data modelling and developing product specifications but related to hydrographic data which could pose a problem for wider implementation.
- One of the present challenges is the lack of experts to contribute to the drafting of product specifications and descriptions of technical services.
- The term "Technical Services" needs to be defined to allow for a common understanding that would assist in providing such information in the various MSs descriptions.
- Trying to harmonize some existing services with the proposed global ones might not be consistent. The example can be pilot booking services through the MS with pilotage services around the world.
- A better coordination is required in terms of the work being undertaken by the NCSR Sub-Committee and the FAL Committee.

- The main challenge is the missing link to technical services as the relation between technical specifications and operational services.
- Interaction between various maritime services is necessary, so that some data needed to be produced only once for several services.
- Among the main challenges, privacy and ethical aspects regarding some data are very important, an example is medical data.
- Additional guidance for the drafting of MSs descriptions, technical services and product specifications should be provided by IMO as there is no prior experience in drafting these documents and there are different interpretations of the level of detail required for the descriptions by stakeholders.
- More certainty is needed in the future on how the MSs in the context of e-Navigation would be implemented, including time frames for when providers should commence delivering services, and how long legacy services should be provided for. Without more structure, the practical implementation of MSs might be haphazard and slow and might result in confusion with an adverse effect on safety.
- IMO cannot proceed work in Sub-Committees without dedicated output from main Committee which slows down the whole procedure and relegates the effects into meetings' agenda of "any other business" which could be very ineffective.
- The detailed critical analysis as presented in [17] will be necessary when test-beds of new services take place.

References

1. IALA Guideline 1115. Maritime Service Portfolios: Digitizing Maritime Services, 1st ed. IALA Working Paper, ENAV-19-14.2.9; International Association of Lighthouse Authorities (2017)
2. IMO FAL 43/20. Report of the Facilitation Committee on Its Forty-Third Session. International Maritime Organization, London (2019)
3. IMO MSC.1/Circ.1593. Interim Guidelines for the Harmonized Display of Navigation Information Received Via Communication Equipment. International Maritime Organization, London (2018)
4. IMO MSC.1/Circ.1595. e-Navigation Strategy Implementation Plan – Update 1. International Maritime Organization, London (2018)
5. IMO MSC.1/Circ.1610. Initial Descriptions of Maritime Services in the Context of e-Navigation; International Maritime Organization, London (2019)
6. IMO MSC.467(101). Guidance on the Definition and Harmonization of the Format and Structure of Maritime Services in the Context of e-Navigation; International Maritime Organization: London, UK (2019)
7. IMO NCSR 7/8. Consideration of Descriptions of Maritime Services in The Context of e-Navigation. Report of an informal meeting of Member States and international organizations acting as domain coordinating bodies for the further development of descriptions of Maritime Services in the context of e-Navigation. Note by the Secretariat. International Maritime Organization, London (2019)
8. IMO NCSR 7/WP.1. Draft Report to The Maritime Safety Committee. International Maritime Organization, London (2020)

9. IMO NCSR 7/WP.4. Consideration of Descriptions of Maritime Services in The Context of e-Navigation (Item 8). Report of the Navigation Working Group. International Maritime Organization, London (2020)

10. IMO Res. A.857(20). Guidelines For Vessel Traffic Services. International Maritime Organization, London (1997)

11. Jonas, M., Oltmann, J.-H.: IMO e-navigation implementation strategy - challenge for data modelling. TransNav Int. J. Mar. Navig. Saf. Sea Transp. 7(1), 45–49 (2013)

12. Weintrit, A.: Development of the IMO e-Navigation concept – common maritime data structure. In: Mikulski, J. (ed.) TST 2011. CCIS, vol. 239, pp. 151–163. Springer, Heidelberg (2011). https://doi.org/10.1007/978-3-642-24660-9_18

13. Weintrit, A.: Prioritized main potential solutions for the e-Navigation concept. TransNav Int. J. Mar. Navig. Saf. Sea Transp. 7(1), 27–38 (2013)

14. Weintrit, A.: Technical infrastructure to support seamless information exchange in e-navigation. In: Mikulski, J. (ed.) TST 2013. CCIS, vol. 395, pp. 188–199. Springer, Heidelberg (2013). https://doi.org/10.1007/978-3-642-41647-7_24

15. Weintrit, A.: The harmonization of the format and structure of maritime service Portfolios. In: Mikulski, J. (ed.) TST 2018. CCIS, vol. 897, pp. 426–441. Springer, Cham (2018). https://doi.org/10.1007/978-3-319-97955-7_29

16. Weintrit, A.: Initial description of pilotage and tug services in the context of e-navigation. J. Mar. Sci. Eng. 8(2), 116 (2020)

17. Zalewski, P.: A critical analysis of IMO S-mode guidelines. TransNav Int. J. Mar. Navig. Saf. Sea Transp. 13(4), 841–846 (2019)

High Availability of the Modern Railway Systems Using the Example of Axle Counter

Przemysław Wołoszyk[(⊠)] and Mariusz Buława[(⊠)]

voestalpine Signaling Polska, Jana z Kolna 26C, Sopot, Poland
{Przemyslaw.Woloszyk,Mariusz.Bulawa}@voestalpine.com

Abstract. Availability of the modern safety systems for railway transport depends on many aspects. The technical solutions used in the designing process have a significant impact on the availability and reliability of the equipment and thus also the availability of the railway system in total. There are many key areas affecting the availability of devices, among others, proper system architecture, power supply, transmission system, software solutions etc. Redundant solutions can be implemented in both the hardware and software/logical layers of the system. The article presents practical solutions used in design of the UniAC2 axle counter system.

Keywords: System · High availability · Redundancy · Safety · Communication · Axle counting

1 Introduction

Safety related systems in railways require high availability to ensure continuous traffic operation. As a consequence, high quality components and proper maintenance are required. The standard EN 50126 defines availability of a product as "ability of an item to be in a state to perform a required function under given conditions at a given instant of time or over a given time interval, assuming that the required external resources are provided" [1]. The standard EN 50129 [2] defines assurance of correct hardware functionality as hardware architecture which achieves the required functionality with respect to reliability, availability, maintainability and safety. In current times, the most variable are the conditions in which the function operates and the requirements for reliability level. Systems for which the requirements specify increased availability are called high availability systems (HA). The increased availability of the system is affected, among others, by the reduction of faults (reliability) and by limiting the effects of a fault.

Technical concepts of availability are base on a knowledge of [1]:

- Reliability in terms of:
  - All possible system failure modes in the specified application and environment.
  - The frequency of the occurrence or the likelihood of each failure mode.
  - The consequences of each failure mode.

© Springer Nature Switzerland AG 2020
J. Mikulski (Ed.): TST 2020, CCIS 1289, pp. 415–425, 2020.
https://doi.org/10.1007/978-3-030-59270-7_31

– Maintainability in terms of:

  – Frequency and time for the performance of planned or unplanned maintenance.
  – Time for detection and identification of the faults.
  – Time for the restoration of the failed system (unplanned maintenance).

– Operation and maintenance in terms of:

  – All possible operation modes and required maintenance (talking into account cost issues), over the system life cycle.
  – The human factor issues.
  – Tools, facilities and procedures for effective maintenance of the system.

The following study addresses selected aspects from above list and does not exhaust the topic of system availability.

1.1 Single Point of Failure

"A single point of failure (SPOF) is a part of a system that, if it fails, will stop the entire system from working" [6]. SPOF shall be eliminated in the systems to achieve high availability. It is not possible to eliminate every SPOF in the system with a reasonable financial investment. It should be also considered that increased weight, size and power consumption are disadvantages of a fault-tolerant design [9].

Risk and impact analysis should be carried out to determine which SPOF is worth eliminating. Additionally, customer requirements or market needs can define it. Evaluation of a potential SPOF includes identification of critical components of a complex system that can cause system failure in case of that component failure of malfunction.

The following pictures present the idea of single point of failure (SPOF). Taking into account common approach to power supply, there are many single points of failure, as it is shown in the Fig. 1.

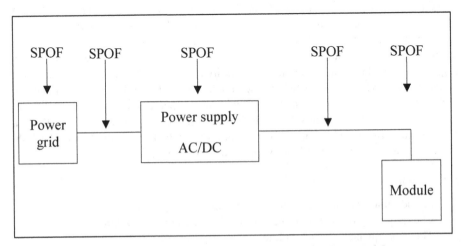

Fig. 1. Single points of failure in a power supply bus [own study]

After availability analysis during the design phase, some of these single points of failure can be eliminated for example by using a redundant power supply (AC/DC converters), as shown in the Fig. 2.

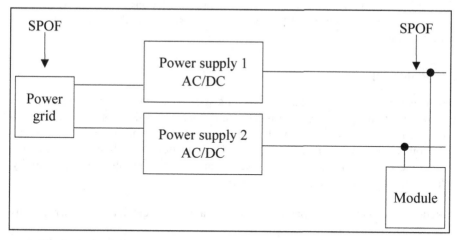

Fig. 2. Redundancy of single points of failure in a power supply bus [own study]

In order to further increase the reliability of power supply in the system, it is possible to eliminate the remaining SPOFs through two power sources or for example a battery backup, as shown in the Fig. 3.

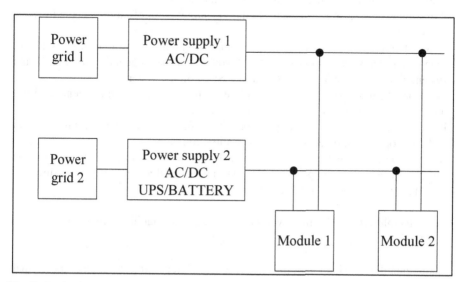

Fig. 3. Redundancy of all components – no single point of failure in a power supply bus [own study]

At the hardware level, SPOF elimination is usually associated with addition of redundant components or modules. This increases the cost, weight, and size of each piece of the device.

At the software level, SPOF elimination can often be carried out based on the same hardware, but with algorithms prepared for redundant solutions.

At the communication level, SPOF elimination is usually based on device redundancy or route redundancy.

1.2 High Availability

"High availability (HA) is a characteristic of a system, which aims to ensure an agreed level of operational performance, usually uptime, for a higher than normal period" [7]. It should be the goal of any system with high availability requirements, such as axle counters or other components of railway systems. The reduction of reliability and availability risks of the system helps to decrease losses of railway system (railway line availability, delays etc.). Those risks can be scaled down by:

- Reduction of a failure number reduces loss of railway system. It improves a reliability of the system in total.
- Reduction of a failure impact reduces loss of railway system. It improves availability of the system in total.

The main principles of systems design to achieve high availability are:

- Minimisation or elimination of single points of failure (SPOF). Specific component malfunction shall not cause failure of the system in total.
- Provision of duplicate components so that no single point of failure is able to cause loss of function.
- Efficient and reliable way to crossover redundant systems or components. Switching time of a component responsible for crossover shall not influence operation of the system. Crossover point shall not be a new SPOF in the system.
- Isolation of failure. In case when a failure occurs, the failing component shall not interfere with the normal operation of the system.
- Provision of degraded mode of operation when a failure occurs. Part of functions can still be in operation, others can perform limited functions.
- Supervision of the technical state of the system. Failure of one component may be invisible for the system operation, but shall be detected and reported to ensure it is fixed before next malfunction occurs.

Other principles, that are directly related to High Availability, are maintainability concepts:

- Maintainability: Reduction of time between repair start and restoration of the normal operation.
- Maintainability: Reduction of logistic delay by proper staff, equipment and spare parts management.

At the system design level, the technique used to improve availability is very often redundancy. Its design requires analysis of failure detection and common cause of failures. Redundant systems are most frequently divided into:

- passive redundancy – HA by excess capacity, for example two redundant power supplies. Failure of one power supply is not considered to be a system failure because normal operation mode is continued and there is no loss of functions or availability.
- active redundancy – HA by automatic detection of failure and automatic reconfiguration of the system. System reconfiguration can bypass the failed component. This method is frequently used in network management.

Another type of redundancy classification is [10]:

- space redundancy – it is related to additional components and functions. It can be classified as:

  - Hardware redundancy.
  - Software redundancy.
  - Information redundancy.

- time redundancy – it is related to additional computation or data transmission. The computation or transmission is repeated and its result is compared with the previous result.

Redundant systems can also be characterised by their downtime. It means that a crossover function can cause a non-zero time to restore function by switching between a failed component and a component in operation. It is possible to design a system with zero downtime, using already known techniques.

Fault tolerance is also related to the concept of high availability (HA). It means "the property that enables a system to continue operating properly in the event of the failure of (or one or more faults within) some of its components" [8].

The aim of a redundant system should be to satisfy all redundancy requirements according to the abovementioned divisions and definitions.

2   High Availability in UniAC2 Axle Counting System

The UniAC2 axle counting system is intended to monitor the track vacancy and sections on railway lines, shunting and marshalling yards with low, medium and high traffic, railway sidings, tram depots and loops, and lightweight railway lines. The UniAC2 system is a new generation, modular solution designed to address high availability requirements of the modern signalling subsystems.

This part describes solutions that increase the availability of the UniAC2 system and its relations with other systems.

Among others, the following techniques were used:

- Power supply redundancy.

- Communication redundancy.
- Functional redundancy at the software level.

To provide redundancy, more components are used in the system. It leads to more complex system and can impact availability negatively because of higher amount of potential failure points. In case of UniAC2 system, the following principle was defined: redundancy implementation shall be as simple as possible.

More detailed description of above mentioned techniques can be found further below.

2.1 Power Supply HA

Power supply can be seen as one of the critical points of any system, therefore power redundancy is widely used in numerous industries. Redundancy solutions have been known for years and have even been implemented as COTS solutions. This reduced the expenditure required, among others, for design, the number of components and, consequently, the final price of the product.

Power supply in axle counter UniAC2 is characterised by:

- Independent power lines on input to the system. E.g. one from power grid, second from battery.
- Independent power supplies in cassette (PW1, PS2). Range 18...72 V.
- Hot swap function of power supplies in cassette.
- Independent power supply buses in cassette (V1, V2).
- Independent inputs on the AXM module with overvoltage, overcurrent protection and isolation.

The chosen solution is an example of passive redundancy. The failure of one power supply does not lead to a system failure because the system is still in operation and there is no loss of functions or availability (Fig. 4).

Redundant power supplies increase availability of the system significantly. In case of a failure, the damaged power supply has to be replaced during repair procedure. The hot swap function allows to replace the damaged component with no loss to normal operation, at the same time providing full availability of the system. The solution with a single backup is known as single point tolerant and it represents the vast majority of fault-tolerant systems. In that kind of systems, the mean time between failures (MTBF) should be long enough to allow the operator to fix system (mean time to repair – MTTR) before the second failure occurs and possible backup fail.

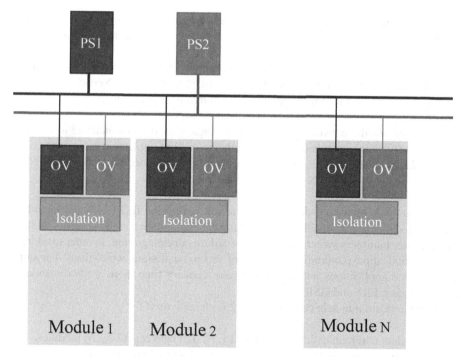

Fig. 4. Redundancy of power supply in UniAC2 [13]

2.2 Communication HA [11, 12]

In modern electronics systems, several transmission systems can be defined as a part of connection between subsystems and also as connection between internal modules and functional blocks. Some of these systems belong to non safety related transmission systems. Safety requirements are generally implemented in safety related hardware and safety related software. Because of that, at the level of "safety related application" and "safety related transmission function" adequate techniques shall be used to keep safety level according to requirements.

In communication subsystems highly reliable network components alleviate the potential for failure of transmission, but also network redundancy is beneficial in order to ensure continuity and avoids disruption of critical communication, as it limits the risk of losing of availability in case of failure.

Redundancy could be implemented [4, 5] as:

– dynamic (standby, serial), or
– static (parallel, workby).

Dynamic redundancy does not actively participate in the control. A switchover logic decides whether to insert redundancy and put it to work. This allows to share redundancy and load, implement partial redundancy and reduce the failure rate of redundancy. On the other hand, such switchover takes time.

Static redundancy with costly total duplication provides seamless switchover, continuously exercise redundancy, increase fault detection coverage and provide fail-safe behaviour.

In order to provide high availability networks, several methods were implemented in many industrial applications. The "Highly Available Automation Networks" selected many redundancy methods that could be divided into two main categories:

– redundancy in the network, e.g. redundant rings, with devices attached to a single bridge only (singly attached devices), while the bridges implement redundancy,
– redundancy in the devices, using devices with two network interfaces attached to redundant networks (doubly attached devices)

The methods above are described in the suite of norms IEC 62439 [3] including Parallel Redundancy Protocol (PRP), implements "redundancy in the devices" method that provides bumpless switchover in case of failure or reintegration. In order to address specific application requirements the set of recommendations were given. For critical real-time applications with requested zero recovery time there are two standards recommended: PRP and HSR.

Communication in axle counter UniAC2 is characterised by:

– Independent communication busses (NET1, NET2) between all AXM modules.
– Independent communication busses with external interlocking system.
– Zero recovery time.
– Redundant protocol – PRP based.

One of the main challenges for the implemented solution is to provide high availability transmission system for communication between all AXM modules over Ethernet network. The individual logic peer-to peer connections ensure the quasi-continuous exchange of states between unrestrictedly defined AXM modules.

PRP redundancy protocol implements redundancy in the devices, through doubly attached nodes operating according to PRP (DANPs).

As a final result, the tailored solution was developed around bus topology with two separate networks MAG_NET1 and MAG_NET2 connecting local and distant AXM modules (Fig. 5), using proprietary UniPRP protocol.

Each AXM module has two ports and is attached to Network 1 (MAG_NET1) and Network 2 (MAG_NET2). Information transferred between AXM modules is sent via both networks in parallel. In case of damage of one network, the second network is enough to deliver messages on time. Redundancy on this level is executed in Black Channel unit. Safety Channel sends one message (MESSAGE), that I doubled on Black Channel level and it is send via MAG_NET1 (MESSAGE1i) and MAG_NET2 (MESSAGE2i). Black Channel on relevant AXM module (receiver) receives MESSAGE1i and MESSAGE2i. The first MessageXi ($X = 1,2$) is transferred to Safety Channel; second message is discarded as a duplicate.

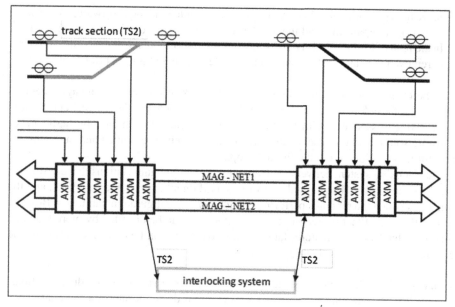

Fig. 5. Redundancy of transmission system [own study]

2.3 Functional HA

To address high availability requirements of the modern signalling solutions, the UniAC2 system consists of unified AXM modules which exchange information over the embedded Ethernet network. On the functional level, several redundant solutions or availability improvements are implemented as a software algorithms.

Among others the following solutions are prepared to improve availability:

- At the protocol level, the chosen solution is based on the PRP (Parallel Redundancy Protocol), mentioned in the previous paragraph. This solution eliminates part of SPOFs and can be considered to be an example of passive redundancy.
- At the level of frame repetition, the implemented solution is "time redundancy", additional network transmissions mean that the loss of a defined number of frames shall not result in loss of system availability.
- At the level of data processing algorithms, the chosen solution allows to restore state of a track section after communication is reconnected, based on the state of that track section defined before the loss of communication and on the locally processed data of the disconnected modules.
- At the level of data processing algorithms, the solution enables processing of selected axle counter functions with the same data but on different modules. It is an example of SPOF elimination.
- At the level of data processing algorithms, the solution allows to separate external interference affecting signals from the track (e.g. stimulation of the wheel sensor located on the road – tramway market) from the real stimulation of the wheel sensors by the wheel.

- In the field of Maintainability, by unifying the modules and their software, a significant reduction in repair time and the number of spare parts needed has been achieved.
- In the field of Maintainability, by storing configurations outside the modules, it is easy to remove faults and replace damaged modules without requiring prior configuration.

The techniques mentioned above reduce the risk of loss in the railway system by reduction of a failure impact. They are related to fault-tolerant design concept. System fault is often associated with the system environment. In such case by hardware or software solutions the impact of the error is imperceptible or limited and the functions are still in operation within the limited scope.

Interlocking system delivers a different kind of redundant solutions that are specific for the local market. The unified software is used on all axle counter modules, and the functions which the modules perform depend only on configuration parameter. Because of that the same functions computing the same data can be operated by more than one module. Thanks to this feature, fault-tolerant solutions can be delivered between axle counting system and interlocking system:

- In case of a node failure, a StandBy module can take over Online module functions. The time of switching function is so short that it does not interrupt the continuous operation of the railway system. The switching function can be configured on the axle counter or on a interlocking system.
- In case of one network failure, the Online module can provide data telegrams via a single network from both safety channels.
- In case of more than one external system, e.g. interlocking system and user panel, a single axle counter module (AXM) is enough to deliver consistent data telegrams to both of them.

3 Conclusion

In a demanding industrial environment, it is not possible to avoid faults. System reliability depends entirely not only on the reliability of its own components, but also on components that cooperate with it or provide a specific service. It can be external power supply, telecommunication devices used in connection with remote devices, existing wiring cables or others. Additionally, interferences occurring in the industrial environment, such as railway market, increase the likelihood of faults.

The reliability of internal components should be a subject to analysis and design, followed by monitoring and continuous improvement. Especially prediction of the ever-increasing level of external interference is crucial for rail system operation. Basing their design only on today's requirements and experiences is insufficient. With the rapidly changing level of technology and the increase in interference from the environment in which they work, it is not possible to provide efficient and highly available operation for the next 20–30 years if one decides to stick only to the current situation.

The reliability of external components should also be analysed and techniques adequate to results should be used. Some of these techniques can lower the risks of system failure (redundant network, power supplies); other can lower impact of the failure (fast reconnection in case of connection lost, robust design).

The supervision of the system by monitoring procedures and functions increases availability significantly by measures such as lowering of logistic delay. The embedded monitoring system of UniAC2 ensures that the diagnostic data registered on the AXM level is collected on the system level by a specialized diagnostic module for the notifications and further analysis.

References

1. EN 50126:2017 EN 50129:2018 Railway applications – Communications, Signaling and processing systems – Safety related electronic systems for signaling (2018)
2. EN 50129:2018 Railway applications – Communications, Signaling and processing systems – Safety related electronic systems for signaling (2018)
3. EN 62439 series. Industrial communication networks – High availability automation networks Part 1–7
4. Hirschmann/Belden: WP1003-White paper. Media Redundancy Concepts. High availability in Industrial Ethernet. http://belden.picturepark.com/Website/Download.aspx?DownloadToken=b427cf97-d5bc-4628-b41a-57d3d2eca706&Purpose=AssetManager&mime-type=application/pdf. Accessed 14 Dec 2019
5. Kirrmann, H., Dzung D.: Selecting a standard redundancy method for highly available industrial networks. In: Proceedings of 2006 WFCS, IEEE International Workshop on Factory Communication Systems, pp. 387–394 (2006)
6. Designing Large-scale LANs – Page 31, K. Dooley, O'Reilly (2002)
7. High availability. https://en.wikipedia.org/wiki/High_availability. Accessed 06 Mar 2020
8. Adaptive Fault Tolerance and Graceful Degradation, Oscar González et al., University of Massachusetts - Amherst (1997)
9. Dubrova, E.: Fault-Tolerant Design, Springer, New York (2013). https://doi.org/10.1007/978-1-4614-2113-9
10. Avizienis, A.: Fault-tolerant systems. IEEE Trans. Comput. **25**(12), 1304–1312 (1976)
11. Wołoszyk, P., Buława, M.: Safe communication for railway transport using the example of axle counter. In: Mikulski, J. (ed.) TST 2019. CCIS, vol. 1049, pp. 83–92. Springer, Cham (2019). https://doi.org/10.1007/978-3-030-27547-1_7
12. Buława, M., Wołoszyk, P.: Transmission redundancy in safety systems for railway transport using the example of the axle counter. In: Mikulski, J. (ed) Management Perspective for Transport Telematics, Springer, Heidelberg, CCIS 897 (2018)
13. UniAC2 axle counting system. Technical documentation

General About Telematics

Management of Processes of the Diagnosis and Treatment of Acute Myocardial Infarction Using Telematics Systems

Lukasz P. Gawinski[1]([✉]) and Remigiusz Kozlowski[2]([✉])

[1] Department of Management and Logistics in Health Care,
Medical University of Lodz, Lindleya 6, Lodz, Poland
lgaw@gumed.edu.pl
[2] University of Lodz, Matejki 22/26, Lodz, Poland
rjk5511@gmail.com

Abstract. In accordance with European standards, every patient with suspected acute myocardial infarction should have a 12 – leads electrocardiographic (ECG) performed as soon as possible to establish a proper diagnosis. The correct interpretation of the ECG record is crucial for the quick qualification of the patient for the appropriate treatment. If ST segment elevation myocardial infarct (STEMI) is diagnosed, the most optimal treatment is performing primary percutaneous coronary intervention (PCI) in no more than 120 min. Network between hospitals with various levels of referentiality linked by efficient ambulance service was introduced in Poland in order to optimize the treatment of patients with STEMI and minimize time delays. The essence of the functioning of this network is the pre-hospital selection of patients with STEMI and their transport directly to the hospital offering 24/7 primary PCI programme, bypassing non-PCI- hospitals. Commercial telematics systems available on the market facilitate the process of diagnosis and treatment patient with STEMI. The system consists of several transmitting stations (modems) located in ambulances, which enable the transmission of ECG to the receiving station situated in the PCI - hospital, which allows to immediately put the correct diagnosis. Modems are coupled with defibrillators, which are necessary to perform 12-lead ECG and collect patient vital signs. Moreover, the system allows the automatic transmission of clinical data and vital signs of the patient, automatic notification (via e-mail, SMS) of all necessary members of medical staff about transport of the patient with infarction, provide an application for mobile devices enabling cardiologist to conduct remote consultations of ECG recordings.

Keywords: Diagnostic process of myocardial infarction · Telematics in cardiology · Management of cardiac diagnostics processes

1 Introduction

The 21st century is a period of dynamic development of computer technology, robotization and digitization. It is also a period of very rapid development of mobile technologies

© Springer Nature Switzerland AG 2020
J. Mikulski (Ed.): TST 2020, CCIS 1289, pp. 429–442, 2020.
https://doi.org/10.1007/978-3-030-59270-7_32

and IT networks. On the other hand, in the same 21st century, the incidence of so-called civilization diseases, to which the World Health Organization has already included coronary artery disease (CAD) for a long time, is increasing. It is estimated that civilization diseases, also known as the 21st century epidemic, cause over 80% of all deaths. The obvious fact is that the development of technology relieves man in many aspects, facilitating his everyday life. Unfortunately, the price we have to pay for it is quite high. Urbanization and industrialization of the environment, air pollution, decreased physical activity, sedentary life style, fast and unhealthy nutrition and a fast pace of life are directly related to the global, rapid increase in the incidence of CAD. The 21st century is also a period of dynamic development of medicine, in particular cardiology. The development leap that has taken place over the last 30 years in the diagnosis and treatment of CAD is huge. Currently, cardiology uses the latest developments in information technology. The dynamic development of this medical discipline would be impossible without the achievements of modern technology. Nowadays, cardiology could easily be called "cardiology of guidelines". Currently, practically every cardiological disease has carefully developed, regularly updated guidelines for diagnosis, treatment and prognosis. The internationalization of these guidelines is also an important highlight. The European Society of Cardiology (ESC), which is responsible for preparation of these guidelines, ensures that every cardiologist in Europe has easy access and can apply the same standards of treatment and diagnosis. This work aims to present the possibilities recommended by ESC to apply modern technologies in the process of diagnosis and treatment of myocardial infarction. Therefore, while selecting this technology we should among others: adjust advanced technologies to the needs; make sure that the new technologies can be easily integrated with the technologies that had already been used and make sure that specialists and servicemen who will set up and deal with maintenance of the new technologies are easily available. These are the necessary conditions to achieve good results from their use [54].

2   Diagnostic and Treatment of Acute Myocardial Infarction

2.1   Coronary Artery Disease - Morbidity and Mortality

CAD and myocardial infarction (MI) as its final clinical presentation is one of the most serious medical, economic and social problems of the 21st century. CAD and stroke are collectively referred to as cardiovascular diseases (CVD) and they are the leading cause of mortality in Europe as a whole, responsible for over 3.9 million deaths a year, or 45% of all deaths. In men, CVD accounts for 1.8 million deaths (40% of all deaths), while in women it is responsible for 2.1 million deaths (49% of all deaths). By comparison, cancer – the next most common cause of death – accounts for just under 1.1 million deaths (24%) in men and just under 900,000 deaths (20%) in women respectively. CAD is the leading single cause of mortality in Europe, responsible for 862,000 deaths a year (19% of all deaths) among men and 877,000 deaths (20%) among women each year. Comparing the CVD mortality burden across individual European countries reveals substantial variation, with a higher burden typically found in Central and Eastern European countries compared to that in Northern, Southern and Western countries. CAD is estimated to cost the EU economy €59 billion a year: 28% of the overall cost of CVD. Of the total cost of

CAD in the EU, 32% (€19 billion) is due to direct health care costs, 33% (€20 billion) to productivity losses and 35% (€21 billion) to the informal care of people with CAD [1]. In Poland, 21,044 men (10.6% of all deaths among men) and 17,494 women (9.6% of all deaths among women) died of coronary artery disease in 2014 (latest available year) [1].

2.2 Pathophysiology of Myocardial Infarction

MI is pathologically defined as myocardial cell death due to ischaemia [2]. Coronary arteries located on the surface of the heart are responsible for the blood supply to the heart. At the end of the 19th century, papers suggesting a link between coronary artery occlusion and MI [3] were published, but it was not until the early 20th century that the first clinical descriptions appeared between coronary artery thrombus formation and associated clinical symptoms [4, 5]. Atherosclerotic processes underlie the development of coronary artery disease (as well as its extreme clinical presentation which is MI). Atherosclerosis is a chronic inflammatory disease of the arteries, characterized by the formation of characteristic changes in the walls of the vessels called atherosclerotic plaques, composed of a lipid core, a thin connective tissue cover (the so-called cap) and inflammatory infiltration cells. The formation of a thrombus blocking blood flow in the coronary artery is the result of rupture or damage to the atherosclerotic plaque. The occurrence of this phenomenon requires the coexistence of at least 3 factors: 1) a stimulus damaging the plaque, which may be an external factor (e.g. increase of blood pressure) or an internal factor (e.g. activation of metalloproteinases digesting the tissue cover of the plaque, secondary to stimulating the inflammatory process in 2) susceptibility of damage to the so-called vulnerable plaque, which causes the injurious stimulus to be able to erode or rupture the connective tissue plaque cover 3) with an adequate tendency to form an intravascular thrombus [6, 7].

2.3 Definition and Clinical Symptoms of Myocardial Infarction

Today, the concept of MI means acute ischaemia of the heart, which results from the global imbalance between oxygen supply and oxygen demand. MI may have a complex and diverse pathophysiology, heterogeneous clinical, electrocardiographic and enzymatic presentation. In clinical conditions, myocardial ischaemia can most often be identified based on the history and electrocardiographic image. Typical symptoms of cardiac ischaemia include chest pain/discomfort radiating to the upper limb, lower jaw or epigastrium when resting, as well as equivalents of ischemic symptoms such as dyspnea or fatigue. Discomfort is often diffuse; is not well positioned and does not depend on body position or movement. However, these symptoms are not specific to myocardial ischaemia and may occur in other conditions such as gastrointestinal, nervous, lung or osteoarticular disorders. MI can occur with unusual symptoms such as palpitations or sudden cardiac arrest, and even without symptoms.

2.4 Classified of Myocardial Infarction

Currently, two main divisions of MI are distinguished, which overlap each other: 1) depending on the pathophysiology 2) depending on the electrocardiographic image.

In everyday clinical practice, the second division based on electrocardiographic image analysis is much more important, as it sets specific methods and standards of treatment in this way. We distinguish myocardial infarction with ST segment elevation (STEMI) and myocardial infarction with non - ST segment elevation (NSTEMI). The mechanism of STEMI is typically responsible for the acute coronary artery occlusion in the process described above. In this paper, we will mainly deal with the logistics and organization of the STEMI treatment, because it is associated with a high pre-hospital mortality rate and requires the implementation of immediate therapeutic procedures. Globally, the relative incidence of STEMI is decreasing, while for NSTEMI it is increasing [8, 9]. Perhaps the most complete European STEMI register exists in Sweden, where the incidence of STEMI in 2015 was 58/100 thousand persons/year [10]. In other European countries, the incidence is 43–144/100,000 persons/year [11]. There is a consistent tendency for STEMI to occur more frequently in younger people than in older people, as well as in men compared to women [10, 12]. Several recent studies have highlighted the reduction in post-STEMI mortality in short- and long-term follow-up, which occurred with more frequent use of reperfusion therapy, primary percutaneous coronary intervention (PCI), modern anticoagulant therapy [13–15]. Nevertheless, the risk of death remains significant; in-hospital mortality among unselected STEMI patients in national registries is 4–12% [16], and coronary angiography registers report that the risk of death within 1 year after STEMI is approximately 10% [17, 18].

2.5 Selection of Reperfusion Strategies

The best form of treatment for STEMI is reperfusion therapy, which is based on restoring the patency of the artery that causes the infarction, the so-called infract-related artery (IRA). With total coronary occlusion, the time that passes from the beginning of the infarction to the restoration of patency in the artery is very important. The sooner this happens, the final myocardial damage is smaller, and the final prognosis is better. The time to intravenous artery opening also affects the incidence of peri-infarct complications (including potentially fatal cardiac arrhythmias, free wall of heart rupture, and ventricular septal rupture). Primary coronary angioplasty is the preferred reperfusion strategy for patients with STEMI within 12 h of onset of symptoms, provided it can be performed appropriately quickly (i.e. within 120 min after diagnosis of STEMI) by an experienced team of invasive cardiologists. Primary coronary angioplasty should be understood as unblocking the infarcted artery with a balloon, stent or other device. In centers performing many PCI procedures, a lower incidence of death is observed among patients undergoing primary PCI [19, 20]. That is why it seems so important to create a national network of highly specialized centers with extensive experience in the treatment of MI. The second form of reperfusion therapy is pharmacological fibrinolytic treatment, which consists of intravenous administration of drugs aimed at dissolving the blockage thrombus in the coronary artery. In the past, several randomized clinical trials have been conducted that have demonstrated that primary coronary angioplasty in experienced centers is definitely more beneficial than fibrinolysis, resulting in reduced mortality, the incidence of recurrent MI and the frequency of strokes (assuming treatment delay is similar) [21, 22].

2.6 Time Delays

According to the current standards of the ESC for the treatment of STEMI [24], the absolute time from diagnosis of STEMI to reperfusion during PCI (i.e. wire crossing of IRA) was set at 120 min. Assuming that the maximum delay from diagnosis of STEMI to administration of a fibrinolytic drug bolus is 10 min, the absolute time to start invasive treatment equal to 120 min corresponds to the relative delay associated with PCI in the range 110–120 min (this is the time consistent with the identified values in studies and registers as the delay limit for choosing PCI instead of fibrinolysis) [23–25]. If pharmacological fibrinolytic therapy is chosen as the reperfusion strategy, the goal is to inject the bolus of fibrinolytics within 10 min from STEMI diagnosis, while the time expected from the patient's first medical contact (FMC) to make the correct diagnosis should not be less than 10 min. The latter requirement set for Emergency Medical System (EMS) coming to the place of a call outside the hospital the task of quickly and correctly interpreting the electrocardiogram (ECG) record, which seems particularly difficult assuming that recently the majority of members of EMS are paramedics with no high level of experience in interpreting ECG. According to the above recommendations, if the estimated time to primary PCI (devoted to transport to the Catheterization laboratory (CL)) is longer than 120 min, administration of fibrinolytic drugs should be considered (if possible even in pre-hospital conditions) and subsequent immediate transport to the PCI -center [26, 27]. Further management of a patient in a hospital who has been given fibrinolytic therapy at place of a call depends on the effectiveness of this treatment: rescue PCI (immediately after the patient is transported to the PCI center) is indicated in the event of fibrinolysis failure (i.e. normalization/reduction of ST segment elevation by < 50% within 60–90 min after administration of the fibrinolytic drug), as well as presence of hemodynamic or electrical instability, increasing ischaemia or persistent chest pain [28], while after successful fibrinolysis, a strategy for routine early PCI is recommended (preferably 2–24 h after fibrinolysis) [29, 30]. In the event of MI occurs in a patient presenting at PCI- center, the time between STEMI diagnosis and the wire crossing should be less than 60 min. The treatment regimen described above for patients with STEMI generally refers to patients whose time from onset of symptoms is not more than 12 h. Where this time is more than 12 h and less than 48 h, the primary PCI strategy should be chosen in patients presenting 1) ECG evidence of ongoing ischaemia; 2) persistent or recurrent pain with dynamic ECG changes, and 3) persistent or recurring pain, including signs of heart failure (HF), shock or malignant arrhythmia.

2.7 Electrocardiographic Criteria for the Diagnosis of STEMI

Analyzing the above guidelines, one can clearly see the importance of fast and proper assessment of ECG in a patient suspected of having MI and the time needed to transport the patient to PCI -center. Each patient with chest pain suggestive of MI should have an electrocardiographic test as soon as possible. If the ECG image is ambiguous, the ECG registration should be repeated and, if possible, the obtained records should be compared with the previous ones. If it is not possible to interpret the pre-hospital ECG at the incident site, it is recommended to transmit the ECG from the registration site to the hospital reference center dealing with invasive treatment of MI [31]. We diagnose STEMI after following ECG changes: 2 or more contiguous leads with ST segment elevation ≥ 2.5 mm in men < 40 years old, ≥ 2 mm in men ≥ 40 years old or > 1.5 mm in women in leads V2 – V3 and/or ≥ 1 mm in other leads (if there is no left ventricular hypertrophy (LVH) or left bundle branch block (LBBB)) [32]. In patients with inferior MI, it is recommended to record right ventricular precordial leads (V3R and V4R) in search of ST elevation in order to detect the accompanying right ventricular infarction [32, 33]. Likewise, ST segment depression in leads V1-V3 suggests myocardial ischemia and confirmation should be considered by showing associated ST-segment elevation ≥ 0.5 mm in leads V7–V9 to detect posterior myocardial infarction. In the case of the LBBB, the electrocardiographic diagnosis of STEMI is relatively difficult. To facilitate this diagnosis, quite complex algorithms have been proposed [34, 35], but they do not provide diagnostic certainty [36]. It seems that one of the best indicators of STEMI is the presence of concordant ST-segment elevation (i.e. in leads with positive deflection of the QRS complex) [37]. Also, the presence of ventricular pacing may prevent correct interpretation of ST segment changes and urgent coronarography may be needed to confirm the diagnosis of myocardial infarction. In patients independent of ventricular pacing, reprogramming of the pacemaker may be considered, which will allow for the assessment of ECG changes during intrinsic heart rhythm, but such actions should not delay invasive diagnostics [38, 39]. It is important to repeat ECG recording or ECG monitoring for dynamic ST segment changes in unclear cases with a high clinical likelihood of MI. It should also be noted that in some patients with acute coronary artery occlusion, for example an occluded circumflex coronary artery [40, 41], acute venous graft closure or left main disease, ST segment elevation may not occur. This results in delayed invasive treatment implementation and worse prognosis. Some of these patients may be identified by extending the standard 12-lead ECG with V7-V9 leads. In any case, the suspicion of persistent myocardial ischaemia is an indication for coronary angiography, even in patients without diagnostic ST segment elevation [42, 43].

2.8 Organization of STEMI Treatment in Networks

In order to optimize the diagnosis and treatment process in accordance with the ESC recommendations, a network of highly specialized centers dealing with MI treatment and performing 24-h, 7 days a week primary coronary angioplasty procedure should been introduced. Optimal STEMI treatment should be based on a system comprising a network of invasive cardiology centers and cooperating regional hospitals connected by an efficient ambulance system. The goal of this system is to provide optimal care while minimizing delays, which will improve clinical outcomes. According to the ESC, such a system should be characterized by: a clear definition of the geographical areas of responsibility of a given invasive cardiology center; pre-hospital segregation of patients with STEMI and transporting them directly to the center of invasive cardiology bypassing non-PCI hospitals or hospitals without a 24 h a day, 7 days a week (24/7) primary PCI programme; after arriving at the appropriate hospital, the patient should be transferred directly to the CL passing the emergency department; patients arriving at a non-PCI hospital and waiting for transport to the appropriate center should be properly monitored and supervised by medical staff; if the ambulance crew did not recognize STEMI and the ambulance arrives at a non-PCI hospital, ambulance crew should wait for the diagnosis to be made and, if STEMI is diagnosed, should continue to transport the patient to the PCI center. To maximize staff experience, primary PCI centers should perform these procedures systematically, 24 h a day, 7 days a week, for all STEMI patients. Hospitals that cannot offer primary PCI 24 h a day, 7 days a week, should be allowed to perform primary PCI in patients already admitted for another reason who develop STEMI during their stay in hospital. The introduction of the well-functioning system described above increases the percentage of patients in whom reperfusion therapy is applied with the shortest possible delay [44, 45].

2.9   The Role of EMS

ESC guidelines place great emphasis on compliance and minimization of delay times. Delay dependent on the healthcare system can be minimized by organizational means relatively easier than patient-dependent delay. EMS is a very important link in this system. The ambulance transport system plays a key role in the logistics process of treating patients with STEMI [46, 47]. It is recommended that all ambulances be equipped with ECG recorders and defibrillators. Ambulance staff should be able to record an ECG and either interpret it or send it to an experienced staff of the Intensive Cardiac Care Unit (ICCU) for evaluation. Paramedics according to ESC guidelines should be trained to administer fibrinolytic drugs [48], because pre-hospital fibrinolysis is recommended when the estimated time from STEMI diagnosis to primary PCI is >120 min [49, 50].

3   The Use of Telematics Systems in Acute Myocardial Infarction

3.1   The Place of Telematics Systems in the STEMI Diagnostics Process- A Practical Approach

Commercial telematics systems available on the market facilitate the process of diagnosis and treatment patient with STEMI. Their primary role in the diagnosis of STEMI is to enable the EMS team to transmit an ECG record of a patient suspected of having a MI to an invasive cardiology center, where this record is analyzed by an experienced cardiologist working in ICCU or in the CL. Early correct diagnosis of STEMI allows to significantly accelerate the patient's transport to the appropriate center (bypassing non PCI hospitals), which correspond to a better final treatment result. After receiving the ECG transmission, the on-duty cardiologist can view the ECG record on the computer monitor or print it and then interpret it (confirm or not STEMI in ECG record). The next stage is the telephone contact with the EMS team present at the place of the incident with PCI center; EMS members provide information on the patient's clinical condition (symptoms, their duration, comorbidities, findings in the physical examination, vital signs), receive confirmation/exclusion diagnosis of STEMI in the ECG records and information as to the further qualification of the patient to the primary PCI strategy. The EMS team discusses by phone the travel time to the PCI center in given atmospheric conditions, administration of appropriate medications (anticoagulants, antiplatelet agents) is ordered. In case of critical ill patients cardiologist from PCI - center consults other necessary rescue operations, indicates the necessity administration of other drugs. If the on-duty cardiologist does not confirm diagnosis of STEMI, the EMS team is directed to ED of the nearest hospital for further assessment of the patient. In some cases, although the ECG has not confirmed STEMI, the patient is directly transported to the PCI center. These are patients with electrocardiographic features of severe cardiac ischaemia other than ST elevations in severe clinical condition (persistent stenocardia, cardiogenic shock, pulmonary edema, malignant cardiac arrhythmias). If the total time from FMC to wire crossing is expected to be longer than 120 min (due to, for example, poor weather conditions, ongoing treatment in CL with a predicted long duration), the on-duty cardiologist consults, discusses and coordinates the administration of fibrinolytic therapy by the EMS team at the scene of the incident. Because currently most EMS teams in Poland are composed of paramedics, the role of an experienced cardiologist who consults by phone and helps the EMS team seems not to be underestimated. After discussing the time of transport, the cardiologist from the PCI center notifies and activates CL, the ICCU and all their members on duty. While waiting for transport patient with STEMI in CL does not start the next procedure (a patient with STEMI should not wait for a free place on the operating table after arriving at the PCI center). Upon arrival at the PCI center, the patient is transported by EMS staff directly to CL, bypassing ED. If the transported patient is in a severe condition or requires mechanical ventilation about the patient's arrival at the PCI center the hospital resuscitation team is also notified. If the patient requires stabilization of vital functions, which for various reasons cannot be performed in an ambulance, these activities are performed by a previously called anesthesiologist in ED rooms (as an exception to the rule about transporting the patient directly to CL) and then is transferred to CL for primary PCI. All the procedures described above with the use of telematics systems are consistent with the guidelines for the treatment of STEMI described above, improving them and thereby increasing the survival rate of patients.

3.2 The Process of Using the Telematic System Physio-Control Lifenet 5.2

Currently, two competing telematics systems are commercially available in Poland. These are Physio-control Lifenet and ZOLL RescueNet Medgate. Their structure and operating principles are similar. In this study, we will focus on the first of these systems for several reasons:

– despite the fact that the scope of functionality of each of these systems is quite similar, one can notice a slight advantage on the Lifenet side,
– the Lifenet system is much more common,
– the author of this work has also been using this system for several years.

Each system consists of a number of transmitting stations (modems), which are located in ambulances. The modems are integrated with defibrillators, which are necessary for 12-lead ECG and collect vital signs of the patient. Another component of the system is the receiving station located in the PCI center (PC computer). With the help of the latter, the transmitted ECG records can be analyzed on the monitor screen or printed. Telematics systems used in cardiology in the last period of time have significantly expanded their capabilities beyond only the possibility of ECG transmission. The author discusses the possibilities of such a system in this work on the example of the latest version of Physio-control Lifenet 5.2. The system's operation is based on Medtronic's defibrillators from the LIFEPAK family. It is a versatile device, which depending on the model may include: a defibrillator, pacemaker, cardioverter, cardiomonitor, capnometer, pulse oximeter, blood pressure monitor. This device is in the equipment of EMS teams and is taken to the place of call to the patient (e.g. patient's home, street). If STEMI is suspected, a 12-lead ECG is performed, the patient's parameters (heart rate, blood pressure, blood saturation) are measured. Currently in many countries Electronic Patient Care Reporting (ePCR) is being introduced. Data in real time can be exported from medical equipment (such as LIFEPAK15 or other machines) directly to the ePCR. For the transmission of clinical data, the communication technology of mobile operators is used; currently the signal is used to connect to the Internet. The data is sent to a central server, which then, after identifying the recipient, sends information about the examination to the recipient. All transmissions are made using the TCP/IP technology [51]. The key and basic components of the system are:

- LIFENET Transmission Subscription - core transmitting subscription for EMS, which allows EMS agencies to get their LIFEPAK device onto the LIFENET System so that it can transmit the clinical date,
- LIFENET Alert Subscription - core receiving subscription for hospitals, which allows PCI hospital to receive clinical date of an incoming patient from the field, either through LIFENET Alert, text messages or emails,
- LIFENET Alert Software included as part of the LIFENET Alert subscription that is downloaded on a hospital's existing Windows® PC and allows PCI hospitals to receive alerts and emergent data related to incoming patients.

The Lifenet system also offers many new innovative tools, applications and capabilities. Using LIFENET Consult Mobile, an interactive iPhone® application, a hospital-based clinician can interact with a remote more experienced physician to speed critical decisions such as identifying a STEMI and rerouting to a PCI facility. LIFENET Adapter technology allows hospitals to standardize on one system and receive 12-lead ECGs from the field regardless of defibrillator manufacturer. The ePCR data integration features of LIFENET 5.2 give the power to capture more information on patient status, including vital signs, patient ID and chief complaint information and then use the simple LIFENET PC Gateway-interface to add that data to their hospital bound 12-lead ECG. LIFENET ePCR automatically capture data from ePCR applications. When medics are ready to submit their final event report to the hospital, LIFENET ePCR Delivery automatically sent data to hospital with every 12-lead ECG via trusted LIFENET connection from the field to deliver as a PDF, which can be easily stored or printed. At the hospital, LIFENET Alert consolidates all EMS transmissions into a single record, quickly providing a clearer progression of patient status. That means more time for planning and preparing the right treatment, more data about patients in pre-hospital environment, faster transfer of care and ensuring that patients are sent to the most appropriate department. And because clinicians already have access to critical prehospital 12-lead data via LIFENET 5.2, there's no need to spend time duplicating processes when the patient arrives at ED. LIFENET PC Gateway Software installed on a computer (i.e., a tablet PC) that can receive information from a LIFEPAK device and send that information to the LIFENET System using the computer's existing Internet connection. This allows EMS teams to either manually enter additional patient information to attach to a 12-lead ECG or data can automatically be attached from ePCR application. LIFENET OnePush Software provides automated protocol activation and team member notifications (all necessary personnel at once, from cardiologist from CL to pharmacy via email, text, or LIFENET Alert), helping clinicians respond more quickly, reduces clinician burdens and decreases workload. Equipment of EMS spends its time away from a central base— in a vehicle, being used to save patients, it can be challenging to manage. Web - based LIFENET Asset is a next innovation feature of Lifenet 5.2 provides a simple dashboard view that makes it easier to track the status of equipment — from location to battery life to usage — upload necessary, software updates, and manage setup options, even across a fleet of devices. LIFENET 5.2 also makes data transmission and analysis from those devices more powerful for EMS teams. LIFENET Connect lets crews utilize their wireless connection to transmit LIFEPAK monitor data directly from the ambulance into CODE-STAT™ software to help strengthen quality assurance and improvement initiatives focused on cardiac arrest response. CODE-STAT is a post-event review software which allows users to play back cases and provides access to continuous ECG data, chest compressions, and cardiopulmonary resuscitation (CPR) statistics and providing clear summary data and detailed case data to give EMS organizations a better picture of their responses to codes. This valuable feedback can dramatically improve efficacy of code response and CPR and assist organizations in determining where to direct training resources, which specific areas to target for improvement, and how they can help their teams meet performance goals. LIFENET Archive and LIFENET Export provide flexible solutions that allow hospitals to export the information they received from the field (12-lead ECG and vital signs reports) into their downstream record management systems. Data can be exported directly into GE MUSE or other applications, such as Philips® TraceMaster, that can import image files [53].

4 Conclusion

Telematics methods are playing an increasingly important role in modern medicine. Cardiology can be called a leader among medical fields when it comes to the use of modern ICT (Information and Communication Technologies). ESC guidelines for the diagnosis and treatment of MI have for several years already foreseen and recommend the use of modern technologies to improve and increase the effectiveness of treatment of patients with MI, which directly results in reducing of the mortality rate of these patients. The use of the Lifenet 5.2 system is an excellent example of application of ICT. Thanks to the innovative technology, LIFENET 5.2 is a system with versatile possibilities that effectively uses telematics technology to increase efficiency throughout the entire medical care cycle of a patient suspected of having MI, and provides critical information to help EMS teams reduce time to intervention. The LIFENET 5.2 system is an excellent tool for EMS teams, enabling the improvement of the response protocol and care for a patient with MI, ensures better efficiency of their work, and allows mutual transfer of relevant information within medical units and to maintaining constant contact while undertaking significant clinical decisions. On the other hand, hospital staff through Lifenet 5.2 receive prior, detailed notification of the patient's transport and a set of invaluable, preliminary data about his condition, necessary to provide him with proper care. Currently in Poland there is a very well developed network of CL with the vast majority of possibilities for ECG transmission. This successful course is caused by, among others also through the use of appropriate forms of inter - organizational cooperation [52]. Further improvement of results will not be possible without improving these technologies and adapting processes to the opportunities they offer.

References

1. Wilkins, E., et al.: European Cardiovascular Disease Statistics 2017. European Heart Network, Brussels (2017)
2. Jennings, R.B., Ganote, C.E.: Structural changes in myocardium during acute ischemia. Circ. Res. **35**(Suppl 3), 156–172 (1974)
3. Hammer, A.: Ein fall von thrombotischem verschlusse einer der kranzarterien des herzens. Wien Med Wschr. **28**, 97–102 (1878)
4. Obraztzow, V.P., Straschesko, N.D.: Zur Kenntnis der Thrombose der Koronararterien des Herzens. Z Klin Med. **71**, 116–132 (1910)
5. Herrick, J.B.: Clinical features of sudden obstruction of the coronary arteries. JAMA **59**(23), 2015–2022 (1912)
6. Bentzon, J.F., et al.: Mechanisms of plaque formation and rupture. Circ. Res. **114**(12), 1852–1866 (2014)
7. Falk, E., et al.: Update on acute coronary syndromes: the pathologists' view. Euro Heart J. **34**(10), 719–728 (2013)
8. Morrow, D.A., et al.: TRA 2P–TIMI 50 Steering Committee and Investigators. Vorapaxar in the secondary prevention of atherothrombotic events. N. Engl. J. Med. **366**(15), pp. 1404–1413 (2012)
9. Ng, V.G., et al.: The prognostic importance of left ventricular function in patients with ST-segment elevation myocardial infarction: the HORIZONS-AMI trial. Euro Heart J. Acute Cardiovasc. Care. **3**(1), 67–77 (2014)
10. Sutton, N.R., et al.: The association of left ventricular ejection fraction with clinical outcomes after myocardial infarction: findings from the acute coronary treatment and intervention outcomes network (ACTION) Registry-Get With the Guidelines (GWTG) Medicare-linked database. Am. Heart J. **178**, 65–73 (2016)
11. Ponikowski, P., et al.: Authors/Task Force Members. 2016 ESC Guidelines for the diagnosis and treatment of acute and chronic heart failure: the Task Force for the diagnosis and treatment of acute and chronic heart failure of the European Society of Cardiology (ESC)Developed with the special contribution of the Heart Failure Association (HFA) of the ESC. Eur. Heart J. **37**(27), 2129–2200 (2016)
12. Di Donato, M., et al.: Effectiveness of surgical ventricular restoration in patients with dilated ischemic cardiomyopathy and unrepaired mild mitral regurgitation. J. Thorac. Cardiovasc. Surg. **134**(6), 1548–1553 (2007)
13. Mega, J.L., et al.: ATLAS ACS 2–TIMI 51 Investigators. Rivaroxaban in patients with a recent acute coronary syndrome. N. Engl. J. Med. **366**(1), 9–19 (2012)
14. Weinsaft, J.W., et al.: Echocardiographic algorithm for post-myocardial infarction LV Thrombus: a gatekeeper for thrombus evaluation by delayed enhancement CMR. JACC Cardiovasc. Imaging. **9**(5), 505–515 (2016)

15. Pöss, J., et al.: Left ventricular thrombus formation after st-segment-elevation myocardial infarction: insights from a cardiac magnetic resonance multicenter study. Circ. Cardiovasc. Imag. **8**(10), e003417 (2015)
16. Solheim, S., et al.: Frequency of left ventricular thrombus in patients with anterior wall acute myocardial infarction treated with percutaneous coronary intervention and dual antiplatelet therapy. Am. J. Cardiol. **106**(9), 1197–1200 (2010)
17. Meurin, P., et al.: College National des Cardiologues Français, Collège National des Cardiologues des Hôpitaux Français, Paris, France. Incidence, diagnostic methods, and evolution of left ventricular thrombus in patients with anterior myocardial infarction and low left ventricular ejection fraction: a prospective multicenter study. Am. Heart. J. **170**(2), 256–262 (2015)
18. Delewi, R., Zijlstra, F., Piek, J.: Left ventricular thrombus formation after acute myocardial infarction. Heart **98**(23), 1743–1749 (2012)
19. Thiemann, D.R., et al.: The association between hospital volume and survival after acute myocardial infarction in elderly patients. N. Engl. J. Med. **340**(21), 1640–1648 (1999)
20. West, R.M., et al.: Impact of hospital proportion and volume on primary percutaneous coronary intervention performance in England and Wales. Eur. Heart J. **32**(6), 706–711 (2011)
21. Zijlstra, F., et al.: Long-term benefit of primary angioplasty as compared with thrombolytic therapy for acute myocardial infarction. N. Engl. J. Med. **341**(19), 1413–1419 (1999)
22. Keeley, E.C., Boura, J.A., Grines, C.L.: Primary angioplasty versus intravenous thrombolytic therapy for acute myocardial infarction: a quantitative review of 23 randomised trials. Lancet **361**(9351), 13–20 (2003)
23. Pinto, D.S., et al.: Hospital delays in reperfusion for ST-elevation myocardial infarction: implications when selecting a reperfusion strategy. Circulation **114**(19), 2019–2025 (2006)
24. Nallamothu, B.K., Bates, E.R.: Percutaneous coronary intervention versus fibrinolytic therapy in acute myocardial infarction: is timing (almost) everything? Am. J. Cardiol. **92**(7), 824–826 (2003)
25. Betriu, A., Masotti, M.: Comparison of mortality rates in acute myocardial infarction treated by percutaneous coronary intervention versus fibrinolysis. Am. J. Cardiol. **95**(1), 100–101 (2005)
26. Bonnefoy, E., et al.: CAPTIM Investigators. Comparison of primary angioplasty and prehospital fibrinolysis in acute myocardial infarction (CAPTIM) trial: a 5-year follow-up. Euro. Heart J. **30**(13), pp. 1598–1606 (2009)
27. Armstrong, P.W., et al.: STREAM investigative team. fibrinolysis or primary PCI in ST-segment elevation myocardial infarction. N Engl. J. Med. **368**(15): pp. 1379–1387 (2013)
28. Gershlick, A.H., et al.: REACT trial investigators. rescue angioplasty after failed thrombolytic therapy for acute myocardial infarction. N Engl J Med. **353**(26), 2758–2768 (2005)
29. Madan, M., et al.: Relationship between time to invasive assessment and clinical outcomes of patients undergoing an early invasive strategy after fibrinolysis for ST-segment elevation myocardial infarction: a patient-level analysis of the randomized early routine invasive clinical trials. JACC Cardiovasc Interv. **8**(1 Pt B), 166–174 (2015)
30. Cantor, W.J., et al.: TRANSFER-AMI Trial Investigators. Routine early angioplasty after fibrinolysis for acute myocardial infarction. N Engl. J. Med. **360**(26), 2705–2718 (2009)
31. Dhruva, V.N., et al.: ST-segment analysis using wireless technology in acute myocardial infarction (STAT-MI) trial. J. Am. Coll. Cardiol. **50**(6), 509–513 (2007)
32. ESC Guidelines for the management of acute myocardial infarction in patients presenting with ST-segment elevation: The Task Force for the management of acute myocardial infarction in patients presenting with ST-segment elevation of the European Society of Cardiology (ESC)European Heart Journal, vol. 39, Issue 2, pp. 119–177 (2018)

33. Lopez-Sendon, J., et al.: Electrocardiographic findings in acute right ventricular infarction: sensitivity and specificity of electrocardiographic alterations in right precordial leads V4R, V3R, V1, V2, and V3. J. Am. Coll. Cardiol. **6**(6), 1273–1279 (1985)
34. Sgarbossa, E.B., et al.: Electrocardiographic diagnosis of evolving acute myocardial infarction in the presence of left bundle-branch block. GUSTO-1 (Global Utilization of Streptokinase and Tissue Plasminogen Activator for Occluded Coronary Arteries) Investigators. N Engl. J. Med. **334**(8), pp. 481–487 (1996)
35. Wong, C.K., et al.: HERO-2 Trial Investigators. Patients with prolonged ischemic chest pain and presumed-new left bundle branch block have heterogeneous outcomes depending on the presence of ST-segment changes. J. Am. Coll. Cardiol. **46**(1), 29–38 (2005)
36. Shlipak, M.G., et al.: Should the electrocardiogram be used to guide therapy for patients with left bundle-branch block and suspected myocardial infarction? JAMA **281**(8), 714–719 (1999)
37. Lopes, R.D., et al.: Diagnosing acute myocardial infarction in patients with left bundle branch block. Am. J. Cardiol. **108**(6), 782–788 (2011)
38. Madias, J.E.: The nonspecificity of ST-segment elevation > or = 5.0 mm in V1-V3 in the diagnosis of acute myocardial infarction in the presence of ventricular paced rhythm. J. Electrocardiol. **37**(2), 135–139 (2004)
39. Sgarbossa, E.B., et al.: Early electrocardiographic diagnosis of acute myocardial infarction in the presence of ventricular paced rhythm. GUSTO-I investigators. Am. J. Cardiol. **77**(5), 423–424 (1996)
40. Krishnaswamy, A., Lincoff, A.M., Menon, V.: Magnitude and consequences of missing the acute infarct-related circumflex artery. Am. Heart J. **158**(5), 706–712 (2009)
41. From, A.M., et al.: Acute myocardial infarction due to left circumflex artery occlusion and significance of ST-segment elevation. Am. J. Cardiol. **106**(8), 1081–1085 (2010)
42. Rokos, I.C., et al.: Correlation between index electrocardiographic patterns and pre-intervention angiographic findings: insights from the HORIZONS-AMI trial. Catheter Cardiovasc. Interv. **79**(7), 1092–1098 (2012)
43. Stribling, W.K., et al.: Left circumflex occlusion in acute myocardial infarction (from the National Cardiovascular Data Registry). Am. J. Cardiol. **108**(7), 959–963 (2011)
44. Implementation of guidelines improves the standard of care: the Viennese registry on reperfusion strategies in ST-elevation myocardial infarction (Vienna STEMI registry). Circulation **113**(20), 2398–2405 (2006)
45. Henry, T.D., et al.: A regional system to provide timely access to percutaneous coronary intervention for ST-elevation myocardial infarction. Circulation **116**(7), 721–728 (2007)
46. Terkelsen, C.J., et al.: System delay and mortality among patients with STEMI treated with primary percutaneous coronary intervention. JAMA **304**(7), 763–771 (2010)
47. Huber, K., et al.: Task Force on Pre-hospital reperfusion therapy of the working group on thrombosis of the ESC. Pre-hospital reperfusion therapy: a strategy to improve therapeutic outcome in patients with ST-elevation myocardial infarction. Eur. Heart J. **26**(19), 2063–2074 (2005)
48. Björklund, E., et al.: Pre-hospital thrombolysis delivered by paramedics is associated with reduced time delay and mortality in ambulance-transported real-life patients with ST-elevation myocardial infarction. Euro Heart J. **27**(10), 1146–1152 (2006)
49. Steg, P.G., et al.: Comparison of angioplasty and prehospital thrombolysis in acute myocardial infarction (CAPTIM) Investigators. Impact of time to treatment on mortality after prehospital fibrinolysis or primary angioplasty: data from the CAPTIM randomized clinical trial. Circulation **108**(23), 2851–2856 (2003)
50. Bonnefoy, E., et al.: CAPTIM Investigators. Comparison of primary angioplasty and prehospital fibrinolysis in acute myocardial infarction (CAPTIM) trial: a 5-year follow-up. Eur Heart J. **30**(13), 1598–1606 (2009)

51. Maciejewski, R., Zubrzycki, J.: Inżynieria biomedyczna Telemedycyna Monografie – Politechnika Lubelska Lublin, pp. 90–92 (2015)
52. Kozłowski, R., Marek, M.: Forms of cooperation with the business environment in the process of technology entrepreneurship development. Res. Logist. Prod. (2083–4942), nr 1/2012, pp. 99 (2012)
53. Product Brochure Physio Control Lifenet 5.2 https://www.physio-control.com/uploadedFiles/Physio85/Contents/Workplace_and_Community/Products/3308272_D_LR.pdf
54. Kozłowski, R., Marek, M.: The identification of difficulties in using advanced technologies in the implementation of projects. Int. J. Bus. Manage. (2336–2197), vol. 3, no 4, pp. 56–57 (2015)

Telematic Support of Management Processes in Diagnosis and Treatment of Acute Myocardial Infarction in Poland

Lukasz P. Gawinski[1](✉) and Remigiusz Kozlowski[2](✉)

[1] Management and Logistics in Health Care, Medical University of Lodz, Lindleya 6, Lodz, Poland
lgaw@gumed.edu.pl

[2] University of Lodz, Matejki 22/26, Lodz, Poland
rjk5511@gmail.com

Abstract. Coronary artery disease is one of the most serious medical challenges of the 21st century. Thanks to the development of cardiology and medical technology, the treatment of myocardial infarction (MI) has become more and more effective in recent years. According to European standards, electrocardiogram (ECG) should be performed as soon as possible for every patient suspected of having a MI. Correct ECG interpretation is crucial for qualifying the patient for the appropriate treatment. If ST segment elevation myocardial infarction (STEMI) is diagnosed, the optimal treatment is primary coronary intervention (PCI) within 120 min since first medical contact with the patient. Patients diagnosed with STEMI should be transported directly to the hospital with the primary PCI program. In order to accelerate and facilitate the diagnosis of MI, telematic systems supporting the management of the diagnostic process have also been introduced for daily use. Lifenet 5.2 is the most common system operating for several years in Poland consisting of a number of transmitting stations (modems) located in ambulances that enable ECG transmission to the receiving station located in the catheterization laboratory, which allows immediate put to correct diagnosis. The modems are connected to defibrillators, which are necessary to perform an ECG and collect the patient's vital signs. This paper describes the process of diagnosis and treatment of STEMI using Lifenet 5.2 in the realities of the Polish health care system with particular emphasis on the key role of the Emergency Medical System, shows strengths of the system, their impact on the development of cardiology and on decrease in mortality rates due to MI, as well as limitations and local problems during the everyday use of this system.

Keywords: Diagnostic process of myocardial infarction · Telematics in cardiology · Logistics of clinical data transmission

1 Introduction

Coronary artery disease (CAD) has become one of the most serious medical problems of society in the 21st century. In addition to purely medical significance, this disease is

© Springer Nature Switzerland AG 2020
J. Mikulski (Ed.): TST 2020, CCIS 1289, pp. 443–455, 2020.
https://doi.org/10.1007/978-3-030-59270-7_33

also becoming a serious economic and social problem [1]. Due to the high incidence of CAD, the costs associated with treatment, payment of disability benefits and sickness benefits are increasing rapidly, constituting a significant burden on the state budget. Mortality due to myocardial infarction (MI) and stroke, which are jointly referred to as cardiovascular diseases (CVD) (their common denominator is the atherosclerotic process involving arteries) in Eastern and Central European countries in recent years has been definitely higher than in Western Europe. Only recent years have brought a significant improvement in this area and a significant reduction in mortality rates due to CVD (comparable to those observed in Western Europe) [2]. The reasons for this decline should, of course, be seen in the greater public awareness of the prevention of coronary artery disease and its risk factors, but it is also associated with a huge scientific and technological leap in the diagnosis and treatment of myocardial infarction. Currently, cardiology is, along with oncology, the fastest growing field of medicine. Modern cardiology is primarily cardiology based on evidence-based medicine. Hundreds of clinical trials that have taken place over the past 30 years have introduced cardiology into a new era of medicine: modern medicine based on hard scientific evidence, medicine based on recent technological and IT advances. Cardiology is one of the few (and probably the only) branches of medicine for which a set of guidelines for the diagnosis and treatment of practically every cardiological disease has been developed. It should be added here that these guidelines are regularly updated and made available free of charge to a wide international medical community. Guidelines for the treatment of myocardial infarction a lot of attention devoted to the use of the latest technological achievements: methods of invasive treatment and technology in the field of broadly understood telemedicine. Poland as a distinctive country of Central and Eastern Europe very quickly introduced to everyday medical practice modern, invasive methods of treatment of patient with MI, as well as telematic systems support decision making process during interpretation of ECG recordings what mostly led to a significantly decrease in the mortality rates of these patients. The use of telematics technologies has helped Polish cardiology achieve a very high global level. Poland can easily be called a leader in the field of Invasive Cardiology not only in Central and Eastern Europe, but also around the world. This paper presents the process of implementing telematics systems in Poland to facilitate diagnosis and treatment of MI, their impact on patients' access to modern, invasive methods of treating CAD, mortality of patients with MI and on the development of generally understood invasive cardiology in this country.

2   CVD Mortality in Europe in Late 20th and 21st Century

Cardiovascular diseases (CVD) remain in 21st century the leading cause of mortality and a major cause of morbidity in Europe. Each year CVD causes 3.9 million deaths in Europe and over 1.8 million deaths in the European Union (EU). It is estimated that CVD has been responsible in recent years for 45% of all deaths in Europe and 37% of all deaths in the EU. In men, CVD accounts for 1.8 million deaths (40% of all deaths), while in women it is responsible for 2.1 million deaths (49% of all deaths). CAD is the leading single cause of mortality in Europe, responsible for 862,000 deaths a year

(19% of all deaths) among men and 877,000 deaths (20%) among women each year. In Poland, 21,044 men (10.6% of all deaths among men) and 17,494 women (9.6% of all deaths among women) died of CAD in 2014 (latest available year) [2]. Considerable inequalities in the burden of these diseases still exist across the region. CVD mortality and prevalence rates are, on average, lower in the European Union (EU) than outside of the EU. Furthermore, among both EU and non-EU member states, rates of CVD mortality and morbidity tend to be higher in Central and Eastern European countries than in their Northern, Western and Southern European counterparts [2]. In the 20th century, these geographical disparities in mortality due to CAD were even greater. In Poland, male mortality rate due to CAD at the end of the 20th century was higher than in most Western and Southern European countries, but definitely lower than in other Central and Eastern European countries. As for the mortality rate of women in Poland due to CAD, it was comparable to the rates achieved in Western and Southern Europe at the end of the 20th century and, as in the case of men, definitely lower than in Central and Eastern European. Trends in CAD mortality in Poland were downward in the 20th century for both sexes. The only deviation from this rule are the years 1998–2000, where a significant, abrupt increase in these rates was observed (similarly for both sexes) (Fig. 1 and Fig. 2). The 21st century brought gradual equalization of CAD mortality rates in Central and Eastern Europe compared to Western and Southern Europe. The dynamics of this process varied in different countries of course, as shown in Fig. 1 (male) and Fig. 2 (female).

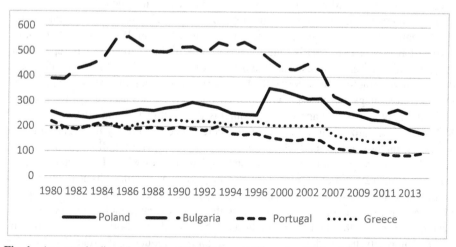

Fig. 1. Age-standardized death rates/100,000 from CAD, males, 1980 to 2014, selected European countries [own study based on [2]]

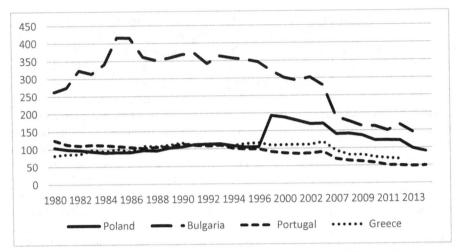

Fig. 2. Age-standardized death rates/100,000 from CAD, females, 1980 to 2014, selected European countries [own study based on [2]]

3   STEMI Treatment Process Logistics in Poland

In accordance with European standards, every patient with suspected MI should have a 12 – leads electrocardiographic (ECG) performed as soon as possible to establish a proper diagnosis [3]. The correct interpretation of the ECG record is crucial for the quick qualification of the patient for the appropriate treatment. If ST segment elevation myocardial infarct (STEMI) is diagnosed, the most optimal treatment is reperfusion therapy, which is based on restoring the patency of the artery that causes the infarction, the so-called infract-related artery (IRA). Primary coronary angioplasty is the preferred reperfusion strategy for patients with STEMI within 12 h of onset of symptoms, provided it can be performed appropriately quickly (i.e. within 120 min after diagnosis of STEMI) in specialized cardiological center. Percutaneous coronary intervention (PCI) should be understood as unblocking the infarcted artery with a balloon or stent. The second form of reperfusion therapy (recommended in cases where PCI cannot be performed within 120 min of first medical contact (FMC)) is pharmacological fibrinolytic treatment, which consists of intravenous administration of drugs aimed at dissolving the blockage thrombus in the coronary artery. In the past, several randomized clinical trials have demonstrated that PCI is definitely more beneficial than fibrinolysis, resulting in reduced mortality, the incidence of recurrent MI and the frequency of strokes [4]. In order to optimize the diagnosis and treatment process in accordance with the ESC recommendations, a network of highly specialized centers (PCI centers) dealing with MI treatment and performing 24-h, 7 days a week primary coronary angioplasty procedure has also been introduced in Poland [5]. In 2018, 163 catheterization laboratory (CL) operated in Poland, of which 95 are formally accredited by the Polish Cardiac Society; in which 613 certified operators (PCI operators) worked [6]. The traditional logistic scheme of treating a patient with MI is based on a chain of subsequent events:

- chest pain of the patient staying at home,
- call for an ambulance,
- performing an ECG at patient's home and suspecting of MI,
- transporting the patient to the nearest Emergency Department (ED),
- ECG recording reanalysis by the physician - confirmation of the STEMI diagnosis,
- telephone contact with PCI center in aim to confirming the patient's transfer,
- transport patient by the EMS to PCI center,
- admitting the patient to ED of PCI center - reanalysis of the ECG recording by the invasive cardiologist and confirmation of the STEMI,
- transport of the patient to the CL and primary PCI procedure.

This way of organizing treatment significantly increases the time to open the IRA. According to the recommendations, the maximum time provided for ECG performance and its proper interpretation is 10 min. This fact poses EMS teams a big challenge of fast and proper interpretation of the ECG record. ESC guidelines recommended EMS teams use the option of teleconsultation with experienced ICCU or CL members to confirm the diagnosis of STEMI [7]. There are currently two commercial systems in Poland supporting the decision-making process for patients with STEMI [8]. The principle of operation and functioning of these telematics systems is similar. In this paper, we will focus on the Lifenet 5.2 system for several reasons: despite many similarities, it seems that the Lifenet system has more advantages and functionality, currently it is the most widely used telematics system in Poland, the author of this work has his own several years professional experience working with this system. Lifenet 5.2 consists of several transmitting stations (modems) located in ambulances, which enable the transmission of ECG to the receiving station situated in the PCI – hospital, where this record is analyzed by an experienced cardiologist working in ICCU or in the CL. Modems are coupled with defibrillators, which are necessary to perform 12-lead ECG and collect patient vital signs. Moreover, the system allows the automatic transmission of clinical data and vital signs of the patient, automatic notification (via e-mail, SMS) of all necessary members of medical staff about transport of the patient with infarction [9]. Next step is a phone call of the on-duty cardiologist with the EMS team present at the place of the event, during which further proceedings are discussed, i.e. in case of confirmation of STEMI, the on-duty cardiologist qualifies the patient for PCI, discusses with the EMS team the administration of appropriate medications (anticoagulants and antiplatelet), specifies estimated time of arrival of the patient directly to the indicated PCI center; in case of a serious condition of the patient, the on-duty cardiologist discusses and supports other emergency medical services necessary to perform on-site. Early correct diagnosis of STEMI allows to significantly accelerate the patient's transport to the appropriate center (bypassing non-PCI hospitals), which correspond to a better final treatment result [10]. It is recommended that if STEMI is diagnosed in pre-hospital conditions and the patient is qualified for primary PCI, the local CL should be immediately notified and activated by the on-duty cardiologist, and then the patient should be transported directly to the CL bypassing the ED of the nearest hospital. CL after notifying about transport patient with STEMI suspends performing new procedures (a patient with STEMI should not wait for a free place on the operating table in the PCI center). If the transmitted ECG does not confirm the diagnosis of STEMI, the EMS team is directed to ED of the nearest hospital for further assessment of the patient. In some cases, although the ECG record does not confirm STEMI, the patient is transported directly to the PCI center. This applies to patients with severe electrocardiographic features of myocardial ischaemia (other than ST segment elevation), in severe clinical condition (persistent coronary pain, pulmonary edema secondary to cardiac ischemia, malignant cardiac arrhythmias). Patient transport to the PCI center for PCI should also be considered in all cases of successful resuscitation of patients after sudden cardiac arrest in non-hospital settings (especially in the mechanism of ventricular fibrillation/ventricular tachycardia without pulse) - regardless of ECG after resuscitation. Considerations regarding the indications for PCI of patients after sudden cardiac arrest exclude beyond the scope of this study. Each time transport to the PCI center of the patient without a typical STEMI image in ECG should be carefully arranged and agreed with the on-duty cardiologist. After arriving at the PCI center patient is transferred directly to the CL, bypassing the local ED, which is associated with shortening the time from FMC to wire crossing by 20 min [11]. Such a management scheme shortens treatment delays, but also reduces mortality among patients [12, 13]. If the patient requires stabilization of vital functions (e.g. due to the deterioration of the patient's condition during transport) these activities are performed by a previously called anesthesiologist in ED rooms (as an exception to the rule about transporting the patient directly to CL) and then patient is transferred to CL for primary PCI. For patients arriving at a non-PCI center, the indicator that should be used to assess clinical performance is the time from arrival at the non PCI center to leave for the PCI center (door-in to door-out time) To speed up reperfusion treatment, this time should be $\leq$30 min [14]. If the total time from FMC to wire crossing is expected to be longer than 120 min (due to, for example, poor weather conditions, ongoing treatment in CL with a predicted long duration, long distance from PCI center), the on-duty cardiologist consults, discusses and coordinates the administration of fibrinolytic therapy by the EMS team. ESC guidelines recommend fibrinolysis at the incident site (in pre-hospital settings) and immediate transport patient with STEMI to the PCI center [15, 16]. To illustrate the above recommendations, ultimately the chain of events in a patient with STEMI should look like this:

- chest pain of the patient staying at home,
- call for ambulance,
- ECG at the patient's home and suspicion of STEMI,
- contact with invasive cardiology center aim to confirm the diagnosis of STEMI and qualify the patient for the primary PCI,
- transport patient via EMS to PCI center,
- admitting the patient to the CL bypassing the ED and primary PCI.

The above recommendations, communication schemes, time delay limits and the place of telematics systems are presented in Fig. 3. All the procedures described above with the use of telematics systems are consistent with the guidelines for the treatment of STEMI described above, improving them and thereby increasing the survival rate of patients [17, 18]. As shown in Fig. 3, EMS teams have a very important role in the diagnosis and treatment logistics of STEMI, which are a link connecting individual elements of the STEMI treatment system.

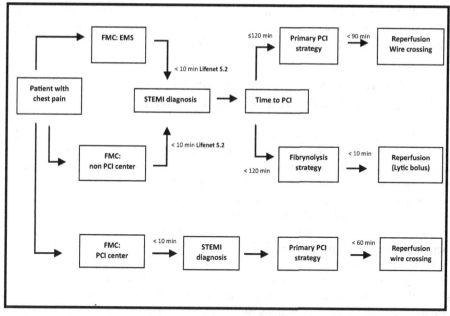

Fig. 3. Logistic diagram of the process of diagnosis and treatment of patients with STEMI, including the recommended maximum time delays and the role of telematics systems. EMS = Emergency Medical System; FMC = First Medical Contact; PCI = Percutaneous Coronary Intervention; STEMI = ST-segment elevation myocardial infarction, based on [5]

It should be noted that the role of EMS teams is not only limited to the transport of patients, but also is directly related to the triage, diagnosis and treatment of patients with STEMI [19, 20]. At present, there are two types of EMS teams in Poland: the specialist type ("S") in a 4-person team (doctor - optimally specialist in emergency medicine, nurse, paramedic, driver-paramedic), the basic type ("P") in a 2 or 3 person team (1 or 2 paramedics, driver-paramedic). All EMS ambulances in Poland (regardless of team class) have the same professional life support equipment: an ECG monitor, defibrillator, respirator, oxygen supply system. The EMS team are well prepared and trained in basic life support (BLS) as well as advanced life support (ALS) activities. A very important element of the rescue system in Poland is the Helicopter Emergency Medical Service (HEMS) operating as part of the Polish Medical Air Rescue (PMAR) founded in 2000. HEMS teams are also very often used to transport patients with STEMI. Today PMAR consists of 21 regional HEMS bases and 1 seasonal HEMS base; 4 bases are open 24 h a day, 9 working at regular hours from 7 to 20, and the other bases are open from sunrise (however not earlier than from 7 am) to sunset (but not longer than until 8 pm). The tasks of HEMS include flying to accidents and sudden illnesses and helping their victims, as well as transporting patients requiring medical care between health care centers. HEMS are equipped with a modern EC 135/H135 helicopter, which is able to reach the site of an accident within 60 km within several minutes. The HEMS team consists of a pilot, a doctor and a paramedic/nurse. Rescue helicopter equipment does not differ from the equipment of the ambulance, and the training of the team meets the highest medical standards. Currently, HEMS is characterized by high standards for medical emergency and 3 min operational readiness. Each rescue helicopter is also equipped with the option of ECG recording transmission to the nearest PCI center.

4   Polish Experience in the Management of Diagnosis of STEMI Using Telematics Systems – Critical Analysis

It should be noted that the first ECG teletransmission in Poland was made in the Kuyavian-Pomeranian Voivodeship in the Clinic of Cardiology and Internal Diseases of the University Hospital in Bydgoszcz as early as December 5, 2003. For the transmission a non-commercial set was used: ECG EHO8 recorder, Nokia 6310i cell phone (GPRS data transfer) and the receiving station was a PC computer (Pentium 4, 3 GHz, 800 MHz FSB, 1 GB RAM) with a Siemens MC35T GSM modem. Today, such a set seems archaic, and it has been several years since then that a rapid development of commercial technologies for the transmission of ECG could be observed. The Kujawsko Pomorskie Voivodship (at the area of which the author of this publication works as a cardiologist) was for many years the undisputed leader in the implementation and dissemination of telematics systems supporting the process of MI diagnosis. One should also not forget about local restrictions and differences as well as the specifics of the Polish health care system, which can reduce the effectiveness of using telematics methods. At present, the purchase of devices and software for ECG transmission is not financed by the National Health Fund. There are no official written protocols sanctioning and forcing the use of ECG transmission in Poland. Each hospital purchases the appropriate equipment from its own resources, and then chooses EMS teams by themselves, equipping them with modems. There is no clear definition of geographic areas of responsibility of particular PCI center in Poland, which may disinform EMS teams, hinder cooperation between the EMS team and the PCI center and thus prolong the transport time of the patient to the appropriate center. Due to the relatively large number of CLs, as well as the presence of commercial CLs, there are paradoxical cases of equipping one ambulance with 2 modems from 2 different PCI centers, as well as transporting the patient to a further away PCI center (having a more closely located center available). Due to the lack of written protocols of action, there are practices of "selecting" less burdened patients and deliberate refusal to admit a serious, problematic patient. There are also cases of transport of patient with STEMI without prior notification to the PCI center (despite the technical capabilities), which can paradoxically lead to a significant extension of the time for wire crossing. Frequent cases of lack of vacancies in the local ICCU or interruptions in the operation of Cl due to unforeseen technical failures lead to the necessity of further transport to the next PCI center. Not informing the PCI center about transport of patient with STEMI may also lead to a prolonged waiting time of the patient at ED due to waiting for a free operation table in CL or the necessity of arriving at the hospital of all team members (in Poland, very often part of the CL team is on non-stationary duty at home, after informing about patient's transport by phone, they arrive at the hospital within several minutes). As presented above, the time spent on ECG recording transmission and telephone conversation with the on-duty cardiologist from the PCI center (despite the clear diagnosis of STEMI by the EMS team) is not a waste of time, on the contrary, it ultimately allows a significant reduction in time to implement PCI strategy. Another problem related to the functioning of telematics systems in the Polish reality are transports of patients to the PCI center after prior disqualification by the cardiologist on duty. Such a patient usually, despite the lack of indications for urgent PCI, remains in the PCI center, leading to a smaller pool of free places in the local ICCU, what may result in the fact that another patient with STEMI is not admitted and must be transported to a distant place PCI center (which significantly reduces its chances of survival). The functioning of EMS teams in Poland needs to be discussed separately. In the Polish EMS, tendencies to limit the number of "S" teams in favor of "P" teams have been visible for several years, which leads to the fact that most members of the EMS teams are currently paramedics or nurses (these are pan-European tendencies). Paramedics do not have sufficient knowledge and, above all, experience in the correct interpretation of ECG records and STEMI diagnostics. The introduction of telematics methods, which allow ECG consultation with an experienced cardiologist, has enabled EMS to achieve a new, much higher standard of medical services in Poland related to the diagnosis and treatment of MI. The role of an experienced cardiologist who consults by phone and helps the EMS team seems not to be overestimated. Undoubtedly, the problem is also unnecessary and unjustified abuse of the Lifenet system by EMS teams. Sending ECG records of patients without typical chest pain is a common reality. Abdominal pain, fainting, palpitations, dizziness, bradycardia are one of the most common causes of ECG transmission to a PCI center. It should be clearly emphasized that the possibility of ECG teletransmission does not mean the possibility of consulting with on-duty cardiologist for any patient who is problematic for the EMS team. In the aforementioned cases, the time spent on ECG transmission is wasting because in some of these cases medical emergency services should be started immediately, on which the patient's survival may depend. The patient must be transported to the PCI center only in the case of STEMI, other patients (even those reporting cardiac problems) can be transported to the ED of the nearest hospital, where they will be provided with all necessary medical assistance. Excessive amounts of unnecessary and unjustified ECG teletransmissions can lead to increase of workload of on-duty cardiologist and at some moments can significantly disintegrate the proper functioning of ICCU. Another problem is the phenomenon of attempts to transfer responsibility for the patient's treatment to the on-duty cardiologist. There are cases of refusals to transport the patient to the hospital by EMS teams explained by the fact that after teletransmission the patient was disqualified from transport to the PCI center by on-duty cardiologist. The fact that the patient does not require immediate PCI and transport to the PCI center does not mean that the patient does not have a heart attack, and even more does not mean that there is no need to transport the patient to the hospital. The decision to transport a patient to nearest ED is always made by the EMS team leader after a taking medical history and performing physical examination. The on-duty cardiologist only consults the ECG record and is unable to determine the necessity or the lack of transport of the patient to the hospital (especially since ECG records of patients with non-cardiac complaints are very often transmitted). It seems necessary to further educate and make members of the EMS teams aware of the indications and applications of the Lifenet system. The author's own observations regarding the functioning of the EMS in Poland indicate that the ambulance staff in the vast majority are not well prepared for the correct using of fibrinolytic treatment (they do not know what the drugs are used, rules of dosage these drugs, they do not know the basic indications and contraindications for this therapy). It should also be noted that in the realities of the 21st century in Poland, taking into account the well-developed network of the CL, fibrinolytic treatment at the place of incidence (e.g. at patient's home) is practically not applicable because the numbers of PCI centers, which can receive a patient with STEMI is so large that the transport time of the patient is very short. An additional factor that does not encourage the administration of fibrinolysis in pre-hospital conditions is the lack of reimbursement of fibrinolytic drugs (given by the EMS teams) by the National Health Fund. Confirmation of these words may be the fact that the author of this study during his 14 years of professional work both in the Intensive Cardiac Care Unit (ICCU), EMS teams as well as in the CL never once gave patients fibrinolytic treatment. The organization of EMS is another problem associated with the use of telematics in the treatment of MI. EMS teams often do not receive permission from the coordinator to transport a patient with MI to a PCI center located outside the operational area of a given EMS team. If the diagnosis of STEMI has not been made by the ambulance crew and the ambulance arrives at a non-PCI-capable hospital, the ambulance should await the diagnosis and, if a STEMI diagnosis is made, should continue to a PCI-capable hospital. Very often, EMS teams do not receive consent from the coordinator to await the decision on further transport. If the decision is made to transport the patient to the PCI center, there is a need to organize an appropriate ambulance, which according to Polish standards remains in responsibility of to the hospital in which the patient is currently located (the hospital cannot use the EMS team). In practice, this means a very large loss of time and a significant extension of transport time to the appropriate center. The use of HEMS in the STEMI treatment process also requires separate discussion. On first sight, it seems to be a very good solution, however, in everyday practice flights of HEMS encounter significant restrictions. Only 4 bases perform night flights (Warsaw, Wroclaw, Gdansk, Cracow), so not the entire area of the country at night is covered by operating range of HEMS; most bases fly only from dawn to dusk (with the helicopter returning time to base being taken into account). Another limitation is the availability of airstrips located at PCI centers. While the majority of invasive cardiology centers have landing sites, only a few centers have in their structure airfields ready to receive a helicopter at night (airfields equipped with artificial lighting). Another problem is the very frequent inability to land a helicopter at the scene of incidence (e.g. a helicopter is not always able to land in the city center). Each commune and city in Poland have a fixed and prepared place that acts as a local field airstrip for HEMS. In the absence of technical possibilities to land at the scene of incidence, the helicopter lands at the nearest field airstrip, and the patient is transported from the house to the airstrip by the EMS team. It should also be added that for safety reasons, helicopter landing in an accidental area or field airport must be secured by the Fire Brigade team at all times. Considering the need to involve many services (EMS team, Fire Brigade team), the need to transport the patient from the scene of incidence to the landing site (in some cases), the need to perform time-consuming safety checks before each take-off and landing (e.g. helicopter external visual control, waiting for the engine to be switched off, etc.) despite the fact that the actual flight time of the helicopter to the PCI center is definitely shorter than the duration of transporting the patient by road transport, overall time of transport of the patient with STEMI by HEMS may be longer than by the EMS team. An additional limitation is the weather conditions, which very often prevent any rescue flights. Consideration should also be given to the relatively long time (compared to EMS teams) of restoring readiness for the next rescue mission (the need to return to the base after each completed mission to refuel).

5 Conclusion

The first successful ECG teletransmission in Poland took place 17 years ago. During this time, the number of PCI centers with a 24 h a day, 7 days a week (24/7) primary PCI programme as well as centers offering the use of ECG teletransmission systems has been growing at an impressive pace. It can be safely said that at present Poland is completely covered by a network of PCI centers which enable telematic consultation of patients with suspected of MI [21]. An evident annual increase in the number of PCI procedures performed has been observed in Poland since 2003, which is undoubtedly due to, inter alia, the broad introduction to everyday medical practice of telematic ECG transmission methods. In 2018, according to the Polish National PCI Registry (ORPKI), the total number of PCI amounted 104,283 (2709 PCIs per 1 million inhabitants per year). Of these procedures, 20.219 was performed for STEMI (19%), 20.666 for NSTEMI (20%) and 26.185 for unstable angina (26%). The rest of the PCI was performed in patients with stable CAD (35%) [6]. Figure 4A shows the number of PCIs performed in Poland in recent years. By analyzing the above data, Poland can be clearly identified as the leader among European countries in terms of the number of PCIs (Fig. 4B).

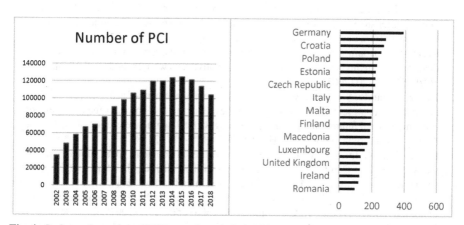

Fig. 4. Left panel: number of PCI procedures in Poland in the years 2002–2018, [own study based on [6]]; Right panel: number of PCI procedures per 100.000 inhabitants (2014; latest available data) [own study based on [2]]

Unfortunately, a significant decrease in the number of these procedures has been observed since 2015. In the unanimous opinion of the experts, this fact is associated with a significant decrease in valuations for PCI procedures by the National Health Fund. Changes in recent years have also affected functioning of the EMS in Poland, making it a well-developed service, well equipped with medical support life device as well as ambulances. Also, technological development in the last decade has made telematics systems more and more efficient, miniaturized, more accessible, easier to use and offer a growing range of service. The results presented in this article show that in the analyzed case all relevant factors were taken into account [22] and the technology was properly selected. The increase in the number of PCIs and the development of cardiology and emergency medicine in Poland translated into a reduction the mortality rate due to CAD (Fig. 1 and Fig. 2). In the 21st century, Poland recorded the largest percentage decreases in CAD mortality rates among countries in Central and Eastern Europe. Despite these undoubted successes, one should still remember about many limitations and problems that telematics systems encounter during everyday medical practice in Poland. In the opinion of the author of this paper, in addition to further technological development and miniaturization of ECG teletransmission systems, should also be taken to educate and make medical personnel aware of the proper use of these devices, and above all to introduce legally sanctioned protocols of conduct and clear definition of geographic areas of responsibility of particular PCI center.

References

1. Hartley, A., et al.: Trends in mortality from ischemic heart disease and cerebrovascular disease in Europe: 1980 to 2009. Circulation **133**(20), 1916–1926 (2016)
2. Wilkins, E., et al.: European Cardiovascular Disease Statistics 2017. European Heart Network, Brussels (2017)
3. Diercks, D.B., et al.: Frequency and consequences of recording an electrocardiogram > 10 minutes after arrival in an emergency room in non-ST-segment elevation acute coronary syndromes (from the CRUSADE Initiative). Am. J. Cardiol. **97**(4), 437–442 (2006)
4. Keeley, E.C., Boura, J.A., Grines, C.L.: Primary angioplasty versus intravenous thrombolytic therapy for acute myocardial infarction: a quantitative review of 23 randomised trials. Lancet **361**(9351), 13–20 (2003)
5. Ibanez, B., James, S., et al.: ESC guidelines for the management of acute myocardial infarction in patients presenting with ST-segment elevation: the task force for the management of acute myocardial infarction inpatients presenting with ST-segment elevation of the European Society of Cardiology (ESC). Eur. Heart J. **39**(2), 119–177 (2018)
6. Dudek, D., et al.: Interventional cardiology procedures in Poland in 2018. Summary report of the Association of Cardiovascular Interventions of the Polish Cardiac Society (AISN PTK) and Jagiellonian University Medical College. Adv. Inter. Cardiol. **15**(4 (58)), 391–393 (2019)
7. Dhruva, V.N., et al.: ST-segment analysis using wireless technology in acute myocardial infarction (STAT-MI) trial. J. Am. Coll. Cardiol. **50**(6), 509–513 (2007)
8. Maciejewski, R., Zubrzycki, J.: Inżynieria biomedyczna Telemedycyna Monografie – Politechnika Lubelska, Lublin, pp. 90–92 (2015)
9. Product Brochure Physio Control Lifenet 5.2. https://www.physio-control.com/uploadedF iles/Physio85/Contents/Workplace_and_Community/Products/3308272_D_LR.pdf
10. Kawecki, D., et al.: Direct admission versus interhospital transfer for primary percutaneous coronary intervention in ST-segment elevation myocardial infarction. JACC: Cardiovascular Interventions, **10**(5), 438–447 (2017)

11. Bagai, A., et al.: Emergency department bypass for ST-Segment-elevation myocardial infarction patients identified with a prehospital electrocardiogram: a report from the American Heart Association Mission: Lifeline program. Circulation **128**(4), 352–359 (2013)
12. Fordyce, C.B., et al.: STEMI systems accelerator project. association of rapid care process implementation on reperfusion times across multiple ST-segment-elevation myocardial infarction networks. Circ Cardiovasc Interv. 10(1) (2017)
13. Stowens, J.C., Sonnad, S.S., Rosenbaum, R.A.: Using EMS dispatch to trigger STEMI alerts decreases door-to-balloon times. West J Emerg Med. **16**(3), 472–480 (2015)
14. Wang, T.Y., et al.: Association of door-in to door-out time with reperfusion delays and outcomes among patients transferred for primary percutaneous coronary intervention. JAMA **305**(24), 2540–2547 (2011)
15. Bonnefoy, E., et al.: CAPTIM Investigators. Comparison of primary angioplasty and prehospital fibrinolysis in acute myocardial infarction (CAPTIM) trial: a 5-year follow-up. Eur Heart J. **30**(13), 1598–1606 (2009)
16. Armstrong, P.W., et al.: STREAM Investigative Team. Fibrinolysis or primary PCI in ST-segment elevation myocardial infarction. N. Engl. J. Med. **368**(15), 1379–1387 (2013)
17. Kalla, K., Christ, G., et al.: Implementation of guidelines improves the standard of care: the Viennese registry on reper-fusion strategies in ST-elevation myocardial infarction (Vienna STEMI registry). Circulation **113**(20), 2398–2405 (2006)
18. Henry, T.D., et al.: A regional system to provide timely access to percutaneous coronary intervention for ST-elevation myocardial infarction. Circulation **116**(7), 721–728 (2007)
19. Terkelsen, C.J., et al.: System delay and mortality among patients with STEMI treated with primary percutaneous coronary intervention. JAMA **304**(7), 763–771 (2010)
20. Huber, K., et al.: Task force on pre-hospital reperfusion therapy of the working group on thrombosis of the ESC. Pre-hospital reperfusion therapy: a strategy to improve therapeutic outcome in patients with ST-elevation myocardial infarction. Eur. Heart J. **26**(19), 2063–2074 (2005)
21. Legutko, J., et al.: Poland: coronary and structural heart interventions from 2010 to 2015. EuroIntervention. 13(Z), Z51–Z54 (2017)
22. Kozłowski, R.: Wykorzystanie zaawansowanych technologii w zarządzaniu projektami, pp. 96–97. Wydawnictwo Uniwersytetu Łódzkiego, Łódź (2010)

Conditions for Implementing Innovating Telemedicine Procedures After Hip Arthroplasty

Karolina Kamecka[1], Per Engelseth[2], Anna Staszewska[1],
and Remigiusz Kozlowski[3(✉)]

[1] Medical University of Lodz, Department of Management and Logistics in Healthcare,
Lindleya 6, 90-131 Lodz, Poland
kkamecka@gmail.com, anna.staszewska@umed.lodz.pl
[2] University of Tromsø, Tromsø School of Business and Economics, Narvik Campus, Lodve
Langesgt 2, 8514 Narvik, Norway
pen008@uit.no
[3] University of Lodz, Faculty of Management, Matejki 22/26, 90-237 Lodz, Poland
rjk5511@gmail.com

Abstract. Telemedicine technology offers a wide range of possibilities for improving various forms of healthcare services. These technologies can support and economize healthcare service processes including medical consultations, preparation for medical treatment and in the post-operative period. The increasing number of older people in developed countries increases the importance of telemedicine as a way to economize the care of the elderly. Domestic healthcare is one such opportunity. This study focuses on the use of this technology as a networking achievement demanding integrated relationships and purposeful interaction to implement and use this technology including focus on use of domestic healthcare of elderly patients after total hip arthroplasty in Poland. This network of actors consists of importantly interaction between patients, healthcare service providers and technology providers. A combination of telematics technology, services theory and contingency theory creates a distinct network approach to understanding domestic healthcare as a particular form of service process provision implying development of the exchange economy to support the services production economy. The aim of the article is to analyze the conditions for innovative telemedicine procedures implementing after total hip arthroplasty. Due to the conducted considerations, a set of fundamental solutions in regards to network implementation and application in home healthcare of Polish elderly patients after total hip arthroplasty will be developed. Conclusions will also concern the potential market of telemedicine solutions for patients after hip arthroplasty in Poland. Attention will also be paid to restrictions on the implementation of new technologies and ways to overcome them.

Keywords: Healthcare service process · Telemedicine procedures ·
Telemedicine technology · Total hip arthroplasty · Value of telemedicine market

© Springer Nature Switzerland AG 2020
J. Mikulski (Ed.): TST 2020, CCIS 1289, pp. 456–467, 2020.
https://doi.org/10.1007/978-3-030-59270-7_34

1 Introduction

Domestic healthcare plays an important role for the use of telemedicine technology and can be supported with various forms of healthcare services. In 2050 every third person in Europe will have more than 60 years old and providing medical care for all those persons will not be possible. Due to lack of medical staff and emigration the number of medical specialists in Poland is very small. Technology can support older in some procedures at home without a need to visit medical professionals personally. These are the main reasons to use telemedicine solutions. The aim of the article is analyses of conditions for implementing innovating telemedicine procedures after hip arthroplasty. Research is conducted within the EU-financed InterDoktorMen project.

2 Conditions for Implementing Innovating Telemedicine Procedures

To study the complexities of on innovating telemedicine procedures after hip arthroplasty we apply, as suggested by Engelseth and Kritchanchai (2018), a combining of contingency theory with ecosystems thinking [9]. Firstly, contingency theory (1967) is applied as our fundamental theoretical approach. Ecosystems thinking refines this approach. Contingency theory implies a process approach to in this case a service production. A fundamental management stance in contingency theory is that there is no best way to organize a corporation [18]. This approach encompasses focus on resource use and transformation; the dynamics of innovating telemedicine procedures after hip arthroplasty. This implies that processes are viewed as fundamentally speaking, environmentally contingent. Conceptually, "context" is this approach the part of the environment direct interaction between the sequences of healthcare service providers. This again implies that "environment" forces not necessarily interacting, but still impacting on healthcare services in a more one-way manner. Figure 3 developed by Engelseth and Kritchanchai (2018) describes this approach:

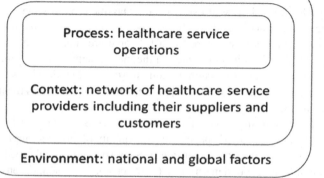

Fig. 1. The healthcare service process as embedded unit of analysis [9]

Process management involves in our case study the actual flow telemedicine procedures after hip arthroplasty. This involves aspect importantly two aspects: (1) the combining of more or less heterogeneous resources to achieve complementarity, and (2), the actors doing and managing this flow of activities, the service operation. As service logistics, innovating telemedicine procedures after hip arthroplasty involves accordingly economizing through redesign this workflow. This, however, is in accordance with figure three not completely straightforward. We cannot proceed with deterministic thinking, following a planning paradigm. Researcher sensitivity to service fulfilment *chaos* is vital. The healthcare service process is viewed in this approach as *emergent* due to its contingencies. Importantly, healthcare service provision; no two such service processes are at any time completely alike. It is complex and depends on features and workings of its environment as a layered phenomenon.

To improve innovate telemedicine procedures after hip arthroplasty we need to elaborate on features of healthcare operations, as a form of service logistics. Research needs therefore to be founded on service industry particularities important in economizing healthcare logistics. Emphasizing "logistics" means focus on the service as a flow. A flow is metaphorical and directs focus to process as a series of transformations. Value in logics is measured in relation to transformation as pooling resources including people to create the service. This is different from physical distribution of goods, where transformation is associated with the transformation of a product in the flow. In services the service output is difficult to measure. The resources that crate the service and how they are coupled together and thereby interact, is measurable.

To analyse the state of a healthcare service process we propose considering features of networked interdependencies. This is a network of people and resources where inter-firm boundaries is regarded as a contextual factor. Within contingency theory Thompson (1967) later, Stabell and Fjeldstad (1998) have developed an approach focusing on the role of power relations in the supply chain that enhances service industry particularities enabling process development schemes better adapted to service [33, 36]. Furthermore, the embedded nature of healthcare in society call for ecosystems thinking [5]. Ecosystems direct attention to features of service sustainability and integrating a range of societal concerns associated with a studied healthcare service.

Services are commonly classified as intangible, heterogenic, inseparable, and perishable hampering according to Spring and Araujo [33] a comprehensive analysis. Fundamental to this critical view of using a static classification of services in academia is that service production demands a different form of organising of the resource structure and processes within this structure [6, 26]. People are fundamental to value creation in services [11, 24]. This is highlighted in the more recent service-dominant logic that highlights the importance of customer value in supply [21]. Service supply chains are according to Sampson and Froehle [32] bidirectional in nature. This means that interaction is a key feature of service supply chains. In service processes the customer provides significant inputs into the production process (ibid.). Sampson and Froehle [32] also point out that from a supplier's perspective the quality of customer inputs in the service process interactions can vary. According to Sampson and Froehle [32], three types of customer inputs can be found in services: (1) the customer person, (2) physical resources such as customer belongings, tools and other tangible objects, and (3) information. These resources are pooled and used in combination to produce a service. In healthcare the customer value aspect is usually not only the patient, but also next of kin. This is especially when the patient is incommunicative due to the illness. In cases of hip arthroplasty, however, it is expected that the patient is a communicative actor the healthcare service providers can interact with.

Sampson and Froehle [32] site empirical evidence of quality issues predominant in the service supply chains including (1) random arrivals, (2) inconsistent specification, and (3) varying input quality that influence service processes as capacity and demand management and quality management. From a Lean perspective Bicheno and Holweg [2] point to typical forms of waste (muda) found in services are represented by (1) delay, (2) duplication, (3) unnecessary movement, (4) unclear communication, (5) incorrect inventory, (6) poor customer service, and (7) transaction and production errors. To support quality service provision tools such as reservation systems, price incentives and promotion of off-peak demand, and customer self-service are may be used. In addition, capacity management involves a mix of resources such as people, tools and goods.

A key feature of the supply chain is that it is a network consisting of multiple interconnected actors [29]. When approaching how to understand the nature of healthcare process contingency in relation to the supply chain context, analysis is dependent on revealing and the analyst thus understanding the nature of this context [7]. One of the key features of any network is the strength of coupling between the network entities. Following Weick [38], network interactions take place through business relationships where this coupling varies on a continuum ranging from weak to strong. The nature of coupling impacts importantly on the loyalty of actors in the network, which then again may be viewed as expression of degree of power and trust; the "network atmosphere" [10]. Following Thompson (1967), a fundamental reason for networking is associated with interdependency between actors. Resources are scarce. Investments have made production resources specialized to a single firm. These actors need to interact to produce. Trading is a fundamental defining feature of the industrial network, the supply chain. Emerson [8] points therefore out power as the fundamental characteristic of network interaction. These supplier or customer relationships can also be characterised as degrees of being imbalanced or balanced. Following Pfeffer and Salancik (1978) supply control is based on a mix of resource ownership, access, use and ability to make the rules regarding resource use [30]. Power is often associated with coercion. Based on the writings of the process-focused sociologist Elias, Stacey [34] argues how power both enables and constrains in production processes in industry. According to Pfeffer and Salancik (1978) and Leonardi et al. [30, 20], interdependencies can be managed, be increased, reduced, or the dominant interdependency in a dyadic relationship changed. Contingency theory is not limited to explaining how production is an emergent phenomenon. Managing interdependencies of the network context is, following contingency theory, the core feature of strategic corporate management. This represents a longer term understanding of producing e.g. services, that it is the context that needs to be invested in to change process.

Interdependencies are impacted by uncertainty which is defined by Burns and Stalker [3] as the ignorance of the person who is confronted with a choice about the future in general, and in particular about the outcomes of which may follow any of his possible lines of action. Interaction helps soothe uncertainty through exchange mechanisms; fundamentally involving information sharing [30]. Mutual adjustment is typical of the reciprocal interdependency that characterises services [33]. Mutual adjustment through human interaction is a time-consuming form of organisation. It is also costly in cases of high salaries. Alternatively, services may be increasingly pooled using mediating technology. This implies increasing standardization in the network. Since services are predominately characterized by reciprocal or pooled interdependence [33, 36], automating service processes entail increasing strategically pooled interdependence by reducing reciprocal interdependence in individual or sets of business relationships. Managing interdependency provides a pathway to increased service process efficiency.

Ecology is fundamental to an ecosystem. Ecology was conceptualised by Haeckel [12] as the science of relations between organism and the surrounding outer world. "Ecosystems" indicate accordingly considering nature, society and business as integrated from a system's perspective. Systems thinking finds its roots in the natural sciences, based on observations of how biological organisms' function. As Capra and Luisi (2014) state that "...nature does not show us any isolated building blocks, but rather appears as a complex web of relationships between the various parts of a unified whole" [5]. Systems are found in nature regardless of the glasses the researcher wears. In sum, an ecosystem understanding of healthcare processes implies using systems thinking encompassing economic, societal and nature concerns; an expansion of systems border that entails increased complexity.

One of the fundamental characteristics of interdependencies as discussed by Thompson (1967) approach is that this lies within systems theory. Ecosystems represents fundamentally system thinking meaning function, interconnectedness and system boundaries are core features when describing phenomena. Thompson's (1967) discussion, is however, limited to systems of industry. This does not encompass a wider scope of society and nature. Healthcare is clearly associated with a societal function. Furthermore, healthcare concerns the human body. Ailments may well be caused or treated by features embodied by the concept of "nature". Thompson (1967, p. 10) states that "...we will conceive of organizations as open systems, hence indeterminate and faced with uncertainty, but at the same time as subject to criteria of rationality and hence needing determinateness and certainty". Management understanding the nature of interdependencies is associated with increasing rationality in decision-making in the network. However, interactions in a healthcare service producing network accounts for only a part of these influences. Following Leonardi et al. [20], interdependency changes subject to incremental and iterative adaptations in the context of the healthcare "supply chain" and a wider social and natural environment. While business systems tend to conceptually be governed by management, ecosystems places weight ion how both nature and society together interplay making the system more self-governed; more out of reach to the manger.

Expanding healthcare services management to regard it as an ecosystem involves taking account of not only interaction in the supply chain network to manage the workflow, but to expand management discourse to encompass also societal and nature concerns. A direct impact of this expansion is not only widening the scope of systemic description and investigation, but also expanding the researched time frame. Since ecosystems are associated with sustainability, this means that the time frame of analytical scrutiny is expanded to considering interests of future generations. Furthermore, an ecosystem will be forming the perspective of the manger be perceived as uncertain and inherently complex. Ecology has its own logic of organising that may be different from that of mangers, e.g. in a hospital. Based on Engelseth and Kritchanchai (2018) management particularities of healthcare services consist of these three service production aspects:

- *Structure*: production pools various interlinked resources in an integrated network structure embedded in society and nature. This describes the *pooled* interdependency.
- *Dynamics*: managing these services demands through resource pooling demands interaction. This represents the *reciprocal* interdependency. The higher the uncertainty in how to configure resource pooling, the higher the reciprocal interdependency. This is the core of production, the activity value-making process.
- *Learning and development*: Service quality is poor much due to the complex nature of services process coupled with weak understanding of managing services as emergent phenomena. This represents the *sequential* interdependency. Learning and development fundamentally follows the timeline of production and is embedded in the network context the actor knows, and the wider unmanaged societal and natural environment. This is the long-term aspect that ensures the quality of production context. Development of capacities, people, tools including information systems, are examples here.

It is the context of "learning and development" aspect that application of telematics is considered. It is important to remember that all these aspects are interconnected. Our case description will therefore describe the structure and then the dynamics of procedures after hip arthroplasty to consider the use of telemedicine technology to develop this healthcare process.

3 Number of Hip and Knee Arthroplasty in Poland

We now consider the empirical realm of this study. Hip arthroplasty takes 64,62% of all joint replacement operations in Poland. Second place takes knee arthroplasty reaching

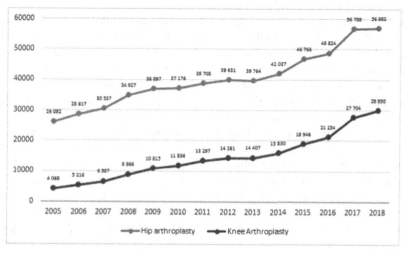

Fig. 2. Number of hip and knee arthroplasty procedures conducted in 2005–2018 in Poland according to realization report from National Health Fund [23]

33,97% in 2018 year. Since 2005 year there is constant increase in realization of total hip arthroplasty procedures in Poland refunded from National Health Fund (NHF), from 26 082 in 2005 year to 56 983 in 2018 year (Fig. 1). In absolute numbers, the highest increase in joint arthroplasty is observed in the case of hip joint.

A hip replacement procedure is more often performed than knee replacement (Fig. 2). For a hip replacement procedure average age of operated woman is 71 years old and 65 years old for man. Also, worth mentioning is that the largest share in total number of operated people were patients aged 60–69.

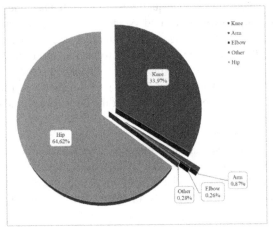

Fig. 3. Percentage share of individual types of arthroplasty procedures conducted 2018 in Poland according to realization report from National Health Fund [23]

In the period from 2005 to 2018 year number of arthroplasty procedures increased as well as costs of those operations. In the mentioned period there was 5 billion PLN spent for hip and knee arthroplasty together.

Healthcare services as a form of operations management (OM), is poorly developed and thus inefficient [13, 14]. Healthcare management involves physical distribution challenges such as inventory management and transportation costs. Healthcare is, however in relation to OM, predominately a service production. Instead of following a flow of goods, a workflow is the essence of transformation in time, place and form. A study by Butt and Run [4] pointed out the weak state of information management infrastructure in hospitals. Patients in this study rarely receive the right service at the right time, indicating flow malfunction. This is much due to poor planning and management supported by insufficient healthcare information systems (HIS). Leng [19] reveals how even though a government prioritises healthcare services hospitals continue to cope with frail healthcare services performance including a long treatment cycle. According to Parker [28]: "Measuring performance is something that all organizations do". This implies that measuring healthcare service performance supports healthcare management in the evaluation, control, personnel guidance, organisational learning and process improvement. Introducing an effective performance measurement system in healthcare entails that quality shortfalls can be detected on a daily and continuous basis more supporting efficiency in quality shortfalls detection and thereby efficient process improvement [31]. It is according to Baker et al. [1] an important aim in healthcare services to improve service performance. Providing healthcare services operations that provide the appropriate service for its recipients is vital to ensure patient value. Haux (2015) therefore states that improving HIS to support healthcare series is therefore a priority in many countries [15]. This study approaches developing healthcare services as a process integration problem. This implies modelling the flow of healthcare services within and between networked actors.

4 Technology Review for Telemedicine Procedures After Hip Arthroplasty

Telemedicine is defined as a technological and organizational solution for patient care, in particular:

– remote contact of a specialist with a patient,
– remote specialist-specialist consultation,
– measurement and data transfer between devices,
– information sent by devices to the patient and/or specialist,

provided that the obtained results of measurements, tests, conversations, analyzes and information sent in an electronic form are recorded. Reimbursed by National Health Fund services in Poland are in the field of cardiological telerehabilitation and teleconsulium in senior care.

Telemedicine thanks to technology develops faster and faster. The field is worth to conduct research because of possibility to prepare better solution which can help doctors and patients. We have a lot of types of technology being used in telemedicine. The most important of those are: Teleconsultation, Teleeducational platform, Alarm devices, E-registration, E-results, Telerehabilitation (example in cardiology) and Teleradiology. Below we try to briefly characterize possible use of those technologies in telemedicine.

Teleconsultation can be performed as simple technological solutions as chats or chatbots. More advanced usage are video consultations – there are more electronic devices needed like cameras, storage servers, internet connection [37]. The most complicated solution are e-offices with results commented online where we need not only technical equipment, but proper organization is a must have. Teleradiology is implemented through remote medical images descriptions. Is possible to use tool to converse Artificial Intelligence to analyze breakage of bones and soft tissue injuries in the technology of 3D being a support for MD [25].

Examples of wearables for domestic healthcare:

– Collapse wrist band (Noomi Case Study, Swedish startup, Nordics Insights 2018) – band equipped with collapse sensor, changes in diet and sleep process ready to analyze behavioral patterns [25].
– AppleWatch – device measurng pulse, blood pressure and temperature, physical activity and detecting atrial fibrillation [39].

- LifeWristband - Furnished with Life Button alarm that connects to the Remote Medical Care Center to call for help.
- ECG recording device with telemedicine function that permits patient geolocation and Holter ECG for longer periods.
- CTG device - Telemedical cardiotocography performed at home.
- CardioVest. - Non-invasive monitoring for early detection of silent atrial fibrillation (AF) detection [41].
- StethoMe® - system that detects abnormalities in the respiratory system relying on medical AI algorithms working with a wireless stethoscope and dedicated application [44].
- High-precision non-contact sleep sensor for professional sleep recording, measuring, analysing and improving personal sleeping habits and recording of heart rate, respiratory rate and movement [40].
- Digitsole connected footwear - smart insoles detecting neurological diseases, indicating how increase performance and warn against injury while physical activity (digitsole.com).

5 The Value of Telemedicine Market in Poland

The value of the global telemedicine market in 2018 was estimated at USD 34.28 billion. At the same it is anticipated that by 2026 this value has a range of up to USD 185.66 billion [35]. The telemedicine sector in Poland is a market in the growth phase. Currently, its value is approximately PLN 44 million (2018) and is expected to increase by 29% till 2023 [22]. Following types of telemedicine procedures are refunded by National Health Fund in Poland [27]:

- geriatric teleconsilium,
- cardiological teleconsilium,
- hybrid cardiological telerehabilitation.

The sector is characterized primarily by: a high level of uncertainty and risk of operations, variable prices, large capital needs to finance operations, which is caused most of all by the introduction of technology and innovation with relatively low competition. Therefore, estimating the costs of using telemedicine tools is not easy, especially in the public system as only a few benefits are financed by the National Health Fund (e.g. cardiological teleconsylium and geriatric teleconsylium). The "reluctance" to finance telemedicine services by the public sector arise, among others, from the economic approach to the valuation of guaranteed services. Telemedicine itself does not generate income but it is worth identifying and estimating the costs of lost benefits and/or financial and time savings. If subsequent telemedicine services were to be included in the guaranteed benefit package, cooperation between service providers and the public sector as well as producers of telemedicine solutions is necessary. Only comprehensive cooperation will allow conducting pilot programs to assess the effectiveness of these solutions, as well as to estimate the actual costs of using telemedicine solutions. According to the National Health Fund data [23], expenditure on health care in 2019 was to be about PLN

95 billion, while the finance allocated for the development and introduction of innovation is marginal. At the same time, it is worth noting that the data from the "Patient in the digital world" report indicate that 60% of patients living in Central and Eastern Europe (with revenues over EUR 300 net per month) declare their willingness to use telemedicine tools such as teleconsultation, telediagnostics, telemonitoring and telerehabilitation. Furthermore, in the literature, the indicated costs of using telemedicine in global terms are only estimated costs due to lack of uniform methodology of comparative research in this area and the fact that the same device can be used for another purpose, and therefore the costs of its use in another case may vary.

6 Conclusion

The case description shows that using telemedicine technology in essence is an emergent process. This implies that a key feature of developing telemedicine use is enabling flexibility in the healthcare service workflow, it production. In practice developing such flexibility may involve using telemedicine technology to support both in preparation for medical treatment as well as in post-operative period. Determining the potential market for telemedicine solutions in Poland are:

- Hip joint is the most common joint replacement. This shows that it is worth taking a closer look especially for this procedure.
- Reports of arthroplasty operations refunded for NHF shows that the number of operated patients increases every year. Due to high cost of procedure and proven impact of i.a. rehabilitation before and after operation, control visits, there is a need to consider implementation of technologies to economize via domestic healthcare influencing on the results of operation and health benefits for patients.
- Waiting list to hip arthroplasty procedure at NHF varies between few weeks and few years [44].
- Third most commonly reported health problem by older people is osteoarthritis. Saying this it is important to mention that the advanced osteoarthritis is the medical indication for joint replacement [43].

Another factors, which are very important in telemedicine implementation are: sociocultural, economical, legal (regulation on the protection of personal data), technological. We must also remember about the limitations of implementing telemedicine technologies such as [16]:

- make sure that the new technologies can be easily integrated with the technologies that had already been used,
- check if the users have sufficient knowledge and skills to operate the new technologies,
- check if users of the technology did not report any defects or if there were no instances of technology's breakdowns.

In order to overcome these barriers, all interested parties should be involved and the potential of universities should be used to support research [17] into the processes of implementing telemedicine processes in specific patient groups such as e.g. patients after hip arthroplasty. In practical terms development should be sensitive to that environmental factors are two-layered as described in Fig. 1. The context represents the, by healthcare institutions, governable environment. It works a s a buffer in relation to uncertainty in the healthcare process itself and wider environmental uncertain such as technology change, epidemics, regulations etc. The context represents a realm of investment in human resources and technology. Given the nature of uncertainty in healthcare service production, this is where healthcare institutions should direct their focus of development. They should not focus on developing the process first, since this will follow investments. They should neither direct focus to changing the wider environment since this is an unruly entity. Rather investments should enable healthcare process responsiveness to the wider environment and healthcare process change.

References

1. Baker, G.R., et al.: Hospital Quarterly 2, 22 (1998)
2. Bicheno, J., Holweg, M.: The Lean Toolbox: The Essential Guide to Lean Transformation. PICSIE Books, Buckingham (2009)
3. Burns, T., Stalker, G.M.: The Management of Innovation, p. 112. Tavistock Institute, London (1961)
4. Butt, M.M., Run, E.C.: Int. J. Health Care Qual. Assurance 23, 658 (2010)
5. Capra, F., Luisi, P.L: The Systems View of Life. A Unifying Vision. Cambridge University Press, Cambridge (2014)
6. Chase, R., Garvin, D.: Harvard Bus. Rev. 67, 61 (1989)
7. Christopher, M.: Logistics and Supply Chain Management (5 ed.), Financial Times Press, London (2016)
8. Emerson, R.: Am. Sociol. Rev. 27, 31 (1962)
9. Engelseth, P., Kritchanchai, D.: Innovation in healthcare services: creating a Combined Contingency Theory and Ecosystems Approach. IOP Conference Series: Materials Science and Engineering 2018; vol. 337. pp. 1–8 (2018)
10. Gadde, L.E., Håkansson, H., Persson, G.: Supply Network Strategies. Wiley, Chichester (2010)
11. Grönroos, C.: Service Management and Marketing: Managing the Moments of Truth in Service Competition. Lexington Books, Lexington (1990)
12. Haeckel, E.: Generelle Morphologie der Organismen. Reimer, Berlin (1866)
13. Hall, R.: Patient Flow. Springer, Berlin (2013)
14. Haszlinna, M.N., Potter, A.: Suppl. Chain Manag. Int. J. 14, 234 (2009)
15. Haux, R.: Int. J. Med. Informatics 75, 268 (2006)
16. Kozlowski, R., Matejun, M.: The identification of difficulties in using advanced technologies in the implementation of projects. Int. J. Bus. Manag. III(4), 56–57 (2015)
17. Kozlowski, R., Matejun, M.: Forms of cooperation with the business environment in the process of technology entrepreneurship development. "Research in Logistics & Production", nr 1/2012, pp. 99 (2012)
18. Lawrence, P.R., Lorsch, J.W.: Organization and Environment: Managing Differentiation and Integration. Harvard University, Boston (1967)
19. Leng, C.H.: Global Soc. Policy 10, 336 (2010)
20. Leonardi, P.M., et al.: How Matter Matters. Objects, Artefacts, and Materiality in Organization Studies, p. 142. Oxford University Press, Oxford (2013)

21. Lusch, R.F., Vargo, S.: Service-Dominant Logic, Perspectives, Possibilities, Premises. Cambridge University Press), Cambridge (2014)
22. Market of temedicine solutions in Poland in 2018. Analysis of the market and growth forecasts for 2018–2023, Raport, PMR (2018)
23. National Health Fund financial plan for 2019. https://www.nfz.gov.pl/bip/finanse-nfz/. Accessed 20 Sept 2019
24. Normann, R.: Reframing Business: When the Map Changes the Landscape. Wiley, West Sussex (2001)
25. Nordic insights, Trends that create future of business. Scandinavian-Polish Chamber of Commerce, Warsaw (2018)
26. Oliva, R., Kallenberg, R.: Int. J. Serv. Ind. Manag. **14**, 160 (2003)
27. OSOZ, Open Health Care System Special report 2018 edition, E-health in infographics. Kamsoft S.A. (2018)
28. Parker, C.: Work Study **49**, 63 (2000)
29. Parsons, T.: Structure and Processes in Modern Societies. The Free Press of Glencoe, New York (1960)
30. Pfeffer, J., Salancik, G.R.: The External Control of Organizations. Stanford Business Books, Stanford (1978)
31. Purbey, S., Mukherjee, K., Bhar, C.: Int. J. Prod. Perform. Manag. **56**, 241 (2007)
32. Sampson, S.E., Froehle, C.M.: Prod. Oper. Manag. **15**, 329 (2006)
33. Spring, M., Araujo, L.: Service and products: rethinking operations strategy. J. Oper. Prod. Manag. **29**(5), 444–467 (2009)
34. Stacey, R.D.: Complexity and Group Processes. Routledge, Milton Park (2003)
35. Telemedicine Market Size, Share & Industry Analysis By Type (Products, Services), By Application (Teleradiology, Telepathology, Teledermatology, Telepsychiatry, Telecardiology, Others), By Modality (Store-and-forward (Asynchronous), Real-time (Synchronous), Others), By End User (Healthcare Facilities, Homecare), and Regional Forecast 2019–2026, Report ID: FBI101067. https://www.fortunebusinessinsights.com/industry-reports/telemedicine-market-101067. Accessed 07 June 2019
36. Thompson, J.D.: Organizations in Action, pp. 101–102. McGraw Hill, New York (1967)
37. Vesterby, M.S.: Telemedicine support shortens length of stay after fast-track hip replacement. Acta Orthop. **88**(1), 41–47 (2017)
38. Weick, K.E.: Adm. Sci. Q. **21**, 1 (1976)
39. Search terms: smart watch. www.apple.com. Accessed 15 Jan 2020
40. Search terms: sleeping sensor SE80. www.beurer.com. Accessed 15 Jan 2020
41. Search terms: remote medical care. www.comarch.com. Accessed 15 Jan 2020
42. Realization of arthroplasty health services in 2018 on the basis of data from the Central Base of Arthroplasty of the National Health Fund. www.nfz.gov.pl. Accessed 15 Jan 2020
43. Information on the situation of the elderly based on surveys of the Central Statistical Office of Poland, Warsaw, September 2018. www.stat.gov.pl. Accessed 15 Jan 2020
44. www.stethome.com. Accessed 15 Jan 2020
45. Search terms: hip arthroplasty, stable mode, urgent mode, voivodship, city. www.terminyleczenia.nfz.gov.pl. Accessed 15 Jan 2020

Author Index

Printed in the United States
By Bookmasters